W9-BVX-675

Global Information Systems and Technology:
Focus on the Organization and Its Functional Areas

P. Candace Deans
Thunderbird-American Graduate School of
International Management

Kirk R. Karwan
University of South Carolina

 IDEA GROUP PUBLISHING
Harrisburg, USA • London, UK

Senior Editor: Mehdi Khosrowpour
Managing Editor: Jan Travers
Printed at: BookCrafters

Published in the United States of America by
        Idea Group Publishing
        Olde Liberty Square
        4811 Jonestown Road, Suite 230
        Harrisburg, PA 17109
        Tel: 717-541-9150
        Fax: 717-541-9159

and in the United Kingdom by
        Idea Group Publishing
        3 Henrietta Street
        Covent Garden
        London WC2E 8LU
        Tel: 071-240 0856
        Fax: 071-379 0609

British Cataloguing in Publication Data
A Cataloguing in Publication record for this book is available from the British Library

ISBN 1-878289-21-7

To our parents —

L.C. and Hazel Deans
Henry and Leah Karwan

Other IDEA GROUP Publishing Books

IDEA GROUP PUBLISHING

SERIES In Global Information Technology Management

Senior Editor:
Mehdi Khosrowpour
Pennsylvania State University

Releases of this series

• **The Global Issues of Information Technology Management**

• **Global Information Technology Education: Issues and Trends**

• **Global Information Systems and Technology: Focus on the Organization and Its Functional Areas**

For more information, or to submit a proposal for a book in this series, contact:

Mehdi Khosrowpour, Senior Editor
Idea Group Publishing
Olde Liberty Square
4811 Jonestown Road, Suite 230
Harrisburg, PA 17109
1-800-345-4332

Table of Contents

PREFACE

As the literature has recently stressed, information systems (IS) and information technology (IT) applications provide the central decision support infrastructure for addressing managerial complexities and developing strategies for operating in a global business environment. Yet, despite the current research emphasis upon strategic concerns, many of the technological and managerial challenges of operating internationally are being addressed by corporations through information technology applications at the *functional levels* of the organization. Subsystems of the firm's overall information system continue to play key roles in the effort to achieve overall system integration and strategic advantage. These major subsystems, which have long included marketing information systems, financial information systems, production planning and control information systems, and human resource information systems, increasingly share databases and information resources while at the same time continuing to support unique global applications. There is little doubt that system design and implementation of strategic global information systems requires a solid understanding of the issues at the functional and subsystem levels.

While keeping in mind the role of the functions, it is also necessary to simultaneously extend the traditional domestic systems models to include international variables and unique information requirements necessary to meet the needs of the global organization. Thus, this book is designed to address the need for an organized examination of issues and technology applications at the functional levels of the organization as they contribute to the firm's global information systems and strategic posture. Topic coverage flows from a broad overview of global business management drivers and global organizational responses to a more focused examination of information subsystem applications of the functional areas of management. The final section ties these themes together with an emphasis on relevant information technology issues that have implications for organizational change and leadership challenges in the changing global marketplace. The level of analysis throughout the book is the organization, whether U.S.-based or foreign, in the context of the international business environment.

In particular, Section I sets the stage for the book by addressing broad issues relevant to globalization of the marketplace and globalization of the organization. This overview addresses both external elements of the global environment as well as those factors that affect internal consistency through functional linkages. The sections that follow then address specific IS /IT applications and issues in the areas of international marketing, finance, accounting, manufacturing and logistics, research and development (R&D), and human resource management. The emphasis in each chapter is on those issues that make the design, development, implementation and management of information systems and technology applications more difficult internationally (i.e., in comparison to a strictly domestic perspective). It should be noted that the finance section is limited primarily to financial services since many of the current research endeavors have been focused in this domain. Also, although R&D is not typically included as a functional dimension, we believe that its significance in global business activity is immense. With the advent of time-based competition, it has become apparent (from the IS/IT standpoint) that the R&D function deserves management attention akin to that traditionally accorded to the line functions of business.

Not surprisingly, research in international, functionally-oriented information systems and technology is scarce. Although a growing number of IS research efforts are examining these issues, much of the important, integrative, interdisciplinary work is being reported by experts in the various business functions. As a result, many of the authors who have contributed to this effort are among the leading innovators in diverse management areas.

Many of the chapters in the book are primarily conceptual and a number of them report upon preliminary research. Since our purpose is to provide the timely reporting of ideas and preliminary work in areas in which the literature is currently scarce, this format provides readers with some background and guidance for further research endeavors and a means by which to obtain information. It represents the first broad-based attempt to extend the concepts of information subsystems to include the international dimensions. At this time we are not aware of any other efforts that address these issues from an interdisciplinary and cross functional approach.

This book fits well with the objectives and overall goal of the Global Information Technology Management Series. The more focused examination of global information systems and applications at the functional levels of the organization represents a natural progression from the broad overview of the first book in the series. The contribution of the current book lies in providing academicians with state-of-the-art knowledge on the topics, further research directions and challenges for an interdisciplinary approach to addressing the global issues of information technology management.

The book targets a similar audience as previous books in this series, i.e., IS academicians and practitioners. However, we believe that the material will interest an even broader audience that includes international business academicians as well as academicians across the functional business areas. It is also intended to provide educational support for executives and middle level management. It is necessary that global managers across all functions in the organization understand the benefits and pitfalls of information technology in order to support a more integrated approach and strategic orientation to international systems development.

The editors would like to thank the contributing authors for their cooperation and responsiveness in preparing revised drafts of their manuscripts. A special note of thanks goes to Robert Kauffman at New York University for his advice on preparing this book and also his help in soliciting and reviewing manuscripts for the section on financial services. The authors wish to acknowledge Dawn Colegrove at the University of South Carolina for her assistance with manuscript revisions and final preparations and Karen Lewis at Wake Forest University for secretarial assistance. For their encouragement, we also thank Dana Johnson, Dean of the School of Business and Accountancy at Wake Forest University, John Mathis, Chairman of the World Business Department and David Ricks, Vice President of Academic Affairs both at Thunderbird - The American Graduate School of International Management, and Bob Markland, Chairman of the Management Science Department at the University of South Carolina. Finally, we thank the editorial staff at Idea Group Publishing - and especially Mehdi Khosrowpour and Jan Travers who have provided an important forum for interdisciplinary endeavors such as this.

Candace Deans
Kirk Karwan

October 1993

SECTION 1

Perspectives on Global Management of Information Technology

This introductory section contains two chapters and serves as the foundation for a more focused examination of functional issues in the sections that follow. The chapters provide a background discussion of information technology management issues in the context of both the firm's external and internal international business environments. In chapter 1, Jim Senn presents an evaluation of the major economic factors that drive international business activity and the resulting challenges that are faced by organizations as a result of their involvement in the evolving global marketplace. He then links these global influences to the specific challenges of managing information technology. In the second chapter, editors Candace Deans and Kirk Karwan, build the argument for increased attention to systems development and information technology applications at the functional levels of the global organization. Their discussion highlights the importance of continually focusing and re-focusing on the strategic implications of the various (international) functional subsystems. They present a framework that suggests that a detailed understanding of these subsystems will be required before global strategic systems integration can be accomplished.

CHAPTER 1

Exploring the Globalization of Business: New Realities with Implications for Management of Information Technology

JAMES A. SENN
Information Technology Management Group (INTEG)
and
Georgia State University

International commerce is, of course, nothing new. Its origins date back many centuries. Along the path from yesterday to today, the world's traders have shaped the politics, the geography, as well as the business of the world. In the process, they have turned international trade into global business. They have been behind the transformation of organizations from regional to national, then multinational, and now to transnational.

Yet international, or global, business is newly discovered in many boardrooms and on a growing number of academic campuses. That such a discovery is important cannot be disputed. Yet understanding the reasons for the increased attention are another matter.

The discussion that follows explores the new realities of globalized business. Economic forces driving globalization are examined through a variety of examples representative of the activities of private sector organizations and governments around the world. This chapter also examines the high-level requirements for success by global firms. The concluding section of the chapter discusses the implications for managing information technology in global organizations. This section's purpose is not to provide answers about how global business can be conducted successfully, but rather to raise issues that will be explored in greater detail in the subsequent chapters of the book.

THE DRIVERS OF INTERNATIONAL BUSINESS

International business is first a matter of economics. Firms are seeking global opportunities because of five overwhelming economic factors: the chance to participate in large markets, the need to spread large cost bases, a need to serve customers, the desire of firms to escape low wage strategies, and the decreased importance of a home-country base.

Participation In Large Markets

It is well known that the principal economic powers of the world—the US, Japan, and Germany—are nations comprised of global traders. The US market of 250 million people is large, but the European Community's 345 million person region is larger. Then again, the Asian region has a still greater population and potential market opportunity. And so it goes. International business is driven by companies constantly seeking larger markets.

Add to this a second factor: the opening of entire regions that have been closed or inaccessible for any number of reasons (e.g., Russia, China, and parts of South America and Africa). Within some of these countries that tried to keep their trading borders closed have since been forced to open them to rejoin world economic processes. Brazil, for example, the largest market in South America, found it could not continue existence under its Law of Similars, legislation which closed the country to import of foreign-made goods.

Third, a new level of economic and political stability is emerging in many regions. As political powers have shifted, markets have become open and global traders have sought entry.

Spreading Large Fixed Costs

The cost of developing new products and services, or even bringing out the next generation of an existing product, is skyrocketing. In the semiconductor industry, when Motorola brought out the 68040 chip, it invested two years of effort and $70 million in research and development. Today, it is evident that the R & D for the next generation of chip will cost at least four to five times that of the last generation.

The information technology sector is not alone when it comes to the need for large research and development expenditures. The story is similar in virtually any industry. The development of a new drug in the 1980s required an R & D investment of approximately $50 million. Today the average R & D cost is more than $275 million. Yet the entire industry is under more scrutiny than ever to determine whether its profit taking is excessive.

To enjoy reasonable profits and recover R & D costs in these and other industries, firmsare being forced to seek international markets. It is likely that this is a long-term, irreversible trend that will affect a growing number of enterprises.

Meeting Customer Expectations

Even if a company does not view itself as a global competitor, it may have no choice but to focus on international commerce because of the need to serve its customers, many of whom themselves may be heavily involved in international business. One of the principle drivers for the expansion of US companies such as the package carriers Federal Express and United Parcel Service (UPS) into international markets was demand from their best customers. Each needed to ship parcels outside of North America with the same level of convenience, accountability, and speed to which they had grown accustomed in local markets. Federal Express and UPS could have foregone the business opportunity, but doing so would have surely created other risks: encouraging their best customers to turn their international business over to competitors such as DHL and TNT. The risks were considered unacceptable, especially in light of growing long-term opportunities.

Escaping The Low Wage Strategy

The level of industrial development in countries demonstrates the impact of wages as an economic driver. As developing countries and their most important industries slide along the continuum from undeveloped to developed, the average wage climbs. A review of wage and salary data from the last several decades shows that countries such as Japan, newly industrialized countries (NICs) like the Republic of South Korea, and now the next generation of NICs (perhaps Mexico, Malaysia, and Indonesia) incur successively higher wages. Comparable patterns are followed in each of these countries:

1. Industries gain a market foothold following a strategy as the low-cost producer based on cheap labor.
2. The companies gain market identity, useful as a basis from which to develop their own brand names.
3. Salaries and wages of workers escalate as the company begins to

enjoy new market opportunities.
4. Low wages cease to be a basis of advantage for the company or the
   country.

If determined to do so, it appears that countries can develop
selected industrial capabilities very quickly. For example, in 1980,
the Republic of South Korea did not have a semiconductor industry.
Today, it is the third country, after the United States and Japan, to
produce advanced types of semiconductor chips. Malaysia, an
emerging industrialized country, was once thought of only as a
supplier of commodity products. Now it is the third largest assem-
bler of semiconductors and is beginning to develop an automobile
industry.

In the long run, neither companies nor countries can compete
exclusively on the basis of low wages. Rather they must seek
participation in world commerce by providing products that, far from
being commodities, are perceived as having meaningful value added.
Selling those products drives countries and their industrial firms
into international markets.

Recognizing the Decreasing Importance of National Origin

People around the world tend to classify companies based on their
national origin, rather than the markets in which they do business,
Yet the leading global firms are reshaping themselves from national
to transnational competitors. A tangled web of international links is
typically the result.

Americans view Honda as a Japanese automobile and Reebok as
an American sneaker. The British view Rover as an English automobile and Adidas as a German sneaker. But, in international business
the home base is often as deceiving as the national ownership of the
enterprise. Honda manufacturers more automobiles in the US than
in Japan, employs more American workers than Japanese, generates more revenues in the US than it does in Japan, and even exports
American-designed and American-made autos to Japan. In the
United Kingdom, Honda also manufacturers many Rover automobiles. Yet because its headquarters is in Japan, it is viewed around
the world as a Japanese firm. The British sneaker carrying the
Reebok label is actually owned by an American company. But the
sneakers themselves are manufactured in Asian factories, often in
the same factories that make products for competitors Adidas and
Nike.

The tangled web of international links is not limited to manufacturing firms. Burger King is owned by the English firm Grand
Metropolitan while Holiday Inn, the American lodging company that
started the roadside motel phenomenon, is a business unit of

Multinational Firms	Global Firms
• Centralized management and decision making	• Decentralized management and decision making
• Hierarchical organization structure with top down managerial authority	• Assigned managerial authority based on know-how and location rather than position in hierarchy
• Country-based focus	•• Regional globalization
• Export orientation in supplying customer needs	• Manufacture throughout the world at the best locations to supply customer needs
• Research and development performed at headquarters	• Research and development performed anywhere in the world where the firm is best served
• Business knowledge internalized	• Business knowledge distributed between parts of the organization and key component and service suppliers
• Manufacturing seeks to drive consumption	• Consumption leads manufacturing

Table 1: How Global Firms are Different

England's Bass PLC. Holiday Inn has more American employees than UK employees and generates more revenue and profit in the US than in the UK. Is Holiday Inn an American company, a British company, or are the question and answer both irrelevant?

Globalization is changing the very meaning of "national company", making it difficult to distinguish between a home and foreign firm. Hence the description *transnational* is often applied: the organization views itself as a single firm that spans many countries, in contrast to the multinational company which has a home country and any number of foreign "daughters" (Drucker, 1989, pp. 124-125).

REQUIREMENTS FOR GLOBALIZATION

Although the leading global companies compete across a variety of industries in many different markets, there is an emerging pattern of strengths that these companies have. This section describes those requirements for successful global competition. (Table 1 summarizes differences between multinational and global firms.)

Be Large, But Lean

It appears that global companies have to reach a critical size to compete successfully with other world businesses. Yet, in addition to being large, they must also be lean. The resizing that many international companies are undergoing is as much a result of global competition as it is weak economic conditions at home, as the following examples suggest:

- IBM, the world's largest computer company, is in a well publicized transition from a 340,000 person company to one of 225,000 employees. It sells around the world and is challenged by competitors who are also changing the foundations of IT around the globe.
- Asea Brown Boveri, which became the world's biggest electrical engineering manufacturer in 1987—a result of mergers—cut its corporate staff from 4000 to have followed, each aimed at making the firm much leaner and more powerful at the same time.
- British Telecom (now officially known as BT) was once the only telecommunications service provider in the United Kingdom. Now it faces formidable internal competition due to deregulation and privatization in the UK. At the same time, BT is expanding throughout the world. Even as it does so, it is substantially reducing the size of the company (the latest wave of downsizing will eliminate an estimated 15,000 jobs) to become leaner even as its markets become larger.

These representative experiences go well beyond the current management philosophy of downsizing and delayering, suggesting that global firms must be large and lean at the same time.

Acquire Technology and Ideas From Anywhere

When companies think of themselves as transnational (or even non-national), they tend to look beyond borders to acquire the best technology available. They also seek to acquire product and process ideas from throughout their organization without regard for national origin. Countless examples are available:

- When Otis Elevator, headquartered in Hartford, Connecticut, recently developed a new line of fast, quiet elevators, it reached out internationally to the extent that
    - Motor drives were designed in Japan,
    - The door system was perfected in France,
    - Electronics were handed in Germany,
    - Small gear components were developed in Spain,
    - Systems integration was performed in Farmington,

Connecticut (*Business Week*, May 14, 1990).

- When Honda decided to begin manufacture of a new compact station wagon, it looked across the world markets it served to find the best location at which to develop the product. In the end, Honda's first station wagon was designed in the company's Marysville, Ohio facility. When the time was right to move from design to production, the Ohio facility was selected at the manufacturing site as well. Hence Honda now *exports* American designed, American made Honda (Japanese) automobiles to Europe and Japan from the United States.
- The IBM Corporation was reported several years ago to have closed all but one of its magnetic media research centers. The one center it maintained was in Japan, far from its New York headquarters, where it felt it was getting the best return on its R & D investment.
- Asea Brown Boveri, formed in 1987 out of the merger of Sweden's Asea and Switzerland's Brown Boveri, has 4000 profit centers around the world, each focusing on products and services it handles better than any other facility. National location is not a principal consideration, but an afterthought (if it is considered at all).

Whether the company is American, Japanese, or of virtually any other national origin, it is increasingly evident that global companies seek to acquire the best ideas and most effective technology from anywhere in the world.

Supply Foreign Markets Locally

As the preceding examples of Honda and Otis have suggested, when companies view themselves as non-national, they become part of the country in which they are based. They do not rely on home facilities for the supply of products, components and parts, but rather rely on the local markets.

As globalization proliferates, the use of local sourcing is becoming widespread. The practices of the Ford Motor Company outside its US home are typical: in supporting its assembly facilities in the United Kingdom, Ford makes or buys over 90 percent of its parts, supplies, and machinery in Europe. Rarely do components come from the US.

Manage Products as Composites

The combination of global linkages, multicountry supply chains, and the sourcing of the best ideas and technologies regardless of national origin has brought about still another increasingly familiar characteristic in today's global business community: products are becoming composites. The following illustration demonstrates how products are often composites of the global services of many nations:

1. In London a high-fashion buyer views a line of clothes devised by a New York designer, placing a large custom order after the viewing.
2. Within an hour after the order, the designer sends, via satellite, the *drawings* for making the clothes to a ground station in Hong Kong. The details are transmitted by a fiber optic ground link to the manufacturing facility where they appear on the very high resolution workstation display of the manufacturing engineer who will take responsibility for the order. By viewing the drawings on the console, the manufacturing engineer determines the best way to transform the drawings into prototype garments.
3. The prototypes are manufactured in a Chinese factory, perhaps using computer-aided manufacturing and flexible manufacturing cells.
4. Designer, buyer, manufacturing engineer, and factory supervisor review the prototype without traveling to a central location. Videoconferencing makes the around-the-globe review possible.
5. With the prototypes approved, manufacturing gets underway. In less than 6 weeks after the order is placed, the finished goods *arrive* in London at the buyer's designated location.

At a growing rate, this manufacturing paradigm is replacing the ways and means of multinationals of the past.

MEETING INTERNATIONAL BUSINESS CHALLENGES

There is a tendency for inexperienced managers to view international business as nothing more than their local business, but on a larger scale. Nothing could be farther from the truth. This section outlines several of the most dramatic challenges. Subsequent chapters of the book describe other challenges in greater detail.

Interconnection Beyond Boundaries

In order for an enterprise to be successful in global business, it must develop the capability (whether at the corporate, business unit, or subsidiary level) to interconnect with business partners and key constituents. Perhaps even more important is the capability to interconnect with customers, suppliers, and government agencies. Firms that cannot interconnect beyond their borders are seriously hindered.

At an international level, the sharing of information is not an option but a requirement. Government agencies want to know about the movement of goods and documents in advance. They are doing their best to fulfill their obligations by participating in an information network. Customs and taxation agencies, as well as insurance brokers, rely heavily on electronic sharing of information.

The Cargonaut and Sagitta systems in the Netherlands or Tradenet in Singapore are typical of those systems with which companies must interconnect when conducting cross-border transactions. Sharing information by way of such systems also reduces process time, since there is no delay awaiting the movement of documents or the location of papers. It also reduces costs and errors resulting from clerical activities.

On the island state of Singapore, whose total volume of trade is three times its gross domestic product, the government must coordinate more than 10,000 international commerce applications per day across more than 20 government agencies. Prior to implementing the highly regarded Tradenet network, anyone seeking to import goods required approximately a half day of time to obtain the necessary approvals. Meanwhile the goods sat. Since the implementation of Tradenet where firms now communicate with the government electronically, 95 percent of all approvals are granted electronically within 15 minutes while the cost of approval is 1/10 of its former cost.

Because of inter-networking, the network *is* the system (and often the success of the business relationship is an outgrowth of the success of the network). The capabilities of the communications network are more important than the computing systems of which the network is comprised. Diverse hardware, software, and communications platforms should always be assumed. Rather than focusing on ways to help business partners acquire the right computing equipment or the right system, IT professionals' primary emphasis must be on achieving the right interconnection.

Meet Differing Legal Requirements

Laws influencing international business vary dramatically between countries, even if they border one another in the same geographic region. Restrictions on the capture, movement, and use of personal information is perhaps the most widely debated issue. But many other subtle issues affect business practice in some countries, including: government mandated employee profit sharing, varying benefit packages, or co-determination whereby employees are guaranteed seats on governing boards.

Accommodate Diverse Business Practices and Customs

That business is a universal practice is a myth. Even in the most basic areas there appears to be more diversity than similarity. Consider the following:

- Since 1945, getting and keeping market share (rather than profit maximization) has driven Japan's global companies. In the West, product prices aredriven by costs and profit: businesses arrive at prices by adding up the costs of product materials, components and assemblies and then adding overhead and profit. In Japan, many companies start with a target market share, estimate the price needed to get that share, and then work backwards, pushing down the cost of components until the target price is met.
- 7-Eleven shops in Tokyo place stock orders every four hours. Warehousing and transport expenses make up 8 - 9% of total product cost—twice the level in America. Streets are clogged by vans delivering small shipments, even a loaf or two of bread. There is little interest in using IT to change these practices.
- In North America, businesses traditionally set budgets every 12 months. In other parts of the world, practices differ dramatically. In a number of countries, for instance, budgets are set every 6 months under a philosophy that shorter budget periods give managers greater control over performance.
- The chart of accounts used to run business units within the bounds of a country often vary dramatically because of laws, taxation, employee benefits, and other government or union imposed requirements in addition to usual and customary business practices.

On top of these differences, the normal amount of work varies tremendously from country to country, directly affecting the management of businesses (see Table 2). In some areas, information technology cannot produce an effect without bringing about change

Work Practice	France	Germany	Japan	United States
• Labor hours (annual)	1675	1655	2160	1975
• % of days absent*	8%	9%	2%	3%
• Number paid vacation days and holidays	35	40	25	23
• Average hourly cost to employer per industrial worker (including benefits and taxes)	$17.79	$26.90	$19.23	$15.89

* Not including vacation or holidays

Source: United States Bureau of Labor Statistics; German Federal Labor Office; John Naisbitt *Trend Letter*

Table 2: Differences in Work Practices Between Countries

because the issues are more culturally based than they are part of business practice. Instead, companies must adjust their systems to accommodate the differences even as they seek to maintain a uniform corporate perspective on performance assessment and reporting.

IT MANAGEMENT ISSUES

Information technology managers must first recognize the role of information technology in international business and how IT has additional attributes when compared to its domestic role. One must also then deal with the additional challenges brought about by global practices.

Recognize The Role of IT

Even the most cursory analysis of international business will quickly reveal that the role of information technology is not one of automation, but rather to unlock business potential. Unless companies competing globally maximize their information technology capability, they have little chance of succeeding in achieving their international objectives or even in preserving their current levels of international success.

From the consumer viewpoint, information technology must assume four strategic roles:

- *Accommodate Local Taste*—World products are not necessarily global products. Flexible manufacturing and customized products are becoming mandatory for competition in the world market. Underlying the means to provide for these is a vast array of IT resources.
- *Enable Local Presence*—As firms expand outside their national boundaries, given the realities of the changing business playing field, they must give greater attention to establishing and supporting a local presence. Information flow among decision makers and various locations is fundamental to this strategy.
- *Compress Business Response Time*—Removing time from business processes is a necessity and not an option. An organization's IT capabilities take on strategic value when they allow the firm to overcome the barrier of response time.
- *Provide A Single Point of Interface*—As trading blocs continue to grow in importance, global firms will find it mandatory to provide across the regions a single presence point honoring all manufacturing, warranty, and service agreements.

Develop Common Systems

Determining whether information technology and systems should be common globally or tailor-made to fit market regions will provoke vigorous discussion between corporate and country units. So will paying for them. The growing importance of accommodating local taste while achieving the levels of effectiveness firms need to compete across many borders also raises a question of uniformity across information systems: should applications be tailor-made to fit local needs or common across markets, thus having a universal design?

More internationally focused firms are emphasizing the use of common systems. Corporate information systems professionals define data standards, processing characteristics, and application interfaces. Local development teams carry out the implementation, giving them ownership and involvement. At the same time, they pass back experience that may influence common system features as the applications evolve.

Create A Suitable Architecture

The need for a coherent architecture is often realized as soon as an enterprise undertakes globalization of its information systems. Yet information technology components will frequently vary from country to country, often because of the importance of supporting the national vendor. In some areas, such as telecommunications, there are few viable options other than to use the nationally designated provider (e.g., the PTT to provide communication lines).

Many firms may find that they do not have a true architecture, but rather a series of incompatible facilities, and worse yet, incompatible application systems. The accrual of long-run business advantages will only occur when firms establish a platform from which infrastructure can be developed—computing, network, data, and software—and on which they can base all applications.

Facilitate Cross-Border Services

Companies often begin their success within national borders and then seek to expand internationally. Seldom is the reason for their success wholly-based on a manufactured product but rather it encompasses a broad range of support services. Customers grow to expect these same services anywhere the company does business. Or, alternatively, the chance of duplicating the firm's success internationally without the identical level of services may be limited.

The IT director typically faces the same requirement, even though customs and practices, laws, and technology platforms differ. In spite of it all, the international firm faces a basic requirement: *Provide all services-everything-across borders, and not just within them.*

Support Work With More People

Expanding internationally brings with it the need to involve a greater number of individuals in formulation of strategies and management of business processes. Yet this can be challenging to even the most seasoned manager. Usually the key participant in the expanded business process is a country manager, area vice president, or comparable executive. Such a senior person is used to being *the* decision maker for the region, having both responsibility and accountability. Likewise, the business unit he or she manages typically has its own planning process. A transition from a multinational to global structure may threaten the country process and country manager, creating tremendous challenges to those presenting an outside viewpoint.

SUMMARY

International business is not an option, but a requirement for many organizations today. Likewise, it is an area of opportunity for countries and entire regions. As discussed in this chapter, in both instances there may be no alternative than to seek and develop international markets.

The deployment of information systems and technology in international commerce, where extended beyond the bounds of traditional organizations, raises new questions for the IT manager in particular and the enterprise in general. How these questions are addressed and answered will largely determine the impact and role that IT will have on the globalization process of the firm.

REFERENCES

Drucker, Peter F., *The New Realities*. New York, Harper & Row, 1989.
"The Stateless Corporation," *Business Week*. (May 14, 1990) pp. 98-106.

CHAPTER 2

Exploring the Globalization of the Organization: New Realities for Information Systems Design, Information Technology Applications, and Strategy

P. CANDACE DEANS
Thunderbird - The American Graduate School
of International Management

KIRK R. KARWAN
University of South Carolina

An array of global business forces are currently working in unison to create an environment of uncertainty and fast-paced change. In order to compete, companies must respond in ways which are alien to their very cultural and organizational foundations. Advancements in information technology (IT) provide an additional element of concern as companies strive to implement IT applications that keep them competitive and at times provide competitive advantage. As firms develop global information systems (IS) and IT applications that complement overall international and strategic goals, the inherent complexities of the international business environment become apparent. A model is presented in this chapter that substantiates the significance of understanding IS/IT applications at the functional levels of the organization as they contribute to the overall strategic goals of the firm. This framework lays the foundation for a more focused examination of the relationships among international busi-

ness concerns and information technology applications developed for each of the functional areas of business.

INTRODUCTION

Organizations are undergoing radical change as a result of their efforts to respond to the changing global marketplace and information technology breakthroughs. In order to meet the challenge and compete in a marketplace with new rules, companies are employing information technologies to reengineer their entire business operations. The evolution of global companies has resulted in the need for new organizational structures and architectures to more adequately support the complexities of operating in a politically, economically, and culturally diverse international business environment. Companies must face the reality of global competition for products and services that in turn requires new strategies, technologies, and leadership responses.

Change is the constant in this emerging dynamic environment. Success will reflect the company's ability to anticipate change, manage change, and respond to change in ways that give the organization a competitive advantage. Solutions to today's organizational problems will need to be addressed through global information technology (IT) applications both at the strategic and functional levels of the organization. In fact, it is our contention that multinational corporations (MNCs) need to pay attention to the ways in which functional issues are being addressed before meaningful integration and strategic decisions can be made. Specifically, systems development by end users in the functional areas of MNCs is leading to solutions that better meet the needs of those utilizing the applications.

In this chapter, we begin with a discussion of general business forces impacting the organization and its strategic position in a global marketplace. We then shift to information technology trends contributing to these changes and their potential for solving global business problems. These global business forces and technological trends are contributing to a greater emphasis on end user involvement in systems development and IT applications. Implications of these influences on strategy and systems planning are then discussed. Finally, we develop a model that extends the domestic conceptualization of functional information subsystems to include the unique information requirements of the international business environment. This extended model contributes a new dimension to current thought in international information systems research and application and lays the foundation for the remainder of the book.

GENERAL BUSINESS FORCES IMPACTING THE GLOBAL ORGANIZATION

As discussed by Jim Senn in the first chapter, there are many global business drivers transforming organizations and influencing strategic decisions. As companies strive to globalize their business operations it becomes necessary to view the business world from a different perspective. Bartlett and Ghoshal (1992) advocate a new management mentality as a key component of the "transnational solution" and one that is necessary for success in the international business arena.

Wendt (1993) describes the emergence of transnational corporations as a major force transforming not only the business world but also the way in which politics and world economies are bound together. He views the transnational challenge as part of the familiar domain of competition, but one of a more fierce kind in which national boundaries are becoming more blurred and the global market is becoming increasingly and relentlessly interconnected. An array of complex issues emerges as executives deal with decisions involving international mergers, strategic alliances, joint ventures, adequate organizational structures and architectures, managerial competence to compete in global markets, and continuous training of the workforce. The destiny of our world is increasingly being driven by these large global companies.

Globalization of Competition

Today, companies compete in a global market. The world is fast becoming one market and competition has become more fierce as companies strive to survive in an international environment unfamiliar to many. Companies must develop the capabilities to serve the global customer anywhere in the world and find ways to access markets all over the world. Many companies must become comfortable in the three major world markets of North America, Europe and Asia. In many cases, it may be necessary to find allies in markets that are difficult to penetrate. Failure to respond to these types of challenges clearly puts the firm at a competitive disadvantage.

As new pressures transform global competitive strategies, companies are reevaluating the adequacy of their organizational structures, management of processes to support worldwide operations, and technology solutions that provide competitive advantage. Stalk, Evans and Shulman (1992) describe today's global competitive game as "less like chess and more like an interactive video game." As Porter (1990) emphasizes, a combination of company strategy and national circumstances are necessary to ultimately achieve competitive advantage.

New Global Strategies

New global strategies are evolving as companies strive to meet the demands of a more competitive marketplace. As stressed by Hamel and Prahalad (1990), simply imitating global competitors in an effort to attain the same cost and quality advantages will not lead to revitalization of company competitiveness. Today's global marketplace demands rethinking many of the basic concepts of strategy. Prahalad and Hamel (1990) advocate core competencies as the focus of corporate strategy and the winning business philosophy for companies today. Stalk, Evans and Shulman (1992) argue that competition based on capabilities better defines the new rules of corporate strategy. The authors conclude that a combination of core competencies and capabilities may represent an appropriate model of strategy for corporations today. These examples are representative of the evolving thought that is defining new rules for developing winning global strategies.

Business Process Reengineering

Reengineering is basically a fundamental rethinking of the organizational objectives and redesign of business operations to meet those objectives. Global market forces provide the impetus for companies to think in new ways about their organizational goals. Information technology breakthroughs provide the means by which to implement solutions to meet new organizational objectives.

Hammer and Clampy (1993) describe the aim of reengineering as a quantum leap in performance rather than as a series of incremental improvements. They argue that the basic theory and foundations upon which the modern organization is founded no longer works in a world of rapid change and global competition. Since the goal of reengineering efforts should focus on creating value for customers, this may mean that companies must rethink their strategies and supporting infrastructure. Reinventing the organization requires a new kind of leadership. Although the process is not easy, the benefits may be substantial. Companies have little choice but to reevaluate their organizations as they strive to survive in the face of fierce global competition.

Global Quality Initiatives

Today's customer-driven economy dictates that companies pay attention to quality. In a global marketplace, customers will buy those products that offer the highest quality at the lowest cost and products and services compete with other products and services from all over the world. As a result, quality initiatives have become an important component of both corporate and international business strategy. In fact, in the global economy, quality is fast becoming the international standard for trade. Dobyns and Crawford-Mason (1991) believe that companies must begin today to develop a quality-based culture simply to remain competitive.

On an international scale, quality systems will provide the means of assuring consistency and conformity in products and services in order to meet varying worldwide standards and customer expectations. The standards that are currently being adopted to meet the needs of global quality systems are the ISO-9000 series of standards. These standards originated in the European Community's (EC) plan to become a single market. They provide the assurance that products moving across national borders will meet defined quality standards regardless of the country of origin. ISO-9000 standards have been adopted by the EC and over 55 nations as their voluntary quality guidelines. More than 600 U.S. company sites were registered to at least one ISO-9000 standard as of December 1992 and the number continues to grow (Breitenberg, 1993). As the importance of the standard is realized and the advantage as a competitive marketing tool is recognized, pressure to become ISO-certified will increase.

Diversity of the Work-force

Cultural diversity in the international workforce is a managerial challenge that has become reality. Understanding cultural differences and responding to these differences effectively has become an important component of management training. No longer is cross-cultural training directed solely for managers who have been targeted for assignments in other countries. Greater emphasis on cross-functional teamwork and project-oriented tasks requires enhanced communication skills in order to effectively deal with people from diverse cultural backgrounds.

A truly global workforce is emerging that has caused major shifts in how and where the world's work is accomplished (Flax, 1992). Labor forces in other parts of the world are highly capable and increasingly well educated. Sophisticated work is being moved to other countries around the globe. There has been an evolution in the labor market from one that is regional to one that is national, and now international (Johnston, 1991).

IMPACTS OF INFORMATION TECHNOLOGY ON THE GLOBAL ORGANIZATION

As companies strive to meet the challenges of customer satisfaction, business reengineering, strategic alliances, downsizing, empowering employees, enhanced teamwork, and an increasingly diverse work-force, information technology provides the vehicle to make things happen. Companies have capabilities today that were not imagined even ten years ago. The global organization can be tied together through electronic mail connections that provide communications capability superior to phone links. Facsimile has quickly become an essential means of global communication. Physical proximity is no longer necessary to achieve the same level of project performance that once required expensive travel time and personal meetings. The companies that gain competitive advantage will be those that use these technological breakthroughs in ways that provide an advantage over the competition.

Telecommunications Technology

Advancements in telecommunications technology have clearly contributed to a more integrated global economy. Communications technologies force organizations to view the world from a different perspective. Today, even smaller companies with international business operations are discovering the advantages of the right investments in telecommunications (Resnick, 1993). Facsimile services, cellular phones, notebook computers, electronic mail, on-line databases, and videoconferencing systems are becoming commonplace in companies around the world.

The reduced price for videoconferencing equipment, for example, is a major breakthrough promoting global business operations. This technology is replacing travel costs and time and many companies are becoming more reluctant to put employees on planes. The benefits are substantial for companies that spend hundreds of thousands of dollars in plane tickets. It is predicted that videoconferencing will soon become as commonplace as fax is today. In fact, many business cards already now show a teleconferencing number along with fax, email and phone. The advantages are particularly apparent for international operations, although, at this point, videoconferencing equipment is barred from entry by local customs rules in some countries and incompatible national phone service standards also present difficulties in other parts of the world (Resnick, 1993).

In summary, telecommunications systems are no longer viewed as providing the firm a competitive advantage. They are simply a cost of doing business today. The key is to find innovative solutions that maximize return on investments.

Wireless Networks / Mobile Communication

Wireless networks are the wave of the future. This technological breakthrough allows the user to communicate, for example, over Internet by adding an antenna type device to a notebook computer similar to using a cellular phone. Information is readily available to the user regardless of location and time. As the technology becomes easier to use, end-user computing becomes commonplace, leading to greater interest in applications development. End users will be encouraged to develop applications to solve their specific problems, thus providing better decision making tools.

Mobile communication technologies are transforming the way work gets done. Cellular phones, for example, make it possible to better utilize time spans that were once wasted. The use of laptops in the field to communicate data and information has provided innovative means by which to become more efficient in operations and responsive to customer needs. Worldwide access to data and information is clearly changing the nature of international business transactions.

Client / Server Technology

Client / server technology is being touted as the IT foundation for the next decade. The client is typically a desktop computer which requests information or services from a server, which may be another PC, mainframe, or other intelligent device. This technology allows computer resources to be utilized more effectively. It is possible for information to be distributed to any client or server regardless of location. A major advantage to the organization is the ability to integrate information systems across the functional dimensions of the organization. Furthermore, this technology allows for the trans-formation of work flows and a means for better meeting the needs of all workers in the organization. As application development is more readily transferred to the end user, faster solutions and changes can be made in order to meet the market demands of a highly competitive, global economy. Client / server computing provides advantages for streamlining business processes, enhancing the cost effective use of resources, empowering workers with better information, and im-proving customer service.

Object-Oriented Technology

Object-oriented programming is also a wave of the future. This breakthrough has simplified the application development process and resulted in faster creation of software. The time savings in development and productivity have been reported to be substantial, although the benefits may go beyond that of time and productivity. The ease of use of this technology will make it possible for those more familiar with business processes to develop appropriate applica-tions. This will lead to improved systems that more closely meet the needs of end users.

End User Computing

As we have noted, current information technology trends are clearly leading to greater involvement by the end user. In an international environment, this may lead to development of better tools for decision making and application development that better address complexities and provide solutions for meeting the specific needs of local markets and customer expectations in those markets. Client /server technology is driving the move toward dispersing applications development to those who implement solutions for marketing, manufacturing and human resources. In the international environment, these applications are being developed to address issues at the functional levels of the organization. Currently, in many companies, information systems applications are being farmed out to those units managing a specific process or function in the company. Current global trends and information technology developments promote a natural progression toward more dispersed development of applications that more adequately meet the needs of an evolving organization.

STRATEGIC IMPLICATIONS AND SYSTEMS PLANNING FOR GLOBAL SUCCESS

Setting up information technology strategies to support the firm's global mission is clearly a complex task. Today, companies are dependent on information technology applications and global networks for survival. Flax (1992) advocates that companies that are successful at managing their IT will also be successful at managing their business strategy worldwide. Information technology can aid in all types of decision making that involve worldwide customer preferences, changing regulations in foreign markets, and political information on countries in which a firm has business operations. Keen (1992) stresses the importance of linking the strategic IT plan with the firm's global IT strategies. These linkages become even more imperative as companies expand their operations to new global markets.

Cultural issues become critical in the development of international systems and support applications. This is an aspect often overlooked by companies with limited experience in the international arena. Information systems and applications developed for one context may not be appropriate or fit the needs of users from other cultures. It is necessary that those involved with the design of international systems and applications be aware of these issues and take the necessary precautions.

Strategic Implications

The design and development of information systems and information technology applications should support the global business strategy of the organization. Information technology has long been recognized as a means by which the firm may attain competitive advantage. Deans and Karwan (1989) provide empirical evidence that substantiates the potential power and perceived role of IT to support the firm's international business operations and strategic initiatives.

Information has become one of the firm's most important assets and, as such, should be treated as an integral component of strategic initiatives. Those companies that learn to access and utilize information most effectively will clearly prosper in the new global marketplace. Effective development and utilization of both external and internal databases will be crucial to effective managerial strategies. Executive Information Systems (EIS) are currently playing a significant role in the utilization of information to support executive level decision making, and particularly, in managing the more complex scope of international managerial challenges.

Flax (1992) provides the following suggestions for IT executives as they strive for success in the global arena:

1. Be proactive in the development of IT applications and systems
2. Consult with senior operating managers all over the world
3. Find the business imperatives first - then link them to the technology
4. Identify the information needed - then develop the system for getting it reliably
5. Develop systems that support the company's real life business needs.

Planning for Global Systems and IT Applications

Establishing a global IT strategic plan that spans the firm's international operations is not without its problems. Recognizing that this plan is essential and attaining top management support are paramount for the success of international IS and IT initiatives. Deans and Karwan (1991) provide research findings that confirm the efforts of many multinational companies to establish information systems planning arrangements for their international business operations. As expected, these efforts are more pronounced in firms with greater international business involvement. The manner in which these initiatives are being implemented, however, varies considerably from one company to another. At one extreme, some companies have established separate departments for their international information systems planning to address the unique concerns associated with setting up communications networks and developing IT applications to support business operations that must incorporate different legal constraints, government regulations, variations in accounting systems, and cultural differences that impact systems development and implementation. Other companies have established a separate international IS group within the corporate information systems department or international business department. In many other companies, the responsibility is distributed to geographical IS managers or managers responsible for local subsidiary operations.

Technological advancements are currently supporting distribution of control and autonomy in the development of IT applications to support foreign operations. Companies appear to be in a learning stage as they experiment with managerial and organizational changes necessary to move toward more autonomous and distributed IT support. Organizational culture, top management support and encouragement, managerial capability, experience with international business activity, and the transfer of technology internationally all play a part in the direction companies take. Tradeoffs vary depending on the industry in which the firm competes and the pace with which the competition forces change.

GLOBAL ORGANIZATIONAL INFORMATION SUBSYSTEMS: AN EXTENSION OF THE DOMESTIC MODEL

Given the current trends toward greater end user involvement in IS and IT initiatives, increased emphasis on application development at the functional dimensions of the organization should be expected. In his IS textbook, McLeod (1993, and earlier editions) describes the information subsystems that support decision making at the functional levels of the organization. According to McLeod, these major subsystems include marketing information systems, manufacturing information systems, financial information systems, and human resource information systems, with information from each of these providing the input for executive information systems that support strategic level decision making. Although this representation is strictly conceptual, McLeod's model recognizes the special information needs of particular functions or departments and how these information systems meet those requirements. The McLeod model defines subsystems along functional lines because this has traditionally been the most typical organizational arrangement. Although information subsystems might also be represented as levels of management, resource flows, or as business processes, such models are less common in practice.

Figure 1 depicts one extension of the original McLeod Model that incorporates additional information requirements specific to the needs of international business decision makers. External data and information that flow into the subsystems and strategic planning systems incorporate information necessary for managing operations outside the firm's home country. Marketing systems, for example, may include information requirements about worldwide consumer preferences and market conditions in various countries. Human resource information subsystems will incorporate additional data on wage fluctuations, expatriate data, and varying payroll systems. International financial subsystems require up-to-the-minute data and information concerning foreign financial markets and interest and exchange rates.

Note in the figure that we have included one area of management that McLeod's model has long overlooked, i.e., that of research and development. As competition has intensified to develop and market new products and as new processes have given rise to competitive advantages in operations, corporations have sought to better manage and provide more effective supervision for their R&D groups. Since the key people in multinational organizations are often dispersed throughout the world, IT is playing the key role in bringing their combined expertise together. For long term profitability and survival, MNCs have not only elevated the R&D function within the organization but are also emphasizing infrastructure development (through IT) for improved R&D.

As depicted in Figure 1, external data may be obtained from the

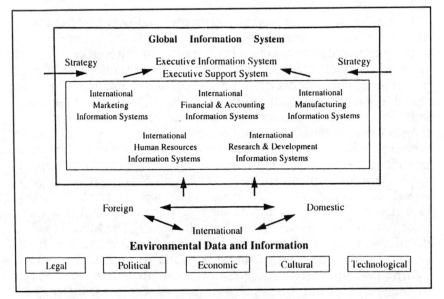

Figure 1: Global Oranizational Information Subsystems

domestic, international and foreign environments in which the firm operates. The domestic environment represents the home country in which the firm resides. The foreign environments include those of all countries in which the firm has operations or has information needs. The international environment represents the interaction of forces among foreign environments and the firm's domestic country. Economic indicators, for example, may be needed for individual countries as well as for the overall international environment. Political, legal, cultural, economic, and technological data are all necessary inputs for decisions in and among given locations of the world.

This model is a conceptual representation that is useful as a point of reference for discussion. Currently, most international information systems research has focused on systems issues from a broad perspective (see, e.g., Deans et.al., 1991, or Ives and Jarvenpaa, 1991). Very little international information systems research has addressed issues at the application and functional subsystem levels. Although the functional subsystem inputs must clearly be integrated to ensure adherence to consistent global strategies, these systems will typically address the unique information requirements and end user needs of the complex international business environment. Information technology applications are usually developed at this level in response to the multitude of unstructured and complex decisions confronting the global firm. Integration is possible only after a detailed understanding is obtained of each of the functional subsystems.

Consider the developments that are occurring in each of the functional areas from the perspective of international business and IT applications:

• Marketing information systems have been recognized for some time as an effective means by which to organize and manage market and customer information. Given the many unique and complex variables specific to the international marketing function, the firm's information systems and technology applications may be utilized as an effective means by which to address the challenges imposed by differences in cultural, economic and technological environments. The decision variables and identified tradeoffs for international marketing problems must be approached from a different perspective than might be the case for a single domestic market.

• In a similar manner, international financial and accounting information systems are playing an increasingly important role in the global arena. Financial markets are highly dependent on a global interlinked network. Accounting systems and IT applications are playing a significant role in addressing the problems associated with different accounting systems, changing currency values, and volatility in exchange rates.

• Global operations provides, through the transformation process, products and services that embody the factors that are critical to success in one or more markets. Those competitive priorities that directly involve manufacturing (as well as services) relate to quality, delivery reliability and speed, cost and flexibility. Production planning and control information systems are being utilized to coordinate the global organization that competes on these dimensions while outsourcing from many countries, producing sub-assemblies in others, and conducting final assembly in yet others. The problems and complexities associated with information technology applications for the international production environment are only now being seriously addressed.

• Research and development is taking on an increasingly significant role in the international realm. Astute organizations have recognized that corporate product and process innovations are the result of a greater and more varied flow of new ideas and expertise among scientists, designers, engineers and managers in different countries. While accelerating the product (and process) development cycle, information technology plays perhaps the key role in making R&D a truly global endeavor. For example, the implementation of CAD / CAM systems has enabled companies to reduce the time required for design review, analysis, and modification and has enabled product and process tests to be coordinated while being undertaken in different countries.

• Human resource information systems (HRIS) have only recently been implemented in many companies and the literature addressing these issues is new. Human resource management is recognized as one of the most important dimensions of international management. On a global scale, there are many unique aspects to managing the human resource function. Human resource managers must design and administer programs for more than one national group of employees. Information technology applications may address solutions to such issue as international relocation and orientation, administrative services for expatriates, host government relations and wage administration.

Despite all these developments, the literature that integrates the international business function and IS/IT is sparse. Academic research that addresses the international dimensions of the functional business areas is extensive and the literature stream in many areas (e.g., international marketing, international accounting, international human resources) is well established. Academic research is also available (though widely dispersed) that addresses information systems and technology issues for the traditional business functions (e.g., marketing information systems, manufacturing information systems, accounting information systems). There is, however, a clear need to better integrate these streams of research thought in an

effort to reflect the realities of a truly global organizational orientation.

The remaining chapters in this book provide research findings and
preliminary work that address these concerns.Taken together, the
chapters provide researchers and practitioners with a base from
which to think about the issues and develop further the concepts
that link the international business functions, strategy, and IT.

SUMMARY

Globally oriented strategies will demand increasingly integrated
and coordinated information systems that link the firm's functional
areas while at the same time respond to unique functional needs.
Dependence on information systems, global communication networks, and information technology applications that provide competitive advantage are now a given. Companies must stay abreast of
technological breakthroughs, new global strategies, and rapid change.
The rules of survival have changed and those that can respond to the
demands of this new world of business operations will be tomorrow's
winners. These are exciting times with unprecedented opportunities
for change not only for business but for academicians that seize the
opportunities to respond to a new era of management.

REFERENCES

Bartlett, C.A. and Ghoshal, S. (1989). *Managing Across Borders*. Boston:
Harvard Business School Press.

Breitenberg, Maureen (1993). "ISO 9000," U.S. Department of Commerce Publication.

Deans, P.C. and Karwan, K.R. (1990). "MIS Planning: Incorporating the
International Dimension," *Proceedings of the Southeast Decision Sciences
Institute*, Columbia, South Carolina, 333.

Deans, P.C. and Karwan, K.R. (1989). "Information Technology, Strategy,
and the Multinational Corporation," *Proceedings of the Decisions Sciences
Institute*, New Orleans, Louisiana, 537-539.

Deans, P.C., Karwan, K.R., Goslar, M.D., Ricks, D.A., and Toyne, B.
(1991). "Identification of Key International Information Systems Issues in
U.S.-Based Multinational Corporations," *Journal of Management Information Systems*, 27-50.

Dobyns, L. and Crawford-Mason, C. (1991). *Quality or Else*. Boston:
Houghton Mifflin Company.

Hammer, M. and Champy, J. (1993). *Reengineering the Corporation*. New
York: Harper Business.

Flax, S. (1992, August-September). "Global IT Without Tears," *Beyond
Computing*, 19-26.

Hamel, G. and Prahalad, C.K. (1990). "Strategic Intent," *McKinsey*

Quarterly, 36-61.

Ives, B. and Jarvenpaa, S. (1991). "Applications of Global Information Technology: Key Issues for Management," *MIS Quarterly*, 33-49.

Johnston, W.B. (1991). "Global Workforce 2000: The New World Labor Market," *Harvard Business Review*, 115-127.

Keen, P.G.W. (1992). "Planning Globally: Practical Strategies for Information Technology in the Transnational Firm," in *The Global Issues of IT Management*, Palvia, S., Palvia, P. and Zigli, R. (eds.). Harrisburg, PA: Idea Group Publishing.

McLeod, Jr., R. (1986, and earlier). *Management Information Systems*, First, Second, Third eds. Chicago: Science Research Associates.

McLeod, Jr., R. (1990, 1993). *Management Information Systems*, Fourth and Fifth eds. New York: Macmillan Publishing Company.

O'Reilly, B. (1992, December 14). "Your New Global Workforce," *Fortune*, 52-66.

Porter, M. (1990). "New Global Strategies for Competitive Advantage," *Planning Review*, 4-14.

Prahalad, C.K. and Hamel, G. (1990). "The Core Competence of the Corporation." *Harvard Business Review*, 79-91.

Resnick, R.(1993). "Plug Into Profits," *International Business*,47-52.

Stalk, G., Evans, P. and Shulman, L.E.(1992). "Competing on Capabilities: The New Rules of Corporate Strategy." *Harvard Business Review, 57-69.*

Wendt, H. (1993) *Global Embrace.* New York: Harper Collins.

SECTION 2

Information Systems and Technology for Global Marketing

The usefulness of marketing information systems (MKIS) as a means for organizing and managing marketing information has long been recognized as an effective tool for the organization's domestic (U.S.) operations. The potential for these systems to support the firm's international marketing function is likewise considerable. Although current literature supporting this contention is scarce, the practical evidence is strong. International marketing managers are clear in their conviction that IT will help them in their attempts to understand and deal in the global marketplace.

In this section of the book, three chapters are included that advance our knowledge and provide supporting documentation for the importance of information systems and technology applications for international marketing activities. These chapters, in combination, give the reader an indication of the breadth of potential and possibilities that abound for the use of information technology to aid in international marketing decision making.

In the first chapter, Kimball Marshall provides an overview of the state-of-the-art of marketing information systems with particular emphasis on their contribution to the international marketing arena. He provides background information for readers less familiar with the external and internal information requirements of marketing information systems in general. He argues that marketing information and information technology applications will contribute to the firm's competitive advantage and support global marketing initiatives.

In the second chapter, Cuneyt Evigen and Tamer Cavisgil take a more focused look at information technology applications for international marketing. In particular, they focus on current applications of decision support systems and expert systems that are in use today to meet decision making needs of international marketing managers. The authors argue that the criteria for expert systems justification are easily met within the international marketing domain. Expert systems may be utilized to facilitate better decision making and reduce the complexities of international marketing, thus enhancing the firm's competitive position.

In the final chapter, Sayester Daser shifts the focus back to a broader perspective and the critical role of information technology in the formation of global markets. She develops a framework that highlights the major environmental determinants of a global market and demonstrates the significance of IT in this globalization process. She uses the European Community (EC) as a case study to illustrate the influence of these forces and the pervasive mature of IT as a catalyst in the process. Companies must be aware of these influences and impacts on their particular operations as they expand in markets throughout the world.

CHAPTER 3

Global Perspectives of Marketing Information Systems: Opportunities and Challenges

KIMBALL P. MARSHALL
Jackson State University

Today, more than ever, organizations depend on advanced information systems and technology to guide the planning, implementation, and control of international marketing programs. This chapter addresses the role of marketing in multinational organizations and how marketing information can contribute to competitive advantage. The chapter then discusses the key components of marketing information systems (MKIS) and the process of MKIS development. Finally, special problems that confront developers of internationally oriented marketing information systems are discussed.

INTRODUCTION

The last half of the 20th century has witnessed numerous changes in modern business practices. Dramatic changes have occurred in government regulation, employee-employer relationships, product availability, transportation systems, finance and banking, and many other areas. Of all the changes that have occurred, two major trends stand out: 1) the development of the global marketplace; and 2) the rise of information systems technologies as the fundamental mechanisms for modern business activities (Hohn, 1986; Deans and Kane, 1992).

As producers of goods and services, today's business firms must develop long term strategic plans and shorter term tactical plans with awareness of international competitors, changing monetary exchange rates, international distribution systems, risks of political instability, and cross-national variations in culture, demography, and technology. For this reason it is important that modern firms develop systematic approaches to monitoring international business environments. Moreover, as more and more businesses become actively involved in international trade, systematic attention must be paid to the development of information systems that will be effective tools for planning, implementation, and control of marketing programs in a global context.

Just as technology has affected other areas of business, technological advances in computer-based information systems have fundamentally affected marketing management (Marshall and LaMotte, 1992; Churchill, 1991; Perreault, 1992; Malhotra, 1992; Curry, 1993; Robinson, 1989; Rubinstein, 1989). Indeed, advances in automatic identification systems, scanner technology, inter-organizational data transfers (Cash and Konsynski, 1985), international on-line data services, electronic mail, and global telecommunications systems are affecting how marketers work and are leading to fundamental shifts in the way market research and market intelligence are carried out.

Today, more than ever, it is critically important that marketers develop systematic approaches to the development and use of information systems to support marketing activities for competitive advantage (Eisenhart, 1988; Keon, 1987; Robinson, 1989; Wiseman, 1988; Bagozzi, 1986; Porter and Millar, 1985). This chapter focuses on how marketing information systems, referred to as MKIS, can support the international marketing activities of the modern firm. We will define a "marketing information system" as "*a formal system designed with the objective of creating an organized, regular flow of relevant information for use and analysis by marketing decision makers*" (Marshall and Lamotte, 1992).

Because the field of marketing information systems is relatively new (Cox and Goode, 1967; Marshall and LaMotte, 1992), as is the field of global information systems (Deans and Ricks, 1991, 1993), much of the discussion must be speculative. Our goal is to establish a foundation for dialogue among marketers and information systems specialists regarding the design and implementation of marketing information systems in a global context. We will use the complex situation of the multinational corporation as our benchmark. The multinational corporation, or MNC, has been defined by several researchers and writers (Deans and Kane, 1992; Phatak 1992) as "any firm that has one or more foreign affiliates or production facilities and is therefore involved in international management" (Deans and Kane, 1992). Although much of our discussion might apply as well to other types of organizations involved in international trade (exporters for example), the MNC has been chosen because it represents one of the more complex, non-governmental types of organizations from the standpoints of marketing management and information systems. The complexity derives from the need to include in strategic and tactical plans and daily operations consideration of multiple business environments, diversity in technological circumstances, and complex organizational forms that uniquely press toward both centralization and decentralization (Deans and Kane, 1992; Terpstra, 1988; Phatak, 1992). Most multinational corporations are large (revenues in the hundreds of millions of dollars), involved in manufacturing, and operate in several counties simultaneously (Phatak, 1992).

To achieve the goal of stimulating dialogue among information systems and marketing professionals regarding the design and development of marketing information systems, this chapter will first direct attention to a review of the basic functions of marketing in an organization and the types of information needed to carry out marketing roles. The major components of an MKIS will then be discussed. Finally, the chapter will consider several special problems that developers of marketing information systems face when designing systems to serve organizations involved in international trade.

THE SCOPE OF MARKETING: AN INTERNATIONAL PERSPECTIVE

If we are to consider how information systems may be developed to facilitate marketing from an international perspective, we must first make clear what is meant by marketing. To many people the term marketing implies advertising and promoting products. To others, marketing means sales. Advertising, promotion, and sales are all part of marketing, but marketing is more than these. Marketing may be thought of as a boundary department linking the organization to its environment in order to create opportunities for exchange. The American Marketing Association (AMA) defines marketing as "*the process of executing the conception, pricing, promotion, and distribution of ideas, goods, and services to create exchanges that satisfy individual and organizational goals*" (Bennett, 1988). This definition is widely accepted (Ferrell and Lucas, 1987) and is similar to definitions used in a variety of standard textbooks (Pride and Ferrell, 1991; Kotler, 1991).

The AMA definition suggests that the role of marketing in the firm is to create exchanges that lead to the fulfillment of the organization's goals. These exchanges take place between the organization and its customers in the environment. Customers enter into exchanges with the organization in order to obtain goods or services, referred to as products, that the firm produces. The set of potential customers for the firm's products is the market. If marketers are to create exchanges, then the product or service offerings of the organization must be superior to those of the competition from the perspective of potential customers. Therefore, the offerings developed by marketers and the tools used to develop the organization's offerings must provide the organization with sustainable competitive advantages in the marketplace (Kotler, 1991; Porter, 1985; Porter and Millar, 1985). To create successful exchange opportunities, marketers must carry out the following activities:

1) identify potential markets that have a basic need for the possible products of the firm and are sufficiently large and represent a sufficient competitive opportunity to contribute to the firm's objectives;
2) create opportunities for exchange by conceiving of products that will be demanded by a sufficiently large number of the members of the potential market;
3) coordinate with others in the firm to assure that the products are appropriately designed and produced;
4) develop appropriate pricing, financing, and transaction terms to allow customers to exchange the product for the resources desired by the firm;
5) develop a communication program to inform potential customers of the product's availability and how it can meet their basic needs; and
6) develop and coordinate a distribution system by which the firm's products are transferred to the geographic locations of target markets, stored, and made available to potential customers, and by which the exchange transactions (sales) can be carried out.

Information Requirements for Competitive Market Advantage

If the objective of marketing is to create opportunities for exchange by developing a sustainable competitive advantage in the marketplace, the key to creating competitive advantage through marketing is information. With proper information, marketing managers can better identify potentially profitable markets and can segment these markets into groups of potential customers with similar needs. Information on competitors can help marketers identify weaknesses in competitors' offerings or distribution systems, or may suggest initiatives that the organization can take that competitors could not easily copy. Information about culture, values, attitudes and lifestyles of consumers or the particular requirements of industrial customers can help the marketer modify current products or create new products that will be more highly valued by the market than competitors' products. Information can help advertising managers to develop promotional programs that will position the organization's offerings favorably in the minds of potential customers. Information regarding the geographic distribution of potential customers and the economic and industrial profiles of specific geographic areas can help the sales manager to develop sales territories and quotas and to plan the size of the sales staff.

Information on the internal operations of the organization will also be valuable to marketers. Product sales data for salespeople and geographic areas can help the sales manager identify overworked or under-performing salespeople and can alert product managers to potential product failures. Data on responses to advertising programs can help the advertising manager better select media outlets. Information on manufacturing costs and processes can help the product manager to reduce product costs or improve product quality. Data from the customer service department can alert the marketer to problems with quality or design and may even suggest new product or market opportunities.

With so many potential competitive advantages to be derived from marketing related information, and so much information to consider in the international marketplace, both marketers and information systems professionals need a model to relate information resources to competitive advantage. Figure 1 draws on two common approaches used in marketing and business strategy. The first is an approach to organizing environmental scanning data used by Montgomery and Weinberg in their 1979 article on strategic intelligence systems that has now become commonplace in discussions of business planning. The second draws on Michael Porter's value chain analysis (1979; 1985; Porter and Millar, 1985) approach to suggest key indicators of internal firm conditions.

External Environmental Data for MNCs

Turning first to environmental scanning, Montgomery and Weinberg suggest that a strategic intelligence system should have three purposes; defensive intelligence, passive intelligence, and offensive intelligence (1979). Defensive intelligence monitors environments to avoid surprises and to verify that the organization's assumptions continue to hold. Passive intelligence provides benchmark data on environmental forces, such as competitors. Offensive intelligence seeks opportunities for the organization. To accomplish these three objectives *a strategic intelligence system should focus on six types of*

Sample External Environments ------------------> Factors	Sample Marketing Strategy And Mix <--------------- Elements	Sample Internal Environment Factors
Competitors		*Inbound*
Multinational		*Logistics*
Industry Structures	Target Markets	Supplier Costs
Firms	Market Segments	*Material Costs*
Host Countries		Inventory
Industry Structures	Product Designs	Storage Costs
Firms	Global vs Custom	
Technological		*Operations*
Multinational	Distribution	Production Cost
Communications	Systems	Inventories
Host Countries	Sales Force	Finished Goods
Communications	Type of Outlets	Labor Supply
Utilities	Transportation	
Computing	Storage	
Production		Outbound
Skills		Logistics
Customers/Non-Customers		Shipping Costs
Multinational	Promotion Plans	Warehouse Costs
Industrial	Advertising Media	
Host Countries	Ad Content	
Industrial	Sales Promotions	
Consumers	Publicity	Marketing
Economic	Public Relations	And Sales
Multinational		Product Sales
Exchange Rates		and Revenue by
Finance		Salesperson
Host Countries	Pricing and	Geo. Area
Inflation	Financing Terms	Wholesaler
Economic Stability	Prices	Retailer
Finance	Credit	Transaction
Political	Return Policies	Records
Multinational		Scanner Data
Treaties		Commission Plan
Organizations	Customer Support	Product Rework
Host Countries	Services	and Repair
Stability	Warranties	Customer
Legislation	Training	Satisfaction
Judicial Courts	Modifications	Customer
Regulations		Requirements
Social		
Multinational		
Communication		Service
Migration		Customer
Host Countries		Service Costs
Cultures		Product
Demographics		Customizations
Religion		Training

Figure 1: Sample International Marketing Information Needs

environments: 1) competitive; 2) technological; 3) customers; 4) economic; 5) political; and 6) social. In each of these areas the managers of the organization must determine the critical issues to monitor based on the nature of the industry, the diversity of markets to be addressed, the nature of products, strategic objectives, and so forth. Parsimony is important in selecting the appropriate issues to consider if the marketing manager and the information systems developers are not to become so overwhelmed with the volume of data available that analysis and interpretation are impeded. As Montgomery and Weinberg (1979) observed "... a word of caution is in order. The problem is not to generate data, but to determine what information is relevant and actionable".

Competitive issues have been carefully studied by business strategy researchers and include structural features of the industry as well as the capabilities and actions of competitors. These include issues such as production costs, economies of scale, extent of product differentiation, capital requirements, distribution channels, power of suppliers, specific competitors' market share, brand recognition, customer loyalty, technological advantages, and so forth. The *technological environment* should also be monitored to anticipate how technological changes may lead to new products, more cost effective production techniques, improved distribution, and enhanced communication, or other changes in the nature of business practices or the structure of the industry. The challenge facing the multinational firm regarding monitoring competitive and technological environments is complicated because other multinational competitors must be considered as well as domestic competitors in each target market country.

As explained by Montgomery and Weinberg (1979), the *customer environment* refers to the markets in which the organization participates including both the organization's current customers and potential customers. Customers provide new product ideas, suggestions for improvements in products and distribution, etc. In one study noted by Montgomery and Weinberg (1979), 74% of 137 innovations studied in two industries were initiated by customers (von Hippel, 1977). Studies of members of the market who choose competitor's products may suggest new ways to gain advantage and may reveal the organizations' weaker characteristics in certain segments. Competitors' weakness may even be revealed. Monitoring customers and occasional primary research studies of non-customers is particularly important to the multinational corporation since the MNC must consider domestic and non-domestic markets simultaneously and must identify market segments with similar needs if it is to develop globally standardized products (Goodyear, 1990; Jeannet and Hennessey, 1992; Czinkota and Ronkainem, 1993). Here also the multiple domestic markets faced by the MNC exponentially increase the intelligence efforts that are required. Customer intelligence gathering is further complicated by language and cultural variations that make data gathering and analysis regarding buyer psychographics particularly difficult (Czinkota and Ronkainen, 1993; Jeannet and Hennessey, 1992).

Economic environments may be the easiest for the multinational corporation to monitor because international monetary exchange rates and banking practices in most developed and developing countries are regularly monitored by private banking services, the United Nations, and many governments. Of course, in some underdeveloped and developing countries many of the economic indicators of specific geographic markets may not be as readily available as in the United States where private information sources such as the Survey of Buying Power (Sales and Marketing Management, 1989) and a variety of information subscription services (Dialog Information Services, 1993; Krol, 1992; Darian, 1989) supplement the public data resources of the federal government. This is changing, however, and in recent years many regional research services have begun operations, particularly in Europe (Bowers, 1990; Dawson, 1989; Jeannet and Hennessey, 1992) and through international organizations such as the United Nations. For a list of possible international data sources including private organizations, professional associations, trade associations, and government associations, the reader may wish to review David W. Stewart's short text *Secondary Research: Information Sources and Methods* (1984). Even when it is difficult to locate data, economic indicators and exchange rates must be monitored to verify the buying power of prospective markets and to assure that domestic costs and prices in the host country will actually translate into expected profit margins.

Perhaps the *political environment* is the most visible aspect of external environments that must be monitored by the international marketer. Whereas the domestic marketer must be concerned with political movements in one country, as well as changing laws, judicial court rulings, and regulations issued by government agencies, the marketer in the multinational corporation must be concerned with these same forces in the multiple markets in which the firm participates. In addition, the MNC marketer must be conscious of a wide range of international agencies and treaties that may impinge on business practices. For example, in 1992 conflict in negotiations between the United States and France regarding oil seed production quotas in the General Agreements on Tariffs and Trade (GANTT) treaty led to threats of sudden changes in US tariffs on french wines. In this case, difficulties in the political environments related to the political power of french seed oil producers led to potential turmoil in the economic environment of international wine dealers. Similarly, in mid-1993 much confusion existed in trade relations among the United States, Canada and Mexico due to political uncertainty in the United States Congress regarding the North American Free Trade Agreement. Continuing negotiations made it difficult for MNCs to plan for possible business developments in Mexico. Of course, in less politically stable areas of the world, the impact of the political environment may be even more volatile.

The *social environment* includes each host domestic country's cultural and demographic characteristics and trends. *Demographic characteristics* such as population size, age and racial and ethnic distributions may be fairly easily obtained for most countries, but it may be difficult to locate demographic information for specific geographic regions within a country. Also, even basic demographic information may be unreliable in less developed nations that lack the technology needed for accurate census estimates or in countries undergoing political upheaval. Significant cultural characteristics include area religions, traditional belief systems and customs, language, as well as formal and informal business practices. These are of particular importance to firms marketing consumer goods but such factors may also affect the development of personal relationships that will be important in industrial markets.

With so much diversity in external environmental information to consider, MNC marketers will be well advised to develop a systematic format for building a country profile database. Such a database should include quantitative indices and coded indicators of qualitative factors that would be included in the profile, but allowance should also be made for text variables that can annotate the profile or elaborate certain environmental trends. Demographic, economic, and many competitor related data items may be expressed in quantitative or systematically coded terms (Hall and Marshall, 1992), but because much environmental data is of a qualitative, text nature, developers of an internationally oriented MKIS should consider applications of computers to qualitative ethnographic data that have been developed by social scientists (Hall and Marshall, 1992). A key challenge facing MNC marketers is to define the relevant factors to include for each country, since the risk of excessive data may be greater than too little data. Therefore, marketers and information systems developers must together develop formal guidelines for selecting items to be included in a country or environment database.

Internal Information

In order to sensitize marketers and information systems developers to internal environmental factors, Figure 1 uses the primary activities of Porter's (1980; 1985) value chain approach to assessing competitive advantage. Although value chain's primary activities and support activities (firm infrastructure, human resource management, technology development, and procurement) were developed as a model to guide the search for competitive advantage, these divisions, and the primary activities in particular, provide a useful checklist for considering internal forces and costs that can direct or constrain an organization's marketing strategy and the elements of the marketing mix. For example, *inbound logistics* refers to how the firm obtains needed resources from suppliers. Suppliers' resources and costs can affect product development and design and influence overall costs for the firm and its specific products. Awareness of these constraints may lead a firm to work with suppliers to reduce costs or may sensitize the marketer to areas in which the firm's products are vulnerable. Similarly, material costs, raw materials or component inventories, and storage costs may suggest marketing opportunities or threats, particularly when competitors have better access to supplies or lower costs for supplies.

The *production operations* of the firm may also suggest competitive advantage or risks. Production costs influence the variable costs of a product and constrain pricing flexibility. If the MNC has operations in several countries, the marketing database should allow the marketer to monitor these costs to determine the lowest cost operations. Inventories of materials and finished goods may suggest the need for special sales promotions in order to reduce inventory levels. If inventories are low, this may alert the marketer to the need to reduce advertising or promotional expenditures until inventories are sufficiently high to justify and support such activities. Similarly, efficient managing of outbound logistics can also produce competitive advantage. A marketer seeking to maximize profit opportunities may need to consider efficiency in physical distribution systems such as shipping and warehousing costs and may wish to direct attention to new markets if physical distribution costs in current markets rise. Declining physical distribution costs may provide the marketer with pricing flexibility.

The internal environment factors associated with *marketing and sales* include the need to monitor unit product sales, prices obtained, and gross margins by product type, geographic area, and even by specific wholesaler and/or retailer. An excellent approach to organizing and analyzing data of this type has been discussed by Dunne and Wolk (1977) as a "modularized contribution approach." This approach suggests the need for careful allocation of costs at each aggregated level of analysis (i.e. retailer, wholesaler, region, country, etc. and by product) and careful monitoring of sales at each level. For this type of analysis it may be useful to organize product and sales data within each country as a series of relational databases. In the United States consumer markets scanner data are widely available to marketers. Such sales data can be matched to allocated cost data to allow detailed assessments of gross margins within product markets, by distribution channel, etc. Scanner data and related forms of automatic recording of specific product sales are becoming more common in most industrialized countries. In less developed countries, such data may not be available.

Service records will also be important to marketing managers since these may provide opportunities to assess product quality and customer satisfaction. Furthermore, marketers may wish to carefully monitor demands for customized products, and special customer training needs. Each of these types of activities may represent both costs and increased customer value.

In sum, a very large number of factors must be considered for effective market management. These factors range over a variety of external environment issue areas including competitor information, technological events and trends, customer and non-customer characteristics, economic trends, political systems, and socio-cultural and demographic factors. Defining appropriate indicators and data requirements to monitor these external environments presents a significant challenge. These challenges increase exponentially with the multinational corporation. When an organization operates in two or more nations, each of these business environmental areas must be monitored as must international events not localized in any one nation. Effective marketing management also requires that the organization's internal environments be monitored. Systematic attention must also be given to ongoing trends in costs, sales, and margins. The development of effective information systems for multinational, even global, environmental scanning requires teamwork among marketing managers and information systems developers in order to select appropriate scanning techniques, and the factors to be monitored, to support the information needs of the marketing function.

MARKETING INFORMATION SYSTEMS

A review of the literature related to marketing information systems reveals that the term is used to refer to a wide variety of activities. Some writers use the term MKIS to refer to computer based sales tools such as lead and prospect tracking, telemarketing systems, or customer support systems (Datapro Reports, 1989; Dobrozdravic, 1989; Eisenhart, 1988; Keon, 1987; Moriatry and Swartz, 1989; Snyder, 1988). Other researchers and practitioners use the term to refer to support systems for market intelligence, planning, and managerial decision making in such areas as pricing, advertising, sales management, or product and sales tracking, sales territory management, etc. (Churchill, 1991; Dyer, 1987; Robinson, 1989). All of these types of computer applications to sales and marketing activities are aspects of marketing information systems and, as such, are possibly MKIS related systems. However, from a systems planning perspective, the starting point should be more comprehensive. For this reason we have adopted Marshall and LaMotte's (1992) definition noted earlier.

A Marketing information system may be defined as a formal system designed with the objective of creating an organized, regular flow of relevant information for use and analysis by marketing decision makers.

Several aspects of this definition should be noted. First, the definition calls for a formal system. This means that a MKIS is not a serendipitous product of ad hoc, end user solutions to short term requests for information or marketing reports. *Rather a MKIS is a deliberately developed system designed with specific managerial objectives in mind and operating via specified rules and procedures that assure data and analytical integrity as well as managerial user efficiency.*

The second requirement of the MKIS is that it is to provide for organized, regular flows of information. This requirement distinguishes MKIS database activities from ad hoc, one time project-oriented data gathering characteristic of traditional forms of market research (Malhotra, 1992; Perreault, 1992; Curry, 1993; Churchill, 1987). This is not to demean the importance of traditional, primary data collection market research projects. Information obtained from such projects should be integrated into the MKIS database system (Malhotra, 1992). *However, the MKIS must be capable of drawing on continually evolving sources of data internal and external to the organization.*

The third requirement of the MKIS definition is that the data provided by the MKIS be relevant to marketing decisions. While this may seem obvious, it implies that *marketing managers must be part of the design effort in order to assure that the MKIS databases are in fact relevant to the issues and activities in which marketing managers are involved.* This involvement of marketing managers is particularly critical with international marketing activities in order to provide efficiency in light of difficulties of obtaining systematic data, the range of countries that may be involved, and the tremendous number of data items (i.e. variables) that might be considered (Cateora, 1987; Terpstra, 1988).

A fourth implication of the MKIS definition is that marketing managers are expected to use the MKIS to carry out further analyses on the data provided in the system. Therefore, *the design of the system must include analytical resources appropriate to the types of decision making processes carried out by the organization's market-ing managers.* These will include statistical and mathematical modeling tools and subsystems for interpreting and reporting find-ings and making recommendations (Bagozzi, 1986; Little, 1979; Malhotra, 1992). Any MKIS development plan must keep in mind that while carefully designed, routine reports may have utility, *the types of questions asked by marketing managers require interactive, ad hoc inquiry and analytical tools* (Little, 1979). Because market planning and control involves interactions with uncertain and changing environments, the information and analytical needs of marketers are changeable and the MKIS must be designed to provide flexibility for inquiry, analysis and reporting.

A final implication of the definition is that *it stresses analysis and decision making, not operational management,* although data derived from operations systems will become part of the MKIS database to be used by marketing managers. This is an important distinction. Operational management systems might include sales transaction systems, systems for tracking salespersons' commissions, systems to govern the logistics of distribution such as shipping orders, warehousing inventories, and stocking stores, and systems to pro-vide customer services and support such as may be involved for warranties, product repair or replacement, or managing customer complaints. These are all marketing related activities but they are typically carried out by other divisions of the organization. Market-ing managers may have responsibility for monitoring these activities and coordinating the various departments to assure that operations flow smoothly, but typically marketing managers will not have direct responsibility over these types of support activities. For example, sales transactions may be the responsibility of a division within the accounting department such as order entry, and shipping and warehousing activities may be treated as a division of the overall production operations or perhaps the sales department. In some cases the sales department may be considered a part of the market-ing department, but in many others sales and marketing are independent and are coordinated by higher levels of senior manage-ment.

Although we are separating operational management from mar-keting management for purposes of this discussion, marketing mangers have responsibilities for monitoring the results of opera-tional activities and for making recommendations regarding changes in tactical plans or operational activities as needed to achieve the organization's goals. Therefore, even where marketing mangers do not have direct line responsibilities for operational activities related to serving markets, marketing mangers will need access to data-bases reflecting trends and statuses of those activities so that they may monitor and evaluate the effectiveness of marketing programs.

Basic Components of MKIS

The essential systems components of a comprehensive MKIS are depicted in Figure 2. At the boundary of the system are potential sources of *data inputs*. These environmental scanning sub-systems are divided into two groups, external environmental scanning systems and internal monitoring systems. These are described as sub-systems because one function of the MKIS is to draw routinely on external and internal data sources in order to feed the ongoing MKIS database. Therefore, it is necessary to identify sources of environmental scanning data and the processes and procedures by which these data will be systematically captured, transmitted to the location of the MKIS database, and incorporated into the MKIS database.

The second set of MKIS components may be considered *operational components* (labelled Database and Systems Operations in Figure 1). For heuristic purposes we have divided these into five types. The first is *system controls*. These are essentially subsystems to assure system and data integrity, security from unauthorized access, internal checks on operations, and general housekeeping activities necessary for the proper functioning of the system on its hardware and software platforms.

The second type of operational component is the *MKIS database management system*. This system includes the continually expanding and evolving data files, and the data dictionary that defines the elements of the data files and their locations, and the variables including their types, formats, locations, possible characteristics and meanings. In conjunction with the system internal controls, the data integrity subsystems include subsystems for bringing new data into the database (i.e. linking to environmental data sources either electronically or through direct keyboard entry), purging unnecessary old data elements, and assuring that data included in the MKIS database meet the definitions specified in the data dictionary. The data access subsystem provides manager users of the MKIS system with access to the needed data items under the guidance of the appropriate system security controls.

User interface systems provides marketing managers with access to the data and analytical tools. The design of these systems is crucial to users' acceptance of the system. Ideally, a common graphical user interface would be developed for most applications and implemented using icon symbols that would be acceptable and meaningful across cultures. This is substantially the philosophy that guided the development of the Apple Macintosh and the Microsoft Windows user interfaces. Such interfaces speed the user's learning curve for the basic system and because the interface is common across most applications, it is easier for users to learn new application programs.   Cross-cultural icons may increase system acceptability in diverse cultures.

A set of *applications systems* are needed to provide marketing managers with *inquiry and analysis* capabilities. Inquiry systems allow managers to monitor product sales, promotional programs, environmental trends, and other issues. Essentially, inquiry systems allow managers to obtain answers to questions of "what is?" or "what has happened in the past?" These are different from analytical

Environmental Scanning Inputs ------------>	Database And System Operations --------->	Possible Application Outputs
Internal Organizational Inputs Sales Summaries	System Internal Controls	Product Management
Transaction Processing System Shipping Records Customer Database Sales Commissions Telemarketing Database Customer Service Accounts Receivables Pricing Standards Inventory Records Etc.	Database Management Systems and Controls Data Files Data Dictionary Data Administrator Data Integrity Data Access Data Communications	Tactical Plans Forecasts Budgets Profit Analyses Communications Budgets Simulations Media Plans Impact Reports
External Environmental Inputs Quota Planning Ad Hoc Market Territory Analysis	User Interface Systems Access Controls User Interfaces Ergonomics	Sales Management Territory Design Sales Forecasts
Research Studies Third Party Reviews Subscription Data On-line Environmental Data Industry Trends Economic Trends Advertising Costs Regulatory Trends Competitor Trends Supply Trends Scanner Data Single Source Data	Applications Systems Fixed Reports Ad Hoc Inquiries Statistical Analyses Simulation Models Expert Systems Qualitative Analyses Forecasting Systems	Channel Assessment Commission Cost Reviews Senior Management Simulate Strategy Financial Modeling Market Assessments Ad Hoc Reviews
Inter-organizational Data Sharing (Business Partners)	Reporting Systems Text Processing Graphics Output Slides and Viewgraphs Electronic Output	

Figure 2: Fundamental MKIS Components

questions that ask "Why?" (Little 1979). Both types of systems are needed. Because marketing mangers will need to monitor trends in different countries, compare trends in product lines, compare sales of different distribution channels, and so forth for a plethora of questions that cannot be completely anticipated, it will be desirable to provide relational capabilities in the design of the databases so that managers can have maximum flexibility in their inquiries. However, given the potential size of the MKIS database system, and the importance of speed to users engaged in interactive inquiries, it may be necessary to balance flexibility and system responsiveness and to develop innovative approaches to inquiries. Mangers will also require a diverse set of analytical decision support tools. Certainly, statistical processing tools with tables, regression, and similar capabilities will be required, but much more advanced analytical tools may also be needed as will simulation modeling, linear programming, forecasting, PERT and CPM systems. Precisely which analytical tools must be incorporated into the main MKIS system and which should be left to end users on networked microcomputers are questions that must be resolved in the planning stage with substantial end user input.

The fifth type of operational system depicted in Figure 2 is *reporting systems* to provide printed and electronic output so that the results of inquiries and analysis can be preserved and displayed to other managers and incorporated in managerial reports. Such systems may involve text processing and desk top publishing, presentation and publication quality graphics, 35 millimeter slide output, and electronic microcomputer-based slide shows, storyboards, computer-assisted instruction, and multinational electronic mail. Here again, it will be important to have substantial input from the intended end users because, ultimately, these systems will be the primary way by which the decision making benefits of the MKIS are transmitted to other decision makers and the rest of the organization.

These environmental scanning and operational systems represent the main components of the MKIS. The successful MKIS will provide marketing managers with effective information and tools to support decision making. The results may affect all marketing functions. As suggested in Figure 2, product managers can benefit through efficiently developed sales summaries, forecasts of the impacts of tactical plans, long term product forecasts, accurate budgeting, and accurate analysis of the profit contributions of each area of the product's marketing program. Similarly, communications managers should be able to use the MKIS to simulate the impact of various promotional programs, and develop more cost-effective media plans. Sales managers may benefit by more appropriate designs of sales territories, sales forecasts (which in turn affect production costs), sales quotas for districts and individual salespersons and accounts, and so forth. The benefits of the MKIS will also extend to senior managers who should be able to use the system to simulate alternative strategy decisions, develop financial models of alternative marketing strategies, more accurately assess the potentials of diverse international markets, and carry out ad hoc reviews of individual programs throughout the global reach of the organization.

ISSUES IN DEVELOPMENT AND PLANNING

The comprehensive market information system objective described in this chapter represents an ambitious challenge even in a domestic environment. In a multinational context, the challenge is even more foreboding because, although the basic challenges are similar, they are multiplied by the number of countries involved and the need for international linkages and coordination. Therefore a systematic approach is needed for the development of the MKIS and for anticipating the special problems that may be presented in a multinational context. In this section we will review the basic challenges of MKIS development in a multinational context and make recommendations for managing these challenges. We suggest three types of generic challenges in developing a multinational MKIS: 1) managing the planning and development of the system; 2) challenges of data collection; and 3) technological challenges related to transborder data flows.

Managing the Planning and Development of the System

An effective MKIS is a continually evolving system.   Senior managers, marketers, and information systems developers will be well advised to define the general parameters of a comprehensive, ideal system, and then to focus on initial marketing information priorities. These priorities can then be developed within the standards established for the MKIS so that future developments will have effective interfaces to the initial modules.   Obviously, the initial planning stages must be guided by a clear vision of the future of the organization in a global context.

Cox and Goode (1967), among the earliest researchers to recognize the strategic importance of marketing information systems, delineated six steps for a systematic MKIS planning process. These steps have been further elaborated by Marshall and LaMotte (1992) in light of technological changes that have occurred:

1. Preparation of the organization which includes: a) developing top management support; b) creating realistic expectations of the

MKIS objectives, limitations, time frames, and costs; c) executing a full marketing review to understand the information needs of marketing managers and the decision making processes in each functional area; and d) appointing an ongoing MKIS team led by a high level administrator to keep the project on tract, overcome internal political battles, and maintain top management support;

2. Development of macro level specifications related to: a) the requirements of intended users including inquiry and analytical decision support tools (Little, 1979) and expert systems (Chandler and Liang, 1990); b) interfaces to other internal systems and to external data sources; and c) user interface and output requirements;

3. Database system design including: a)interfaces to internal and external data sources; b) approaches to systematizing and coding unsystematic data and managing qualitative data (Montgomery and Weinberg, 1979) with consideration of maintaining the lowest practical level of aggregation and flexibility for user defined hierarchial analysis; and c) data and software independence so that the resulting databases will effectively serve the input requirements of a variety of analytical decision support and expert systems tools;

4. Development of MKIS components and user interfaces including: a) system internal controls; b) database systems and controls; c) applications systems; and d) user interface and reporting systems as noted in Figure 2. User interface specifications are particularly critical and should include such topics as the responsibilities of users' positions, how the MKIS will affect decision making, computer literacy and anxiety, and cultural prejudices related to work tools and roles, and current computer tools with which users are familiar;

5. Prototype development and phased implementation which includes involvement of intended end users in the design of prototype interfaces and output systems and the use of modular design and programming techniques that will allow interfaces to be adjusted and the users to adapt to one capability at a time;

6. Marketing usage and future modifications including efforts to monitor user satisfaction, identify and resolve bugs, user training and ongoing user support, and ongoing study to anticipate new MKIS needs and/or modifications of the existing system to adjust to changing organizational goals or processes and changes in the environments.

While these six stages outline the basics of a systems planning and development project, they do not convey the full complexity confronting a multinational organization. Firms operating in several countries present special problems for planning, implementing, and managing a global approach to MKIS. Although a variety of problems could be suggested, we will here focus on three: autonomy of foreign operations; access to common hardware and software; and socio-cultural variations in skills and working methods that may affect MKIS operations.

The degree to which a firm operating in several countries allows each country's management autonomy may complicate the MKIS planning and development stages. For example, if management in each country has substantial autonomy it may be difficult to assure and maintain each country's operations' endorsement and cooperation with the MKIS planning effort. Furthermore, the greater the autonomy of each country's operations, the more likely that the respective marketing managers may follow different decision processes and depend on different data. On one hand, the MKIS should reflect the marketing decision processes of the organization, but, on the other, parsimony and standardization should be sought when possible if it can be achieved without reductions in effectiveness.

Another type of problem faced by the developer of a global MKIS for a MNC may be the availability of common hardware or software platforms across countries (Deans and Kane, 1992). Variations in available hardware and software may affect the types of decision support modules that can be implemented, thus reducing the utility of a standardized MKIS in certain countries.

Since the success of the MKIS will depend on the acceptance of the system by the intended users, a multinational planning effort must consider socio-cultural variations among managers and marketing analysts in different countries. Literacy levels may vary, particularly if English is to be the standard language for MKIS modules. In less developed countries, more advanced analytical tools may not be understood. Cultural issues related to status and work roles may affect whether senior managers are willing to use what some might initially see as a "clerical" tool.

Other cross-cultural managerial issues related to MKIS planning could be suggested, but these adequately illustrate the need for the development effort to consider the special nature of business operations in each country. Even when the MNC has adopted a global strategy, country specific issues must be considered in the design of MKIS operations that will be carried out in the field. One approach to resolve the complexities of multinational management of the MKIS planning and development effort may be to establish "home office" goals, objectives, and data requirements as a model for subsidiary operations in other countries. Domestic managers in the specific countries of operation may then be called upon to develop their own plan with the constraint that their systems provide appropriate data inputs to the home office system. The home office can then provide consulting support for the development of the MKIS of each country. In this way domestic autonomy can be protected such that the MKIS development effort and final system is consistent with the specific MNC's management style, technical hardware and software capabilities, and socio-cultural circumstances. This approach is also consistent with the trend toward de-centralized data processing through distributed systems among multi-national corporations observed by Deans and Kane (1992).

Data Collection Issues

The adequacy of a MKIS is constrained by the quality of the data on which it is able to draw. *The fundamental issues related to data quality are availability, timeliness, validity, comparability, accuracy, and reliability over time, across organizations, and across national boundaries.* As discussed earlier in this chapter, the MKIS will draw on internal and external environmental data. Because of the dangers of including inappropriate or erroneous data in the MKIS, which may lead to inaccurate analyses and unsound business decisions, it is vital that procedures be in place to assess data quality (Rice and Mahmoud, 1984).Assuming that adequate transaction processing and internal accounting systems are available in each country of operation, the necessary internal data can be expected to be available (although as we shall discuss in the next section, transmission of these data across national boundaries to the central office may be problematic). External environmental data may be more problematic.

External environmental data can take two forms; secondary data or primary data. *Secondary data* are data that were originally collected for another purpose, but are available in some form and may be applicable to the researchers' current purpose. *Primary data* are data that are collected for the first time for the explicit purpose at hand. For example, government census reports on the population of a country are a form of secondary data when used by a marketer to assess the sales potential of a country. An example of primary data would be the data from a survey of customers carried out to assess customer satisfaction. Both secondary and primary data are important to marketers in the planning, implementation and monitoring of marketing programs.

The international marketer will depend heavily on secondary data resources for most environmental monitoring activities. Frequently used data sources may include publications of the United Nations, international trade associations, host governments, and a variety of private international data subscription services (Stewart, 1984; Dialog Information Services, Inc., 1993; Czinkota and Ronkainen, 1993). Secondary data can be of great benefit to the researcher, but can also present problems. The precise information needed by the marketer might not be available, and if it is available in one country, it might not be available in another. Even when the desired information is available, secondary data may be old, having been produced several months or years earlier. For example, the United States Census is taken only once every ten years and the results may not be fully available for several years after it is taken.

The problems of validity and comparability of data are closely related. *Validity addresses whether the data measures what the researcher expects it to measure.* If, for example, a government report refers to the number of wholesalers in a country, is the government definition of a wholesaler in this report the same as would be used by the market researcher? Related to validity is the problem that secondary data often do not precisely fit the issue with which the researcher is concerned or the format that the researcher desired. Sometimes, the international market researcher must "interpret" such data as is available even though he or she recognizes that the data might not precisely refer to the issue at hand. *Comparability refers to whether secondary data on a topic obtained from different countries or organizations are measured, computed, or reported in the same way.* Comparability may suffer because of different definitions of terms or because of different ways of measuring or reporting data. This may especially be a problem in international research because different governments may report such things as census data, business statistics, educational data, and so forth using different categories, indices, methods of calculation, and so forth. Therefore, data that are available from different countries might not be easily compared. For example, it may be difficult to compare the number of wholesalers or industrial suppliers in the United States with the number in Japan since these terms may have different meanings in these two countries. Because comparability of secondary data can be a serious problem in establishing a database for an MKIS, formal procedures should be developed to adjust the data to comparable formats or to warn users of the system of discrepancies.

Accuracy and reliability of secondary data should also be of concern to the international market researcher (Czinkota and Ronkainen, 1993) *Accuracy refers to how precisely the measurement is carried out.* For example a survey may produce an estimate with a large margin of error. *Reliability refers to whether the measurement and reporting technique would produce the same results each time the measure is taken if the thing being measured has not changed.* Governments and other producers of data may differ in their ability to accurately and reliably measure social, cultural, business, or economic conditions (Ramachandran, 1991; Vukmanic, Czinkota, and Ricks, 1985), and in some countries it may not be uncommon for reported data to be distorted for propaganda purposes. Procedures must be put in place to verify the integrity of secondary data before it is recorded as part of the MKIS. One method of assessing whether reported data are accurate or reliable is to seek two or more sources. If different sources provide similar estimates, the researcher can have more confidence in the data.

Because the market researcher has greater control in the collection of primary data, many of the problems described above are less likely to occur However, primary data collection projects in the international context may present problems as well. Differences in cultures and languages may create problems of validity and comparability because questionnaires and other data collection instruments may have to be translated into several languages (Terpstra 1988). One way to verify that translations are accurate would be to translate the data collection instrument into a second language and then have it retranslated into the original language by another translator. The retranslated version may then be compared to the original.

Field primary data collection may be more difficult in less developed nations than in developed nations. Less developed nations may not have the communications and transportation infrastructures needed to reach the intended respondents. High levels of illiteracy may create further problems in using conventional techniques to administer questionnaires or interviews Response rate problems may be accentuated since large numbers of sampled respondents may not be accessible. Another problem in less developed countries may be locating sufficient numbers of skilled data collectors and clerical staff to adequately carry out the field checks and central office checks needed to prevent "non-sampling" errors such as mistakes in recording, coding data, or entering data. However, when such research is needed to provide information to the MKIS database, sufficient planning, realistic funding of the project, and careful project management following sound research practices can assure high data quality.

Technological Issues for International Data Flows

Even when the developers of the MKIS have obtained cooperation from the various country managers and have arranged for capturing internal and external information needed by the MKIS, the information must be transmitted to the home office. This brings us to the third set of generic challenges in developing an international MKIS, transborder data flows. Transborder data flows (TDFs) refers to the movement of data across national boundaries and may be problematic in at least three ways: 1) technological communications problems; 2) cost issues related to host country PTT (postal, telegraph, and telephone agencies) charges; and 3) host country and international regulations.

Deans and Kane (1992) have provided an excellent overview of the diverse political, legal, technological and historical issues that underlie the current status of TDFs. They note that the term "transborder data flow" is used in both narrow and broad ways. In the narrow definition the term refers to data that are explicitly stored and transmitted via computer. The broader definition considers a TDF to be all data and information that cross a national border in any way or form. Although the narrow view is most often used, the broader view is gaining acceptance with the spread of various electronic technologies. For this reason, MKIS developers should consider the broad definition when assessing the issues that may affect the transmission of data to the home office and the global sharing of MKIS data among marketing managers in different countries.

From a technological standpoint, the MKIS developer must be concerned with whether the computer and related data collection and transmission operations in a country's local domestic office are adequate for effective transmission at reasonable speed and whether the transmission form will be acceptable to the host system in the home office. When the MNC has full control over both the home computing systems and the remote systems, this may not be problematic. However, some countries may require that computers used locally must have been produced locally (i.e. Brazil restricts the use of foreign computing equipment). Moreover, local transmission systems regulated by the domestic PTT system might not provide adequate transmission quality to allow high speed transmission, or lines might not be available for extended periods at the time that the data are to be transmitted. In general, however, technological problems can be solved, although perhaps at the cost of reducing the amount of data transmitted or the timeliness of the data.

The costs of TDF may be substantially higher than internal communications for several reasons. These include requirements that locally produced data processing equipment be used, high tariffs on international communications and on data transmission in particular, possible taxes on data, or excessive charges for data lines (Deans and Kane, 1992). Typically, these costs should not be completely allocated to the MKIS since some costs will be incurred simply to maintain the domestic operation. However, where special data lines are needed, or where tariffs or taxes specifically target data, MKIS planners will have to weigh the benefits of elaborate and timely data against the incremental costs of transmission. Careful planning of the MKIS data requirements, and the aggregation level of the desired data can help to limit costs so that these may not be a significant issue. Still, TDF costs should be considered in the MKIS planning process.

Perhaps the most significant issues faced by MNCs developing or operating international marketing information systems will be domestic laws and regulations that may limit the types and volume of data that can be transmitted due to concerns over privacy rights of citizens or concerns over national security or sovereignty. These issues may be as serious in developed countries as in developing or less developed countries. Over thirty nations already have laws affecting TDFs and many others are considering regulations. This includes such developed nations as France (The Data Processing, Data Files, and Individual Liberties Act) and Sweden (the Data Act of 1973). Differences in laws among host countries further complicate matters. Even when laws governing TDFs are not in place, MNCs may encounter problems with government officials for exporting economic information that might be considered commonplace in a western society such as the United States but may be deemed politically sensitive elsewhere. Even in western societies pressures may build for restrictions on the flows of market related information as the strategic value of information is recognized. (Deans and Kane, 1992).

SUMMARY

In summary, business today is carried out in an international context and organizations must plan their activities with consideration of global business environments. Marketing information systems represent a tool by which information systems professionals can facilitate achievement of their organization's goals by providing marketing managers with regular flows of relevant information and flexible inquiry and analysis tools to support marketing decision making. Marketing has been presented as that area of the organization whose goal is to create opportunities for successful exchanges between the organization and its potential customers. Marketing seeks to develop competitive advantage in the marketplace by developing, implementing, and monitoring effective strategic and tactical programs guided by high quality information. Marketing information systems include systems for monitoring external and internal business environments, systems for developing and maintaining dynamic databases, flexible inquiry, analysis and reporting tools, and systems to assure the integrity of the marketing databases and operational components.

The development of an MKIS is a significant effort and the challenges are substantially greater for the multinational corporation. The special challenges facing developers of an internationally oriented MKIS include unique managerial problems related to coordination of operations, data collection and processing, and transmission of data across national boundaries. One approach to addressing these problems may be to provide managers in host counties with substantial autonomy over the development of local MKIS within standards and guidelines that will assure conformity to the data requirements of the central MKIS. This can allow a MKIS to reflect the marketing decision making process of the MNC and allow it to be adapted to the environmental circumstances of the host countries. After data have been collected and initially processed on local computer systems, they may then be transmitted to the MNCs central system within the limitations of local regulations and technological constraints governing transborder data flows. As the central MKIS database is developed, the information that it contains can be shared and used by corporate managers and by marketing managers both in the home office and each country of operation.

REFERENCES

Bagozzi, Richard P. (1986), *Principles of Marketing Management*, Science Research Associates, Chicago, IL.

Bennett, Peter B., Ed. (1988), *Dictionary of Marketing Terms*, American Marketing Association, Chicago, IL.

Boone, Louis E., and Kurtz, David L. (1989), *Contemporary Marketing, Sixth Edition, The Dryden Press*, Chicago, IL.

Bowers, Elena (1990), "Powerhouses Tear Down Europe Borders," *Advertising Age*, June 11, s-14-16.

Cash, James I., and Konsynski, Benn R. (1985), "IS Redraws Competitive Boundaries," *Harvard Business Review*, Vol. 63, No. 2 (March-April), 134-142.

Cateora, Philip (1987), *International Marketing*, Richard D. Irwin, Homewood, IL.

Chandler, J. S., and Liang, T. (1990), Developing Expert Systems for Business Applications, McGraw-Hill, New York, NY.

Churchill, Gilbert A., Jr. (1991), *Marketing Research: Methodological Foundations, Fifth Edition*, Dryden, Chicago, IL.

Cox, D. F., and Good, R. E. (1967), "How to Build a Marketing Information System," Harvard Business Review, Vol. 45, No. 3 (May-June), 145-154.

Curry, David J. (1993), *The New Marketing Research Systems*, John Wiley and Sons, New York, NY.

Czinkota, Michael R. and Ronkainen, Ilkka A. (1993), *International Marketing, Third Edition*, The Dryden Press, Chicago, IL.

Darian, Jean C. (1989), "Estimating Market and Sales Potential Using a Dialog Data Base," in Dyer, Robert F., and Steinberg, Margery S., eds., *Proceedings of the 1989 AMA Microcomputers in the Marketing Curriculum Conference*, American Marketing Association, Chicago, IL, 74-82.

Datapro Reports (1989), *Marketing Information Systems*, McGraw-Hill, New York,NY.

Dawson, Donna (1989), "Booming Reports," *Marketing*, December 14, . 37.

Deans, Candace P., and Kane, Michael J. (1992), *International Dimen-*

sions of Information Systems and Technology, PWS-Kent Publishing Company, Boston, MA.

Deans, Candace P., and Ricks, David A. (1993), "An Agenda for Research Linking Information Systems and International Business: Theory, Methodology and Application," *Journal of Global Information Management*, Vol. 1, No. 1 (Winter), 1-14.

Deans, Candace P., and Ricks, David A. (1991), "MIS Research: A Model for Incorporating The International Dimension," *The Journal of High Technology Management Research*, Vol. 2, No. 1, 57-81.

Dialog Information Services, Inc. (1993), *Dialog Database Catalog, January 1993*, Dialog Information Services, Inc., Palo Alto, CA.

Dobrozdravic, N. (1989), "Computerized Lead-tracking Analysis Makes Direct Marketing More Effective," *Marketing News*, Vol. 23, No. 11, 27-28.

Dunne, Patrick M. and Wolk, Harry L. (1977), "Marketing Cost Analysis: A Modularized Contribution Approach," *Journal of Marketing*, July, 83-94.

Dyer, R. F. (1987), "An Integrated Design for Personal Computers in the Marketing Curriculum," *Journal of the Academy of Marketing Science*, Vol. 15, No., 2, 16-24.

Eisenhart, Thomas (1988), "Faced with Limited Resources the Computer is Becoming a Key Tool in Staying Close to the Customer," *Business Marketing*, Vol. 73, No. 5, 49-56.

Ferrell, O.C., and Lucas, George (1987), "An Evaluation of Progress in the Development of a Definition of Marketing," *Journal of the Academy of Marketing Science*, Vol. 16, No. 3, 17.

Goodyear, Mary (1990), "Bold Approaches to Brave New Worlds," *Marketing Week*, March 23, 52-55.

Hohn, Siegfried (1986), "How Information Technology is Transforming Corporate Planning," Long Range Planning, Vol. 19, No. 4, 18-30.

Jeannet, Jean-Pierre and Hennessey (1992), Hubert D., *Global Marketing Strategies, Second Edition*, Houghton Mifflin Company, Dallas. TX.

Keon, E. F. (1987), "Making MKIS Work for You," *Business Marketing*, Vol. 72, No. 10, 71-73.

Krol, Ed. (1992), *The Whole Internet User's Guide and Catalog*, O'Reilly and Associates, Inc., Sebastopol, CA.

Kotler, Philip (1991), *Marketing Management: Analysis, Planning, Implementation and Control, Seventh Edition*, Prentice-Hall, Englewood Cliffs, NJ.

Little, John D. C. (1979), "Decision Support Systems for Marketing Managers," *Journal of Marketing*, Vol. 43, Summer, 1979, 9-26.

Malhotra (1992), "Shifting Perspective on the Shifting Paradigm in Marketing Research: A New Paradigm in Marketing Research," *Journal of the Academy of Marketing Science*, Vol. 20, No. 4, 379-387.

Marshall, Kimball P., and Lamotte, Stephen W. (1992), "Marketing Information Systems: A Marriage of Systems Analysis and Marketing Management," *Journal of Applied Business Research*, Vol. 8, No. 3 (Summer), 61-73.

McCarthy, Jerome E., and Perreault, William D., Jr. (1993), *Basic Marketing: A Global Managerial Approach*, Irwin, Homewood, IL.

Montgomery, David B. and Weinberg, Charles B. (1979), "Toward Strategic Intelligence Systems," *Journal of Marketing*, Vol. 43, Fall, 41-52.

Moriatry, R. T., and Swartz, G. T. (1989), "Automation to Boost Sales and Marketing," *Harvard Business Review*, Vol. 89, No. 1, 100-108.

Perreault, William D., Jr. (1992), "The Shifting Paradigm in Marketing Research," *Journal of the Academy of Marketing Science*, Vol. 20, No. 4, 367-

375.

Phatak, Arvind V. (1992), *International Dimensions of Management, Third Edition*, PWS-Kent, Boston, MA.

Porter, Michael E. (1979), "How Competitive Forces Shape Strategy," *Harvard Business Review*, March-April, 137-145.

Porter, Michael E. (1980), *Competitive Strategy: Techniques for Analyzing Industries and Competitors*, The Free Press, New York, NY.

Porter, Michael E. (1985), *Competitive Advantage*, The Free Press, NY.

Porter, Michael E., and Millar, Victor E. (1985), "How Information Gives You Competitive Advantage," *Harvard Business Review*, Vol. 63, No. 4 (July-August), 149-160.

Pride, William M., and Ferrell, O.C. (1991), *Marketing Concepts and Strategies, Seventh Edition*, Houghton Mifflin Company, Boston, MA.

Ramachandran, Kavil (1991), "Data Collection for Management Research in Developing Countries," in Smith, N. C. and Dainty, P., eds., *The Management Research Handbook*, Routledge, London, GB.

Rice, Gillman and Mahmoud, Essam (1984), "Forecasting and Data Bases in International Business," *Management International Review*, Vol. 24, Fourth Quarter, 59-70.

Robinson, P.J. (1989), "High Time to Exploit Applied Science in Marketing in the Knowledgeable '90's," *Marketing News*, Vol. 23, No. 11, 11-12.

Rubinstein, E. (1989), "Food Manufacturers Discover Value of Intelligence Systems," *Marketing News*, Vol. 23, No. 11.

Sales and Marketing Management (1989), 1989 Survey of Buying Power, August 7.

Snyder, C. (1988), "Bigger sales, Better Marketing: The Potential of Creative Computing," *Business Software Review*, Vol. 7, No. 8, 24-29.

Stewart, David W. (1984), *Secondary Research: Information Sources and Methods*, Sage Publications, Newbury Park, CA.

Terpstra, Vern (1988), *International Dimensions of Marketing, Second Edition*, PWS-Kent Publishing Company, Boston, MA.

von Hippel, E. (1977), "Has A Customer Already Developed Your Next Product," *Sloan Management Review*, Vol. 18, Winter, 63.

Vukmanic, Frank G., Czinkota, Michael R., Ricks, David A. (1985), "National and International Data Problems and Solutions in the Empirical Analysis of Intra-Industry Direct Foreign Investment," in Erdilek, Asim, ed., *Multinationals as Mutual Invaders*, Croon Helm, London, GB.

Wiseman, Charles, *Strategy and Computers*, Dow Jones-Irwin, Homewood, IL, 1988.

CHAPTER 4

Promise of Decision Support Systems for International Marketing Executives

CUNEYT EVIRGEN
S. TAMER CAVUSGIL

Michigan State University

Expert knowledge is extremely scarce and decisions are particularly complex in international marketing. There are many critical decisions such as the decision to go international or not, selecting market(s) for entry, selecting foreign distributors, joint venture partners, etc. Hence, international marketing offers an appropriate domain for development of useful expert system applications (Cavusgil, 1990). On the other hand, a number of steps can be identified in the internationalization process of companies. Companies would be making different types of decisions at each of those steps and would have different needs for assistance. Expert systems applications can help companies make strategic choices more systematically. The underlying theme in this chapter is that expert systems methodology can be applied to international marketing decisions with fruitful results. A comprehensive project aimed at developing such applications is described and current applications in international business are briefly presented.

INTRODUCTION

In recent years, there has been a growing interest in expert systems research, and in particular, expert system applications in various business domains. Among these, international marketing has proven to be a fruitful domain generating interesting applications such as CORE, Country Consultant, PARTNER, FREIGHT, PRODUCT, and NEGOTEX (Cavusgil and Nason, 1990; Cavusgil, Mitri and Evirgen, 1992; Mitri, et.al., 1991; Ozsomer, et. al., 1992; Rangaswamy, et. al., 1989). This interest is due to the usefulness of expert systems in enhancing knowledge dissemination and managerial decision making.

Expert system applications are particularly appropriate for international marketing decisions due to scarcity of expertise and complexity of decisions (Mitri, et.al., 1991). In this chapter, an overview of expert systems will be provided first, followed by a discussion of the use of expert systems in international marketing. Then, a framework for involvement in international business will be described. It will be argued that this framework can be used to develop expert system applications for international marketing. Finally, a comprehensive research project currently underway at the Expert Systems Laboratory of the Center for International Business Education and Research at Michigan State University aimed at developing such systems will be described along with various applications which have been developed.

The main objective of this chapter is to demonstrate the use of expert systems in international business and marketing decisions. It will be argued that international marketing offers a very suitable domain for expert system applications that would generate fruitful results. Another objective is to illustrate the usefulness of the framework used to structure development efforts of such systems for international marketing. Finally, the chapter aims to illustrate the promise of expert systems for international marketing executives.

WHAT ARE EXPERT SYSTEMS?

A variety of definitions and descriptions of expert systems are offered in the literature. According to Newquist (1986), expert systems are computer programs that mimic human logic to solve problems (cited in Mentzer and Gandhi, 1992, p.73). Such systems represent one type of application of artificial intelligence (AI) technology (Luconi, Malone and Scott Morton, 1986).

Waterman and Hayes-Roth (1982) define an expert system as "a computer program that uses the experience of one or more experts in some problem domain and applies their problem solving expertise to make useful inferences for the user of the system" (cited in Mentzer and Gandhi, 1992, p.73). Rangaswamy, et. al. (1989)'s definition is very similar with the exception that they specify a single expert being the knowledge source. If more than one expert or source is involved in supplying the knowledge, then such systems are referred to as knowledge-based systems (Luconi, Malone and Scott Morton, 1986).

Although there is no commonly agreed definition of expert systems, there seems to be a consensus that expert systems are computer programs, applied within a specified domain, that incorporate the knowledge of experts in that domain, and make that knowledge available to nonexperts to aid in solving problems within that domain. They differ from traditional computer applications by the use of heuristic reasoning (Luconi, Malone and Scott Morton, 1986). They are also a class of innovative tools to express and disseminate knowledge (Cavusgil, 1990). Remus and Kottemann (1986) also point out that an expert system "attempts to induce or deduce new knowledge using the system's *a priori* knowledge, inferred knowledge and real world data" (p.408).

Finlay, Forsey and Wilson (1988) classify expert systems into management information system (MIS) or decision support systems (DSS). In the former type, the outcomes are all specified, exhaustive and mutually exclusive, whereas in the latter type they are not required to be specified, exhaustive or mutually exclusive. In describing a DSS, Finlay, Forsey and Wilson (1988) state that: "Here there is no 'right' answer. Knowledge is difficult to elicit; little of it will have been documented; some of it will never even have been unambiguously articulated. The expert system will be providing insights to the user..." (p.935). The focus of this chapter is on decision support systems.

Facts and heuristics comprise the knowledge of an expert system (Mentzer and Gandhi, 1992). "The 'facts' constitute a body of information that is widely shared, available, and agreed upon by experts in the field. The 'heuristics' are rules of thumb that are used by experts to make judgments on the basis of their own beliefs and experience" (Mentzer and Gandhi, 1992, p.73).

An expert system typically has two main components: the knowledge base and the inference engine (Luconi, Malone and Scott Morton, 1986). The knowledge base contains the rules and facts. These include definitions of the objects and variables related to the application domain and the relationships among them (Rangaswamy, et. al., 1989). The inference engine, on the other hand, contains the inference strategies, and it processes the elements of the knowledge base to solve a particular problem within the domain (Mentzer and Gandhi, 1992; Rangaswamy, et. al., 1989).

Interaction with the user is achieved through the user interface program or protocol. During such interaction, which we will call "consultation", the inference engine infers the user's responses and the system's queries using the facts and rules stored in the knowledge base (Mentzer and Gandhi, 1992).

Basic Requirements of Expert Systems

Rangaswamy, et. al., (1989) suggest three basic requirements that expert systems should satisfy: First of all, the system should be able to represent the accumulated knowledge and expertise in its domain of application in such a way that this knowledge and expertise is accessible and usable by a computer. Secondly, the incorporated knowledge and expertise should be usable in different ways. For example, the system should be able to refer to particular elements of the knowledge base and request additional information to solve a problem. Third, the system should be user-friendly.

In regards to user-friendliness, the system should have WHAT, WHY, HOW and WHAT-IF features. These features refer to the system's capabilities to clarify its questions, to justify the presence of the questions, to explain its reasoning and to allow the user to play what-if games, respectively. In fact, one of the distinguishing characteristics of expert systems is their ability to explain their own reasoning (Buchanon and Smith, 1989).

Validation Issues

Validation of the expert system is a vital stage in its development (Rangaswamy, et. al., 1989). The effective use of expert systems and their widespread acceptance depend on the quality of output produced by such systems. To ensure high quality of output, the expert systems have to be validated before being used in real life situations. Any kind of validation methodology would entail validation of both the knowledge base and the inference engine. Hence, rigorous and scientific validation methodologies and procedures need to be developed and implemented. Two such methodologies have been suggested in the literature for two different types of expert system architectures (Evirgen, et. al., 1992; Ozsomer, et al., 1992).

USE OF EXPERT SYSTEMS IN INTERNATIONAL MARKETING

In terms of the desirability of developing expert systems, Cavusgil (1990) notes that there are three dimensions that need to be considered: feasibility, justification and appropriateness. Feasibility requires that experts within the domain of application exist, are accessible and can articulate their expertise and that a consensus on solutions can be reached. These criteria are very challenging to meet and require a great deal of commitment and investment for both the experts and the system developers. Justification for developing expert systems would be achieved if the solution has high payoff, expert knowledge is scarce and expertise is needed in many locations. Finally, appropriateness condition requires the task to be of manageable size, to require heuristic solutions and to have practical value. Applying these conditions, Cavusgil (1990) concludes that expert systems are particularly desirable in a domain where there is little or no established theory. International marketing, in particular, is one such area where expert system development can lead to potentially useful applications.

Expert system applications are particularly desirable within the domain of international marketing. The criteria of feasibility, justification and appropriateness are easily met within that domain (Cavusgil, 1990). Expert knowledge is extremely scarce and fragmented in international marketing. Moreover, the complexity and uncertainty of the international marketing environment makes expertise that much more valuable and needed. Expert systems can preserve and disseminate scarce expertise, and make this expertise readily available to novices or less experienced people who are involved in international marketing (Ozsomer, et.al., 1992).

The complex and uncertain environment of international marketing offers many challenges to companies. There is also a tendency among many companies to focus on domestic operations and to overlook great international business opportunities due to various attitudinal, informational or operational barriers (Cavusgil, 1980). Expert systems in various areas of international marketing would help to reduce the complexity and to overcome these barriers significantly as educational or training tools. Through interacting with such systems and accessing their knowledge bases, the users can learn about international marketing decision areas and criteria. Such systems can be tailored to the user, be very practical and provide a very concise and efficient training tool for managers.

Ozsomer, et. al. (1992) note that expert systems can facilitate better, more effective and quicker decision making and thereby enhance the competitiveness of organizations. Through using expert systems, the users can capture the whole domain of the problem they are dealing with. This becomes particularly important in international marketing due to the complexity and uncertainty of the environment. There are a lot of different factors that play into international marketing decisions. The expert system will point to the relevant and critical dimensions to consider and provide a systematic approach to the problem under consideration. No matter what its domain of application is, an expert system will "have an impact on an organization's ability to achieve its objectives, as well as on overall performance" (Ozsomer, et.al., 1992, p.25).

10 STEP ROAD MAP TO SUCCESS IN FOREIGN MARKETS: A FRAMEWORK FOR EXPERT SYSTEM DEVELOPMENT IN INTERNATIONAL MARKETING

Companies are faced with a number of unique challenges when they attempt to internationalize their activities. Great success in the domestic market does not necessarily translate into great success in international markets. The complexity and uncertainty of the international business environment necessitates careful strategic assessment, planning and implementation. Miller (1993) has proposed the 10 Step Road Map[1] to success in foreign markets as a systematic framework to take a company through the internationalization process.

Miller (1993) notes that the 10 Step Road Map is based on extensive first-hand experience with both small and large companies and breaks the internationalization process into three main phases, namely assessment, planning, and implementation. Each of these phases involves taking a number of strategic steps and all together they form the 10 Step Road Map. Figure 1 shows the different steps in the Road Map and the issues dealt with at each step.

The assessment phase is where the company takes on an internal evaluation of where it is and where it is going. The objective is to assess the feasibility and appropriateness of getting involved in international business for the company. The first two steps in the Road Map are taken in this phase. Step 1 is the assessment of the company profile and Step 2 involves the assessment of the readiness of the company to export.

Planning is the second main phase which involves three steps tapping into planning issues that need to be considered and taken care of before moving on. The objective is to make sure that the necessary groundwork is done before major resources are committed and a sound strategic plan is in place for successful involvement in international business. Step 3 involves the assessment of global opportunities, Step 4 involves global strategic planning and budgeting, and foreign market entry plans are developed in Step 5.

The final five steps in the Road Map take place in the third phase of the internationalization process—implementation. In this phase, the company makes the necessary moves to go outside and implement the strategic plan that has been developed in the previous phase. The individual steps focus on specific aspects of the implementation phase of the internationalization process. Step 6 involves the identification, selection and contracting of various foreign partners such as distributors, licensees, joint venture partners, etc. The standards and regulations in effect in the foreign market are evaluated in Step 7. Identification, selection and contracting of support service providers such as freight forwarders, banks, etc. is

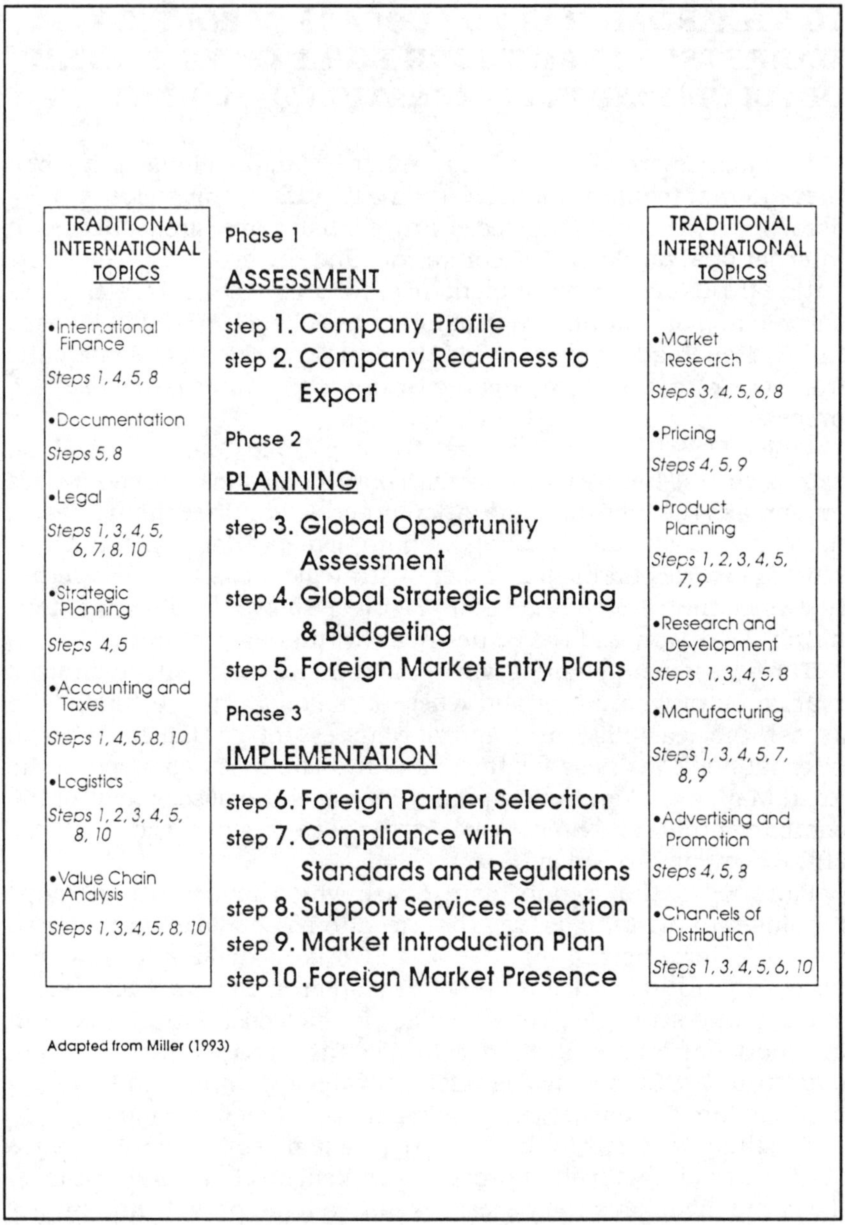

TRADITIONAL INTERNATIONAL TOPICS		TRADITIONAL INTERNATIONAL TOPICS
•International Finance *Steps 1, 4, 5, 8* •Documentation *Steps 5, 8* •Legal *Steps 1, 3, 4, 5, 6, 7, 8, 10* •Strategic Planning *Steps 4, 5* •Accounting and Taxes *Steps 1, 4, 5, 8, 10* •Logistics *Steps 1, 2, 3, 4, 5, 8, 10* •Value Chain Analysis *Steps 1, 3, 4, 5, 8, 10*	Phase 1 **ASSESSMENT** step 1. Company Profile step 2. Company Readiness to Export Phase 2 **PLANNING** step 3. Global Opportunity Assessment step 4. Global Strategic Planning & Budgeting step 5. Foreign Market Entry Plans Phase 3 **IMPLEMENTATION** step 6. Foreign Partner Selection step 7. Compliance with Standards and Regulations step 8. Support Services Selection step 9. Market Introduction Plan step 10. Foreign Market Presence	•Market Research *Steps 3, 4, 5, 6, 8* •Pricing *Steps 4, 5, 9* •Product Planning *Steps 1, 2, 3, 4, 5, 7, 9* •Research and Development *Steps 1, 3, 4, 5, 8* •Manufacturing *Steps 1, 3, 4, 5, 7, 8, 9* •Advertising and Promotion *Steps 4, 5, 8* •Channels of Distribution *Steps 1, 3, 4, 5, 6, 10*

Adapted from Miller (1993)

Figure 1: 10 Step Road Map to Success in Foreign Markets

carried out in Step 8. Step 9 involves developing the market introduction plan and finally, Step 10 is establishing a physical presence in the foreign market.

Miller (1993) emphasizes that the 10 Step Road Map is not a set of rules to follow, but rather provides a useful framework to follow for success in foreign markets. He also adds that the Road Map is not necessarily a one-way, neat path leading from one step to the next. In fact, companies may jump around from one step to another to take advantage of opportunities that may arise such as getting a sales order at a trade fair.

The 10 Step Road Map is also a useful framework to develop expert system applications in international marketing. The companies deal with different issues and have different needs at each step and are faced with different kinds of strategic marketing decisions to make. Hence, expert system applications for use at each step in the Road Map would aid the companies for success in foreign markets.

SOME EXPERT SYSTEM APPLICATIONS IN INTERNATIONAL MARKETING

Among others, international marketing decisions provide attractive platforms for development of fruitful expert systems applications (Cavusgil, 1990). In fact, in a comprehensive research project, a group of researchers at Michigan State University, Center for International Business Education and Research (MSU-CIBER) is involved in developing expert system applications in various decision areas within the domain of international business and in particular international marketing. These computer software programs developed by using artificial intelligence (AI) methodologies incorporate the knowledge and experience of seasoned international business executives as well as empirical research findings on international business operations.

The 10 Step Road Map (Miller, 1993) can be used as a framework to describe how the different expert system applications developed at MSU-CIBER can be used by companies. Each of the current applications developed can be used at one or more steps in the Road Map to aid in decision making at that step. Next, these applications developed will be briefly described pointing out where within the Road Map they would fit.

CORE^2 (COmpany Readiness to Export)

According to the 10 Step Road Map (Miller, 1993), for a company new to international business, the assessment of company readiness to export is one of the first steps for success in foreign markets. This requires an analysis of the desirability and feasibility of exporting for the company. Cavusgil and Nason (1990) note that there are two dimensions that need to be evaluated at this initial stage which are organizational readiness and product readiness to export.

Organizational Readiness

Organizational readiness refers to an internal evaluation of the company to assess whether the company is organizationally fit and ready to start exporting. As an organization, the company has to be ready to take on the challenge of exporting. This necessitates having the necessary resources, being motivated enough and being committed to exporting. In other words, the company must be ready to commit enough resources for successful exporting. In particular, exporting should not be seen as a side activity, but, rather must be considered as a major area of business by top management.

Product Readiness

Product readiness refers to evaluating the product under consideration to assess its suitability and potential for exporting. Hence, the variables to be considered under product readiness focus on the product itself and the potential export destination. These are related to the characteristics of the product and the market under consideration. Issues considered are whether the product is 'right' for exporting and whether the market(s) considered as export destination(s) is (are) 'right' for the product.

CORE is a microcomputer software application that can assist in the self examination of company readiness to engage in export activity. It provides an assessment of both organizational and product readiness to export as well as a tutorial on the basics of exporting. The most current version available is CORE III.

Structure of CORE

CORE evaluates a company's readiness to export along the dimensions of organizational readiness and product readiness. These dimensions are then further divided into subdimensions. In other words, CORE is structured along a hierarchy of dimensions where each subdimension is evaluated through the user's responses to a set of questions related to them.

Organizational readiness is analyzed in terms of three subdimensions, namely motivation, commitment, and firm characteristics, resources and growth rate. Product readiness, on the other hand, is analyzed through two subdimensions, namely product characteristics and product market fit.

Based on the user's responses to the set of questions asked, CORE generates ratings of a company along the two main dimensions—organization and product readiness. Ratings are also generated for each subdimension analyzed. The company's strengths and weaknesses in the context of exporting are identified and presented to the user along with a report including recommendations for the company.

CORE has been developed on the basis of substantial research into the success factors in exporting that discriminate successful exporters from non-exporting companies or unsuccessful exporters. It also reflects the collective opinions of numerous experts and seasoned international business executives. Since its introduction in 1986 as a D-Base III based decision support tool, CORE has gone through significant improvements. The original software is now replaced by the second generation program-CORE III.

CORE III incorporates the experience and the feedback obtained from hundreds of users of the original tool. The current version is no longer a D-Base application and is now programmed as an 'expert system' using artificial intelligence techniques and offers many technical capabilities. It has been developed with the objective of simplicity and user friendliness and does not require computer proficiency on the part of the user. The system is developed for IBM compatible PCs or networks.

Uses of CORE

First of all, CORE can be used by individual companies in evaluating their readiness to export in a systematic and objective way. Second, it can be used as a training tool by export assistance agencies in preparing their client companies for successful export market entry. Third, CORE can be used as an educational tool in seminars and workshops designed for potential exporters.

Despite the short period since its introduction in 1986 and limited publicity, CORE has been acquired by hundreds of users both in the U.S. and abroad. The U.S. Department of Commerce adopted CORE in 1991 as a principal training tool. In a project known as the Export Qualifier Program, the U.S. and Foreign Commercial Service of Commerce is currently working on incorporating CORE into its field offices throughout the country. Similarly, the U.S. Small Business Administration has adopted this software as a training and decision support tool for use nationwide. CORE has also been adopted by state export assistance agencies as well as individual companies in countries such as Australia, Ireland, Thailand, Turkey, Norway, France, and Canada. It has also been translated into Thai, Chinese and Turkish and different country versions have been developed. The International Trade Center (UNCTAD/GATT) has also adopted CORE in its export development programs for developing countries. It is also very important to note that the successful experience of CORE has been instrumental in developing other expert system applications within the domain of international business.

Country Consultant[3]

One of the most critical tasks facing companies engaged in international marketing is evaluation of different foreign markets and selecting the one(s) to enter (Evirgen, Bodur and Cavusgil, 1993). This necessitates having reliable, relevant and up-to-date information about various characteristics of the market(s). Cavusgil, Mitri and Evirgen (1992) note that uncertainty is a significant factor in foreign market selection decisions and information helps to reduce this uncertainty. Such information is absolutely needed during the planning phase in the 10 Step Road Map. Moreover, up-to-date and reliable information on the foreign market(s) selected is also needed to supplement decisions made in the other steps.

"Information on the demographic, political, economic, cultural and legal environments as well as information on market entry conditions and information on the market structure (in aggregate or disaggregate form) are highlighted in the literature as key information requirements in country selection" (Cavusgil, Mitri and Evirgen, 1992, p.25). Moreover, information about these characteristics also tends to be different for different industries and entry modes making information needs a multidimensional problem.

The Country Consultant is an intelligent knowledge base that incorporates factual information coming out of secondary research, executive insights, decision rules and international business and marketing guidelines. It contains processed judgmental knowledge about foreign markets as well as practical guidelines (Evirgen, Mitri and Cavusgil, 1993). Hence, the Country Consultant can be used at any step along the Road Map since different types of information about the foreign market(s) will always be needed. However, it would be particularly very useful during the planning phase which includes Steps 3 through 5. The system is designed to operate on IBM-compatible PCs.

Structure of the Country Consultant

Information in the Country Consultant is organized in terms of four concept types. These are market feature, entry mode, industry, and market. Each piece of information is tied to one particular combination of market feature, entry mode, industry and market. For example, information on health standards (market feature) for licensing (entry mode) pharmaceuticals (industry) in Germany (market).

The Country Consultant has two forms of knowledge representing the stored information: judgments and guidelines. Judgments are evaluative statements giving the user an assessment of the current situation and future direction, whereas guidelines are descriptive in nature. Each judgment refers to one and only one concept combination as described above. The judgments indicate how "good" or "bad" the current situation is and whether it is getting better or worse. Each judgment has a confidence level associated with it indicating the reliability level of the presented assessment. Moreover, textual information coming out of secondary sources on which the judgment is based is provided to the user. Guidelines, on the other hand, contain information in text form for different concept combinations. Information presented covers issues such as how to do business in that country, contact places, culturegrams, negotiation guidelines, etc. The structure of the Country Consultant is presented in Figure 2.

The Country Consultant is also an intelligent knowledge base with its intelligence stemming from its inferencing capabilities. If there is no judgment pertaining to the particular concept combination requested by the user, the system can be asked to infer a judgment based on other judgments already stored in the knowledge base that are conceptually close to the original request.

Some additional features of the Country Consultant include getting knowledge base statistics, defining inferencing strategy, comparing judgments across any of the concept types (feature, industry, entry mode or market), doing keyword search, and defining the scope of the queries.

Uses of the Country Consultant

Cavusgil, Mitri and Evirgen (1992) suggest a variety of different uses for the Country Consultant: The Country Consultant fills in the need for processed information on foreign markets. It "provides to the user ready-to-use information by compiling the relevant data and information presented in published documents or reports and supplementing this with expert consultation" (p.30). The system is also designed to be able to adjust to different needs of any company interested in going international or selecting a foreign market for entry. Furthermore, marketing managers will be able to use their time more efficiently by accessing the Country Consultant since the information they need would be presented to them in a user-friendly software form. The Country Consultant also helps companies to structure their market research studies on foreign markets. Evirgen (1992) also suggests that the information contained in the judgments can be coded to test a causal model for foreign market attractiveness. Finally, the tool can be used in the classroom in international business or international market research courses as supplementary material. Instances of educational usage of the tool have been reported elsewhere (Bhargava, et. al., 1993)

CEVAL (Candidate EVALuator) Applications

Candidate Evaluation Shell: CEVED and CEVAL[4]

A number of expert system applications have been developed using a task-specific expert system shell, namely Candidate Evaluation which has two components. The **C**andidate **EV**aluation **ED**itor (CEVED) is the development environment, and **C**andidate **EVAL**uator (CEVAL) is the run-time module and includes the inference engine and the user interface.

CEVED can be used to represent four main types of objects: dimensions of evaluation, contextual questions, evaluative questions and recommendation fragments (Mitri, 1991). Dimensions refer to the constructs of the evaluation model being implemented. These are related to each other in a parent-child relationship forming a tree-structured dimension hierarchy. A weighted linear model is used along this hierarchy to generate scores for the dimensions. The overall score of a parent dimension is based on a linear-weighted sum of the scores of its children dimensions. The context questions allow the weights of the dimensions to be adjusted based on the context. There is a set of evaluative questions associated with each lowest-level dimension in the hierarchy. The score of a lowest-level dimension is the linear weighted-sum of the scores of its evaluative questions. The scores of the questions are determined through the responses of the user. Finally, the dimension ratings (or scores) are tied to and trigger recommendation fragments. Thus, CEVED is used to develop the knowledge base.

CEVAL, on the other hand, is what the user interacts with to evaluate a pool of candidates. It presents the context and evaluative questions to the user, processes his/her responses, and presents a final recommendation to the user based on the dimension ratings. Figure 3 shows the structural components and flow of knowledge in the CEVED/CEVAL system.

So far, the CEVED/CEVAL shell for expert system development has been used to develop three modules that involve selection of various types of foreign 'partners' along the 10 Step Road Map. Among these, PARTNER is used for international cooperative venture partner selection; FREIGHT is used for freight forwarder selection in exporting; and DISTEVAL is used for foreign distributor selection. Next, these modules will be briefly described.

PARTNER[5] (Collaborative Venture PARTNER Selection)

In today's highly competitive and volatile global environment, companies are strongly motivated not to go alone (Ohmae, 1989). In

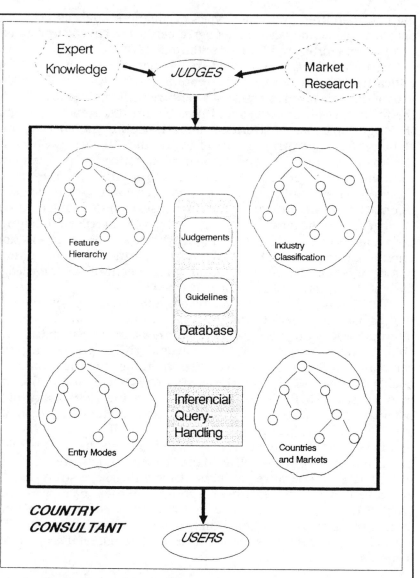

Judge enters information based on expert knowledge and market research findings. User queries the system for information, which triggers inferencing process. Semantic networks aid in knowledge organization and inferencing.

Figure 2: Structural Components and Information Flow of Country Consultant©

this regard, there has been growing interest in international cooperative ventures among firms. These ventures are more than arm's-length or open market transactions, but fall short of merger including joint ventures and other types of alliances such as licensing agreements, technology transfer agreements, joint marketing agreements, etc. (Porter and Fuller 1986; Root 1988).

International cooperative venture partner selection is one of the critical decisions to be made when entering such a venture. There are a lot of risks involved in entering a venture with another firm due to the prevailing uncertainties and possible misfits. Hence, selecting the "right" partner is of critical importance for the success and viability of a cooperative venture of any nature. That's why Step 6 in the Road Map involving the decision of selecting the partner(s) to work with is a very critical step that needs to be taken with great care.

Nevertheless, limited attention has been given to the issue of international cooperative venture partner selection (Geringer, 1991). Geringer (1991) suggests to distinguish between partner-related and task-related criteria in developing a typology of partner selection criteria. Geringer's (1988, 1991) model of partner selection criteria has been central in the conceptual development of the knowledge base of the expert system to be described.

PARTNER is an interactive microcomputer expert system module that assists managers in the analysis and evaluation of potential international cooperative venture partners in a systematic and objective way (Evirgen, 1993). It is particularly designed to help the companies at Step 6 in the Road Map when they may be looking for such partners. PARTNER can be used with IBM-compatible PCs. The module provides feedback to the user on the desirability of a potential cooperative venture partner based on an evaluation of its attributes on key dimensions.

It is important to note that a variety of different names are used in the business world as well as in the academic literature to refer to international cooperative ventures. Among these are strategic alliances, collaborative ventures, corporate linkages, coalitions, etc. PARTNER is equally applicable to any form of cooperative agreement/arrangement between firms in international business. We have chosen to refer to such ventures as *international cooperative ventures*.

Structure of PARTNER

PARTNER evaluates a potential cooperative venture partner in terms of partner-related and task-related criteria. These two dimensions are further subdivided into subdimensions. Hence, PARTNER is structured along a hierarchy of dimensions representing parent-child relationships (Evirgen, 1993).

Partner-related selection criteria refer to those variables that are relevant qualifications of the partner which are not specific to the type of operation, but that affect the risk(s) faced. These allow an assessment of the efficiency and effectiveness of the partners' cooperation. Partner-related criteria are examined along six subdimensions, namely partner characteristics, compatibility of business philosophies, motivation, commitment, reliability, and property rights protection.

Task-related selection criteria refer to those variables that are relevant for the venture's viability in terms of its operational requirements. Hence, these variables are specific to operational resources and skills related to the venture. Task-related criteria for the potential partner are also examined along six subdimensions. These are potential partner's financial resources, marketing resources, customer service, R&D and technical resources, organizational resources, and production resources. Production resources dimension is further subdivided into production facilities and assets, production workforce and government incentives for local production.

Geringer (1991) has found that relative importance of task-related criteria are contingent upon the strategic context of the venture. Context questions enhance PARTNER's adaptability to different venture contexts. These questions are designed to determine the context of the venture under consideration which may be R&D and technology-based, production-based, etc. Context questions function to automatically adjust the weights and/or ratings of the individual dimensions based on the user's responses.

There are also a couple of evaluative questions which operate as quick reject questions included in PARTNER. These questions are extremely critical questions in evaluating potential international cooperative venture partners. When the user answers one of these questions, a warning message may be triggered depending on his/her response. At that point, the user has the options of either getting out of the program or continuing with the rest of the questionnaire. The warning messages are there to alert the user to extremely unfavorable conditions regarding a potential cooperative venture with the candidate you are evaluating.

PARTNER does not demand any degree of computer proficiency from the user other than simple keyboard familiarity. The software has been developed for simplicity and user-friendliness. It has the WHAT, WHY, HOW, and WHAT-IF features noted as requirements of expert systems above (Rangaswamy, et. al.,1989). There is an explanation message for each dimension, context question and evaluative question in the system. Moreover, the user can query the system to find out why a dimension received a particular rating, or why a particular recommendation is made. PARTNER also allows the user to compare a number of candidates simultaneously and play what-if games.

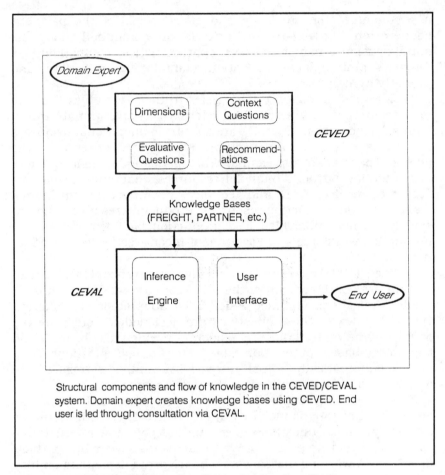

Structural components and flow of knowledge in the CEVED/CEVAL
system. Domain expert creates knowledge bases using CEVED. End
user is led through consultation via CEVAL.

Figure 3: CEVED-CEVAL Candidate Evaluation Shell

Uses of PARTNER

PARTNER is designed as an interactive decision support system to
aid managerial decision making. It can be used to evaluate and
compare a number of potential international cooperative venture
partners, and help in selecting the most suitable candidate. PART-
NER helps the managers in a number of ways. First of all, the
questioning process and the hierarchy of dimensions alert the user
to the critical issues and dimensions involved in the partner selection
process. Thus, it serves a pedagogical as well as a training purpose.
Second, the tool provides a systematic and objective evaluation as
well as simultaneous comparison of potential cooperative venture
partners. Third, recommendations are provided by the module in
regard to each of the candidates both on overall assessments and on
individual dimensions of evaluation.

PARTNER is especially useful to companies (a) that are new to international cooperative ventures by identifying the critical factors that need to be considered in selecting a venture partner or (b) that currently have entered international cooperative ventures by assisting them to evaluate new potential partners for other ventures and/ or to reevaluate the existing partners.

PARTNER can be used by government agencies at the federal or state level in preparing their clients for international cooperative ventures. Companies can use PARTNER as a competitive learning tool as well. Through being exposed to the types of questions they must be thinking about, the users are better equipped for negotiations.

Moreover, PARTNER can also be used by international business consultants who consult companies on selecting cooperative venture partners. Finally, PARTNER can be used as an educational tool in international business and marketing classes by academic institutions.

FREIGHT[6] (FREIGHT Forwarder Evaluator)

There are a number of support services that companies might decide to use to facilitate their exporting. Step 8 in the Road Map involves the selection of support services to use and providers of those services. One such service is provided by international freight forwarders. These are intermediaries that facilitate the movement of goods from the exporting country to the importing country. They provide services such as arranging for carrier and commercial documentation, license requirements, customs clearance, freight insurance issues, transportation of goods (via air, sea/ocean and/ or surface).

A rather complex set of documentary requirements needs to be fulfilled during the process of exporting and importing. The companies also need to be fully informed about any changes in the trade and customs legislation both in the exporting and importing country. Moreover, any delays in product delivery may lead to irrecoverable losses. It is extremely important that your goods arrive at the export destination undamaged, on time, and in the right amount. Selection of a freight forwarder is thus a very critical strategic decision to be made when the exporter decides to use such a service. The objective is to select the freight forwarder that will fit your needs best.

FREIGHT is designed to aid the decision maker(s) in evaluating and selecting international freight forwarders that would fit their needs best (Ozsomer, Mitri and Cavusgil, 1993). It is an interactive microcomputer expert system module that runs on IBM-compatible PCs. The module is particularly directed for use at Step 8 in the Road Map where the company would be selecting support services. It gives the user feedback on the suitability of a potential freight forwarder for the exporter based on its evaluation of the forwarder on six key criteria.

Structure of FREIGHT

FREIGHT evaluates a potential international freight forwarder in terms of six strategic criteria. Similar to other CEVED/CEVAL applications, FREIGHT is also structured along a hierarchy of dimensions representing parent-child relationships (Ozsomer, Mitri and Cavusgil, 1993).

There are six major criteria used in selecting foreign distributors which are expertise, specialization, responsiveness and attention, efficiency and reliability, communication and information, and finance. Hence, FREIGHT evaluates potential freight forwarders on these dimensions. Two of these dimensions are further divided into subdimensions similar to the case of PARTNER. The dimension called specialization is divided into two subdimensions which are product/service specialization and geographical specialization. Similarly, finance dimension is divided into two subdimensions which are pricing and financial position.

Through hypertext, some phrases in the texts of dimension, question, and recommendation explanations are linked to *additional information segments* called *tutorials*. Hence, the user is able to refer to this tutorial for any term or phrase that s/he is unfamiliar with in the context of international freight forwarding. FREIGHT also makes use of quick reject questions as described in the section on PARTNER above.

Uses of FREIGHT

FREIGHT can be used by exporters to systematically evaluate and compare the capabilities of a number of potential international freight forwarders and aid in selecting the one that fits its needs best. It helps exporters to select the most appropriate international freight forwarder for their type and volume of business by providing an assessment of the level of fit between the exporter's needs and the forwarder's offerings. Export assistance agencies can use FREIGHT in preparing their clients for exporting. The nearly 2,000 members of the International Federation of Freight Forwarders Association (FIATA) can benefit from FREIGHT by using it to identify their strengths and weaknesses vis-a-vis competitors. Finally, FREIGHT can also be used as an educational tool in the classroom and a training tool in the companies.

DISTEVAL[7] (DISTributor EVALuator)

The success of a company in international business depends very much on how well its distribution system works. This system is the key link between the company and its foreign customers. When considering entry into foreign markets, choice of the channel structure to use is one of the critical decisions facing the company. Selecting a foreign distributor and working with it is one of the typical choices made by the marketing executive. In particular, if the exporter lacks financial resources to market its product in the foreign market and/or is not familiar with the foreign market, working with a foreign distributor may be better to enter the market. If the company will be working with the distributor, the selection process is similar to that of selecting a partner. Hence, distributor selection is also one of the decisions made at Step 6 in the Road Map.

Selection of a foreign distributor to work with is a very critical task if that route of channel structure is chosen. There are a number of risks involved in the decision such as getting 'locked in' with an undesirable distributor, developing a future competitor, etc. In some countries especially it is next to impossible to break a distributor agreement once it is set without incurring great losses.

DISTEVAL is an interactive microcomputer expert system module that assists managers by providing systematic and objective analysis and evaluation of potential foreign distributors. It is particularly designed to help the companies at Step 6 in the Road Map when they may be looking for such partners. It is different from PARTNER since it specifically addresses issues of concern in foreign distributor selection rather than in international cooperative venture partner selection. DISTEVAL can be used with IBM-compatible PCs. The module provides feedback to the user on the desirability of a potential foreign distributor based on an evaluation of its attributes on five key dimensions.

Structure of DISTEVAL

DISTEVAL evaluates a potential foreign distributor in terms of five strategic criteria. Similar to other CEVED/CEVAL applications, DISTEVAL is also structured along a hierarchy of dimensions representing parent-child relationships.

There are five major criteria used in selecting foreign distributors which are commitment, financial and company strengths, marketing factors, product factors and facilitating factors. Among these, commitment, and financial and company strengths are extremely critical. The other three criteria relate to the marketing capabilities of the distributor, its knowledge of the product and the market and some facilitating factors that would help a smoother relationship to develop. These five criteria are the dimensions in the hierarchical structure of DISTEVAL.

Uses of DISTEVAL

DISTEVAL can be used by companies to evaluate and compare a number of potential foreign distributors and help in selecting the

most suitable candidate. The tool can be used as a training instrument by export promotion agencies in their efforts to help their
clients to select foreign distributors. DISTEVAL can also be used to
supplement the Agent/Distributor Program offered by the U.S. and
Foreign Commercial Service. Moreover, DISTEVAL can be used by
training institutions offering international business certificate programs and seminars. Since it is a practical application which
requires and facilitates user involvement, DISTEVAL exercise is an
ideal tool for management's deliberations of foreign intermediaries.
Finally, DISTEVAL can be a supplement to teaching materials for
international marketing classes at colleges and universities.

BUDGET[8] (BUDGETing and Pricing Tools for the International Marketer)

BUDGET is a decision support system developed by the International Business Centers at Michigan State University. It is actually
not intended to be an expert system, but rather a decision support
tool to aid in decisions regarding budgeting, export price quotations,
pricing, and marketing mix sensitivity analysis.

As Miller (1993) notes, BUDGET is ideally suited for Steps 4 and
5 in the Road map, but can be used any time after Step 1 as well. If
it is used earlier, it can then be refined as the company moves
through the other steps. When used earlier, BUDGET can help to
develop a vision of the risks and rewards of going international.

Structure of BUDGET

BUDGET consists of four interrelated modules: (1) Budgeting for
entry into foreign markets; (2) Export price quotation; (3) Export cost
calculation, sales estimation and break-even analysis; and (4)
Marketing mix sensitivity analysis.

The budgeting module is used to prepare alternative budgets
including all budget items that must be taken into account in doing
international business. A case study of a hypothetical company is
also included in the module to serve as a guide to any company as
it expands into international markets. The export price quotation
module is developed to aid international marketers in preparing
export pricing quotation proposals quickly. Thirdly, the module on
export cost calculation, sales estimation and break-even analysis is
designed to calculate manufacturing costs and the export cost for
your product as well as a sales estimation, and the break-even point.
Finally, the marketing mix sensitivity analysis module is designed to
help managers perform what-if analyses on the marketing mix
variables. The module uses marketing mix elasticities in performing
the analyses and constructing the graphs.

All the modules of Budgeting and Pricing Tools for the International Marketer are Lotus 1-2-3 spreadsheets and require the use of WYSIWYG application of the Lotus 1-2-3 v3.1 software. The modules are menu driven and require only minimum knowledge of Lotus 1-2-3 software.

Uses of BUDGET

This decision support system is designed to serve the needs of a broad range of users. The module is both instructive and practical. The beginner users will find BUDGET very useful in understanding the basics and components of doing business overseas by working through the pricing issues and export price quotation modules. More advanced users will find the sensitivity analysis for the marketing mix variables interesting and helpful, especially through its graphs and tables. The expert users will benefit from the "what-if" scenario analyses and the enhanced graphical capabilities. BUDGET can also be used as an educational or training tool by referring to the sample cases for budgeting incorporated into it.

CONCLUSIONS

Expert system applications in a variety of domains have gained much interest in the last few years (Ozsomer, et. al., 1992). Among these domains, international marketing has proven to be a very suitable domain. This is mainly due to the fact that expert knowledge is very scarce and hard to locate in international marketing. However, it is possible to identify the areas where such knowledge would be needed and the 10 Step Road Map, proposed by Miller (1993), can be used for that purpose. This framework breaks the internationalization process into three phases—assessment, planning and implementation—and identifies a number of steps a company would be most likely to go through. There are different types of knowledge and expertise needed at each of these steps which point to potential areas for expert system applications.

Such an approach has been taken in a comprehensive expert system development research project at MSU-CIBER. The goal of the project is to develop expert system applications within the international marketing and business domain to help managers in their decision making. In this chapter, after a brief discussion of what expert systems are, the use of the international marketing domain for expert system applications is discussed. This is followed by the description of the 10 Step Road Map proposed as a framework for success in foreign markets and the applications developed at MSU-CIBER. Each of these applications is designed to help managers in their decision making in different areas of international marketing. These applications have generated a lot of interest among academicians, students and international business executives.

There are many benefits that would be achieved through developing expert system applications in international marketing. Efficient and effective dissemination of expert knowledge is facilitated through the use of expert systems. Such systems preserve and disseminate the knowledge of the expert(s) in the domain of application. Furthermore, they help the managers to make fast, efficient and effective decisions. Since each application captures the whole domain of the particular problem investigated, they can be used as educational tools in the classrooms and/or as training tools in companies. In short, decision support systems promise a lot for international business executives.

ENDNOTES

[1] The 10 Step Road Map to success in foreign markets is copyrighted by Myron M. Miller, 1990.

[2] CORE is copyrighted by S. Tamer Cavusgil.

[3] The Country Consultant is copyrighted by Michigan State University.

[4] For a more detailed discussion of the Candidate Evaluation shell and the approach to designing task-specific architecture in developing expert systems, see Mitri (1991).

[5] PARTNER is copyrighted by Michigan State University.

[6] FREIGHT is copyrighted by Michigan State University.

[7] DISTEVAL is copyrighted by Michigan State University.

[8] BUDGET is copyrighted by Michigan State University.

REFERENCES

Bhargava, V., Evirgen, C., Mitri, M., & Cavusgil, S.T. (1992). Using an Intelligent Database in the Classroom: The Case of the Country Consultant, *Journal of Teaching in International Business*, V. 4(3/4), 17-37..

Buchanan, B.G. & Smith, R.G. (1989). Fundamentals of Expert Systems. In A. Bann, P.R. Cohen and E.A. Feigenbaum (Eds), *The Handbook of Artificial Intelligence*. vol 4, Addison-Wesley Publishing Group, Inc.

Cavusgil, S.T. (1980). On the Internationalization Problem of Firms, *European Research*, 8:(6), 273-281.

Cavusgil, S. T. (1990). Expert Systems in International Marketing. In Bearden, et al. (Eds), *1990 AMA Summer Educators' Proceedings*, American Marketing Association, 336.

Cavusgil, S.T. & Nason. R. (1990). Assessment of Company Readiness to Export. In H. Thorelli & S.T. Cavusgil (Eds.), *International Marketing Strategy*. Pergamon Press, 129-139.

Cavusgil, S.T., Mitri, M. & Evirgen, C. (1992). A Decision Support System for Doing Business in East Block Countries: The Country Consultant,

European Business Review, 92:(4), 24-34.

Evirgen, C. (1992). A Causal Model for Foreign Market Attractiveness: Use of a Decision Support Tool as the Knowledge Base, In Leone, *et al.* (Eds.), *Proceedings of the 1992 AMA Summer Educators' Conference,* abstract, 208.

(1993). Use of Expert Systems in International Marketing: An Application for Cooperative Venture Partner Selection, working paper presented at *the 23rd Albert Haring Symposium,* Indiana University, Bloomington, Indiana.

Evirgen, C., Mitri, M., Bhargava, V. & Cavusgil, S.T. (1992). A Sequential and Dynamic Testing Methodology for Validating an Intelligent Database System. In Leone, *et al.* (Eds.), *Proceedings of the 1992 AMA Summer Educators' Conference,* 481-487.

Evirgen, C., Bodur, M., & Cavusgil, S.T. (1993). Information Needs of Exporters: An Empirical Study of Turkish Exporters, *Marketing Intelligence and Planning,* 11:2, 28-36.

Evirgen, C., Mitri, M., & Cavusgil, S.T. (1993). Using Expert Systems in International Business: The Case of an Intelligent Knowledge Base - The Country Consultant©, Chapter in *Utilizing New Information Technology in International Business,* Karakaya and Kaynak, (Eds.), forthcoming.

Finlay, P.N., Forsey, G.J. & Wilson, J.M. (1988). The Validation of Expert Systems- Contrasts with Traditional Methods, *Journal of Operational Research Society,* 39 (10), 933-938.

Geringer, J.M. (1988). *Joint Venture Selection: Strategies for Developed Countries,* Westport, Conn.: Quorum Books.

Geringer, J.M. (1991). Strategic Determinants of Selection Criteria in International Joint Ventures, *Journal of International Business Studies,* First Quarter: 41-62.

Luconi, F.L., Malone, T.W. & Scott Morton, M.S. (1986). Expert Systems: The Next Challenge for Managers, *Sloan Management Review,* 27 (Summer), 3-14.

Mentzer, J.T. & Gandhi, N. (1992). Expert Systems in Marketing: Guidelines For Development, *Journal of the Academy of Marketing Science,* 20 (1), 71-80.

Miller, M. (1993). The 10 Step Road Map to Success in Foreign Markets, *Journal of International Marketing,* 1 (2), 89-106.

Mitri, M. (1991). A Task Specific Problem Solving Architecture for Candidate Evaluation, *AI Magazine,* 12 (3), 95-109.

Mitri, M., Yeoh, P., Ozsomer, A. & Cavusgil, S.T. (1991), "Expert Systems in International Marketing," *Proceedings of the 1991 AMA Microcomputers in the Marketing Education Conference,* (August), 164-175.

Ohmae, K. (1989). The Global Logic of Strategic Alliances, *Harvard Business Review,* March-April: 143-154.

Ozsomer, A., Mitri, M. & Cavusgil, S.T. (1993). Selecting International Freight Forwarders: An Expert Systems Application, *International Journal of Physical   Distribution and Logistics Management,*V. 34(3), 11-21.

Ozsomer, A., Evirgen, C., Mitri, M., & Cavusgil, S.T. (1992). A Framework for Validating Expert Systems in International Marketing, *Marketing Intelligence and Planning,* 10 (9), 25-34.

Porter, M.E. & Fuller, M.B. (1986). Coalitions and Global Strategy. In M.E. Porter, (Ed.), *Competition in Global Industries.* Boston, MA: Harvard Business School, 315-343.

Rangaswamy, A., Eliashberg, J., Burke, R.R. & Wind, J. (1989). Developing Marketing Expert Systems: An Application to International Negotiations, *Journal of Marketing*, 53 (October), 24-39.

Remus, W.E. & Kottemann, J.E. (1986). Toward Intelligent Decision Support Systems: An Artificially Intelligent Statistician, *MIS Quarterly*, December, 403-410.

Root, F.R. (1988). Some Taxonomies of International Cooperative Arrangements. In F.J. Contractor & P. Lorange (Eds.), *Cooperative Strategies in International Business*. Lexington, MA: Lexington Books, 69-80.

CHAPTER 5

The Role of Information Technology in Global Marketing: The Case of the New Single Market of European Community

SAYESTE DASER
Wake Forest University

Information technology has a critical role to play in the formation of today's global markets. The environmental determinants of a global marketplace may be analyzed in terms of government, infrastructure, cultural values and technology advances. Information technology pervades its influence through all these four forces. A case study of the developments in the new single market of European Community (EC) illustrates this point.

INTRODUCTION

There is an irreversible trend toward globalization in today's borderless world economy. It is hard to determine where one country market ends and the other begins. The diversity in business operations and relationships challenge the fortress mentality. International competitors sell to other international competitors and they join other competitors for mutual sustainable success. Customer attitudes in the developed world seek the "best value for the money" and/or the "best service" or the "quickest response that adds value."

It is estimated that 75 per cent of the world Gross Domestic Product and 70 percent of the world trade are concentrated among the global "triad" powers (NAFTA, EC and ASEAN). The biggest challenge to internationally minded businesses is not whether to globalize but how to do it.

The basic purpose of this chapter is to discuss a conceptual framework regarding the environmental determinants of the global marketplace. It will then explore how the forces in information technology (IT) prepare this globalization trend by way of applying it to the case of the newly emerging Single Market in European Community.

CONTEXTUAL DETERMINANTS OF A GLOBAL MARKET

As can be seen from Figure 1, Sheth (1990) has viewed the basic marketing task in the global marketplace as overcoming the perceptual, procurement, and performance gaps between providers (sellers) and users (customers).

As providers learn to position their goods and services appropriately to meet the similar biogenic and psychographic expectations of users around the globe, the perceptual gaps between providers and users will no longer have to be identified in terms of differences across international markets.

In a global market area, the managerial tool of "intermarket segmentation" provides a means to cater to "subnational" markets which exhibit perceptual similarities across international markets. Thorelli and his research collaborators (1975 and 1989) point to the importance of an "information-prone" consumer segment in various developed markets as a key construct in global marketing.

Procurement refers to the acquisition of needed resources, goods and services. As competitive sellers and customers cross traditional geographic borders to buy and to sell, national market boundaries are disappearing. The borderless economy is emerging in large part as a consequence of global sourcing and global competition.

Performance gaps may be overcome when sellers really "listen to and understand" their customers. Furthermore, in the actual delivery of both product and service benefits, sellers not only have to meet but exceed customers' expectations.

Significant similarities may exist among segments of users from

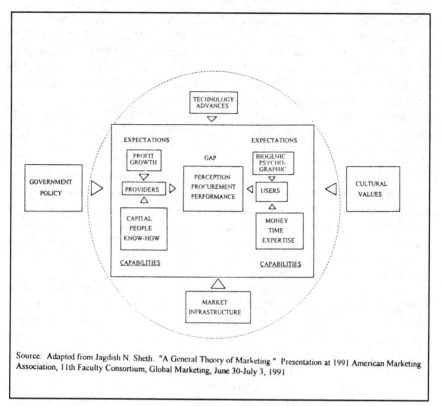

Figure 1: Determinants of Global Marketplace

different countries as gaps in their life-styles, tastes, and resulting behavior narrow. As the economic world becomes globalized, differences in market expectations and capabilities may be expected to vary more within a country market than between country markets. Therefore, it will be highly advantageous to develop marketing opportunity by looking at similar market segments that cut across geographic frontiers on a global basis (Sheth and Eshghi 1989, Ohmae 1990, Lamont 1991).

This section will attempt to highlight the four environmental determinants of a global market environment (Figure 1). It will be seen that information technology has a critical role to play in the globalization process. The next section will apply this framework to the case of a newly emerging global market in the European Economic Community.

(1) Government

In global markets governments play a big role as the largest customer and/or gatekeeper which provides market access and as regulator of marketing action to create and build markets.

Governments also realize that military power counts for much less, and economic power much more in today's global competitive advantage. This basic shift in government policy from political to pragmatic economic imperatives is due in large part to technology and the need to encourage innovation and efficiency in different sectors of the economy (Drucker 1989).

Governments have always had a strange relationship with technology. They are typically slow to recognize the implications of technological advances and quick to assert control over them once they do.

There have been a wave of deregulation and privatization of state-owned monopolies, the opening up of public procurement to competitive suppliers in information technology, and deregulation of major industries like telecommunications, transportation and broadcasting in many markets around the world. These have been favorable developments which have the potential to open up freer markets around the globe.

Governments also sometimes distort competition by subsidizing and granting exclusive rights to state-owned firms for the supply of basic services such as telecommunications, transport or utilities. Restricted competition in information technology and related sectors can result in poor quality service, little innovation and high prices.

According to the recent World Bank Development Report (1991), the key factor which will contribute to growth in the Third World nations is market liberalization. Governments of developing countries need to invest more in human capital and intervene less in industrial and agricultural pricing, focus on improving infrastructure and reduce tariff and non-tariff barriers to trade. Such developments are most likely to contribute to the growth of their economies and their ability to participate in global trade.

(2) Infrastructure

Availability of adequate distribution, information/communication network facilities in a marketplace are the basis of modern marketing activity. Establishing "information superhighways" and electronics infrastructure is one of the most challenging prerequisites for globalization. These have revolutionalized marketing processes and practices (Muroyama and Stever 1988, Jussawalu 1989, Charles 1989).

As can be seen in Figure 2, transportation and communication costs have tumbled over the past 60 years. The cost of sending cargo by sea has more than halved in 1990 dollars. The average cost of air transport is now only a sixth of what it was in 1930. A three-minute transatlantic call now costs barely 1 1/2% of what it did 60 years ago. These decreases in cost have helped to boost world trade and to

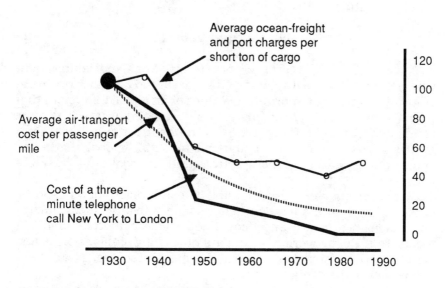

Source: Institute for International Economics

Figure 2: Transport and Communication Costs (1930 = one hundred 1990 dollars)

prepare the globalization of markets.

As hierarchical organization structures become flattened, information networks serve as infrastructure to connect research and development design studios, manufacturing job shops and sales offices to operate concurrently as process-oriented teams to manage everything simultaneously.

Knitting networks extend over to partnerships with suppliers and customers. Market acceptance of information networks by both consumers and organizational users have also been great. For example, cellular systems are introduced in newly emerging markets of Eastern Europe and they become a staple in their second year of introduction.

Businesses seeking to create global information links with their branches and/or customers utilizing the networks of several countries face a multitude of political and administrative problems. They also have to cope with vastly different tariff structures.

As governments have a vested interest in this area and as investments in infrastructure are very high, this area has attracted global strategic alliances of many forms -- technology licensing arrangements, formal joint ventures, or informal collaborations between competitors. This has been an added important stimulus for globalization.

(3) Cultural Values

There is a historical controversy in international marketing about whether a company's marketing strategy should be based on cross-cultural differences in norms and values or on global influences that reflect similarities between customers in global markets. The more recent conceptual literature tends to emphasize intercultural similarities across international markets to define global marketing opportunity. (Marketing Perspectives and International Business Conference, 1992)

Global media and programming like television news, sports, music, movies and advertising, newspapers (Wall Street Journal) and magazines create an effect, known as "mainstreaming." It means that the network of media are promoting similar norms and values in the global village. This is also loosening government controls over the media.

Satellite transmission in Europe allows the same advertisements to be run on a Pan European basis (O'Guinn et. al 89,9). Global brands are not limited to Coca Cola and Levi Jeans. Today, IBM, British Telecom and Anderson Consulting are aiming to develop uniform, high quality image through global positioning.

Information technology is said to play a key role in driving user values toward similarity in markets around the globe. Differences in user tastes will continue to remain critical, however, in determining the satisfaction that users experience and the success that marketers enjoy.

Globalization does not mean homogeneous values but similar segments of values across international markets which share similar expectations, benefit satisfactions and lifestyles.

Opportunity lies in "thinking globally and acting locally" so that successful products and services travel internationally with a minimum change in their positioning. As such marketing strategies might provide for a global reach that might provide a universal image and important economies of scale while some adaptation to local market conditions is almost always necessary. A good product and universally appealing communications program, just like a well-known piece of art or literature, will transcend international borders with a "Mona Lisa" effect.

(4) Technology Advances

Rapid development around the world has become possible with rapid developments in technology. With advances in technology, the time required to achieve substantial changes in the quality of life has shrunk steadily. Starting in 1885, Japan took 34 years to double its per capita output. Beginning in 1977, China doubled living standards in only a decade.

The merging telecommunications, computing office automation and consumer electronics industries are collectively described as the "information technology" sector. The use of these technologies are revolutionizing interorganizational relationships and business practices. A new concept of "relationship marketing" links providers and users without the time and place barriers of doing business. Revolutions in fax, 800 numbers, overnite delivery, new satellite, fiber optic and wireless technologies have all opened up new avenues for global reach.

Since the IT sector has the potential to be the driving force in the formation of global markets, the next section will be devoted to a review of developments in the IT sector. The European Community will be used as a case study of a global marketplace.

DEVELOPMENTS IN GLOBAL INFORMATION TECHNOLOGY: THE CASE OF EUROPEAN COMMUNITY

Two decades ago, IT was identified as the engine of the third industrial revolution in succession to steam and electricity. Industry estimates have forecast that by the year 2000, the IT sector (semiconductors, computers and consumer electronics) would generate $1,000 bn. a year in sales (See Figure 3). This would represent 10 percent of the world gross domestic product, up from 5 percent in 1989.

The IT sector is extremely critical for its underpinning of many other markets which use IT, including telecommunications, automobile, financial services and other service industries. The European Commission estimates that this sector already conditions or influences 60 percent of all employment in the EC.

IT sectors have enjoyed a robust growth of about 20 percent a year or more over the last decade. In 1992, however, the overall growth in semiconductor sales were projected to average less than 11 percent, computers about 5 percent and consumer electronics sales were projected to be flat (Cane 1992).

According to industry sources, unless the market grows by at least 15 percent a year, it becomes difficult for companies to afford the research and development cost and risk of innovation for the next

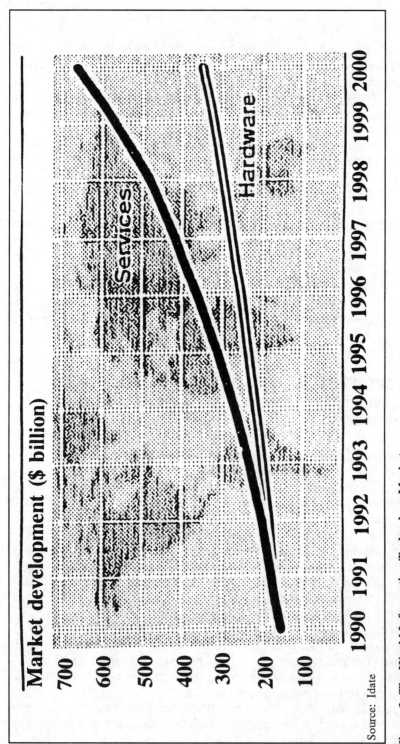

Source: Idate

Figure 3: The World Information Technology Market

generation of IT products. International strategic alliances are the wave of the future to meet the increasing cost of new technology. One half of all recent global strategic alliances have been in the area of IT. (Terpstra 1993).

The world recession and the market maturity stage of the IT business on the hardware side have been responsible for the falling prices of semiconductors and computers.

In previous recessions, companies continued to invest in IT, especially in the US, in the belief that it would improve their efficiency and competitiveness. This time, the simple efficiencies have already been achieved and there is little faith that further investment will bring improved performance. (Dahlman 1992).

As the world information technology market fast approaches maturity on the hardware side, services are expected to enjoy much higher growth. (See Figure 3) There will be an increasing trend toward products and services that provide high added value rather than the production of commodities such as memory chips and basic personal computers. Services such as facilities management -- operating a customer's computer systems and new uses of automation as in intelligent road systems, environmental monitoring, health care fields and mobile telecommunications, will enjoy accelerated growth.

Role of Information Technology in New Single Market of European Community

The new Single Market program of European Community is launched in January 1, 1993. Its basic purpose is to achieve European economic integration through the completion of the "internal" market, which means undistorted freedom of movement within the EC for goods, services, capital and people.

With nine official languages, EC represents a culturally diverse population base of 350 million consumers. It enjoys comparatively high living standards and well developed communications and distribution infrastructure in its national markets. With its flexible geographical borders, EC remains at the forefront for globally minded executives.

As potentially the largest domestic market in the free world, the single market is much more than the sum of the 12 Member States. The "global village" in the New Europe covers the European Economic Area between EC and EFTA, the larger Germany and the opening markets of central and eastern Europe.

If an international firm can exploit the synergies and advantages created by the single internal market in Europe, then it will use the competitive advantages gained as a leverage to penetrate the other global "triad" markets.

In the high technology area, major goal of EC is to overcome the technological slippage of EC firms against their North American and Japanese competitors. EC Commission in 1988 identified three main targets for research - improving competitiveness, improving quality of life and concentrating on basic research (see Figure 4).

The European IT industry has long blamed its weaknesses on two main problems: One is inadequate R&D. The European industry is more often a follower than a leader in successful product innovation.

Second, producers blame the lack of a large, homogenous home market that U.S. and Japan enjoy. As a proportion of Gross Domestic Product, spending on most types of products—from chips to computer equipment—is still lower in Europe than in the US and Japan, and European business users are slower to adopt IT innovations.

Information Infrastructure as Catalyst for the Single Market

European governments have realized that efficient operation and competitive leverage of the internal market in EC cannot be realized without a "European information and electronic nervous system" in place.

EC Commission has appropriately fixed its gaze on the liberalized and harmonized IT infrastructure. The provision of a dedicated communication and information infrastructure will multiply the advantages of the single market as a result of the following factors (Nakamoto 1992):

• As pan European businesses grow, demand for information and communication systems capable of spanning national borders will also grow.
• As the geographical scope of the market grows to include the less-developed Eastern and Southern parts, there will need to be greater reliance on information systems to disseminate information across wider business networks.
• Financial institutions will boost their IT capability as pan-European banking and other financial services (electronic payments and clearing systems) take off.
• As competition intensifies, manufacturers will consider adopting computer-integrated manufacturing and distribution systems as well as computer-assisted design facilities.
• As travel throughout the EC increases, there will be a surge in demand for mobile telephones, radio pagers and digital personal communicators.

The challenge will be to focus on better integration of existing networks, backed up by technical and regulatory standardization and by better overall interworking between them. Also, future networks will have to be designed in a pan-European single market context.

Deregulation of the telecommunications sector is also crucial to the development of the information market in Europe. The industry is pervaded by monopolies and price distortions.

The EC ended public monopolies over the supply of telecoms equipment in 1990, followed by telecoms services such as electronic mail in 1991. Outside rivals like AT&T are challenging the telephone monopolies known as PTT's (postal, telephone and telegraph services) by introducing snazzier services at lower prices. Most lucrative sectors have included data transmission, leased telephone lines, video conferencing and information lines.

Except for Great Britain, voice communication which represents at least 85% of total revenue (estimated $134 billion) of the telecommunications services sector is still under public monopolies. The EC Telecommunications Council has agreed to fully liberalize basic telephone services in at least six of the 12 member states by January 1, 1998.

The greatest stride in deregulation of telecommunications has been in progress towards a common set of standards and the opening up of public procurement. Deregulation of and growth of satellite channels (even with moderate advertising revenues) will serve to enhance the communication infrastructure in Europe.

Governmental IT Strategy to Build Framework for Competition

EC Commission has taken several measures to strengthen the European IT industry in the 1980's. These ranged from trade protection to subsidized collaborative research programs and encouragement of cross-border mergers and strategic alliances.

There was sufficient evidence that suppliers' costs in Europe were higher due to the differing technical standards and fragmented structure in information and telecommunications networks. European IT companies also argued that their US and Japanese competitors were better equipped to absorb these costs because they have already built up large sales volumes at home. However, there was also growing evidence that higher prices in Europe reflected more than just the extra costs of doing business there. For products from computers to video recorders, European pre-tax prices were twice or more than in the US.

One explanation was that the American and Japanese suppliers which dominated European sales of products such as computers have pursued profit maximization rather than market share. Instead of challenging the prices set by the market leaders, European producers have also chosen to shelter under them.

In consumer electronics and microchips, which have seen fierce price competition, the EC has repeatedly resorted to protective anti-dumping tariffs to shelter threatened European producers against their Japanese rivals. These measures have raised prices of some products by as much as 50 percent.

Higher prices have only served to dampen demand and discourage European business customers from exploiting the full potential of IT to improve productivity and innovation in products and services.

Collaborative framework programs in Research and Development were launched in the 1980's. These programs made it possible to concentrate research activity on a few selected strategic industries (see Figure 4.) "Information and communications technology" sector benefited the most from this research collaboration.

The most significant IT research consortium is the European Strategic Project for Research in Information Technology (ESPRIT). This program was established in 1984 to provide experience to European companies to collaborate on pre-competitive research in basic technologies attempting to introduce worldwide standards. It was hoped that working together in basic research might inspire companies to also collaborate in bringing innovative and competitive products to the market. This hope was never realized.

When the Ecu 7 bn ($8.82 bil) ESPRIT program concluded at the end of 1992, its formal evaluation concluded that "one-third to one-half of the projects appear to have produced little of industrial value" and that "continuation of ESPRIT as presently conceived would not serve the best interests" of IT industry or the economy. (Business Europe, 1992, 12/4).

The program's failure pointed to the fact that it is very difficult for multi-sector basic research programs to be successful if they do not have industrial applications close to the market. ESPRIT failed to persuade leading IT companies to work together on product planning, production or marketing closer to the market in fear of sharing commercial secrets.

Based on these experiences and the need to recuperate the long-term industrial competitive position of EC on the world market, the EC commission has unveiled a new five-point strategy for the entire IT sector (Business Europe, 1991, 03/22):

(1) In order to promote EC technology and help Europe become competitive in world markets, it will create a second generation of EC-sponsored framework research, development, and technology programs.
(2) It will stimulate demand for European products and technology, particularly by investing in trans-European networks (TEN's) for telecommunications systems, energy and even transport infra-

structures. TEN's promote compatible systems and technologies across Europe.

(3) Stressing that "lack of training" is one of "the most important handicaps in Europe" for creation and use of new technology, the

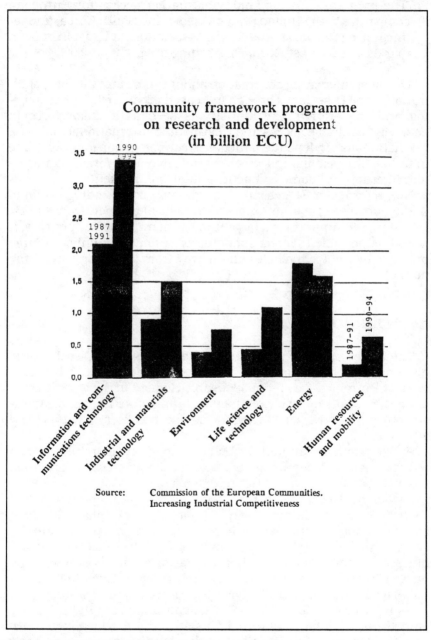

Figure 4: Community Framework Programme on Research and Development

strategy calls for action at all levels of education and for the creation of a "network of excellence composed of academic and industrial teams geographically located throughout the Community."

(4) The program calls for improving market access for European companies in the United States, Japan, and South Korea, and for integrating European Free Trade Association and East European markets into a vast European trading area.

The most interesting observation about this strategy is the globalization of the IT sector. Through increased productivity, restructuring and cooperation, the industry is seen as a major force in achieving equitable access and treatment in international markets. The nationalist, independent theory of technology appear to be giving in to cooperative alliances which may even include foreign competitors in order to become competitive in global markets.

New reforms for EC research and development funding signal to the importance of market-oriented industrial competitiveness. By lessening the support for a large number of multi-sector projects, it would be possible to focus spending on a limited number of large projects for key technologies all the way from the laboratory to the market.

CONCLUSIONS

The above analysis attempted to show that the IT sector—the merging telecommunications, computer, semiconductor and consumer electronics—is an indispensable element in the globalization of markets. This can be explained in terms of its impact on infrastructure and advances in technology as a source of competitive advantage.

As governments attempt to better manage their industrial and technological policies for global competitive contest, information technology will have a priority role to play.

Global marketing does not mean marketing of products and services in a standardized way. A global marketplace does not assume homogeneous users. It does mean, however, that similar segments of users who share similar cultural values may be addressed from a common positioning platform. The emerging target market in a global marketplace is likely to be "information prone" users who share similar lifestyles, attitudes and motivations.

As the irreversible trend toward globalization continues, EC will emerge as a global platform in itself and the globally minded organizations will feel the need to develop presence in and draw expertise from all of the global Triad powers—Japan and North

America as well as EC.

In the case of EC, the full benefits of the Single market provisions of "free movement of goods, services, people and capital" may not be realized unless they are extended to the information and electronic environment.

As EC moves towards closer integration, fiercer price competition can be expected. As global competitors, including Japanese and US companies, move more deeply into the European market and produce more of what they provide in large local plants, they will need high sales volumes to be profitable. Economies of scale due to globalization will be greatly appreciated. European providers will be under greater pressure to increase efficiency, speed up product innovation and broaden their base beyond traditional, geographically defined national markets.

Multinational companies will be engaged in pan European financing, procurement, logistical planning and customer service programs. They will engage in harmonizing European price lists. If information technology is not used to the fullest, such development in the 1990's will be severely limited. Cost conscious mentality will be of paramount importance to success in the new marketing environment of the 1990's in Europe. Marketing management will be under greater pressure to lower costs and increase customer service at the same time. This will require a change in management philosophy from a "product" orientation to a "marketing" orientation.

If marketing-oriented management is to "think globally and act locally," effective MIS (marketing information systems) is a must. This will enable suppliers to gather enough information from current and potential users about their product and service expectations. Advances in IT will facilitate "interactive marketing" which seeks to deal with the best customers regardless of their geographic location through long-term, value-added relationships.

Global marketing enables brand programs to travel through international borders with a centralized positioning strategy. Strong local management will still be needed to implement tailored sales and customer service programs close to the market.

Global print or broadcast media may be expected to emerge in Europe. These will have to enter new markets with maximum flexibility leaving room for a creative angle in each market.

Direct response programs and satellite television home shopping networks will also be spreading in Europe.

For policy makers at both EC and national levels, the challenge will be to adapt to rapid changes which are blurring the frontiers of IT. The structure of Europe's IT industry is becoming increasingly international, due to the growth of global alliances and of local investments by companies based elsewhere.

There will be an increasing trend toward cooperative international strategic alliances among competitors in the IT area. Driving this trend are three major forces: the increasing cost, complexity and risk of developing new technologies; coverage of global markets and the need to incorporate Eastern Europe and the former Soviet Union; governments' encouragement of joint ventures to develop access to sources of technology.

Strategic alliances will be aimed at enhancing strengths, rather than addressing weaknesses. For example, Europe's weaker players in industries like semiconductors would strengthen their competitive position better than joining stronger global alliances where complementary competencies might be emphasized.

In the future, the test of government policy may lie less in how effectively it supports the production of IT than how it encourages its applications. Government sponsored research consortia do not serve a real purpose unless they bring about cooperation in bringing innovative and competitive products to the market that serve real needs.

REFERENCES

Business Europe. (1992, December 4). New York NY: Business International Corporation.

Business Europe. (1993, March 29-April 4), pp. 2-3. New York NY: Business International Corporation.

Cane, Alan (1992). A Hiatu for the High-Tech Dream, *Financial Times*, August 12.

Charles, D., Monk, P. & Sciberras, E. (1989). *Technology and competition in the international telecommunications industry*, London: Printer Publishers.

Chipello, C. (1989). More Competitors Turn to Cooperation. *Wall Street Journal*, June 23, B1.

Dahlman, C. & Mody, A. (1992). World Bank Report on Global Information Technology.

Directorate-General for Audiovisual, Information, Communication and Culture. (1992, July). *Competition policy in the European Community*. Brussels.

Directorate-General for Audiovisual, Information, Communication and Culture. (1992, March). *Increasing industrial competitiveness*. Brussels.

Directorate-General for Audiovisual, Information, Communication and Culture. (1992, March). *Trans-European networks, commission of the European Communities*. Brussels.

Drucker, P. (1989), *The new realities*. New York: Harper & Row.

Drucker, P.F. (Autumn 1986). The Changed World Economy. *The McKinsey Quarterly*, 2-26.

Geake, E. (1992). Europe switches on electronics, *New Scientist*, January 25, 133 (1805) 25.

Gilbert, X. & Strebel, P. (1986). Developing competitive advantage. *The handbook of business strategy*, 83-84.

Hooper, L. (1992, July 13).   IBM, Toshiba, Siemens, form venture to develop DRAMs for next century. *Wall Street Journal*, B8.

International business intelligence.   (1989)   *1992 - Planning for the information technology industries.* London: Butterworth & Co. Ltd. and Eurifi plc.

Jussawalla, M., Okuma, T. & Araki, T. (Eds.) (1989). *Information technology and global interdependence.* New York NY: Greenwood Press.

Levine, J. (1992). Look who's helping defend fortress europe. *Business Week*, February 17, No. 3252, 131.

Marketing perspectives and international business. Papers presented at conference on Perspectives on International Business: Theory, Research and Institutional Arrangements, University of South Carolina, May 21-23, 1992.

Nakamoto, Michiyo (1992). The barriers are falling, *Financial Times*, March 17.

O'Guinn, T. et al. (1989). The cultivation of consumer norms. In Thomas K. Scrull, (Ed.), *Advances in consumer research*, (16), Provo, Utah, Association for Consumer Research, 779-785.

Ohmae, K. (1990), *The borderless world.* New York NY: Harper Business.

Muroyama, J. H. and Stever, H. G., (Eds.) (1988). *The globalization of technology: International perspectives.* Washington DC: National Academy Press.

Robinson, Richard D. (1986). Some new competitive factors in international marketing. In S. Tamer Cavusgil (Ed.), *Advances in International Marketing*, (1), Greenwich, Connecticut: JAI Press, Inc., 1-20.

Sheth, J. N. (June 30-July 3, 1991). A general theory of marketing. Unpublished Presentation at 1991 American Marketing Association, 11th Faculty Consortium on Global Marketing.

Sheth, J. N. (1992). Emerging market strategies in a changing macroeconomic environment *International Marketing Review*, (in press).

Sheth, J. N. & Abdolrezza, E. (Eds.) (1989). *Global marketing perspectives*, Southwestern Publishing Company, Cincinnati, OH.

Terpstra, V. & Simonin, B. (1993). Strategic alliances in the triad. *Journal of International Marketing*, 1(1), March, 4-25.

Thorelli, H.B., Lim, J.S., & Ye, J. (1989) Relative importance of country of origin, warranty and retail store image on product evaluations. *International Marketing Review*, 6(1), 35-46.

Thorelli, H.B., Becker, H., & Engledow, J. L.   (1975) *The information seekers - An international study of consumer information and advertising image.* Cambridge MA, Ballinger.

World Bank Development Report. (1991).*The Challenge of Development.* Oxford University Press.

Zachary, P. (1992, July 29). High-tech firms find it's good to line up outside contractors. *Wall Street Journal*, A1.

Section 3

Information Technology in International Finance Services

Introduction by

ROBERT J. KAUFFMAN

The application of information technology in the international financial services arena has increased dramatically in the last ten years as international banks and securities firms have expanded their operations to the far corners of the globe. In the meantime, however, developments such as the Black Monday stock market crash in New York and the bursting real estate bubble in Japan have prompted specialists in international financial services to become increasingly aware of another need: to employ information technology to monitor risk in their global operations. Others, meanwhile, view technology as a means *non-pareil* to achieve a competitive advantage in changing markets, even if it only a a few second decrease in response time to lock in a profitable trade. And still others regard technology as the means to build the kind of globally integrated product delivery and operational capability that yields a high level of service quality, enables rapid product innovation and introduction, and helps to control operating costs.

The commonality among these diverging views may not be obvious but it is highly significant: global financial services in the 1990s is an industry made possible by information technology, regardless of the specific ways it is employed by firms that wish to maximize their profitability. This section showcases four papers that will introduce the reader to a variety of themes and applications of information technology in international financial services.

In the first chapter, Professors Raj Aggrawal and James Baker discuss the findings of a survey of international banks about the perceived role and effectiveness that SWIFT — the Society for Worldwide Interbank Financial Telecommunications — plays as the primary telecommunications infrastructure for international electronic payments. SWIFT was formed in the mid-1970s by a group of European and American commercial banks, who were interested in substituting the lower costs of a new technology and a new standard for the existing higher cost, unformatted and lower quality telex and leased-line transmissions.

Since then, SWIFT has been largely successful in standardizing the formats that are used by international banks to transmit information related to letters of credit and documentary collections, lending and repayment, treasury management-related funds concentration, investment and disbursement; and foreign exchange trading and investment. Today, industry observers can hardly imagine a world without SWIFT. Its role has not only been to manage the costs, risks and security issues associated with international funds transfer. SWIFT also acts as a circulatory system for the ebb and flow of world payments, enabling firms that actively carry out international lending, funds movement and financial market investments to operate effectively.

In the following chapter, Bruce Weber, a specialist in electronic financial market architectures and operations, offers useful travel information for the reader who would like to go on a fast-paced tour of the major international financial markets. During the last decade, the financial markets have also undergone a transformation that has been driven by multiple forces. First, cost pressures (as trading volumes have mounted) have forced exchanges to figure out ways to increase capacity and process the load more efficiently. Second, computerization at member firms has created pressures for different kinds of exchange services, including, for example, 24-hour market operation, and trading in futures and options on securities and custom-designed "baskets" of financial instruments.

A third force is the investing public. They have increasingly demanded markets that are fairer to a range of investors, rather than biased in favor of large institutions and market insiders. In other cases, the development of a national financial market that enables concentration and redeployment of capital from an increasingly wealthy work force within an economy (as was the case with countries such as Taiwan, South Korea and Singapore) is a desirable goal by itself, and a "ground zero" start offers an excellent opportunity to select the "right" market architecture. As the author points out, the outcomes in terms of market performance have not always measured up to what the designers had in mind. But in almost every case, the quality of markets has improved (in terms of better liquidity and market depth, reduced volatility and more transparent operations) where information technology has been used to re-engineer the price discovery and trade execution process. Accompanying some of these changes, exchanges have also made a conscious effort to package and broadcast market information back to the market, creating additional impetus for market efficiency.

The third chapter in this section was contributed by Arun Bansal, a specialist in the area of financial risk management information systems at a major Wall Street securities firm. He considers the ways in which firms which operate in the global financial markets can control their exposure to a variety of risks through information technology.   Economic growth in other nations, the performance of domestic and foreign firms overseas, central bank and governmental policies affecting trade and international capital flows are all unpredictable to a certain extent. Firms must monitor the relevant information, predict the direction and the impact of changes on their portfolios, and be ready to react instantly when market conditions become adverse.

As an example of the risks that these firms face and the potentially beneficial role for information technology in this area, consider an institutional investor who wants to develop a sound strategy for deploying invested funds in overseas money and securities markets. Interest rate parity theory, based on well-accepted principles in financial economics applied to international markets, states that any difference which occurs in the spot rate and the forward rate of a foreign currency can be explained in terms of variations in the rates of return on securities of similar risk in the countries whose currencies are used to form the exchange rate. Acknowledging interest rate parity in international financial services forces the investor to recognize and understand the extent of linkages like this between domestic money and stock markets, and the market for a country's currency. If the investor has not taken these linkages into account, the return on the invested funds will always under-perform a portfolio that is optimized to take them into account.

In fact, the world is even more complex: there are normally multiple markets for a country's currency, and multiple countries whose domestic money and stock market are linked to rate changes in the foreign country. Information technology's role is to act as a net for the relevant data, and then a sieve that pulls out the useful information so that risk managers, foreign exchange traders and international lenders can make sense of it and implement policies that protect the firm against excess risk, yet still earn money.

The final chapter in this section proposes an evaluative framework for senior managers in international financial services firms who are considering undertaking projects that re-engineer money market or securities market trading operations. The research, conducted by Vasant Dhar, Katherine Duliba and Rob Kauffman in the context of a larger project sponsored by the United States Council on International Banking, describes several "waves" of information technology investment that span from automation of core operational processing in international banking to integration and control of global trading operations. The authors argue that in the current phase, the key to improving international banking performance in trading operations will center on the integration of such technology-driven capabilities as market intelligence gathering and pre-trade analytics, combined with innovative products and nearly instantaneous response to market changes on behalf of treasury management clients.

An implication of the framework that the authors propose is that it would be a mistake for senior managers to view efforts to re-engineer trading operations primarily to achieve "per transaction" cost reductions. Productivity, in the usual sense, is not the most important goal here. Instead, senior managers need to consider how information technology can be employed to shift market conditions in their favor, to reduce the risk associated with operating in markets that span time zones, national borders and different regulatory and rate environments, and to deliver a level of service quality that the competition finds hard to match. In this view, the outcomes of efforts to re-engineer trading operations can be viewed in terms of productivity metrics whose output component is "quality-adjusted", "opportunity-adjusted" or "risk-adjusted"

The author gratefully acknowledges the U.S.-Japan Business and Economics Research Center at the Stern School of Business, New York University for generous support of my work with the editors and the authors of this section of the book. The author also wishes to thank Dan Taylor, President of the United States Council on International Banking, New York, for sponsoring "Project 1990s: The US Council on International Banking's Study of Information Technology Investment and International Banking Performance."

CHAPTER 6

Evaluation of Global Electronic Funds Flow System:
The Society for Worldwide Interbank Financial Telecommunications (SWIFT)

JAMES C. BAKER
Kent State University

RAJ AGGARWAL
John Carroll University

This chapter contains an empirical study of the Society for Worldwide Interbank Financial Telecommunications (SWIFT). SWIFT is an international cooperative owned by more than 200 U.S., Canadian, and European banks and which serves more than 3,000 financial institutions worldwide. It utilizes computer technology to transfer the instructions underlying interbank funds flows. This system offers clients a very fast, secure, low cost means of transmitting such instructions with the use of standardized message formats. In 1990, a new expanded version, SWIFT II—in the planning stages for several years—was placed in service.

The chapter reports on the organizational and operational framework of SWIFT as well as a survey of SWIFT user banks regarding their utilization of the system, why they became members, what changes they believe should have been made in SWIFT I, their opinions of SWIFT II, what problems they perceive in SWIFT II, and what future strategies they believe should be formulated for successful international funds flows.

INTRODUCTION

Since the 1963 cover story in *Business Week* concerning the advent of the multinational corporation (MNC), international business operations have grown tremendously. In order to facilitate such growth in international trade and investment, a large stateless vat of money known as the Eurocurrency market has evolved from a system of Eurobanks operating globally. This US$4-trillion money and capital market has facilitated cross-border funding of multinational corporate operations.

Global markets for financial instruments as well as for their derivatives have blossomed to the point whereby, for all intents and purposes, one worldwide financial market now exists. Funds transfers in these global markets must be accomplished by systems or methods such as the Clearing House Interbank Payments System (CHIPS), Fedwire, telex, and others. Such electronic banking systems have globalized retail banking operations and, in the process, have made international operations safer, faster, and less costly for all customers of banks, be they individuals at the retail level or MNCs at the wholesale level.

The wholesale financial payments system can be divided into one tier through which high-value payments move and another through which low-value payments move. High value payments or their instructions flow through three major interbank funds transfer systems: CHIPS—the Clearing House Interbank Payments System, SWIFT—the Society for Worldwide Interbank Financial Telecommunications, and Fedwire—part of the U.S. Federal Reserve System. On the other hand, low-value payments move through the checking system and, for recurring payments, the ACH—Automated Clearing House (Steiner and Teixeira, 1990, p. 144).

SWIFT does not, at present, transfer funds but does transmit the instructions for such transfers from one bank to another. It is a multinational, multicurrency, interbank message system which offers more than 70 types of standardized messages. Nearly 80 percent of its transactions involve payments (Steiner and Teixeira, 1990, p. 148). After 16 years of actual live service, SWIFT has evolved into one of the least cost, most secure, most rapid means for transmitting payments instructions.

In addition to facilitating funds flows between wholesale customers—banks and international corporations—SWIFT has had a significant impact on the retail banking industry. The system has resulted in more rapid service, better intra-bank communications, reduced costs, improved services, more standardization, an improvement in international banking relations, greater efficiency, and improved cash flows than the banking system has achieved with other systems to date.

Many banks use several shared and third-party private networks such as SWIFT, MasterCard International, VISA International, and ATM networks. These systems are used for more than just transmission of data. In addition, banks use them for gathering, selecting, formatting, and processing data, performing other operations, or facilitating the sending and receiving of many kinds of messages, such as credit authorization and validation or for payments and settlements (OTA, 1992, p. 10).

By 1991, SWIFT operations had made a significant impact on international financial transactions. It had captured a substantial portion of the world's payment-related transactions conducted by commercial banks, having been recognized as a very important communications platform by international banks. During 1990, a total of 332 million messages were processed through SWIFT. More than 3,000 financial institutions in 72 countries subcribe to SWIFT for its services (Hock, 1991).

SWIFT has been recognized for its success and global importance. In 1991, SWIFT received one of the four Computerworld Smithsonian Awards. These prestigious awards are given to honor technological achievements measured as landmarks in humanity's effort to make the world a safer, saner place. SWIFT received its award for the finance, insurance, and real estate category (Margolis et al., 1991).

SWIFT has pioneered successfully in the field of global payments transmission. Because of its status and the entrepreneurial efforts by SWIFT to create a global network connecting the leading financial institutions, the authors believe that it should be the focal point of an objective study performed externally. Thus, the objectives of this chapter are: 1) to discuss the evolution and current operations of SWIFT and the new system, SWIFT II, and 2) to present the results of a global study of SWIFT member and user banks designed to evaluate their present use of SWIFT and to measure their opinions about the new system.

Two major limitations can be suggested by the authors. First, we have had little or no cooperation from SWIFT management. We did, however, obtain a large amount of information from queries sent to SWIFT users. Second, the evaluation study of SWIFT I was completed before SWIFT II was implemented. Some of the objections raised by query respondents have been satisfied by the system now in place. Some of the problems were previously reported by the authors (Aggarwal and Baker, 1991).

SWIFT I

Organizational Aspects

Historical Background

The idea for SWIFT stemmed from the need to reduce time, labor, and cost of international banking transactions coupled with pressure for services offered by U.S. bank branches in Europe. As a result, representatives of 36 banks from seven countries met in late 1970 and produced a feasibility study for an international electronic banking network.

The study produced a proposal for an organization, SWIFT, which was established in 1973, incorporated in Belgium with headquarters in Brussels, as a non-profit cooperative to be jointly-owned by 239 charter shareholder banks from 15 different countries. SWIFT went operational in 1977 with 519 member bank shareholders (O'Connor, 1985). In its first year of operations, the SWIFT network accounted for 10 million messages sent (Byler and Baker, 1983). Figure 1 offers a graphic example of the growth in the number of member banks, member countries, and bank user locations.

Organizational Framework

SWIFT, as a non-profit, bank-owned cooperative, has a complicated administrative and political structure. It is governed by an annually-elected board comprised of persons from countries each of whose member banks generate more than 1.5 percent of total message traffic. A country which generates more than six percent of total annual message flow volume may nominate two members to the board. These nominees are elected by member banks at an annual meeting. Smaller countries may combine their message volume to gain board representation to the disadvantage of major countries. In mid-1987, only West German banks (10.43 percent of total message traffic) and American banks (18.68 percent of total message traffic) had more than 10 percent of total shares in SWIFT, while 7-9 percent of the shares were owned by Italian and Swiss banks, respectively. Japan's 86 member banks own fewer than three percent of total shares since Japanese banks, despite their global significance and size, make little use of SWIFT facilities.

Operations

Growth of Volume

Growth of SWIFT operations has resulted in expanded demand for resources as well as expanded needs of customers. In short, all

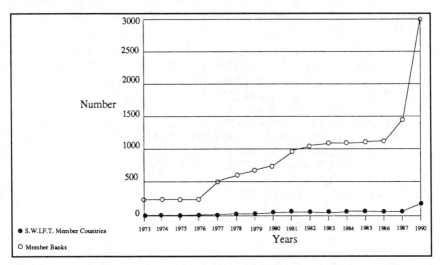

Figure 1: S.W.I.F.T. Member Countries and Users

initial expectations of daily transaction volume, the number of members and users, and revenues have been exceeded. For example, management estimated that 1987 volume was 156 million messages transmitted (Moore, 1986). Approximately 30 million more messages were transmitted in 1988 than in 1987 (Shale, 1988). About 75 percent of this message volume was between North American and European banks while some 18 percent of all traffic was transmitted solely between U.S. banks. Current daily volume capacity was increased from 900,000/day to 1,460,000/day in mid-1988. This was accomplished by increasing the number of switches located in the Netherlands and the United States to seven. This capacity compared with SWIFT's highest peak-day traffic of 1,120,000 messages gave the system a reserve factor of 30 percent (Shale, 1988). From such volume, SWIFT was able to generate turnover of US$200 million in 1988 (Moore and Kok, 1989). By the advent of SWIFT II in 1990, SWIFT daily volume was near its capacity (Hock, 1991).

Types of Transactions

SWIFT can transfer both domestic and international transaction messages. These include, among others, customer transfers, foreign exchange confirmations, bank transfers, and letters of credit.

Message Standards

A key service developed by SWIFT involves message-text standards enabling member banks to communicate through a common language which is computer readable, allowing each bank to auto-

MT 100 CUSTOMER TRANSFER
MT 200 BANK TRANSFER FOR ITS OWN ACCOUNT
MT 202 BANK TRANSFER IN FAVOR OF A THIRD BANK
MT 205 BANK TRANSFER EXECUTION
MT 210 NOTICE TO RECEIVE
MT 300 FOREIGN EXCHANGE MESSAGES
MT 320 FIXED LOAN/DEPOSIT CONFIRMATION
MT 330 CALL/NOTICE LOAN/DEPOSIT CONFIRMATION
MT 350 ADVICE OF LOAN/DEPOSIT INTEREST PAYMENT
MT 400 ADVICE OF PAYMENT
MT 410 ACKNOWLEDGEMENT
MT 420 TRACER
MT 430 AMENDMENT OF INSTRUCTIONS
MT 500 ORDER TO BUY
MT 501 ORDER TO SELL
MT 521 RECEIVE AGAINST PAYMENT
MT 531 CONFIRMATION OF RECEIPT AGAINST PAYMENT
MT 580 CEDEL MESSAGE
MT 700 ISSUE OF A DOCUMENTARY CREDIT
MT 740 AUTHORIZATION TO REIMBURSE
MT 940 CUSTOMER STATEMENT MESSAGE
MT 950 STATEMENT MESSAGES
MT n90 ADVICE OF CHARGES, INTEREST AND OTHER ADJUSTMENTS
MT n91 REQUEST FOR PAYMENT OF CHARGES, INTEREST, ETC.
MT n92 REQUEST FOR CANCELLATION
MT n95 QUERIES
MT n99 FREE FORMAT MESSAGE

Source: *S.W.I.F.T. User Handbook*/Volume 6-Standards (Hulpe, Belgium: Society for World-wide Interbank Financial Telecommunications, 1983).

Figure 2: Selected SWIFT Message Types

mate the handling of account transactions and reconciliation. Such automation has reduced bank personnel cost while permitting each bank to handle greater volume with greater speed. Selected message formats are shown in Figure 2.

SWIFT Users

The issue of what institutions may use SWIFT services has divided SWIFT membership. At first, only commercial banks could use the system. This became one of the first major issues which SWIFT management faced. The issue still has not been fully resolved. Pressure was applied to permit non-bank financial institutions and brokers to join SWIFT, especially from the securities industry itself.

At the 1987 Annual Meeting of SWIFT, permission was granted to brokerage houses, central depositories, and securities exchanges to join SWIFT.   In late 1988, the Big Four securities firms in Japan—Yamaichi, Nomura, Dai-Ichi, and Nikko—applied for membership in SWIFT (Shale, 1988). By 1989, some 43 of these firms had become subscribers (Murphy, 1989c). Money brokers were accepted as a new category in 1989 but trust companies, providers of custodial services, and investment management institutions were rejected. Morgan Stanley, for example, went on-line in 1988 as did four exchanges including the International Stock Exchange of London and the Chicago Mercantile Exchange (Arend, 1989). U.S. brokers adopted SWIFT standardized message formats as a strategy to cuts costs and improve global cross-border securities transactions (Ioannou, 1991).

However, the largest issue involved international funds management firms. At the 1991 SWIFT Annual Meeting, 32 percent of the membership voted against admitting this category ("SWIFT Busters. . ., 1992). The large U.S. banks led the opposition to this group of financial institutions. Use of the SWIFT system would give the international funds managers a better choice of custodian as well as standardized formats, and lower costs and risks. These mutual funds must now process their payment orders through a broker to a bank to another bank to another broker to a customer—with additional costs and counterparty risks at each step (OTA, 1992). The funds managers have threatened to bypass custodians altogether with the possible result being disintermediation (Rudnick, 1992) or fragmentation of the industry (Timewell, 1991).

Technical Aspects

Essentially, SWIFT makes use of telecommunications technology and highly standardized message formats. It incorporates a packet switching technique allowing participating banks to use different terminal speeds and equipment on a network which leases lines, for example, from various postal, telephone and telegraph authorities in member countries.

SWIFT operates by means of a system of regional processing units (RPUs) through which encrypted messages are sent. These messages are transmitted through a central processing unit (CPU) by means of satellite transmission to another RPU where they are decoded and sent on to the receiving bank. The sending and receiving banks are members of SWIFT and use keys or codewords to send and receive messages. These keys are frequently changed for security reasons. SWIFT messages instruct one bank to make a payment. The bank then transfers funds from one account to another on its books and because these messages are accepted by banks as authentic and authoritative, banks consider SWIFT as a form of electronic funds transfer system (OTA, 1992)

Security and Authentication

A unique SWIFT feature is the authentication of messages. A test calculation is permitted by the system based on the entire money transfer message rather than solely on the amount of money ("Chase Manhattan Bank's . . .," 1977). Authentication is the foundation of the primary SWIFT objective of a highly secure environment for its members. Its security system is comprised of a multi-level combination of physical, line, operations, and procedures security. For example, access is restricted to authorized users. The performance of these users is monitored to detect procedural and message format errors. Messages accepted for delivery are protected from loss by mutilation.   Finally, the message is encrypted at the regional processor before transmission to the operating center over a highly secure leased international circuit.

The public or private lines through which messages may pass on their way to the RPU represent the only portion of the network not totally secure. SWIFT does recommend encoding of messages before they reach an RPU but, because of cost considerations, few banks have believed such encoding to be necessary. This gap in security, no matter how narrow, might be breached with the use of a personal computer in the hands of a knowledgeable hacker, although inside information about security keys would probably be necessary. For example, a scheme to steal US$70 million from First National Bank of Chicago through wire transfers to Vienna, Austria, was foiled when the bank employees who furnished confidential code words needed for money transfers by computer were apprehended.

The following is a representative procedure for assuring security of SWIFT message transmissions. An operator calls up on a terminal screen that an inward payment has come over the SWIFT network from abroad. After a few minutes of keypunching, the operator decides whether to process the message, checks the account number, releases it—the traditional bank signature, debits the payment bank's account and credits the receiving bank's account. The beneficiary and account cannot be altered. The computers are programmed not to accept a payment before its due date. Each transaction is authenticated electronically for each digit and character. In addition, each operator has a specific number and code word so no outsider can intercept a message.

Advantages of SWIFT

Speed
Another SWIFT objective is the speed by which a message is transmitted. The advantage of increased speed is that settlement of accounts in a single day is permitted. Electronic transfer of a SWIFT

message, for example, between Tokyo and London can be accomplished in as little as 3.2 seconds (Sharkey, 1982). Use of such technology can eliminate the 16-hour float process, estimated to cost banks more than US$1 billion annually in lost interest revenues (Buyer, 1983).

Cost

Cost has been an important incentive for banks when considering membership in the SWIFT network. A member bank incurs a cost of about $60,000 in addition to a membership fee to tie into the system. Per message cost was reduced from Bfr 18 at the beginning of 1987 to Bfr 17 one year later (Moore and Kok, 1989). This represents a significant reduction from telex or wire transfers which may cost as much as US$6.00 or more for each message.

Convenience

SWIFT is a very convenient system. Its facilities can be used 24 hours per day. Many markets, e.g. the foreign exchange market, operate on this basis. A system which is available to international financial institutions and markets and their customers offers a convenience necessary to global financial transactions and payments.

SWIFT II

Motivation

An improved SWIFT system was necessitated for several reasons. Competition, for example, from both non-members and members had increased. Independent communications companies such as GEISCO (General Electric Information Services, a General Electric subsidiary), Reuters, and others had increased their market share in the financial services sector. Major banks had developed networks of their own, thus diverting interbank traffic. Some of these were among SWIFT's largest members. Only 35 member banks do 50 percent of SWIFT volume and these are among the world's largest banks. A few of these banks have developed funds and message transfer systems internally and, thus, come in competition with their own SWIFT operations.

Issues in the Introduction of SWIFT II

SWIFT had already developed a number of special services to enhance its standardized message formats. Among these are the MT 940 balance reporting message for cash management, a European

Currency Unit (ECU) netting procedure, a NOSTRO account reconciliation package for different currencies, and the selling of integrated hardware and software packages to members. The ECU netting service, run in co-operation with the Bank for International Settlements in Basel, Switzerland, has been quite successful with more than 3,000 daily messages sent (Moore and Kok, 1989). Despite these services, major competition has surfaced in several areas, e.g. from voice/data circuits in intrabank high-volume communications areas and external communications systems, including Western Union and ITT.

In addition to competition from international communications services and banks, including member banks, SWIFT is threatened with direct competition from European postal, telephone, and telegraph authorities which can provide secure, flexible, reliable telecommunications systems that can quickly collect, sort, and transfer messages both domestically and internationally. One example of a national attempt to compete with SWIFT, especially on cost terms, is the French SIT, the Systeme Interbancaire de Telecompensation, which began a pilot stage in 1988 and became fully operational during 1989. This is an automated cash transmission system. A driving force for development of SIT stemmed from the need for large French banks to pay twice for a SWIFT message as well as for the amortization cost of the software to the central bank. Thus, SIT will transmit messages for a few centimes each, a cost found to be less than that charged by the SWIFT system (Ferrand, 1987).

Finally, a political threat to SWIFT's operations could present itself in the form of protectionism. If economic conditions deteriorate in a given SWIFT member country, the country might resort to nontariff barriers including restrictions on the flow of information across national borders. The current Uruguay Round of the General Agreement on Tariffs and Trade (GATT) may alleviate this problem, since its agenda includes discussion of services for the first time.

Operations and Technology: The Changes to SWIFT

Planning

SWIFT management began to plan in 1982 for a new system, SWIFT II, to improve its present operations with more capacity and flexibility. The new system offers member banks a decentralized network architecture incorporating a "transaction processing" approach. Such a system enables member and user banks to incorporate a variety of processing application functions for national or regional services. Such an approach provides greater flexibility for banks in processing operations and substantially increases overall system capacity.

Technology

The new system included Burrough's A9 processors running central control systems, slice processors for message storage and forwarding, regional processors for handling local protocol conversions, and new user terminals. Thus, this system was designed to enhance flexibility, capacity, service, and security. Several technical problems in hardware and software development delayed introduction of the system ("SWIFT II Transition," 1987). During its early development stage, some doubted whether SWIFT II would ever be implemented, at least as originally planned (Tate, 1985).

Implementation and Advantages of SWIFT II

The advantages of the proposed system enhances SWIFT services to its members. For example, not only will capacity be increased, the system will: 1)be more user friendly offering easier access to smaller banks, 2) handle longer messages, 3) have longer on-line storage—up from 10 days to four months, and 4) return messages to the sender which are incorrectly coded (Tate, 1985).

SWIFT management reaffirmed the commitment to a SWIFT II system upgrade. After successful production control testing during 1988 of the 978 SWIFT II functions programmed into one million lines of code (Moore, Kok, and Naacamuli, 1989), SWIFT executives approved the next test phase—Network Acceptance Testing—which was completed in early 1989. Operational testing was then accomplished during the next eight months (Moore and Kok, 1989).

Progress, although behind schedule, was made in the implementation of the new system. By late 1990, 39 banks had moved to a full SWIFT II mode. It was announced that the new system would concentrate on SWIFT's expertise in communication services, electronic data interchange, and matching and netting systems in various fields (Kok, Drummond, and Cerveau, 1990).

The new, but revised, system was launched in 1990, three years behind schedule. While the original SWIFT had been designed to handle 300,000 messages/day and had reached the 1.3-1.5 million message/day level in its operations, SWIFT II will have unlimited capacity with the installation of new Unisys processors in the operating centers. It was able to service all 3,000 subscribers by mid-1992 (Crockett, 1990).

The new system has incorporated some innovative changes in the new services offered to its subscribers. The new Interbank File Transfer (IFT) is designed to support the transmission of high volume data and includes security features as well as the ability to handle automated bulk data transfer (Horwitt, 1992). The IFT service will use the Stratus XA2000 Series 200 computer enabling financial institutions to automate the flow of general business information in addition to payment-related messages ("SWIFT Selects. . ., 1990). In addition, Northern Telecom's DPN-100 data networking system adopted by SWIFT will enable the system to route data more quickly, more simply, and with less blockage at the intermediate nodes than was the case with traditional systems (Drynan, 1991).

PROBLEMS FACING SWIFT

The SWIFT concept has been confronted with several challenges to its managers. In addition, some external commentary has been critical of SWIFT, its operations and organization. These challenges and criticisms will be discussed in the next sections.

Challenges to SWIFT Managers

A number of challenges have confronted SWIFT management. These include external competition, the large bank/small bank dichotomy, international funds managers, rising costs, Africa, and SWIFT's own managerial competence. First, SWIFT faces external competition from specialist network operators (Jones, 1992). Some of these have been discussed in a previous section. Second, SWIFT must reconcile the aims of large user banks which generate the bulk of SWIFT operations with those of smaller banks (Jones, 1992). The issue of how to bring international funds managers into the network has implications for the global securities and custodial business (Jones, 1992). The issue of rising costs in international financial payments can be met, so says SWIFT management, by increasing customer service. This will be met by new services such as netting, electronic data interchange, and the Interbank File Transfer function, ("S.W.I.F.T. Outlines. . ., 1991).

SWIFT operations in Africa pose special problems. The continent has low telephone penetration, slow network growth, suboptimal reinvestment of profits, and widely varying national network infrastructures. Ingenuity and persistence will be essential strategies for global network managers of companies operating in Africa (Shetty, 1991).

Finally, a more ominous problem confronting SWIFT may be the way its management is perceived in the way it formulates and implements its objectives. For example, it was reported in 1989 that many of the original SWIFT II functions which management had planned had disappeared from future planning. The apparent failure of the SWIFT Executive Committee to realize its own objectives may be a reflection about how well SWIFT is actually operated (Murphy, 1989b).

External Evaluations of SWIFT

SWIFT has been evaluated occasionally by external observers as well as its subscribers. A number of concerns have been identified. The U.S. General Accounting Office (GAO) has found three areas of concern ("GAO Sees. . ., 1990). These are lack of independent internal audits made by SWIFT of its operations, potential problems with computer capacity, and problems with the planned replacement system. Some of these concerns have been or will be alleviated. The use of new Unisys processors in the operating centers may add unlimited capacity. And the launch of the revised SWIFT II system may eliminate some of the problems which occurred during its planning stage.

Many users lost confidence in the whole concept of SWIFT II and the ability of SWIFT management to produce it during the late 1980s (Murphy, 1989a). The cancellation of SIONA, the planned users' "insurance policy" for switching from SWIFT I and the transfer of its US$9.9 million of resources to the SWIFT II system was seen by many users as a potential liability to them. The SIONA safeguard plan would have transferred SWIFT I software to new Unisys A-series computers which the SWIFT II system uses (Murphy, 1988). Users upset with this change believed SWIFT management erred by engaging in internal development work of which it had no prior experience.

THE STUDY

SWIFT has been such a success during its first decade of operations that competitors and member banks have tried to emulate it. Little or no evaluation of SWIFT's operations has been published and in light of the proposed new system, such a study seemed warranted. The objective of the remainder of this chapter is to report the findings of that study by the authors.

The Sample

A sample of 1,079 SWIFT bank users was selected from the stockholder list published by SWIFT in 1985. These banks were located in 51 different countries. The geographical breakdown for the surveyed banks was as follows: Europe 622, North America 148, Latin America 138, Asia 127, and Middle East/Africa 44.

The Survey Instrument

A survey instrument was designed to elicit responses from subscriber banks about the major concerns they perceived after experiencing the SWIFT network and its operations. Measurement of these variables is necessary in order to properly evaluate the efficacy of such a global network to its users. These variables include message types sent by them and their volume, title of person responsible, costs, message errors, transmittal time, customer acceptance of SWIFT services, opinions concerning what countries and user-types to add to SWIFT II, banks' initial reasons for joining the SWIFT network, what new software packages and services should be added, changes in SWIFT suggested by respondents, and long-range or strategic challenges to the system.

Some of these variables are sufficiently important to be singled out. For example, user message volume is important because users receive rebates based on their usage. Transmittal cost is lower as a user increases volume. Measurement and identification of errors may explain why message cost and security of this system is more valuable. Measurement of transmittal time is important because this also is a determinant of cost, especially in a world of volatile foreign exchange rates.

The Response

A total of 142 SWIFT user banks returned usable responses to the survey. These respondents were located in 36 different countries. In addition, 30 unusable responses were received. The reasons for the unusable nature of these responses included: incorrect address resulting in no forwarding of the questionnaire, member bank not yet on-line, or the bank was no longer a member. No bank responded with the typical "against corporate policy" response. The unusable responses were eliminated from the original sample of 1,079 banks, thus making the sample size 1,049 for purposes of this study. Thus, the 142 responses received represented a usable response rate of 13.5 percent. In terms of country of origin, the most frequent responses were from: the United States (25 banks or 17.6 percent of total responses—23.1 percent of U.S. banks queried), Italy (18 banks or 12.7 percent of total responses—14.1 percent of Italian banks queried), France (9 banks or 6.3 percent of total responses—13 percent of French banks queried), and Belgium (8 banks or 5.6 percent of total responses—33.3 percent of Belgian banks queried).

In addition to these data on responses, some interesting returns can be noted. For example, six of nine SWIFT banks queried in the Philippines responded as did five of 12 in Thailand, three of six in Greece, and each of the sole SWIFT member banks in Jordan and Kuwait, respectively. On the other hand, only nine SWIFT banks from among the 138 located in Central and South America responded (6.5 percent). One reason for this small response rate from

Latin American banks may have been the language barrier incurred from an English-language survey instrument. However, several letters were received from Latin American banks which were listed, as long ago as 1985, among SWIFT member banks and, in every case, the respondent bank had not yet committed to on-line SWIFT operations. Lack of technology seemed to be the factor most often given as the reason for this delay by Latin American banks.

Although the response rate, percentage-wise, is relatively small, the returns in terms of countries and representatives were adequate for statistical analysis. Several reasons may be given for the low response rate. The English-language questionnaire, as was mentioned, was mailed to banks in many non-English speaking countries. Many foreign nations consider this area of financial information communications to be highly secretive in nature. Many banks may not have understood the non-SWIFT related "objectivity" of an academic study and may have assumed it was not approved by SWIFT. In fact, SWIFT officials did query the authors about questions they received from member banks concerning the authenticity of this study, i.e., whether it was approved by SWIFT officials. Correct, up-to-date addresses may have been a problem, especially in developing countries. In addition, the appropriate officer within the bank may not have received the instrument.

However, it must be recognized that this study includes a large non-response. The non-responses were not tested for bias. Thus, the major limitation of the results of this study may be that a significant non-response bias may be present.

Demographic Data About Respondents

Respondents were asked to furnish information about their bank on a voluntary basis. For example, 89.4 percent of the respondents reported the total asset size of their bank. The respondent banks ranged in size from US$2 million to US$200 billion in total assets. The vast majority of banks (95 percent) had total assets of US$50 billion or less, with 50 percent of all respondents having US$3.1 billion or less.

Banks were asked to report the number of countries in which they operate. Of those responding, answers ranged from one to 50 countries with slightly more than half of those responding having operations in no more than two countries.

Banks were asked how many SWIFT terminals each operated in the home country or worldwide. Most banks have only a few terminals in their home country, with 81.3 percent reporting less than four terminals in the home country, although one bank reported as many as 60 terminals. Most banks (67.9 percent) do not have terminals in a foreign country, although the remaining respondents to this query reported having from one to 62 terminals worldwide.

THE FINDINGS

Message Types and Volume

Message Types

The sample SWIFT user banks were asked several questions concerning what message types they generally transmitted, their message volume, and other related questions. With regard to the types of messages sent by respondent banks, the frequency of message types reported is shown in Table 1. The respondents reported using a total of 798 different categories of message types. Thus, respondents sent or received, on average, 5.6 different message types.

Message Types	Frequency*
Interbank Transfers	239
Customer Transfers	142
Documentary Credit	92
Advice of Payment	69
Foreign Exchange	50
Confirmations of Debits and Credits	42
Statement Messages	35
Reimbursements, Discrepanies, Discharge, Acceptance, Refused, etc.	25
Netting	23
Loan/Deposit	23
Queries, Answers, Free Format	22
Acknowledgement, Tracers, Instructions, Amendments	18
Order to Buy or Sell, Confirmations to Buy or Sell, Deliver, Receipt Against Payment	16
Balance Reporting	2
Total	798

*Frequencies total more than number of respondents because each message type listed here contains more than one message sub-type. For a breakdown of SWIFT message types, see *SWIFT User Handbook*/Volume 6-Standards, Issue Date 1 July 1983, available from Society for Worldwide Interbank Financial Telecommunications, Hulpe, Belgium.

Table 1: SWIFT Message Categories Used by Respondents

Global Telex Service

Banks were asked whether they use the SWIFT Global Telex service, a SWIFT attempt to compete with regular telex. Only 8.5

percent of respondents reported using this service. Of the eight banks which reported Global Telex volume, two reported more than 11,000 messages per month whereas five other banks reported monthly volume in this service ranging from 25 to 3,000 messages.

Message Volume

The survey asked banks to estimate their message volume through SWIFT facilities. Respondent banks reported a range of from seven messages to 8,000 messages sent daily. The message volume reported most frequently by respondents were 100 messages/day (10 banks) and 200 messages/day (10 banks).

Person Responsible

SWIFT users were asked what title is used to designate the person in the bank responsible for SWIFT operations. Several titles were given for this position but, after some judgment calls by the authors, most of the titles were divided between those connoting a supervisory position and those signifying a technical position. Almost 62 percent of the respondents designated this position to be a supervisory officer whereas 22.5 percent referred to the position as technical.

Size of SWIFT Staff

Banks were asked how many persons were authorized to operate the SWIFT terminal. The responses ranged from two to more than 100. Most respondents reported relatively small staffs. In 80 percent of the cases, 11 or fewer persons are authorized to operate the SWIFT terminal. It would seem that the larger the staff, the higher the chance for a security problem.

Funds Transfer Messages

SWIFT banks were asked what percentage of SWIFT messages were instructions for funds transfers. In most cases—60 percent— banks reported that more than 50 percent of their messages were to facilitate funds transfers. In 18 percent of the responses, more than 80 percent of SWIFT messages were to facilitate such transfers.

Message Problems

Message Errors

Several questions were asked SWIFT user banks about message errors or other malfunctions in their utilization of the SWIFT system.

Banks were asked whether an error or malfunction in the transmission of a message had ever resulted in lost revenues for their firm. More than 87 percent reported that no such losses had been incurred by their bank. When asked what percentage of SWIFT messages contain some type of error, e.g. unauthorized message, improper use of message type, electronic malfunction, incorrect spelling/dollar amounts, or unclear instructions, some 99.1 percent of the respondents reported from zero to 25 percent of their message transmissions on the SWIFT system had contained some error or malfunction. In 21.1 percent of the cases, no such errors or malfunctions had occurred. More than 70 percent—71.3 percent—reported incurring five or fewer errors or malfunctions since being on-line with SWIFT. The implications of these responses seem to be that message errors may have happened more often than has been publicly reported and that banks may have incurred losses of revenues which may also have been unreported.

Banks were asked whether they had ever received messages with confusing, incomplete or inaccurate information or if such messages had been improperly routed. Exactly 50 percent of the respondents answered that such had occurred. These respondents were asked what percentage of messages were of such a nature. The responses to this query ranged from one percent of the messages in 32 banks to 50 percent in one bank. Banks receiving confusing, incomplete, or inaccurate messages were asked how much time elapsed until the correct message was received. The responses ranged from less than one day in 11 banks to seven days in three banks. Slightly more half of such respondents—37 banks—reported a delay of 1-2 days before a correct message was received. However, only 8.5 percent of the respondents reported that they had ever decided against sending a message on the SWIFT network because of concern about errors. An even smaller number of banks—seven—had ever decided against sending a message on the SWIFT network because of security concerns.

Transmission Time

Banks were asked to estimate the transmittal time to receipt for an average message. If the bank is logged on to the system, 35.2 percent reported a few seconds. Another 15.5 percent reported transmittal time to be from a few seconds up to one minute. Only five percent of respondents reported that transmittal time, when logged on, has taken longer than a few minutes. The overall average of transmittal time, including the operation of logging on, was reported to be less than one minute by 43 percent of the respondents. Slightly more than one-third of the responding banks—35.9 percent— reported a preference for faster response time/transmission time.

The MT 940 Message Format

SWIFT user banks were queried about their utilization of the relatively new MT 940 message format permitting transmission of customer financial statements. Only seven percent reported using this message type. Of the remainder, less than 20 percent reported plans to introduce this message format in the near future. When the banks reporting usage of the MT 940 message format were asked to rate customer acceptance of this service on a 5-point scale (1 = highest, 5 = lowest acceptance), the service did not seem to rate a very strong customer acceptance. Perhaps SWIFT subscriber banks using the format have had too little experience with it to show much more than a neutral response to such a query.

Adding New Member Countries

User banks were asked what new countries they would most like to see added to country membership in SWIFT. The vast majority—73.9 percent—responded that specific new countries should be added. Among the most frequently mentioned countries desired by user banks to be added were: Arab, African, and East European nations, Russia, India, South Korea, and the remaining Latin American countries not now members. In 1989, Kuwait, the former German Democratic Republic, and Turkey were added to SWIFT membership. South Korea has also joined since then.

Adding Non-bank Users

User banks were asked whether they favored adding non-bank users to the SWIFT network. With the exception of credit card processors—a function performed by many bank affiliates, SWIFT members generally opposed addition of non-bank users to the SWIFT network. User banks seemed to be neutral with regard to adding stockbrokers to the network. A total of 34 banks agreed to their addition while 36 banks disagreed. The remainder were neutral. With regard to corporate treasurers, only 10.6 percent agreed to their addition whereas 30.3 percent disagreed. More user banks were opposed—33.8 percent—to addition of non-bank, non-broker financial companies than were favorable—19.7 percent. These conclusions by respondents, in general, are in opposition to recent SWIFT decisions to permit non-banks to join the system. Finally, more user banks favored adding credit card processors—28.9 percent—than opposed their membership—19.0 percent.

SWIFT Membership Determinants

Banks were asked several questions to determine their reasons for joining the SWIFT network. Among the various determinants were cost savings, security, system reliability, competitive environment, and greater access to international transactions.

Cost Savings

SWIFT users were equally divided when asked whether cost savings was a primary factor for their decision to join SWIFT. Sixty-seven user banks—47.2 percent—said cost savings was a primary factor for joining SWIFT whereas 68 banks—47.9 percent—said it was not. When asked whether overall equipment cost had increased since the bank became a user, 56.3 percent responded positively. Slightly less than half—48.6 percent—stated that operating costs had increased since they joined SWIFT, although 43.7 percent answered that such costs had not increased. However, of those banks reporting equipment and operating costs to have increased, 62.7 percent did not consider such increases to be too excessive.

Security and Reliability

The vast majority of SWIFT user banks—73.2 percent—responded that security was a primary factor for their decision to join the SWIFT network. Related to security needs, 85.9 percent reported that reliability was a primary factor in deciding to join the network.

Competitive Environment

Banks were asked whether the competitive environment was a primary factor in their decision to join SWIFT. More than 80 percent reported in the affirmative. In fact, most bank officials, when interviewed in connection with other studies, have stated that the need to be competitive in the transfer of funds, especially electronically, is a major strategic factor for bank management.

International Access

Banks were asked whether greater access to international transactions was a primary factor for their decision to join SWIFT. A total of 114 banks—80.3 percent—responded that this was a primary factor.

Summary

Banks were asked to rank the five factors discussed above in order of importance—from 1 = most important to 5 = least important—in their decision to join the SWIFT network. The factor cited most often as most important was competitive environment—28.9 percent. Security was cited by 25.3 percent—as the most important factor. Bankers responded in 17.6 percent of the cases that cost was most important while 14.1 percent of the respondents offered access to international transactions as the major reason for SWIFT membership, and 12.7 percent responded that reliability was most important.

Float Reduction and Security Execution

Banks were asked whether SWIFT had enabled them to reduce float or idle cash balances. Nearly 60 percent responded in the affirmative. With regard to security execution, however, 42.3 percent of the respondents answered that such transactions were not executed more quickly through SWIFT whereas 38.0 percent answered that quicker securities execution has been possible through the SWIFT network.

SWIFT Software Packages

Banks were queried about which software packages made available from SWIFT were found to be most helpful. Among the packages most often mentioned were the following: traffic reconciliation, payments, mainframe link, fund transfers, and bank files. Banks were also asked what new software packages should be developed or provided by SWIFT. Among those mentioned most were: an automated traffic reconciliation, credit and collections, a package to store repetitive messages, authentication key administration, packages equipped with the Hitachi protocol, brokers' notes, standing orders, among others. Some of these packages were mentioned by respondents to the first part of this query, i.e., which packages are most helpful. Thus, one might infer from such answers that not all SWIFT member banks had available all software packages provided at that time by SWIFT.

Additional SWIFT Services

Banks were asked what services should be added by SWIFT which are not now provided. Among the answers given to this query are the following: client cash management system, standard format for guarantee issuance, facsimile, access to news, dealing system, bulk data transfers, exchange of authentication keys on-line, transfer file, access to bank data, education courses in the native languages of user banks, software permitting communication with other systems, ability to control the quantity of characters of sent messages, and interfaces between SWIFT and application systems.

SWIFT II

The sample banks were asked if they were acquainted with the SWIFT II program. Although 68.3 percent answered in the affirmative, a surprising 30.3 percent reported they were not familiar with SWIFT II. Banks familiar with SWIFT II were asked what the new system could do for them which is not now possible. Among the responses were the following: delivery instructions—MT 047, user acknowledgements, better message check, faster response time, increase of retrieval time from 14 days to six months or less, enhancement of systems and procedures, interfacing of SWIFT to telex, more flexibility within member organization, the ability to cancel a message after approval prior to receipt by the receiving bank because of last minute change of instructions, provision of integrated backup, remote workstations, better control through more strict application of codes, increased security and capacity, more message types, and more fields.

Several members responded, interestingly, that little or no change would result from SWIFT II. Some small banks stated that their volume was too small to benefit from the new system. In fact, they believe their operations might even be complicated by the changes. Overall, most banks either offered no comment or did not even respond to this question.

SWIFT Impact on Retail Banking

Bank officials were asked what impact they thought SWIFT had had on retail banking in their country. Among the most frequently mentioned impacts were: more rapid service, better communications, reduced costs, improved services, more standardization, improvement of international relations, greater efficiency, and improved cash flows. Thus, it would appear that SWIFT has had a significant impact on retail banking operations from an international standpoint.

Changes Recommended in SWIFT

SWIFT members were asked what changes they would recommend in SWIFT. Among the changes recommended were: more words allowed per message, less expensive training courses, better local technical support, better election process for directors, improvement in the participation of Spanish-speaking countries, addition of more countries, improvement in reliability, ability for users to reduce idle cash balances, quicker response to network faults, and lower annual costs and support fees.

Major Technological and Strategic Challenges to SWIFT

Bank users were asked what they believed to be the major technological and strategic challenges facing SWIFT over the next five years. Among the responses were the following: expansion of network to non-bank financial firms, SWIFT II introduction, software improvement, security, competition, lower costs, connection of additional countries, development of a super computer to support the system, ability to handle all transfers, and a mainframe link between member banks.

SUMMARY AND CONCLUSIONS

SWIFT has performed so well during its first decade and a half of operations as a worldwide interbank system for transferring instructions underlying funds flows that it has: 1)incurred competition from other financial communications services firms, national organizations such as the French SIT, and from its own bank members; and 2) implemented a new improved SWIFT II system, although not as elaborate as originally planned. SWIFT has become one of the most secure, rapid, reliable, and cost-effective systems for assisting global business operations. It has had a major impact on international banking.

The responses to this study confirmed most or all of these characterizations of SWIFT. However, they have also pointed out that problems are present. Many smaller banks which responded to the study do not believe that SWIFT II will benefit them. In fact, some think the new system may even complicate their operations.

Hardware development problems delayed introduction of the new system until 1990. In fact, reasons were given for abandoning SWIFT II altogether. The delay in its introduction only gave more time for other competitors to implement new programs, thus rendering SWIFT less effective, no matter what improvements the new system may provide.

Worldwide deregulation of financial institutions and markets coupled with the liberalization of such areas, especially in the developing countries, has fostered the development of a single global market for money. The operations of the various institutions and markets making up this single monolith will be facilitated by improved worldwide electronic systems designed to transfer funds and financial instructions in the shortest time possible, for the lowest cost possible, and with maximum security, flexibility, and reliability. The results of the study reported in this chapter and its further analyses should foster improvement in SWIFT and enable it to meet the major technological and strategic challenges which face it during its next decade of operations.

REFERENCES

Aggarwal, Raj and J.C. Baker (1991). SWIFT as an internal Funds Mechanism: User Satisfaction and Challenges in *Advances in Working Capital Management,* Yong H. Kim and Kenkat Srinivasan, vol. 2. Greenwich Ct: KAI Press Inc., 271-292.

Arend, Mark. (1989, January). SWIFT Speeds Up as Broker/Dealers Join. *Wall Street Computer Review.* 6, pp. 16-19, 79.

Buyer, Martha. (1983, May). Telecommunications and International Banking. *Telecommunications.* 17, p. 45.

Byler, Ezra U. and James C. Baker. (1983, September-October). S.W.I.F.T.: A Fast Method to Facilitate International Financial Transactions. *Journal of World Trade Law.* 17, pp. 458-465.

Chase Manhattan Bank's Evolving Money Transfer System. (1977, June). *Banking.* 69, pp. 46-58, 100.

Crockett, Barton. (1990, September 17). SWIFT2 Completion Adds Needed Capacity. *Network World.* 7, pp. 27-30.

Drynan, David, and David Jeanes. (1991). Global Data Networking with DPN-100.   *Telesis.* 93, pp. 36-45.

Ferrand, Tim. (1987, August). SIT: A Guaranteed Clearing System at Reduced Cost. *Banker International,* pp. 8-10.

GAO Sees Wire Security Gaps. (1990, May/June). *Journal of Cash Management.* 10, pp. 70-74.

Hock, Tan Lee. (1991, August 15). SWIFT Eyes Asia's Emerging Markets. *Asian Finance.* 17, p. 14.

Horwitt, Elisabeth. (1992, April 13). Bank Net Service Calls for X.400 and More.   *Computerworld.* 26, p. 66.

Ioannou, Lori. (1991, August). Brokers Are Doing It for Themselves. *Euromoney,* pp. SS6-SS9.

Jones, David. (1992, January). Getting to Grips with Swift. *Banking World.* 10, p. 34.

Kok, Bessel, Peter Drummond, and Jacques Cerveau. (1990, November/December).   A Report on the Status and Future of S.W.I.F.T. *World of Banking.* 9, pp. 14-17, 28-29.

Margolis, Nell, Susan Nykamp, Donald St. John, Clinton Wilder, Carol Hildebrand, Jean S. Bozman, Maryfran Johnson, Kim S. Nash, and Michael Fitzgerald. (1991, June 17). Awards Praise the Human Touch; The 1991 CW Smithsonian Winners. *Computerworld.* 25, pp. 89-91.

Moore, Robert W. (1986, Fall). Large Value Payments Systems. *Journal of Bank Research,* pp. 232-243.

Moore, W. R., and Bessell Kok. (1989, March-April). S.W.I.F.T.—Today and Tomorrow: An Update on S.W.I.F.T. SIBOS. *The World of Banking.* 8, p. 9.

Murphy, Paul. (1989, April). And with One Bound... *The Banker.* 139, pp. 21-22.

Murphy, Paul. (1988, December). Not So SWIFT Off the Mark. *The Banker.* 138, pp. 55-57.

Murphy, Paul. (1989, November). Banking tomorrow: A Day in the Life Of. *The Banker.* 139, pp. 136, 139.

Murphy, Paul. (1989, September). Banking tomorrow: The Ice Cube Cometh. *The Banker.* 139, pp. 86-92.

O.Connor, James H. (1985, September 19). S.W.I.F.T. Payments System Eyes Change with Mixed Feelings. *American Banker,* p. 2.

Office of Technology Assessment. (1992). *U.S. Banks and International Telecommunications.* Washington, D.C.: Office of Technology Assessment.

Parry, John. (1987, February). Bank Communications System Delayed. *American Banker,* p. 2.

Rudnick, David. (1992, February). Global Custody: In for a Bumpy Ride. *Euromoney,* pp. 73-76.

S.W.I.F.T. Outlines Its Strategies and Its New Services. (1991, November/December). *World of Banking.* 10, pp. 16-18.

Shale, Tony. (1988, November). Swift but Not silent. *Euromoney,* p. 78.

Sharkey, Betsy. (1982, October 11). Bermuda Banks to Begin Wire Transfers. *Business Insurance,* p. 28.

Shetty, Vineeta. (1991, October 14). African Net Quality Tests Users' Mettle (Part 1). *Network World.* 8, pp. 33-35.

Steiner, Thomas D., and Diogo B. Teixeira. (1990). *Technology in Banking: Creating Value and Destroying Profits.* Homewood, Illinois: Irwin.

SWIFT Selects Stratus for Data Service on Its Global Network. (1990, October 11). *Computing Canada* (Canada). 16, p. 65.

SWIFT II Transition. (1987, December). *ABA Banking Journal.* 79, p. 112.

SWIFT Busters Strike Out. (1992, May). *The Banker.* 142, pp. 44, 46.

Tate, Paul. (1985, October 15). Clipping SWIFT's Wings. *Datamation.* 31, p. 42.

The Great Electronic funds Shuffle. (1982, June). *Institutional Investor.* 16, p. 88.

Timewell, Stephen. (1991, August). Global Custody: Last of the Dinosaurs? *The   Banker.* 141, pp. 34-39.

What will S.W.I.F.T. II Mean to Your Bank. (1986, September). *ABA Banking   Journal.* 78, pp. 44-45.

CHAPTER 7

Information Technology in the Major International Financial Markets

BRUCE W. WEBER
New York University

Financial markets perform a seemingly simple function: facilitating the transfer of securities into cash, or cash into securities. Closer inspection of the activities and the information intensity of a trading floor or a dealing room reveals great complexity. Information technology (IT) plays a crucial role in supporting market activities, and no trader today could operate without real-time data services, and computer-based analytical tools. Market information about prices, interest rates, transactions, investor supply and demand, and company and economic news is at the heart of any trading operation. Consequently, the major international markets from Tokyo to Zurich are making increased use of information technology. While IT is capable of making physical marketplaces and trading floors obsolete, no consensus is emerging on the design of an integrated global financial market, and many technological and regulatory issues remain unsolved. Multiple, fragmented markets may be a consequence of the lack of coordination. This chapter highlights the technologies that are revolutionizing international financial markets. The future direction of financial markets will be charted by automation and systems, and IT's influence on banks, securities firms, and the markets themselves will continue to be a subject of debate and controversy.

INTRODUCTION

Financial markets around the world are in the midst of a dramatic transformation. Regulatory and market barriers have fallen, and automation continues to restructure trading processes, lowering the costs of transacting and monitoring financial markets. Observers have declared "The End of Geography" in financial markets[1]; location plays a greatly diminished role in investors' decisions. International market integration is occurring at a rapid pace, and globalization is no longer a buzzword; it has arrived. It is not unusual to hear of a British broker placing a Japanese conglomerate's Deutschmark-denominated securities with a U.S. pension fund manager as part of an underwriting arranged by a subsidiary of a Swiss bank in Luxembourg. To hedge the risk of adverse shifts in currency values or interest rates, the investor may simultaneously execute trades in a screen-based market, such as Globex. These global financial activities provide benefits through increased investor diversification, lower costs of company funding, and increased competition across market participants.

Such transformations do not occur without upheaval and discomfort for some market participants. The move to global markets has heightened competition, and financial technology often leads to low-margin, undifferentiated products (Clemons and Weber, 1991). The return on capital for member firms of the London Stock Exchange between 1987-1990 was **negative** 2 percent. Employment in the U.S. securities industry has fallen from 262,000 in 1987 to 224,000 in 1992. Responding effectively to the changes and pressures will be the hallmark of successful firms and expanding market centers in the coming years. While information technology threatens some sources of profits, it also creates opportunities and a means of reacting to market challenges. For instance, episodes of intensified market volatility such as the October 1987 and October 1989 price breaks have lead to the development of increasingly sophisticated risk management systems. Technology has spawned "financial engineering", the packaging of sophisticated, hybrid financial instruments tailored to investor needs.

This chapter surveys the technologies and computer innovations that are transforming financial markets worldwide. Indicative of the changes, the most advanced information technology on the New York Stock Exchange (NYSE) floor in 1964 was a standard annunciator board on the wall, similar to those used in roadside diners to alert waitresses that customer orders were ready.   The board notified members by their badge number of incoming telephone orders.   In a 5-hour trading day, floor traders often walked 15 miles. In contrast, today's foreign exchange market is based on screen price displays and traders operating from well-equipped dealing rooms.   Over a third of all foreign exchange trades today are executed on-line via screen "conversations" among market participants spread across the globe.

Although commercial applications of computers expanded rapidly in the 1960s and 1970s, primitive communications systems were unable to handle the intricacies of trading. Markets required face-to-face contact on physical trading floors, or extensive telephone searches of brokers and dealers. Nineteenth century technologies such as the telephone and the stock ticker increased the outside exposure of trading, but until recently the need for floor markets was unquestioned.[2] Today's more advanced information systems can perform many of the market's informationally intensive functions such as matching buyers and sellers, finding prices at which trades should occur, and processing transactions. Many capital markets today function as networks of linked trader terminals, and a number of firms operate global communications networks for sharing data on positions and activities, and for serving clients without regard to location. Responding to their customers and competitive pressures from information vendors that have established trading networks, traditional floor-based stock exchanges and futures markets have undertaken significant automation projects.

Firms operating in financial markets are among the most intensive and innovative users of information technology. Securities firms in the U.S. spent $7.5 billion on IT in 1991, or about 20 percent of their noninterest expense. Other types of organizations using IT extensively are investment institutions, information vendors, and the market regulators. Information vendors supply data to market participants using advanced telecommunications networks and satellites to speed transmissions around the globe. The exchanges themselves spend a large percentage of their operating budgets on technology for information retrieval and trading support. A third of the NYSE's 1990 budget of $300 million was spent on systems and technology.   London's International Financial Futures Exchange (LIFFE) market devotes 35 percent of its operating budget to information technology.   The Securities and Exchange Commission (SEC), the industry regulator in the U.S., is currently phasing in its Electronic Data Gathering, Analysis and Retrieval system (EDGAR) for on-line filing of public disclosure documents from corporations and investment managers. EDGAR will cost $75 million, and by mid-1996 will replace paper filings, which total 10 million pages per year from the 14,000 companies registered with the SEC.

Financial Basics: Instruments, Investment, and Market Infrastructure

Financial markets exist as a complex of securities and instruments, investor decision-making, and a financial infrastructure to support trading and trade processing. These are detailed below.

Instruments. Anything of value can be traded, and merchants, marketplaces, and bazaars have existed since the dawn of civilization. *Financial markets* facilitate the transfer of money into financial instruments, which are *issued*, or sold to investors by companies to raise capital, or by government bodies to borrow funds. Most traded instruments fall into one of several standard categories. While a large company may manufacture many products in various sizes, colors, and configurations, its securities will be standardized into a narrow range by the type of *claim* they represent for the investor.

- *Common stock* or equity is an ownership share in a firm's profits and net worth. Equity holders receive dividends, and vote on corporate actions.
- *Bonds or fixed income obligations* represent loans or contractual claims to a specified stream of repayments. The typical bond pays interest up to the *maturity* date, when the face value or *principal* is returned. Bonds are issued by government bodies and companies.   Notes and bills are similar to bonds, but have shorter maturities. Bills mature in a year or less, and notes have an original maturity of 1 to 10 years.
- Markets also exist for *physical commodities* like gold, oil, and agricultural products, and for foreign *currencies*.

Markets differ depending on the timing of the asset's transfer. Often, a transaction occurs today for a financial instrument that the purchaser may not own until some months or years into the future.

- In *cash or spot markets*, ownership of the traded instrument is transferred immediately. Purchasing 100 shares of Intel stock at $118 today means that 100 Intel shares will be added to the buyer's account and $11,800 will be credited to the seller's funds on the settlement date (5 days after the trade in the U.S.).
- *Options* contracts confer the right to buy or sell an asset or financial instrument at a specified *strike price* during the contract lifetime, which ends on the option's expiration date. For instance, the purchaser of a *call option* on Intel with a strike price of $120 expiring in two months has the right to buy 100 Intel shares at $120 up to the expiration date regardless of Intel market price. If Intel's share price rises, the value of this option will increase. The option expires worthless if Intel's price is below $120 at expiration.

- In **forward or futures markets**, a price and a **delivery date** sometime in the future are specified. On the delivery or expiration date, ownership transfers and the pre-agreed price is paid by the buyer and received by the seller. For instance, an investor may buy a $1 million futures contract in April at a yield of 5.0% for December delivery of 90-day Treasury Bills. On the delivery day in April, the seller delivers a T-Bill having 90 days to maturity, and the buyer pays the present value of $1 million discounted at 5.0%, or: $1,000,000 - (0.050*1,000,000)*90/360 = $987,500.

Futures markets developed to meet the needs of farmers and food merchants to protect or **hedge** themselves against adverse fluctuations in agriculture prices caused by weather and crop cycle uncertainties. Trading typically occurs in open outcry trading pits with prices shouted out and good "as long as the breath is warm." Today's largest futures exchange, the Chicago Board of Trade (CBOT), was founded in 1848. With futures, farmers could lock-in a price for crops at the beginning of the growing season, and food producers could be certain of a supply of materials at a fixed cost. **Financial futures** were introduced for foreign currencies in 1972 at the Chicago Mercantile Exchange (CME). Today, financial futures on bonds, interest rates, stock indexes, and currencies are the most heavily traded futures contracts. Future trading has grown in part due to the lower costs of trading futures compared to the cash market instruments. A study by Prudential Portfolio Managers in London showed the cost of buying and later selling a stock position to be 1.9 percent of the position value. For a similar position, a round trip trade in futures cost 0.054 percent.[3] With futures, investors can gain exposure to a market, or layoff some of the risk of their positions quickly and cheaply. In order to maintain the exposure, however, the futures contracts need to be *rolled over* at their expiration date (every 3-6 months on average), leading to another trade and set of transaction costs.

Futures and options are called **derivative** securities because their prices are based on, or are derivative of, the cash market price for the **underlying** asset. The derivatives markets are among the most rapidly growing financial markets. Volumes at the CBOT and the CME, the world's two largest futures markets, tripled between 1982 and 1992. In the same time period, the managed futures industry in the U.S. has grown from several million dollars to $21 billion under management. Warrants, swaps, swaptions, commercial paper, rights, convertible bonds, and several other financial instruments are actively traded, but will not be described here.

Investment. Investments are made in expectation of attractive, positive returns, but any investment entails risk. Stock prices fluctuate according to market conditions, and the company's profits and prospects. Bonds prices vary according to interest rates in the economy, and changes in the creditworthiness of the issuer. Bonds are subject to **default** when worsening business conditions make it impossible for an issuer to meet its obligations. Hence, bonds with a greater likelihood of default pay a higher interest rate.

Technology can improve the management of risk, but it will not eliminate market price fluctuations. Some observers believe that financial markets are excessively volatile, and that reducing transactions costs through automation only exacerbates volatility by promoting superfluous trading. The evidence on market inefficiencies and excess volatility is inconclusive. Analysis of NYSE prices since 1840 showed that between 1980 and 1990 prices were only slightly more volatile than in the 1970s, but were less volatile than in the 1920s, 1940s, and 1890s.[4] Since systems can increase participation and information access, a move toward screen-based 24-hour markets may have the effect of reducing price shocks and volatility.

Investors typically **diversify** their investment portfolio by holding a range of securities. The value of diversification was quantified by the Nobel prize-winning economist Harry Markowitz in the 1950s. Markowitz demonstrated that a diversified portfolio had a higher expected rate of return or a lower variance (risk) of return than an undiversified portfolio.[5] The landmark **Capital Asset Pricing Model** (CAPM)[6] followed from Portfolio Theory, and established that rational investors will expect a return from any security i that is proportional to its risk as measured by its **beta**, $_i$. Beta is the *undiversifiable* risk of investing in asset i, and is measured by $_i = \text{Cov}(i,M)/\text{Var}(M)$, where Cov(i,M) is the covariance of returns on security i with returns on the entire market, M, and Var(M) is the variance of returns on the market. Beta reflects a stock's volatility, and is the amount that investors expect the stock price to change for each 1 percent change in the market. A beta of 1.5 implies that a 1 percent change in entire market is expected to result in a 1.5 percent change in security i's price.

Vendors and in-house systems groups have developed information technology to support all stages of the securities investment process.

Market infrastructure. The keys to a well-functioning financial market are **capital**, **people**, and **technology**. Capital in a market is the sum of the financial resources that back the banks and securities firms that participate in the market. Greater levels of capital raise creditworthiness, enable participants to bear greater risks, and lower the chances that market participants fail to meet their financial obligations. People in a market contribute skill and ingenuity in bringing together those companies and governments seeking to raise funds, with those individuals and institutions seeking to invest wealth. While financial resources are crucial, the adage "the assets walk out the door at the end of the day" applies to

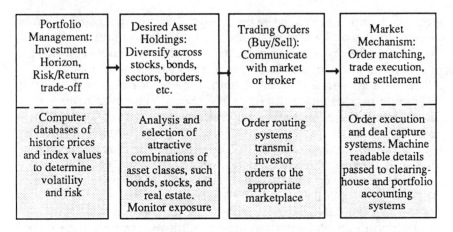

Figure 1: Flow Diagram of Securities Investment Decisions and examples (shaded) of Portfolio Management Technology

firms operating in financial markets.

In only a few advanced expert systems applications is technology used to displace human trading judgment. However, systems have replaced face-to-face and person-to-person contact as the principal conduits of information in modern financial markets. In the past, markets existed only when people gathered in one physical place. Twenty stock exchanges were operating in Britain in 1900, but in 1973 all trading was consolidated in London. Markets today can reach out to a vast collection of customers, and consolidate diverse opinions from any point on the globe, and at any time of day. Technology has also increased the *back-office* efficiency of the securities industry. In many markets, tedious trade settlement paperwork has been replaced by computerized book entry for transferring ownership, and electronic funds transfer for moving payments.

Liquidity is the principal measure of a market's attractiveness. The **liquidity** of a market or a financial instrument is measured by the ease and the economy of transforming cash into the security, and back again at prices that reflect the asset's fair value. Amihud and Mendelson (1991) identified four transactions costs that lower a security's liquidity:

(1) Bid-ask spread is a cost resulting from the difference between the best price to sell and to buy in the market.
(2) Market impact costs are incurred when a large trade can only be completed with a price concession by the investor.
(3) Delays and search costs are incurred when an investor seeks better trading terms by postponing a trade and trying to find an interested counterparty.

(4) Direct costs commissions are paid as a percentage of the value of a trade. For instance, institutional investors paid an average of 6.3 cents a share on average for trading U.S. equities in 1992 according to Greenwich Associates. This reflects a substantial drop from 1977's average of 11.5 cents, and 1987's of 7.1 cents.[7]

Low transactions costs improve trading and market liquidity. This allows securities ownership to shift easily so that capital flows efficiently from investors to expanding businesses.

Technology in Financial Markets

History. In 17th century Britain, trading companies such as the East India Company issued securities to finance shipbuilding and dock construction in London, and to pay for long voyages that returned tea, spice, and silk for England's home markets. U.S. financial markets were organized to enable the trading of former colonies' revolutionary war debts. Scandals and frauds were prevalent in the early stock markets. Shares were issued in 1720 in London by the South Sea Company, which proposed to open up trade and markets for new commodities in South America and the Pacific. The price rose from £128 to £1,050 between March and September, but then collapsed, leaving the shares nearly valueless by December when promised dividends failed to appear.

The London Stock Exchange originated in New Jonathan's Coffee House when an entrance fee was imposed on traders in 1748 to keep out "riff-raff". The participating brokers formally established London's Stock Exchange in 1773. The forerunner of the New York Stock Exchange was formed 19 years later by the Buttonwood agreement of twenty-four brokers to establish an orderly market and to share trading information. A minimum commission of 0.25% was set (and maintained until 1975), and members agreed to give preferential treatment to one another. Fixed commissions, along with the restrictions and licensing mandated by the agreement, had the effect of creating a profitable cartel for the traders that took part. An outside, "curb" market remained, and later became the American Stock Exchange.

The formation of organized securities markets led to official market information. Newspaper-published stock prices in New York first appeared in 1815. The telegraph was invented in 1838 by Morse and Vail, and was quickly used to transmit prices between New York and Philadelphia and New Orleans, replacing horse and train journeys that delayed the news from half a day to a week. As Garbade and Silber (1978) demonstrated, the Transatlantic cable, which in 1866 established telegraph communication between New York and London, affected pricing and changed trading practices in those cities' currency, stock, and bond markets. Time lags of 20 days were reduced to minutes, and the average absolute price differences for identical securities traded in the two cities' markets dropped 69 percent from their previous levels. The electromechanical stock ticker (1867) and the telephone (1876) were also rapidly adopted by market participants, and enabled financial markets to extend their reach and importance in the economy. New York-based brokerage houses that established a presence in other parts of the country to serve retail investors became known as "wirehouses" for their reliance on telegraph communications.

Insider trading takes flight

An early case of windfall profits from trading with *inside, nonpublic information* occurred when Nathan Rothchild received advanced news via carrier pigeon of Wellington's defeat of Napolean at Waterloo in 1815. Rothchild bought shares at low prices from uninformed and anxiety-racked traders in London, and made his family's fortune from having received the favorable news first. Since the timeliness of a trader's news relative to fellow traders makes the difference between fortunes and losses, technology that speeds the flow of price-sensitive information has always found ready application in financial markets.

The commercialization of computers in the 1950s greatly increased access to financial market information. Quotron introduced on-line inquiries for stock market information in 1960. Brokers anywhere could enter a 4-letter code for a stock, and receive the last trade price, daily volume of shares traded, and the current price quotes. Previously, only reported prices of current trades were available on the ticker; consolidation and querying of historic prices was not possible. Information systems also streamlined the archiac after-trade settlement and clearing process. In 1967, rising trading volumes and paper-based settlement systems caused a "back-office crisis", which forced U.S. stock markets to close on Wednesdays during the last six months of 1968. The subsequent computerization of settlement procedures enabled exchanges to cope with the surging trading volumes of the 1970s and 1980s.

Economic Effects of IT. Microeconomic theories of financial markets are built on the assumption of costless trading and freely available information. In fact, transactions costs are significant. Trading in financial markets may involve paying brokerage commissions and other direct trading costs, subscribing to information and research services, and bearing the risk of price changes during the delay between making an investment decision and the eventual execution of the trade. Information technology, however, lessens the importance of time and distance in securities trading, and reduces transactions costs and frictions by opening up markets to additional participants and increasing competition. Research into the general effects of IT on industries has shown that electronic markets allow customers to search and compare many products at low cost, thus heightening competitive pressure among suppliers (Malone et al., 1987)(Bakos, 1991). Thus, the overall effect of IT is to bring financial markets closer to microeconomic ideal, and maximize the economic benefits provided by market activities.

Market clearing through an equilibrium price formation model is the foundation of market theory. Applied to securities markets, the pricing model is a frictionless trading mechanism based on a call-type, *Walrasian auction*. In a Walrasian auction, an equilibrium price is reached through an iterative process known as *tâtonnement* in which buyers and seller indicate their net demands for all securities at all combinations of prices. But the Walrasian auction is an abstraction, and practical difficulties in operating such a procedure prevent its application in actual securities markets. Instead, markets use trading mechanisms to convert investors' orders to buy and sell into prices and executed trades. An *order* is the basic processing element in trading. It specifies to buy or sell a certain number of securities, contingent perhaps on other events or conditions in a market. For instance, a *limit order* may specify the purchase of 5,000 shares of Motorola at the limit price of $60 or less. If the shares can only be purchased at a price higher than $60, the order goes unexecuted. A *market order* instructs the broker to trade at the best available price in the market.

Whitcomb (1985) identified a range of different market structures used in stock markets around the world. Although details can vary, markets differ on two principal dimensions. First, markets may facilitate **continuous trading**, or **batch or call trading**. In a continuous market, such as the New York Stock Exchange, trades can execute at any time at the quoted bid and offer prices. The bid price in a continuous market is the price at which investors can sell securities, and will be somewhat less than the offer price at which they can purchase securities. The difference between the highest bid quote and the lowest ask or offer quote for a security is called the **bid-ask spread**, and is a transaction cost paid by investors. In a call market, a single price is set at the time of the clearing to most closely equate supply and demand. All orders indicating a willingness to buy at that price or higher, or to sell at that price or lower, are executed. The London gold market operates as a twice daily call market, and the daily opening price for stocks on the NYSE is set by a call market procedure guided by the specialist. The second distinction is between **auction markets** and **dealer markets**. In an auction market, investors' orders are "exposed" to the market, and trades occur directly between investors at an agreed price. In a dealer market, competing dealers or market makers post bid and offer prices at which investors can trade. Auction markets are termed **order-driven**, and dealer markets are **quote-driven**.

Automation in Financial Markets: Functions and Benefits

Automation serves a number of functions in financial markets, yet most markets are incompletely automated and retain some manual functions. The following market functions are amenable to automation:

- Information systems play an **order collection** role in the processing of trading instructions in investors' and traders' offices. With an electronic system, once an order is entered details such as size, limit price, and time are accessible for an investor's control and measurement purposes, and for transmitting to a chosen market system.
- Systems for **order routing** direct an order entered by a trader to the appropriate market. The DOT system (Designated Order Turnaround) was introduced in 1976 for order routing on the NYSE. The system enables NYSE member firms to electronically route market orders and limit orders from their offices anywhere to the specialist post on the market floor, bypassing the floor broker's booth. In 1992, 78 percent of NYSE orders arrived via DOT. The remainder arrive via phones to floor traders' booths.
- **Price determination** is often supported by systems that aggregate the orders submitted to a market. The Arizona Stock Exchange (AZX) is a screen-based market for trading stocks after the close of the New York Stock Exchange floor. The system uses a single price call auction mechanism to find a price at which the quantity to buy equals the quantity to sell.
- **Order execution** systems electronically match buy and sell orders in a market, and **order confirmation** systems route electronic verifications of a trade to the participants involved. Reuters' Dealing 2000 system electronically matches buy and sell orders in the foreign exchange market. Details of executed trades are then transmitted back to the trade participants for confirmation. No more than several seconds elapse between order entry to final trade confirmation.
- Systems are used for **trade reporting** and **surveillance** purposes. In the case of a fraud or market manipulation investigation, an audit trail of trades can speed investigations. The NYSE's StockWatch unit, for example, uses computers to monitor trading

activities and to warn of unusual activity, which will be investigated by the staff.

- Systems **disseminate market information** more broadly. The Consolidated Tape System (CTS) was introduced in 1976, and imposed unified trade reporting rules, and facilitated ticker publication of last sale information occurring in any of eight U.S. stock markets. Previously only NYSE and American Stock Exchange (AMEX) trades were reported on the ticker. The CTS informs a far broader audience of all trading activity on the NYSE, AMEX, the five regional stock exchanges, and the OTC market.

Information technology has many benefits in financial markets. First, **visibility** is increased, enabling investors to monitor the market, and to time the execution of their trading strategies. Systems provide the ability to handle increased volumes of business, and contribute valuable **economies of scale**. In automated markets, greater trading volumes lead to fractional increases in overall costs, and a lowering in per transaction costs. **Integration** and international linkages can be achieved with systems that share information between markets and enable participants to pass their positions from one market to another. A number of markets including the Chicago Mercantile Exchange and the Singapore International Monetary Exchange (SIMEX) have automated facilities for "mutual offset". With mutual offset, a position in one market can be used to offset the margin required in another market. For instance, a 15 contract long position acquired in Chicago in T-bond futures, which is offset by a short position of 10 contracts of the same instrument in Singapore, requires margin to be put up for just the **net** position of 5 contracts. Settlement efficiency is enhanced with systems. The number of questioned trades (QTs), don't knows (DKs),

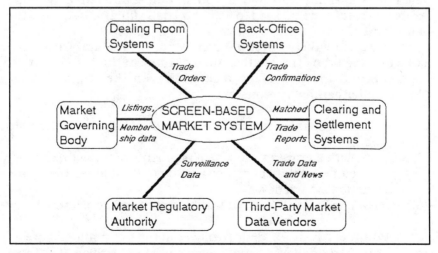

Figure 2: Information Flows in Automated Financial Markets

and fails drops when trading is automated and trade details are captured electronically, reducing costly exception processing.

Constituents in Screen-based Markets. Screen-based securities markets serve many stakeholders including investors, securities firms, and listed companies, as well as the securities exchange or vendor providing the market systems. The organizations that play operational or informational roles in screen-based markets are illustrated in Figure 2.

To succeed, an automated, screen-based market requires cooperation among a number of organizations, the setting of technical standards, and integration of multiple information systems. As markets have globalized and drawn more dispersed participants, achieving cooperation has become more challenging.

Screen-based Global Financial Markets: The Foreign Exchange Market

Today's most active and most automated global market is in foreign currencies. Billions of U.S. dollars are exchanged daily for Japanese Yen (¥), British pound sterling (£), Deutschmarks (DM), Swiss Francs, Canadian Dollars, French Francs, and other currencies. A dollar-yen exchange rate of 116.75 means that $1 buys 116.75 yen, or that ¥1 is worth 0.857¢.

As active as it is, the foreign exchange market has only a 20 year history. To stabilize the world economy after World War II, leaders of major nations met in 1946 in Bretton Woods, New Hampshire and agreed to a system of fixed exchange rates centered on the dollar with a gold standard that pegged the dollar at $35 an ounce. The agreement collapsed in August 1971 under the weight of a U.S. balance of payments deficit, and a weakening of the dollar, which made convertability into gold at $35 an ounce untenable. Foreign exchange rates were allowed to float, and daily fluctuations were the norm by 1973.

Exchange rates between two currencies are a function of a number of factors including the relative interest rates in the two countries, inflation, and the flow of payments between the two countries. Holding all other factors constant:

(1) falling interest rates in one country will cause its currency to decline in value
(2) a nation with a growing balance of payments deficit with another country can expect its currency's value to decline relative to the other nation's currency
(3) increasing inflation in one country lowers the value of its currency

FX Volumes. In 1992, daily turnover in the international foreign exchange (FX) market was estimated at close to $1 trillion. The three major financial centers are credited with the following daily FX volumes:

($ billion)	March 1986	April 1989	April 1992
London	$90	$187	$303
New York	$58	$129	$192
Tokyo	$48	$115	$128
TOTAL	$196	$431	$623

Source: Bank of England, *Quarterly Bulletin*, November 1992

Table 1: Daily Foreign Exchange Trading Volumes

Significant FX trading also occurs in Singapore (fourth, with $80 billion traded daily in 1992), Zurich, Toronto, and Hong Kong.

FX Trading Technology. The FX market is dominated by the world's largest banks, most of which trade currencies 24 hours a day from technologically sophisticated dealing rooms in the major financial centers. There is no market floor for institutional spot market trading of currencies.

The FX trader's desk contains an abundance of information systems and data feeds, which together have an annual cost of $30,000 to $50,000. There are four primary components of the trader's desktop technology.

(1) The desk will typically house a **high density telephone system** with speed-dialing access to twenty or more outgoing phone lines, display keys for counterparties, and buttons for muting the phone and setting up multiparty conversations.
(2) **Real-time market data** is provided by screens displaying market information provided by third-party vendors such as Reuters and Telerate.
(3) **Computer-based analytics** are often used to chart prices, and analyze relationships among financial instruments and economic data. Analytics software is either purchased as a package from a vendor, or is developed in-house.
(4) Both traders will enter the order into their firm's record keeping or **on-line transactions processing** systems, and later the dollar and yen funds will be electronically transferred from one account to another via an electronic funds transfer system such as FedWire if the traders are U.S.-based, or decide to clear the trade in the U.S.

The 1973 introduction of the Reuters Monitor, which displays competing bank dealers' foreign exchange quotes, spurred the development of the foreign exchange market. The widely dispersed

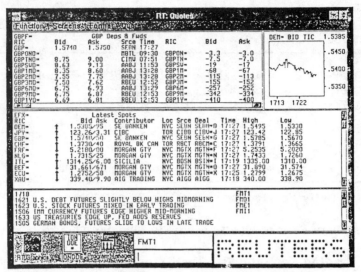

Figure 3: Reuters Terminal with Composite Display of British Money Rates, a Price Chart, Foreign Exchange Rates, and News

market that emerged following the Bretton Woods breakdown needed some way to display its prices. Banks and other firms supplied their prices to Reuters' central system, and the subscribers received consolidated market information and news supplied by Reuters correspondents around the globe. Foreign exchange trades have traditionally been effected over the phone. For instance, a bank representing a multinational customer desiring yen to pay a Japanese supplier will phone a dealer displaying an attractive offering quote for yen. In a short conversation, the bank's trader will identify him or herself, confirm the quote for the intended trade, and agree to the quantity and price. The dealer will read back details of the trade such as "I sell you 50,000,000 yen at 116.7500 for $428,265.52."

About 177,000 Reuters terminals were installed around the globe in 1990, up from just 55,000 in 1985. Each terminal can access 73,000 pages of continuously updated financial news and market prices. In 1981, Reuters introduced Dealing, a "conversational" or interactive electronic dealing system that enables subscribers to negotiate and execute FX trades over their terminals. For the first terminal at a site, Monitor costs $1,800 a month and Dealing is $5,400. There were about 16,500 Dealing terminals in use in 1992. It is estimated that half of world's spot FX trades were executed electronically over the Dealing trading system.[8]

Transactions Cost Illustration

Q: How much would be paid in round-trip transactions costs for converting $100,000 into Deutschmarks, and back to dollars using the indicated spot market prices?

A: Reading from the top line of the middle screen, a customer can sell dollars at the bid quote and receive 1.5385 DM for each dollar sold. The customer can buy dollars with Deutsch Marks from a dealer who will pay 1.5395 DM for each dollar purchased.

Buy @ 1.5385: 153,850.00 DM   **Sell @ (1/1.5395)=$0.6496: $99,935.04**

Transactions (spread) costs = $100,000 - $99,940.96 = $59.04

By making markets more transparent and accessible, one effect of screen trading is to narrow bid-ask spreads, and reduce transactions costs. In the example above, the spread is (1.5395-1.5385)/ 1.5390 = 0.065%, which is narrow, and an indication of the FX market's size and efficiency.

Assessment. The foreign exchange market has become a successful screen-based market for a number of reasons. FX is a 24-hour market with participants dispersed around the globe. Coming into existence in 1971, it lacked a floor market tradition, and the technology at the time was sufficient to deter attempts to develop a floor market in currencies. Finally, the FX market is an inter-institutional, wholesale market that is only loosely regulated by supranational organizations such as the Bank for International Settlements (BIS). The participants are sophisticated financial institutions, requiring little of the supervision and protection necessary in other markets with greater numbers of individual investors. Hence, the market operates without the extensive cooperative arrangements that would be required in other markets.

An International Survey

Financial markets around the globe have introduced technology to enhance the visibility of trading, and extend their reach to global participants. Improved information and market access has fostered the growth in cross-border trading volumes. The activities of non-domestic investors grew dramatically in the 1980s. Between 1980 and 1990, U.S. investors' trading activity increased five-fold in overseas equities, and twenty-fold in overseas bonds. Foreign investors traded fifteen times more U.S. equities in 1990 compared to 1980, and thirty times more U.S. bonds.

In addition to facilitating the growth in cross-border trading, many markets have been pressured to automate in response to competitive threats from other financial centers. International investors are mobile, and will withdraw from markets with rigid and opaque trading mechanisms. For instance, the 1986 deregulation and opening up of the London Stock Exchange attracted trading in many continental securities to London, and forced other European ex-

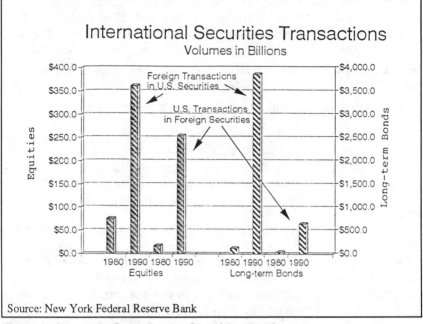

Figure 4: **Growth in Cross-Border Securities Trading**

changes to increase the visibility of their markets, and to enhance their trading systems.

Europe. The six largest European stock markets traded a total of about $6 billion daily in 1991. This is comparable to the daily volume of $6.3 billion on the NYSE in 1991.

United Kingdom. The U.K. stock market is the largest in Europe, and its trading volume in international (non-U.K.) equities is the largest in the world. London is also the largest currency dealing center in the world with $303 billion in daily turnover according to the Bank of England. London's current status as a leading international money center reflects a reversal from a weakening position between 1950 and 1979. Up to October 1979, government exchange controls restricted the conversion of pounds to other currencies and prevented most British investment outside of the U.K. At the time, the London Stock Exchange was closed to non-U.K members, and imposed high, fixed commissions. Trading in major British companies was flowing into New York, where they traded as American Depository Receipts (ADRs). Subsequent financial deregulation in Britain and growing trade and financial flows within the European Community have revitalized London's status as a financial hub.

U.K. Domestic Equities. On October 27, 1986, the London Stock Exchange (LSE) was deregulated and restructured by the *Big Bang* reforms (Clemons and Weber, 1990). Big Bang was the result of a 1983 settlement reached with the British Government's Office of Fair

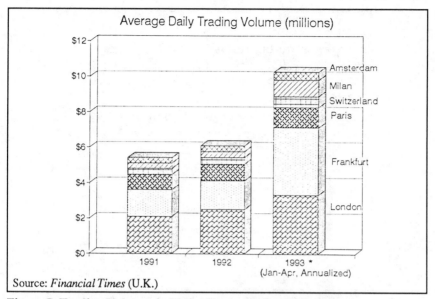

Source: *Financial Times* (U.K.)

Figure 5: Trading Volumes in Major European Stock Markets

Trade to end a lawsuit over restrictive practices and anti-competitive rules by the Exchange. The Big Bang changes abolished a fixed commission rate schedule, and permitted firms to operate in *dual capacity* as a broker-agent **and** as market makers trading for their own account with customers. A 30 percent limit on outside ownership of member firms was removed, and Exchange membership was opened up to overseas firms. Finally, Stock Exchange Automated Quotations (SEAQ), a screen-based market mechanism, was introduced to support the new Exchange operations. In the figure, four of the seventeen market makers are bidding £13.03 to buy ICI shares, and four other market makers are offering £13.08 to sell. The bid-ask spread of 5 pence, or 0.4% is considered tight, and indicative of a liquid and competitive market.

The London Stock Exchange operates as a competing dealer market. In each stock there are a number of dealers, or market makers, that provide bid quotes (the price at which they will buy shares from customers), and ask quotes (the price at which they will sell shares to customers). The SEAQ system has one "page" for each issue that displays all market makers registered in that security with their bid and ask quotes. There is also an indication of the number of shares the market maker is willing to commit to at those prices. For instance, 50x50 means 50,000 shares bid and 50,000 shares offered, and 1L means 100,000 shares. By negotiating over the phone, a trader can usually buy and sell in larger quantities than those shown, and market makers will often agree to trade at prices different than those on the screen.

SEAQ was modeled on the NASDAQ (National Association of

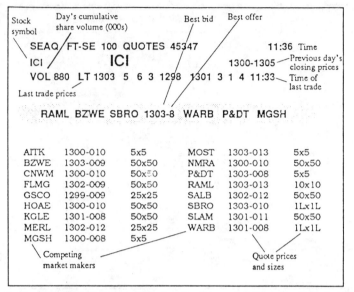

Figure 6: Sample SEAQ Screen Display for Imperial Chemicals Industries

Securities Dealers Automated Quotations) market in the U.S., which was introduced in the U.S. in 1971 as a screen display of trading prices for OTC stocks. Prior to NASDAQ, OTC prices were conveyed via "pink sheets" that were distributed daily. The pink sheets listed dealers and their indicative quotes. NASDAQ and SEAQ enable dealers to be geographically dispersed. In fact, several SEAQ market makers are located in Edinburgh, Scotland, and several SEAQ-International market makers operate out of dealing rooms in Paris and Frankfurt. SEAQ information is displayed on computer screens, and investors, or brokers acting on behalf of investors, contact and make trades with dealers over the telephone. The inside quotes displayed on the SEAQ screen also called the *touch* represent the best bid and offer available in London, and are prominently displayed, double sized, in a yellow strip at the top of the SEAQ screen for each stock. The intent is to give a rapid and accurate indication of the price at which the next trade in any share could be expected to occur. Once a trade is executed the details of price and number of shares are transmitted to the Exchange, which then publishes the stock's cumulative trading volume and the prices of the most recent transactions on the screen above the yellow strip.

London: Overseas Equities. In 1985, the London Stock Exchange introduced SEAQ International, a screen-based dealer market for the shares of foreign companies. The Exchange succeeded in establishing an active international market for trading of non-U.K. securities away from their home exchanges. The growth in trading volume on SEAQ International has outpaced that of the U.K. domestic stock market.

Average Daily Trading Volume (in billions)	1983	1987	1991	1992	1Q 1993 Annualized
SEAQ International (non-UK)	nil	£0.433	£1.12	£1.30	£1.85
SEAQ (Domestic stock market)	£0.445	£2.06	£1.42	£1.71	£2.21

Source: London Stock Exchange, *Financial Times* (U.K.)

Table 2: International and Domestic Equities Trading in London

London is the most global stock exchange today, listing about 760 non-U.K. stocks, compared with 121 foreign stocks traded on the NYSE.[9] London attracts more than two-third's of all equities trading that occurs outside of the stock's country of origin, according to the Bank of England. There were 49 firms operating as market makers on SEAQ-International in January 1993.

Although daily trading volume of domestic stocks in New York and Tokyo is far greater than in London, trading volume of overseas securities on the New York Stock Exchange averaged just $441 million (£250 million) a day in 1991, and on the Tokyo Stock Exchange, it was just $77 million per day in 1991.

	Domestic Listings 1991	Average daily trading volume in domestic shares 1991 ($ million)	Non-Domestic Listings 1991	Average daily trading volume in non-domestic shares 1991 ($ million)	As a percentage of total market trading volume
London	2,243	2,318	725	1,992	46.2%
New York	1,678	6,278	108	441	6.6%
NASDAQ	3,917	2,938	278	114	3.7%
Tokyo	1,614	3,384	125	77	2.2%
Germany	649	1,620	570	48	2.9%
Paris	449	468	236	18	3.7%

Source: London Stock Exchange, *Financial Times* (U.K.)

Table 3: Extent of Cross-Border Trading in Major Stock Markets

The success of SEAQ-I has come mostly at the expense of less liquid and more costly bourses in Continental Europe. SEAQ-I turnover in some shares is often far greater than in the stock's home market. Table 4 indicates the volume of SEAQ-I trading in London relative to totals on the home markets.

Home country of stock	SEAQ-I Trading Volume: Daily Average in 1991 (millions)	As a percentage of the home market's trading volume
Netherlands	$165.6	50.3%
Sweden	$100.0	45.0%
France	$244.8	26.7%
Switzerland	$125.2	25.8%
Germany	$500.0	12.2%

Source: London Stock Exchange, *Financial Times* (U.K.)

Table 4: SEAQ-International Trading Volume in Continental European Stocks

The Paris, Amsterdam, Stockholm, and Frankfurt markets have responded in an effort to regain volume in their domestic shares. Market authorities in those countries have modernized their markets and enacted reforms aimed at lowering costs and repatriating trading volume. For example, in the fourth quarter of 1991, trading volume in the 18 leading Swedish stocks was 8.4 percent higher in London than in Stockholm. Hence in December of that year, the 7-year old two percent turnover tax was repealed, and some volume has returned to Stockholm. In 1992, volumes in both markets were up, but the Stockholm exchange had 12 percent more turnover than London in those 18 stocks.

London: Futures and Options. The London International Financial Futures Exchange (LIFFE) opened in September 1982, and in 1992 merged with the London Traded Options Market (LTOM) and moved to a new facility with 25,000 square feet of trading space. In November 1989, LIFFE introduced its Automated Pit Trading (APT) system, which simulates open outcry trading on a screen for LIFFE members. APT operates from the close of the floor market at 3:00 p.m. to 6:00 p.m., and averaged 5,000 contracts a day in 1992, or about 4 percent of the LIFFE total of 130,000 per day.

Germany. The 1989 fall of the Berlin Wall and the reunification of the country have had a massive impact on the economy. The country is undeterred in its plans to establish "Finanzplatz Deutschland", an international financial center in Germany. Reforms have been implemented, and new trading technology has been developed to improve the international competitiveness of the German markets. Screen-based trading has been introduced. In January 1991, a transaction tax of 0.10% to 0.25% of the value of a transaction was repealed. Agreement was reached in October 1992 to launch a centralized German stock exchange, the *Deutsche Börse*, to consolidate trading now spread across Frankfurt and seven regional markets. Trading is planned for the 30-50 most frequently traded equities and bonds in a fully-electronic screen dealing system.

The technological showpiece of the German financial markets is the Deutsche Terminbörse (DTB). Inaugurated in January 1990, the DTB cost $85 million to develop. It is a fully computerized exchange for futures and options contracts. In November 1990, the DTB launched its Bund (German Government Bond) futures contract to compete with the active, floor-based LIFFE Bund market that opened in 1988. In spite of technological advantages e.g., 2 second execution turn-around vs. 10 or more seconds on LIFFE the DTB had just 30% of Bund futures trading volume in early 1993, with the rest remaining on LIFFE. Another electronic market, IBIS (Interbank Information System) was introduced in December 1989 for screen-based trading of German equities. IBIS cost DM16 million ($10 million), and extended the three hours of operations of the Frankfurt floor market. IBIS was later acquired by the Frankfurt Stock Exchange. In September 1991, IBIS accounted for 12 percent of the Frankfurt's trading volume in the 30 blue-chip stocks in the DAX index. Overall, trading volume on IBIS averaged just 300,000 shares daily in 1991, or less than 10% of London's SEAQ-I volume in German stocks.

France. The French financial markets underwent a "petit bang" series of reforms in the late 1980s. Commissions were unfixed, and in 1988, banks were allowed to purchase stockbrokerage houses. The Paris Bourse introduced the CAC system (Cotation Assistée en Continu) for electronic trading in July 1989. CAC is based on the CATS system, which was developed in Toronto to provide order-driven trading based on a continuous open order book. In 1990, Relit, an advanced, $105 million settlement system was implemented. Relit took four years to develop, and "dematerialized" settlement, moving all ownership records to electronic form, and prompting the destruction of 40 tons of French share certificates. A turnover tax of 0.15% to 0.30% of the value of any transaction is expected to be abolished. IBM is among the most active stocks on the automated foreign section of the Paris Bourse, and averaged 3.5 FF million ($0.5 million) a day in trading value in 1991, compared to about $200 million in daily trading on the NYSE.

Switzerland. SOFFEX (Swiss Options and Financial Futures Exchange), an electronic trading and clearing system for derivative instruments, opened in May 1989. Recognizing the success of SOFFEX and the likely demise of their floor markets, the Basel, Geneva, and Zurich exchanges formed the Association Tripartite Bourses, which is developing a screen-market based on Sun Microsystems SPARCstations.

North America Canada. Toronto is Canada's principal financial center. The Toronto Stock Exchange (TSE) handles 75 percent of the total value of trading on Canada's five exchanges. The TSE traded 117 million shares a day (C$1.2 billion) on average in 1992, up 25.5 per cent from 1991. The second and third largest markets are in Montreal and Vancouver. In 1977, the TSE introduced the Computer Assisted Trading System (CATS).[10] At the time, the market floor was fully occupied, and CATS provided a means of expanding capacity at low cost. The original plan was to offer screen-based trading in less active stocks. In 1990, 840 of the 1,650 listed securities and 22 percent of the TSE's trading volume were on CATS. Facing the renewal of the lease on the floor market in February 1992, 80 percent of the 72 TSE member firms voted to close the trading floor in late 1993, saving C$30 million a year.

United States. The U.S. financial markets are among the largest and most advanced in the world. The two largest equities markets in the world are the NYSE and NASDAQ. The U.S. Treasury bond market is the largest securities market in the world.

U.S. Equities. The Securities Exchange Act of 1934 created a regulatory structure for the U.S. securities industry to guard against fraud and the excesses that were exposed in the October 1929 crash. The Securities Exchange Commission (SEC) was established to oversee markets and securities firms. Only minor revisions were made to the industry's regulatory structure until 1975. The Securities Act Amendments of 1975 overhauled the 1934 Act, and provided a Congressional mandate for the SEC to develop a *"National Market System"* (NMS) for transacting and trade settlement. After some initial disagreements, NMS was interpreted as a call for upgrading systems and establishing linkages, but not a call for a fully computerized securities market. It has, however, led to the introduction of many important market information systems.

• The National Securities Clearing Corp. (NSCC) was created in 1976 from the merger of the clearinghouses of the NYSE, the AMEX, and the NASD. In cooperation with the Securities Industry Automation Corporation (SIAC) and the Depository Trust Company (DTC), the NSCC instituted computerized book entry transfer of securities ownership, and electronic funds movement for trade payments.

• The Intermarket Trading System (ITS) implemented in 1978 to link the five regional exchanges and the OTC market. Orders can be routed between markets, off-exchange upstairs dealers, and trades can be executed over ITS.

Stock exchanges in the U.S. are competing to attract order flow from each other. Several regional exchanges offer automated execution systems for small orders that guarantee the best ITS price with faster execution time than on the NYSE floor. *SelectNet* allows NASDAQ members to send buy and sell orders to other members' terminals, and has filed for SEC approval to begin trading in NYSE-listed stocks. In private, bilateral "conversations", orders can be accepted in part or full, and on-screen price and quantity negotiations can occur between traders. The NYSE called for an inquiry of SelectNet because it circumvents SEC rules on information disclosure by not disseminating the prices on the system widely enough.

U.S. Futures and Options. The Chicago Board of Trade and the Chicago Mercantile Exchange are the two largest derivatives exchanges in the world. The CBOT and the CME traded an average of 600,000 and 525,000 contracts daily in 1992. The most active contracts on the CBOT are U.S. Treasury bond futures, while futures on the Standard & Poor's 500 stock market index are the volume leaders on the CME. Rapid growth in overseas derivatives exchange is diminishing the dominance of the Chicago markets. Combined

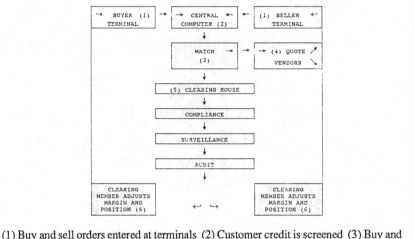

(1) Buy and sell orders entered at terminals (2) Customer credit is screened (3) Buy and sell orders are matched based on price and time priority (4) Trades are executed instantaneously and data updated (5) Confirmed trades are sent to the clearing system for settlement processing (6) Clearing member firms settle for buyer and seller account.
Source: Chicago Mercantile Exchange

Figure 7: Globex Trading

CBOT-CME volumes accounted for about 43 percent of the world's exchange-traded derivatives volume in 1992, which is down from 55 percent in 1990.

The Chicago exchanges are using IT to maintain their international position. *Globex* was initiated by Reuters and the CME with tremendous fanfare in September 1987. Under pressure from members that saw duplicate development as wasteful, the CBOT abandoned its competing Aurora project in March 1991, and joined Globex as a sponsor. Globex was developed at a cost of $80 million, and opened in June 1992. It is not a 24-hour market, and only operates after the 2:30 P.M. close of the Chicago floor markets. Trading hours are 6:00 P.M. to 6:00 A.M., but plans exist to add a 2:30 P.M. to 4:00 P.M. session.

In March, 1993 Globex was handling 3,500 contracts a day via 300 linked terminals, up from 1,800 contracts daily in the month after the launch. Hence, Globex accounts for just 0.3% of the volume of the two floor markets.

U.S. Off-Exchange Markets. U.S. exchanges have long competed vigorously for trading volume. Most major stocks trade actively in several markets. Market participants refer to the NYSE and the AMEX as the *first market*. The five regional exchanges (Boston, Philadelphia, Cincinnati, Chicago, and San Francisco) are considered the *second market*. The *third market* is made up of dealers trading over the telephone from offices using NASDAQ screen prices. The *fourth market* is direct trading between institutional investors. Technology has led to a proliferation of third and fourth market

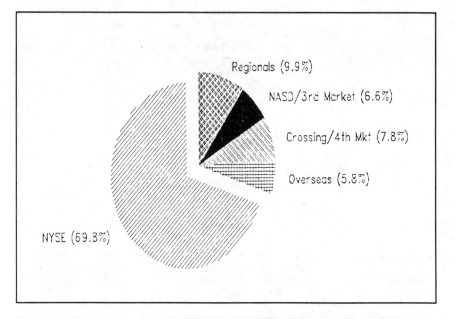

Regionals (9.9%)

NASD/3rd Market (6.6%)

Crossing/4th Mkt (7.8%)

Overseas (5.8%)

NYSE (69.3%)

Figure 8: Market Share of Trading Volume in NYSE-Listed Equities Third Quarter 1991

trading systems, which have proven to be attractive to investors and traders. Equities trading away from the NYSE in NYSE-listed stocks is increasing. In 1980, just 12 percent of *reported* trading in NYSE-listed stocks occurred off the NYSE floor. In 1992, it was 18.2 percent. Reported trade volumes miss an estimated 10-20 million shares a day that are traded in overseas stock markets, or on electronic crossing networks. The following distribution of trading volume is based on available data and estimates.

Burton Malkiel's *A Random Walk Down Wall Street* (1973) popularized the notion that active stock picking was unlikely to lead to investment performance that is consistently better than the return on the broad market as measured by indexes. Detailed studies of the investment performance of fund managers made clear that the majority were generally unable to achieve even the returns registered on the benchmark unmanaged indexes of the market. As a result, "passive management" and "indexation" have become increasingly popular. Such strategies require holding the securities in an index, and trading baskets of the stocks in that index at as low a cost as possible. Today, an estimated 30 to 35 percent of institutional equity holdings in the U.S. are passively managed index matching funds. A September 1989 survey[11] of 36 of the largest U.S. pension funds with assets totaling $259 billion found 34% of their domestic equities holdings were indexed, a 4% increase from 1986. Passive fund managers have become important users of off-exchange trading systems. A number of third and fourth market trading systems

Trading System Type	Mechanism/Basis for Trading Price	Examples (Introduction date) Pricing, Owner, *Daily TradingVolume estimates*
Crossing Network	Batch trading based on closing prices from NYSE or mid-spread of NASDAQ	The Crossing Network (1986) Run by Reuters, 1 cent per share, *3.5 million shares*
Single Price Auction	Call auction. Price set by intersection of supply and demand curves from submitted orders	Arizona Stock Exchange, AZX, (orig.: SPAWorks, 1991) 0.88 cents per share. 94 institutions, *450,000 shares*, 3% fill, 21 million peak day
Portfolio Crossing	Use volume weighted average price of day's trading. Trades in morning and around noon.	Posit (1986) 2 cents per share. Run by Jefferies/ITG, used by 80 institutions managing 80% of US pension fund assets. Traders must enter orders for at least 10 stocks. Orders not exposed. *5 million shares*
Order Matching	Continuous open order books. The order books contain investors' orders ranked by price and time of arrival. Used to trade individual shares or portfolios.	Instinet (1969) Run by Reuters, 1 cent per share, *16 million shares* Quantex (1990) 3-4 cents per share Run by Jefferies/ITG, used by 47 institutions, *3 million shares* MatchPlus (1991) Run by Morgan Stanley, *200,000 shares* SelectNet (1990) Run by NASDAQ, *200,000 shares* after-hours, *10 million shares* during U.S. market hours
International Off-Hours Markets	Screen display of market-makers' quotes for U.S.-listed stocks	SEAQ International, U.S. Section (1985) Run by London SE, indicative quotes, *5-10* million shares NASDAQ Intl (Jan 1992) 3:30 am to 9:00 am N.Y. time, firm quotes, *100,000 shares*
<u>NYSE</u> <u>Responses</u> Crossing (Fixed Price) Session I	(Crossing sessions initiated in June 1991) Enter orders from 4:15 pm to 5:00 pm, to cross at NYSE closing price at 5:00 pm	Member firms enter orders from institutional clients, *110,000 shares traded per night* (1/93-6/93). About 10% of orders execute.
Crossing (Basket) Session II	Paired (prearranged) orders for 15 or more stocks with value greater than $1 million are executed when received Operates from 4:00 pm to 5:15 pm.	*8.7 million shares per night* (1/93-6/93) with peak of 57 million No user commissions or fees.

Table 5: Off-Exchange Trading Alternatives in the U.S.

compete for orders with floor-based exchanges.

Several lessons are emerging from the U.S. experience with aggressive inter-market competition for order flow. Transactions costs to investors have generally fallen, but the multiplication of electronic market systems and the varied level of information disclosure in some trading mechanisms make it difficult for investors to assess the quality of the trade prices. Liquidity and the precision of price discovery are greatest when trading is centralized. Thus, the growth in trading systems that "bypass" the central marketplace may lead to costly duplication and inefficiencies. The NYSE argues that off-exchange trading systems "free-ride" on the prices discovered in the floor market, but contribute little to the costs of operating the exchange. Some observers fear "competitive fragmentation" and a tiered marketplace with securities trading in different prices in different places, leaving only the most sophisticated traders to know where to obtain the best price. The SEC is currently reviewing these market fragmentation issues.

Asia. The Asian financial industry is dominated by Japan. Success of Japanese companies in international markets, and a high saving rate have led to vast pools of investment capital. The Japanese financial markets are the largest in Asia, and nine of the world's twenty largest banks are Japanese.

Not included in figure are the consolidated Australian Stock

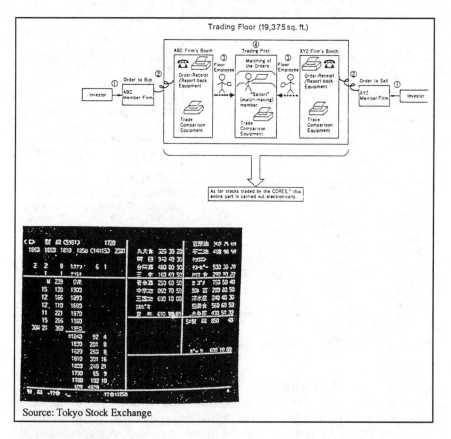

Source: Tokyo Stock Exchange

Figure 9: Trading on the Tokyo Stock Exchange -- Floor Trading Process and CORES Screen Display

Exchanges, which had daily trading volume of $187 million in 1991, or slightly greater activity than the Hong Kong market.

Japan. The Tokyo Stock Exchange (TSE) was the world's largest equities market in 1988, but in 1992 placed third behind the NYSE and NASDAQ. The TSE's average daily trading value was about $3.5 billion in 1992. After rising at 20 percent annually between 1980 and 1990, prices in the Japanese stock market entered a prolonged slump in January 1990. The market index has fallen by half, and trading volumes are 60 percent below their peak levels from 1988.

The TSE's trading mechanism is an agency auction overseen by a "*Saitori*", a special class of TSE member, that matches submitted orders, and smooths price swings by calling trading halts when an imbalance of buy and sell orders exists. TSE stocks have "price collars" that specify the maximum allowable price movement in a day. When these limits are reached trading stops and can continue only at prices within the limits. In contrast, NYSE specialists are expected to facilitate a continuous, "fair and orderly" market by trading as a principal for their own account. The TSE introduced the Computer Assisted Order Routing and Execution System (CORES) in 1982. CORES is modeled on Toronto's CATS. Floor trading has remained for the 150 most active issues, and CORES accounted for 44 percent of the TSE's volume in 1989.

The CORES screen is broken into three sections. On the right hand side is a display of prices for a number of stocks and the index. On the left hand side is detailed information on a single stock. The top left section displays the name of the stock, its maximum allowable trading range for the day, and market orders and market-on-close orders. The lower left section is limit order book, which in this case displays a bid of ¥1,840 for 9,200 shares and an offer price of ¥1,850 for 36,000 shares with another 20,600 shares available at ¥1,860.

The Japanese financial industry has moved in derivatives traded belatedly. The Tokyo International Financial Futures Exchange (TIFFE) opened in June 1989. In February 1991, the Fully Automated Computer Trading System (FACTS) was completed. About 5,000 contracts were traded daily in 1992, placing TIFFE among the ten largest derivatives markets in the world.

Dragon Countries. Singapore, Hong Kong, Taiwan, and Seoul (Korea) are the financial capitals of the four Dragon countries. These countries experienced rapid economic growth and development in the 1980s. While the financial markets in these countries are not large by New York-London-Tokyo standards, they are growing rapidly. The use of trading technology varies from market to market. In Taiwan's market, for instance, share prices are posted on a chalkboard, and traders use binoculars to monitor changes.

China. The financial markets in China have tremendous potential, but also carry enormous risks. China's financial industry is developing rapidly, but with little leadership or regulation. In 1992, fifty companies were listed on the Shanghai and Shenzen exchanges up from 15 in 1991 and daily trading volumes were $68 million in 1992 compared to $7 million daily in 1991. The current speculative frenzy may hinder capital formation in the long term unless government regulations are introduced. As commercial and property laws are written, accounting standards are established, and technology improves, the Chinese markets will grow and attract greater global interest.

Technology Issues in International Financial Markets

Advances in data processing and communications technology, and the opening up of markets, have increased the flow of financial information around the world. This has attracted investors into overseas markets that previously lacked visibility, and restricted market entry and competition. Developments in trading networks and international cross-listings of securities that have heightened competition for trading volumes, are forcing antiquated exchanges to respond. Many observers foresee a unified global financial market based on screen trading. Despite optimistic forecasts for integrated, 24-hour securities markets, this vision is many years off. A number of barriers exist to technology that could support an integrated global financial market. These hurdles include inertia and the critical mass required to establish liquidity in a new trading mechanism, vested interests, regulatory discord, and IT development costs in an industry contending with declining margins.

Critical Mass. In markets, a "network externality" exists because liquidity is a self-reinforcing characteristic of trading; the greater the level of trader participation, the more liquid and attractive the market. Developing liquidity in a new trading system requires a critical mass of users. Yet adoption is more likely the greater the system's liquidity. This paradox is reflected in the comments of a partner in a major Wall Street firm regarding the 1991 introduction of NASDAQ International for trading U.S. stocks between 3:30 a.m. and 9:00 a.m. New York time: *"People may not use it because it's not very active, but if it becomes more active, then they'll use it."*[12] Most evidence about intermarket competition indicates that order flow is retained by the market that already has the greatest liquidity and depth. The director of financial markets at a French bank pointed out "people don't care what medium they trade through, as long as it has the business."[13] Experience has shown that when an off-hours market is introduced, its liquidity is limited, and investors prefer to wait for the particular domestic market to open.

Some observers believe that "in the long run, automated trading systems offer a richer mixture of the market information and the anonymity necessary for trading than either the crowd or the telephone."[14] Although automated markets are technically feasible, trading systems do not create markets; public buying and selling, and in some cases dealers or specialists, are required to create liquidity and a viable market.

In rare instances traders have demonstrated an ability to move their activities to an alternative market when it appears advantageous. The primary and secondary markets for Eurobonds quickly moved from New York to London after 1963, when the Kennedy administration imposed the Interest Equalization Tax (IET), lowering investors' returns on such bonds by about one percent. London did not offer a different trading mechanism; the market remained an over-the-counter market. Yet because trades are physically settled certificates need to be delivered to a clearinghouse or to the contra-party the market derives operational benefits from a single locale, and the relocation of the Eurobond market represented a tacit collective decision to move trading to an alternative center. The IET was repealed in 1974, but the market has remained in London. Trading volume in Eurobonds in 1992 was about $7 billion a day, up from $6 billion in 1990, according to the International Securities Market Association (ISMA).[15]

In other cases, trading mechanisms that appeared to offer technological advantages were ignored by traders and remained illiquid. Many attempts to create alternative markets for securities have failed; the Cincinnati Stock Exchange (1983), Ariel (1974) in the U.K., Boss in Germany (1989), and Intex (1984), a Bermuda-based automated futures exchange, are examples of electronically-supported trading mechanisms that failed to attract liquidity and never seriously challenged the dominance of established, floor-based markets.

Vested Interests. Computer-based market systems enable traders in diverse geographic locations to interact, discover prices, and execute trades through a trading screen. The result is a new market structure without the time and geographic limitations of participating in floor-based stock exchanges. In many screen-based markets, investors are capable of trading directly with each other, bypassing the traditional role played by dealer intermediaries. Since the existing, dominant structure for securities trading in most countries involves a profitable intermediary role similar to the NYSE specialist, established participants may resist change. Furthermore, firms that are earning inadequate returns on capital are not willing to cooperate and support trading technology project that could further reduce margins.

New markets often operate as open limit order books, which are visible to market participants, who can enter limit orders, or trade immediately by matching an existing order. It is often argued that without the necessity of paying the intermediaries' costs, investors will reap larger gains from trade and higher market quality will result. However, this neglects the potential value of intermediation. Market makers with a continuous market presence, such as specialists on the New York Stock Exchange, may improve the quality of the market at a cost less than the value of the service (Weber, 1991). Intermediaries stabilize prices by buying or selling as principals when the net order flow is imbalanced, and also contribute by maintaining a "fair and orderly" market.

The Eurobond market has resisted attempts to introduce real-time screen prices. A proposed system, Eurex, was rejected by the self-regulatory body and trade association for Eurobond dealers in 1983. Since then, several refined proposals have been spurned by dealers in the market. The banks that trade in the market feel their ability to trade profitably would be compromised by too much transparency. Vested interests strive to maintain the current market mechanism, which is telephone search of dealers, who can quote comfortably wide bid-ask spreads.

Discordant Regulations. To achieve an integrated global market requires unified regulatory policies. In fact, regulations vary considerably from country to country, and are often self-serving responses to national rivalries. Despite the efforts of international coordination committees, an inconsistent pattern of regulations exists. Many countries have established of *mutual recognition*, or *reciprocity agreements*, whereby one country's firms can sell financial products to another's domestic investors, and vice versa. Such bilateral access agreements are useful, but illustrate the protective stance taken toward financial markets in most countries. Until regulatory authorities begin to converge on a global standard, markets will remain multi-domestic rather than global.

The changes in global markets have prompted the reexamination of regulations to ensure the international competitiveness of a country's or a region's financial sector. The U.S. financial markets are undergoing thorough study. Recent studies of policy issues include "Securities Trading: SEC Action Needed to Address National Market System Issues" by the General Accounting Office (1990), "Electronic Bulls and Bears" by the Office of Technology Assessment (1990), and the Securities and Exchange Commission's Market 2000 study, due in late 1993.

The twelve member nations of the European Community (EC) are seeking to harmonize regulations and financial services access. The idea of a single market for securities trading has not taken hold because of contention about its market structure and regulation. A system to electronically link EC stock markets was approved in 1989. The system was termed PIPE for Price Information Project Europe, and a company named Euroquote was established to develop the network. The objective was to publish the prices of 200 or more securities on a new list of European blue-chip stocks. In

1991, the project stalled when EC exchanges admitted their conflicting objectives for PIPE, and declined to inject $15 million in capital into the project.

Cost and inexperience with technology. Some observers argue that markets are highly sophisticated processors of information and signals. Given such complexity, it is not evident that screen-based trading currently offers a more attractive market design than one based on face-to-face interaction. Mark Harding, the head financial markets group at Clifford Chance, a law firm, said "I do not think anyone has found a computerized system, which is user friendly or simple enough to take the place of open outcry trading." Skeptics point out that a market may appear to be an easily-automated transaction process, but it is also a complex price discovery mechanism.

Furthermore, initiatives to develop more sophisticated market systems are expensive. Globex cost $80 million. The DTB cost $85 million to develop. The London Stock Exchange abandoned its TAURUS settlement system in March 1993, after spending £75 million and encouraging the industry to incur costs of £325 million in developing interfaces and connections to the planned systems.

CONCLUSIONS

Information technology enhances a market's ability to perform valuable economic functions: providing liquidity and channelling investment funds into productive uses. Across the globe, trading processes are being restructured, and automation continues to lower the costs of transacting and monitoring financial markets. Technology, sweeping changes in regulations, and investor interest in cross-border diversification, are driving up international trading volumes. Competing for trading volumes, network providers such as Reuters, and the major international exchanges are increasing their use of information technology. In a number of markets, screen-based trading has taken the place of physical marketplaces and trading floors. Experience shows that information technology not only threatens some sources of profits in the securities industry, but also creates opportunities and a means of reacting to market challenges.

International market integration is occurring, but in a haphazard way. Today's "global financial market" is actually multiple trading structures, and firms with a patchwork of local expertise in many markets. Progress toward uniformity of regulations and market practices is spotty, and the design of an integrated global financial market remains clouded with many technological and regulatory issues unresolved. Fragmented markets that impose inefficiencies and require expertise in local practices may be a consequence of lack of agreement on the structure of an integrated financial market. The consolidated, worldwide exchange is illusory. "The End of Geography" remains an elusive goal.

The trading systems of the near future will likely be global routing systems that connect and maintain consistent prices across multiple markets internationally. Regulators will continue to seek coordination among markets to reduce risks and inefficiency. Indexation and passive investing will grow. More risk management activities and derivatives trading are likely. All of these strategies require extensive IT investments and systems capabilities on the part of firms, and advanced market technologies provided by exchanges and trading network providers. Clearly, responding effectively to the changes and pressures will be the hallmark of successful firms and expanding market centers in the coming years.

ENDNOTES

[1]   See O'Brien, R. *Global Financial Integration: The End of Geography*, Royal Institute of International Affairs, Pinter Publishers, London, 1992.

[2]   Among the earliest proposals for electronic trading were Fischer Black's "automated specialist", described in 1971, and Mendelson's Automated Trading System (Black, 1971), (Mendelson, 1972). Researchers have since suggested a number of other electronic means for facilitating markets and securities trading (Peake, Mendelson, Williams, 1979), (Amihud, 1985), (Schwartz, 1989).

[3]   Waters, R. "U.K Insurance Groups See a Brighter Future in Derivatives", *Financial Times*, 21 December 1992, p. 19.

[4]   "Safer than It Looks", *The Economist*, 4 August 1990, p. 63.

[5]   Markowitz, H.M., "Portfolio Selection", *Journal of Finance*, Vol. 7, pp. 77-91, March 1952.

[6]   Sharpe, W.F., "Capital Asset Prices: A Theory of Market Equilibrium under Conditions of Risk", *Journal of Finance*, Vol. 19, pp. 425-442, September 1964.

[7]   Reported in "Inside the Buy Side", *Investment Dealers' Digest*, 15 March 1993, pp. 20-23

[8]   See Gandy, T. "Monopoly Mayhem", *The Banker*, February 1993, pp. 56-59, and "Banks Retaliate in Dealing-Room War", *Euromoney*, May 1993, pp. 87-90.

[9]   "Daimler's Arrival Marks New Spirit at U.S. Securities Agency", *Financial Times*, 1 April 1993, p. 17.

[10] Versions of CATS are now in use in stock markets in Tokyo, Paris, Brussels, and Madrid.

[11] Committee on Investment of Employee Benefits, "Survey of Pension Fund Investment Practices", Financial Executives Institute, Morristown, NJ, 1990.

[12] Newman, A. and Torres, C. "SEC Will Vote on Plan to Allow Early-Hours U.S. Stock Trading", *Wall Street Journal Europe*, 9 October 1991, p. 15.

[13] "Frankfurt Fights to Regain Bunds", *Financial Times*, November 26, 1990,

p. 21.
[14] Cohen, et al., 1986, p. 66.
[15] Data reported in "Dull can be Dynamic", *Financial Times*, 27 May 1993, p. 21., and "Complaints about Poor Liquidity", *Financial Times*, 21 December 1992, p. 19.

REFERENCES

Amihud, Y. and Mendelson H. (1985). "An Integrated Computerized Trading System" in *Market Making and the Changing Structure of the Securities Industry*, Amihud, Ho, and Schwartz (eds.), Lexington Books.

Amihud, Y. and Mendelson H. (1988). "Liquidity, Volatility and Exchange Automation", *Journal of Accounting, Auditing & Finance*, Fall, pp. 369-395.

Bakos, Y. (1991). "Information Links and Electronic Marketplaces: The Role of Interorganizational Information Systems in Vertical Markets", *Journal of Management Information Systems*, 8(2), pp. 31-52.

Black, F. (1971). "Toward a Fully Automated Exchange", *Financial Analysts Journal*, July-August, pp. 29-44, and November-December. pp. 25-29.

Clemons, E. and Weber, B. (1990). "London's Big Bang: A Case Study of Information Technology, Competitive Impact, and Organizational Change", *Journal of Management Information Systems*, 6(4), pp. 41-60.

Clemons, E. and Weber, B. (1991). "Information Technology and Changing Nature of the Financial Services Industry,", *Proceedings*, IFIP TC8 Conference on Collaborative Work, Social Communications and Information Systems, Helsinki, Finland.

Cohen, K., Maier, S., Schwartz R., and Whitcomb, D. (1986). *The Microstructure of Securities Markets*, Prentice-Hall, Englewood Cliffs, N.J.

Garbade, K. and Silber, W. (1978). "Technology, Communication and the Performance of Financial Markets: 1840-1975", *Journal of Finance*, 33(3), p. 819-831.

Malone, T., Benjamin, R. and Yates, J. (1987). "Electronic Markets and Electronic Hierarchies: Effects of Information Technology on Market Structure and Corporate Strategy", *Communications of the ACM*, June, pp. 484-497.

Mendelson, M. (1972). "From Automated Quotes to Automated Trading: Restructuring the Stock Market in the U.S.", New York University Bulletins Nos. 80-82.

Peake, J., Mendelson, M. and Williams, R. Jr. (1979) "Toward a Modern Exchange: The Peake-Mendelson-Williams Proposal for an Electronically Assisted Auction Market", *Impending Changes for Securities Markets -- What Role for Exchanges?*, Bloch, E. and Schwartz, R. (eds.), JAI Press.

Scarlata, J. (1992). "Institutional Developments in the Globalization of Securities and Futures Markets", *Review*, Federal Reserve Bank of St. Louis, January/February, pp. 17-30

Waters, R. (1990). "Rawlins Points to Hybrid System", *Financial Times*, October 2, p. 12.

Weber, B. (1991). *Information Technology and Securities Markets: Feasi-*

bility and Desirability of Alternative Electronic Trading Systems, unpublished dissertation, University of Pennsylvania.

Whitcomb, D. (1985). "An International Comparison of Stock Exchange Trading Structures" in *Market Making and the Changing Structure of the Securities Industry*, Amihud, Ho, and Schwartz (eds.), Lexington Books.

CHAPTER 8

International Risk Management Systems: Continuing Improvements and Future Directions

ARUN BANSAL
Bear Stearns & Co., Inc.

Financial firms on Wall Street and elsewhere are increasingly becoming aware of greater opportunities for financial investments in international markets. However, with the potential for higher returns in global markets comes a higher risk of losing all or a significant part of these investments. Increased uncertainty in doing business globally, unstable and uncertain political and economic environments and exchange rate fluctuations are just a few factors that may influence returns. This chapter summarizes different kinds of international risks that an investor may be exposed to and describes how information technology is helping international investors manage risk. The chapter also examines how the key advances in information technology will shape the process of risk management in the future.

INTRODUCTION

Financial risk inherent in an investment reflects the upside potential of return as well as the possibility of downside loss and is measured by the variance of the investment's historical returns.

Until the October 1987 crash of the stock market, this was the only concept of risk that was found within standard finance textbooks. Prior to the crash, not many investors thought that it was possible for their seemingly "safe" investments in financial securities to lose more than half their values in just one day. In addition, while the Crash was a powerful blow to several investment bankers and brokerage houses, some bad international loans to Latin America in late 80s brought several major banks to the verge of bankruptcy.

A relatively prolonged recession in the early 90s, coupled with the above two disasters shook investors' confidence considerably and proved crucial for increasing the importance of risk management in financial investments. Many financial firms took initiatives to identify, measure and monitor risks faced by the firm. Today, in successful financial firms, there is usually a risk manager (a person or computer software) that constantly evaluates the risk in all or at least a portion of trades that are made by a trader.

As a part of their effort to neutralize excessive risk and diversify their portfolios, many investors look for international securities. The total investment risk consists of (Doherty, 1985):

(1)   an unsystematic or firm-specific risk; and
(2)   a systematic risk.

According to the capital asset pricing model, only the firm specific risk can be eliminated by diversification in a domestic market (Haugen, 1987). However, if international securities are included in a portfolio, it is possible to even diversify the systematic risk (Lessard, 1974). Although global portfolios consisting of international securities can help to diversify the total risk, they entail other risks which also need to be identified, measured and controlled.

It is commonly perceived that additional risk in international business arises from an uncertain political environment, economic uncertainty, risk of nationalization, exchange rate fluctuations and cultural differences among different countries (Ting, 1988; Tran, 1980). These different dimensions of risk can be grouped under a single umbrella of *country risk*. Another example of how risk can vary with the country is the state of technological advancement achieved by the recipient country. For example, an investment by a multinational computer firm may bear low risk if the country in which the firm operates is technically advanced or is committed to be so.

In this chapter, we first discuss the types and sources of significant international risks that a financial investment may be exposed to. We then illustrate how international risk is usually managed, and how information technology (IT) plays an important role in international financial risk management. We analyze the contribution of IT along four dimensions: data, analytics, report generation and hardware and we then study how advances in IT have affected each of these four dimensions. Finally, the chapter concludes with a brief description of how risk management could change in the future due to expected improvements in technologies that support this process.

INTERNATIONAL RISK: TYPES AND ORIGIN

The risk faced by international traders can be differentiated from the risk faced by international manufacturers. Traders do not have production facilities in a foreign country. Thus, traders usually face cash-flow exposures due to exchange controls and currency inconvertibility, bureaucratic impediments, and perhaps the impounding of money or investments resulting from acts of war, insurrection, and military blockages. On the other hand, multinational firms with capital or manufacturing investments abroad face risks to both fixed assets and cash flows. These risks include the uncertainty about the relative costs of labor and material, local content requirements, joint venture pressures, probability of expropriation or nationalization, and anti-multinational factions in the government that advocate such measures (Hertz and Thomas, 1984).

The total exposure to international risk is also dependent on the geographical region where the investment is made. While a trader in Eastern Europe needs to worry about converting payments into hard currency, the same may not be true for an investment in the western part of Europe.

Risk and Type of Industry

International risk also varies with the type of industry one invests in. In general, if the investment is in a firm for which markets are stable, and where production and demand is predictable, the risk is relatively low. In contrast, if the investment is made in commodities for which production is highly dependent on the vagaries of weather or the limitations of natural resource discovery, a higher investment risk should be assumed.

Exchange Rate Risk

Before an investment is made in a foreign country, an investor is required to acquire that country's currency in the amount of the investments and the additional transactions costs involved with making the investment. On sale of the security, a U.S. investor needs to convert the proceeds back to U.S. dollars. Fluctuations in foreign exchange rates can have a potentially large impact on the total rate of return to a foreign investment (Haugen, 1987). This variation in return is known as the *currency risk* or the *exchange risk*.

Other Sources of Risks

In addition to international risks, an international investment is also exposed to some domestic types of risks. Market risk, interest rate risk, credit risk and operational risks are a few examples of these.

Market risk is associated with unpredictable price changes of a financial security. *Interest rate risk*, on the other hand, arises from interest rate fluctuations that render the return on financial assets uncertain. Another source of international risk is the *credit risk* associated with defaults in repayment of loans (Doherty, 1985). *Operating risk*, which stems from frequent changes in or discontinuance of a revenue stream against a continuing level of fixed cost expenditures can be linked to the political and economic stability of a country. The more stable the country is, the lesser will the probability of significant operating losses.

RISK MANAGEMENT

Three basic stages are required to manage the risks involved in international financial investments:

(1) *identification* and *classification* of all types of risks;
(2) *measurement* of the risks by using the forecasted probabilities of all possible events that can affect the return on investments; and
(3) the *control* and *monitoring* of these risks for the entire life of the investment.

The identification and classification of risk involves a process of collecting information pertaining to the characteristics of the business. For example, a brokerage firm, which has made large investments in Deutsche Marks (DM), is mainly exposed to the risk of exchange fluctuations. Apart from this risk, the business also faces a market risk and interest rate risk. If the investment was made in a fixed income security, a credit risk may also be involved.

How big or small each of these risks is can be ascertained by using relevant present and past information and a set of rules to analyze this information. The accuracy of such measurements, of course, will depend on the accuracy, relevance and completeness of information acquired and also on how good the rules are.

After the risk has been identified and measured, there is a need to control the excessive risk and monitor it on a continuous basis. Portfolio theory suggests policies that can help to diversify the excessive investment risks (Haugen, 1987). Any such strategy should be continuously studied and monitored because the total investment risk may change rapidly with time.

INFORMATION TECHNOLOGY IN RISK MANAGEMENT

Information technology plays a very important role in each of the three stages of risk management. With the help of developing technology, international risk management is becoming easier to assess and monitor. For example, a portfolio manager today can gather up-to-the-minute information on any international security. Declining costs of computer memory and significant increases in computer processing speeds have made it possible to analyze large volumes of historical data in less than a minute. Furthermore, an increasing use of state-of-the-art technologies, such as artificial intelligence, neural nets, fuzzy logic, genetic algorithms and parallel processing are making it possible to identify and manage the global investment risk on a real-time basis (Bansal, 1993).

Consider, for example, an international option on the Japanese Nikkei index. If the investment is made in US dollars, at least four types of risks are involved with this option: market risk, the interest rate risk, the exchange rate risk of Japanese Yen versus US dollars, and the country-specific risk of Japan. To track the market risk, traders need real-time data feeds that carry information on the Nikkei index. Then using computer models, a trader can analyze the possible deviation in the value of this option with the change in the market value of the index. Similarly, the interest rate fluctuations that affect the market value of options can also be tracked on a real-time basis and used in the option valuation model to measure the changing investment risk. The exchange rate risk can be analyzed by studying foreign exchange fluctuation and forecasting them in the future. Finally, the country-specific risk is identified and managed by obtaining data on major economic and political events concerning Japan.

It is not surprising, thus, that many international investment and brokerage houses are spending more on information technology to make the business of risk management easier and more reliable. Many banks and other financial institutions, such as Barclays de Zoete Wedd (BZW) bank in Tokyo, have recently shown their commitments to information technology by investing a significant amount of money in acquiring new systems or enhancing the existing ones. BZW recently invested in computerized software called Quantec, a system that can analyze risk both on a global asset allocation and individual market basis (Enderle, 1991). The Quantec optimizer assesses the risk of each international market by measuring the volatility and correlation of historical returns. Thus, Quantec helps in designing an optimal portfolio, one where the total risk for any specified return is the lowest or, conversely, the return for a specified level of risk is the highest.

Given the importance of information technology to the business of risk management, we look at some of the existing technologies and suggest how they can be modified or used to manage risk at the international level.

Existing Information Technologies

An information system for risk management can be divided into four components:

(1) a data component that characterizes the input data feeds and the historical data;
(2) a modeling component that either analyzes the current risk in the investment or forecasts future risk, based on the current and historical information;
(3) a reporting component that describes and presents the evaluation of risk to the user; and
(4) a hardware component that controls the data storage and processing capabilities.

In this chapter, we will concentrate only on the first three components of a risk management information system and show how the advances in each of these components can be extended to make a global risk management system more efficient.

The Data Component

The ability to obtain timely information is a very important requirement for a sound financial risk management strategy. Today, a range of data vendors specialize in the business of providing information to investors. Reuters, Knight-Ridder and Dow Jones are just a few examples. Some investors build specialized software that provides customized data to users as per their requirements.

The advancement in communications technology has made the process of data gathering and distribution faster. In many organizations today, the data is gathered by a central server, processed at a central location and then distributed to a number of client locations. By using data sockets, data can be transferred across different types of systems on a real-time basis.

Centralized storage of data and its distribution from a single point ensures stronger control. At the same time, by maintaining only a single copy of the database the problems of data redundancies can be eliminated, resulting in lower data costs for the firm. However, centralized control of data also causes several problems. The response time to maintain data-related problems has been reported to be relatively poor in centralized data control situations. Another problem is a lower flexibility to modify the incoming data to suit an end-user. Different users need different data items and at times, in different forms. Having a single copy of data and centrally controlled distribution makes it harder to fine-tune the data as per a user's needs.

Two strategies are suggested to offset the problems involved with a centralized control of the database. The *first* option is to connect several servers together in a client-server architecture. Thus, a trader can pull the required data from anywhere in the world by requesting his server to track the data from the nearest available source. The copy of the data is maintained either at its source or at a back-up destination. This way decision-making is decentralized with an ability to pull the data from a central place (if needed).

The *second* strategy is to let different servers be connected together via a mainframe. This way the risk calculations can be performed in a distributed fashion with an option to aggregate risk at the firm level with the help of the mainframe. In a global setting, the placement of the centralized control is an important issue. It mainly depends on factors, such as the place where the total exposure of the firm is managed. The other factors that may influence the decision include: the distance of the proposed site from the place of the trade, and economical factors such as the cost of communication, people and other resources.

Either of the two strategies are used by firms today to manage international investment risk. Using the second strategy, portfolio managers can combine the powers of different types of systems - workstations, minicomputers and mainframes - to obtain a very-powerful architecture. Such a combined architecture will enable graphical simulations on workstations, powerful communications capabilities on minicomputers and faster execution of mathematical models on mainframes and supercomputers. However, this approach is costly and may not be particularly cost-efficient for small investment firms. The alternative of a distributed architecture may permit cheaper transfer of data across different servers, but does not provide very powerful execution of models and high data transfer speeds.

Another criterion to select either of the two strategies is the fault-tolerance of the architecture. In the first approach, if one or more servers fail, only the local transactions will suffer. The other connections should still continue to work and may use different communications channels to bypass the inactive connection. On the other hand, in a centralized form of data transfer, if the central system does not function, then data transfer across other sites will not work, unless a back-up arrangement is planned before-hand. Thus, depending on the chances of such a failure and the effect of data transfer losses on the operations of a firm, a firm may decide to choose one alternative over the other.

In international risk management application, there are two levels at which risk is usually managed: at the local level and at the firm-wide level. Specifically, each international location has its own risk management unit which generally manages risk on a real-time basis and, at the "end-of-the-day", calculations are transferred to the corporate headquarters for assessing the total exposure of the firm to all types of risk. In this environment, the presence of a central computer is needed, and thus the second (distributed) architecture is generally adopted. If any of the servers fail, the loss of transactions and data is limited to a particular location.

Data Distribution and Its Use

Data on international investments may be used by different investors in different ways. For example, one investor may look at the prices of a foreign stock in order to calculate its volatility for possible future investments while another may have already invested in the stock and is now interested in monitoring its price on a real-time basis. For varying uses of the same data, most investors keep multiple copies of the data sets, thus adding to unnecessary costs for the firm. A more efficient approach would be to keep a well-designed database management system so that the needs of different investors could be satisfied by using the same data set. Thus, the investor who needs the data feeds for calculating the historical volatility would be given just that and no more and the investor who wants real-time prices will be able to pull the data on prices (but not on volatility) at regular frequent intervals as desired. Under this database design, only a few persons would be given the permission to update or delete the data. Further, if a data item is altered manually, all related data items will be appropriately updated too. Another characteristic of this database would be that each data item would allow only a certain number and types of permissible operations. For example, an investor would never be allowed to multiply two "cusips" (which is a security identifier) or include a foreign currency that cannot easily be encashed in U.S. dollars in a portfolio that should have high liquidity.

Most of the above requirements of a good database management system can be satisfied by using an object-oriented database management system. In an object-oriented database design, there are two related concepts: a class and an instance (Chin and Chanson,

1991). A class is a template from which some entities can be created to encapsulate data with some operations and properties that are associated with the data. These entities are called *objects*. For example, if living beings are considered a class, both animals and plants can be considered objects with their own properties and certain permissible operations. The animals may have a brain while the plants may not. Similarly, the animals may be permitted to have feelings, but not plants. An instance is an example of the objects that belong to the same class.

Using object-oriented technologies, each remote foreign risk management site (a trader's workstation or server) may be considered an object, belonging to a particular class. If the trader is considered a novice, he or she will only be permitted to invest in low-risk securities. If, at any time, the trader wants to invest in high-risk securities, the system would not permit it and would give an option to the trader to transfer the request to his or her manager, who belongs to a different class and has the option to invest in high-risk securities. Each class will be allowed to access different kinds of information from the same database. Thus, a high level manager will only be supplied aggregated information since he or she has no functional need for detailed data. On the other hand, a trader will be given an access to real-time data feeds. As a result, by giving the appropriate level of data access to different investors and controlling the total risk in their position, a system should be able to manage risk effectively at each level.

An open question related to the data component of a risk management system is the quality of data. Recently, Bansal and Kauffman illustrated a technique to analyze the impact of bad data on the process of risk management. They considered three aspects of data quality: accuracy, frequency and response time. Using fundamental principles from economics, the research showed that data quality affects risk diversification, which ultimately exposes the firm to yet another type of risk -- the risk of having bad information. This risk is much more relevant in international settings because the quality of data can vary greatly in an international market. Imagine, for example, the risk a firm could have been exposed to by investing in a Russia, if the information on the Russian coup was not available in the market instantly. Since the risk is generally higher (and sometimes unknown) in foreign investments as compared to domestic ones, the issue of data quality gains increased importance.

Bansal illustrates a number of techniques that can be used to mitigate the effect of bad data on risk management. Although he chose the context of investments in mortgage-backed securities, the same principles can be applied to the case of investments in foreign securities. One technique to detect data quality problems is to use data dependencies and certain set of heuristics to detect data anomalies. For example, if it is commonly known that an increase in GDP (Gross Domestic Product) generally leads to an increase in consumer confidence unless unemployment is high, and the given data shows an increase in GDP but no increase in consumer confidence and low unemployment, then the data on one or more of these three indicators (unemployment, consumer confidence or GDP) may be bad. Research in this area provides a mechanism to associate with each such inference and detect data problems.

The Role of Analytical Models for Risk Management: Further Advances

Analytical models are an important component of risk management. The process of risk management can only be as good as the models used in the process. Analytics are used to identify, measure and monitor the risk in international investments.

Analytics for Risk Identification

To identify risk, investors are increasingly using pattern recognition, artificial intelligence, fuzzy logic, genetic algorithms and neural nets techniques.

Pattern recognition involves analysis of current or historical data on prices, yields or other measures of security performance to detect signs for a significant change in risk. One example of a successful use of pattern recognition in international investments is TARA (Technical Analysis and Reasoning Assistant), a system developed by Manufacturers Hanover Trust in New York City in 1989-1990. The system helps to identify patterns associated with foreign exchange movements and identifies possible currency risk in FX investments.

The biggest problem in risk identification is the amount of data that a trader has to go through in order to arrive at some meaningful conclusions pertaining to risk. Rule-based systems are being used to parse enormous amounts of data to extract only meaningful information from them. For example, an artificial intelligence system can parse all the political news of a country and filter out the information that directly or indirectly affects a trader's investments. Some of these systems (e.g., CONQUEST) match the profiles of individual traders with the semantics of a news item to detect if it is relevant for a particular trader (Addison, Feder, Nelson and Schwartz, 1993).

Rule-based systems have also been used to measure the credit risk in a loan (Keyes, 1990). This is achieved by screening the borrower's past debt payment history and several other indicators that predict if the borrower will be able to pay back the loan or not.

Another technology in detecting and measuring the total risk in international investments is neural nets. Neural nets imitate the human reasoning process by using a complex network of sensory units called *neurons*. Although the term is taken from biology, these neurons are not as complex as human neurons are. Neurons are simply nodes that take as input some data, process these and produce output information that can be used by other neurons (Lippman, 1987).

Neural nets can be used to classify investments into one of several categories of riskiness. They are first trained on sample data and continuously fine-tuned until they are able to replicate the results for the sample data satisfactorily. Then, the current data is supplied to the net and the risk classification is obtained. Although other statistical techniques can be used to classify risk in investments, (e.g. discriminant analysis and regression techniques), researchers have shown that neural nets have performed better at predicting financial indicators, and thus the risk associated with financial investments (Dutta and Shekhar, 1988; Cosset and Roy, 1990).

Bansal, Kauffman and Weitz (Bansal, Kauffman and Weitz, 1993) showed that predictions based on neural nets help to create more efficient hedges than the predictions based on simple linear regression models, even when the input data quality is not very good. Although their research was done to evaluate the prepayment risk in mortgage-backed securities, a similar approach can be used to investigate the impact of bad data on currency and other types of international risks. In fact, in the context of international risk management, the study gains more importance because there is a higher probability of data being inaccurate, and not being delivered on time when it is obtained from many different international sources. Table 1 provides some of the significant differences between neural nets and standard statistical techniques (such as regression).

Risk Measurement: The Use of Analytical Models

The simplest types of analytics used in risk measurement are the spreadsheet-type calculators, which use the historical volatility of securities to predict their future price fluctuations. However, to calculate the risk in any derivative instruments, the relationships between the underlying securities and the derivative instruments need to be evaluated. One simple example is the Black-Scholes analytical model used for evaluating options. The model is one of the most widely used analytics in the finance industry to price both domestic and international options[1].

Using the model, a risk manager can evaluate the changes in his total position in any option corresponding to changes in the price of the underlying security. Thus, the model can be used to quantify total investment risk at any time in the future. Of course, to

	Neural Net	Regression and other statistical techniques
Non-Linear Relationships Between the Input and the Predicted Data	Non-linear relationships between the input and the predicted variables are easier to specify.	Te nature of the model, e.g., quadratic, polyno-mial or cubic, is needed to make statistical generali-zations or predictions.
Adaptation with Time	Keeps adapting itself incrementally as newer test examples are generated.	With every new piece of information, the model needs to be specified again and retested.
Speed of Learning	Can be controlled by changing the learning rate. The user has the option to decide how accurate he or she wants to be.	The speed of statistical generalization (which some may prefer to call learning) is controlled by the algorithm. The degree of accuracy can be specified by indicating the level of statistical confi-dence desired.
Explanation of results	Results from a neural nets are difficult to be explained. Many scientists consider it a "blackbox" still.	Regression coefficients are better understood and can be easily compared against user expectations.

Table 1

determine the total risk, one may still need to predict the prices of the underlying security in the future. These predictions can be made by using techniques such as neural nets and statistical regression as described above.

For securities other than options, derivative models similar to Black-Scholes can be employed. Thus, combining the calculations from all these models, one may be able to determine how the value of a certain portfolio will vary with the price variations in the underlying instruments, thus giving an indication of the total risk a portfolio may be exposed to.

Many impacts of political events in an international market are not always predictable with absolute certainty. For example, if a trader invests in oil futures and there is a war in the Gulf, the trader may assume that the prices of oil will go up in the world market. However, he or she cannot be absolutely certain of this, because there may be other consequences of the war that may drive prices lower. Thus, at the very best, a trader will be able to make a recommendation with a degree of certainty. Information technology professionals have developed a technique—*fuzzy logic*—to deal with such situations of uncertainty. Fuzzy logic allocates probabilities to each major event and then combines these probabilities to arrive at the most likely impact of a particular political or economic event.

The strength of a risk management system lies in its ability to assess and measure the risk accurately and in a timely fashion. Since financial markets may swing widely and are generally considered chaotic, it is not very surprising to see investment firms lose big amount of money in fractions of a minute. Hence, the ability to measure risk instantly is considered necessary to preserve a firm's assets.

By doing parallel processing, many analytical computations can be speeded up. To assess the prepayment pool in mortgage-backed securities and to find efficient hedges, Zenios reports the use of a Thinking Machines, Inc. "Connection Machine CM-2" parallel computing architecture (32,000 processing elements) that takes advantage of recent advances in algorithms for stochastic programming to solve this problem in real-time.

The Use of Analytics in Monitoring and Controlling Investment Risk

Once the risk is identified and measured, it is either neutralized completely by investing in other financial securities or at least minimized by diversifying the risk across a breadth of investments. This diversification process is commonly known as *hedging*. In hedging, an investor makes another investment in addition to the original one such that the risk in the second investment complements the risk in the first investment. For example, one may hedge an investment in call options by short-selling (selling without any physical transfer of securities) the common stock of which the option is a derivative. Since the value of the call option increases with an increase in the price of the common, the combined position will have a reduced risk. The risk in the resultant hedge can be significantly neutralized, if the number of options and common stocks are appropriately selected.

Another mechanism of risk diversification is to invest in businesses which show inverse relationships in variations of returns with corresponding variations in common environmental and political factors. For example, if an investor decides to invest in the umbrella business, he or she may also choose to invest in the golf ball business because both the businesses respond to weather fluctuations in different ways. When it rains, the sale of umbrellas will go up, boosting the firm's returns, but reducing the sale and the profits of the golf ball company. Thus, by choosing investments wisely, an investor may be able to limit part of his investment risk.

Information technology can be used to design analytics for improving the efficiency of hedges (i.e., minimizing risk for a specified

level of return or maximizing returns for a given level of risk).
Dynamic hedging tools that suggest how the hedges should be
formed and altered on a real-time basis are also available in the
market. However, the value of most of these automated tools
depends on the underlying analytics used to calculate the risk and
to make market predictions.

The capability to perform parallel computations can be very
helpful for designing an automatic hedging scheme for risk control.
The selection of optimal investments from a pool of several available
ones can be extremely time-consuming, especially when millions of
alternative investments are available all around the globe and each
of these potential investments possesses its own unique characteristics of risk and return.

Another objective of combining individual assets may be to match
a company's assets and liabilities. Sometimes, the firm has to
balance its cash in-flows and out-flows for at least some time in the
future. The technique of making sure that the in-flows match the
out-flows, is called *gap management* and is another dimension to be
considered in the selection of an optimal combination of securities.
To manage this selection of securities on a real-time basis, the
capability to perform parallel computations can prove to be very
beneficial.

Genetic algorithms are an emerging information technology that
is being used widely to optimize allocation of assets in a portfolio.
These algorithms are most suited for application where optimization
is either not possible or is very time-consuming. In this algorithm,
a number of assets are included and the risk and return of this
portfolio are then calculated. Next, the Darwinian principles of
natural selection are used to select and "breed" the assets that
perform the best and weed out the ones that perform the worst.
Continuing this technique iteratively, an optimal allocation of assets
can be achieved that also satisfies an investor's financial goals
(Goldberg, 1989; Welstead, 1993).

While control helps to prevent major losses in the future, it should
not be considered a one-time event. A manager needs to continuously assess and control the risk during the life-time of an investment. Knowing the maximum possible loss in a trader's portfolio, a
manager can use available and simple computerized analytics to set
automatic limits on investments by a specific trader depending on
his or her experience.

Reporting Risk: The Potential for Technological Innovations

The third and the last component of a risk management system is
the reports generation component. Generally, two levels of risk
management reports are available: a detailed description of risk in

all individual investments and an aggregated risk at varying levels (unit, department or firm).

While an individual trader needs to know the risk that he or she is taking with each invested dollar, the senior management is only interested in the aggregated amount of risk. Thus, a trader is generally provided the risk reports on a real-time basis, whereas the manager is usually given the "end-of-the-day" assessment of the risk exposure of each trader, unit, department and the firm. A trader usually gets an on-line report on the risk that he or she is exposed to. The manager gets a graphical or numerical report on paper or an electronic device.

With the continuing advancements in computer-based graphical capabilities, there are many options which a trader can select to be informed about his or her investment risk. For example, some systems provide audible signals to inform a trader that he or she has crossed a pre-defined level of risk, while others may provide a scheme of colors to distinguish abnormal risk levels from normal ones. A graph that depicts the total risk with variation in time can be another alternative to report the exposure to risk. Establishing automatic locks on investments, if the exposure to risk goes beyond a pre-specified level, and informing the trader accordingly via a flashing message on the screen is yet another way of reporting the risk entailed in an investment.

In addition to these reporting forms, there are risk calculators available, which with the touch of a button can present the risk assessment to a trader in both numerical and graphical form. Some of these systems provide the freedom to a trader to select the reporting form that best suits his needs. Reports to the managers are generally summarized with sophisticated graphics that illustrate the incremental risk taken by an individual or the department in a given day.

In the international setting, risk reports should be suitably translated by computers for non-English speaking individuals. Different cultures may prefer different graphical presentation methods and may prefer different color codes.

COST AND BENEFIT ISSUES

Most risk management systems are expensive to build and maintain. Each component of a risk management system requires the specialized knowledge of IT professionals. A respectable system, for example, needs most advanced communication technologies, advanced database management systems, state-of-the-art analytical models and appealing graphical presentations.

In general, the total cost of a risk management system can be broken into two types: fixed and variable costs. Fixed costs include one-time costs of hardware and the software for the system. The variable costs include the cost of periodic maintenance, monthly costs of data acquisition, and the costs of personnel that maintain the system. In addition to these costs, there are opportunity costs, i.e., the costs of not having the best risk management system available and losing business to competitors because poor risk management services were provided. Similarly, if the risk was not managed properly, the losses that are expected may be counted as an opportunity cost. Note that the opportunity costs for the firm that has the best available risk management system are the minimum possible.

Computerized risk management systems have two types of benefits: direct and indirect. While the direct benefits result in the savings or gains for the firm in hard currency, the indirect benefits contribute to the firm by increasing the productivity of traders by automating several aspects of risk management and allowing them to attend to the other needs of the business. Indirect benefits may also take the form of an increase in the motivation of traders and portfolio managers, because their jobs are made easier and less routine in nature.

CONCLUSIONS

International risk management is clearly more complicated than its domestic counterpart. International investments are subject to the economic and political risks of the countries in which they originate, exchange rate fluctuations complicate decision making, and the risks associated with domestic investments—market, interest rate, credit and operational—do not disappear. Fortunately, growing technological research and systems have contributed to making the job of the global risk manager easier.

Investment firms usually employ risk management systems to identify, measure and monitor international risks. Since a vast amount of data is available in the financial markets, risk managers rely on information technology to prune these data to recover only the meaningful information.

Risk management systems can be divided into four components: data, analytics, report generation and hardware. In this chapter we have described how the first three components have benefitted from advancements in information technology. We especially discussed research in areas, such as artificial intelligence, communications, parallel processing, neural networks, object-oriented databases, genetic algorithms, fuzzy logic, hypertext and graphical presentations.

Given the link between the progress in these advanced technologies and risk management, the process of risk management is certain to be transformed in the next few years. Research in the area of telecommunications, for example, has made it possible to transfer data almost instantaneously. With the promise to wire every house in the United States with fiber optic cables, further changes in financial service management are imminent.

Research in neural nets has notedly gained in momentum, especially after a number of Wall Street firms showed their support for this technology in the early 1990s. One of the problems with neural net modeling has been the selection of relevant input variables. However, researchers have recently demonstrated the use of genetic algorithms to make the search for input variables more efficient (Montana and Davis, 1989).

Some hardware manufacturers, such as IBM and SUN, have announced their intentions to produce more systems with parallel processing capabilities. The operating systems that support parallel processing, (e.g., Solaris) are gaining recognition with users who want to see still higher computation speeds.

Object-oriented technology is also becoming more popular in the global finance industry. There are suggestions today to encapsulate traders themselves as objects, with each trader having the capability to trade a limited number or types of securities. The aggregated risk for all the traders in a group can then be combined at the superclass level. An object-oriented computerized security arrangement like this would also help to control the sharing of "confidential" information among traders, thus enforcing trading ethics throughout the firm.

In summary, the field of international risk management is gaining a great deal by exploiting the advances in information technology. With the development of faster and more cost-efficient means to provide information to investors, the ways in which international risk is managed are likely to both change and improve.

ENDNOTES

[1] A stock or index option is of two types, a *call* option and a *put* option. The holder of a call (put) option has the right to buy (sell) the stock or the index for which the option is written at a predetermined price and date (or earlier if the option is an *American* option).

REFERENCES

Addison, E., Feder J., Nelson, P. and Schwartz, T. J.(1993). Extracting and Disseminating Information from Real-Time News. In the Proceedings of the Second International Conference on Artificial Intelligence Applications on Wall Street, Roy S. Freedman (Ed.), New York City, New York, 14-18.

Bansal, A.(1993). Gauging the Impacts of Data Quality on the Performance of Risk Management Technology. Unpublished dissertation, Leonard N. Stern School of Business, New York University.

Bansal, A., and Kauffman, R. J.(1991). Risk Management and Data Quality: An Information Economics Approach. Working paper, Center for Research in Information Systems, Stern School of Business, New York University.

Bansal, A., Kauffman, R. J., and Weitz, R.(1993). Comparing the Forecasting Performance of Regression and Neural Nets When Data Quality Varies. Working paper, Center for Research in Information Systems, Stern School of Business, New York University, also forthcoming in the *Journal of Management Information Systems*, Summer 1993.

Chin, R. S., and Chanson, S. T.(1991). Distributed Object-Based Programming Systems, *Computing Surveys*, 23(1), 91-124.

Cosset, J. C., and Roy J.(1990). Forecasting Country Risk Ratings Using a Neural Network. In *Proceedings of the Twenty-Third Annual Hawaii Conference on System Sciences*, Kailua-Kona, Hawaii, 4:327-334, IEEE Press.

Doherty, N. A.(1985). *Corporate Risk Management.* New York: McGraw-Hill Inc.

Dutta, S., and Shekhar, S.(1988). Bond Rating: A Non-Conservative Application of Neural Networks. In the *Proceedings of the Second International Conference on Neural Networks*, IEEE, 443-450.

Enderle, F.(1991). The Cost of Change. In J. Lederman and K. Park (Ed.), *The Global Equity Markets*, Chicago: Probus Publishing Company, 575-592.

Goldberg, D.(1989). *Genetic Algorithms in Search, Optimization, and Machine Learning.* Reading: Addison-Wesley.

Haugen, R. A.(1987). *Introductory Investment Theory.* Englewood Cliffs: Prentice-Hall.

Hertz D. and Thomas, H.(1984). *Practical Risk Analysis.* New York: John Wiley.

Keyes, J.(1990). *The New Intelligence: Artificial Intelligence Ideas and Applications in Financial Services.* New York: Harper Business.

Lessard, D. R.(1974). International Diversification and Direct Foreign Investment. In D.Eitman and A. Stonehill (Ed.), *Multinational Business Finance*, Reading: Addison-Wesley, 274-287.

Lippmann, R. P.(1987). An Introduction to Computing with Neural Nets, *IEEE ASSP Magazine*, 4-22.

Montana, D. and Davis, L.(1989). Training Feedforward Neural Networks Using Genetic Algorithms. In the Proceedings of the Eleventh International Joint Conference on Artificial Intelligence.

Ting, W.(1988). *The Political Economy of International Oil and the Underdeveloped Countries.* Beacon Press.

Tran, V.Q.(1980). *Foreign Exchange Management in Multinational Firms.* UMI Research Press.

Welstead, S.(1993). Financial Data Modeling with Genetically Optimized Fuzzy Systems. In the Proceedings of the Second International Conference on Artificial Intelligence Applications on Wall Street, Roy S. Freedman (Ed.),

New York City, New York, 286-293.

Zenios, S. A.(1990).   Massively Parallel Computations for Financial Planning Under Uncertainty, Report 90-11-10, HERMES Laboratory for Financial Modeling and Simulation, Decision Sciences Department, The Wharton School, University of Pennsylvania.

CHAPTER 9

Re-Engineering Trading and Treasury Operations in International Financial Services

VASANT DHAR
KATHERINE A. DULIBA
ROBERT J. KAUFFMAN

New York University

Maximizing business value of investments in hardware, software and telecommunications technologies that occur in the trading and treasury operations of an international bank requires senior management to evaluate the extent to which the technology infrastructure enables the bank to perform a number of key functions. These include: formulating effective trading strategies, pricing financial instruments accurately and rapidly, being able to respond to changing market conditions, processing transactions cost-effectively, resolving inquiries quickly, and moving to support emerging corporate treasury products. After a decade of rapid growth in investment levels, senior managers now emphasize refining, rationalizing and integrating trading and treasury technology architectures to support improved global financial risk management, better capital utilization, and higher transaction volumes. This chapter examines how senior managers can accomplish these goals by re-engineering pre-trade, trade execution and post-trade business processes. It presents a framework that utilizes basic concepts from management science and microeconomics to illustrate the variety of impacts that re-engineering can have on improving firm revenues and controlling or reducing costs. It also presents a series of managerial recommendations based on the framework.

INTRODUCTION

Background

During the late 1970s, Walter Wriston, then chairman of Citicorp, characterized commercial banking as a fast-paced "information business". Nowhere is this observation more true than in the arena of international financial services. Every day, billions of dollars exchange hands, reflecting the many transactions that must be processed to support international lending, trade finance, and money market trading and corporate treasury operations. Although each of these areas has grown during the last decade, especially notable are the changes associated with the trading and treasury business, where the lightning pace of the business and the extent of the financial risks involved place a heavy emphasis on information. Trading income from foreign exchange operations among the large money center banks, for example, increased anywhere from 40% to 1350% between 1979 and 1988. Meanwhile, the banks invested heavily in trading and treasury information technologies (IT) to support this large increase in transaction volume, and to improve reaction time in rapidly changing markets. In 1988, U.S. commercial banks were estimated to have spent almost $1 billion on trading systems *alone*, with *total* systems expenditures amounting to about $5.3 billion. See Tables 1 and 2.

Throughout this period of aggressive investment, it became increasingly evident that the application of the variety of new technologies would ultimately need to be refined, rationalized and integrated to enable the banks that invested in them to continue to reap high payoffs, as their competitors caught up by installing their own proprietary applications and value-added vendor solutions. As one industry observer commented: "In the 1980s, trading floors ... looked like 'spaghetti junctions', as banks rushed to buy the latest hot box of electronic tricks" (*The Economist*, October 3, 1992, p. 24). Relatively little thought was being given at the time to creating the basis for a common or integrated set of trading and treasury platform

Money Center Banks	1979 ($MM)	1988 ($MM)	Increase (%)
Bank of America	90.2	122.0	40
Bankers Trust	16.6	153.9	830
Chase Manhattan	77.0	249.7	230
Chemical	9.9	143.2	1350
Citibank	113.6	616.0	440
First chicago	11.2	148.6	1230
Manufacturers Hanover	16.1	103.0	540
J.P. Morgan	35.9	186.8	420

Source: Adapted fromSmith and Walter, 1990, p. 350.

Table 1: Foreign Exchange Trading Income of Major U.S. Banks

Line of Business	% of Total
Transaction Accounts	43
Trading (i.e. $954 million)	18
Lending	15
Funds Transfer	5
Cash Management	4
Information Services	4
Master Trust/Custody	2
Stock Transfer & Corporate Trust	2
Other	7
Total (=$5.3 Billion)	*100%*

Source: Steiner and Teixeira, 1990, p. 80.

Table 2: U.S. Commercial Banks' Wholesale Systems Expenses by Line of Business, 1988

technologies. With the relatively high margins that were available for firms that beat their competitors to market with new financial products, everyone was too busy making money to concentrate on *maximizing the business value* of their information technology investments.

New Attitudes: Risk Management, Reaction Time and Profit-making

But since the market crash in October 1987, and with the overall slowdown in domestic and international economic growth, attitudes on Wall Street have changed considerably. New opportunities are fewer and further between, more firms are going after them, and it takes a more sophisticated, cost-effective technological approach than ever before to turn them into profit. As a result, today greater emphasis is placed on the effective management of financial risk, ensuring that capital is efficiently allocated and utilized, that client and counterparty risks are properly estimated, and that all of the elements of a trading operation —from front office sales and analysis to back office transaction processing and settlement—are "in synch".

Profitability and performance in trading and treasury operations, like almost all other primary commercial bank lending functions, are subject to systematic market risk (foreign exchange rate fluctuation, import-export trade volume effects, central bank monetary policy shifts, changing interest rates, etc.) and the specific risks (cash flow problems, credit and bad debts, fraud and failed deals, etc.) associated with client firms. As a result, one important use of information systems is to identify and to quantify those risks. In trading and treasury operations, however, the extent of the financial risks may only become apparent when individual positions are aggregated. Some positions may be differentially sensitive to changing market indicators, while others may move in tandem with each other. Still others may be offsetting, acting as natural hedging instruments for each other.

Although managing and controlling the financial risk of an international commercial bank's trading and treasury portfolio is *necessary*, there is widespread recognition on the part of senior managers in international financial services firms that it may not be *sufficient*. Instead, *reaction time* is often what distinguishes the high profitability firms that lead the industry from the hard-charging also-rans. One case in point is Morgan Stanley Japan, an arm of the international investment banking firm that is headquartered in New York City. Morgan Stanley invested $35 million in developing a trading system which would be faster than any other system on the street in Tokyo. Why? So that the firm is able to react faster than its competitors, on each trade, taking advantage of arbitrage opportunities that other firms are not able to act on. As one of the firm's traders in Tokyo told an interviewer, "... two or three seconds make the difference between profiting from opportunities and just watching them whiz by" (Adrian and Kelleher, 1993, p. 1).

FROM CORE BUSINESS PROCESS AUTOMATION TO GLOBAL SYSTEMS INTEGRATION: EVOLVING ARCHITECTURES FOR INTERNATIONAL BANKING

To understand the opportunities that changes to existing trading and treasury platform architectures can create for firms that undertake re-engineering projects, it is useful to establish a basis for understanding where most firms are today, and how they fit into the context of the international financial services industry. We can do this by examining four phases of automation, the rationale behind them, and the kinds of strategies that they have enabled the firms to pursue. The four phases include:

(1) creating systems that automate core business functions;
(2) deploying customer-driven systems that leverage core automation to generate new sources of revenue;
(3) enhancing customer-driven systems so that they enable the firm to control and balance risk and reward; and,
(4) integrating core business process automation, customer-driven systems and mechanisms for controlling risk and improving profitability so that they can deliver seamless, high quality services on a global basis.

Phase 1 —Core Business Process Automation

The first phase of IT investment in the industry involved systems that were first constructed in the 1960s and early 1970s to support the high cost, largely manual operations in several business areas. These include: electronic funds transfer and telecommunication; deposit processing and international deposit services; international trade services, letters of credit and documentary collections; lending, credit evaluation and asset management; and trading and treasury management. Even then, the investments were made with competitive cost pressures in mind. American international banks were profitable and expanding rapidly overseas, and automation of international business operational processing paralleled other efforts that were made at the time to automate domestic corporate and retail operational processing.

Cost reduction pressure became an increasingly important concern as the international banking business became more complex in the mid-1970s. But, by then, investments in each of the areas remained uneven. Trading operations remained largely manual in global trading and treasury management services. Automation for international funds transfer, however, was progressing rapidly, preparing the way for the coalition of European and American banks that formed SWIFT, the Society for Worldwide Interbank Financial Telecommunication, as a standards organization to promote standardized, cost-effective solutions to mounting telecommunications costs. Other major efforts were devoted to setting up bank-wide transactions processing, customer information databases and account reporting information systems. Core business process automation provided a tremendous amount of operational performance information to senior management, and it streamlined the process of conducting periodic audits of bank profitability.

Phase 2—Customer-Driven, Value-Added Systems

These systems were later built on top of the existing core business process automation. They were meant to extend the set of capabilities that enabled better operational reporting within the bank to its customers *outside the bank*. Efforts to deploy this second generation of international banking systems began in the mid-1970s, and extended well into the mid-1980s. During this time, transaction processing information systems were enhanced to capture data on transaction processing in real-time so that they could be reported to clients, who were just beginning to practice intra-day treasury management of the international source demand balances. And, the international funds transfer business was transformed by the emergence of SWIFT, and the willingness of banks around the world to adopt its standards for financial telecommunication.

Automation in trading and treasury operations during this time increased the firms' responsiveness to changing markets, through the purchase of video market data feeds and direct telecommunications and systems links to overseas offices in important markets. But because there was relatively little pressure from senior management to control costs and focus on integrating systems, the usual practice among the large international commercial banks was to build (and only rarely buy) isolated systems to support trading on an instrument-by-instrument basis. As a result, most banks' trading platform systems remained fragmented well into the 1980s: databases were not integrated, applications could not talk to one another, and most important, key trading systems did not feed data to senior management for risk management purposes in a very usable format. Given the extent of the fragmentation, it would later become very costly for the banks to achieve further integration to improve managerial control.

Phase 3— Consolidated Financial Risk and Profitability Management Systems

The next round of investments was built on a solid, but fragmented foundation of existing core automation and the customer-driven, value-added systems. Investments in this area began to occur in the early 1980s. In this phase, the earlier core business process systems, along with the customer-driven systems, were linked to the banks' *internal control* systems. In trading and treasury operations, senior managers increasingly realized the need to monitor and to adjust positions in response to breaking economic news, interest rate and foreign exchange price changes, intra-bank capital allocation policy changes, and changing counterparty risks. This also led to a new emphasis on developing performance and risk management metrics that could be applied to a variety of instruments, yet deliver consistently reliable and useful information to senior management. Efforts in this area were justified in large measure by changing perceptions of what was required to achieve solid profitability: many had come to believe that high profitability could only be achieved through business tactics that emphasized avoiding lower margin lending and trading in markets and in instruments that entailed excessive risk. In instances where a firm was exposed to risk, the presence of adequate controls became even more important.

Phase 4—Globally-Integrated International Banking Systems

An added complexity that international financial services firms face is achieving integration on a global basis. The challenge of deploying globally-integrated systems is perhaps the greatest challenge of all. Cost-effective strategic product delivery systems for the mid to late 1990s will require integration across multiple business operating environments, across different currencies, across different technical environments, and also across different regulatory environments. They will require more vision from senior management than ever before, because the scope of the international banking business has changed dramatically in the last five years. Margins are thin everywhere, speed is of the essence, comprehensive control is mandatory, and getting the information technology infrastructure right can make or break profits in trading and treasury operations.

Current Status

The current status of many large money center banks with respect to the four phases we have described reflects some mixing of the stages. International commercial banks rarely have the time or resources to focus on "everything at once." Instead, their IT architectures have been built up piecemeal, reflecting the competitive demands of participation in specific businesses. As a result, it is not uncommon for a firm to be simultaneously implementing customer-driven applications to support business in one area, while seeking to refine risk management practices and extend them to the range of its global operations. For example, in one firm we recently visited, efforts were underway to deploy expert systems for foreign exchange trade error evaluation and multiple instrument hedge position creation and risk management, in support of specific business objectives. Meanwhile, senior management was conducting a comprehensive and critical review of the information technology platform for the entire portfolio of customer-driven systems related to trading and treasury. The purpose of the latter effort was to determine how to re-engineer the IT architecture to enable object-oriented design concepts to be incorporated in the next generation applications.

In fact, a cottage industry of conferences and seminars has sprung up of late, indicating the extent of the interest in the industry to find workable solutions to re-engineering trading and treasury operations for the global banking environment of the 1990s. Similar pressures are felt by bankers who specialize in credit evaluation and lending, and other international banking functions. On the credit side, bad debts as a percentage of total bank assets in the U.S. increased from 2.24% in 1989 to 3.03% in 1990. In the absence of effective information systems that could have helped to control the mounting bad debts, federal regulators have called for the banks to set aside additional reserves for bad debts. David Gibb, a senior vice president for credit quality and information technology at the Canadian Imperial Bank of Commerce, comments: "[I]f the crisis has served one purpose, it has alerted the banking industry to the neglect of MIS by commercial credit operations" (Caldwell and Violino, 1991, p. 10). Managing financial risk is a major weakness in several business areas represented in international commercial banking— and one that cannot be adequately addressed in the absence of improved integration of core automation, customer-driven systems, and risk and profitability management applications.

We now turn to a more detailed consideration of the hardware, software, and telecommunications technologies with respect to which re-engineering projects can be undertaken to improve pre-trade, trade execution and post-trade operations in the trading and treasury business process.

PRE-TRADE, TRADE EXECUTION AND POST-TRADE PROCESSES

There are several ways to understand trading and treasury business processes for the purpose of improving performance. One way is to focus on the *content* of the trade. The treasury and trading business can be studied by segmenting the business according to product lines. For example, traders can trade Treasury bills, mortgage-backed securities, or foreign exchange. The key question is: What is being traded? This focus is important when trying to determine the contribution of each product line to the bank's total profits.

Another way to understand the treasury and trading process is to analyze the *process* of performing the trade. Here, the focus shifts to the work and procedures and the flow of work that occurs when something is traded. The emphasis is on *how* the product is traded. The key questions are: How does trading work, and how are the workflows changed? A third complementary perspective is to examine the participants or *actors* that populate the trading process.

The related questions that this perspective suggests are: How do the actors' responsibilities change, and how are the relationships among actors changed? The last two can be combined to form a useful perspective for senior management to adopt when re-engineering of business processes is of interest. In particular, with increasing integration of intra-firm operations already underway, a careful reconsideration of the boundaries of the organization can expose new ways of creating new business opportunities and simplifying workflows at the same time. In this chapter, our focus is on the *process* of trading and how the *actors' roles* in that process are changed; *what* is being traded is of secondary importance. We will describe the overall process of trading and the key participants in each phase.

A practical breakdown has been suggested by practitioners in finance to describe the process of trading in terms of three time-dependent sets of activities (Green, 1993; Waters Information Services, 1991):

(1) *Pre-trade processes* occur before the trade is made, for example, pricing or swap analysis, price change forecasting, or position hedging evaluation.
(2) *Trade execution processes* are required in order to initiate, process and complete trades.
(3)   *Post-trade processes* occur after the trade is made, but are necessary to ensure that the appropriate adjustments are made on a firm's books, that funds are transferred into or out of the appropriate accounts to effect settlement, and that any errors that result in inquiries are resolved.

Figure 1 depicts this breakdown and lists the various sub-processes that are associated with each of the major processes.

Pre-Trade Processes

Pre-trade processes include all those activities which occur prior to the trade of a money market instrument. They include the following:

- client needs assessment, credit allocation decisions,
- identification of counterparties for trades, and
- valuation and risk analysis.

Assessment of customers' needs and credit allocation decisions are based on background research and constant contact with customers. These decisions determine what services the traders can perform for the customers. The identification of a counterparty is

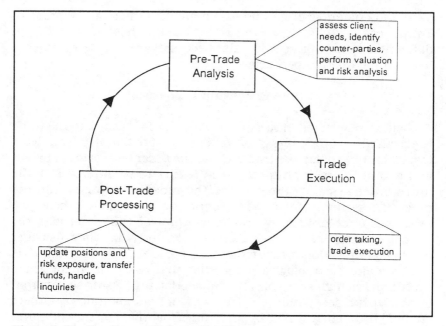

Figure 1: Trading Process Information Flow

essential to complete a trade. The search for a counterparty could be initiated by the trader (say, in response to a request by another trader), or by a member of the "sell-side" team—beginning with the relationship lending officer or the treasury product specialist —who initiate contacts with customers.

Finally, *analytics*—a term used widely in the industry to mean computer-based support for quantitative problems in trading— provide the basis for improving trading decisions. The input to the analytical systems is a wide range of market indicator data (Waters Information Services, 1991). Analytical systems provide the trader with the ability to build models, to perform on-line position analysis with relevant customer and potential counterparty information, to implement real-time risk management of customer portfolios and trader positions, and to create graphical and numerical reports that offer insights into the sensitivity of trading or hedging strategies to changes in market indicators.

International banking introduces additional complexity into the above processes by requiring traders and management to track additional variables. First, banks must continuously value their portfolios in real-time and keep databases consistent in order to be able to "pass the book" from one office as it closes to another in a different geographic market, as the market opens up. Second, for management to keep in touch with the impact of developments in the firm's markets on specific businesses and bank customers, global, local and customer profit and loss statements need to be created. Third, because there are country-specific risks related to trading in different national markets, it is also necessary to track developments in real-time in other countries.

Trade Execution Processes

Trades are effected in two parts: an order is taken, and the trade is executed. Historically, these processes were handled by at least two different people: the trader wrote the order on a piece of paper, and another person physically took it over to be entered into the firm's order system. From there, the order was routed into the execution system. Today, the technology has enabled these two processes to be unified. Workstations provide the trader with the capability to enter trades, check for errors and edit. They also offer on-the-spot position measurement capabilities.

The major technological capability that is required for trade execution is a high speed on-line transaction processing system that is able to process trade entries from the workstations. Orders credited through arbitrage opportunities identified by the computer can be routed automatically. The function of the system is to create a "time-stamp" for the trade as an event in the bank's business, and to send a notice to the market that the event has occurred. In the absence of such notification, the opportunity for another competitor to make the trade still exists. In practice, on-line screen-based trading systems are very fast. Currently, designing an effective transaction processing system requires reaction time in the one to two second range.

Post-Trade Processes

Post-trade processes include the following:

- updating positions and risk exposure,
- transferring funds,
- handling inquiries and one-of-a-kind requests.

Position update occurs after an order has been effected, and the trade has been time-stamped and sent to the market. A number of calculations are performed to update customer and counterparty positions, the trader's position, and apply them to the bank's aggregate position. As a result of these calculations, post-trade processing also enables the computation of useful quantitative information for risk management purposes, including instrument, customer and market exposures. Most banks calculate these at the end of the day. However, some banks are moving towards operating on a real-time basis.

The *flow* of *funds* and settlement procedures are based on the trade. In some cases, the trades only require book entries: banks often promote trades between customers, and they often act as the counterparty to the customer's trade. In cases where the counterparty is the client of another bank, money market trades are completed by the movement of funds through domestic money market bank funds transfer networks such as CHIPS (the Clearing House Interbank Payment System) in New York or CHAPS (Clearing House Automated Payment System) in London, or through notification via SWIFT for later settlement. This part of the process is usually called "clearing".

The final major component of post-trade processing is *handling customer inquiries*. It is important for an international commercial bank to operate a high quality, low error trade transaction processing system. Of course, some errors will inevitably occur. However, when they do, computerization can support inquiry handling by enabling a customer service representative to do an on-line trace through a trade transaction's audit trail, correct the part that is in error, and enable the relevant updating information to be passed to the bank's other customer account and intra-day position information systems. It is imperative for the bank to be able to resolve problems quickly; when they aren't resolved, the bank will incur two costs. First, when the trade finally is corrected, the bank must "back value" funds that were incorrectly applied or that were not received by the customer. This represents a real expense to the bank, and is a function of the dollar value of the underlying transaction, the current funds rate, and the number of days the position is in error. Second, trades processing operations that are prone to making errors attract fewer customers in the long run, which reduces operating scale. This can force pricing changes, which may also cause the bank to lose customers.

Actors in the Trading Process

Table 3 presents an overview of the participants in each of the stages of trading. The major participants in the pre-trade phase are the lending or marketing officer, the senior credit officer, the treasury product specialist, the customer, and the trader. The first two are responsible for bringing to the bank customers who require trading and treasury services. The lending officer makes proposals for the allocation of credit (actually scarce capital resources) so that the bank can trade on behalf of the customer. The credit officer has the authority to decide how to allocate capital. The treasury product specialist acts in an advisory role, in conjunction with the lending officer and the trader, to create value maximizing short-term and long-term treasury strategies. The treasury product specialist is

Processes	Key Actors
Pre-Trade	lending officer, credit officer, treasury product specialist, customer, trader
Trade Execution	customer, trader, counterparty, order taker
Post-Trade	risk manager, funds transfer manager, customer service representative

Table 3: Key Actors in the Trading Process

often responsible for suggesting what kinds of trading activities the customer should engage in, performing quantitative analysis and research to determine how customer positions should be hedged, and so on. The trader and the customer are also direct participants in this process; the former can offer insights on the feasibility of a treasury management and trading strategy, based on deep knowledge of how markets operate, while the customer must inform the trader about important events in its business operations that require changes to the firm's position.

The major participants in the trade execution are the customer, the trader, and the counterparty (which is often the bank itself). In executing the trade, the trader may directly enter the trade into the computer system, which is known as screen-based trading, or the trader may pass the trade on to an order taker, who enters the trade and routes it to the next point in the process.

Finally, in the post-trade phase, the key actors are those responsible for analyzing the effects of the trade, and facilitating the full execution and follow through. In this phase, the risk manager evaluates the risk associated with the new positions. Funds transfer managers play a role in the post-trade process in that they are responsible for any movement of funds that the trade execution requires in order to settle. Customer service representatives provide information to customers and auditors, and collect information from customers, often to resolve errors.

Identifying actors' roles is useful in understanding the workflows involved in trading operations. For example, instead of just generally knowing what pre-trade processes are, one can identify the tasks and the actors which comprise this process, and thus understand the workflow at a more detailed level. After understanding the workflow, role identification and analysis can then help to determine re-engineering opportunities by raising the following issues: Is the role necessary? Can it be combined with another role? Can it be "exported" to the customer or supplier? Can the role be eliminated altogether? We return to this point in the re-engineering section of this paper. First, however, we discuss the hardware, software, and telecommunications and data feeds that are common to modern trading and treasury operations.

RE-ENGINEERING OPPORTUNITIES FROM HARDWARE, SOFTWARE AND TELECOMMUNICATIONS TECHNOLOGIES

The information technologies that global trading and treasury operations in international banking use can be grouped into three broad categories: hardware, software, and telecommunications and data feeds. Some of the capabilities that the different technologies offer may appear to be obvious and trivial to implement, but very often implementation is problematic because of the constraints imposed by existing systems. For example, traders would often like to pull data off a screen display of market indicators, and use it in the context of a workstation-based spreadsheet money market instrument pricing model. But this is only possible if the data source is digital, and if the bank has a data stream capture device that can move data from the screen and into a spreadsheet. Let's examine what opportunities there may be for firms to re-engineer their existing trading and treasury operations in terms of these three categories of technologies.

Hardware

International trading and treasury operations use a wide range of information technology hardware. In the 1960s and 1970s, *mainframes* were the primary focus for transaction processing and customer account reporting. This continues to be the case, but usually mainframe processing capabilities are supplemented by fault-tolerant minicomputers that maintain a steady stream of processing that enables trade-related data to reach the market. Mainframes have been the traditional number-crunchers that banks use to post and clear the high volumes of trades that are executed daily. As we noted earlier, high-speed on-line transaction processing is a basic requirement for trading and treasury support. But mainframes are also used for handling databases of financial data that are typically stored on direct access storage devices (**DASD**) so that they can be called for use in analytical models and for other forecasting purposes.

Although mainframes are fast and powerful, they are not nearly fast or powerful enough to solve highly complex analytical models in real-time. Merrill Lynch, for example, bought a *massively parallel supercomputer* to do pre-trade analysis related to the pricing of mortgage-backed securities (**MBS**), a money market instrument that became increasingly interesting to bank portfolio managers and traders in the mid-1980s (Michaels and Jenna, 1992). The challenge in MBS pricing involves estimating prepayment cash flows that occur over time as an interest rate moves stochastically through a "binomial lattice" of potential interest rate paths. When interest rates fall, borrowers refinance mortgages to obtain the lower rates, reducing the payback for a money center bank that holds the mortgage debt in its *securitized* or MBS form. Assuming that the life of a typical mortgage is about 30 years, and interest rates and prepayments are tracked on a month to month basis, the number of potential scenarios that might obtain is 2^{360} (Zenios, 1991). In practice, a mainframe would take days to solve this kind of problem, effectively eliminating the opportunity for Merrill Lynch to participate in this business. By bringing in a massively parallel system (where several thousand scenarios can be explored simultaneously), the firm has increased the functionality of its system. Merrill Lynch also believes that it can take advantage of more trading opportunities from the increase in speed (Michaels, 1992). Other firms in the securities industry are reported to have applied supercomputing solutions, including Prudential Securities, which has been using them since 1988 (Michaels, 1992), and the Union Bank of Switzerland (Kang and Zenios, 1992).

International financial services firms are also able to increase their cost effectiveness by moving some of their analytics, including statistics, graphics, modeling, and hedging, off mainframes to *workstations* and to *personal computers*. Senior managers note that workstations offer more "economic MIPS". Cost is not the only concern though. Developing mainframe processing schedules in a large international bank involves sorting through the priorities of the many competing business units, all of which are in search of cheap and reliable processing. Ivy Schmerken, a senior editor with an influential industry periodical called *Wall Street & Technology* (previously known as the *Wall Street Computer Review*), comments on the move to distributed processing:

> *Wall Street's vintage back-office systems are a messy patchwork quilt of incompatible minis and mainframes that make it difficult to consolidate a firm's positions, credit exposure and capital allocations across global markets. By distributing the processing on workstations, positions can be updated in real-time right at the trader's desk, so that risk managers don't have to wait for several hours for mainframe reports. (Schmerken, 1992b, p. 84)*

Traders prefer workstations over personal computers, because workstations operate about two to five times faster than the fastest personal computers. As a result, trading platform technology designers increasingly moved the analytics to workstations towards the end of the 1980s and the early 1990s. Workstations predominantly use reduced instruction set computing (**RISC**) chips, which are faster and more economical than the microprocessors used in personal computers, especially for data-intensive numerical computations. Merrill Lynch, for example, has deployed about 1500 Sun Microsystems workstations (Schmerken, 1992a, p. 61).

An important hardware infrastructure design decision is the choice between *proprietary solutions* and *open systems*. The trend today is against proprietary hardware and operating systems. Companies such as Rich Inc. (owned by Reuters Holdings PLC) and Micrognosis (a subsidiary of Control Data Corp.), which previously enjoyed the profitability benefits of dominating the markets for proprietary trading floor hardware and software solutions, are now challenged by the growing industry-wide call for open systems, exemplified by *open* hardware like Unix workstations and microcomputers.

As banks continue to modernize their trading systems, the move to consolidated digital feeds and workstation analytics is evident. This also requires computational power on the trader's desk, a large windowed display format, and a mouse-driven or push button data entry interface to supplement the keyboard. With multiple windows -- each displaying their own data feed -- and consolidated analytics, a trader workstation's windows become "windows on the world markets". Such consolidation will also offer cost savings: every time a market data vendor develops something new, the bank no longer will need to bring in new hardware to support it. No bank wants to be locked into and limited to one firm's products: the trading and treasury business, and the set of hardware technologies that can be used most effectively to support it, are changing too rapidly.

Software

Although the hardware platform is an important investment for an international commercial bank, what really makes it pay off for the bank is the software that it can run, providing decision support, trade execution and inquiry support services, and retrieval of relevant information about the world from market data. The trading and treasury services that a bank can offer are dependent upon the capabilities of the software and hardware mix; more complex pricing algorithms and financial instrument analytics can be designed precisely because the capabilities of the hardware are growing. The major firms have invested a substantial amount of time and money in software to support trading, in part because such investments are viewed by senior management as giving the firm leverage to increase non-interest revenues. In some banks, the rapid deployment of new software to support trading in new instruments and the offering of new financial products has created businesses where there were none before.

Just as there is a trend towards open systems in computer hardware, there is also a trend towards open systems in software to support international trading and treasury functions. Software applications can be classified in one of two ways:

Proprietary applications software is usually developed in-house or on a customized, outsourced basis, where the explicit intent is that the software will produce competitive advantage for the firm.

Open applications result from joint development undertaken by a group of firms who form an alliance, or by an industry outsourcing firm that works with an industry firm to create a non-proprietary solution, that can later be resold to other firms, so that the price to early purchasers will reflect development costs that can be spread over multiple firms.

Proprietary software includes *programmed trading* applications, which are essentially financial strategies of a firm which have been programmed into a computer. In programmed trading, several transactions are executed at the *same* time; for example, several currencies, or their futures or options, can be bought or sold, in varying quantities. The New York Stock Exchange defines programmed trading as "the simultaneous purchase or sale of at least 15 different stocks with a total value of $1 million or more" (*Wall Street Journal*, March 17, 1993, p. C15). An important application of programmed trading concepts is to implement arbitrage strategies. Arbitrage strategies take advantage of mispricing which may occur between a currency on one exchange, and futures or options of that currency on another exchange. The trader has the computer programmed to do two things:

(1) to recognize an arbitrage opportunity, and,
(2) to execute certain trades based on that opportunity.

The program monitors market data and initiates the trades.

Due to the magnitude of the investment required to develop trading and treasury infrastructure software and programmed trading applications, the adoption of industry standards for software development and software alliances has become increasingly attractive. Some firms have actually sold or licensed their own in-house systems to defray the costs. For example, The First Boston Corporation, a New York City-based investment bank, licensed a computer aided software engineering (**CASE**) tool called High Productivity Systems (**HPS**) to Kidder Peabody, an industry competitor with a greater focus on retail securities trading, to defray the $120 million cost of developing the CASE tools and an entirely new set of trades processing architecture software (Banker and Kauffman, 1992).

In addition to being cost-effective, another potential benefit of open systems is that they allow for a modular and flexible software architecture, which accommodates new approaches to software engineering that emphasize software object reuse and object-oriented design (Karimi, 1990; Apte, Sankar , Thakur and Turner, 1990). Software design and object reuse opens up the possibility of "win-win" cross-industry alliances. One such example is the alliance involving six firms, including Financial Technologies International (**FTI**), a New York City-based software design consultancy, IBM, and four financial services firms (Pierson, Heldring & Pierson; U.S. Trust; Wilmington Trust; and Wachovia Bank). These firms have jointly developed several common, *software alliance applications* (including portfolio accounting, customer information, access security, corporate actions and income collection, transaction entry and maintenance, organization information, financial instrument and price information, and payment processing) and several proprietary applications (including performance measurement, analytics, customer workstations, customer reporting, and tax services) (Rolandi, 1993). The financial services industry participants in the software alliance benefit from not having to invent the same wheel four times; and, they can also benefit from their proprietary applications developed jointly with IBM and FTI.

Telecommunications and Data Feeds

Walter Wriston, in his recent book entitled *The Twilight of Sovereignty: How the Information Revolution is Transforming our World*, comments:

> *The new world financial market is not a geographic location to be found on a map but, rather, more than two hundred thousand electronic monitors in trading rooms all over the world that are linked together. (Wriston, 1992, p. 62)*

More than any other single transformational force, the advent of modern, real-time and low cost telecommunications has become the glue that holds the world markets together.

There are two aspects of telecommunications which are critical to trading and treasury operations: the "data highways", that is, the cables that connect the vendor data feeds to the traders' screens, and the "voice highways", that is, the cables that connect the traders' clients and other traders to the trader's phone system. Waters Information Services (1991) points to *high-density key telephone systems* as the primary technology enabling voice communications,

```
WORLD SPOT CURRENCY MARKET  COPR 1989 TELERATE  PAGE 263
          [LAST FIVE UPDATES IN EACH CURRENCY]
```

PAGE	BANK		YEN		GMT
3652	D G BANK	FFT	144.05	-15	16:53
3693	NAT WEST	LDN	144.05	-15	16:51
6252	BERGEN BK	BER	144.00	-10	16:51
3150	RBC	TOR	144.05	-15	16:51
0513	UBS	ZUR	144.00	-10	16:50
HI	0:25 144.73-		143.95	14:52	LO
PAGE	BANK		DMK		GMT
3530	ANDELSBANK	COP	1.6685	-92	16:53
3327	AKTIVBANK	VEJ	1.6682	-89	16:53
3540	CR SUISSE	ZUR	1.6675	-85	16:53
3150	R B C	TOR	1.6670	-80	16:53
3552	D G BANK	FFT	1.6680	-90	16:53
HI	0:13 1.6950-		1.6645	14:52	LO

```
NEW TTS USERS: MIDLAND, HAMBROS, CHASE NY,RABOBK UTRECHT, CA LYON PAR,MBISHI NY
01/08  11:41  TREASURY ANNOUNCES TAX AND LOAN CALLS, RESULTS . . . . . . . . . 4142
01/08  11:42  =GILTS: CONFUSION ON BUYBACKS RESUPRECTS MARKET JITTERS . . .4234
01/08  11:45  GILTS ENDING ON 3/4 AMID CONFUSION OVER GILTS BUY-IN POLICY . . 4158
01/08  11:46  STOCKS MOSTLY LOWER AS MARKET DRIFTS: DJIA UNCHANGED . . . . . 4116
01/08  11:47  NYMEX 1989 TRADING VOLUME -2-: PLATINUM VOLUME OFF 13 . . . 31765
01/08  11:49  OAPEC SAYS COOPERATION WITH EC PROMOTES EURO-ARAB TIES . . . 31825
```

Source: Waters Information Services, 1991

Figure 2: Telerate Page of Data

and they should be considered as a basic trading room technology. Trading platform phone systems handle anywhere from 40 to 120 lines, enable programmable and automated dialing to one of many potential locations (most often traders at other banks) and provide instantaneous identification of the firm from which an incoming call originates. Traders often hold multiple conversations at once—spanning the full range of the international markets to obtain relevant information—with the outcome of transactions involving millions of dollars depending on what transpires in the conversations. A trader's work is mentally and emotionally demanding, and the work environment is often hectic, literally bubbling with information obtained in phone conversations or via screen-based information sources.

The largest firms track the market by acquiring real-time data on specific market indicators, including Treasury bill and bond rates, foreign exchange spot and forward prices, and prices on options and futures. They also track real-time news from other markets, where new developments can influence money market prices. Data feeds are usually of two types: video and digital. *Video data feeds* are video images (based on analog signals) of pages that contain data about the market or a group of financial instruments in a fixed format. Video pages cannot be decomposed into individual elements, in the same way that a television viewer would be unable to pull product prices off of a televised advertisement and insert them into a spreadsheet program. *Digital data feeds,* on the other hand, can be manipulated to support computations for real-time financial decision modeling and early warning alarms of key changes in the market.

Examples of digital data sources relevant to a money market bank's trading and treasury functions include the Chicago Board Options Exchange, and the New York Stock Exchange, as well as market-specific services from firms such as Reuters, Telerate, ILX, Nikkei and Dow Jones. These "quote vendors" (as they are often called by industry practitioners) consolidate data from the exchanges, from central banks worldwide, and from governmental or private sector sources, and repackage it for digital transmission.

An example of a Telerate screen, which displays foreign exchange quotes, is shown in Figure 2. As well as numeric data, there is also textual news data at the bottom of the screen. The largest international commercial banks also purchase specialized data sets for infrequent or customized analyses.

David Leinweber, chief scientist at Integrated Analytics, a firm specializing in the development of pre-trade applications that are embedded in financial market trader workstation software, comments about the importance of high quality data in the context of "intelligent" securities trading systems:

> *All data feeds are subject to errors and delays. When these arise at the primary feed provided by exchanges or NASD (the National Association of Securities Dealers), they will generally be passed on without correction by the providers of the feeds. Other errors and delays can arise from causes internal to the secondary feed distributor, such as line problems, radio interference, and queuing delays in processing. Published reports cite instances of one feed lagging another by up to one minute. In the absence of accurate time stamping at the point of origin, the feed integration system must take the responsibility for selecting the most timely data. Obvious transmission errors need to be detected and corrected. Human users will spot these errors, but it is inefficient to require each and every analytic tool in the trader's arsenal to verify the same data repeatedly. (Leinweber, 1989, p. 313)*

In summary, there is already an extensively installed base of technologies that make up the infrastructure of trading and treasury operations. We now present a new conceptual framework to characterize re-engineering opportunities, with the ultimate goal of identifying ways that international financial services firms can better leverage information technology to improve their business performance.

RE-ENGINEERING TRADING AND TREASURY: AN EVALUATIVE FRAMEWORK FOR SENIOR MANAGEMENT ACTION

Senior executives in international commercial banking talk about re-engineering in the same terms as the most well-known industry consultants. Re-engineering primarily means obliterating, to the furthest extent possible, all "non-value-added" activities that occur in the business. In practice, this means eliminating a task, job, role or operational process if it does not add to the revenue stream of the bank in a direct or indirect manner, or if it adds costs that are not deemed essential to support the operation. Based on the case studies that are cited in the industry press, operational cost cutting, for example, in international funds transfer, loan review, check processing and letter of credit operations is the most often pursued goal. This normally results in improved operational performance and productivity measures, such as funds transfer inquiries resolved per inquiry staff member, operational errors as a percentage of total transaction throughput, or the number of letters of credit or documentary collection transactions processed per clerk.

The emphasis placed on the role of technology is one of *substitution*: rising variable costs can be replaced with a fixed cost technological component that gets the job done as well (or perhaps even better) at a lower (or nearly equal) cost. In this section, we will consider the following question: Given that re-engineering efforts can be aimed at either cutting costs and increasing efficiency, or achieving product and service differentiation to leverage revenues, which of these offers the greater opportunity in the trading and treasury arena?

We can answer this question by employing perspectives derived from a framework for understanding re-engineering in terms of two elements:

(1) the *re-engineering objective function*, and the constraints within which senior management can attempt to optimize it; and,
(2) the *business value levers* that senior managers have at hand to affect the business outcome measured by the objective function.

We will now examine each of these in greater detail.

Primal and Dual: Formalizing Revenue and Cost-Driven Re-engineering Alternatives

Management science, operations research and managerial economics suggest avenues along which it might be possible to construct a formal evaluative framework in which to analyze the re-engineering opportunities in trading and treasury operations. An analyst should begin by asking the basic question: What is the objective function that re-engineering efforts seek to optimize? In our view, there are two general approaches that parallel the ideas we have already expressed above, and which we will call *primal side re-engineering* and *dual side re-engineering*. The terms come from the primal and dual problems that are often the subject of basic analysis in introductory texts in these areas (See, for example, Varian, 1985). They are based on the idea that a rational managerial decisionmaker will undertake actions that seek to maximize the expected value of the firm, subject to the contents of a set of constraints that match the business, operational and managerial environments in which decisionmaking occurs.

Primal side re-engineering seeks to solve the *primal problem*, which broadly focuses on revenues as a means to deliver profits:

Maximize Profit = (Unit Price - Unit Cost) * Units Sold

Subject to: Total Costs ≤ Corporate Operating Budget

The operating budget acts as a constraint within which senior management can adjust two key variables that deliver revenue: units sold and unit price. Applying this idea to trading and treasury operations, primal side re-engineering efforts basically are meant to create leverage on these two variables. They are meant to assist traders and sales professionals to effectively price the money market instruments in which they deal, and to provide the right services and products so as to generate transaction volumes that match the firm's operational scale. Primal side re-engineering, then, is re-engineering undertaken to support the trader as a seller. Done well, for example, the pricing can be adjusted to create aggressive, business-attracting margins, or to meet the demand for high margin trades that other competitors are not able to do competitively. We will shortly investigate the content of the leverage that can be created via *business value levers*, and how the objective function results can be improved.

Dual side re-engineering treats the cost-related variables by providing a solution to the *dual problem*, which can be stated as follows:

Minimize Total Costs = Unit Costs * Units Sold

Subject to: Profit ≥ Targeted Managerial Profit

Here, targeted profitability (perhaps set by the senior manage-

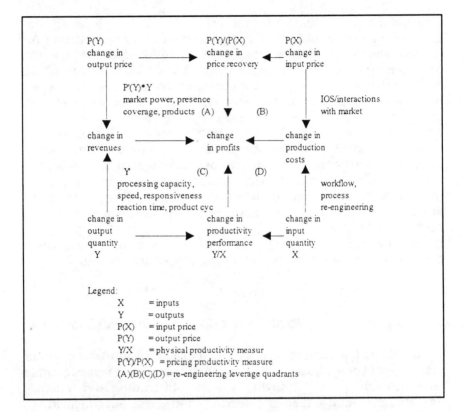

Figure 3: American Productivity Center Profit Variance Matrix Applied to Classify Re-engineering Business Value Levers

ment committee outside of trading and treasury operations) is identified in terms of the firm's business plan, and represents a real goal to which management's actions and results can be compared. Cost minimization in this context is only rational to the extent that the business activities that are supported continue to generate sufficient revenues to enable the business to meet its stated goals.

Thinking about what re-engineering efforts can do for the firm— in terms of the primal and the dual problems—provides a natural analogy to the real simultaneity in which trading and treasury business decisionmaking occurs. It is not possible, for example, to offer trading and treasury services that are highly innovative and very attractive to potential clients, and thus are likely to generate new revenues for the bank, if there is no assurance that marginal revenues (inconclusive of the various risks to which trading activities are subject that will increase expected costs) will be positive. Similarly, an obvious candidate for cost cutting in trading and treasury is the elimination of the order taker. But substituting technology that enables the trader to make a trade by entering it directly into a system via keystrokes, manipulating a mouse or using voice recognition, must be shown to deliver real cost advantages over the human intermediary and not adversely affect other aspects of the business process that ensure quality and provide second checks for errors.

Let us formalize our discussion of the leverage points that are available to senior managers to achieve improved results on the primal and the dual sides in trading and treasury operations.

A Re-engineering Action Leverage Matrix

Using the primal and dual problem analogies opens up a range of useful perspectives that have been employed for analyzing profitability and cost engineering problems elsewhere. One that is especially interesting is a framework that was originally proposed by the American Productivity Center to explain profit variance in terms that reflect the change in productivity (the dual side) times the change in price recovery (the primal side) (American Productivity Center, 1981; von Loggerenberg and Cucchiano, 1981-82). Here we will employ a similar framework to define and analyze the effects that re-engineering can have on trading and treasury profitability variances, as shown in the *re-engineering action leverage matrix* of Figure 3 below.

Decomposition Analysis Approach

Figure 3 depicts traditional accounting analysis in its most aggregated form in the center row, in which changes in profits are evaluated as changes in revenues (the output side) and changes in production costs (the input side). Re-engineering efforts, however, produce more subtle, less readily aggregated effects on the trading and treasury process. To understand the levers that are offered to change profitability, we need to further decompose the changes in revenues and production costs into changes in prices (of the inputs and outputs) and quantities (also of the inputs and outputs).

For example, by focusing on the bottom row, the analyst is able to discern the separable impacts of changing the technical efficiency of production. Re-engineering can increase output quantity while holding the operational inputs fixed, or it can decrease the input quantity while holding output fixed. Similarly, the top row focuses the analyst's attention on the elements of primal side price recovery. Re-engineering efforts that affect price recovery are perhaps of greatest interest to management: a bank that operates as a market leader in the trading of a specific financial instrument possesses special power to turn the market in its favor through the force of its own moves. As a buyer in the market, the firm is likely to be able to change the input prices that it observes, while as a seller it may also have the power to influence the prices at which it can turn trades around on behalf of its clients. (We are not arguing against the efficient markets hypothesis here; our contention is that firms that are able to discover different information earlier, and then act on it, can generate input and output price leverage and market power that will improve their price recovery.)

Column-wise analysis offers additional insights. In contrast to traditional managerial accounting analysis, one can think of changes in profits as being driven (still in aggregate, but now somewhat more descriptively) by changes in productivity and changes in price recovery. The leftmost column focuses on how re-engineering efforts can influence the revenue output side, through changes in the output quantity and changes in the output price. The rightmost column relates changes in input quantity and changes in input cost to arrive at total costs.

Thus, the right quadrants (B) and (D) focus on reducing production costs of trading and treasury products through decreasing the price (such as the cost of funds) or quantity of the inputs. The left quadrants (A) and (C) focus on adding value through an increase in output or through value-added differentiation that results in higher prices or new products.

Quadrant Opportunity Analysis

We think that significant opportunities for re-engineering trading and treasury operations exist in quadrants (A) and (C) on the left hand side. This is especially interesting because this view contrasts with the usual goal of cutting production costs. This is often mentioned in press reports of mergers and acquisitions involving large banks. For example, NationsBank intends to save $400 million, from reducing its annual operating costs, through merging with C&S/Sovran (Crockett, 1992). Chemical had saved $50 million by the end of April, 1992 (Lipin, 1992), and intends to save another $525 million by the end of 1993 (Gullo, 1993), from consolidating its operations with Manufacturers Hanover Corp. Our view also contrasts with the moves towards big dollar outsourcing contracts, such as Continental Bank. "[T]o cut costs and remain competitive, the big Chicago bank [Continental] has been quietly automating certain trust functions through outsourcing (Fraser, 1993, p. 12A)."

Re-engineering activities that affect output price (quadrant A) and output quantity (quadrant C) emphasize different aspects of the IT platform. The lower left quadrant (C) captures speed, reaction time, capacity and other important elements that enable transaction volume to be brought to the bank. Decreasing reaction time allows a bank to increase its trading volume by seizing more opportunities— recall that Morgan Stanley Japan executed more trades because it was faster than its competitors. Re-engineering efforts here can buy lead time and short-term revenue gains, but long-term, the technologies that must be invested in here tend to become commodities. They are adoptable by all competitors, in time as the technologies become cheaper and more readily implemented. So senior managers should recognize that the barriers to re-engineering imitation are probably quite low—low enough so that the business value benefits are temporary gains only, and not the building blocks of sustainable competitive advantage. However, even though the benefit may only be temporary, this does not mean that the bank should not invest in these technologies—it may be necessary to invest simply to keep up with the competition.

Re-engineering efforts that occur in the upper left quadrant (A) affect output prices. A change in output price can only be obtained when the technological enhancements to a bank's trading and treasury operating capabilities lever market power, market coverage, and new product delivery. Changes in this quadrant deal with the trading and treasury infrastructure, not as commodity technologies that are easily imitated, but as an integrated "value platform" that exploits the unique blend of expertise, capabilities and other resources available within the firm (Kauffman and Lally, 1993). *Even though the information technology may be considered to be a commodity, the value platform is not: it is unique to every firm.*

Re-engineering the activities in quadrants (A) and (C) invariably requires changing the roles of the actors involved in the process; the roles are usually either eliminated, enhanced, or offloaded to the customer or supplier. In order to increase market coverage and new product delivery, quadrant (A) activities, roles must be enhanced. For example, to increase market coverage, the role of the sell-side lending officer or treasury management product specialist will broaden to incorporate the change in coverage. In addition, these agents' roles will also increase in depth; as new treasury and trading products are introduced, the sell-side will need to be able to represent the bank's new product capabilities. In the pre-trade phase, the sell-side actor will need increased access to information and analytics in order to proactively assess client's needs and to identify how they may be met through the increased diversity of products. In quadrant (C), the role of the risk manager is enhanced. Because processing capacity increases and reaction time decreases, the risk manager will be able to perform more sophisticated analytics in the same amount of time.

The potential results of re-engineering efforts undertaken in quadrants (B) and (D) are also worthwhile to point out. The usual interpretation of what impacts re-engineering can deliver is found in quadrant (D). Gains are made by eliminating redundant and non-value-added tasks; however, we again must emphasize that such gains may not deliver sustainable competitive advantage. They must be coupled with simultaneous actions on the primal side to ensure that business volume will materialize.

Re-engineering workflows, quadrant (D), also alters the roles of the actors in the treasury and trading process. For example, unnecessary checkpoints, and the roles associated with them, can be eliminated. Data entry and validation become part of the role of the trader. For instance, voice recognition technology is being tested to help the trader enter and verify trades. In fact, the data entry role of the trader can also be taken up by the client (the client becomes the trader) if access to the bank's trading system is provided to the customer. Re-engineered post-trade processes yield simplified processes and fewer errors. In addition, if customers are provided access to the trading system, they can then perform their own inquiries. In effect, part of the service role, typically performed by customer service representatives, is off-loaded to the customer. Fundamentally, as with quadrants (A) and (C), this functionality requires an integrated IT platform that is easily linked to the customer.

The benefits of re-engineering activities undertaken in quadrant (B), where changes are made to affect input prices, are somewhat harder to predict. Examples of changes in this quadrant include intra-firm high-speed voice and data communications linking the firm's traders in different markets. A second aspect is efforts that enable interorganizational information systems to be put into place. A recent example is the Chicago Board of Trade's (CBOT) GLOBEX electronic trading system. GLOBEX enables foreign exchange trading to continue outside the normal hours that the primary markets are in operation in the United States. The reason that we believe that the benefits of re-engineering may be harder to predict in this quadrant is that the impacts of a single firm's re-engineering actions may be constrained by the extent to which other firms are re-engineering. For example, Chase Manhattan Corp. is trying to re-engineer its swaps trading process. It is trying to convince other banks to join together to establish a clearinghouse to trade currency and interest-rate derivatives (Layne, 1992). The success of this re-engineering effort depends on the willingness of the other banks to join the clearinghouse. When firms do join together, industry standards normally emerge, creating beneficial externalities that can drive input costs down for all market participants in the same way and formalize the manner in which everyone conducts business.

Although such externality or standards-based re-engineering may not yield competitive advantage for any single firm, the industry as a whole will produce more valuable services to its consumers. In this regard, Breshnahan's (1986) characterization of IT investments in the financial services industry as yielding "spillover" benefits is especially fitting: re-engineering efforts, when aggregated across firms which are responding to similar developments in hardware, software and telecommunications technologies, can lead to the restructuring of the industry as a whole. The move to truly global trading and treasury management on behalf of multinational corporations and banks, and the changing technological landscape that has made it possible, are bellwether developments that indicate the real power and long-term potential of re-engineering in the industry.

TIMING, RISK AND RE-ENGINEERING PLANNING CHOICES: SOME MANAGERIAL RECOMMENDATIONS

The re-engineering action leverage matrix that we discussed above is intended to assist senior managers to conceptualize where the paybacks from re-engineering are most likely to arise in trading and treasury operations. It suggests a number of guidelines and ideas for senior managers that they may find useful. Our first two guidelines are the most obvious:

Guideline #1:   *Take into account that re-engineering efforts in trading and treasury operations can yield both primal and dual side impacts, and that the gains can vary in their magnitude and their expected duration.*

Guideline #2:   *Don't justify or gauge the benefits of re-engineering solely on the basis of accounting profits: revenues less costs; employ the price recovery margin and productivity metrics to decompose the impacts and evaluate the key business value levers that enable the firm to optimize its re-engineering objective function.*

Salomon Brothers, for example, re-engineered its front and back office operations to save $30 million to $60 million a year. The firm migrated its trading systems from costly mainframes to cheaper workstations (Schmerken, 1991).

In addition to looking at the levers emphasized in the action matrix, senior managers should be concerned about how to manage the re-engineering process to minimize the risks associated with bringing in the new hardware, software and telecommunications technologies. Our remaining guidelines point out the importance of timing and risk, and how they should be treated in managerial planning choices related to re-engineering of trading and treasury operations.

Guideline #3: Recognize the multiple sources of risk associated with implementing new technologies called for in re-engineering programs, especially in terms of the adequacy of the technical skill base and managerial know how within the organization.

Some re-engineering efforts in the trading and treasury arena stretch the available technical and human resources in ways that are wholly unexpected. One example from our own work is The First Boston Corporation's investment in a $120 million "New Trades Processing Architecture". It required the firm to construct its own computer aided software engineering (**CASE**) tool, when a study commissioned by the firm's chief information officer found that there were no available tools to cost-effectively accomplish software development to support global trading (Banker and Kauffman, 1991).

Other concerns include market and technical risks. During the late 1980s, there were a number of firms that placed bets that IBM's advanced PC-based operating system, OS/2, was going to be the dominant operating system in a few years time. Early trading and treasury platform investments were subject to the market risk that OS/2-compatible software would not emerge rapidly enough to bring the firms adequate payback for their early OS/2 investments. And, there was also the technical risk that the operating system would not develop along the trajectory that IBM projected, causing whatever investments were made to be rapidly obsolete. The record shows, of course, that Microsoft's WINDOWS has largely prevailed, even though there is enough of an installed base to have made OS/2 viable for additional development.

Guideline #4: Keep in mind that investments in IT that re-engineer the trading and treasury operating infrastructure are really capital expenditures whose greatest potential payoffs can arise in ways that are planned and managed, and also in ways that are altogether unforeseen.

Investments in infrastructure often yield benefits that cannot be predicted with any degree of precision (Weill, 1993). The development of a flexible IT-based trading and treasury infrastructure creates an "information technology option" for the firm which invests in it (Benaroch and Kauffman, 1993; Dos Santos, 1991; Kambil, Henderson and Mohsenzadeh, 1993; Kauffman, 1993). An information technology option can be exercised by the firm that invests in infrastructure or a new technology, and then later learns how to reinvest, building on top of the infrastructure to create a new capability that would not be possible in the absence of the infrastructure or the learning that occurred. As we pointed out earlier, senior managers in the industry can be reasonably sure that some of these unforeseen applications will come from further reducing "information float" in trading and treasury operations. Thus, a platform that enables "just-in-time everything" is important as the ultimate objective; not having this capability can lead to serious competitive disadvantage down the road.

Guideline #5:   Re-engineer the trading and treasury platform to balance the potential benefits of enhancing "reach" and "range".

Keen's notions of "reach" and "range" are useful here (Keen, 1991; Keen, 1993). Just-in-time functionality on the trading platform is aimed at enhancing range, by enabling information to be shared across the family of applications that enable an international bank to deliver trading and treasury services. For example, one of the goals of Salomon's re-engineering effort was to provide position information to traders across existing incompatible systems (Schmerken, 1991). The business value of current information is evident in so many ways: in rational pricing, in arbitrage identification and programmed trading, in real-time position risk management, and intra-day funds control for trading customers. The benefits are spread across the pre-trade, trade execution and post-trade processes.

It also makes sense to make investments that enhance reach, that is, enabling your systems to deliver their services to "anyone anywhere". For example, some of the pre-trade activity aimed at prospecting for new clients and identifying counterparties to trades, and interest rate and currency swaps could be enhanced by enabling customers to "connect" to the pre-trade system and post information about instruments in which they might be interested. (The logical extension to this idea is a third-party electronic market for a broader array of treasury services, which would create a major challenge to commercial bank servicing, in the same way that the new electronic securities markets are creating concerns among the old guard at the American and New York Stock Exchanges.) The goal here should be to support the process of more efficiently finding hedging and complex trading transaction counter-parties, and to establish first mover advantages by enhancing reach using the IT platform. Post-trade systems, where information is communicated to the debit and credit parties in trading transactions, and funds transfers are made, require seamless links to other bank operating systems including: databases that feed treasury management workstations deployed in corporate treasurers' offices, and the transaction advice and funds movement systems.

Guideline #6: In the absence of certainty about rapidly evolving industry standards for hardware, software and other related concerns, re-engineer to build a viable and broad "base" to hedge your bets in the "market for standards".

As the industry press and knowledgeable observers suggest (Slater, 1993), the standards in trading and treasury operations, unlike check processing and electronic funds transfer, have yet to emerge. As a result, there is really no such thing as an "open system", and senior managers invariably have to gamble on which hardware vendors have the staying power, which technologies will reach critical mass in installed base, and which software packages will emerge as the industry choices.

The solution here is to keep investing in the broadening base of technologies that will define open systems five years from today: SNA and OSI at the network level, TCP/IP at the LAN level, client-server systems, SQL server databases, X.400 mail, and so on. The general guideline for management in deciding whether a base technology should be invested in is whether there is a reasonable expectation that the installed base will reach critical mass in the near future, if it has not reached that point already. This leads to a related recommendation:

Guideline #7: The main issue is balancing timing and risk: committing to a standard or platform too early entails unacceptable technical, organizational and market risks; committing too late can mean certain failure if "functionality risks" make it impossible to compete.

The costs of dealing with the failure of an infrastructure technology in treasury and trading, like an on-line transaction processing system failure, can be staggering. For example, the recent explosion in the World Trade Center shut down the money market activities of many foreign banks located there (Iida, 1993a; Iida, 1993b). Reliability and fail-safe backups, however, are expensive. The obvious solution to this problem is to build in redundancy, both on-site and off-site, and re-engineer to enable a smooth transition that will sustain operating capabilities in the event of business disruption. Maintaining service capabilities in the money market in the event of a failure is crucial, and the potential adverse effects of any disruption are only compounded by the tight cross-market, cross-border and cross-time zone linkages that are at the heart of the international banking business.

CONCLUSION

Knowing how much to invest in information technology and re-engineering, and how to invest it, is a difficult decision for senior managers in the financial services industry. Doing cost/benefit analyses for individual applications can overlook integration and connectivity problems which invariably occur after the individual applications have been developed. On the one hand, trying to evaluate infrastructure investments is difficult since they often lead to yet unforeseen benefits; on the other hand, justifying infrastructure investments by hoping that they will lead to benefits down the line is naïve.

We have provided some structure to this decision in treasury and trading operations in three ways. First, breaking down the process into three sub-phases delineates the various activities involved and how they are carried out. In deciding whether and how to re-engineer, management must ask itself which sub-process it wants to concentrate its resources on. Re-engineering pre-trade processes will result in satisfying a customer's needs better. Errors and reaction time will decrease if management concentrates on redesigning trade execution processes. Re-engineering post-trade processes can improve customer satisfaction as customer inquiries can be answered in real-time, and can improve risk management as instrument, customer, and market exposures can be calculated more and more frequently, towards real-time calculation.

Second, examining the technology platform will reveal the sophistication of the existing system, and the extent of the re-engineering that will need to take place to meet management's goals. For example, the move to real-time decision-making requires faster hardware: is a supercomputer necessary, or will a network of workstations suffice? In addition, senior managers need to decide whether they want to develop their own proprietary systems, or buy an open system. Regarding data feeds, a firm may have a video data feed coming in, but want a digital data feed so that it can process the information with its own systems.

Third, using a re-engineering action leverage matrix highlights some of the variables that management has control over to change. These variables include the prices and quantities of the inputs and outputs. The matrix highlights price recovery margins and productivity metrics, as well as the usual accounting metrics of changes in revenues and production costs.

ACKNOWLEDGMENTS

The authors wish to acknowledge a number of individuals who offered advice to help us shape the ideas presented in this paper. At the top of our list is Brian Slater, Vice President, Global Bank Technology, Chemical Bank, New York, who hosted multiple visits to the bank's money market trading operations, and generously fielded our questions; his answers helped to shape our views of the potential that re-engineering has in trading and treasury. We also appreciated ongoing inputs from Robert Mark, Managing Director, Global Risk Management, Chemical Bank, who convinced us that re-engineering in trading and treasury doesn't just apply to physical workflows: it also involves changing management-trader and market-firm relationships. Rich Rolandi, Vice President, Financial Technologies International, shared with us his broad knowledge of re-engineering, as it applies to trading and treasury data architecture; some of the themes that we have discussed relate to standards-based re-engineering developed as a direct consequence of our meetings with him. We acknowledge Dan Taylor, President, *United States Council for International Banking*, for ongoing sponsorship of *Project 1990s: The US Council on International Banking's Study on Information Technology Investment and International Banking Performance*. The member firms of this industry organization comprise the field study sites for this research. Finally, Vasant Dhar and Robert J. Kauffman would like to acknowledge the following organizations, which provided financial support for this research: IBM Corporation; Nippon Electric Corporation; and The Salomon Brothers Center (for research in finance and financial markets) and the United-States Japan Business and Economics Research Center, Stern School of Business, New York University. Any errors in this document are the sole responsibility of the authors.

REFERENCES

Adrian, J., and Kelleher, K. (1993). Speed Drives Morgan Past Other Brokers in Tokyo, *International Herald Tribune*, 1, 13.

Apte, U., Sankar, C. S., Thakur, M., and Turner, J. (1990). Reusability Strategy for Development of Information Systems: Implementation Experience of a Bank. *MIS Quarterly*, 14 (4), 421-431.

Banker, R. D., and Kauffman, R. J. (1992). Measuring the Development Performance of Computer Aided Software Engineering (ICASE): A Synthesis of Field Study Results from the First Boston Corporation. In *Software Engineering Economics*, T. Gulledge (ed.), New York, NY: Springer Verlag Publishers.

Banker, R. D., and Kauffman, R. J. (1991). Reuse and Productivity: An Empirical Study of Integrated Computer Aided Software Engineering at the First Boston Corporation. *MIS Quarterly*, 15 (3), 375-401.

Banks and Technology: Cure-all or snake oil? *The Economist*, 325 (7779), 1992, 21-24.

Benaroch, M., and Kauffman, R. J. (1993). An Illustrative Assessment of Option Pricing Methods Applied to the Evaluation of Strategic Investments in Information Technology. In process.

Brennan, P. J. (1992). More Quotes for the Buck, *Wall Street & Technology*, 9 (6), 44-47.

Breshnahan, T. (1986) Measuring the Spillovers from Technical Advance: Mainframe Computers in Financial Services. *American Economic Review*, 76 (4), 742-755.

Caldwell, B., and Violino, R. (1991). Underdeveloped Assets: MIS Scrambles As Banks Find They Lack the Systems Needed to Monitor Risky Loans, *InformationWeek*, 312, 10-11.

Davenport, T. (1993). *Process Innovation: Reengineering Work through Information Technology*, Boston: Harvard Business School Press.

Davenport, T., and Short, J. (1990). The New Industrial Engineering: Information Technology and Business Process Redesign, *Sloan Management Review*, 31 (4), 11-27.

Fraser, Bruch. Continental Turns to Outsourcing for Corporate Trust. *American Banker's Management Strategies*, 158 (11), 12A.

Green, C., First Manhattan Consulting Group. (1993). Reengineer the Retail Securities Business to Improve Client Service and Productivity. In *Technology Integration & Re-Engineering for Trading Operations*. Institute for International Research, New York.

Gullo, K. (1993). Chemical, Hanover Branches To Be Unified by March 22. *American Banker*, 158 (38), 1, 6.

Hammer, M. (1990). Re-engineering Work: Don't Automate, Obliterate, *Harvard Business Review*, 68 (4), 104-112.

Hanley, T., Rosenberg, J., DiArista, C., Krahmer, E., Ross, M. (1986). Technology and Banking: The Implications of Strategic Expenditures, New York: Salomon Brothers, Inc.

Hultman, C. W. (1990). *The Environment of International Banking*. Englewood Cliffs, New Jersey: Prentice Hall, Inc.

Iida, J. (1993a). Trade Center Blast Halts Financial Firms. *American Banker*, 158 (39), 3.

Iida, J. (1993b). Trade Center Blast Leaves Many Banks Scrambling for Space. *American Banker*, 158 (40), 3.

Kambil, A., Henderson, J. and Mohsenzadeh H. (1993). Strategic Management of Information Technology Investments: An Options Perspective. In Banker, R. D., Kauffman, R. J., and Mahmood, M. A. (Eds.), *Strategic Information Technology Management*. Harrisburg, PA: Idea Group Publishing.

Kang, P., and Zenios, S. A. (1992). Complete Prepayment Models for Mortgage-backed Securities, *Management Science*, 38 (11), 1665-1685.

Kauffman, R. J. Pricing Information Technology Options: Application to a Trading Expert System. In R. J. Kauffman, R. M. Mark and B. W. Weber, *Information Technology and the Financial Markets: Design and Managing Today's Trading Platform*. Homewood, IL: Business One Irwin Publishers, forthcoming.

Kauffman, R. J., and Kriebel, C. H. (1988). Measuring and Modeling the Business Value of Information Technology. In Strassmann, P. A., Berger, P., Swanson, B., Kriebel, C. H., and Kauffman, R. J. (Eds.), *Measuring Business Value of Information Technologies*. Washington, DC: ICIT Press.

Kauffman, R. J., and Lally, L. (1993). A Value Platform Perspective on Customer Access Information Technology. Working paper, Center for Research in Information Systems, Stern School of Business, New York University.

Karimi, J. (1990). An Asset-based Systems Development Approach to Software Reusability. *MIS Quarterly*, 14 (2), 179-198.

Keen, P. G. (1993). Information Technology and the Management Difference: A Fusion Map. *IBM Systems Journal*, 32 (1), 17-39.

Keen, P. G. (1991). *Shaping the Future: Business Design through Information Technology.* Boston, MA: Harvard Business School Press.

Layne, R. Chase Seeking Partners to Set Up Clearing House for Swaps Trading. *American Banker*, 157, 1, 16.

Lipin, S. Chemical, NationsBank Claim Savings From Mergers Are Ahead of Schedule. *Wall Street Journal*, April 27, 1992, B9.

Michaels, J. (1992). Merrill's "Super" Strategy, *Wall Street & Technology*, 10 (4), 17-22.

Michaels, J. (1992). Unparalleled Performance, *Wall Street & Technology*, 9 (8), 81-84.

Rolandi, R., Financial Technologies International. (1993). Back- and Middle-Office Systems: Coordinating All the Pieces across Functional & Product Lines. In *Technology Integration & Re-Engineering for Trading Operations.* Institute for International Research, New York.

Rummler, G. and Brache, A. (1990). *Improving Performance: How to Manage the White Space on the Organization Chart.* San Francisco: Jossey-Bass Publishers.

Schmerken, I. (1992a). Bullish on Savings, *Wall Street & Technology*, 9 (8), 60-69.

Schmerken, I. (1992b). Distributing the Back Office, *Wall Street & Technology*, 9 (9), 83-94.

Schmerken, I. (1992c). Middle Office Closes Trading Gap, *Wall Street & Technology*, 9 (12), 18-27.

Schmerken, I. (1991). Salomon's Systems For The 21st Century, *Wall Street & Technology*, 8 (9), 15-26.

Schwartzman, S. (1992). The Automated World Explorer, *Wall Street & Technology*, 9 (10), 39-50.

Smith, R. and Walter, I. (1990). *Global Financial Services*, New York: Harper Business.

Steiner, T. and Teixeira, D. (1990). *Technology in Banking: Creating Value and Destroying Profits*, Homewood, Illinois: Business One Irwin.

Total Performance Measurement. (1981). Houston, TX: American Productivity Center.

Stigum, M. (1990). *The Money Market*, Homewood Illinois: Dow Jones-Irwin

Varian, H. *Microeconomic Analysis: Second Edition.* New York, NY: John Wiley, 1986.

Venkatraman, N. (1991). IT-Induced Business Reconfiguration *The Organizational Transformation.* In M.S. Morton (Ed.), *The Corporation of the 1990s: Information Technology and Organizational Transformation.* Cambridge, England: Oxford University Press.

von Loggerenberg, B. J., and Cucchiano, S. J. (1981). Productivity Measurement and the Bottom Line. *National Productivity Review*, 1.

Waters Information Services. (1991). *Market Data and the Trading Room: A Survey of Concepts, Systems and Vendors*, Binghamton, New York.

Weill, P. (1993). The Role and Value of Information Technology Infrastructure: Some Empirical Observations. In Banker, R. D., Kauffman, R. J., and Mahmood, M. A. (Eds.), *Strategic Information Technology Management.* Harrisburg, PA: Idea Group Publishing.

Wriston, W. (1992). *The Twilight of Sovereignty: How the Information Revolution is Transforming our World.* New York: Charles Scribner's Sons.

Zenios, S. A. (1991). Massively Parallel Computations for Financial Planning Under Uncertainty. In J. Mesirov (Ed.), *Very Large Scale Computing in the 21st Century*. Philadelphia, PA: SIAM.

SECTION 4

Information Systems for International Accounting

Although the chapters in Section 3 were focused primarily on the specific concerns of international financial management that relate to financial services, we return in this section to the issues that confront corporate managers in dealing with the globalization of their operations. In particular, the next two chapters deal with the difficulties of the accounting function as the multinational corporation attempts to reconcile differences in procedures and requirements across entitities in an array of countries. Both pieces in this section conclude that developments in information technology hold the key to "success" in effective international accounting management.

In the next chapter, Jim Gauntt offers first a brief tutorial on accounting issues, standards, and how information systems and technology have long supported both transaction processing and financial reporting systems. He then outlines how international accounting variations lead to a number of specific difficulties in attempting to standardize reported data and information. He points out that international accountants tend to discuss "harmonization" rather than standardization as a reasonable goal" in most multinational settings. The chapter concludes with a discussion of the implications for the distribution of accounting information systems activities, in light of current realities in both the accounting profession and the availability of information and communications technologies.

In the second chapter of this section, Terry Campbell, Veronique Duperret-Tran, and Terry Campbell II similarly argue that differing accounting standards across borders make difficult the lives of international financial managers and accountants. The authors then suggest that this puts more pressure on information systems to provide even better information or, as they say, in a manner that is more integrative, instantaneous, intelligent, and intense than most exisiting systems. They further argue that the key driver of success in most firms will be the willingness and ability of the financial/accounting executive(s) to integrate technical and managerial responsibilities, in the sense that the options to change procedures and systems that are provided by new information technologies must be understood at the functional level. This particular chapter draws heavily from published case studies and upon the experiences of corporate managers who have participated in programs and worked with the faculty at the International Institute for Management Development (IMD) in Lausanne, Switzerland.

CHAPTER 10

Accounting in a Global Environment - An IS Perspective

JAMES E. GAUNTT, JR.
University of Arkansas at Little Rock

As companies move into the global marketplace, they find a wide variation in the accounting standards which are used in different countries. In the absence of a global set of accounting standards, it becomes necessary to consider the comparative standards which exist in each country where the firm conducts operations. This chapter explores the areas where accounting standards vary most widely, using the perspective of the information systems which support the accounting function. In considering this, the comparative accounting standards which affect transaction processing systems (i.e., those systems which process the routine activities of a company) are considered first. Next, the comparative accounting standards are considered which primarily affect only financial reporting systems. This approach affords considerable insight into the need to tailor accounting information systems to specific countries. Finally, the distribution of the international accounting function and the technology associated with it are discussed.

INTRODUCTION

The accounting function is supported in many companies today by sophisticated information systems (IS). The problems addressed by these information systems become more complicated when company operations are performed at more than one location, and increase further in complexity when company operations become global in scope. This chapter explores, first, the implications of variations in accounting standards which exist in the global environment on the information systems which support the accounting function, and, second, the complications which arise from the distribution of processing of the accounting function and the systems which support it to the outlying locations of a company.

Variations in accounting standards are analyzed in the context of the information systems which support the processing required by the accounting cycle. The chapter begins with a review of that cycle, discussing the dichotomy of accounting entries between those created by routine transaction processing and those accounting entries which are recorded only at the end of the reporting period.

The dichotomy between transaction processing and the end-of-period entries becomes a useful tool to analyze how accounting requirements change as company operations cross national lines. The accounting standards which vary most widely among countries are identified. They are classified at to whether they affect the transaction processing systems or the end-of-period entries. Each of the variations in accounting standards is also discussed in terms of its effect on the accounting system.

The significance of the focus on end-of-period entries as the primary point of variation in accounting standards is, first, the realization that many IS modules, when properly designed, can be readily transported across national lines, and second, the realization that changing a small number of end-of-period accounting entries can allow the ready re-statement of financial records in accordance with alternative accounting standards. The distribution of the accounting function and the associated information system processing is then discussed using the value chain concept developed by Porter (1985). The discussion begins with the general problems of the distribution decision and then considers factors which apply in a global environment.

IS SUPPORT OF ACCOUNTING

The Accounting Cycle - An IS Perspective

To understand the information systems which perform the accounting functions of businesses, it is important to understand the concept of the accounting cycle. The accounting cycle is the processing cycle of the economic events which affect a firm. The cycle begins with the occurrence of those events and continues through their reporting in the financial statements of the firm. It includes recording, summarizing, and posting. The reporting cycle varies among businesses from a weekly cycle to an annual cycle, with a monthly cycle common.

Because of the heavy volume of routine transactions, the accounting cycle depends on the *transaction processing systems* which are developed to handle these events. The frequent transactions which occur include, as examples, the sale of goods and the payment for goods and services. Transaction processing systems are typically designed to record and summarize transactions efficiently and accurately on an on-going basis throughout the reporting period. At the end of the reporting period, prior to the preparation of financial statements, the transactions from each of the (sometimes many) transaction processing systems are summarized and posted to the company's accounting records. Concurrent with routine transaction processing, but with a much lower frequency, data about non-routine transactions is also recorded. Non-routine transactions are those which do not occur frequently enough to justify developing special processing systems. Examples of non-routine transactions include issuance of stock or long term debt.

In addition to the accounting entries which result directly from transactions, the accounting system must also recognize certain economic events external to the company which affect its financial position. These external events do not result from transactions. Instead the entries reflect either the passage of time or some condition in the economic environment. As a result of the passage of time, for example, a liability may increase in order to pay interest on a loan. As an example of a condition in the economic environment, significant assets of the company such as inventory may experience a loss in value. The accounting entries which are made to reflect these events are called *adjusting entries*. Theoretically, both the adjusting entries and the entries for non-routine transactions could be made on an on-going basis. However, as a practical matter, they are usually made at the end of the reporting period.

After the accounting entries from transaction processing systems and from the end-of-period have been recorded, summarized and posted, the financial statements are created. These financial statements may be the traditional financial statements used by external investors, may be reports generated to assist management, or may be reports which are required by law.

Transaction Processing Systems

When accounting information systems are automated, the recording and processing of routine transactions are assisted by specialized transaction processing systems. These systems also then perform the summarization of those transactions for the accounting records. On a *financial reporting* cycle, which can vary from weekly to annually, an information system typically also provides for the recording of adjusting entries and the entries for non-routine transactions, the posting of those entries to the accounting records, the posting to the accounting records of the summarized entries from the transaction processing systems, and the creation of the financial reports.

With the automation of the accounting function, transaction processing systems have been extended in many companies beyond a passive accounting function to operational systems. Operational systems assist the processing of transactions from their initiation until entry in the accounting records. Consider, for example, the typical point-of-sale system used in retail stores. These systems use some form of optical reader to enter data about a transaction into an information system in a directly machine-readable form. Such systems are efficient and reduce the potential for a variety of transaction errors.

End-of-Period Entries

End-of-period entries are usually made directly into the financial reporting systems mentioned above. Because there are usually few end-of-period entries, most financial reporting systems maintain the specific identity of each entry when it is posted to the accounting records. These entries typically fall into one of three categories: first, allocation entries, which allocate an expenditure to the periods which it benefits; second, accrual entries, which record expected expenditures or revenues which should be associated with the current period; and third, contingency entries, which provide for probable future expenditures associated with the current period.

Where a company has a significant number of fixed assets, the depreciation calculations to allocate cost over the useful life of these are frequently automated. Such fixed asset systems maintain records of asset acquisition, choice of depreciation method, useful life, and other identifying data. Such a system creates a summary end-of-period entry which is entered into the financial reporting system.

In the case of the other end-of-period entries, an accountant typically performs calculations outside the accounting systems to construct the entries. In many cases, the entry—allocation, accrual, or contingency—is determined by complex accounting standards.

The technical nature of the calculations, the low frequency of the entries, and the judgment involved do not make automation of these entries desirable.

CREATION OF ACCOUNTING STANDARDS

Uses of Accounting Information

The reports produced by accounting systems are used by three classes of users: the external investor, the government, and management. The emphasis on financial accounting requirements—reporting to the external investor—in introductory courses can mask the importance of the other two areas. However, each of these users has a stake in the accounting standards used in creating those reports.

In the United States, the needs of the external investor are protected by the conventions known as Generally Accepted Accounting Principles (GAAP). In developing the standards which compose GAAP, the assumption is made that an external investor is not a part of company management and needs information to assist in making investment decisions. The standards which dictate the information to be made available to these investors have been established over time by several standard-setting bodies. The current group responsible for review and changes to GAAP is the Financial Accounting Standards Board - the FASB. The FASB is an independent body with representation from industry and the public accounting profession.

In the United States the second user of accounting information, the government, affects accounting information in three areas: the reporting required by the Securities and Exchange Commission (SEC) for certain public companies; the reporting required by business income tax returns; and the record-keeping required for employees by the personal income tax laws. The SEC requires, for companies which fall under its purview, reports which include not only the GAAP financial reports mentioned above but also additional or slightly different information.

The government also requires business tax returns prepared using accounting methods which differ in several areas from those required by GAAP. The differences in accounting methods which exist between GAAP and income tax reporting fall in two areas: first, for tax purposes, there are areas where incentives exist to influence certain decisions of firms into directions which are socially or economically desirable; second, differences exist in the choice of acceptable accounting method which affects the timing of revenues and expenses. Short term provisions to encourage certain corporate behavior serve a useful purpose. Further, these do not pose major problems in information collection in the accounting systems. The timing differences, on the other hand, pose a problem in that different accounting methods may be used in the preparation of tax returns than the methods which are used in preparation of financial statements.

Finally, the US government requires certain withholdings and record-keeping for employees in the payroll transaction processing system in accordance with federal and state income tax laws. Changes in levels and rates of withholding are made yearly. In addition, the treatment of certain fringe benefits has varied over the years.

The presentation of accounting information for the third user—management—is currently an art rather than a science, and those companies which have refined their accounting systems to support management decisions have enjoyed a strategic edge over companies with more traditional systems. In many cases, management reports involve extracting or summarizing data from the GAAP accounting records. However, management may also benefit from reports which include data not required for accounting purposes—such as the time of day when transactions took place. Further, management may wish to base its decisions in some cases on alternative accounting methods different from either GAAP or federal tax requirements. An example of this latter would be the use of market value rather than historical value of assets. Effective management reports frequently require the collection of information not needed by the accounting systems in addition to a query or reporting capability.

Limitations of Accounting Standards

The intent of GAAP is to provide information for the external investor. It is assumed that the external investor requires financial information which would allow that investor to make responsible decisions. However, once financial information is made public, it is also available to the competitors of a firm. Consequently, the accounting standards stop short of disclosure which might affect a company's competitive advantages. In setting standards, there is a constant balancing between the interests of individual companies and the interests of the investor.

Further, certain biases are built into accounting standards. To prevent an aggressive management from overstating income, the standards reflect, first, the principle of conservatism, and, next, the basis of historical cost. The principle of conservatism means that the accounting records will reflect losses early and gains late. The use of historical cost means that, in some cases, cost figures which are badly out-of-date will be used in making investment decisions, or worse, in making management decisions.

In the recent literature, a number of authors (Elliot, 1992, Elliot and Jacobson, 1991) plead for an overhaul of financial accounting standards to improve usefulness not only to the investor but also to management. At this time, however, the IS specialist must take the financial accounting requirements as fixed and can work only to improve the quality of information presented to management.

INTERNATIONAL ACCOUNTING VARIATIONS

The company moving into the global environment encounters a first level problem in dealing with the accounting for a foreign branch office or subsidiary in the financial statements of the parent company. United States GAAP covers the requirements for this reporting. Each account in the foreign financial statements must be converted to US currency, using conversion factors which differ for class of balance sheet or income statement account. The resulting financial statements are then consolidated with the statements of the parent company into a single set of statements.

The foreign subsidiary problem is straight-forward compared with the requirement to issue financial statements in a foreign country. No universal set of accounting standards exists which is used in all countries. Consequently, a knowledge of the comparative accounting standards is required for the countries where financial statements must be issued. While there have been several attempts to develop a standard setting body which would issue global standards, no accepted body currently exists. Furthermore, not all countries have a single body with the impact of the FASB.

This part of the chapter will, first, review current attempts to create international accounting standards. Next, it will discuss the problems which cause the variations in the accounting standards used in different countries. Finally, the "typical" variations in accounting standards will be identified which affect transaction processing systems, the end-of-period adjustments, and reporting.

Attempts to Create Global Standards

Current efforts to reduce the variation in accounting standards have shifted to the goal of harmonization rather than standardization of the standards. Harmonization recognizes that there will be variation in accounting standards between countries. However, to be able to use the financial statements from different countries, it is desirable to be able to reconcile the differences in the accounting standards which were used in the creation of these. As this harmonization occurs, it may be possible to reduce the differences in the accounting standards themselves.

There are currently three bodies acting to develop this harmonization: the International Accounting Standards Committee (IASC), the United Nations, and the European Economic Community (EEC). The IASC was formed in 1973 to work for the harmonization not only of accounting standards, but also of regulation. As of 1992, 31 standards had been issued by this group. Compliance with these standards remains voluntary, and only with support of the professional associations will there be acceptance of these standards.

The United Nations established an Intergovernmental Working Group of Experts on International Standards of Accounting and Reporting following the recommendations of a 1976 report. The group is not a standard setting body, but is working to consider whether the UN should promulgate accounting standards. However, in 1986, the United States withdrew from this group, at least in part because of the overlap between its charter and the IASC.

Finally the EEC has issued directives which address the comparability of financial statements for companies within the EEC. These directives leave the implementation to individual countries. As these important industrial nations move to harmonize their standards, there will likely be an impact on non-EEC countries.

Comparative Accounting Problems in the Global Environment

In the absence of a single, widely accepted authoritative body which sets international accounting standards, it seems appropriate to look at the way accounting standards are set in individual countries. In the United States and many other industrial nations, accounting standards are set by some combination of government, professional societies, and independent standard setting bodies which decide what accounting methods are acceptable practice. In other countries, no national accounting standards exist, creating an assortment of financial reports which vary dramatically with the accounting methods used.

Even in the industrial nations, the form of national tax laws affects accounting information in many ways, with many of the accounting methods used for tax purposes varying from those used for financial reporting. Consequently, it is important that the company in a global environment recognize the variations in national tax laws as well as accounting standards as it moves into new countries.

The following sections identify several areas where accounting standards vary and discuss how the accounting information system is affected by these variations. Belkaoui (Belkaoui 1993) identifies several areas where national accounting standards are most likely to vary. These areas were the basis for the following classifications.

Comparative Accounting Differences Which Affect
Transaction Processing

There are relatively few major differences in international accounting standards which affect the routine processing of transactions. Even in those cases where differences exist, the alternatives are well-defined.

Research and development costs are intended to benefit future periods, and should, if the funds are used wisely, create an asset. However, the potential exists for costs which should be charged to the current period to be classified as R&D cost. The effect of this would be an overstatement of income. Consequently, R&D costs are required by GAAP to be treated as an expense of the current reporting period under most conditions. The accounting standards used in some countries require these expenditures to be treated as capital investments which create assets.

Long term leases may, as an economic reality, transfer enough benefits of ownership to the lessee as to be equivalent to the purchase of an asset, with an associated loan to finance the purchase. Under GAAP, leases which meet certain conditions are required to be treated as capital leases. Leases which are very similar to these capital leases can be structured to violate the conditions, and are consequently treated as operating leases. Under the accounting standards used in some countries, all leases are treated as operating leases; alternately, in other countries, leases are capitalized which meet the intent but not the technical criteria of GAAP. In Japan, for example, the requirements for capital leases are set by the tax law, and leases are carefully structured to avoid this classification. Leases which would require capitalization in many countries are treated as operating leases.

Inventory costing under GAAP may be done using any of several historical cost methods—LIFO, FIFO, weighted average, or specific identification. All of these options may not exist under the accounting standards used in some countries. Further, under other accounting standards, valuation may be based on measures other than historical cost - replacement value, for example, or the NIFO (Next-In, First-Out) method used by management in some industries.

In each of these cases, at the point of recording, the alternative accounting method can be identified or the alternative accounting classification can be readily determined. In fact, a flexible approach to the design of the transaction processing system can allow preparation of financial reports according to whichever method is desired. In most cases, the only affect on transaction processing systems are the accounts which are charged for certain expenditures. In only a limited number of cases would the revenue-related systems be affected by accounting variations.

- The variations in R and D affect only the accounts to which expenditures are charged.
- For the lessee, again the lease accounting standards affect only the accounts to which expenditures are charged.
- The sales system is only affected for lessors who deal in capital leases.
- As a practical matter, many inventory systems utilize a FIFO costing system. At the end of the year, adjustments are made to convert to LIFO, if necessary.

One category of non-routine transaction that varies in its accounting treatment is that of equity issues. EQUITY ISSUES which pose problems are those which combine characteristics of debt with an equity interest in future earnings. Treatment of these issues strictly as equity means that no interest is charged against period income. National accounting standards vary as to the tests applied to determine how to account for these transactions. In the case of equity issues, transactions are recorded in the financial reporting system and are not summarized with other transactions in a transaction processing system.

Comparative Accounting Differences Which Affect End-of-Period Entries

The differences in international accounting which affect end-of-period entries primarily affect two areas - cost allocations and contingencies. *Cost allocations* involve the allocation of past or expected future costs over the periods which those costs benefit. The depreciation of fixed assets has already been mentioned.   Under United States GAAP, other areas of cost allocation are goodwill, deferred income taxes and future pension payments. The GAAP pronouncements associated with each of these areas differ from standards which exist in some other countries.

- In some cases, depreciation methods which are acceptable under GAAP may not be allowed.
- Goodwill is created when a company acquires another company at a price which exceeds the fair value of its assets. GAAP requires that this goodwill be amortized over time. Under other national standards, this goodwill is retained on the balance sheet or may be charged against equity accounts immediately. In the United Kingdom, for example, it is rare to amortize goodwill.
- Deferred income taxes and pension liabilities are covered by extremely technical pronouncements which attempt to assure that a company recognizes likely future liabilities. Many alternative approaches exist for each of these areas which are used in other

countries. The predominant practice in most other countries is to accrue taxes currently payable. However, deferred income taxes which result from timing differences are not recognized by many Japanese companies, for example.

Contingency estimates are established to record probable (but not certain) future payments which are associated with the current period. The best example is the estimated settlement for a pending legal action against the company.

In terms of both cost allocation and contingencies, the accounting standards which have developed are quite technical and tend heavily toward conservatism. That is, they would record expenses in the present reporting period which would reduce the current period income. Further, each of these areas requires calculation outside the accounting systems before an accounting entry is made. Consequently, they have little direct affect on the associated information systems.

Comparative Accounting Differences Which Affect Reporting

Certain differences in accounting standards have almost no effect on information systems. These differences affect accounts which are shown on the balance sheet. Once the appropriate entry is made, these account balances are subject to little change.

The *basis of presentation* is the cost basis which is used for the financial statements—historical cost as opposed to some measure of current market value. In the United States, the cost basis is historical cost unless evidence exists that the value has been impaired and the original cost basis should be reduced. There are nations where a current cost basis is used.

Foreign currency translation requires restatement of certain transaction in terms of another currency. When cash is received or disbursed in a foreign currency, a company makes this exchange at current translation rates. However, the associated asset or liability may have been entered into the accounting records at a different rate, resulting in a possible gain or loss on the transaction. The translation factor which must be used varies under GAAP according to complex rules. The rules may be different under other national standards.

Consolidation reporting is the incorporation into a parent company's financial statements of certain financial information for subsidiaries which are wholly or partly owned by the parent company. The US requires the consolidation of subsidiary companies under certain technical criteria. These criteria could be more or less stringent in other countries. In some countries subsidiaries which are consolidated under GAAP might simply be shown at historical or market cost. Consolidation is significant because a subsidiary of a corporation may have a level of debt or other difference in its structure which would be concealed if the subsidiary were shown as an asset at its historical cost. Most countries do not require the consolidation of subsidiaries which are not homogeneous with the parent in capital structure, such as a financing subsidiary. Japan does not require consolidation of subsidiaries with parent company financial statements.

Minority ownership may be shown in several ways depending on the accounting standards in a particular country. This interest, the value attributed to stockholders outside the family of companies in the financial statements, may be shown at cost, at current market, or some other method.

A *combination of interests* occurs when two companies enter an agreement to combine into a new entity. In some cases, this is treated as a purchase by the dominant company. In other cases, the combination is treated as a mutual pooling of interests. In the case of a pooling of interests, the entities are merged at their book values. In the case of a purchase, the assets of the purchased company must be re-valued at a fair market value. Outside the US, only Australia recognizes pooling of interests.

In many of these cases which affect reporting, the accounting entry is made only once, when the account balance is entered, and no further information systems processing is required. In the other cases, it is likely that the accountant creating the financial statements would perform a calculation outside the information systems and no permanent entry would be made.

Legislated Differences Which Affect the Accounting Systems

The major barrier to a unified set of international accounting standards may well be the variation in the national income tax structure across nations. There is a wide variety of accounting methods required by the tax laws. In fact, the difference in income reported by companies for income tax purposes and for financial reporting purposes creates a serious accounting problem in dealing with the timing differences in tax payments which result from the difference between the income figure calculated for tax purposes and that calculated for financial statements.

It should be reiterated at this point that the variations in national income tax systems affect the transaction processing systems perhaps more than variations in the international accounting standards. Each of the issues raised previously regarding accounting standards not only causes variations in financial reporting, but also is a source of possible variations in the accounting methods required for corporate income tax calculation. Further, variations in requirements for individual income tax withholdings will mean that payroll transaction processing systems will almost always need to be changed to reflect variations across national lines.

MULTI-LOCATION IMPLICATIONS FOR ACCOUNTING IS

When a company performs some of its activities at a location away from its primary or home base - i.e., remotely - the decision must be made as to which support functions will be performed at that location and which at the central location. In IS vocabulary, this decision affects the "distribution" of processing. This issue, through not necessarily a simple one even for domestic companies, can be quite complex in support of global operations. This section of the chapter discusses some of the issues involved in this decision, focussing on the information systems and technology which support the accounting function.

The concept of distribution affects all functions of a company and is not unique to the IS area. In discussing the decision of distribution of information systems required by companies at remote locations, it is important to consider the different forms and levels of involvement which may exist at those locations - i.e., the distribution of primary and support activities which are conducted. An additional factor in the distribution decision is the legal organization of the remote location. The following discussion will explore these issues and their implications for the case when the remote location is in a different country.

Activities Conducted at Remote Locations

The structure used by Michael Porter (Porter 1985) in his "value chain" model of a company provides a useful tool for considering the range of operations conducted remotely. Porter identified "primary" activities which a company must perform, including sales, production, and service. In most cases, the justification for the remote location is to improve the linkages between one or more of these primary activities and the customer or vendor base. This point is most apparent in the international context.

In many cases, a remote location of a company performs only a limited range of operations—either one of these primary activities, or possibly a combination of service in conjunction with either sales or production. In other cases, the remote location may perform a full spectrum of the company's activities—all three of the primary activities identified above as well as "secondary" activities including firm infrastructure, human resources, technology development, accounting, information systems, etc. In this case, the remote location becomes almost a scaled-down version of the larger entity.

As activities become wider in scope, it becomes increasingly likely that business would benefit from the operational support which transaction processing systems provide. For example, if marketing is conducted at the remote location, it may be desirable to distribute transaction processing for sales and cash receipts to the location. If the production activity exists at the remote location, it is more likely that the payroll transaction processing system will be distributed.

In the cases where only limited activities are performed at a remote location, it is very likely that much - possibly all - of the accounting function will be performed at a central location. Alternatively, where the remote location represents the full range of primary activities, it is more likely that at least part of the accounting function will be "distributed" to that remote location. In these cases, varying accounting standards and country specific technology issues can impact both the accounting function and support systems.

Given the domestic (US) data communications network, distribution of the transaction processing capability to remote locations does not require complete distribution of processing. For domestic companies, a refinement of the distribution of processing has developed. With reliable high speed data communications, terminals are often located at remote locations which communicate with a central computer installation. Increasingly, companies capture data about transactions at remote (i.e., foreign) locations and perform some or all of the processing of those transactions at the central location.

Legal Organization of Remote Location

The legal organization of the remote location also influences the distribution of the accounting and information systems functions. We can identify three levels of legal organization: first, a branch location of the company; second, a separate, wholly-owned subsidiary of the company; and, third, a separate partially-owned corporation.

For a branch location of the main company, such as a sales office, the distribution of processing for the accounting and information systems functions can be based on efficiency of activity and on the need for current information.

When the remote location is organized as a separate corporation, even wholly owned, government requirements may make it less feasible to conduct significant activities at a central location. For a separate corporation which is not wholly owned, it seems likely that the accounting and information systems activities will be conducted at the remote location.

Complications in a Global Environment

In the global environment, a more general approach to the

distribution decision is needed. Three important factors can be identified which must be considered: first, the trade-off between the cost of the support activity and the level of service which can be provided at each location; second, the choice which the company makes between local autonomy and central control; and, third, the local economic and regulatory environment.

Furthermore, the decisions to distribute or centralize the information systems activity and the accounting activity are not independent. Many information systems—the transaction processing systems, for example—directly affect accounting records. This close relation makes it desirable for accountants and information systems personnel to work closely together, whether at a remote location or at a central location.

With respect to levels of cost and service in a global corporation, the distribution decision must consider several additional factors: the available data communications network, the pool and cost of available workers, and the IT equipment available. In the United States and in Western European countries, there is a combination of sophisticated data communications networks, and, in many cases, a selection of carriers available to deal with. However, in most countries, the data communications infrastructure is not sophisticated enough to support the distribution of processing which may be available for domestic locations. Further, in most countries data communications is controlled by a government-owned company which controls the postal service, the telephone systems, and the telegraph system —P T&Ts (Deans and Kane, 1992). In these countries, data communications reliability may suffer, and service may be delayed with respect to new installation and repairs. Uncertainty with respect to data communications would be the key factor in favor of distribution of processing to the remote location. Otherwise, a failure of data communications would leave the remote location without support.

An additional factor which must be considered is that of the availability and cost of the skills needed to perform the support activities at the remote location. Availability of skilled, reasonably-priced personnel at the remote location would be an additional factor which would favor distribution of the support activities to the remote location. In countries such as India, college educated professionals in information systems and accounting are readily available for salaries which may be 15-20% of the level of their US counterparts. Returning to the previous discussion of the variation in accounting standards, skilled accountants would most be needed to support the accounts payable/cash disbursement transaction processing system, the payroll system, and the end-of-period entries.

The question of autonomy of operations becomes a significant factor in many countries. In some countries, legal restrictions make it necessary to perform some activities locally which might otherwise be performed centrally. Even where regulation does not force it, good corporate citizenship may make it extremely desirable to distribute many activities. Further, the distribution of infrastructure activities to a remote location for other reasons may make it necessary to allow more local autonomy in the global environment than would be allowed in a domestic location.

A factor related to the problems of data communications is the existence of laws in some countries which place severe restrictions on the movement of data across national borders. In Scandinavian countries and in some Western European countries, personal data transmitted across national lines would be considered an invasion of privacy. In these countries, laws have proven to be a barrier to the distribution of support activities to the home location.

As a result of many of these additional factors, the multinational corporation is likely to distribute the financial reporting and the accounting support of that function to the foreign operations.

CONCLUSION

Information systems which support the accounting function consist of two major elements: transaction processing systems which support the routine business of a company, and the financial reporting system which summarizes the period activity and creates financial reports. When these systems are analyzed in the context of the accounting standards which are most likely to vary across national borders, it is apparent that the impact of variations of global accounting standards is minimal on all of the transaction processing except the payroll system. Most of the variations in accounting practice affect only the end-of-period financial reporting system. For those examples where there are effects on transaction processing, the variations in accounting across national borders are comparable in scope to the variations in practice which are necessary to maintain accounting records to support the calculation of the company income tax.

When the factors which affect the distribution of activities are considered, the distribution decision is usually similar to that involved at domestic locations. There would be, however, more reason to distribute information systems processing to remote locations when those locations are located in foreign countries, primarily because of legal considerations and the reliability of data communications. In the case of higher level accounting functions, these activities are often more likely to be distributed to foreign locations than to domestic locations because of the need for specific technical knowledge about local accounting standards.

REFERENCES

Amenkhienan, Felix E., *Accounting in the Developing Countries: a Framework for Standard Setting*, UMI Research Press, 1986.

Belkaoui, Ahmed Riahi, *Accounting Theory*, Dryden Press, 1993.

Cash, James I., F. Warren McFarlan, James L. McKenney, and Lynda M. Applegate, *Corporate Information Systems Management*, Irwin, 1992.

Deans, P. Candace, and Michael J.Kane, *International Dimensions of Information Systems and Technology*, PWS Kent, 1992.

Drucker, Peter E., *New Realities*, Harper and Row, 1989.

Elliot, Robert K., "The Third Wave Breaks on the Shores of Accounting", *Accounting Horizons*, June, 1992 pp. 61-85.

———— and Peter D. Jacobson, "US Accounting: a National Emergency", *Journal of Accountancy*, November, 1991, pp. 54-58.

Gensler, Philip J. and David G. Chou, "Managing Global Information Systems", *Information Executive*, Fall, 1991, pp. 35-37.

Ives, Blake, and Sirkka L. Jarvenpaa, "Applications of Global Information Technology - Key Issues for Management", *MIS Quarterly*, March, 1991, pp. 33-49.

Martin, James, *Telecommunications and the Computer*, Prentice Hall, 1990.

Mueller, Gerhard, Helen Gernon, and Gary Meek, *Accounting an International Perspective*, Irwin, 1991.

Porter, Michael E., *Competitive Advantage*, Free Press, 1985.

————, *Competitive Advantage of Nations*, Free Press, 1990.

Schroeder, Richard G., Myrtle Clark, Levis D. McCullers, *Accounting Theory Text and Cases*, Wiley, 1991.

CHAPTER 11

Ideal International Accounting Information Systems: Integrative, Instantaneous, Intelligent and Intense

TERRY CAMPBELL
International Institute for Management Development (IMD)

VERONIQUE DUPERRET-TRAN
International Institute for Management Development (IMD)

TERRY CAMPBELL, II
Wake Forest University

Ideal accounting information systems are the target against which firms must judge their accounting systems and the relevant benefits and costs to determine how close and how fast to approach the ideal. As the alliterative title of this chapter suggests, management and other stakeholders expect the accounting information system to perform integratively, instantaneously, intelligently, and intensely! While we make no claims to have found the "ideal" system, we have observed each of these dimensions expressed as critical performance criteria of contemporary information systems. Many of these items have been mentioned in the literature and, more importantly, beyond the literature. We have been privileged to have seen each of the performance criteria in use in today's multinationals. The ideal system is not one that is a static goal but one for which internationally[1] competitive firms will strive. Our intention is to provide ideas, evidence, and suggestions about the ideal accounting information system in the broadest possible context.

INTRODUCTION

Integrating reality into strategy and into accounting and other information systems is not something for the faint of heart to attempt. Numerous chief financial officers (CFOs) and chief information officers (CIOs) have gone down this path, either wandering or for evermore lost. For internationally oriented firms there is little choice but to move towards the ideal, however defined (see, for example, Banker, Kaufmann, and Mahmood, 1993). Naturally, the CFO and CIO of a domestic firm know many of the issues and perils of such adventures; but none know it better than those brave souls who venture on to the international scene.

Global capital markets, differential accounting standards, currency markets, hedging strategies, international financial derivatives markets, international transfer pricing, consolidations, segmentation issues, and internal reporting for decision making set up what appear to be impossibly solvable situations. Yet, we find numerous examples of firms which make progress in narrowing the gap from the actual to the "ideal". Of course, any of the ideas, evidence, and suggestions we make are subject to the "law" that what gets published on these topics is out of date immediately. Yet, we intend to suggest what may become key elements of the future in this area.

In respect of the ideal, we build an argument for the overall scenario in which international accounting information systems must survive and succeed. To do this, we begin at an overall level of the global capital markets, move to multinational units, to strategic business units (SBUs), and on to local operations. At each level, it is important to keep an emphasis on the *international* aspect of accounting information systems.

In this context, we then claim that systems must be integrative, instantaneous, intelligent, and intense. Management is under increasing competition for efficient and effective operations which has resulted in the necessity for teams. These teams are cross-functional and bridge the gaps between functions and countries, thus requiring *integrative* international accounting information systems. The drive for competitive efficiency and effectiveness also results in the need for immediate feedback and availability. With immediacy comes the need for decision making aids in the form of decision support systems (DSS), executive information systems (EIS), and even forms of expertise up to and including neural networks. Immediacy[2] in such systems becomes *instantaneous* in international accounting information systems.

As management continues this drive for competitive advantage, DSS, EIS, and other such systems increasingly rely on and/or are inextricable linked to the accounting information system. Management expects the expertise, suggestions, and routine decisions to be built-in to the systems. Regardless of the perspective that managers must exercise in their final judgements, systems are becoming increasingly *intelligent.*

Competitive advantage also moves management to respond to a variety of pressures including, but not limited to, time pressures, resource pressures, rapid changes, and facing the unknown future that requires long term perspectives with shorter and shorter "generations" of products, processes, and services. This volatility means that systems, including the international accounting information system, become even more *intense.*

Specifically, in this chapter, we examine the overall phenomenon of increasing globalization with special emphasis on its impacts on financial reporting, external and internal. Next, we provide several specific examples of selected examples of implementation. Finally, we offer a dual view of the likely tomorrows based on either increasing homogeneity or increasing heterogeneity. Within this duality, we note that the ideal international accounting information system (IIAIS) is inseparable from other systems and other functions. Thus, the IIAIS has impact on all decisions including organizational ones. Given this influence, we argue that the IIAIS is an important strategic information asset.

GLOBALIZATION TRENDS

We take a number of trends as the basis for long term change in the content and role of accounting information systems in international firms (see, for example, Bradley, Hausman, and Nolan, 1993). These trends include global capital markets, differential accounting standards, currency markets, hedging strategies, international financial derivatives markets, international transfer pricing, consolidations, segmentation issues, and internal reporting for decision making. The relative rate of change is a function of many variables. Campbell and Umanath (1991) and Umanath and Campbell (1993) have outlined the variables and influences on differential rates of diffusion for information technology (IT) in order to assist managers in understanding the alternative approaches to be taken. Their work is outlined in Figure 1 which depicts an adapted version of their more complete model. For our purposes, the restricted model reveals the categories of variables and denotes the longitudinal perspective that managers must have relative to strategy formulation and resource deployment.

In Figure 1, we attempt to depict a scenario that shows the multiple influences of societal and organizational dimensions. In addition, the changes over time in the "current IT state" are made evident. The roles that "diffusion of IT" and "strategy formulation and resource deployment have are depicted in part[3] but suffice it to say that the arrows (influence) of each would extend to both societal and organizational dimensions. Practicing managers[4] have been exposed to this particular model in numerous instances and have contributed greatly to its development.

As we have explored[5] international accounting information systems, it has become increasingly evident that the model in Figure 1 provides important insights into the key phenomena. More specifically, we have been able to leverage the model in specific terms with accounting in the larger sense of including external reporting, internal reporting, and ad hoc reporting. This has been done in the context of the MACROS[6] (Management Accounting Communications Reporting Organizational Systems) model used for outlining the various levels that financial reporting may take (Campbell, 1992). Figure 2 provides a summary of the categories of MACROS reporting alternatives.

This approach attempts to represent financial reporting at three levels: external, operating performance of segments, and internal

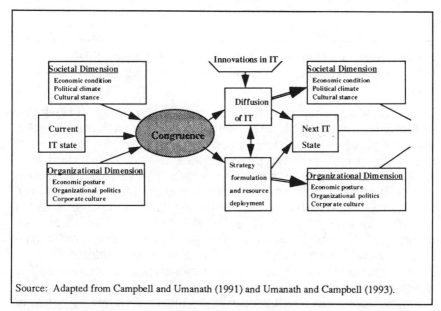

Source: Adapted from Campbell and Umanath (1991) and Umanath and Campbell (1993).

Figure 1: A Dynamic Model for Managing Diffusion of Information Technology

FOR: Taxes Creditors Employees Shareholders Stakeholders
BY: BOARD of Directors and Executive Management including Chief Financial
Officer

External Reporting -- Financial Statements + ('+' indicates the discussion, analysts
meetings, ideas, stories, and the complete set of information sources used)

    Consolidations
    Currency Translations
    Intracompany Transfers
    Joint Ventures and Alliances

FOR: Operating Performance in Total and by Segments
BY: Controllers, Treasurers, Finance and Control Executives

    Strategic Business Units
    Divisions
    Geographic
    Customer

FOR: Internal Reporting
BY: Controllers, Cost Accountants, Plant Accountants

    Profitability Analyses (Cost Analyses)
    Operating Performance Measures (including non-financial measures)
    Ad Hoc Reports

Figure 2: Summary of MACROS Financial Reporting Alternatives[18]
**Management Accounting Communications Reporting Organizational
Systems**

reporting. Most other more detailed examples of financial reporting
fit nicely within this tri-level classification. At the external reporting
level, we point out that these reports are provided to a broad set of
stakeholders with different perspectives but who share a need for a
fairly narrow set of reporting alternatives in order to strive for a
degree of efficient comparability and understandability. In addition,
at this level and at all levels, the need for explaining the business idea
or story is vital, thus the use of the "+" sign. At this level,
consolidations, currencies, and costing (intracompany transfer pricing) are handled, eliminated, translated, and consolidated.

The next level is the operating performance of segments. The
segments of an organization may be described as strategic business
units, divisions, by geographic area, in terms of customer types, or
by any other meaningful way of decomposing results. Within the
relevant segments, management and the readers of such statements

must find a mechanism for improved communications as the standards for segment reporting, either internal or external, are not as clearly defined as the standards for generally accepted accounting principles or international accounting standards. Thus, it is not uncommon for the larger multinationals to comment that they are in compliance with more than 30 sets of accounting standards. The obvious implication is one of duplication and, at the very least, some obfuscation of the underlying economic phenomena. On the other hand, the use of information technology has permitted several organizations to maintain the multiplicity of systems and maintain a degree of order and transparency, at least internally.

The internal reporting level has the broadest possible set of reporting alternatives; in fact, there are no limitations on what a firm might choose to do internally, subject to benefit/cost analysis of the alternative system. Profitability analyses are the primary internal reporting routines and with the simultaneous advent of information technology and of activity based analysis (or some variant of it), most management analyses that are requested may indeed be done. Of course, the necessity of a business reason for the report remains central to the decision to conduct the analysis. Given the increase in international business, accounting systems for internal reporting are under pressure to match the growth in order to provide timely information for decision making. As organizations struggle in the competitive arena to find the right organizational structure, size, and segmentation, management expects accounting systems to change in parallel. In addition, the use of all kinds of other information in conjunction with accounting information is an accepted way of life. These other kinds of information include non-quantitative varieties.

Given these perspectives as background, we now turn to the globalization trends in more detail. We expect these trends to provide insights into the present situation and offer some guidance on the direction that ideal accounting information systems will take in the future.

Global Capital Markets

The year 1993 marks an event regarding accounting information systems and financial reporting where Daimler-Benz (the holding company for Mercedes-Benz) will begin reporting their financial results in sufficient compliance with US generally accepted accounting principles (GAAP) as interpreted by the SEC (Securities and Exchange Commission) to offer Daimler-Benz shares on the New York Stock Exchange. This event occurred October 5, 1993 when the shares begin trading on the New York Stock Exchange. Daimler-Benz believes that the firm's equity position can only be enhanced by such a listing; indirectly, this means there is a positive benefit-cost ratio (European Report No. 1876, 17 July 1993). This event may be partially explained in the context of Figure 1. A combination of societal and organizational dimensions came together in such a way as to cause or at least facilitate the decision for "GAAP" compliance.

This is not the last word or even a beginning of a surge of companies coming into SEC compliance; but, it is a signal that, when necessary, an international firm can adjust its accounting information systems to the marketplace. Freund (1993) argues that the example is a unique case and represents an action that actually does not need to be undertaken. Freund was chief economist for the New York Stock Exchange from 1976-85 and argues that the SEC has outgrown its usefulness. His final argument is that such firms need to ". . . abide by America's anachronistic accounting standards, . . . strangle US markets and do irreversible harm to the US as the world's dominant financial center". We view these arguments as fairly strong and worthy of consideration. The facts of the present situation are that Daimler-Benz is proceeding as planned with other multinationals with which we communicate watching with interest, and even with a degree of optimism that the experience gained will transfer in some way to their long term consideration of a similar listing.

Choi and Levich (1990) examined the effects of international accounting diversity on capital markets. As might be expected the results were ambiguous. Choi and Levich concluded that finding a consensus will not be easily done. The choices proposed ranged from multiple principles, to reciprocity, to the IASC (International Accounting Standards Commission), to EC standards, to other forms of harmonization. In the end, Choi and Levich note that the relative size of the US market and its sophistication provide some opportunity for leadership in standard setting.

Japan is the next leading stock market in terms of market value of domestically traded shares. Yet, their securities markets are anything but the standard setter. Terawasa (1993) argues that the key success factor for Japanese financial markets is the creation of an ". . . autonomous Securities and Exchange Commission on the US model". Expanding upon this argument, Terawasa notes that unless action is taken, ". . . Japan will further isolate itself from its trading partners".

Moving to the EC, we find that 12 countries have 23 Stock Exchanges (*Economist*, 19 June 1993) compared to the USs eight stock exchanges and seven futures and options exchanges. The argument is that the eventual use of electronics and some degree of harmonization of accounting standards will re-structure the EC exchanges into a more efficient and transparent set of financial markets. Firms facing this possibility are searching for a common set of accounting standards in order to be listed on each of the exchanges selected. The obvious implication that "electronics" will drive the system is clear. More importantly, even if alternative reporting standards are maintained, the accounting information system of the future (maybe, the present) will permit multiple reporting at a reasonable cost.

So, global financial markets with alternative accounting standards are presaging a potential revolution in two ways: (1) electronic markets with alternative reporting requirements may be handled with help keys or other decision aids (with geographical separation not an issue), and (2) given alternative reporting requirements, firms find that automating the alternative presentations under different rules are less onerous than originally thought. Note, specifically, the Daimler-Benz case above. The ideal accounting information system will include the opportunity for flexible financial reporting.

Differential Accounting Standards

With the diffusion rates of technology (including accounting information systems, technology, and learning) differing in numerous and substantial ways, it is of little surprise that global accounting standards (see, for example, Mueller, Gernon, and Meek, 1994) have not been met with overwhelming acceptance and enthusiasm. The International Accounting Standards Committee (IASC) was founded in 1973 in a wave of optimism that harmonization of accounting standards would occur in 5 to 10 years. Some 20 years from this beginning, relatively little progress has been made in approaching a set of accounting standards that an international firm may apply uniformly (Emenyonu and Gray, 1993). See Table 1.

Several firms have moved to IASC standards as they are established; yet, even in these firms, a careful reading of the accounts indicate that IASC standards are used along with other standards. Thus, an "ideal" international accounting system must allow for these differences. Efforts at reconciliation have been undertaken by various interested parties. One such example provided by the Centre for International Financial Accounting Research (CIFAR) indicates that, under CIFAR standards, the net income of German firms increases by 40%, Swedish by 60%, and Japanese firms by 12%; while the net income of Swiss firms decreases by 8%.

Emenyonu and Gray (1992) examined accounting measurement practices in France, Germany, and the UK in six areas: stock valuation, depreciation, goodwill, research and development, valuation bases for fixed assets, and the treatment of extraordinary/exceptional items. In summary, their study, ". . . yielded results that are not very encouraging to those concerned to eliminate or reduce differences in measurement practices . . . ." (p. 56). Of the six measurement practices examined, depreciation had the lowest degree of harmony! Given the lack of harmony on an item of such

Index	1971-72	1992-93	% change
Consolidation method	0.0963	0.9269	862.5
Investments in Associates	0.7784	0.9376	20.4
Treatment of goodwill	0.6865	0.5441	-20.7
Rate for translating income statement of subsidiaries	0.5417	0.7039	29.9
Treatment of Translation differences	0.5377	0.5063	-5.8
Treatment of Exchange differences	0.2323	0.8136	250.2
Method used to assign cost to inventories	0.3853	0.2825	-26.7
Measurement basis for recording inventories	0.6781	0.7564	11.5
Definition of market value	0.6164	0.6990	13.4
Cost basis for recording property, plant, equipment	0.7629	0.7906	3.6
Gains/losses on disposal of property, plant, equipment	0.7093	0.9777	37.8
Method of accounting for depreciation	0.3294	0.2295	-30.3
Method of valuing long-term investments	0.8471	0.6088	-28.1
Gains/losses on disposal of long-term investments	0.5803	0.9889	85.9
Method of valuing current investments	0.5731	0.7662	33.7
Gains/losses on disposal of current investments	0.6999	0.9914	41.6
Method of accounting for borrowing costs	0.9426	0.3843	59.2
Basis for providing for deferred taxes	0.7732	0.2321	-70.0
Method of treating deferred taxes	0.4005	0.3953	-1.3
Accounting for extraordinary and exceptional items	0.9401	0.9950	5.8
Treatment of research expenditures	0.3592	0.9465	163.5
Treatment of development expenditures	0.4125	0.9098	119.5
Determination of the cost pensions	0.9524	0.4882	-48.7
Treatment of past service costs/experience adjustments	0.9439	0.8501	-9.9
Method of accounting for long-term contracts	0.6670	0.5933	-11.0
Method of treating government grants	0.7300	0.6300	-16.0
Average Harmony Index Score	**0.6230**	**0.6903**	**10.8**

Source: Emenyonu and Gray, FINANCIAL TIMES, July 2, 1993

Table 1: International Accounting Harmonisation: 1971/72 - 1991-/92

general interest and of such specific impact on both the income statement and the balance sheet, we suggest that an ideal system will provide for instantaneous and intelligent comparisons regarding depreciation across countries. Of course, the entire litany of alternative standards makes for an increasingly "alert" ideal system.

Foreign Currency, Financial Instruments, and Hedging

Global capital markets and differential accounting standards concern the financial reporting aspect of accounting systems. The foreign currency aspect is a point of contact for reporting and for decision making. The reporting issues are of the usual nature surrounding the recognition and translation of international transaction and their impact on the financial statements. The decision making aspect is of intense interest to the accounting/finance decision maker charged with the responsibility of managing the exposures via hedging, derivatives, or other forms of financial instruments (McKie, 1989).

The Institute of Management Accountants[7] (IMA) has issued a formal statement (Statement Number 4-Q) regarding the *Use and Control of Financial Instruments by Multinational Companies* (1992). This statement outlines the significant responsibilities of the accounting function in managing the complexity of such transactions as: financial instruments for investing and borrowing, hedging risks in foreign exchange, and hedging risks in commodity operations. Thus, the ideal accounting information system will include elements of instantaneous and intelligent responses for management.

Globally Green

As if the above elements of the trend are not sufficiently challenging, the environment surfaces as an additional topic which must be included in an ideal accounting information system. As society increasingly recognizes the inextricable linkages on "Spaceship Earth", stakeholders are demanding an accounting. Unfortunately, no or few standards have emerged. But, one may easily speculate that the accounting information system and those managers responsible for it will emerge in the limelight to assist stakeholders in understanding the situation. Reasonable speculation suggests that this issue will emerge as one of the more volatile ones for international firms reporting on their global operations.

Campbell and Duperret-Tran (1993) developed a compilation of articles ("Lean, Mean, and Green") regarding the phenomenon of environmental responsibilities from the societal perspective to the environmental audit report (Eco-management Directive in the EC) and finally to specific case examples of firms engaged in environmental audits as well as firms making capital budgeting decisions. Finally, over 100 executive participants were engaged in a discussion and feedback session on the responsibilities and opportunities with respect to the environment. As the discussion evolved, it was evident that the vast majority of the executives are in support of the societal responsibilities of management for the environment. In addition, they felt that the accounting system was an integral part of the decision process for them to carry out their responsibilities. Finally, when confronted with the "opportunity" to be made responsible for the environment for their business, less than 10% were interested; the vast majority felt that it was a losing proposition for their careers. To the extent that this initial effort at increasing executives' understanding of their responsibilities may suggest current attitudes, we note that the role of the accounting system is felt to be critical. Thus, the ideal international accounting information system will assist management in measuring this phenomenon.

Summary of Trends

Our literature search, applied research, and consulting assignments indicate that globalization trends are increasing the need and potential availability of ideal international accounting information systems. Globalization of capital markets, consumer markets, and societal responsibilities up to and including the environment suggest an integral role of accounting information systems for survival and success of international firms.

The next section examines several firms and their responses to the demands to find the ideal accounting information system. Our intention is not to exhaustively provide examples of international accounting information systems and technology, but rather to highlight a number of key issues.

INTERNATIONAL ACCOUNTING INFORMATION SYSTEMS: SELECTED EXAMPLES AND CASE STUDIES

International firms do not wait for the ideal accounting system or technology to be discovered; rather, they move forward on a variety of fronts to make sense out of the situation in such a way as to find competitive advantage, success, or survival. Our intentions as stated above are to provide some selected examples and case studies for consideration in thinking about the ideal international accounting information system. We do note that the examples and cases provided are representative of numerous examples that are publicly available; i.e., none of these required permission for the release of proprietary data. We include a consumer goods company, an industrial goods company, a technology company, and a retail company.

Consumer Goods Company[8]

One of the largest consumer goods manufacturing companies (48 plants in 59 countries with 195,000 employees in 1990) made a strategic decision to move the information technology investment from a supporting role to an enabling one for competitive advantage.

Integral to this effort is the necessity for the accounting system to evolve in parallel. As the industry changed over time, it was increasingly evident that the information systems would be critical in both marketing and manufacturing information. Marketing information was needed all the way through the business system to and from the point of sale. Manufacturing information was needed to allocate production across plants and countries. Within this context, the accounting information systems help management in decision making in a more *integrated* manner across functions, countries, and product lines. Such an endeavor required not only proper strategic planning but in-depth operational plans on such mundane things as the various protocols for electronic data interchange (EDI). The resulting systems had to respond to two opposing forces: standardization and personalization (Oliff, p. 4). These opposing forces may be met most efficiently and effectively by information technology. Further consideration must be given to the impact of these changes on decision making, decision makers, and involved elements of the business system from suppliers to customers. This particular firm is oriented to all aspects of the ideal information system from the global capital markets to the environmental responsibilities to the internal decision making: i.e., its intended systems are international, integrative, instantaneous, intelligent, and intense.

Industrial Goods Company[9]

A large international petrochemical company (sales over $10 billion with 51 manufacturing plants in 22 countries and supplied customers in over 100 countries) initiated a benchmarking study of information technology within the chemicals division. The chemicals division was composed of basic chemicals, polymers, and performance products. Thus, the information technology was needed to provide information for products that were essentially commodities (when low delivered cost wins) as well as performance products (where high perceived value wins). The various elements of the successful information system address each of these key success factors in different but complementary ways.

The benchmarking results indicated that a significant challenge was presented to management in that there were examples of leading edge uses of information technology that appeared to offer improvement opportunities. These opportunities were in: sales and customer service, computer research support, plant management systems, process and product design, sales-marketing-manufacturing-distribution, decision support, communications, systems support, and human resources (Oliff and Marchand, 1993, p. 16). That is, the entire business could benefit from information technology.

For our purposes, we note the primary benchmark in sales and customer service to be the Electronic Data Interchange (EDI) with suppliers and customers. The integration of the accounting systems with the EDI system permitted significant improvements in processing productivity and in customer service. This effort was not without cost as numerous technical requirements needed to be met; but the overall assessment was that the investment was beneficial to the company. The primary benchmark in decision support was in financial analysis; we emphasize this benchmark because it goes to the core of an ideal accounting system. Unless the ideal accounting system provides data in a timely and appropriate fashion for analysis and decision making, all the benchmarks in the world will not prove beneficial.

In reviewing the other benchmarks, we find that efficiency gains or effectiveness improvements are the keys to success. In fact, each of the other benchmarks uses financial analysis in one form or another to justify the investment. Management has consciously taken the decision to analyze the ". . . costs of doing business in markets rather than the costs of information management or information technology alone" (Oliff and Marchand, 1993b, p.5). Continuing in this vein, management must lead the effort in using information technology for ". . . setting business strategies, capital and expense budgets, and annual priorities world-wide" (Oliff and Marchand, 1993b, p.5). With these goals and responsibilities, management is intensely interested in the accounting system that helps make the decisions from an integrated perspective and then assists in monitoring the implementation of the decisions. Elements of short term and long term planning appear in the recommendations, capital and expense budgeting decisions are included, and effective monitoring systems are put into place.

Strategy in a Technology Firm[10]

With sales growth rates in the range of 30-40% per year, this technology company needed a financial system to match. Internal management reports had grown to 1,700 pages; data quality was a concept not an operational reality; general ledgers had grown to 55 with 18 different accounts payable systems; and corporate was the ultimate repository of financial information. The solution chosen was to move to financial management centers in geographic areas in which the operating companies "owned their data" and provided summary reports to corporate. The trade-off for the operating companies was to engage in a structured planning exercise to define the chart of accounts to have common definitions. This allows corporate, if necessary, to "drill down" in a particular country or operation as necessary. Operating managers may select data and view it in a decision-friendly fashion without going to corporate for a special report.

The technology firm here organized elements of their ideal accounting information system to be instantaneous for the decision makers at the local level subject to globally accepted definitions. Their goal was to gain effectiveness and efficiency; they argue that, ". . . quality of information is far superior . . . .". Plus, the closing of the books occurs two and one-half weeks earlier so "we get to management and Wall Street earlier". Finally, "We cut 150 data-gathering jobs at corporate" (Ryan, 1989, p.46). This technology firm oriented its ideal accounting information system to an integrated strategic view away from centralized control at corporate while still keeping the focus on performance.

Accounting and Strategy in a Technology Company[11]

As the world's largest technology firm, the use of technology to address the ideal accounting information system at IBM seems an appropriate choice. Yet, upon examination of six key accounting applications (general ledger, fixed assets, intracompany - US, inter-company - worldwide, accounts receivable, and accounts payable), IBM discovered 315 separate systems to handle these **basic accounting** functions. In essence, they were confronting the primary issues that most of their customers were facing: slowly changing systems, inefficient consolidation, expensive development and maintenance costs, and very little management information. By late 1991, the systems were down to 36, support employees reduced by 20%, while world-wide revenue increased by 300%. An important estimate is that the company expects to save more than $300 million by removing clerical staff and redundant systems. Terms used to validate the investment include "internal rate of return", bottom line", and "business decision making".

This has caused some changes in the controller's functions. The controller is:

- much more involved in the business decision,
- focused on financial, non-financial, quantitative, and non-quantitative information, and
- reducing the clerical and other accounting workload.

To accomplish this, the financial executives needed to overcome resistance to change, tradition, obstacles, outright counter implementation, and other typical events that occur during significant change. More importantly, the idea that the controller's staff become a visible increment of value to the organization is reinforced by, ". . . the controller's office will add value to the business or it won't exist" (Andros et. al, 1992, p. 31). Note that the driving force for the controller's office in adding value is the potential of information technology. In summary, the example suggests that the controller (financial executive) either leads or gets out of the way in building an ideal accounting information system.

Retail Company

In the UK, retail stores found that the government's macroeconomic policies during the late 1980's dramatically affected their opportunities for sales and profits. High interest rates and a decline in consumer confidence led to significant declines in opportunities for retailers. One retail chain focused their attention on improving the use of the accounting information system as a technical tool and as a motivating function.

From the technical side, the retail group intensified their focus on key pricing and inventory uses. The accounting information system was the integrative tool that allowed all levels of managers in all functions, including the retail store manager, to speak a common language in striving to accomplish group goals. For longer term decisions such as closing a store, the accounting information system is again the tool of choice.

From the behavioral side, the fact that each store is a "semi-autonomous" unit provides an opportunity for incentive compensation. The incentives are based on achieving goals and targets for the year, month, week, day, or other variation including specific product sales. All employees participate in such systems. If the system is not in control, the results can only lead to inaccurate results, erroneous decisions, and dysfunctional behavior as distrust of the system begins.

In a fiercely competitive world of retailing, this firm argues that it is developing an ideal accounting information system to give guidance to employees and managers along with incentive compensation. Indeed, such a system is intense.

The examples above are representative of the variety of accounting information systems that are currently being used and/or developed to meet management's needs.   In each case, we have tried to comment on the underlying elements relative to the need for having an ideal accounting information system: these systems will be integrative, instantaneous, intelligent, and intense.

LIKELY TOMORROWS

As we attempt to assess the likely tomorrows, we intend to draw on the overwhelming practical evidence that we see in the literature, in the media, and in contact with hundreds, if not thousands, of international executives annually. We find their discussions focused both on doing what financial executives have always done AND on doing it better, more efficiently, and more effectively. Managers continually argue that only information technology offers them the opportunity to succeed professionally. They define professional success in terms such as "understanding the business", "challenging the business plan in a rational manner," "being the most credible person in the organization," "initiating change," "motivating people," and "leading the organization in ethical and professional behaviors".

We tend to agree with the overall thrust of these comments but note that the ultimate responsibility for the finance function rests with the financial executive. Therefore, as the function itself becomes more technical (even to the point that "financial engineering is an accepted term), the technical requirements will continue to increase. At the same time, management expects the financial executive to move into a more managerial and strategic role. To the extent that the executive is able to do this, integration of technical and managerial responsibilities will in great part rely on information technology. Whether the changing and changed organization will be "transformed" in dramatic ways is not the issue; the real issue is that neither the organization nor the accounting function will ever be the same. The real task is then to move forward in a way that information technology enables the finance executive to strive for and find the ideal accounting information system. The choice is not automatic, but rather requires a conscious decision.

In this chapter, we have considered two views (among many) of likely tomorrows. In either case, we have found that the ideal international accounting information system is inseparable from other systems and functions and has impact on all decisions, thereby requiring significant organizational change.

The two views are in direct response to the overall changes in reporting needs of global firms. If changing reporting needs lead to increased fragmentation or heterogeneity in reporting rules, etc., the increase in transaction costs of dealing in global economic events will drive the ideal international accounting information system to minimize transaction costs. On the other hand, if changing reporting needs lead to increased homogeneity, then capital markets will become even more global. Therefore, the goal of the ideal international accounting information system will be to help the business and then minimize transaction costs. In either tomorrow, the ideal international accounting information system will help the business and minimize transaction costs as it fulfills the key success factors of integration, instantaneity, intelligence, and intensity.

ENDNOTES

[1] We note that the term international may be replaced by transnational, multinational, multi-domestic, or other such terms; the primary efforts in finding a definition that is satisfactorily stable eludes academics and is of considerably less concern to practicing international managers.

[2] Building models for international firms encourage accounting information systems to provide, "...real-time information supporting the management and control of business operations in an international firm" (Kasanen, Lukka, and Siitonen, 1993).

[3] Rather than overly complicate the diagram for this chapter, we chose to explicate the multiplicity of interactions here.

[4] These practicing managers have been from all functional areas and over 100 countries; we believe the model provides insights for both theory and practice.

[5] We used literature searches, information interviews, consulting assignments, and discussions with participants at IMD in several executive education programs.

[6] MACROS, as an acronym for the overall description of financial reporting, has been well received as a beginning discussion point for understanding financial reporting's various dimensions.

[7] We recognize the emphasis placed on financial reporting in this paper and we posit that the issues within management accounting reporting are significant as well. In fact, the statement 4-Q mentioned here is issued by management accountants. Another issue driving the ideal international accounting information system is one where governments become interested: i.e., international transfer pricing. Clearly, government taxing authorities have become interested in such mundane transactions as transfer pricing. An ideal international accounting information system will provide management with insights into alternative scenarios.

[8] See "Nestle, S.A. - Fitting Information Management Strategy with Competitive Restructuring", M.D. Oliff, 1992.

[9] See "Exxon Chemical: Competitive Benchmarking of Information Technology", M.D. Oliff and D.A. Marchand, 1992.

[10] See "DEC's Decentralized Financial System Puts Strategy above Controls", B.J. Ryan, 1989.

[11] See "Reengineer Your Accounting, The IBM Way", D.P. Andros, J.O. Cherrington, and E.L. Denna, 1992.

REFERENCES

Andros, David P., J. Owen Cherrington, and Eric L. Denna, Reengineer Your Accounting, The IBM Way, *Financial Executive*, July/August 1992, pp. 28-31.

Banker, Rajiv D., Robert J. Kauffman, and Mo Adam Mahmood, *Strategic Information: Technology Management - Perspectives on Organizational Growth and Competitive Advantage*, Idea Group Publishing, 1993.

Bradley, Stephen P., Jerry A. Hausman, and Richard L. Nolan, *Globalization, Technology and Competition: The Fusion of Computers and Telecommu-*

nications in the 1990s, Harvard Business School, 1993.

Campbell, Terry L. and Veronique Duperret-Tran. Lean, Mean, and Green: Environmental Roles for Financial Executives, Unpublished working paper, IMD, Lausanne, Switzerland, 1993.

Campbell, Terry L. and Narayan S. Umanath, Global Diffusion of Information Technology: A Causal Analysis and Ramifications for Strategy Formulation, *Proceedings of the Symposium on the Management of Management Information Systems,* October 2/3 1991, Grenoble, France.

Choi, Frederick D.S. and Richard M. Levich, *The Capital Market Effects of International Accounting Diversity,* Dow Jones-Irwin, 1990.

Emenyonu, Emmanuel and Sidney Gray, Elusive Harmony, *Financial Times,* July, 2, 1993, p. V.

Emenyonu, Emmanuel N. and Sidney J. Gray, *EC Accounting Harmonization: An Empirical Study of Measurement Practices in France, Germany and the UK,* Accounting and Business Research, Vol. 23, Nr. 89, pp. 49-58, 1992.

European Report, Company Law: Daimler-Benz New York Listing May Impact on EC/US Talks on Accounts Standards, *European Report/Economic and Monetary Affairs,* July 15, 1993, pp. 2-2.4.

Freund, William C., That Trade Obstacle, the SEC, *The Wall Street Journal,* August 30, 1993, p.10.

Institute of Management Accountants, Practices and Techniques: Use and Control of Financial Instruments by Multinational Companies, *Statements on Management Accounting,,* Statement Number 4-Q, June 30, 1992.

Jack, Andrew, Still Too Many Variations for Global Harmonization, *Financial Times,* May 7, 1993.

Jones, M.J., Accounting Information Systems: Their Behavioral Role, *Management Accounting,* Vol. 67, June 1989, p. 66.

Kasanen, Eero, Kari Lukka, and Arto Siitonen, The Constructive Approach in Management Accounting Research, *Journal of Management Accounting Research,* Volume 5, Fall 1993, pp. 243-264.

McKie, Stewart, The Multi-Currency Marketplace: Is Your Company Up To It?, *Financial Executive,* May/June 1989, pp. 30-33.

Mueller, Gerhard G., Helen Gernon, and Gary K. Meek, Accounting: An International Perspective, *Richard D. Irwin,* 1994.

Oliff, Michael D., Nestlé S.A. - Fitting Information Management Strategy with Competitive Restructuring, IMD Iinternational, Lausanne, Switzerland, GM 480, 1992.

Oliff, Michael D. and Donald A. Marchand, Exxon Chemical: Competitive Benchmarking of Information Technology, IMD Iinternational, Lausanne, Switzerland, GM 479, 1993a.

Oliff, Michael D. and Donald A. Marchand, Teaching Note for Exxon Chemical: Competitive Benchmarking of Information Technology, IMD Iinternational, Lausanne, Switzerland, GM 479, 1993b.

Ryan, Bruce J., DEC's Decentralized Financial System Puts Strategy Above Controls, *Financial Executive,* July/August 1989, pp. 42-46.

Terasawa, Yoshio, Break Japan's Finance Bureaucracy, *The Wall Street Journal,* July 15, 1993.

The Economist, Too Many Trading Places, *The Economist,* June 19-June 25, 1993, pp. 21-23.

Umanath, Narayan S. and Terry L. Campbell, Global Diffusion of Information Technology: A Causal Analysis and Ramifications for Strategy

Formulation And Resource Deployment, *Proceedings of the Annual Meeting Decision Sciences Institute*, San Diego, CA, 1990, November 1990.

Umanath, Narayan S. and Terry L. Campbell, Differential Diffusion of Information Systems Technology in Multinational Enterprises: A Research Model, Forthcoming in *Information Resources Management Journal.*

SECTION 5

Information Technology for Global Manufacturing and Logistics Management

Although international business research studies and textbooks are replete with discussions of "international operations", very few of them actually delve into the details of what goes on in the field of operations management. The details of how products are produced and distributed and the systems to support these activities are left typically to practitioners and academics in the functional area known in business schools as Production/Operations Management. A number of researchers in this field have increasingly become involved with corporations which are trying to systematically manage production and distribution activities on a global basis. As they have found, information technology is the catalyst which is making it possible for managers to arrive at effective and even "optimal" solutions to global production and distribution problems.

Despite the fact that the Production/Operations function has a long history in forward-looking corporations of employing up-to-date information technologies to solve ongoing problems and facilitate planning, Information Systems researchers have long neglected the specific issues that confront operations managers. In this section of the book, we have included five very different chapters that reflect the wealth and breadth of international operations and distribution activities that are affected by ongoing developments in information technology. These run the gamut from day-to-day activities in scheduling, sourcing, tracking, and inventory management, to intermediate term issues in forecasting and the management of demand, to long-term (and more strategic) issues involving process choice and production systems design.

Elliott (Chip) Minor and Martha Larkin point out in the first chapter that the issues of manufacturing planning and control systems and technology, though at the heart of research efforts in (domestic) manufacturing, have not been adquately addressed in the context of the multinational corporation. With the aid of a number of case study situations, the authors identify how each of the IS/IT solutions to classical planning and control problems are made more complex in the global setting. The next chapter, written by Frank DuBois and Erran Carmel, notes that a systematic, IT-based approach to related manufacturing and distribution problems will be necessary to reduce lead times and promote the effectivenss of a multinational corporation competing on the dimension of time. The issues are illustrated with a discussion of Black and Decker's successes and failures in attempting to connect the various (often multinational) stages of its value chain.

The third chapter in this section, by Paul Swamidass and Charles Snyder, deals with the issue of computer integrated manufacturing (CIM). Despite the fact that CIM has been discussed conceptually and implemented in part by a large number of corporations over a ten (or so) year period, real success stories are only beginning to unfold. Swamidass and Snyder point out that global competition is forcing companies to integrate and network the various components of their manufacturing operations, employing many technologies in order to increase flexibility and thereby compete in a variety of markets and on a number of dimensions. Interestingly, the main difficulties in implementing CIM across national boundaries are likely to center on human rather than technological aspects.

The final two chapters in the section discuss the impacts upon logistics and distribution, both present and future, of two very specific information and communications technologies. First, Rob Handfield, Steven Walton, Ann Marucheck and Allison Wilkins focus upon electronic data interchange (EDI) as a way for multinational firms and alliances of organizations to establish sourcing relationships. Using data obtained from a survey of the National Association of Purchasing Managers, the authors project substantial future growth in the use of EDI as a result of global firms striving to enhance competitiveness. In the final chapter of the section, Giampiero Beroggi and Al Wallace describe the yet unrealized potential of satellite tracking systems to improve transportation logistics in terms of delivery and safety. Current and anticipated satellite tracking systems in Europe and the United States are discussed.

CHAPTER 12

Information Technology and Global Operations Integration, Planning, and Control

ELLIOTT D. MINOR III
Virginia Commonwealth University

MARTHA LARKIN
Broughton Systems, Inc.

The role of global information systems (IS) and information technology (IT) has received very little attention at the production and operations functional level. This chapter focuses on identifying the role of information technology in integrating, planning and controlling global manufacturing and operations functions. There is a clear need for empirical research to further identify and confirm key issues, and to compare the uses of manufacturing and operations related IS/IT methods.

INTRODUCTION

The focus of this chapter is on the role of information systems and information technology in multi-national corporations (MNCs) from a production and operations management perspective. Specifically, the role of information technology in integrating, planning and controlling the manufacturing and operations function will be explored. While researchers have explored the IS/IT needs of MNCs, the question of how these needs relate to manufacturing and operations has received little attention.

Prior research suggests that domestic and multi-national corporations do not face all the same issues in their use of information systems and technology. Deans, Karwan, Goslar, Ricks, and Toyne (1991) note that managers strongly believe there are issues that are unique to MNCs. In their study, respondents indicated that many of their concerns were the direct result of operating in foreign countries, and not just the "distance-related" problems of operating multiple business units. Issues that were understandably identified as unique to MNCs included local cultural constraints, currency restrictions, and export restrictions. IS/IT related issues identified in the Deans et al. study included data security, integration of technologies, central versus decentralized processing, and computer integrated manufacturing (CIM). While these concerns are also relevant to domestic manufacturers, they take on even more significance in the global environment.

The operations management literature has not explored global operations management to the extent that a set of purely "global" IS/IT issues can be identified. Studies of this type are needed, and would be a contribution to the operations management literature. The literature does, however, offer clues as to what these issues are. In this chapter, IS/IT related issues of global manufacturing and service operations will be explored.

Globalization and the Manufacturing and Operations Function

The impact of globalization has been felt throughout the firm, particularly at the functional level. Today's manufacturers are under intense pressure to improve quality, reduce costs, accelerate product development, and reduce manufacturing lead times. Firms find that these pressures intensify as they move from the domestic to the global environment. Like an athlete who moves from the local arena to Olympic contention, manufacturers who choose to compete in the global market face a new and formidable set of competitors.

A primary qualification for competing in the global manufacturing environment is the ability to develop, produce, and deliver goods faster than the competition. The need to improve speed of response is the driving force behind some of the most current concepts in manufacturing. Product development teams have become popular in the U.S. because they permit faster product development. Concepts such as computer integrated manufacturing (CIM) and flexible manufacturing systems (FMS) are being adopted by manufacturers worldwide as a means of eliminating superfluous transactions, and reducing manufacturing lead times.

The common denominator among initiatives to improve the speed of product development, manufacture, and delivery is the need for *accurate, relevant, and timely information.* Time-based manufacturing requires the collection, processing, and dissemination of a vast amount of information. Without the ability to rapidly process information, manufacturers cannot successfully compete in an environment where time is at a premium.

The importance of information to the global manufacturing and operations function is difficult to overstate. Drucker (1990), suggests that Japanese manufacturers view the development and control of information as their highest priority for the near future. Creation of knowledge and control of information is necessary to develop new and innovative products and the processes necessary to manufacture them.

Overview of the Chapter

The primary objective of this chapter is to suggest and explore IS/IT issues that are of concern to the manufacturing and operations function of the global firm.

IS/IT Issues that have strategic implications will be addressed first with the discussion focusing on the flow of information among remote sites, and the integration and coordination of global operations efforts. The role of IS/IT in these efforts will be discussed, and will be complemented with the experiences of several multi-national manufacturers. Following this, production and control related issues will be discussed, with a focus on the role of IS/IT in the integration of production, operations, and other business functions. Afterwards, comparative statistics on the use of IS/IT related technology in U.S. and Japanese manufacturing will be explored. Finally, concluding remarks will be presented along with some suggestions for further research.

STRATEGIC ISSUES: OPERATIONS COORDINATION AND INTEGRATION

Coordinating and integrating the operations of multiple plants and distribution facilities is of primary concern in the global manufacturing environment. The integration of operations efforts affords the firm the opportunity to operate as a "system" rather than as an uncoordinated collection of independent entities.

Although there are many approaches to global operations integration, the trend appears to be toward giving individual business units as much flexibility as possible. The role of top management is coordination, including the collection and dissemination of information. For example, the management of Zurich (Switzerland) based ABB (Asea Brown Boveri) views its collection of multi-national businesses as "a federation of national companies with a global coordination center" (Taylor, 1991). Managers of ABB's 50 or so "business areas", located throughout the world, are given a great deal of latitude to run their businesses. The relatively small size of their business units gives them the ability to focus on flexible and time-based manufacturing. This makes them responsive to and competitive in the many diverse markets they serve. Information learned as a result of innovation in one business unit is collected and passed to others. For a general discussion of integrating global operations, the reader is referred to McGrath and Hoole (1992).

In the remainder of this section, IS/IT issues related to plant location strategies, product design and development, forecasting, demand management, and production allocation will be considered. The advantages and disadvantages of centralized versus decentralized processing of information, as well as the impact of standards on the transfer of operations related information, will also be addressed.

Plant Location Strategies

Research that is relevant to the plant location strategies of MNCs has appeared in the literature. Swamidass (1990) reported the results of a comparative empirical study of the plant location strategies of US and non-US manufacturers in the United States during the period 1973 to 1983, and how these strategies changed over time. Haug (1992) modeled the transfer of production from domestic to foreign sites in the case of "high technology multinational enterprises". Neither study investigated the role of IS/IT.

It is likely that there are IS/IT related variables in the plant location decision not identified in previous studies that are more relevant to multi-national manufacturers than domestic manufacturers. Intuitively, issues identified by Deans et al. (1991) such as transborder data flow restrictions, level of information technology sophistication in the country, and price and quality of telecommunications are relevant issues for the multi-national manufacturer. The experience of a US-based manufacturer illustrates that the quality of telecommunications in the host country is an important issue:

Hamilton Beach / Proctor-Silex, a well-known manufacturer of household appliances headquartered in Richmond, Virginia, located one of its plants in Juarez, Mexico. The company's mode of communication with its other plants, located within the US and Canada, was a Wide Area Network (WAN) that was based on the public telephone system of each country. The telephone system of Mexico, however, was not of sufficient quality to be used. The system was not reliable and lacked data integrity.

The solution used to communicate with the plant was to install a microwave tower on both sides of the U.S. - Mexican border, and to directly connect the towers to local plants using privately owned communications equipment. Although the solution accomplished the objective of linking the plant into the company's network, it was expensive and time consuming to implement, and required on-going technical support to keep it operational.[1]

Product Design and Development

Product design and development is a complicated task in the global environment. It is unlikely that a single design of most products and services will suit the tastes of all markets. McGrath and Hoole (1992) suggest the joint development of "core products" designed such that they can be modified and adapted to suit the tastes of local markets.

The concept of a core product may not be applicable in all circumstances. Tastes in clothing, for example, tend to be country and market specific. Apparel manufacturers such as Turin (Italy) based Gruppo GFT find they benefit from giving their subsidiaries considerable latitude in designing clothing for specific markets (Howard, 1991).

Global operations require that designers, who are often long distances from each other, be able to share information and technology. For example, Davenport and Short (1990) note that design teams at Ford Motor Company have members from around the globe. Because they have standardized design systems and data structures, however, the team members are able to easily and quickly share their designs. Digital Equipment uses an extensive world-wide electronic mail network to permit their designers and engineers to easily communicate with each other (McGrath and Hoole, 1992).

Forecasting, Demand Management, and Production Allocation

Forecasting is the development and dissemination of product and service forecasts. Demand management is the practice of influencing levels of demand through pricing, promotions and other strategies. Demand management is desirable in some cases as it reduces the variability of demand, which in turn, permits more level capacity loads. The manner in which production is allocated among multiple facilities has a substantial impact on manufacturing costs, speed of delivery, and other measures.

McGrath and Hoole (1992) note that global forecasting requires a system which is capable of gathering information at the local level, integrating the information, and then disseminating it back to the local level. Although there are non-technical issues involved in any type of forecasting, global forecasting necessitates the rapid electronic flow of information among a variety of sources. Compatibility among communication systems and the quality of the technological infrastructure are among the issues that affect the ability to collect and disseminate data.

The ability to manage demand and balance production among multiple facilities likewise requires considerable information. Manufacturers are finding that proximity to markets is an important consideration when allocating production. Consumers are often inclined to buy products from "local" manufacturers. Proximity to markets also permits faster response and shorter lead times (Faltermayer, 1991). As manufacturers become more market specific, information systems must be able to handle a diverse range of information from diverse locations.

Centralized Versus De-Centralized Information Processing

A key question at the strategic operations level is the degree to which information is centralized versus distributed. At one extreme, all information may emanate from or be channeled through a central facility. The facility must have the capacity to handle all the information that flows through it. Centralized processing may slow down the flow of information, and may hamper the flexibility to respond to the many contingencies and country-specific needs of remote manufacturing locations.

At the other extreme, information may be generated at any remote site and flow freely among remote sites. While this approach allows for flexibility, coordination of information flows and duplication of effort can be a problem. For a general description of the benefits of centralized versus de-centralized information processing, the reader is referred to Von Simson (1990).

What follows is a description of how one large US multi-national manufacturer channels information through a central system:

The manufacturing plants of Reynolds Metals Company are located all over the world. One of the plants provides raw materials to a Ford Motor Company manufacturing plant in Detroit, Michigan. The Reynolds plant is located near the Ford plant, and has a computerized manufacturing system installed on its own computer. Non-manufacturing related business functions such as accounts receivable, accounts payable, and general ledger are performed on a central computer at the company's headquarters in Richmond, Virginia.

Although the two computers operate independently for some functions, they work together using information exchange to achieve others. For example, when a shipment is leaving the Reynolds plant for the Ford plant, information about the shipment is electronically sent from the Reynolds plant to the Reynolds's headquarters, where it is then forwarded to a central computer at Ford. Ford's central computer in turn forwards the information to the Ford plant's computer so that they may receive the raw materials without the usual paperwork and delays that are often involved in the receiving procedure. This enables Ford to benefit from the use of a just-in-time (JIT) inventory management methodology.[2]

The blend of centralization versus decentralization of information processing for global manufacturers should reflect competitive priorities, and the degree of contact with and needs of the markets they serve. For example, Deans et al. (1991) note that, relative to financial service operations, manufacturers appear to favor more decentralized systems. They explain that this may reflect the fact that manufacturers are more likely to employ local workers from all walks of life, which involves them more in the full range of the host country's culture.

The competitive priorities of manufacturers continue to evolve toward the ability to quickly develop and produce goods and services that are increasingly customized to suit local markets. The more this occurs, the more likely that manufacturers will move towards decentralized information processing. As an example, Gruppo GFT, the Italian apparel manufacturer gives its GFT USA subsidiary in New York and its Riverside, Massachusetts manufacturing plant a great deal of autonomy in terms of product design and manufacturing. Their autonomy allows them to adapt and respond very quickly to the US market. The two US sites are linked by an automated production planning system which is used to schedule production at the Riverside plant. The managers of Gruppo GFT view themselves more as coordinators of information than as controllers, and are able to encourage and capitalize on local innovation (Howard, 1991).

Protocol, Standards, and Data Transfer

The successful implementation of electronic transfer of engineering and manufacturing data requires an appropriate infrastructure for data transfer as well as standardized data formats. Value Added

Networks (VANs) are the most common carriers of information that is transmitted through electronic data interchange (EDI). VANs are networks that provide value-adding services to their underlying transmission facilities such as Electronic Mail and EDI message forwarding. Availability of networks that are compatible and reliable facilitate the flow of design, engineering, and manufacturing related information. Consider, for example, how IBM makes use of its electronic information transfer capabilities:

> IBM is a multinational firm with manufacturing and non-manu-facturing facilities located around the world. The communica-tions network that IBM has in place enables activities such as these to occur:
>
> Electronic mail can be sent from any IBM facility to any other IBM facility, anywhere in the world.
>
> Electronic Data Interchange is conducted between manufac-turing facilities, and their customers and suppliers. Financial data is sent from divisions around the world to the corporate headquarters in Armonk, New York for evaluation and consoli-dation.
>
> Research and development information is exchanged between divisions so that future manufacturing and marketing strate-gies can be developed.[3]

PLANNING AND CONTROL: INTEGRATING PRODUCTION FUNCTIONS

Information systems and technology play an important role in the planning, scheduling, and controlling of manufacturing operations. One of the first substantial applications was in the use of material requirements planning (MRP) systems. MRP systems define end-products in terms of their component parts and sub-assemblies, and specify when production and purchasing must begin in order to complete products on schedule. Other facets of the planning and control process include scheduling the production of end products, planning capacity needs, and product sequencing, scheduling, and expediting. IS/IT plays at least some role in all of these functions.

Relatively recent initiatives to improve planning and control efforts include the application of just-in-time (JIT) related concepts to improve the flow of products on the shop floor. Daniel and Reitsperger (1991) note that information flows are critical in JIT systems in order to compensate for lack of "slack" resources such as work-in-process inventory and buffer stocks.   Other initiatives include highly automated flexible manufacturing systems (FMS) which are totally dependent on information systems and technology. For a general discussion of computer technology in planning and control, the reader is referred to Smith (1989).

The focus of this section is on integrating functions that are associated with planning and control beginning with a discussion of the role of standards at the production planning and control level. The concept of computer integrated manufacturing will then be addressed followed by a discussion of process re-design.

Standards: Operator Interfaces

IT standardization is of special concern to the production and operations management function at the production planning and shop-floor control levels. For example, consider the IT related issues involved in the programming and operation of coordinate measuring machines (CMM). CMMs are used to measure and inspect assemblies and parts for a variety of features, and improve the accuracy, flexibility, and productivity of measuring and inspection tasks (Groover, 1987). There is currently no universally accepted standard for transferring information from the design process, where specifications are set, to CMMs, although efforts are underway.

Computer-Aided Manufacturing International (CAM-I) has developed DMIS (Dimensional Measuring Interface Specifications), the purpose of which is to specify a direct interface between computer-aided design and manufacturing systems (CAD/CAM) and CMMs (Genest, 1990). DMIS defines a standard format for programming specifications from CAD/CAM systems directly to the CMMs that use the specifications to monitor performance during the manufacturing process. DMIS permits the operator/programmer to export data from CAD/CAM to the CMM module. The DMIS standard has been adopted in the US, and is under review in Europe.

A related problem that is applicable to CMMs and similar equipment such as Numerically Controlled (NC) machines is the lack of standard programming languages. NC machines can be programmed to perform sequential operations without user intervention. They are an essential component of flexible manufacturing systems where fabrication operations such as boring, drilling, and honing are common.

Planning and documenting the sequences of steps to be performed by NC machines is called "part programming". Groover (1987) notes that over 100 NC part programming languages have been developed since research on programmable machines began. No one language has been uniformly accepted by all manufacturers of all machines.

Lack of a standard language or interface has serious consequences for manufacturing. Time must be spent to train operators in the languages of the machines they operate. A standard interface between the part programming language and the user would allow operators to devote less effort to programming, and more to production. CAM-I is overseeing the development of a graphical standard operator interface (SOI). This interface is intended to establish a standard user-friendly interface between the programming software used to program machines, and the operators who program and run them (Genest 1990).

Computer Integrated Manufacturing

Computer integrated manufacturing is defined by Smith (1989) as follows:

"...computer integrated manufacturing uses an integrated computer system to plan, execute, and control all activities of a manufacturing enterprise from design of the product to its delivery to the customer."

According to this definition, CIM is a corporate-wide system intended to integrate functions such as design, production, purchasing and delivery, as well as accounting, financial, and administrative functions under a single computer-controlled umbrella. The *concept* of CIM is not new, nor are software applications that attempt to integrate and coordinate manufacturing functions with other business functions. For example, the computer software product "BPCS" (Business Planning and Control System), a product of System Software Associates Inc., contains modules to automate functions such as Order Entry, Inventory Control, Master Scheduling, Forecasting, Warehouse Management, Accounts Receivable, Accounts Payable, General Ledger, and more. The integration of modules is intended to improve efficiency by sharing inventory data, customer data, financial data and other relevant information.

The role and effectiveness of any CIM effort is related to the degree of integration that is achieved among functions. Melnyck and Narasimhan (1992) define four classes of CIM, depending upon the degree of integration that has been achieved. The degree of integration ranges from "functional", where only the manufacturing functions have been integrated to "channel", where all activities of the firm are integrated *and* there is formal integration between the firm and its customers (forward integration) and vendors (backward integration). Melnyck and Narasimhan note that the higher the degree of integration, the more emphasis shifts from the product to the process, i.e., the more suited the CIM is to products whose traits are not well known in advance and are primarily manufactured to order. In global manufacturing, where diverse markets, customized products and intense time pressure are common, a highly integrated CIM would seem to be the most effective. It also follows that the higher the degree of integration, the more critical is the role of information flows.

Goldhar and Lei (1991) describe CIM as one of the "distinct features" of fast-response global manufacturing. They cite several successful implementations of CIM among MNCs, including Allen-Bradley, General Electric, Ingersoll Milling Machine Company, and Panasonic Bicycle Company. Other MNCs having experience with CIM include McDonell Douglas and Motorola (Yoder, 1990). There is little other research to date that addresses CIM in a global context or the role of IS/IT in the global CIM environment. An exception is a study by Huang and Sakurai (1990) who visited 18 Japanese manufacturing plants that make extensive use of CIM. They found that the Japanese managers of these plants consider reduction of labor costs as the most substantial contribution of CIM. The next highest rated contributions were improvement of product quality and improvement of production flexibility, respectively.

The results of the Huang and Sakurai study suggest several research questions. The pressure to produce a wide range of products for diverse markets implies that improving production flexibility is a more critical concern for global manufacturers than reducing labor costs. One question is the degree to which CIM delivers the flexibility and responsiveness it is intended to provide, and the role IS/IT plays in achieving flexibility. Several respondents in the Huang and Sakurai study reported not being satisfied with the flexibility provided by their systems. Huang and Sakurai suggest that the reason for the dissatisfaction is primarily IS related in that the flexibility of such a system is a function of the software that controls it. Not surprisingly, the respondents identified software design and development as one of the most difficult and time consuming tasks in implementing CIM. Avishai (1989) also noted that development of software was a major concern and expense in the implementation of CIM at a major U.S. manufacturer.

A second question concerns the manner in which systems are designed and selected, and the manner in which software is developed. Huang and Sakurai noted that U.S. companies tend to rely heavily on outside consultants in designing and selecting systems whereas all of the Japanese manufacturers in their study had performed these tasks in-house. Japanese manufacturers are at least perceived to be more adept at managing highly integrated and automated technology than their U.S. counterparts. An appropriate research question is the degree to which CIM implementation is related to the manner in which systems and software are designed and developed.

Finally, Huang and Sakurai's respondents cited issues that were primarily technological in nature as the major impediments to CIM. Yoder (1990), who focused on CIM among U.S. manufacturers, suggests that "people" issues - more so than technological issues - are the primary impediment. More comparative research would help researchers to better understand how experiences with CIM implementation can be expected to vary among different manufacturing regions.

Process Re-Design

Process re-design and re-engineering can be defined as a methodical approach to analyzing processes, the objective being to eliminate ineffective and/or inefficient processes. Process re-engineering is an important component of any process integration effort, such as CIM.

One of the goals of time-based manufacturing systems, such as just-in-time, is to eliminate all but the essential transactions required to produce and deliver goods and services. Unnecessary or redundant transactions require time and resources, and have a negative impact on cycle time and customer service. This is especially true in the global manufacturing company. The manual entry of data from a printed form, for example, provides a significant source of potential errors and time delays. Information technology is at a point where manual order entry is no longer necessary. Rather, information may be gathered by means such as bar coding and optical scanning. The advantages include increased processing speed and a lower margin of error.

Some transactions may be eliminated outright. Consider how the clothing manufacturer Benetton has eliminated the need for requisitions to replenish stock in its retail outlets. Benetton has been defined as "essentially an extremely intelligent information-feedback loop, tying cash register data directly to robotic sewing machines" (Unruh 1991). Once an hour, a mainframe sweeps the bar code information at Benetton's various points of sale and signals robotic fabric-cutting sewing machines 6000 miles away to produce schedule and produce replacements. Then, they bag it, put a bar code on it and send it on its way.

Elimination of transactions is complemented by re-thinking the flow of transactions, inventory, and material through the process. It serves to point out that information systems and technology, in and of themselves, are not enough. Successful companies are able to identify useful and critical data flows and information needs, and eliminate the rest.

Davenport and Short (1990) provide an extensive discussion of the role of information technology in business process design. They note that information technology is an integral and essential part of process re-design, and should be considered early in the re-design process. It is important to consider the capabilities and limitations of information technology early on as these capabilities can and should influence process redesign. IT is also an enabler in process re-design. Certain aspects of re-design are not possible without the information collection and processing capabilities of IT.

COMPARATIVE STATISTICS

Most of the IS/IT issues that have been discussed in previous sections of this chapter are assumed to be relevant to all multi-national manufacturers without regard to their country of origin. The limited amount of research that is available suggests that the perceived importance of and experience with IS/IT in manufacturing applications varies among geographical regions.

Giffi and Roth (1992), for example, included manufacturing technology questions in their comparative study of Japanese and US manufacturing. Responses from 900 manufacturing executives were reported. Several observations are suggested by the results:

The authors of the study noted that the majority of respondents in both Japan and the US did *not* indicate an average or greater "degree of experience" for most applications of state-of-the-art technology. In spite of this, there was substantial interest in both countries in concepts such as value analysis/value engineering and computer-aided design.

Japanese manufacturers' "degree of experience" was as high or higher than that of their US counterparts in most applications of state-of-the-art technology.

Japanese and US manufacturers perceived differences in the importance of certain IT/IS to future success. For example a considerably larger percentage of Japanese respondents identified computer-aided design, engineering, and process control as having "above average importance to future success"

The authors of the study suggested that the Japanese perception of the importance of technology may reflect their concerns over the future availability of Japanese labor for the manufacturing sector.

Another comparative study that has been reported in the literature is that of Daniel and Reitsperger (1991). Based on a sample of electronics manufacturers in the US and Japan, the authors concluded that management information systems in Japan better reflected the strategies of JIT than did those of US manufacturers.

More studies such as the two described above would help researchers to better understand the role of IS/IT in the production and operations function. Studies that include other manufacturing regions such as Europe and Pacific Rim countries would also be a contribution to the literature.

CONCLUSIONS AND SUGGESTIONS FOR FURTHER RESEARCH

The purpose of this chapter has been to identify and discuss IS/IT issues that are important in integrating, planning and controlling global manufacturing and operations functions. It is clear that domestic and multi-national manufacturers do not face all the same issues in their use of information systems and technology. Global manufacturers face intense pressure to improve quality, reduce costs, accelerate product development, and reduce manufacturing lead times. The need to be responsive and innovative, and to serve a range of diverse markets simultaneously, is driving current initiatives in manufacturing such as computer integrated manufacturing and flexible manufacturing systems. Each of these initiatives shares the critical need for accurate, relevant, and timely information.

There are many opportunities for researchers interested in further exploring IS/IT issues in the context of production and operations. The most crucial need is for *empirical* research. There are few published studies that in any way investigate IS/IT issues and their relationship to global manufacturing and operations. Empirical research would help to identify the key issues. *Comparative* empirical research would help to identify how IS/IT issues vary among different regions of the world.

A number of IS/IT related issues in need of further research have been suggested in this chapter. These include issues such as the degree to which data processing is centralized versus de-centralized, standards and methods for data transfer, and the development of standardized part-programming languages and operator interfaces. In general, there is a need for research on how IS/IT activities are and should be organized vis-a-vis the manufacturing and operations needs of the organization. A study by Jarvenpaa and Ives (1993) explores alternative IT designs in the global environment. More research of this type is needed with particular emphasis on the manufacturing and operations function.

Planning and controlling issues relevant to manufacturing and operations include the role of IS/IT in plant location, demand management, production allocation, and product design and development. Relevant issues include the degree to which concepts such as CIM meet the needs global manufacturers. One question, as noted earlier, concerns the extent to which CIM delivers the flexibility and responsiveness it is intended to provide, and the role IS/IT plays in achieving this flexibility.

Researchers should also consider how global IS/IT issues vary between manufacturers and service organizations. Most research indicates that the strategies and concerns of service organizations differ from those of manufacturers (see, e.g., Anderson, Cleveland, and Schroeder, 1989). Deans et al. (1991) specifically noted that IS/IT issues appear to vary between *multi-national* manufacturing and service organizations as well.

ENDNOTES

[1] Interview with Terri Hechler, Hamilton Beach/Proctor-Silex, Data Communications Specialist, Interview, October 1, 1992.

[2] Interview with Bruce Chambers, Reynolds Metals, EDI Coordinator, Interview, September 10, 1992.

[3] Interview with Chad Nystrom, IBM, Senior Marketing Representative, Interview, November 1, 1992.

REFERENCES

Anderson, J.C., Cleveland, G., & Schroeder, R.G. (1989). Operations strategy: a literature review, *Journal of Operations Management*, 8(2), 133-158.

Avishai, B. (1989). A CEO's common sense of CIM: an interview with J. Tracy O'Rourke, *Harvard Business Review*, January-February, 110-117.

Daniel, S.J. & Reitsperger, W.D. (1991). Management control systems for J.I.T.: an empirical comparison of Japan and the U.S., *Journal of International Business Studies*, Fourth Quarter, 603-617.

Davenport, T.H. & Short, J.E. (1990). The new industrial engineering: information technology and business process redesign, *Sloan Management Review*, Summer, 11-27.

Deans, P.C, Karwan, K.R., Goslar, M.D., Ricks, D.A., & Toyne, B. (1991). Identification of key international information systems issues in U.S.-based multinational corporations, *Journal of Management Information Systems*, 7(4), 27-50.

Drucker, P.F. (1991). Japan: new strategies for a new reality, *The Wall Street Journal*, Wednesday, October 2.

Faltermayer, E. (1991). U.S. companies come back home, *Fortune*, December 30, 106-112.

Genest, D.H. (1990). SOI: a path to global manufacturing, *Quality*, August, 49-51.

Giffi, C.A. & Roth, A.V. (1992). *Winning in global markets: survey of U.S. and Japanese manufacturing*. Cleveland: Research report by Deloitte & Touche Manufacturing Consulting Services.

Goldhar, J.D. & Lei, D. (1991). The shape of twenty-first century manufacturing, *The Journal of Business Strategy*, March/April, 37-41.

Groover, M.P. (1987). *Automation, production systems, and computer integrated manufacturing.* Englewood Cliffs NJ: Prentice Hall.

Haug, P. (1992). An international location and production transfer model for high technology multinational enterprises, *International Journal of Production Research,* 30(3), 559-572.

Howard, R. (1991). The designer organization: Italy's GFT goes global, *Harvard Business Review,* September-October, 28-44.

Huang, P.Y. & Sakurai, M. (1990). Factory automation: the Japanese experience, *IEEE Transactions on Engineering Management,* 37(2), 102-108.

Jarvenpaa, S.L. & Ives, B. (1993). Organizing for global competition: the fit of information technology, *Decision Sciences,* 24(3), 547-580.

McGrath, M.E. & Hoole, R.W. (1992). Manufacturing's new economies of scale, *Harvard Business Review,* May-June, 94-102.

Melnyck, S.A. & Narasimhan, R. (1992). *Computer integrated manufacturing: guidelines and applications from industrial leaders.* Homewood IL: Business One Irwin.

Smith, S.B. (1989). *Computer-based production and inventory control.* Englewood Cliffs NJ: Prentice Hall.

Swamidass, P.M. (1990). A comparison of the plant location strategies of foreign and domestic manufacturers in the U.S., *Journal of International Business Studies,* 2nd Quarter, 301-317.

Taylor, W. (1991). The logic of global business: an interview with ABB's Percy Barnevik, *Harvard Business Review,* March-April, 90-105.

Unruh, J.A. (1991). Pirates and Pioneers, *Unisphere,* January 1991, 38.

Von Simson, E.M. (1990). The 'centrally decentralized' IS organization, *Harvard Business Review,* July-August, 158-162.

Yoder, S.K. (1990). Putting it all together: computer-integrated factories are said to be the savior of industry. But can anyone make the system work?, *The Wall Street Journal,* Monday, June 4.

CHAPTER 13

Information Technology and Leadtime Management in International Manufacturing Operations

FRANK L. DUBOIS
The American University

ERRAN CARMEL
The American University

As international market opportunities expand and the costs of information technology falls, the ability of multinational enterprises (MNEs) to integrate information technology-based solutions to manufacturing and distribution problems increases. The purpose of this chapter is to discuss the components of an idealized model of an international manufacturing and distribution system and to illustrate this model by examining the progress that a major U.S. industrial and consumer goods manufacturer is making towards reaching this goal.

INTRODUCTION

The effective management of international manufacturing and distribution activities (of which leadtimes are a major dimension) is a critical component of a multinational firm's competitive advantage

[Giunipero and Moncza 1990; Deans and Kane 1992]. The use of information technology (IT) to enhance this advantage offers opportunities to study the interactions between the use of IT and the extent to which manufacturing and distribution performance is improved in an environment of time-based competition (Stalk and Hout 1990, Bower and Hout 1988). For the purpose of this chapter, we draw attention to actions that organizations can take to reduce the lead times involved in supplying their customers. In the next sections of this chapter we discuss the forces operating on firms to reduce lead times and then move on to the discussion of an idealized model of a global manufacturing and distribution system. In the final two sections we discuss the international manufacturing and distribution operations of the Black and Decker Corporation and the progress that they are making in moving towards this idealized model in their international activities.

THE ENVIRONMENT OF GLOBAL OPERATIONS

Most manufacturing processes are by nature separable into distinct operational stages (or components of the value chain) whose execution can be performed in a location different from that of the eventual market. If managed well, disaggregation of the manufacturing processes across national boundaries can provide an organization with numerous benefits not available to firms that limit their activities to only one country. Operations can be placed in areas where local factor endowments are most amenable to that stage of the process; labor-intensive operations in low wage areas for instance. Factory "focus" can be enhanced as a result of manufacturing specialization in a particular function or process leading to greater economies in manufacture (Skinner 1974). Spatial separation of manufacturing stages may also permit greater responsiveness to the characteristics of the local market when final assembly operations are located close to end-user markets. From the corporate perspective, dispersal of manufacturing activities into different nations offers benefits through financial and tax system arbitrage (Kogut 1985, Aggarwal and Soenen 1989).

On the negative side, the dispersal of manufacturing activities entails the assumption of much greater levels of risk. In the case of transborder shipment of parts and components to other stages of the production process, orders may not arrive on time, orders may be incomplete or quality problems may compromise later stages of the process that depend on reliable delivery of zero defect components—especially in a Just In Time (JIT) type of manufacturing environment. One or more of these contingencies may result in an avoidable disruption in the manufacturing process leading to lost customer goodwill, lost sales, higher costs and the possible degrading of the organization's viability. This is coupled with the reality of doing business with the so called "super-retailers" or major retail chains such as K-Mart and Wal-Mart in the U.S. who are putting pressure on suppliers to squeeze inventory out of the supply chain to reduce costs while simultaneously demanding superior service levels. Wal-Mart, for example, targets its operating and selling expenses at 15% of sales compared to 28% for Sears, Roebuck & Company (Business Week, 1992). Many analysts cite this as a major reason for Sear's recent problems.

In responding to these pressures, numerous consumer goods companies have instituted systems to compress delivery times and increase responsiveness to customers needs: VF Corporation reduced its restocking time from 80 days two years ago to 4-7 days today (Information Week, 1992); the apparel manufacturer Levi Strauss has organized a system known as LeviLink with its major customers to reduce resupply times. As such, a critical component of a firm's manufacturing and distribution strategy is the development of an information system capable of tracking the status and capabilities of the various parts of the system (Roche 1992). This is especially critical given the aforementioned benefits that can arise from careful coordination of activities located in different regions of the world.

INTERNATIONAL MANUFACTURING STRATEGY

The extent to which disruptions in a production process can be tolerated without significant cost penalties is directly related to an organization's manufacturing strategy. Wheelwright (1978) suggests that manufacturing strategy is dependent on a firm's differential focus on the dimensions of cost, quality, dependability and flexibility. The extent to which these dimensions are prioritized defines the firm's manufacturing strategy which in turn leads to the adoption of one or more types of international manufacturing configuration. Depending on the firm's experience and commitment to developing international markets its international manufacturing configuration(s) may range from the use of stand-alone, export-oriented facilities to a globally dispersed configuration involving vertical integration of spatially separable components of the manufacturing process (DuBois, Toyne, and Oliff 1993).

Organizations prioritizing low manufacturing costs in their manufacturing strategies, for example, are more likely to adopt strategies that incorporate the use of "offshore" locations in low wage countries, at least for the labor-intensive stages of the manufacturing process. When flexibility and dependability are priorities, low wages may take a backseat to preferences for locations that offer close proximity to

1. __Home Country Manufacturing__: A centralized strategy consisting of almost all manufacturing taking place in the company's country of origin with a high degree of global sourcing taking place through third parties. Sales representatives or joint ventures/licensing agreements are used to gain access to foreign markets.

2. __Regional Manufacturing__: This strategy takes the view that the world is composed of various regions having essentially common characteristics (similar markets, common distribution requirements, government policies) and develops manufacturing operations in these areas at either the product or component level.

3. __Coordinated Global Manufacturing__: This is the classic strategy for taking advantage of low labor costs. This strategy typically leads to the firm having separate manufacturing facilities for lower level components and subassemblies. Outputs are then transferred to other facilities for final assembly.

4. __Combined Regional and Coordinated Global Manufacturing__: This involves a mix of the second and third strategies with component and subassembly manufacturing in low cost regions and final assembly in regions close to markets.

Source: Adapted from McGrath, M. and R. Bequillard (1989) International Manufacturing Strategies and Infrastructural Considerations in the Electronics Industry. In __Management of International Manufacturing__ (ed.), K. Ferdows. Amsterdam: North Holland p. 24.

__Table 1: Manufacturing Configuration Strategies__

major customer markets. As such, the choice of which manufacturing configuration strategy to adopt will dictate the scale and scope of information technology requirements.

No matter what sort of international manufacturing configuration is used, centralization of manufacturing coordination is mandated by the need for coherent and consistent administrative mechanisms to control parts and components flows from sources both internal and external to the firm. Information technology needs then are a function of the complexity of the manufacturing environment. The more complex the international manufacturing configuration, the greater the amount of risk that something will not happen according to plan and the greater the need for a sophisticated decision support system to coordinate activities; especially in time-critical competitive environments.

AN IDEALIZED MODEL OF A GLOBAL MANUFACTURING AND DISTRIBUTION INFORMATION SYSTEM

"The ideal integrated logistics and information system is one in which minutes after an aluminum patio chair is purchased in Topeka, another shovel full of bauxite is thrown into a rail-car in Shandong province." [Hypothetical Chinese Proverb]

The above proverb illustrates the pressures facing a typical multinational manufacturer engaged in global competition. In the past, inventory stocks and lead times provided buffers between the manufacturing function and the customer. Twenty years ago there was just no other way to prevent discontinuities between stages of the supply chain. Because of the lag between when information became available and when it could be used as an input to decision making, businesses built up inventories in anticipation of future sales. During periods of strong economic growth, optimistic sales forecasts led manufacturers to produce as if these conditions would continue indefinitely. If sales were lower than expected, manufacturers were left with excess stock to dispose of in some way. Hence, the economic effects of recessionary periods were exacerbated; layoffs occurred, unemployment rose, industrial output dropped, and other sectors of the economy were drawn into the downturn. Since most manufacturing operations were notoriously inflexible in dealing with changes in the demand environment, there was little that organizations could do to increase responsiveness to changes in demand.

In the 1980s, with the advent of better and less expensive information technology resources, improved telecommunications infrastructures, and increased pressure from more efficient competitors in Asia and Western Europe, this dynamic began to change. As a result of the influential work of numerous academics (notably Hall and Schonberger) many western businesses have adopted a Just-in-Time manufacturing philosophy as a solution to the competitiveness problems that they confronted during the 1970s and early 1980s. Key to the successful implementation of this philosophy is the timely exchange of information between upstream and downstream stages of the manufacturing process[1]. This philosophy has percolated outward from the factory floor—where its implementation has dramatically reduced inventories and lead times as well as asset and workforce requirements—to encompass an increase in linkages with organizations external to the enterprise.

For a typical manufacturer this means information linkages not only with suppliers but with customers leading to dramatically better performance of the manufacturing and distribution functions. Unfortunately, as manufacturing activities have become more international in scope over the last two decades, numerous complications have arisen for organizations attempting to integrate activities across national boundaries. Previous research has highlighted four issues that must be addressed in developing an effective global manufacturing and distribution information system: centralization of data for decision making, data management, organizational changes and external relationship changes (Roche 1992, DuBois, Toyne, and Oliff 1993).

These four issues are the foundation for a more detailed list of nine characteristics that make up an idealized model of a global manufacturing and distribution information system:

- **Centralized coordination of information flows**. For a multinational corporation this implies a significant investment in hardware, software and telecommunications infrastructure.
- **Total logistics management**. All transportation, ordering, and manufacturing systems are integrated. Order change notices trigger a cascading series of modifications to production schedules, logistics plans, and warehouse operations. For organizations composed of more than one business unit there must be a mechanism whereby transportation resources can be shared across different businesses both within and across national boundaries.
- **Global inventory management**. The ability to locate and track the movement of every item no matter where located.
- **Global sourcing**. The consolidation of the purchasing function across organizational lines so as to prevent duplication and to take advantage of quantity discounts through order aggregation. This might also permit component standardization across different business units.
- **Intercompany information access**. There must be a means of allowing access to production and demand information residing in organizations on both sides of the value chain: both upstream and downstream.
- **Data interchange**. The ability to exchange data between affiliates and non-affiliates through standard telecommunications channels and information protocols.
- **Data capture**. The ability to acquire data about an order at the point of origin and to track products during movement and as their characteristics change. Innovations in bar coding and laser scanning technology have allowed significant advances in this area.
- **Transformation of the business from within**. This has been discussed elsewhere (Senge 1992, for example). From the perspective of IT design, what is critical is the development of managers

able to see the "big picture" and to suppress parochial instincts in favor of systemwide optimization. Top-level commitment and leadership coupled with a realistic means of measuring performance is essential.

• **Improvements in supplier-customer relationships** to justify investments in Electronic Data Interchange (EDI) linkages. This applies to both upstream (suppliers) and downstream (customers) linkages. The scope and size of the commitment will be in direct relation to the scope, size and number of transactions between the two parties.

Figure 1 illustrates the linkages between the various components of this idealized model. In this figure, information flows are separated from product and material flows to show how the centralization of information technology activities allows better coordination of activities in different locations. In the model, all international manufacturing activities would be coordinated by a centralized headquarters data management and analysis function. This function would have

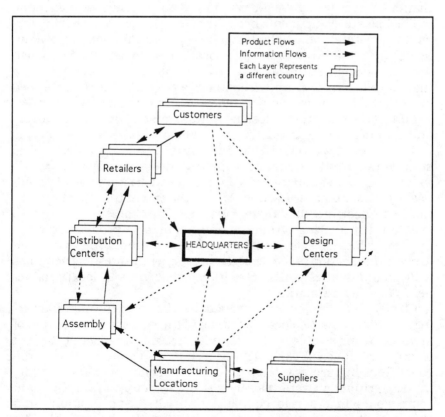

Figure 1: An Idealized Model of Information and Product Flows in an MNE

access to all information necessary to adjust production schedules to correspond to consumer demand at all locations. It would also have access to information concerning the availability of transportation assets between stages of the manufacturing and supply chain. As customer demand information became available, it would be disaggregated by product line and dispersed into organizational functional areas where appropriate. This information would be available on a daily basis and used as inputs into the production planning process used at the individual plant level. Manufacturing schedules and loading could then be easily adjusted upward and downward to correspond to actual rather than anticipated demand (making allowances for leadtimes).

In the diagram, the manufacturing and assembly functions are separated into two areas to reflect the realities of actual practice and the efficiencies possible by focusing activities in those plants that have a comparative advantage in performing certain activities. It is often the case that, because of differing capabilities across manufacturing facilities, there is some transhipment of subassemblies and components from one plant to another. For example, one plant in the manufacturing system might provide all other plants with injection molded plastic components because of the expense of providing this equipment to all other plants. Another scenario might involve an assembly plant in a low wage location such as Mexico which assembles components imported from a capital-intensive plant in a high wage location. Output from the low wage plant is then shipped back to the high wage country where major markets are located[2].

Linkages between the design centers, customers, headquarters and manufacturing locations are meant to illustrate the varying influences on new product design and introduction. In a prototypical situation such as this, changes in product design and features evolve in response to customer needs, financial constraints, and capabilities of the manufacturing function. To the extent that there is more than one design center there must be a mechanism designed to facilitate the sharing of information about new product developments in other markets. Ideally, design centers should be structured to avoid duplication in the design of components and subassemblies while simultaneously maximizing responsiveness to local product needs in different markets.

Efficient information and product flows between the manufacturing function and suppliers are critical to the successful execution of manufacturing strategy. This includes not only strategies designed to support Just In Time deliveries but also initiatives towards concurrent engineering of new products. In concurrent engineering, the design function works closely with outside suppliers of parts and components in order to couple new product specifications and characteristics more closely to those which are already available. The objective is to maximize the use of already existing inputs in new products or, when preexisting inputs are not available, to involve outside suppliers as early as possible in the design phase of the new product.

The customer/retailer/distribution center linkage offers an opportunity to reduce the amount of time that it takes for inventories to be replenished. As discussed in an earlier section, retailers at the cutting edge of inventory management have established point-of-sale hookups back to distribution centers so that inventory levels can be monitored and orders triggered based on real consumption as opposed to anticipated consumption trends. In the ideal situation, manufacturers can track sales of different products in different markets and can adjust production schedules and marketing programs in response to consumer demand. This linkage gives a manufacturer the ability to rapidly respond to any changes in demand that may take place.

The idealized model discussed above represents a utopia that, at present, few organizations have achieved. Aside from the expense of developing such a system there may be numerous institutional and infrastructural barriers that need to be removed before more organizations fit the above profile. In the next section we discuss the progress that the Black & Decker Corporation is making towards this ideal.

INTERNATIONAL MANUFACTURING AND DISTRIBUTION AT BLACK & DECKER

Company Background

The Black and Decker Corporation (B&D), based in Towson, Maryland, has during its 80-year history grown to become the world's largest manufacturer of hand tools. Largely as the result of an aggressive acquisition strategy during the 1980s, sales growth has been strong. Presently, B&D ranks number 109 in the Fortune US 500. International sales accounted for approximately 45% of total revenues of $4.7 billion (1991). $1.4 billion in revenues come from Western Europe, $.7 billion from other countries. Several acquisitions over the last 10 years have served to redefine the Black and Decker name in the minds of consumers.

The purchase of General Electric's Housewares division in 1984 put B&D into a new business sector with toaster ovens, irons, coffee makers, can openers and cordless vacuums. Acquisition of the Emhart Corporation in 1989 effectively doubled the size of the company and gave B&D complementary product lines in plumbing equipment (with Price-Pfister) and security hardware (with Kwikset locks) but also presented the firm with the problem of effectively integrating Emhart's many other business units into the B&D hierarchy.   Other business units acquired through Emhart have been or are in the process of being sold to work off debt undertaken to finance the original acquisition (approximately $4 billion).

Black and Decker is the seventh most widely recognized brand name in the USA (Fortune 1992) and is known primarily for its manufacture of power hand tools and accessories for the consumer do-it-yourself market.   The firm recently branched out into the professional power tool segment with a premium line of tools sold under the Dewalt brand name. B&D has been involved internationally since 1918 beginning with sales representatives in Russia, Japan and Australia.   In 1922 it opened its first manufacturing facility outside the U.S., in Canada.

Two major goals guide B&D design of an integrated manufacturing and distribution system:

(1) The ability to inform the customer within 4 hours whether or not demand can be met; and,
(2) to deliver a customer order to the nearest distribution center anywhere in the world within 5 days of order receipt.

Information Systems

Spending on information systems is approximately 2% of sales or $100 million. A major focus in North American operations in recent years is the implementation of a "Quick Response" system to handle accounts with major customers in the U.S., Canada and to a lesser extent, Mexico.   Data centers are located one each in Maryland, Ontario, and Mexico. Several smaller centers are located in Europe, which are gradually being consolidated into one centralized location in Spennymore, England. A small data center is located in Singapore to handle manufacturing and distribution requirements from that location.   Only the U.S. and Canadian data centers are tightly coupled.   In addition to manufacturing and distribution some product design systems (Computer Aided Design) permit cross-national collaboration via satellite. This is expected to increase in the future as all design centers adopt a common design system.   The Information Systems function is organized in a mixed fashion, with some units reporting by product orientation and others reporting by country.

Because of its position as a dominant manufacturer in both housewares and hand tools, B&D has been an early partner with its major retail customers in developing a Quick Response and Electronic Data Interchange (EDI) strategy to minimize inventory levels and lead times while keeping customer service levels high.   A

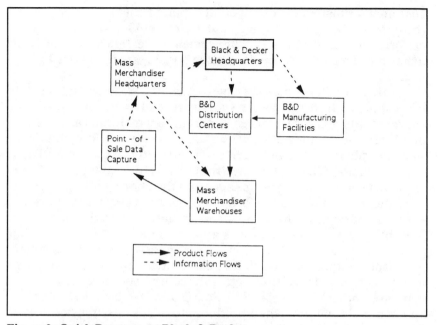

Figure 2: Quick Response at Black & Decker

program with Wal-Mart, for example, has reduced delivery cycle times by a factor of 2 with no compromise in service levels.

Figure 2 illustrates how the Quick Response system for North America operates. At the retail level, Point-Of-Sale devices capture data on sales quantities and continuously update inventory levels. When inventories reach a certain preestablished level an order is triggered to Black & Decker to replenish inventories at the customer's warehouse. Since none of B&D's manufacturing facilities are equipped to hold finished goods inventories, customer orders are processed through centrally located distribution centers spread around the U.S. Finished goods inventories are required to be held off-site because manufacturing facilities are organized around the product's motor size; products using different size motors (e.g., drills or power saws) are consolidated at a centralized "mixing' facility rather than being shipped directly from the plant to the customer.

An interesting feature of this system is the use of electronically transmitted Advance Shipping Notices to advise customers of discrepancies between what was ordered and what is being shipped. Prior practice dictated that customers did not know what they were going to receive until the order was actually delivered. As a result, undelivered merchandise was backordered or the unfilled portion of the shipment was canceled. The new system allows customers to more accurately adjust replenishment plans in anticipation of shipment arrivals and there is now less likelihood of backorders being canceled. In another innovation with a major customer, the customer's finished goods inventory management is delegated directly to B&D. This arrangement is, of course, subject to strict performance constraints but illustrates the extent to which some major retail customers are delegating some responsibilities to suppliers.

On the supplier side, B&D has enlisted its major suppliers in programs that have resulted in significant lead time reductions. One aspect of this program involves imported raw materials and components. Rather than waiting for orders from B&D before shipment, some suppliers are now staging inventories in the U.S. in anticipation of orders. The use of Electronic Data Interchange (EDI) has improved communications linkages and the sharing of manufacturing schedules and other information between B&D and its major suppliers and is permitting better coordination of production plans. Presently, this program involves approximately 150 suppliers that provide over 50% of B&D's parts, component, and subassembly purchases. Shipping costs have been reduced by coordinating raw materials and finished products shipments between different vendors and other B&D plants. For example, the B&D plant in Singapore shipping finished products to a U.S. distribution center might consolidate shipments with another Singaporean manufacturer supplying raw materials to a U.S. B&D manufacturing facility. Loads are then broken up at the U.S. distribution center and the raw materials dispersed to the appropriate manufacturing facility. Previously, no shipments would leave the Singapore factory until there was a full container load of product. Use of this consolidation technique has cut 2 to 3 weeks from lead time between the U.S. and the Far East.

Similarly, in Western Europe, where there is shipment of finished product in both directions—from European plants to the North American markets and from North American plants to the European market—there have been innovations in the way transatlantic shipments are coordinated. Previous practice involved shipments directly to a country-specific European distribution center located in the eventual consuming market. Again, this compromised the speed with which full container loads of products could be assembled and shipped to the final market. The new system involves consolidating European requirements at the US distribution center and shipping to a pan-European distribution center in England. Shipments are then "blown - out" and disaggregated into the requirements for each individual European market. The identical system is now used for shipments from European facilities back to the U.S.

Impediments to Global Integration

At present, other opportunities for improvements in Black and Decker's manufacturing and distribution system in Western Europe are hampered by numerous structural and institutional impediments. Despite the ongoing implementation of the Europe 1992 program with its goal of eliminating all trade barriers between the 12 members of the community, it is perceived that information-technology based enhancements to intra-community product and material shipments lag advances that have been made in North America by three to five years. The reasons are numerous and are useful in illustrating the extent to which country specific differences in business practice and infrastructural considerations inhibit economic integration.

To begin with, the telecommunications infrastructure is still very fragmented between countries. This serves to impede information flows and development of EDI systems until such time that pan-European data transmission standards are adopted and implemented and the cost of intra-community communications falls. The eventual deregulation of the communications industry should lead to improvements in this area. In addition, Point-of-Sale devices are not in widespread usage in most of Europe. This exacerbates the "gap" between when sales information is generated and when it is available as an input to decision making in the manufacturing and distribution system.

The structure of retail establishments is also different in each country. There are still no true pan-European mass merchandisers. Each country is characterized by different retail structures and differing philosophies about customer service needs and accompanying distribution methods. Product and packaging standardization is also not uniform. The German market, for example, imposes much stricter standards for electromagnetic shielding than other community members. As yet, a pan-European product has not been developed. Similarly, language differences between countries mandate different requirements in terms of packaging.

Two other inhibitors to integration exist at the beginning and end of the information/product loop depicted in figure 1. The order process is such that orders "hit the system" anywhere from 1 to 13 weeks after being placed. Only then can the system begin responding to them. The other inhibitor is at the final link in the loop; the movement of product from distribution center to retail outlet. In Europe, this link is controlled by independent jobbers who are not connected to the IS structure and whose schedules cannot be tightly controlled. Finally, although border crossings have been streamlined and much paperwork and documentation eliminated, the development of pan-European trucking and freight services is still in its infancy.

In spite of all these difficulties, B&D is optimistic that the loops connecting the various stages of the value chain will begin to close in Europe and Asia and between these locations and North America. One non-IS factor may accelerate this cycle, at least for Europe:

B&D's manufacturing plants are now operating over capacity and any incremental additions to output levels are pushing more and more manufacturing into underutilized European plants.

CONCLUSION

The purpose of this chapter was to present an idealized view of a global manufacturing and distribution system incorporating a centralized information technology management function. Customers in the global marketplace are becoming increasingly intolerant of the inefficiencies that result from ineffective management of product distribution. In an effort to improve product distribution, more and more businesses are taking steps to facilitate the flows of information between dispersed stages of the value chain. As shown in the illustration of Black and Decker's global information and distribution system, advances are incremental as systems are better managed and coordinated to reduce inefficiencies. To some extent, the idealized model is captured within B&D's Quick Response system though only for North American operations. The trans-ocean/cross-border aspects of the ideal model are still distant for most firms—not because of the information technology limitations (which are still extensive), but because of the economics of sourcing, manufacturing and assembly. The idealized model represents a situation that is to be strived for. Cost constraints and the inability to justify benefits prevent its adoption by many firms. However, as we see from B&D's North American Quick Response system, major improvements in parts of the system can lead to dramatic payoffs over the long term. For operations in other geographic regions (such as Western Europe) numerous obstacles remain for the large scale adoption of a hybrid system such as this.

ACKNOWLEDGMENTS

We warmly appreciate the cooperation of several senior managers associated with the Black & Decker Corporation in this research.

ENDNOTES

[1] Upstream refers to those stages closest to the source of raw materials and components, downstream to those closest to the final consumer.

[2] In current North American practice, these are known as Maquiladora operations. Most are located along the U.S. - Mexico border and operate under the aegis of U.S. and Mexico tariff regulations permiting reimportation of components with duty applied only to value-added in Mexico.

REFERENCES

Aggarwal, R. & Soenen, L. (1989). Managing persistent real changes in currency values; The role of multinational operating strategies, *Columbia Journal of World Business*, 24(3).

Baxter, Andrew. (1993). Delivering the goods, *Financial Times*, January 18, page 6.

Benjamin, R.I. and Blunt, J. (1992). Critical IT Issues: The next ten years, *Sloan Management Review*, Summer, v.33(4).

Bower, J.L. and Hout, T.M. (1988). Fast cycle capability for competitive power, *Harvard Business Review*, Nov - Dec.

DuBois, F., Toyne, B. and M. Oliff. (1993). International manufacturing configuration strategies: Studies in four industries, *Journal of International Business Studies*, 24(2).

Business Week. (1992). Clout, *Business Week*, December 21, 1992, 66.

Eurich, J.P. and Roth, G. (1990). EDIF Grows Up, *IEEE Spectrum*, November.

Giunipero, Larry C. and Robert M. Moncza. (1990). Organizational approaches to managing international sourcing, *International Journal of Physical Distribution and Logistics Management*, 20(4), 3-12.

Hall, Robert W. (1983). *Zero Inventories*. New York: Dow Jones-Irwin.

Information Week. (1992). 500: The biggest and best users of information technology, *Information Week*, September 21.

Kogut, Bruce. (1985). Designing global strategies: Profiting from operational flexibility, *Sloan Management Review*, Fall, 27-38.

McGrath, M. & Bequillard R. (1989). International manufacturing strategies and infrastructural considerations in the electronics industry. In K. Ferdows (Ed.), *Management of International Manufacturing*. Amsterdam: North Holland, 23-40.

Porter, M. (1982). *Competitive Advantage*, New York: The Free Press.

Roche, Edward M. (1992). *Managing Information Technology in Multinational Corporations*. New York: MacMillan.

Rochester, J.D. (1989). The strategic value of EDI, *I/S Analyzer*, 28(8).

Senge, Peter (1991). *The Fifth Discipline: The Art and Practice of the Learning Organization*. New York: Doubleday.

Shonberger, Richard J. (1982), *Japanese Manufacturing Techniques*. New York: The Free Press.

Skinner, W. (1974). The focused factory. *Harvard Business Review*, 52(3), 113-121.

Stalk, G. & Hout, T. (1990). *Competing against time: How time based competition is reshaping global markets*. New York: The Free Press.

Wheelwright, S.C. (1978). Reflecting corporate strategy in manufacturing decisions. *Business Horizons*, 21(February), 57-66.

CHAPTER 14

Integration and Flexibility: The Promise of CIM for Global Manufacturing

PAUL M. SWAMIDASS
CHARLES A. SNYDER
Auburn University

Time-based competition calls for many changes in manufacturing. Primarily, successful time-based competition in domestic or global manufacturing requires integration of the manufacturing facilities, suppliers and customers. Computer integrated manufacturing (CIM) is a powerful tool for achieving this integration whether limited to one plant or many plants scattered across the globe. The extent of integration and flexibility that CIM can offer are illustrated using examples from Xerox and Oldsmobile.

According to a study conducted in 1990 (Swamidass, 1992), only about five percent of manufacturers were extremely skilled in the use of CIM. The low success rate with CIM adoption is due to the complexity, and time and effort required in implementation. This chapter uses current examples to highlight the problems faced by CIM users; the key problems being incompatibility between hardware and software, lack of skilled personnel to implement CIM, and the massive cultural change required. Naturally, these problems are magnified in the international context. Yet, the growth of CIM use in global manufacturing is inevitable. CIM is the technological answer to a number of problems arising from the far flung operations of global manufacturers.

INTRODUCTION

Global manufacturing is now a reality. Globalization in sourcing, production and marketing ". . . looks at the whole world as being nationless and borderless" (Sera, 1992, p. 89). One can make a distinction between multinational manufacturing and global manufacturing (Gopal, 1986). While multinational manufacturing may emphasize local production for each foreign market, global manufacturing takes a world perspective in which goods, capital and people move freely (Gopal, 1986; Sera, 1992).

In this chapter we address the issue of how global firms can engage in time-based competition. We show that enterprise integration and enterprise flexibility are the keys to time-based competition for global manufacturers. Next, we show how CIM promises to provide both integration and flexibility in manufacturing, using the example of an automaker. We then discuss how the implementation of CIM will need to overcome several hurdles, and highlight these problems as they have arisen in companies.

Regardless of the difficulties with CIM implementation, CIM is here to stay. If anything, CIM implementation will grow rapidly. A recent survey (Swamidass, 1992) of nearly 400 US manufacturing facilities of the members of the National Association of Manufacturers showed that 4.9 percent of manufacturing facilities are extremely skilled users of CIM but 20.3% (i.e., one in five) plan to excel in the use of CIM. We predict that, with the growing interest in CIM and with the emerging awareness of the problems of implementation, the difficulties with applications will decline in the years to come. It is readily apparent that CIM is essential to the success of global manufacturers engaged in time-based competition and operating multiple facilities in many countries.

THE CHALLENGE: TIME-BASED COMPETITION

It is argued by some that Japanese manufacturers' strategies have evolved over four decades from a low-cost strategy, to a scale-based strategy, to a focused manufacturing strategy, and now to a time-based strategy using flexible factories; the last being the most formidable of them all (Stalk and Hout, 1990). Time-based competition is impossible without a flexible factory that is part of a flexible enterprise. Flexible factories have the following characteristics:

(1) they compete on the basis of a high-variety of products and not high volume.Their product variety is always expanding.
(2) they use short production runs without compromising on cost.
(3) they use simple scheduling procedures.
(4) growth comes through flexibility.
(5) their response time to changes anywhere is very short.
(6) their lead time for manufacturing and for new product introduction is very short.
(7) their up-time for equipment is high.
(8) they compete based on focus without specialization.
(9) they use cell-based manufacturing as frequently as possible.
(10) they are engaged in time-compression in everything they do.
(11) they are able to innovate more rapidly.

The flexible firm is engaged in reducing cycle time continuously. In a typical organization, cycle time is made up of sales, order entry, design, engineering, pre-manufacturing, material procurement, manufacturing, storage, distribution and delivery. For a typical product, the actual operation time is usually less than five percent of the overall cycle time. To shorten the cycle, most of the reduction in time must come from activities that occur before or after the manufacturing operation. These activities are information dependent and are tied to various functions in the organization.

Global manufacturers are generally large in total sales and market share. Market shares are constantly under attack from other global as well as local manufacturers in every nation where they manufacturer and/or sell. Today, engaging in time-based competition is essential to the success and growth of global manufacturers. US manufacturers are realizing that developing a flexible enterprise consisting of flexible factories needed for time-based competition is slow and difficult. The magnitude of the problem becomes larger in the context of global manufacturers operating multiple manufacturing facilities in a number of countries.

THE BENEFITS OF INTEGRATION AND FLEXIBILITY

What determines success in global manufacturing? From the emerging literature, we can ascertain at least two important factors for successful global manufacturing. Consider the following quote:

> ... a multinational's new scale advantage comes from increased interaction *across* functions. When companies globalize the design process, for example, they may also create products that

are easier to manufacture. And when companies globalize purchasing, manufacturing is no longer tied to a specific plant, and designers are not limited by local suppliers.

A multinational of the future, fully integrated yet still flexible, may supply its component plants with raw materials from a single source; standardize the manufacturing process in British, German and American final assembly plants; enter customer orders into a worldwide order fulfillment system so that products are assembled in and distributed from the most convenient site; and install a sophisticated electronic network that links product designers, demand analysts, and production planners at all facilities." (McGrath and Hoole, 1992, p. 102)

As this quote stresses, integration with flexibility will be the key to success. Flexibility is the desired goal and integration is the tool by which flexibility can be attained in global operations.

The Case of Xerox

Consider the Xerox Corporation, which put integration to work in its global enterprise. In the late seventies, Xerox was a multinational with operations throughout the globe where each "company controlled its own suppliers, assembly plants, and distribution channels. . . The managers of these scattered plants gave little thought to how each one fit into the overall production plans of Xerox and rarely communicated with each other" (McGrath and Hoole, 1992, p. 95).

In the early eighties, Xerox was the market leader in the copier business but competitive pressures began to change that. The Cannon Corporation of Japan began to globalize its production with new design and manufacturing facilities in Europe and the US; until then, Cannon had primarily been an exporter from Japan. The rising competitive pressures caused Xerox to respond with a strategy of global integration. The following were the specific steps taken by Xerox to increase its position (McGrath and Hoole, 1992):

1. It consolidated raw materials sources and used a central purchasing group to cultivate high-quality, low-cost components for global operations, reduced number of suppliers from about 5,000 to about 400, and reduced purchasing overhead costs from 9% of material cost to 3%.
2. It created a new product-delivery process that standardized procedures and employed functionally and geographically integrated teams. Each product team managed the design, sourcing of components, manufacturing, distribution and customer service on a global basis.

3. It adopted global standards for basic processes applicable to all operations, e.g., databases for managing materials.
4 It adopted common business practices but tailored to local needs, e.g., JIT programs.
5. It also created common metrics and goals for plants to follow. This enabled product cost and inventory data to be compared across factories which led to better balancing of production and the utilization of excess inventory saving $20M in a two year period.
6. It adopted site-specific processes only for limited systems that must conform to local needs, e.g., government reporting requirements.
7. It created multifunctional, product-focused teams to integrate the supply chain across international boundaries. The effort is credited with saving $500M in worldwide inventories.
8. It integrated its product delivery system by creating a distribution center for spare parts for the US, Canadian, and Latin American markets. This helped the consolidation and shrinking of safety stocks, saving millions of dollars per year.

The benefits of this integration were felt in five areas: product development, purchasing, production, demand management, and order fulfillment. Altogether, the benefits enabled the firm to introduce new products more rapidly, reduce manufacturing cycle time and increase the overall flexibility of the enterprise. This particular case is a good illustration of how integration and flexibility, the keys to time-based competition, go together.

THE PROMISE OF CIM

Computer integrated manufacturing can be a valuable tool for accomplishing integration and flexibility in global manufacturing in an interconnected network of manufacturing facilities. The original CIM concept, which has evolved in many different forms, has many competing definitions. The following definition, which is rather comprehensive, captures most of the espoused concepts.

"CIM usually consists of such technologies as computer aided design and manufacturing (CAD/CAM), robotics, materials handling and automatic identification, machine vision, materials requirements planning (MRP), flexible manufacturing systems (FMS), communication network, and the just-in-time (JIT) philosophy as well as many systems that are outside of traditional industrial automation categories. Marketing, purchasing, engineering, production planning and control, finance, personnel, and strategic planning, as well as other functional

We visualize the domain of CIM to be

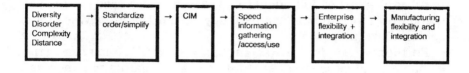

Figure 1

areas not directly concerned with the manufacturing process, must be integrated if CIM is to be successful" (Snyder and Cox, 1988; p. 198).

The process of planning for and implementing CIM in global manufacturing imposes standardization and rationalization upon the critical differences in functions, factories, hardware, software, and national standards, to bring about an order, compatibility and simplicity to a complex system that defies both order and simplicity. The promise of CIM in global firms is integration and flexibility through improved as well as quicker information capturing, information access, and information use by a network of factories and vendors across many nations.

Integration through CIM occurs not only by the integration of all the separate automated islands that are connected to each other, but by the integration of vendors and several manufacturing and non-manufacturing facilities of the manufacturer into a "single unit." Integration through CIM can be made to occur across product lines, functions and facilities that are spatially far apart.

Flexibility through CIM can be realized as enterprise flexibility whose subsets are manufacturing flexibility, marketing flexibility, and other functional area flexibilities. Manufacturing flexibility helps manufacturers to respond to changes in the marketplace with rapid changes and/or improvement in the product design, engineering, quality, manufacturing cycle-time, manufacturing processes, and so on. The strategic importance of flexibility in manufacturing is well documented in the literature (Swamidass, 1988, Swamidass and Newell, 1987).

A framework of CIM in the global firm is offered in Figure 1. It is elaborated upon in the subsequent sections of this chapter. This framework shows that the manufacturing environment is composed of diversity, disorder, complexity and distance between facilities. Therefore, before CIM can be implemented, there is a strong need for standardization, simplification and increased order. (This is highlighted in the Xerox example described above where, before integration could be accomplished, standardization had to occur in a number of areas.) Additionally, with CIM there is a need to consider standardization and/or compatibility of hardware, software and communication.

Furthermore, as indicated in the figure, once CIM is in place in the global setting, it should speed information gathering, increase access to information across boundaries, and generally increase the use of data and information. Finally, the figure depicts that the free flow of information on a timely basis across the firm is the key to enterprise flexibility and integration, as well as manufacturing integration and flexibility.

The Case of an Automaker

One case of successful implementation of CIM in a large automobile manufacturing environment is described here to acquaint the reader with the potential of CIM as well as to elaborate upon the framework in Figure 1. This example is based on a complex but predominantly U.S. operation of Buick-Oldsmobile-Cadillac (Hyduk, 1992). It displays the intricacies of complex manufacturing in a CIM environment. The goal of CIM here was to develop a "smart factory" that links all the islands of automation for maximum integration and flexibility. Very specific components of CIM were created to address integration and flexibility as described below.

Integration: The integration promised by the CIM system from the customer to the final assembly in this case is captured in Figure 2. The figure documents how a customer order placed at a dealership 2000 miles away will cause vendors to produce and ship to the assembly plant and cause the vehicle to be assembled, tested and shipped without human modification of the order; the customer, in effect, controls the specific processes in various plants. In the case of today's major automobile manufacturers, vendors are often located across national borders. According to one study (Swamidass and Kotabe, 1993), European and Japanese multinationals manufacturing in the US source 30% of their components from their home country. Another study (Swamidass, forthcoming) notes that current trends indicate that economic and non-economic forces are conducive to increased import sourcing of components used in manufacturing.

Integration at the assembly level links the on-board car computer

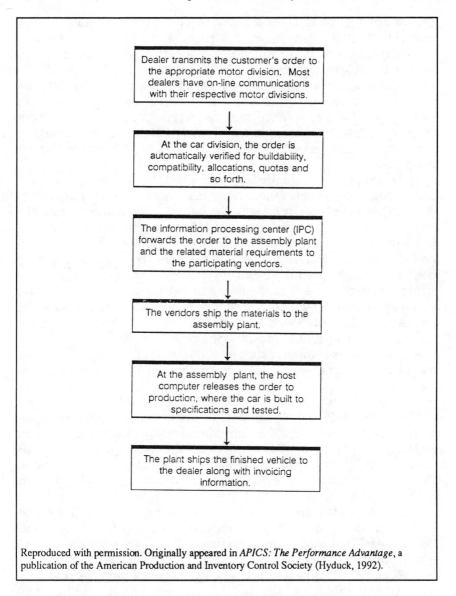

Dealer transmits the customer's order to the appropriate motor division. Most dealers have on-line communications with their respective motor divisions.

At the car division, the order is automatically verified for buildability, compatibility, allocations, quotas and so forth.

The information processing center (IPC) forwards the order to the assembly plant and the related material requirements to the participating vendors.

The vendors ship the materials to the assembly plant.

At the assembly plant, the host computer releases the order to production, where the car is built to specifications and tested.

The plant ships the finished vehicle to the dealer along with invoicing information.

Reproduced with permission. Originally appeared in *APICS: The Performance Advantage*, a publication of the American Production and Inventory Control Society (Hyduck, 1992).

Figure 2: Integration through CIM in Auto Manufacturing

of every car on the assembly line with the cell controller, which is linked to an area computer, which in turn is linked to the plant host computer; thus, the vehicle on the line is linked to the plant computer. The integration of production, planning and control is accomplished through three distinct systems:

a. **Manufacturing information database** (MIDB): "Once a day the plant host computer downloads data in the MIDB, the central depository for all data necessary to control production. MIDB ensures that all shop-floor and plant systems have access to common data about current build requests. The system contains vehicle build specifications..." (Hyduk, 1992, p. 28).

b. **Manufacturing support system** (MSS): It provides "parameters to production equipment and facilities using a centralized procedure to store, retrieve and document programmable-device memories...The system feeds data from the MIDB to the plant-floor controllers and robots" (Hyduk, 1992). This is an example of a cell controller.

c. **Assembly line diagnostic link** (ALDL): "ALDL verifies and documents the quality of the vehicles leaving the plant. It interfaces with MIDB to extract vehicle build information. Then it tests the engine's electronic control module (ECM) to verify that it is working properly. ALDL forwards test results electronically to other computerized systems. This data is used in shipping, planning and quality control systems" (Hyduk, 1992).

Flexibility: The key to flexibility in manufacturing in this case was a local area network (LAN) that supported flexible assembly by linking flexible subassembly systems. Overall flexibility in the enterprise was attained through four system goals.

a. **Multivendor connectivity**: Different manufacturer's host computers, programmable logic controllers, vehicle inspection systems, and other subsystems are all linked together. Multivendor connectivity increasingly requires global networking.

b. **Open standards**: To promote future network expansion, open standards were used. The manufacturing automation protocol (MAP), which uses an IEEE 802.4 token passing protocol, was adopted for factory applications. In the global implementation of CIM, open standards take on increased importance for the success of the required linkages.

c. **Universal terminal access**: This ensured access from host systems from any plant-floor terminal for efficient and timely plant-floor control. In global manufacturing firms, this control occurs across national borders.

d. **Reconfiguration flexibility**: "The network topology and configuration required flexibility to allow efficient and timely modifications and equipment/system mobility throughout the plant. This would support plant-floor changes, such as mode changeovers" (Hyduk, 1992).

This case demonstrates the specific actions that are needed to attain integration and flexibility in one enterprise through the use of CIM. Although, each company must address its quest for integration and flexibility individually, the goals and expectations for CIM should not vary significantly from one firm to another. The automobile industry is increasingly a global industry, requiring cross-border implementation of CIM. Consider the fact that Japanese automakers assemble approximately two million automobiles in the US, and that BMW will soon be assembling cars in South Carolina; these foreign assembly plants in the US depend heavily upon home countries for component supplies (Swamidass and Kotabe, 1993).

REALIZING CIM IN GLOBAL FIRMS

Although, CIM has been touted as a major breakthrough, it has not been successfully implemented by large numbers of firms. As Davidow and Malone (1992) have pointed out, CIM has often been a costly fiasco--usually because the implementing firm did not make the sweeping cultural or organizational changes that are required. Since most of these cases of improper implementation were in domestic manufacturing locations, it is easy to conjecture that the cross-cultural implementation of CIM in global environments will present a complexity that is likely to be an order of magnitude greater. As has been discovered by researchers investigating CIM implementation, the problems today are most likely to center on the human aspects rather than the technology (see, e.g., Davidow & Malone, 1992; McGaughey, 1991; Snyder & Cox, 1989).

Changing the Old System

It must be recognized that a truly integrated manufacturing system based on CIM will destroy the old patterns of communication and human interactions. The "old" organization has been character-ized by a bureaucratic structure. The old structure is typically functionally organized and the people who operate the functions have been stacked in silos with a minimum of contact with those who inhabit other silos. It is common to see functional areas supported by tailored systems to satisfy one function **alone**.

This specialization of systems has inhibited cross-functional communications to the point of reducing the effectiveness of the enterprise as a whole. The personnel in these so-called silos may easily tend to think in "them" versus "us" terms. For example, if a customer complaint about a product is received by sales personnel, they can be quick to point back to manufacturing to lay blame upon the production function. In turn, the manufacturing personnel may point to engineering, who may blame research and development, and so on.

Many authors have noted that organizations must make funda-mental changes to compete in the changed environment. For example, Peters (1988) and Drucker (1988) have written that, to be successful, the drastically changed organizations of the future will require extensive computer integration. There are efforts underway in firms aimed at changing their corporate culture so that the entire team of personnel required to conceive, design, manufacture, market, and support a product will work in a cooperative rather than an adversarial mode. Properly implemented, CIM should help to accomplish this goal.

We argue that the CIM philosophy can transform organizations for the new environment. CIM forces cross-functional approaches and it requires that the old functional silos be demolished so that relevant skills and resources may be coordinated in an integrated fashion. On the other hand, changing the old culture is very difficult and may prevent the successful implementation of CIM in global as well as domestic enterprises.

Challenges to Implementing Global CIM

The success of CIM has been traced to three distinct phases; planning, implementation and operation (McGaughey, 1992). Because of the standardization that CIM imposes in an environment that is seemingly beyond standardization, the process of planning and implementing CIM in the multinational operations context can be an extremely demanding task. Once installed, the operation of CIM should be "relatively" easy, at least in comparison to the first two phases. The planning and implementation of CIM is a dynamic process through which the system is constantly upgraded to meet new challenges of integration through new and emerging technologies and techniques.

A great deal has been written about the problems that a firm may encounter in CIM implementation. For example, Snyder & Cox (1989) have examined three major categories of problems: 1) management, 2) technical, and 3) human resource. They have further delineated specific problems and/or issues under each major category. The article cited contains a compilation of problems and issues gleaned from an extensive literature review. Rather than simply reiterate these issues, it is our aim to focus on those issues that take on greater importance in the global environment. Some of the problem areas that deserve extra attention for global CIM are:

CIM perspective

For the successful implementation of CIM, it is necessary to clearly communicate the CIM perspective to the personnel of the firm. In the global firm, this need is even more critical if the distributed locations are to be properly integrated. If we take, for example, the case of a microelectronics manufacturer that has operations in 14 locations around the world, the task of communicating the CIM philosophy must be translated into relevant and consistent terms so that the personnel working for the company's plants in Singapore, Ireland, Mexico, Scotland, Thailand and in seven widely separated states in the US will have consistent views. Without this important underpinning, the efforts to develop and implement a successful global CIM will be difficult.

Cultural differences

Many US manufacturers who have moved into the multinational arena have been ill-prepared for the obstacles imposed by cultural differences. Many try to preserve the differences, e.g., as in the case of Xerox discussed earlier. With CIM, some things just cannot be done the way they have always been done. When implementing CIM the corporate culture undergoes drastic changes. If we are dealing with global CIM implementation, the magnitude of the changes across many cultures makes it a formidable task. To ignore these cultural issues is to invite mis-interpretations and reduce the success of CIM. Employees in every country have subtle differences in perceptions, customs and taboos that can be hidden traps for the managers engaged in implementation. Davidow and Malone (1992) state that the content of CIM is 20 percent technological and 80 percent cultural. This judgement reinforces the relative importance of understanding and carefully managing the cultural aspects of CIM implementation.

Compatibility of technologies to be integrated

Usually the technologies that CIM brings together are quite varied. This variation can be higher when integrating systems in many countries and may result in many kinds of compatibility problems. For example, various computer systems could have difficulty in being connected because of the differences in their operating systems. Network protocols may be so different as to present a formidable barrier to achieving integration. In some cases, CIM implementors have concluded that trying to integrate diverse systems is simply too formidable a task and have had to resort to operating the various sites as independent modules, thus sacrificing some of the potential benefits of CIM.

Telecommunications requirements and capabilities

There is no way of making global CIM a realistic possibility without reliable telecommunications. Managers who wish to implement global CIM must carefully plan the required telecommunications components to make systems function in an integrated manner. The determination of telecommunications needs must incorporate an assessment of existing capabilities. Among the factors for analysis are the modes, capacities, speed, and reliability of the alternatives. The implementor of global CIM should fit telecommunications requirements and capabilities into a meaningful architecture.

Network architecture

Specifically, the firm must place its global CIM network within its overall **network architecture**. Network architecture is defined as "...an overall plan that governs the design of the hardware and software components that make up a data communications system" (Martin & Leben, 1988, p.42). We would extend this definition to include the firm's voice communications as well. According to Snyder (1991), the concept of network architecture should include the set of design principles and the system philosophy that forms the basis for linking the nodes of the entire organization. Managers must examine the telecommunications alternatives in each location.

Frequently, manufacturing sites are located in developing countries that have inadequate telecommunications infrastructures. In these cases, the firm may be forced to build and operate its own telecommunications facilities, bypassing the inadequate facilities of the host nation. Another important consideration is the need to comply with onerous regulations when using a host nation's facilities. Many firms have resorted to building their own satellite telecommunications systems to avoid reliance on sub-standard host nation systems. It is important to analyze the impact of such systems on the overall architecture.

Security and disaster recovery

There is no question about the increased exposure to the risk of losing critical manufacturing data when operating in a global telecommunications-based environment. When operating CIM in a configuration that must link diverse modules located in several countries, the vulnerability of the underlying technologies must be assessed and the consequences of lost data determined so that adequate protection can be provided. Not only must the protective measures be installed, but they need to be tested to insure that they work as advertised. In addition, since there can never be 100 percent security, a firm needs to establish disaster recovery procedures and test them periodically. Despite the great advances in reliability of computer-based systems and telecommunications facilities, we hear all too often of disasters that cause serious interruptions in service. This means that the firm operating global CIM must plan for such contingencies. Guidance for performing such analysis and planning can be found in the risk analysis literature. Since CIM is based on information technology, managers should find the specific risk management methodologies surrounding the deployment of information technology discussed by Rainer, Snyder, and Carr (1991) particularly useful.

Cross-cultural sociotechnical CIM user

Not only must the personnel operating in a global CIM environment work across traditional organizational boundaries, they need to work in teams that are geographically distant; e.g., as in the Xerox example cited earlier. In many cases, CIM teams will be from different national cultures as well as different corporate cultures peculiar to each location. The potential for great diversity means that it is important to understand the team and its members from a complex sociotechnical perspective. We recommend that there be a development of profiles of the various CIM users in order to fully understand the ramifications of multi-cultural teams and develop training programs to facilitate the smooth working of such teams as part of the human resource development function of the corporation.

Training and education needs

One of the major obstacles to success in implementing new technologies is the lack of understanding of the objectives, benefits, and individual impacts of the new technologies. While it is rather obvious that personnel who will operate or use CIM must be trained in the specific modules that they are to be involved with, the need for more general, broad education about the CIM philosophy and its importance to gaining or maintaining competitive advantage is often left to chance. We maintain that this sort of education is much needed in a domestic CIM implementation, and is essential in global CIM. The proper educational level can set the stage for success and serve as a critical component in insuring that the human resources have the necessary knowledge to reap the **integration and flexibility** benefits of CIM. Top management's responsibility is to ensure that proper planning and implementation of training occurs at all manufacturing sites.

Logical implementation plan

CIM needs to be logically planned and implemented. The planning for global CIM takes on a much more complex character because of the geographic, time, language, and cultural differences. The cycle time for planning and implementing a good size CIM is *many years*. The many steps involved in planning and implementing a successful

CIM are outlined by Snyder and Cox (1988).

CIM IMPLEMENTATION EXPERIENCES

Since, CIM implementation experiences in manufacturing are spotty, we provide specific case examples of how implementation could suffer and how one might avoid those problems.

Case 1: This company that manufactures aircraft is known for implementing advanced manufacturing technologies. The manufacturing in this company occurred at two major domestic locations. At the time it was reported, CIM implementation was only 30 percent complete but the manufacturer's experience reveals two major problems that either slow down implementation or actually reduce the effectiveness of CIM. As is typical, the aircraft manufacturer had international partners for several subassemblies and major components. This global dispersion exacerbated the difficulties in implementing CIM.

The incompatibility of hardware and software in the two locations was caused by the following:

(1) Hardware included IBM mainframes for CAD and process planning, Unisys mainframes for shop orders and master scheduling, DEC VAX minicomputers on the shop floor, DEC PDP minicomputers for control of machine tools, Tandem computers for tracking, NCR Tower minicomputers, microcomputers and HP workstations for CADAM, and a Cray supercomputer on the network. The gateway between IBM and Unisys has been particularly difficult.
(2) Operating systems included VM, VMS, Pick, and others. The variety of systems contributes to difficulties in integration.
(3) Communication and network architecture included Ethernet, DECNET, SNA, TCP/IP and others.
(4) Software included extensively modified packaged software, applications developed in-house, and much off-the-shelf software for specific tasks.
(5) The CIM environment included engineering, material procurement, finance, labor and other areas of the company.

The results in this case are noteworthy. Several data flows remain manual and CIM installation is not particularly extensive in relation to the size of the firm. The lessons from this manufacturer concerning CIM implementation may be stated in terms of the following proposition.

Creating CIM around existing hardware and software seriously damages or reduces CIM effectiveness andincreases the time it takes to implement CIM.

Case 2: This case involves a tire manufacturer's experience with the implementation of CIM. This firm has global operations in Europe, the US and Canada. The major issues in the implementation of CIM were:

(1) Hardware in the CIM network included IBM mainframes, DEC minicomputers, and various microcomputers.
(2) The communications network included a satellite providing linkages between manufacturing facilities in the US, and an SNA gateway between the company's IBM and DEC environments. The plants have a broadband network installed with about 800 nodes on the network.
(3) Software was mostly developed in-house to meet flexibility requirements with some highly modified off-the-shelf packages.
(4) The CIM environment covered marketing, engineering, R&D, product technology information, bill of materials, and a closed-loop planning environment that tied together corporate level planning with manufacturing and shop floor planning.

The result in this case is also an interesting one. Implementation in the US is ahead of the European plants by about 18 months. The major problem here was in finding skilled personnel with experience in integrating and networking the various systems. Internal training caused start-up problems and delay in the implementation of the CIM system. As a result, we would summarize this case with the following proposition.

The success of CIM implementation is a function of the technical personnel needed for networking and integration.

CONCLUSIONS

This chapter stresses that the importance of using CIM lies in the integration and flexibility that it offers to global manufacturers. Although currently quite formidable, CIM implementation is expected to get easier in the future. One study by Swamidass (1992) shows that nearly one in five manufacturers in the US (in SIC classifications 34-39) plan to excel in the use of CIM while only 5 percent are currently extremely skilled in its use. Thus, we are likely to see rapid growth in the implementation of CIM. This growth in adoption will create needs for more skilled personnel (to perform the integration and networking) and more hardware and software suitable for easier implementation. Overall, the trend is clearly towards growth; manufacturers who hesitate to implement CIM may well be left behind by the competition.

In the competitive environment faced by global firms, time-based competition is increasingly deciding which enterprises survive and which ones fail. One emphatic conclusion from this chapter is that time-based competition will likely be waged using CIM since it offers integration and flexibility, both essential ingredients to successful global firms.

REFERENCES

Davidow, W.H. and Malone, M.S. (1992). *The virtual corporation*. New York: Harper.

Drucker, P. (1988). The coming of the new organization, *Harvard business review*, 66, 1, 45-53.

Gopal, C. (1986). Manufacturing logistics systems for a competitive global strategy. *Information strategy: The executive's journal*. Fall, 19-24.

Hyduk, S.J. (1992). Systems integration provides the answer for multiple systems operation, *APICS--The performance advantage*, 2, 11, November, 27-30.

Martin J. and Leben, J. (1988). *Data communication technology*. Englewood Cliffs, NJ: Prentice-Hall.

McGrath, M.E. and R.W. Hoole. (1992). Manufacturing's new economies of scale. *Harvard Business Review*, May-June, 94-102.

McGaughey, R. (1991). The critical success factors of computer integrated manufacturing, Unpublished doctoral dissertation, Auburn University.

Peters, T. (1988). Restoring American competitiveness: Looking for new models of Organizations, *The academy of management executive*, 2, 103-109.

Rainer, R.K., Jr., Snyder, C.A., and Carr, H.H. (1991). Risk analysis for information Technology, *Journal of management Information systems*, 8, 1, 129-147.

Sera, K. (1992). Corporate globalization: A new trend, *The academy of management executive*, 6, 1, 89-96.

Snyder, C.A. (1991). CIM Networking: Promise and Problems, *International Journal of production economics*, 23, 205-212.

Snyder, C.A. and J.F. Cox. (1989). Developing computer integrated manufacturing: Major issues and problem areas. *Engineering costs and production economics*, 17, 197-205.

Stalk, G. Jr., and Hout, T.M. (1990). *Competing against time*. New York: The Free Press.

Swamidass, P.M. (1988). *Manufacturing flexibility*, monograph #2. Plano, Texas: Operations Management Association.

Swamidass, P.M. (1992). *Technology on the factory floor*. Washington, D.C.: National Association of Manufacturers.

Swamidass, P.M. (forthcoming). Import sourcing dynamics. *Journal of international business studies.*

Swamidass, P.M. and M. Kotabe (1993). Component sourcing strategies of multinationals: An empirical study of European and Japanese multinationals. *Journal of international business studies,* vol. 24(1), 81-99.

Swamidass, P.M. and W.T. Newell (1987). Manufacturing strategy, environmental uncertainty and performance: A path analytic model. *Management science,* 33, 4, 509-524.

CHAPTER 15

International Purchasing Transactions Through Electronic Data Interchange Systems

ROBERT B. HANDFIELD
Michigan State University

STEVEN V. WALTON
ANN S. MARUCHECK
ALLISON McKINNEY WILKINS
University of North Carolina at Chapel Hill

Manufacturing organizations are undergoing a metamorphosis from national entities to "stateless organizations" which operate in a global arena. Improved information technologies such as Electronic Data Interchange (EDI) provide the means for domestic firms to electronically span time and distance barriers to establish trading relationships with global suppliers. This chapter examines the nature of EDI technology in global sourcing networks, its associated benefits, and the issues surrounding successful EDI implementation. Data from a survey of members of the National Association of Purchasing Managers are analyzed to determine the trends in global sourcing through EDI. The results indicate that although the global diffusion of EDI as a technology is currently limited, improvements in communications infrastructure will accelerate the use of EDI as an information link in global sourcing relationships.

INTRODUCTION

The increasing level of globalization occurring in manufacturing operations within the last decade has brought many new changes in organizational structure and capabilities. A new breed of "stateless enterprise" has emerged which operates in many different countries and which no longer recognizes the limitations imposed by national borders. These firms often progress through stages of internationalization which evolve in a dual interplay between the development of knowledge about foreign markets and global operations, as well as an increasing commitment of resources to foreign markets (Johanson and Vahlene, 1990). Motivated by the need for reduced costs, access to state-of-the-art technology, improved quality products, and production flexibility, these stateless enterprises seek to take advantage of their global manufacturing networks by assigning design and sourcing responsibility to the appropriate international business units, and in later stages, seeking to integrate and coordinate international strategic business units (Monczka and Trent, 1992).

Within the context of these global sourcing strategies, recurring problems such as long lead-times, increased inventories, time zones, and barriers to communication often hinder the effectiveness of the relevant business transactions, and thus threaten the firm's ability to realize desired strategic benefits from globalization (Handfield, 1992). To overcome such barriers to global sourcing implementation, firms are increasing their efforts to globalize their information technology networks. Specifically, Electronic Data Interchange (EDI) technology is often used to span the distances between distribution centers and monitor and control logistical transactions. For instance, a domestic firm in the grocery industry has been able to reduce its inventory levels and decrease the downtime related to unreliable deliveries through the use of EDI. One of its EDI suppliers, a German firm, delivers 83 percent of shipments within 20 days of order placement. As the buying firm demands short lead times and high delivery reliability, EDI is a necessity for its global suppliers. This example illustrates how these systems are profoundly changing the way global corporations communicate and relate with one another.

This chapter describes the nature of EDI technology in global sourcing networks, the associated benefits, and the implementation issues. This is followed by a discussion of recent trends in the levels of diffusion of this technology, based on a set of interviews with EDI managers at several large multinational organizations and a survey returned by 100 members of the National Association of Purchasing Managers conducted in 1991. Some of the trends discussed include the level of EDI use, the barriers to implementation, and the role of supplier partnerships in the implementation of this emerging global information technology.

THE TECHNICAL ELEMENTS OF EDI

Traditional information flows between buyers and suppliers often necessitate a lengthy sequential process composed of a multitude of steps required to support the servicing of the order as well as the actual fulfillment of the order. Examples of these information flows include transmission of product specifications from buyer to supplier, submission of bids, acceptance of contracts, inspection and receiving documents associated with shipments, accounting audits, and submission of payments. As is often the case with interfirm communication, most of the effort of managing these information flows involves completing time-consuming paperwork and managing the paper-based documents associated with the information exchange, including engineering drawings, purchase orders, etc. Some of the problems which occur within these traditional information flows include increased transaction time, low accuracy caused by data-handling errors, high utilization of staff time and resources, and increased uncertainty in the form of both mailing and processing delays.

Electronic Data Interchange is a computer-based technology designed to support the interorganizational electronic exchange of common business documents and other related information. When used by buyers and suppliers, EDI can help eliminate many of the steps involved in traditional information flows. In order to adequately implement the physical EDI system, three basic components must be present (Emmelhainz, 1990):

- A "standard" form (EDI standards)
- A translation capability (EDI software)
- A mail service (EDI network).

EDI standards include the basic rules of formatting and syntax used to describe the EDI transmission. These standards provide guidelines for which documents can be communicated electronically; what information is included within these documents; what sequence the information should follow; and the meaning of individual pieces of information. EDI standards also describe the various computer settings (baud rate, protocol, etc.) that must be used to transmit and receive the EDI document.

Originally, EDI communication standards were developed by individual industries as their members began adopting EDI. The Transportation Data Coordinating Committee (TDCC), for example, was formed in 1968 to develop EDI standards for the air, motor, rail, and water industries. In the United States, several other industry-specific standards have been adopted, although progress in the development of standards varies from industry to industry. Industry associations have facilitated the development of standards in those industries where the level of interfirm cooperation is high and there is an absence of influential firms pushing for proprietary standards (Gupta and Neel, 1992). Other industry-specific standards have been adopted in the grocery industry ("Uniform Communications Standard") and in the warehouse industry ("Warehouse Information Network Standard" or "WINS"). However, in 1978 the American National Standards Institute (ANSI) recognized the need for a global, cross-industry standard and later formed the Accredited Standards Committee (ASC) X12 to develop this standard. Within the X12 standard, each document in the transaction is referred to as a "transaction set" and has both an X12 document number and a transaction set identification. For instance, a purchase order would be identified with a document number of X12.1 and a transaction set identification of 850; while a shipping notice would be identified with a document number of X12.10 and a transaction set identification of 856. Other standard documents such as invoices and requests for quotes would have similar electronic identifications.

The ANSI X12 standard is quickly being adopted by both domestic and foreign organizations, including companies in Canada and Australia where X12 also is the predominant standard. The development of X12 and other cross-industry standards lowers the barriers to entry associated with the use of EDI, making it easier for firms of all sizes to implement and use EDI. In a global context, the development of cross-industry standards, such as X12 or the UN/EDIFACT standards in Europe and Asia, should promote EDI as a platform for the international communications of a diverse group of transactions. Using this global communications technology for purchasing-related transactions, such as the purchase order, should facilitate the development of a true global marketplace for buyers and suppliers.

The second element of EDI is translation capability. Within most companies, the internal format of business documents does not conform to the X12 standard. Therefore, the computer system must be able to translate this internal format into the externally defined and accepted X12 format. This capability is achieved through interpreter software. Since EDI crosses organizational boundaries, both the buyer and the supplier in the EDI relationship must have translation capabilities.

The final component of the EDI system is the electronic mail service. Transmission is usually in the form of either a direct network or a third party provider. A direct network is a link between computers through modems. This alternative works well when there are a limited number of trading partners involved. However, when a firm has many trading partners, a third party network avoids traffic problems which occur, such as maintaining open lines, time transactions, and maintaining security over transmissions. Such a "value-added network" (VAN) serves as an intermediary "post office" for the partners. A "mailbox" for the sender and receiver is maintained, into which all electronic transmissions can be transferred simultaneously. The network then sorts each transmission into the appropriate mailbox. The trading partners then check their mailboxes at agreed upon times to retrieve the electronic transmission. A further advantage of VANs is that in the absence of industry-specific standards, EDI systems with incompatible formats may communicate. VANs have promoted the rapid diffusion of EDI in different industries by providing easier transmission of information than previously possible; however, as there are service fees associated with VANs, they may be more expensive to use than direct

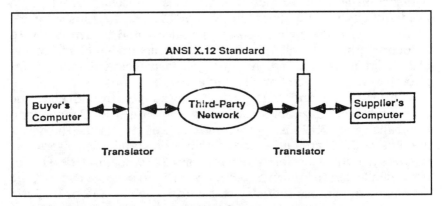

Figure 1: EDI Data Flows for a Typical Company

networks. Several companies offer EDI VAN service, including General Electric (GEIS), Sears (SCC) and BT Tymnet.

The process which occurs when a buyer and supplier go through an EDI transaction ideally progresses in the following manner, as depicted in Figure 1. The computer in the buying company monitors the real-time inventory status of the item purchased through EDI using technologies such as bar code scanners. When, according to a pre-defined reorder criterion, it is determined that there is a need to order more of the item, the application program notifies the translation software. An EDI purchase order is created and released against a pre-negotiated blanket amount, and the purchase order is sent electronically to the supplier. The supplier's computer receives the order and the EDI software translates the order into the supplier's format. A *functional acknowledgment* which indicates receipt of the order is automatically generated and transmitted back to the buyer. In many instances, the trading partners have agreed that the supplier will electronically create and transmit a purchase order (P.O.) acknowledgment indicating the availability of the item. The buyer's computer updates its purchase records automatically when it receives this P.O. acknowledgment.

The computers of the two trading partners continue swapping relevant business documents related to this purchase order until the purchase order is reconciled (eliminating the need for a manual accounting audit) and the funds for the transaction are electronically transferred to the supplier's bank. Within this automated process, there are fewer instances where manual data entry is required. In traditional information flows, each step would require that paperwork be completed and filed by clerical staff. Thus, EDI allows fewer opportunities for errors, no mailing or physical transmission delays, fewer clerical costs, and saves a lot paperwork!

It is important to note that not all EDI users achieve this level of EDI use. In fact, Emmelhainz (1990) has shown that most organizations fall into one of three categories of EDI implementation:

Level 1 - transmit only one or two different documents to a limited number of trading partners, and EDI is handled by only one department in the company.

Level 2 - communicate with a large number of trading partners across a number of industries, and many departments are involved.

Level 3 - completely immersed in EDI, which is a way of business, and internal corporate functions are restructured to get the most from EDI.

This framework of levels of EDI implementation is consistent with the findings of other researchers in other areas of information technology (Cooper and Zmud, 1990). However, the framework does not address the different types of benefits that might be achieved at each of the three levels of EDI implementation.

BENEFITS OF EDI IMPLEMENTATION

As a technology, EDI is relatively immune to a number of the technical implementation problems which have tended to plague other information technologies. Many firms have found EDI to be a turnkey technology with an excellent record for reliability in system performance. The literature is replete with examples of the potential benefits from EDI use in both global and domestic contexts. They include: lead time reduction, reduction in raw material inventories through more frequent deliveries, reduced warehousing, improved delivery reliability, improved production scheduling, lower transaction costs, better customer service, and better response to changes in retailer demand through Point of Sale (POS) integration (Kandel, 1990). However, whether a firm can actually achieve these benefits is dependent on the implementation process. There are four critical issues which should be addressed in a successful EDI implementation:

- Integration of EDI with other computer applications
- Inducement of trading partners to use EDI
- Personnel training
- Expected versus realized strategic benefits.

Each of these issues will be discussed within the context of an initial exploratory study involving in-depth case analyses of ten firms which were using EDI (McKinney and Marucheck, 1991).

Integration of EDI with Other Applications

Many argue that the key to strategic advantage in EDI is not merely moving data electronically between computers, but in creating partnerships with other firms through the sharing of information about forecasts, production schedules, and planned inventory levels. The degree to which a firm's EDI system is integrated with other information systems in the firm has a major impact on the benefits the firm itself can realize and its potential for information sharing with trading partners. Integration of information systems implies that there is no redundancy in data processing (i.e., output from EDI, or any computerized file, is not rekeyed as input into another application program). Although many firms have integrated EDI with their inventory management systems, innovative examples of integrated EDI systems include EDI/EFT (Electronic Funds Transfer) where funds are electronically transferred to the supplier as the remittance to an electronic bill which was generated when the shipment is received; this process was described in the previous section. Another innovation is EDI/EGI (Electronic Graphics Interchanges) where graphics and drawings are interchanged between buyer and supplier often in the context of new product development and the bidding process (DeFosse and Barr, 1992).

EDI has helped to facilitate the trend toward "off-shore outsourcing" whereby domestic firms are likely to source the parts and labor needed in the manufacture of products to capable suppliers abroad (O'Reilly, 1992). EDI has helped to reduce the magnitude of problems associated with international communications, information delivery, time zone delays, and documentation which have long plagued international purchasing transactions. With these problems mitigated, the outsourcing firm can then realize cost advantages by tapping into global suppliers who not only enjoy lower labor costs but also have well-trained workforces. It should be further noted that integrated applications like EDI/EGI allow the global outsourcing of design work to areas of the world which have a surplus of highly educated engineers and computer programmers. Thus, the impact of integrated EDI applications is currently producing opportunities for global manufacturing and is likely to do the same for services as they are internationalized.

Table 1 presents the findings from the case studies of EDI implementations in ten firms. The firm, its industry, and the integration of the EDI system are presented in the first three columns. The table very clearly indicates that the six firms which had integrated their EDI system with other computerized applications felt that they had received benefits from the use of EDI; the other four firms which had failed to integrate EDI with their other systems universally felt they had received no benefits from EDI. In fact, in non-integrated EDI applications, firms often realized lower delivery reliability, increased lead times, and higher inventory levels as a result of errors created in the manual processing of EDI-generated orders. Although additional time and resources are consumed in the development and implementation of integrated application programs, they may be regarded as a "down payment" toward achieving beneficial EDI trading relationships which can be extended globally.

Inducing Suppliers to Use EDI

In order to reap the benefits of EDI (particularly transaction cost reduction), a firm must have a sufficient number of trading partners using EDI. However, many have argued that EDI use seems to provide more benefits to the buying firm than to the supplier; hence, there may be a reluctance on the part of suppliers to invest in the technology unless it is obvious that an EDI relationship is the only way of providing the customer with the service it expects. Thus, the burden falls on the buying firm to convince suppliers that adopting EDI is in their best interest.

One manifestation of this effect is the proliferation of hub programs where large corporations systematically encourage, and sometimes even coerce, their suppliers into adopting EDI (Samuelson, 1989). A voluntary approach to EDI is where the buying firm gains acceptance and voluntary commitment from suppliers through educational programs and seminars about EDI in a cooperative effort. Such cooperation between trading partners can lead to increased benefits for both firms (Monczka and Carter, 1988).

However, in a number of industries, coercive approaches to EDI have been the norm. There are three different types of coercive influence that firms use on trading partners: threats, promises, and legalistic pleas (Frazier, Gill and Kale, 1989). Threats are suggestions or implications that negative sanctions (i.e., loss of business) will be applied if the partner fails to adopt EDI. Promises are more palatable coercion where the firm agrees to provide specific rewards (i.e., price discounts or more favorable credit terms) contingent on

EDI adoption. Legalistic pleas are the use of agreements or contracts which require the trading partner's compliance in using EDI. Often these coercive mandates can result in a backlash which creates resistance on the part of the trading partner to EDI and a very poor trading relationship (Skagen, 1989).

Table 1 indicates that the firms who implemented EDI on a voluntary basis (see column 4) all realized benefits from EDI use, and all but one firm who was coerced by a trading partner into using the technology felt that they had received nothing from their efforts. It is notable that several of the firms that were coerced into EDI use were members of either the automotive or the textile industry. Both of these industries have aggressively pursued Just-in-Time strategies mandating frequent deliveries from suppliers through EDI-based transactions. These industries are also characterized by extensive off-shore sourcing. Several major firms in both of these industries have refused to trade with suppliers not using EDI. Follow-up interviews revealed that coercion tended to produce suppliers who would implement an EDI system which could minimally satisfy the demands of the trading partner. The result was often an non-integrated EDI system which did not provide the firm with any realizable benefits, and further, was not a suitable platform to expanding trading relationships internationally.

Personnel Training

As one of the intended goals of EDI is the reduction of personnel costs, particularly through the reduction of clerical staff, the implications of EDI on human resources are profound. Several studies have shown that one of the major impacts of EDI is the redistribution of work activities performed within the purchasing department. Buyers' time may be reallocated from lower level activities like filling out purchase orders, follow-up with suppliers, expediting, and order status communications to more professional activities, including strategic planning, supplier evaluation and selection, make or buy decisions, negotiation planning, and cost management activities (Carter and Fredendall, 1990). As will be discussed later in the chapter, supplier selection becomes more complex in an international sourcing environment and requires greater professionalism on the part of the buyer. Early user involvement and training within the purchasing department in anticipation of these changes in responsibilities seems to be a critical factor in assuring that implementation is successful (Emmelhainz, 1987).

Although EDI training is often concentrated in the purchasing department, there may be workers in other areas of the firm, such as warehousing and distribution, who will need training to understand how EDI will impact their work and to realize the opportunities for

Firm	Industry	Integration of EDI [1]	Voluntary or Coercive	Expected Benefits	Realized Benefits
A	Textiles	I	Voluntary	Reduced Inventory	Reduced lead times Improved quality Less clerical work Reduced inventory
B	Auto	NI	Coercive	None	None (Costs have increased)
C	Textiles	I	Voluntary	Reduced costs	Reduced lead time
D	Fiber	I	Voluntary	Reduced costs	Reduced inventory levels Less paperwork
E	Apparel	I	Voluntary	Reduced costs	Better forecasting Better planning Lower clerical costs
F	Apparel	I	Coercive	Faster order processing	Reduced lead times Marketing tool for attracting customers
G	HVAC	NI	Coercive	None	None (Paperwork has increased)
H	Auto	NI	Coercive	None	None
I	HVAC	NI	Coercive	Clerical savings	None
J	Textiles	I	Voluntary	Reduced paperwork	Reduced lead times

[1]   An EDI system which is integrated with at least one other computer application is denoted I. Otherwise, the system is denoted NI.

Table 1: Benefits Achieved by EDI Suppliers

job enrichment (i.e., additional responsibilities, quality control) which may emerge. However, several cost-conscious firms have recognized that not all workers who interface with suppliers and customers need EDI training. Workers, who will lose their current jobs because of EDI implementation, may be excluded from training initiatives if they are not identified as intended users of the technology. Successful EDI implementation depends on anticipating the need for personnel training in order to gain acceptance for EDI by the workers who must directly interface with the system and to communicate the changes in job roles and responsibilities which will result from the new technology.

Expected versus Realized Benefits

The findings in Table 1 indicate that often the expected benefits of EDI are considerably more modest in scope and more tactically oriented than the realized benefits. Expected benefits cited by the firms were often reduced costs in the form of decreased personnel costs and less paperwork. However, frequently these cost reductions were not realized. The reallocation of work from clerical duties to more professional activities in the purchasing department often requires hiring workers with higher education levels and more experience, particularly in international sourcing. Thus, any reductions in clerical costs may be negated by the higher salaries commanded by a more professional workforce. Further, there may be a need to hire additional specialists who are responsible for implementing, maintaining, and developing the EDI system. Thus, a reduction in personnel expenditures may not be realized on a global basis.

The same result may be true of an anticipated reduction in paperwork. Electronic processing of customer orders may reduce the amount of paperwork generated in traditional purchasing activities. However, in the complex arena of international sourcing, management may use the EDI system more frequently to produce ad hoc reports and collect additional data, and in essence, generate more paperwork (Gupta and Neel, 1992).

Finally, Table 1 shows that for the successful EDI users, the realized benefits were unexpected, more strategic, and less tangible in nature. These firms leveraged time savings in order processing activities and the availability of better information from trading partners in two ways. First, they streamlined their business processes associated with order fulfillment. Second, they worked at forging stronger relationships with their customers. The results of these two strategic initiatives are better customer responsiveness and enhanced competitiveness. Often the realized benefits of EDI transcended the purchasing function and provided advantages for the operations and marketing functions as well. This finding is illustrative of the concept of electronic integration where successful EDI users have used technology to change the nature of their relationships with trading partners in order to achieve competitive advantage in the global marketplace (Venkatraman and Kambil, 1991).

EDI IMPLEMENTATION PROCESS IN GLOBAL SOURCING NETWORKS

Introducing EDI into a global sourcing network first requires a careful analysis of current and future procurement requirements. In an initial implementation of EDI, the greatest benefits (lower inventory, reduced lead time, etc.) often occur for purchased components that are considered "critical". Such critical items generally can be identified on the basis of one of the following attributes: cost, price volatility, technical complexity, difficulty in sourcing, ease of substituting an alternative item, procurement lead time, role in differentiating the product, and purchasing time consumed. These critical items, whether components or Maintenance, Repair and Operations (MRO) items, clearly have the greatest potential to provide significant cost savings in inventory, lead-time, and procurement efficiency when EDI is successfully implemented. In addition to the types of items to be procured using EDI, the firm must also consider which supplier(s) of these items are to be approached for EDI implementation. After the supplier is chosen, the process of EDI implementation is undertaken. This process is shown in Figure 2.

The supplier selection process generally involves an explicit or implicit weighting of various criteria. As more and more firms solicit bids from international sources, the task of supplier selection becomes more complex. Initial screening of those suppliers actually using EDI has been facilitated by the publication of reliable sources of names of companies currently using EDI (many yellow pages and trade registers list those suppliers that are currently using EDI). However, after potential suppliers are identified, systematic selection criteria need to be established. Through interviews with firms currently involved with EDI, the authors have identified several criteria important in supplier selection, including supplier willingness to implement EDI, willingness to absorb part of the EDI costs, volume of trading with the supplier, and the anticipated ability of the supplier to successfully implement EDI. The suppliers considered by the firms included only those firms which had established performance records in terms of quality, cost, delivery, and product/process technology, or which supplied a critical item. Other criteria such as degree of R&D and financial stability may also play an

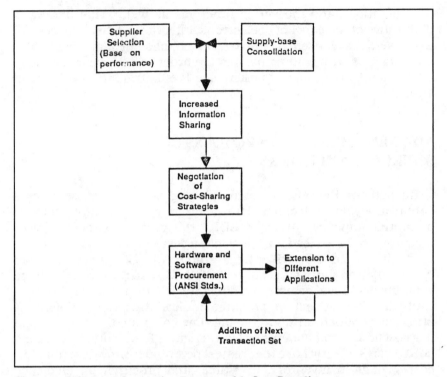

Figure 2: EDI Implementation Process with One Supplier

important role in selecting suppliers. These efforts are usually part of an executive-level strategy of supply-base consolidation, which strives to reduce the number of vendors in a supply pool in order to develop closer working relationships.

Once a reduced set of suppliers is selected, a potential EDI partner is identified. Partnership implies that an increased level of data and information sharing must occur; this includes production schedules, forecasts, capacity projections, and anticipated design/engineering changes. Once the information set to be shared has been established, negotiations should focus on the terms by which the cost of EDI implementation will be shared. Typically, these costs might include allocation of hardware and software costs, costs of using a third party network, and costs of data transmission. Once these terms have been established, on-going efforts to extend the information shared to other applications should proceed. In conjunction with increasing the information that is shared among the existing transactions and applications, this on-going effort should also focus on implementing the next transaction set with the selected trading partner.

RECENT TRENDS IN GLOBAL EDI NETWORKS

A recent study of 97 firms provided information on current trends in EDI implementation as practiced in the United States. After the initial instrument was pre-tested at ten firms in the U.S. (Handfield, 1992), the survey was mailed to 500 American-based purchasing managers who are members of the National Association of Purchasing Managers (NAPM). The surveys were returned by 108 respondents, of which ten were unusable (19.6% response rate). The remaining 97 companies were all manufacturing firms, of which 54 were using foreign sources, and 43 were sourcing domestically. Of these firms, only seven extensively used EDI, although many others were at various stages of implementation. A breakdown of the sample by industry of the purchasing firm, and the location of the supplying firm is presented in the endnote.

In general, the EDI partners were located overseas , in Japan, Europe, and Asia. Only two of the seven EDI suppliers were in the United States. This suggests that one major group of benefits of EDI is in the realm of global sourcing. While local suppliers may be reached more easily by telephone, buyers dealing with foreign suppliers often have to overcome problems such as different time zones, language difficulties, elaborate documentation, and other "technical barriers". These technical barriers range from the "shape of electrical plugs to the packaging for butter to the content of beer." (Cram-Martos, 1992) The recent adoption of the United Nations EDI standard, UN/EDIFACT, by most of the European Common Market member countries has prevented inconsistent EDI standards from becoming another technical barrier to international EDI implementation. With cross-industry standards evolving, EDI provides a common platform for electronic communication. In addition, EDI eliminates the need for complicated customs documents, which are in many cases transmitted electronically as well.

Table 2 illustrates some other patterns evident among both EDI and non-EDI users. In general, EDI is used in situations where materials represent a high percentage of total costs and supplier lead-times are very long. This result agrees with the prior observation that the greatest benefits of EDI occur when implemented with suppliers of critical items, with the criticality being determined by factors such as cost, lead-times and the availability of alternate sources of the item. In addition, EDI can make significant inroads into time compression for these long lead-time items. The benefits achieved include reduction of on-hand inventory of such items, and smaller delivered lot sizes (which is often required for Just-in-Time). One firm interviewed by the authors reduced international delivery times from one of their suppliers to the point where 83% of all deliveries from this supplier were made within twenty days of order

	EDI Firms	Non-EDI Firms
Materials Cost (% of Total Cost)	68%	53%
Delivered Lotsize (Day's Inventory)	7.7	32
Onhand Inventory (Week's Supply)	2.1	5.0
Supplier lead-time (Weeks)	12.3	8.7
Sales of Buying Company (Millions US $)	4720	1168

Note: No tests of statistical significance were performed on these data because of the skewness of the sample.

Table 2: Patterns Seen in EDI Firms vs. Non-EDI Firms

generation.

Another trend which is evident from Table 2 is the fact that firms currently using EDI tend to be much larger than those not using EDI. To some extent, this indicates that EDI firms may have greater leverage over their suppliers. For instance, if a firm encounters significant employee resistance or other barriers to EDI implementation, this can be overcome by top management communicating directives to both the supplier and employees to cooperate with the EDI implementation team rather than using coercive tactics as previously discussed. The fact that larger firms are involved with international EDI may further indicate that currently only larger firms have the resources to effectively pursue international sourcing strategies, and thus, be in a position to effectively transfer EDI technology to internationally sourced items.

In addition to the size of the firm, there are many other barriers to international EDI implementation. These other barriers include a lack of willingness to change existing purchasing processes, and a fear that the present supplier relationship will be damaged. In some cases, buyers are afraid to share proprietary data with international partners and are concerned over the legality of documents exchanged. Also, when electronic data sharing is possible in a trading relationship, there may be a concern over loss of control and authorization, because EDI will eliminate the paper audit trail. However, many EDI systems have control mechanisms which are being used to protect data integrity including system editing features, built-in passwords, real-time recording of transactions, and data encryption codes.

CONCLUSIONS

This chapter has provided an overview of some of the key attributes of EDI, as well as an assessment of recent implementation factors and trends in global sourcing networks. Although the extent of diffusion of this particular technology is somewhat limited, it is increasing rapidly across industries and across international borders. While many global sources (particularly those in developing countries) suffer from a lack of communications infrastructure, the growth of fiber optic technology on a worldwide basis should result in a comparable growth in the use of EDI. In order to remain competitive in global markets, firms will need to coordinate their global sourcing strategies with their information technology strategies, and will need to make continual efforts to promote effective communication links among these external manufacturing bases. Although the road to full implementation is often long and arduous, the benefits of such global linkages are essential to sustained competitiveness.

ENDNOTE

Industry of EDI Buyer and Number of Representatives in this Sample:
Industrial Equipment - 29, Electronics - 21, Consumer Goods - 14, Steel - 9, Chemical - 8, Pharmaceutical - 7, Computers - 5, Automotive - 4
Location of EDI Supplier and Number of Representatives in this Sample:
USA - 43, Japan - 19, Europe - 17, Asia - 15, Latin America - 3

REFERENCES

Carter, J. & L. Fredendall (1990). The Dollars and Sense of Electronic Data Interchange, *Production and Inventory Management Journal*, 31(2), 22-25.

Cram-Martos, V. (1992). EDI and the European Common Market, *EDI World*, 3(11), 32-34.

Cooper, R., R. Zmud (1990). Information Technology Implementation Research: A Technological Diffusion Approach, *Management Science*, 36(2), 123-139.

DeFosse, S. & T. Barr (1992). Implementing EDI/EGI will Reduce Time to Market, *Industrial Engineering*, 24(8), 30-31.

Emmelhainz, M. A. (1987). Electronic Data Interchange: Does It Change the Purchasing Process?, *Journal of Purchasing and Materials Management*, 23(4), 2-8.

Emmelhainz, M. A. (1990). *EDI: A Total Management Guide.* Agawam,

MA: Penfield Productions.

Frazier, G.L., Gill, J. D. & Kale, S. H. (1989). Dealer Dependence Levels and Reciprocal Actions in a Channel of Distribution in a Developing Country, *Journal of Marketing*, 33(1), 50-69.

Gupta, Y. & G. Neel (1992). The Origin of EDI and Changes Associated with its Implementation, *Industrial Engineering*, 24(8), 25-29.

Handfield, R. (1992). International Purchasing in Foreign and American Multi-National Firms *Proceedings of the 1992 International NAPM Conference.*

Johanson, J. & J-E. Vahlene (1990). The Mechanism of Internationalisation, *International Marketing Review*, 7(4), 219.

Kandel, J. (1990). Improving Inventory and Production Management Through EDI, *Production and Inventory Management Journal*, 31(2), 32-35.

McKinney, A. & A. Marucheck (1991). The Effect of Environmental, Technological, and Human Resource Factors on the Success of Electronic Data Interchange: An Exploratory Study, *Proceedings of the Decision Sciences Institute 1991 Annual Conference*, 1220-1222.

Monczka, R. & J. Carter (1988). Implementing Electronic Data Interchange, *Journal of Purchasing and Materials Management*, 24(2), 2-9.

Monczka, R. & R. Trent (1992). Worldwide Sourcing: Assessment and Execution, *International Journal of Purchasing and Materials Management*, 28(4), 1-15.

O'Reilly, B. (1992). Your Global Work Force, *Fortune*, 126(13), 52-66.

Samuelson, R. (1989). EDI Holds the Promise of Faster Document Transfer, *The Office*, November, 38-40 and 46.

Skagen, A.E. (1989). Nurturing Relationships, Enhancing Quality with EDI, *Management Review*, February, 28-32.

Venkatraman, N. and A. Kambil (1991). Electronic Integration, *Sloan Management Review*, 32(2), 33-43.

CHAPTER 16

Global Logistics Using Satellite Technology for Monitoring and Control

GIAMPIERO E.G. BEROGGI
Delft University of Technology

WILLIAM A. WALLACE
Rensselaer Polytechnic Institute

Global logistics is beginning to benefit from the potential of satellite tracking systems. Centralized facilities can monitor the environment for new business opportunities or hazards threatening the successful completion of field operations, and take action to capture benefits or mitigate damages. We present a conceptual model of satellite tracking and identify the generic tasks of the real-time dispatcher and the variables of transit control. Reported benefits show that satellite tracking can improve transportation logistics and safety on a national, international, and even intercontinental basis.

INTRODUCTION

Global logistics, the world-wide movement and storage of goods, is becoming a significant strategic component in the value-added chain. However, three major trends pose new challenges to the transportation and storage of goods on a global basis. The first challenge is the need for improvements in infrastructure and increased capacity for rail, road, and barge shipments; the second is the deregulation of the transportation industry in Europe by the European Community (EC) and in America by the Intermodal Surface Transportation Efficiency Act of 1991 (ISTEA); and the third, the commercialization of advances in computer and communications technologies.

Advances in information technology are giving rise to "virtual transit," the ability to find, identify, and control goods enroute by such means as hand-held scanners and integrated data bases. While real-time monitoring of goods moving around the world using a network of personal computers was a short time ago considered futuristic, the concept has now become commercially feasible, and perhaps even a competitive necessity.

We will limit our discussion by focusing on the use of satellite-based information and communications technology and its capability for global identification, positioning and communications. We further constrain our presentation to the operational tasks of monitoring and control. Although we recognize the need to address strategic concerns, such as investments in advanced information technology for distribution, one cannot begin to make effective strategic decisions about new technology until one understands its value in an operational environment.

We will first discuss the present state of the system of global logistics in the context of today's turbulent business environment—with particular emphasis on the European situation. The new challenges due to the merging of markets are accompanied by new constraints imposed by policy makers both nationally and in the European Community. These constraints include a trend to modal-split (road, rail, inland-water, and sea shipments) and stringent regulations to assure safety and environmental compatibility. Maintaining competitiveness requires, therefore, coping with these constraints by employing advanced information and communications technologies with integrated intelligent decision support capabilities.

We will then review present and anticipated advances in satellite technology, showing how these will support decision making in the management of global logistics systems. Managing goods in transit requires location and identification, a process of "sensing," and control. Control is the process of sensing the present and taking action to achieve the desired state—a process that requires "reasoning." The processes of sensing and reasoning involve the gathering and structuring of data, and then processing of data into information for decision making. The sensing process in global logistics management involves monitoring coupled with communications, and display for interaction with management. Reasoning is the control that is extended by management in ensuring that the logistics system meets its goals of efficiency, effectiveness, and safety in the movement and storage of goods.

We will present and apply a transit control paradigm for managing global logistics. It will delineate generic tasks of sensing and reasoning. The variables of the control model will be categorized into classes of flexibility. An integrated system of satellite technology and decision support will be proposed to support the transit control paradigm. Experiences from the trucking industry and first results from research and ongoing pilot studies in Europe and the US are also reported.

TODAY'S GLOBAL LOGISTICS

Global logistics involves owners of goods, shippers, and transportation companies. The goods are moved on one or more modes from origins to destinations. Transport can be local, national, international, intercontinental, and even global. The goods moved are diverse and include agricultural products, foodstuffs, minerals, fuels, petroleum products, ferrous and non-ferrous ores, metal products, fertilizers, chemicals, machinery, manufactured products and miscellaneous. Some of these products fall under the classes of "hazardous materials" or "extremely valuable," and call for special handling requirements.

There are several thousand world-wide shipping companies using air, road, rail, and water shipment, and, in many cases, having to utilize modal-split. Shipping companies are not necessarily identical with the forwarders (shippers) of the goods. Some shipping companies use multiple shippers to combine modes efficiently, in spite of technical and legal constraints. In addition to these constraints, there are several geographical hurdles to be taken. A large concern in Europe, for example, is the Alps crossing in the North-South arterial from Frankfurt, Germany to Rome, Italy—a major European transit corridor.

The road and rail systems in Europe have not significantly changed over the past two decades, even though the number of vehicles and vehicle miles steadily increased. This increase in traffic has extended the planned capacities of European airports, roads, and rail systems. It is therefore not surprising that an investigation of the European transport system by the group Transport 2000 recognized the necessity to harmonize national transport policies and regulations including modal-split and construction of a Pan-European rail system (Teleroute, 1991).

Concurrent with the recognition that the transportation systems are becoming strained beyond capacity is the need for a nation or a community of nations to compete effectively in the global economy. The globalization of the US economy is illustrated graphically by the data in Figure 1.

The level of trade, as shown in the figure by merchandise imports and exports, approximately doubled during the 1980's. Therefore, an integrated transportation system that can deliver a product "in a timely fashion, at a reasonable cost, and without damage is an important objective" (Turnquist and List, 1992). Of course, we should also add to this the words "in a safe and secure manner."

Another fact of global business is the development of the integrated global manufacturing system—with its requirement for Just-In-Time (JIT) production. This requirement has at least two important implications for global logistics: (1) the need to provide on-time materials from suppliers to manufacturing, assembly, and distribution facilities, resulting in an integrated supply-chain management system (Council of Logistics Management, 1990), and (2) the ability to respond rapidly to any breakdown in the system, from an accident that spills hazardous materials to an equipment failure within a plant. In these cases there could be economic loss, environmental degradation, and hazards to workers and the citizens.

An integrated global system would seem to resolve these difficulties and provide the service needed for global logistics. Although we are seeing a movement toward multi-modal freight shippers, for example, the combination of many competing individual firms and differing national policies and standards makes the integrated system a vision for the future.

In today's logistics system, a dispatcher is unable to take advan-

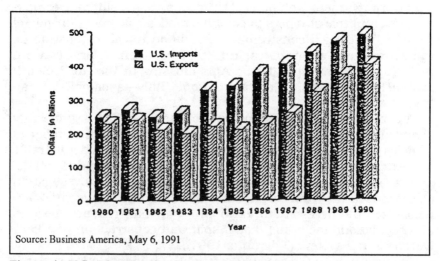

Source: Business America, May 6, 1991

Figure 1: U.S. Merchandise Imports and Exports

tage of sudden changes in the location and character of demand when dealing with truckload shipments. Another problem is the high rate of empty returns coupled with the steadily increasing transport volume. This trend worsens the conflict in urban areas between freight transport and passenger transport (Périssard, 1993).

As indicated above, a significant impact on national and international logistics is the increasing amount of small loads that need to arrive just-in-time (JIT). In Switzerland, for example, the number of trucks up to 3.5 tons increased between 1976 and 1986 by 68%, while the number of heavy trucks over 3.5 tons increased by only 2.2%. Smaller trucks are more flexible and are not subject to as many restrictions and curfews (e.g., in regard to weight limits on certain roads, or night and weekend transport).

Today's global logistics is facing various new challenges and opportunities. The growing problems affect efficiency and services. New markets provide business opportunities but also pose new difficulties. Advances in communications and computing technologies can both improve present operations and facilitate the transition to an integrated logistics system. Shipping companies and forwarders have been experimenting with technological advances such as satellite tracking systems that allow a centralized headquarters to monitor the position and status of all mobile units in real-time.

SATELLITE TRACKING AND GLOBAL LOGISTICS

The trend towards globalization of production and consumption and the need to envision world markets require a comprehensive approach to logistics. Any such approach must be built around modern communications and computing technologies, including electronic data interchange, computer networks, and mobile communications. Technologies that are being commercialized include satellite tracking systems, communications systems, and electronic cargo bourses (Sheffi, 1991). The concept of satellite tracking is illustrated in Figure 2.

Cargo can move on a transportation system, as a container either in a truck or on a train, on a ship between continents, or on inland water-ways, or some combination of these. The position of the cargo and of the vehicles is periodically recorded in a world-wide coordinate system. Sensors installed on the cargo and in the driver compartments collect various data about the cargo (e.g., temperature or pressure), the vehicle (e.g., amount of fuel left, condition of brakes), and the driver (e.g., hours driving since last break, communications). These data are then transferred via a communications system to the headquarters and fed into a computer. The data are then transformed into acoustic signals (voice) or visualized on the

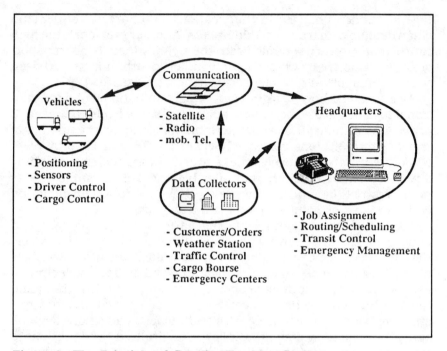

Figure 2: The Principle of Satellite Tracking Systems

dispatcher's monitor. A geographical information system is used to display the transportation network, identifying the position of the cargo and its past and anticipated route. Communications by the dispatcher can be initiated, for example, by clicking on the icon representing the vehicle on the screen.

The Tasks

The generic tasks of the dispatcher and the variables of control have been identified elsewhere (Beroggi and Wallace, 1991). The process of transit control can be generalized as one of assessing current conditions, identifying any potential for immediate change to those conditions, comparing both to a desired state, and if there is a gap, taking action to bring the present or future state in concordance with the desired state (Wallace, 1989). Therefore, the generic tasks can be grouped into sensing and reasoning. Sensing refers to data collection about the vehicles and the environment-affected performance of the shipments. It is supported by external data collectors, such as weather stations, traffic control units, cargo bourses, and emergency centers. Reasoning consists of job assignment, routing and scheduling of the shipments, transit control during the shipment to change operations if necessary, and emergency response in cases of disruptions.

The generic tasks and the variables of transit control are summarized in Figure 3. The generic tasks consist of sensing, and reasoning by the headquarters, and intervention by the drivers or specialized units in case of changes. The first aspect of sensing refers to obtaining requests from customers. This can be accomplished by questioning electronic cargo bourses or by monitoring the customer's operations and determining the company's requirements. The second aspect of sensing is to monitor the locations of the vehicles and their status on a screen. The third aspect of sensing is to monitor the environment for any changes that could improve or worsen the ongoing operations.

Reasoning includes analyzing data and making decisions in a time constrained environment under uncertainty. Incoming data are often unreliable and incomplete. The dispatchers at headquarters must make decisions while the operations are in progress. Reasoning addresses three major tasks. First, orders must be assigned to vehicles in such a way as to minimize transportation time and reduce the number of empty shipments. Second, changes of operations in response to a sudden onset of events that either threaten the successful completion of the shipment or represent unanticipated orders that could result in additional profits, must be evaluated and forwarded to the drivers. And finally, actions to effectively and rapidly respond to vehicle failures, such as breakdowns, must be determined and forwarded to the appropriate response unit.

Advances in computing technologies are providing a variety of tools to support the reasoning process. We envision a dispatcher to be able to manage simultaneously many cargo units, moving in different modes. In order to do so, we propose that a traffic management control center have workstations with a large flat screen for projection of the transportation network and visual monitoring by center personnel. Reasoning is supported by decision aids incorporating scheduling algorithms and extensive databases. The capability exists for an electronic bourse for a company or, at the very least, communicating in real-time with a regional bourse, to match demands for deliveries with available vehicles.

The decisions made by the headquarters are implemented either on the vehicles by changing their routes and delivery priorities or by emergency units designed to assist the vehicles and the cargo. If the proposed decisions cannot be implemented, the headquarters must investigate alternative courses of action.

A shipment is considered to be successful if it is on time and conducted safely. Timeliness is measured in terms of customer satisfaction and the resulting economic gains. Safety refers to internal safety of the drivers and the cargo as well as the external safety of the population and environment. External safety is especially crucial for hazardous material shipments. A shipment can

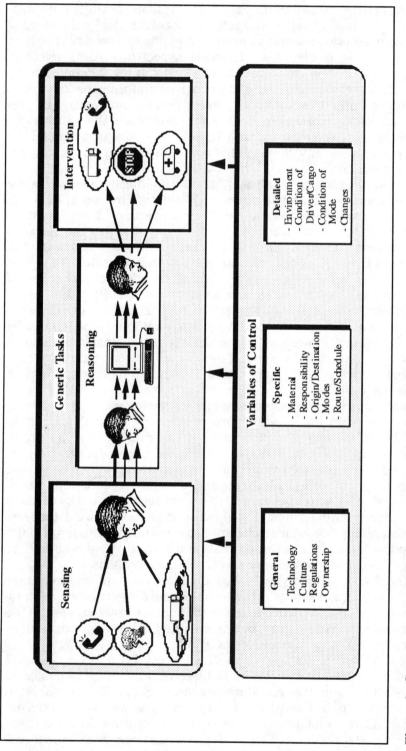

Figure 3: Generic Task and Variables of Control for Satellite Tracking.

become costly if its safety is reduced or if delays occur. A shipment can provide additional benefits if changes in demand can be met without increasing costs, i.e., rerouting to pick up additional freight.

The variables of control affect the generic tasks. They are identified at three levels: (i) general, (ii) specific, and (iii) detailed. General variables of control are the technology, culture, regulations, and ownership. They change very seldom and if they do, they do not affect on-going shipments. General variables have to be considered strategically. Specific variables of control can affect the planning phase of individual shipments but not the operation itself. For example, hazardous cargo needs special care, some modes need special provisions, and for some schedules, special vehicles must be employed. Finally, detailed variables have an impact on the operations. Sudden weather changes can force a truck to reroute to safer roads, fatigue might force a driver to stop, and problems with the vehicle can result in delays. Although we are concerned in this chapter with the detailed or operational variables of control, we recognize the hierarchical dependency of the various levels. Decisions made on, for example, the use of advanced information technology will effect a firm's ability to plan shipments and control their transit. It is our contention that we need to understand the impact of a general or specific variable of control on the operations of a transportation system in order to assess its costs and benefits.

Existing and Anticipated Systems

Satellite tracking systems were introduced in the late 1980's in the United States. They were promoted by promising a competitive advantage over trucking companies that rely on traditional systems. The only communication between dispatcher and long-distance shipments was, at that time, the phone system. Drivers had to report back to headquarters by calling from a public phone. This required unnecessary stops and lost time. In addition, this one-way communication made the dispatcher dependent on the drivers and drivers dependent on the availability of a public phone. The result was, in the case of emergencies such as break downs, an inability for the driver to contact the headquarters or police for immediate help.

Shortly after the first satellite tracking systems became commercially available, the US trucking company Schneider acquired 5,000 satellite positioning units to monitor its truck fleet. This acquisition was made without any empirical assessment of potential benefits or risks. At about the same time, the US Department of Energy began monitoring, via satellite, shipments of radioactive materials. The major reason was to improve emergency response in the case of an accident. The potential benefits were demonstrated in an transportation emergency exercise (Analysas Corporation, 1992).

There are several companies in the communication business that offer access to a satellite tracking system, the best known being OmniTracs in the US and EutelTracs in Europe. Other companies provide communications links between headquarters and mobile units based on satellite or radio systems, and the software for the computer system at the headquarters. The best known satellite communications system between headquarters and mobile units is Inmarsat C.

Satellite tracking systems are commercially available as closed systems or as combined positioning/communications systems (Jacobs et. al., 1991). Closed systems provide positioning, communications, and management at a central location in one package. Examples are OmniTracs and EutelTracs. They consist of two satellites; one for massaging and one for positioning. A network management computer transfers messages of up to 2,000 characters in length via satellite between a company's headquarters and its vehicles. The system allows the mobile unit operator (driver) to save and recall up to 256 lines of messages. Positioning accuracy is a few hundred meters. The system is around the clock in service, providing almost real-time communications between the headquarters or control center and a fleet of vehicles.

Open system approaches are based on the Global Positioning System (GPS). It is maintained by the US Department of Defense and available free of charge for commercial and private use. Positioning data are transferred to a headquarters location either via satellite (e.g., Inmarsat C), radio, or mobile phone.

A completely integrated system for global communications is expected to happen before the start of the 21st century with the global phone system Iridium being developed by Motorola. The Iridium system, consisting of 77 satellites, will permit any point-point communication on a global scale, without a processing center or waiting times.

EXPECTED AND REPORTED BENEFITS

The expected benefits of employing transit control in global logistics are somewhat obvious. Of major importance are both the economic and strategic benefits. Customers are now requiring timely, reliable shipments in order to utilize a just-in-time production and distribution system. Any slippage in schedules is costly, with the result a loss in future sales for the shipper. However, shippers can use real-time data to take responsive actions to changes in order and inventory conditions. This capability has a major impact on the traditional patterns of ordering supplies, shipping products, and maintaining inventories. In addition, transport requirements with regard to size and frequency of shipments alter significantly.   The resulting improved service in terms of reliability of transports and meeting of deadlines is becoming as important as cost to the customer.

Another aspect of transit control is the need for the transportation industry to recognize the potential for (positive) environmental impacts. For example, transit control will permit increasing optimal assignment of vehicles to demands, resulting in fewer empty loads and, therefore, miles traveled (with a related reduction in environmental degradation).   Customers with environmentally sensitive cargo will also require that shippers emphasize safety. Transit control can improve safety by rerouting vehicles in hazardous conditions. In cases of a vehicle breakdown, response can also be managed more effectively.

Satellite monitoring may also be used to track vehicles carrying valuable cargo, and notify appropriate law enforcement authorities in case of disruption of service. The issue of driver and cargo security has already become extremely important as vehicles move from the newly emergent nations of Eastern Europe.

An open question is the impact of transit control on driver satisfaction.   There are serious concerns among the drivers as to whether satellite tracking systems can enhance the working environment or whether they limit the freedom of driving.   However, drivers do acknowledge the benefits in the transportation of hazardous or valuable cargos.

Morlok and Halowell (1989) reported on the benefits of using advanced satellite tracking systems.   Cost reductions were reported due to an increase in load factor, reduction in fuel consumption, less communication time, lower telephone charges, better use of vehicles (less empty shipments), and reduction of out-of-route shipments. Service improvement was obtained because customers could be warned in cases of delays, and perishable hazardous cargo could be tracked from the headquarters, and inoperative vehicles could be provided faster service. In addition, the ability to alert drivers about bad weather or other conditions that could change planned routes was also recognized as beneficial to the shippers and customers.

A recent joint TRANSCOM (Transportation Operations Coordinating Committee) and ATA (American Trucking Association) demonstration using real-time traffic information concluded that fleet productivity could be increased, that customer service and the driver's environment could be improved, and that costs to shippers would be reduced. In addition, unusual events and accidents could be handled more efficiently (Batz, 1991). The biggest advantage, in fact, seemed to stem from the possibility of rerouting vehicles in cases of nonrecurring events (e.g., congestions).

Many different pilot studies are being conducted in Europe

(Visser, 1991). The 3-year EC DRIVE project is conducting seventy-two projects all over Europe. The costs of about 120 Mil. ECU are shared between industry, universities, and government agencies. The goal of the DRIVE program is to establish directives for use of information and communication technologies throughout Europe (Keen, 1992). Other comparable programs in Europe are Eureka, Prometheus, Carminat, and Europolis. Results are expected in the near future from the pilot studies in the third phase of DRIVE, due to be completed in 1994 (Combi Box, 1988).

SUMMARY AND CONCLUSIONS

Global logistics managers currently face a number of major problems, the resolution of which could result in rewarding opportunities. In many cases, traffic load is reaching full capacity; new markets are attracting more business; national policies are pushing shippers to switch to rail transport; and advanced information and communications technologies are providing the basis for true global transportation.

In this chapter we have presented a conceptual model of satellite tracking that changes the focus from just planning a shipment to include monitoring the shipments performance and taking action in cases of unexpected events. The generic tasks of the dispatcher at a central location were identified as sensing and reasoning with the variables of control being general, specific or detailed. Various benefits of using real-time control have been noted from practical experience and pilot studies. However, taking advantage of these potential benefits requires an investment by the shipping companies and forwarders. Recent economic slowdowns in both Europe and the US have dampened the enthusiasm of trucking companies to experiment in this sector, and they are continuing to rely on traditional and available means. However, according to J. Larkin from Alex Brown & Sons, the ever increasing concern for environmentally responsible manufacturing and logistics in both Europe and the US may force the shipping industry to implement satellite tracking technology, regardless of whether it can be economically justified (Kerver, 1989).

REFERENCES

Analysas Corporation, (1992). Transcom Overview. Prepared for the US Department of Energy.

Batz T.M., (1991). The Utilization of Real-Time Traffic Information by the Trucking Industry. IEEE Transaction on Vehicular Technology, 40 (1), 64-

67.

Beroggi G.E.G. and Wallace W.A., (1991).   Closing the Gap -Transit Control for Hazardous Material Flow. Journal of Hazardous Materials, 27, 61-75.

Business America, May 6, (1991), p. 3.

Combi Box, (1988). Rationelle Gütertransporte/Kombinierter Verkehr: Von Box zu Box, Direkt und Wirtschaftlich. Schweizerische Handelszeitung, Separatdruck aus Nr. 46.

Council of Logistics Management, (1990). 1989 Proceedings. Oakbrook, IL: Council of Logistics Management.

Jacobs I.M., Salmassi A., and Bernard T.J., (1991). The Application of a Novel Two-Way Mobile Satellite Communications and Vehicle Tracking System to the Transport Industry, IEEE Transaction on Vehicular Technology, 40 (1), 57-63.

Keen K., (1992). European Community Research and Technology Development on Advanced Road Transport Telematics, 1992-1994, Traffic Engineering and Control, April, 263-267.

Kerver T., (1989).   Qualcomm's Gambit in Ku-Band Mobile, Satellite Communications, June.

Morlok E.K. und Halowell S.F., (1989). Reported Benefits of Advanced Vehicle Tracking and Communications Systems, Mobile Satellite Project, WP 89-8-1, Department of Systems, University of Pennsylvania, Philadelphia.

Périssard J., (1993). Written communication: Department of Economic Affairs, International Road Transport Union, Geneva, Switzerland.

Sheffi Y., (1991). A Shipment Information Centre, The International Journal of Logistics Management, 2 (2), 1-12.

Teleroute, (1991). Transport in Europa-Rapport. Teleroute 5.

Turnquist, M.A. and List, G.F., (1992). Charting a Course for Intermodal Policy and Research, University Transportation Research Center, Region III, US Department of Transportation.

Visser A.R., (1991). Development of Land Mobile Satellite Services in Europe, Journal of Navigation, 44 (2), 224-232.

Wallace W.A., (1989). Command and Control: A Team Problem Solving and Decision Making Process, RADC/COE, Griffiss AFB, New York, 13441-5700.

SECTION 6

The Impact of IT on Innovation and Global Research and Development

The world of competitive priorities has been turned on its ear by corporations which have increased their market shares and profitabilities by bringing newer and more desirable products to market in very short periods of time. Global automakers, for example, have shortened their product development cycles over the last 15 years from 8 or so years to something approaching 3 years. This has been accomplished with a combination of better procedures and increased coordination among (typically) disparate groups in most corporations (i.e., marketers, production managers, product designers, researchers, engineers, etc.) Information and communications technologies have again played the key role in making all of this possible.

Customers, of course, do not buy products or services simply because a corporation is "innovative". On the other hand, since "first comers" to the market often enjoy tremendous market share advantages when their products are desireable, even smaller corporations feel the pressure to monitor research developments vis-a-vis consumer preferences. Furthermore, many advances in corporations take the form of "process innovations", where new and improved ways of production allow firms to increase their capabilities in terms of the dominant competitive priorities (e.g., better quality, quicker delivery, or lower cost). In the context of the global marketplace, this adds more than one level of complexity to the tasks of overburdened managers. It is clear that technology-based tools will be needed to increase the efficiency and effectiveness of corporations trying to compete and survive in a world where "time" now has a broader connotation than "manufacturing lead time".

The literature on innovation is a burgeoning one. In this section of the book we include three chapters which, in total, give some indication of the breadth of current issues as well as a clear indication that advances in IT are making the new realities possible for the MNC. In the first chapter, Alexander von Boehmer observes that research and development in global organizations is really couched in a broader area that may be termed "technology management". He notes that the strategic dimension of R&D recognizes that corporations must also concern themselves with the external acquisition and external use of technological knowledge as well as the establishment of R&D capability. This chapter also points out that global corporations have a vast array of hurdles to overcome in the IT area before the R&D function will be truly integreated across national borders.

In the second chapter, Alok Chakrabarti examines in greater detail the role of information technology in global R&D. Marketing in certain countries, producing in others, and designing/developing in another or some combination of these is a formidable, integrative endeavor. As the author points out, current R&D executives are cautionsly optimistic about the potential for IT to make their jobs in the global corporation "doable".

The final chapter of this section differs somewhat from the other two but makes a very important contribution to the discussion. Xiaobo Wu, Weiqiang Wang, and Qingrui Xu from the People's Republic of China write about how corporations in developing countries must take advantage of information technologies simply to ensure that they may gain competitive advantage even as "late-comers" to the marketplace. Japanese corporations have long proven that primary innovation - totally new products or processes - are not a necessary condition for profitability. Secondary, incremental changes in process and product technologies often bring even greater long term profits. Although the authors do not emphasize this point in the context of the generic multinational corporation, the lessons are clear. The global R&D organization is responsible for both the incremental and radical changes that sustain corporations, and IT is the "potential weapon...to gain new sources of advantage".

CHAPTER 17

Information Systems for Global Technology Management

ALEXANDER VON BOEHMER
University of Kiel

Based on an analysis of the tasks performed and decisions made in the management of technology (which will be defined to include research and development), an integrated information system for global technology management is outlined. The requirements for such a system are deduced from the information needs of technology management. The second part of the chapter then reports on empirical studies which investigate technology management information systems currently in use. These studies have shown that information systems are employed for a great variety of applications ranging from project planning and control systems to formal budgeting systems. However, these applications seem not to be integrated into a comprehensive information system. In the final section of the chapter, the implications of new developments in the design and implementation of technology management information systems are discussed.

INTRODUCTION

In a world of global competition, shortening product life cycles and of decreasing product development times, technology has become a strategic variable to sustain the competitiveness of companies (Friar & Horwitch, 1986). The timely access to new technological knowledge constitutes one of the driving forces behind the increased decentralization of research and development (R&D) activities. Companies are setting up R&D facilities in foreign countries in order to be more responsive to local demand or to tap into centers of excellence (De Meyer & Mizushima, 1989; von Boehmer, 1991; von Boehmer, Brockhoff & Pearson, 1992; Brockhoff & von Boehmer, 1993). Overseas R&D activities are performed through wholly-owned subsidiaries either in self-standing R&D facilities or in R&D facilities in conjunction with production or marketing activities. Joint ventures, strategic alliances and other forms of R&D agreements constitute additional modes of global R&D activities. Thus, global R&D networks have emerged with a diverse set of information flows[1].

Many studies have pointed to the importance of communication for problem solving in R&D (Allen, 1977). Face-to-face communication is increasingly complemented by electronic communication, with recent advances in information technology being the key factor in this development.

Accessing different sources of technology is an important task of technology management. In addition to the acquisition of technological knowledge, the management of technology is concerned with managerial decisions on the storage, retrieval and use of this knowledge (Brockhoff, 1992). Among others, the technology manager is involved in planning and control activities. To increase the efficiency and effectiveness of R&D operations and to provide tools and information for the management of technology, information systems are deployed, i.e., systems that collect, process and diffuse information with electronic support. Comprehensive and task-adequate information systems may enable or facilitate problem solving in technology management.

This chapter addresses the following questions:

1. What are the requirements for a system to facilitate the management of technology on a global basis?
2. What kind of information systems currently exist and how are they used?
3. How could the existing systems be changed and what are the management implications of developments in information technology?

The chapter is divided into three parts. The first part outlines the informational needs of an integrated technology management information system. Based on a description of the tasks of technology management, we illustrate the requirements for such an information system. The complex situations of multinational corporations are taken into account. The second part gives an overview of empirical studies which investigate the employment and utilizations of different types of information systems. The findings are compared with the requirements for an "ideal" information system, and differences between the desirable state and the existing situation are identified. In the concluding section, potential developments and their implications for technology management are discussed.

INFORMATIONAL NEEDS OF INTEGRATED SYSTEMS

In order to depict the desirable characteristics of a comprehensive, integrated global information system, we first describe and analyze the tasks performed and decisions made in technology management. In the second step, we derive the information necessary to carry out these tasks. Finally, we deduce from the information needs the requirements for a comprehensive technology management information system.

Tasks of Technology Management

Technology management is concerned with supplying and generating technological knowledge and providing the management capabilities for doing so. The latter includes planning and control activities as well as solving organizational and human resource issues[2].

Technology management is frequently assumed to be identical with R&D management. It encapsulates, however, much more than the R&D function in that it also includes the external acquisition and external use of technological knowledge. Obtaining a license or the purchase of other companies are examples of external acquisitions of knowledge. They constitute alternatives to generating knowledge in-house through R&D activities. Similarly, an external use of knowledge exists if a company grants a license on an in-house development to someone outside the corporation (Brockhoff, 1992). Global technology management implies that both the internal as well as the external acquisition and use of technological knowledge is taking place across national boundaries, i.e. multinational corporations compete globally for sources of technology.

R&D management is generally comprised of the tasks of planning, control, and organization (Brockhoff, 1992). To derive the key information needs of these, in the next three sub-sections we will first elaborate on the specific tasks of

- R&D planning and control,
- R&D organization, and
- the external acquisition and use of knowledge.

The discussion in the sections on the information needs of R&D management— i.e., R&D planning and control, and R&D organization—are based on the study by Möhrle (1991).

R&D Planning and Control

R&D planning and control is frequently divided into strategic, operative and tactical planning and control (Brockhoff, 1992). Strategic planning and control refines and operationalizes the R&D objectives, evaluates technological trends and decides on the set of technologies to focus on. One of the fundamental decisions in this respect is the location decision, which for many internationally operating companies is a decision of whether to locate R&D activities outside the country of the headquarters of the corporation. The R&D budget is determined at the operative level. Finally, tactical R&D planning and control deals with R&D projects, i.e., their selection, evaluation and termination (Möhrle, 1991). It is evident that moving from the strategic to the tactical level goes along with shorter planning intervals and more detailed contents of the plans. Also the people involved in the planning and control activity vary with the different levels. Corporate and R&D top management are involved on the strategic level, whereas R&D project leaders and R&D managers have more of an input at the tactical level.

Table 1 lists the information needs for the different tasks performed by R&D planning and control. The information needs are shown in terms of type of information and specific information content.

The table points out that, in addition to the R&D function, other functional areas such as marketing, manufacturing, human resource management and cost accounting will be involved in providing necessary information. This illustrates how complex planning and control can be when R&D is performed and coordinated across multiple countries.

R&D Organization

The task here is to determine the organizational structure of both the R&D function as well as R&D projects. The R&D function may be organized around, for example, scientific disciplines, product lines or the degree of applicability. For a global corporation to be responsive in the area of product development, R&D organization must promote sharing of ideas and open communication. Another issue is the question of centralized vs. decentralized R&D activities. R&D projects are usually embedded in the organization of the R&D function unless the project is very large. For the decisions on the organizational structure the information shown in Table 2 is needed.

Task	Type of information	Specific information content
Strategic	• general R&D objectives	• goal object, attributes, time, dimensions
	• characteristics of technological fields	• interdependencies, possibility for technical substitution
	• performance measures of technologies	• limitation, substitution, cost
	• potential of technologies	• applications, diffusion over time
	• know-how on technologies	• current level, stability
	• R&D personnel	• areas of expertise, quantity, quality
	• R&D budget over time	
Operative	• financial situation of company	• resources, expected profits
	• expenditures in a specific period	• investments (excluding R&D)
	• financial requirements of R&D	• facilities, projects, technologies
	• R&D production function	• input/output factors (e.g. patents) and their functional relationship
Tactical • generating new project ideas	• customer needs	• complaints, suggestions, results of customer surveys (focus groups)
	• new products and processes	
	• specific R&D objectives	• goal object, attributes, time dimensions
	• new technological developments	
• project evaluation and selection	• project idea, technical	• description of technical project goals
	• technological attractiveness of idea	• existing know-how, patents, appropriability
	• market attractiveness	• potential sales
	• financial situation of company	• resources, expect profits
	• cost of project	• qualitative and quantitative resource requirements
	• available R&D capacity	• human resources, equipment
	• required R&D capacity of project	• human resources, equipment
• project planning and control	• project outcome	• qualitative and quantitative success measures
	• projected & actual activities of project	• task descriptions
	• sequence of activities	• PERT chart, bar chart
• project termination	• progress of project	• performance, time, cost
	• know-how of project team	• description of available and potential capabilities
	• estimated market potential	• sales
	• behavior of competitors	• actions taken
	• feasibility of manufacturing	• know-how, resources
	• legal restrictions, standards and norms	• benchmarks

Table 1: Informational needs for R&D planning and control

Type of information	Specific information content
• tasks to be performed	• requirements of projects, project plan
• human resources	• availability and qualification
• organizational structure of company	• organization chart

Source: Based on Möhrle (1991).

Table 2: Informational needs for organizing the R&D function

External Acquisition and Use of Technological Knowledge

Keeping track of the technological developments outside one's own company is an important task of technology management and may help "to increase warning times before the introduction of innovations by competitors" (Brockhoff, 1991, p. 91). This task may be accomplished by a systematic competitor technology analysis (Brockhoff, 1991). In a number of cases, foreign R&D facilities function as listening posts collecting information on technological developments of competitors, suppliers and other institutions in the local environment (von Boehmer, 1991). Various indicators may be used to provide the sought after information. See Table 3.

In addition to the monitoring activity, information on the transfer of technology is important as well. For example, if a license agreement is signed or R&D cooperation established, the means of technology transfer between the partners need to be specified. Similarly issues arise with the external use of in-house R&D results.

For the make-or-buy decision, i.e., internal or in-house R&D vs. external acquisition of the required knowledge, a picture of external sources of technology and the means of transferring the technology are necessary.

Requirements of Information Systems

In the preceding section we have seen that quite a large number of different indicators and types of information on technological developments (both within a corporation and outside its organizational boundaries) are necessary to perform the tasks of technology management. If information systems are to be used effectively to satisfy the complex information needs, a number of requirements will need to be met.

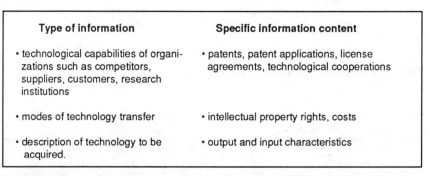

Type of information	Specific information content
• technological capabilities of organizations such as competitors, suppliers, customers, research institutions	• patents, patent applications, license agreements, technological cooperations
• modes of technology transfer	• intellectual property rights, costs
• description of technology to be acquired.	• output and input characteristics

Table 3: Informational needs to manage external acquisition and use of technological knowledge

- Since several indicators regarding technological developments, global markets and competition may easily be overlooked due to the weakness of their signal, data collection should be complemented by data analysis. Methodical knowledge seems to be necessary to detect such signals (Brockhoff, 1989).
- The emergence of information grave yards should be avoided. Information that is not needed should be removed from the system as its storage induces costs. The information should constantly be monitored and, if necessary, be modified as the tasks of technology management and the corporation may change over time.
- Aggregation of information is important. Not all levels of management need the same information. Different levels of R&D management have already been pointed out: strategic, operative and tactical. The higher levels in the hierarchy require more aggregated, general information. On the operational level detailed information related to a specific point in time is needed to support daily work. An adequate supply of information may also avoid information overload.
- As mentioned above, the R&D function exchanges information among many locations and with other functional areas in the corporation. This implies that an information system must take these interfaces into account. In the case of corporations with overseas R&D facilities, additional information flows exist between the parent company (headquarters) laboratory and the overseas subsidiaries as well as among the subsidiaries. Information systems for such multinational corporations are marked by a relatively high degree of complexity.

EXISTING INFORMATION SYSTEMS

Having outlined the desirable state of a technology management information system, we now turn to the existing situation for such systems. This part of the chapter gives an overview of empirical studies which investigate the employment and utilization of different types of information systems. The systems currently in use are then compared with the requirements stated above. The set of differences is then identified and discussed.

The presentation of the empirical studies is, however, accompanied by a number of caveats:

- None of the studies described here has directly investigated information systems for technology management as defined in this chapter. One study focused on R&D information systems (Möhrle, 1991). The other studies may be divided into two groups: those concerned with the use of computers in R&D and those looking at the application of quantitative methods in R&D.

- An explicit investigation into multinational corporations has not yet been carried out. However, the samples of several studies tend to include a number of multinational corporations. Case & Pickett (1989), for example, collected data from Fortune 500 companies, many of which are qualified as multinational corporations. Thus the global dimension of technology management is partially captured.

- Most of the studies were conducted several years ago. With the rapid developments in information technology, it seems fair to assume that the results of the studies do not fully represent the current situation.

Types and Their Utilization

Information Systems

The most detailed and comprehensive study was conducted by Möhrle (1991). His broad definition of R&D management captures an extensive part of the tasks of technology management. In his interviews with 34 electronics companies in Germany he identified five types of R&D information systems: single project information systems, program information systems, cost accounting information systems, computer-aided design (CAD) systems and external databases (see Table 4).

Single project information systems support R&D managers in the planning and control of single projects. Such systems foster the communication with other functional areas by exchanging information on the project activities. Although this type of system has received quite some attention in literature, it was used in only 38% of the cases. Compared with the potential applications of this system, the companies in Möhrle's sample were making only limited use of this system.

Program information systems are applied at a more aggregate level than single project information systems. They contain information on a project as a whole and comprise a set of projects. The project evaluation and selection decisions, the project termination decisions and the cost and time management of all projects belong to the main tasks of program information systems. Möhrle (1991) reported that only 7 of the 34 (21%) companies employed such a system, with little use of its project evaluation capabilities.

More than two-thirds (71%) of the companies were working with cost accounting information systems, a result which was expected since such systems are commonplace in a number of other functional areas. Möhrle (1991) observed, however, that not much use was being made of cost accounting systems for planning purposes.

Existing Information Systems _Feature_	Single Project Information Systems	Program Information Systems	Cost Accounting Information Systems	CAD Systems	Databases
Application	Tactical planning and control of R&D projects	Selection of project ideas, control of projects within a program	Retrospective cost accounting with R&D project as costing unit	Improvements of processes and quality, rationalization	Identification of technological trends, low utilization of patent databases
User	Project leader, project members, collaborators in manufacturing and marketing	Head of R&D, project leader, top management, chief financial officers	Head of R&D, project leader and members, top management, cost accountants	Members of project, members of manufacturing	Project leader and members, head of R&D
Structure of Information	Information on every single activity and the sequence of activities	Differs from company to company	Information on various cost items	Relevant and required technical information, no uniform structures	Rather simple structure, difficult to obtain information on interrelations
Output	PERT charts, bar charts, lists of activities	Plan of required capacity, documents for project control	Overview of various cost items	Fairly different depending on application	List with information from various databases
EDP Aspects	Mainframe and micro computers, only purchased software, wide range of software	No standard software available, only in-house developments	Company-wide computer system, standard software	Computers with special peripherals, software bought, lack of standards	Minor hardware equipment necessary, modem, telephone network
Frequency of Use (in percent of sample size, 34 Electronics Co.)	38%	21%	71%	91%	65%

Table 4: Results of the study of Möhrle (1991) on R&D information systems

The cost accounting information system consisted only of historical monetary data.

The more technical oriented information needs are met by CAD-systems and databases. The former system was applied by 91% of the electronics companies, the latter by two-thirds. As other authors have noted (Brockhoff, 1989), companies are making too little use of databases.

In summary, Möhrle (1991) identified great inter-firm discrepancies regarding the utilization of technology management information system components. Information systems with a strong technical orientation are widely used. The same applies to cost accounting systems. Single project and program systems, however, were employed in only a few companies. A number of the features and capabilities of the five R&D information systems were not fully utilized by the companies. In addition, the five systems are configured as stand-alone systems, with few attempts made to create integrated systems. Although, the findings are based on data from only one industry, the electronics industry in Germany, they are likely to be representative of many other types of organizations.

In fact, we know from anecdotal evidence that in the software industry the need for shorter product development times has lead to the establishment of international programming teams. Once the working day of the team members in Asia ends they hand their programming results over to their European colleagues. Similarly, American software engineers receive the daily output from the European facility. A company-wide electronic network (information system) enables the transfer of the project details and the communication among R&D facilities. This example stresses the importance of information systems for the competitiveness of technology driven multinational companies.

Use of Computers in R&D

In the last decade, the studies by Morse, Ong & Pearson (1984), Rossini & Porter (1986)[3], Rossini, Porter, Jacobs & Abraham (1988) and Case & Pickett (1989) have investigated the use of computers in R&D. See Table 5. In their study on 176 organizations in Britain, Morse, Ong & Pearson (1984) grouped the various computer applications into management, experimentation, modelling/design/simulation, analysis/calculation, and information handling. The control and analysis of experiments proved to be the most common application for computers. A similar result was also obtained by the other three studies. Although, the importance of computer applications for experiments was not identified by Möhrle, this discrepancy may be attributed to the fact that these studies covered various industries other than electronics. R&D activities in the electronics industry may not be dominated as much by "pure" experimentation activities.

Rossini & Porter (1986) and Rossini, Porter, Jacobs & Abraham (1988) surveyed the Industrial Research Institute (IRI) companies at three different points in time: 1974, 1984 and 1986. 67 companies participated in all three studies. The major computer applications in order of importance were: laboratory automation, statistical analysis, database management, modelling and simulation. In 1986, close to 60% of the senior managers had a terminal on their desk. Management employed computers mainly for budgeting, program and project management and communications. Over the course of the three studies an increase in artificial intelligence and expert system applications was observed. This trend is projected to continue in the future.

The respondents to the most recent survey of Case & Pickett (1989)—74 "Fortune 500" companies—anticipated a similar trend[4]. The majority of the companies in the sample employed computers for statistical analysis, CAD, process control and project management. The companies see a need for improving the integration and global networking of the current applications. In addition, they are concerned with the security of the databases and systems - an issue which has been ranked highly in other international studies as well (Deans et al., 1991).

The results of the empirical studies suggest that the main applications of computers in R&D are for the control of experiments and the statistical analysis of data. In addition, management uses computers for budgeting, project management and communication. In summary, the computer is used more as a sophisticated and powerful calculator rather than as an integrated information system. The limitations, in terms of promoting global competitors through quicker product and process development, are clear. Corporations with a world-wide R&D network often attribute specific roles to their overseas R&D facilities. For example, such facilities may function as centers of excellence or have the worldwide responsibility for a specific product or product line (world product mandate). The need for coordination and communication—and thus the need for deploying information systems—to avoid unwanted duplication of effort is apparent. Competitive pressure may foster the integration and networking of computers to establish necessary technology management information systems.

Quantitative Methods

Three empirical studies have been conducted in recent years on the use of quantitative methods in R&D. They differ with respect to the country of origin, sample size and the research method (see Table 5). These studies provide additional information on how components of technology management information systems are used.

Research focus	Study	Sample	Research method	Description
R&D information systems	Möhrle (1991)	34 electronics companies in Germany	interviews	Five categories of IS are identified: 1. single project IS, 2. program IS, 3. cost accounting IS, 4. CAD systems, 5. databases. Most companies employ 3.-5.; some companies use 1.., only a few 2. In most cases the IS exist as stand-alone systems, few IS are integrated.
Computers in R&D	Case & Pickett (1989)	74 *Fortune 500* co.	questionnaire	Most companies use computers for statistical analysis, CAD, process control and project management. Expert systems, artificial intelligence and decision support systems are expected to be of interest in the future. Respondents expressed the need for improvements for better integration and networking. They indicated concern with the security of databases and systems.
	Rossini, Porter, Jacobs & Abraham (1988)	126 Industrial Research Institute co., 71 also in Rossini & Porter, 1986, various industries	questionnaire	Management uses computers for budgeting, program and project management and communications. Computer applications include laboratory automation, statistical analysis, database management, modelling and simulation. In the future artificial intelligence, expert systems and communications seem to be increasing in relative importance.
	Rossini & Porter (1986)	158 IRI companies, various industries	questionnaire	Results similar to Rossini, Porter, Jacobs & Abraham (1988).
	Morse, Ong & Pearson (1984)	176 organizations in Britain; 77% public, rest industrial sector, various industries	questionnaire	Computer applications are grouped into management, experimentation, modelling/design/simulation, analysis/calculation and information handling. Computers are mostly used for the control and analysis of experiments. Of secondary importance are CAD systems, followed by network analysis and financial modelling.
Quantitative methods in R&D	Thoma (1989)	7 automotive companies in Germany	questionnaire as well as interviews	The study focuses on the application of quantitative methods for the evaluation of R&D projects. Most companies employ methods used in cost accounting and financial analysis. Checklists are commonly used.
	Watts & Higgins (1987)	65 British companies in first, 37 in second phase, various industries	two phases, questionnaire	For project selection most respondents make use of checklists and project profiles. Risk analysis is less common. Very few companies employ mathematical programming techniques. For project planning and control half the companies use bar and Gantt charts. A low usage of more complex techniques (e.g. network techniques) is found.
	Liberatore & Titus (1983)	36 R&D managers in 19 *Fortune 500* companies	interviews	Financial models and Gantt charts are widely used. Limited usage is observed for decision trees, network analysis, checklists and scoring models. In most cases the familiarity with a quantitative method is higher than its usage.

Table 5: Empirical studies on R&D information systems and the use of computers and quantitative methods in R&D

Liberatore & Titus (1983) interviewed 36 senior R&D managers in 29 "Fortune 500" companies on the use of quantitative methods for tactical R&D planning and control. Both the familiarity with a method as well as its usage were of interest. The quantitative methods under consideration belonged to the following categories: financial methods, risk assessment techniques, formal budgeting systems, scheduling and control techniques, mathematical programming models, behavioral models and subjective evaluation. Financial models and Gantt charts are widely used. Limited usage was observed for decision trees, network analysis, checklists and scoring models. In a number of cases the companies were familiar with a method but were not employing it. There is apparently quite some room for increasing the utilization of these methods and for integrating these tools across multiple locations.

In a two phase questionnaire study, Watts & Higgins (1987) requested information from senior R&D managers in Britain on the selection and evaluation of R&D projects and on the planning and control of R&D projects. The first part on project selection and evaluation included the categories financial methods, risk assessment techniques, formal budgeting systems, mathematical programming models and subjective evaluation in the study by Liberatore & Titus (1983). Compared to the US data, the British data show the following order of importance: checklists and project profiles, financial methods, and risk assessment techniques. The second part of the Watts and Higgins study, regarding project planning and control, revealed that bar and Gantt charts were employed in half the companies with a low usage of more complex techniques.

Thoma (1989) investigated quantitative methods for the evaluation of R&D projects in seven automobile companies in Germany. Most companies employed methods used in cost accounting and financial analysis. As in other studies, checklists were frequently used.

In summary, the studies on quantitative methods clearly show that existing methods are not fully utilized despite the fact that companies are familiar with most of these. Apparently, individual, organizational, and technological barriers to the implementation of these approaches exist.

The Resulting Picture

In describing the existing situation of information systems for technology management, this chapter has drawn on empirical studies on R&D information systems, on the use of computers in R&D and on the application of quantitative methods in R&D. A somewhat murky picture of the current situation is apparent:

- *Content*
    - Single project information systems are widely available; but with different degrees of utilization.
    - Information systems with a strong technical orientation are widely used.
    - Existing information systems are limited to provide support for the tasks of R&D management. Many of the aspects of technology management are typically not fully covered.
    - Industries differ with respect to the importance of computers used for monitoring and controlling experiments and for the statistical analysis of data.
- *Usage of available technical potential*
    - The capabilities of existing systems are not fully utilized.
- *Usage of familiar techniques*
    - A great discrepancy exists between the familiarity and usage of methods.
- *Integration*
    - Few attempts have been made to integrate existing technology management information systems or components of such systems. The need to improve the integration and networking has been expressed by industry. In general, industry recognizes that this is a glaring weakness in its attempts to integrate diverse markets and complicated R&D organizations, across national boundaries.

INFORMATION SYSTEMS BEYOND ROUTINE: A CONTRADICTION?

Over the last couple of years, we have seen electronic communication substituting for face-to-face communication. On the other hand, for problem solving in R&D face-to-face communication has been identified as an important factor for success (Allen, 1977). In the R&D domain, little is known about the effects of substituting face-to-face communication with electronic media. Based on Hauptman's (1986) distinction of innovative and routine information, de Meyer (1991, p. 55) observes "that the capacity to share innovative, problem-solving information was dependent on the nature of the R&D work, including its analyzability and complexity." It remains to be seen whether advanced information systems, which are able to represent and process unstructured information in an interactive mode, will overcome the communication problems caused by the complexity and uniqueness of the information needed in R&D.

However, even in a world of such sophisticated information systems, it is not certain that all aspects of problem solving will be fostered by the use of electronic media. It has been shown that companies benefit greatly from informal inter-firm technology transfers (Schrader, 1991; Schrader & Sattler, 1993). These transfers might be hindered by channeling them through electronic media. De Meyer (1991) argues that face-to-face communication is needed to build up confidence, and that this will decay over time if only electronic communication is present.

In summary, this chapter calls for a better utilization of the existing information technology potential. However, at this point, this potential should not be overestimated. The idiosyncracies of technology management and R&D may limit useful designs of information systems. Good examples of integrated, global R&D/ technology management systems are probably several years away.

ENDNOTES

Remark: The author wishes to thank Stephan Schrader for his helpful comments.

[1] Neo (1991) outlines how information technology can help multinational corporations resolve issues such as coordination and responsiveness.
[2] For an overview of the managerial aspects of the invention and innovation process, see Roberts (1988).
[3] The results of the study are described in more detail in Porter & Rossini (1986).
[4] Recent developments which are to a large extent based on expert systems seem to support the respondents' outlook. For example, Reminger (1990, 1991) presents an expert system for the support of strategic technology planning, Wilkinson (1991a, 1991b, 1991c) developed a system for project evaluation. Pickett & Case (1991) argue that some expert systems do not seem to be easily integrated in R&D or corporate information systems for technical reasons.

REFERENCES

Allen, T.J. (1977). *Managing the flow of technology.* Cambridge/ Massachusetts: MIT Press.

Brockhoff, K. (1989). *Schnittstellen-Management: Abstimmungsprobleme zwischen Marketing und Forschung und Entwicklung.* Stuttgart: Poeschel.

Brockhoff, K. (1991). Competitor technology intelligence in German companies. *Industrial Marketing Management*, 20, 91-98.

Brockhoff, K. (1992). *Forschung und Entwicklung: Planung und Kontrolle.* 3rd edition. Munich, Vienna: Oldenbourg.

Brockhoff, K. & von Boehmer, A. (1993). Global R&D activities of German industrial firms, *Journal of Scientific & Industrial Research*, 52 (6), 399-406.

Case, T.L. & Pickett, J.R. (1989). R&D information systems, *Research-*

Technology Management, 32 (4), 29-33.

Deans, P.C., Karwan, K.R., Goslar, M.D., Ricks, D.A. & Toyne, B. (1991). Identification of key international information systems issues in U.S.-based multinational corporations, *Journal of Management Information Systems*, 7(4), 27-50.

De Meyer, A. (1991). Tech talk: How managers are stimulating Global R&D communication, *Sloan Management Review*, 32 (3), 49-58.

De Meyer, A. & Mizushima, A. (1989). Global R&D Management, *R&D Management*, 19 (2), 135-146.

Friar, J. & Horwitch, M. (1986). The emergence of technology strategy: A new dimension of strategic management. In: M. Horwitch (Ed.), *Technology in the modern corporation*. New York: Pergamon Press, 50-85.

Hauptman, O. (1986). Influence of task type on the relationship between communication and performance. The case of software development, *R&D Management*, 16 (2), 127-139.

Higgins, J.C. & Watts, K.M. (1986). Some perspectives on the use of management science techniques in R&D management , *R&D Management*, 16 (4), 291-296.

ERRATA ADDENDUM

ea Group Publishing regrets that the following references were inadvert-
tly omitted from Chapter 17 [Information Systems for Global Technology
anagement] of *Global Information Systems and Technology: Focus on
e Organization and Its Functional Areas.* For your convenience, please
ace this page after page 360 in the book.

Liberatore, M.J. & Titus, G.J. (1983). The practice of management science in R
D project management, *Management Science*, 29 (8), 962-974.

Möhrle, M.G. (1991). *Informationssysteme in der betrieblichen Forschung und
twicklung.* Bad Homburg: DIE Verlag Schäfer.

Morse, G., Ong, C.H. & Pearson, A.W. (1984). Computers in R&D; A brief report
a survey of UK R&D establishments, *R&D Management*, 14 (4), 261-267.

Neo, B.S. (1991). Information technology and global competition, *Information &
nagement*, 20, 151-160.

Pickett, J.R. & Case, T.L. (1991). Implementing expert systems in R&D, *Research-
chnology Management*, 34 (4), 37-42.

Porter, A.L. & Rossini, F.A. (1986). Current and future uses of the computer:
dustrial R&D in the United States, *R&D Management*, 16 (4), 279-289.

Reminger, B. (1990). *Expertensystem zur Unterstützung der strategischen
chnologieplanung.* Berlin: Schmidt.

Reminger, B. (1991). How to manage technology by an expert system. In D.F.
caoglu & K. Niwa (Eds.), *Technology management. The new international language.*
rtland/Oregon: IEEE, 554-561.

Roberts, E.B. (1988). Managing Invention and Innovation. *Research-Technology
anagement*, 31 (1), 11-29.

Rossini, F.A. & Porter, A.L. (1986). Who's using computers in industrial R&D —
d For What, *Research Management*, 29 (3), 39-44.

Rossini, F.A., Porter, A.L., Jacobs, C.C. & Abraham, D.S. (1988). Trends in
mputer use in industrial R&D, *Research-Technology Management*, 31 (5), 36-41.

Schrader, S. (1991). Informal technology transfer between firms: Cooperation
rough information trading, *Research Policy*, 20 (2), 153-170.

Schrader, S. & Sattler, H. (1993). Zwischenbetriebliche Kooperation: Informaler
formationstransfer in den USA und Deutschland, *Die Betriebswirtschaft*, 53 (5),
7-606.

Thoma, W. (1989). *Erfolgsorientierte Beurteilung von FuE-Projekten.* Darmstadt:
eche-Mittler.

von Boehmer, A. (1991). Global R&D activities of US multinational corporations.
me empirical results. In D.F. Kocaoglu & K. Niwa (Eds.), *Technology management.
he new international language.* Portland/Oregon: IEEE, 135-140

von Boehmer, A., Brockhoff, K. & Pearson, A.W. (1992). The management of
ternational research and development. In P.J. Buckley & M.Z. Brooke (Eds.),
ternational business studies - An overview.* Oxford: Blackwell, 495-509.

Watts, K.M. & Higgins, J.C. (1987). The use of advanced management techniques
R & D, *OMEGA International Journal of Management Science*, 15 (1), 21-29.

Wilkinson, A. (1991a). Developing an expert system on project evaluation, Part
Structuring the expertise, *R&D Management*, 21(1), 19-29.

Wilkinson, A. (1991b). Developing an expert system on project evaluation, Part
Structuring the system, *R&D Management*, 21(3), 207-213.

Wilkinson, A. (1991c). Developing an expert system on project evaluation, Part 3:
he managerial questions raised by the work, *R&D Management*, 21(4), 309-318.

CHAPTER 18

Information Technology for R&D in Global Business[1]

ALOK K. CHAKRABARTI
New Jersey Institute of Technology

Information Technologies are having significant beneficial impacts in research and development (R&D) organizations and decision processes. These technologies are making it possible for scientists, technicians, marketing professionals, and customers to effectively communicate across national boundaries with one another about new products and processes. This chapter outlines the role of IT in R&D organizations, discusses how decisions in R&D are affected by the new technologies, and describes the key organizational issues and concerns about global R&D. Much of the reported information was obtained through detailed interviews with R&D managers in three large multinational corporations.

INTRODUCTION

To understand the implications for the impact of information technologies in research and development (R&D) organizations, one should recognize that the main functions of scientists and technical persons revolve around the generation, processing and communication of information. The ultimate output from an R & D organization is information—information about a product, process, material or some advancement in the basic knowledge base.

Figure 1 shows a simplified view of the innovation process

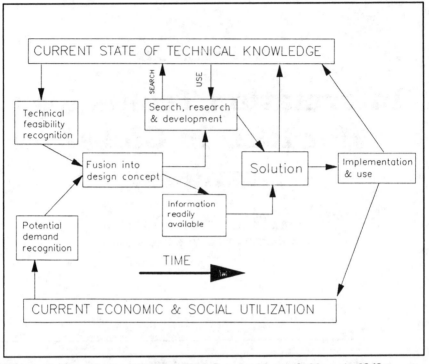

Figure 1: The Process of Innovation *Source: Myers & Marquis 1969*

following Myers and Marquis (1967). According to this view, innovation requires information exchange with both the technological and the socio-economic environments. The technological environment provides the necessary technical foundations for understanding the various technical opportunities and specific solutions. The socio-economic environment provides the information about market conditions, and the need for new products and processes. The input from the latter is critical in developing the corporation's competitive strategy within which technology is one of several key elements. Scientists and technologists who work on the development of new products and processes are users of information from the environment; they contribute to the knowledge base by advancing the state of the art in technology, as solutions to problems are developed.

Figure 2 elaborates on the idea of interaction between the two environments and how the various functional units interact in the process. This interaction process involves both scientists and marketing professionals who are the sentinels of market and economic conditions. The state of the art of technology, which provides the foundation for the activities of the scientists and engineers, can be divided into two categories; the proprietary knowledge base which is available to organizational members only, and the knowledge base

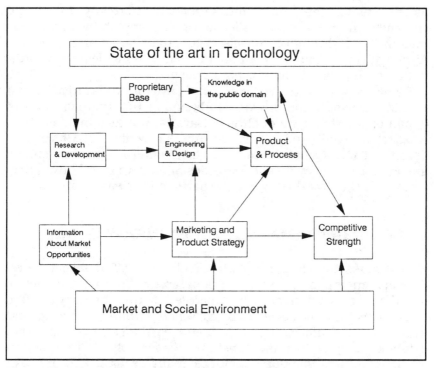

Figure 2: Information exchange in technology development process

existing in the public domain. People involved in research, engineering, design, and manufacturing activities draw from the stock of knowledge in both domains. They also contribute to these knowledge bases through their output.   For example, when a scientists is awarded a patent, he or she is contributing to the knowledge base in the public domain. Only a fraction of the knowledge generated in corporate settings is made available to the public.   Most of the information remains proprietary.

One can readily understand the complexity of the problem which R&D and marketing professionals face in this process, as corporations engage in the global market place. Globalization of the business increases the complexity of the customer base as well as the other forces of competition. Simultaneous understanding and tracking of the changes in various facets of technology and market conditions are becoming the major challenges for people involved in the innovation process.

Consider the example of a multinational such as Unilever. It is in the business of multiple consumer and food products and is located in both developed and developing countries. Keeping track of the changes in food habits, availability of raw materials, changes in regulations and regulatory processes, etc. in diverse countries such as the United States, the United Kingdom, Germany, India, and Holland is indeed, a great challenge. Unilever maintains many R&D organizations through the aegis of its subsidiaries and divisions. Although the divisions are autonomous to varying degrees, coordination of their work must be accomplished.

Similarly, the auto designers in Tokyo or in Stuttgart must consider not only the driving conditions of the crowded cities of Japan or the rolling autobahns of Bavaria, but also the deserts of Arizona or Saudi Arabia and the freezing winters of Chicago or Toronto. To be successful in their global enterprise, the scientists and engineers in Toyota and Mercedes must develop effective interfaces with their marketing counterparts in far away locations.

ROLE OF INFORMATION TECHNOLOGY IN R&D

To discuss the role of information technology (IT) in research and development organizations in the global context, one needs to define first the scope of information technologies. In this chapter we define IT as "all technologies used in the *collection, storing, processing,* and *transmission* of information including voice, data and images". This definition emphasizes the functional aspect of the information technology and, therefore, includes many technical means. Although computer technology occupies the pivotal role here, recent advances in the fields of optoelectronics, sensors, imaging, communication, etc. have created unprecedented opportunities in information technologies.

The emerging trends in the impact of information technologies include: (a) the increased use of electronic data interchange, (b) new communications paths opening among people, machines, buildings and other inanimate objects, and (c) dual market structures for different size companies (Diebold, 1988). Firms have followed different paths in implementing electronic data interchange (EDI) for strategic objectives: (1) following the lead of suppliers or customers, (2) using EDI to take on new roles in the supply chain, (3) using innovatively to develop new products and services, (4) tying in trading partners by linking electronically with them, and (5) using time-based advantages of EDI to outperform the competition (Holland, Lockett and Blackman, 1992). Since R & D is a significant component in the competitive strategy of a firm, one must deploy these and other available advances in information technology in the management of the R&D function.

The environment of organizations in the post-industrial society is different from that of organizations in the industrial society characterized by mass production and trading based on colonial traditions (Huber, 1984). The post-industrial society is characterized by :

Features	Electronic Messaging System	Executive Presentation System	Executive Information System	Group Decision Support System
Sender	One	More than one	One	More than one
Target	One or more	Group	One or more	Group
Purpose	Sharing information	Communicating with a group	Monitoring information from internal and external sources	Contributing, evaluating, prioritizing and participating in decision making
Benefits	To overcome spatial and temporal barriers	To facilitate sharing of complex information	To gather, filter, synthesize, organize and store information	To remove communication barriers in group meetings

Table 1: Computer based communication systems and their features
(Adapted from Huseman and Miles, 1988)

- more information and an increasing knowledge base;
- more and an increasing complexity of organizational relationships;
- greater and increasing turbulence in the environment;
- more frequent and faster decision making capability of organizations.

Since R & D organizations are always at the forefront of the changes in technology as both initiators and reactors, they are among the organizational areas most likely to be affected by the new demands of the post-industrial society. The various information technologies, including computer and communications technologies, are playing an important role in new organizational designs to help meet the challenges. For example, computer-based communications systems have opened up new opportunities for facilitating communication and decision making. Table 1 provides a detailed comparison of electronic messaging systems (EMS), executive presentation systems (EPS), executive information systems (EIS), and group decision support system (GDSS) in terms of their scope.

In my recent discussions with three large global organizations, I have found that information technology is implemented in R & D organizations in different ways. Organizations have found different scopes for the use of IT in their variety of activities. The intensity of the use also differs among organizations. Here are some examples.

Two of the organizations have used E-mail (electronic mail), as an "enabling" technology to facilitate communication between their development people in various parts of the corporation as well as their customers. E-mail has greatly enhanced their ability to respond to their customers in terms of both speed and quality. Both of these companies are in the chemical industry and are active on a global basis. One of them is headquartered in Europe while the other is in the US. Communication is indeed, a great concern and their ability to respond to customers in solving technical design problems is a major competitive tool.

In one organization, the use of electronic voice mail has improved the quality of communication as it has provided the capability to communicate on a real-time basis as well as to provide the emotional component of the message. Voice mail has also provided the capability to broadcast a message to a group of people simultaneously, thus increasing the efficiency of communication. Electronic bulletin boards have provided an effective medium for exchange of ideas among scientists in another organization. The bulletin board has replaced many of the regularly scheduled meetings formerly used to facilitate the innovation process.

Bibliographic databases have now become indispensable in libraries, with both technical and commercial information now available. One organization has focused on intensive use of computer technology in building its information resource center. While the other two firms extolled the virtues of other uses of information technology, this company focused on the storage and retrieval of text, data and images in computers. Since this organization is a manufacturer of parts and components, it is important that information related to technical specifications, design data, and manufacturing processes are available. Of course, communication is important and this organization is one of those that intensively uses e-mail facilities.

Although these examples are drawn from three isolated sample companies, it is possible to generalize from what has been reported elsewhere. Table 2 summarizes what is known about the use of information technology in the R&D function along with potential benefits to the process of innovation.

IT IN R&D DECISION MAKING PROCESSES

The R&D Life Cycle

The characteristics of R&D decisions are dependent on the stages of the technology development cycle. Ford and Ryan (1981) have identified six stages of this cycle as follows:

R&D MANAGEMENT FUNCTION	INFORMATION TECHNOLOGY APPLICATION	BENEFIT
Communication	E-Mail Voice Mail Teleconferencing Bulletin boards	Improved communication
Storage & retrieval of text, data and images	Bibliographic databases	Efficiency of operation
Simulation and Modeling	Molecular modeling Simulation exercises	Understanding the technical problem Research planning Cost effectiveness
Control of experiments	Automatic data collection Smart interface with equipment Control of experiment	More productivity Less cycle time
Design	Computer aided design	Flexibility Speed
Decision making	Decision support systems	Involvement of more people Availability of information

Table 2: Examples of Use of IT in R&D

(1) *technology development:* this stage begins with the identification of a potentially beneficial technology. The firm continues further development contingent on the availability of resources and its strategic fit with the organization's mission.

(2) *technology application:* this involves application of the technology in some tangible product form which will have commercial significance. Selling and licensing can be the effective means for this.

(3) *technology launch:* this stage involves introduction of the technology to market as embodied in marketable products.

(4) *technology applications growth:* this stage marks the objective of sales maximization through applications in diverse products and markets.

(5) *technology maturity:* at this stage the market conditions become mature along with the technology. The firm can expect little competitive advantage from the technology and the competitors have either mastered the technology themselves or are ready with alternatives.

(6) *degraded technology:* this is the last stage at which the technology sees the end as it has reached universal exploitation.

The nature of decisions facing an R&D executive will vary according to the life cycle of the technology. Table 3 provides a summary of the various factors involved in the different decisions to be made for technologies at different stages of their life cycle. As may be observed from the table, the nature of decisions varies with the various stages. The extent of involvement of people from the various functional units as well as other external groups organizations (such as customers) also varies throughout the cycle. Communications technology is often an integral part of this process. Organizations have been involved in implementation of the communication technology for this purpose with varying levels of intensity.

R&D Decisions and IT

Information technologies can have significant beneficial impact in the R&D decision processes of both managerial and technical domains. Managerial decisions include R &D project selection, project monitoring, project control, project termination, and the allocation of resources of various types among projects. Most of the decisions in R&D involve certain levels of risk and uncertainty. Managers cannot afford to deal with obsolete information. Moreover, information from different sources adds to the complexity. Information technology can be described as "enabling" technology for decision making purposes; it "enables" a manager to make better decisions.

For technical personnel (engineers, scientists, designers), information technologies have opened new avenues of decision making. As mentioned earlier, a technical person has to know about the stock of knowledge existing in his or her field related to a specific problem. Bibliographic databases and bibliometric analyses can help the technical person to store, organize and retrieve information efficiently and effectively. Modeling and simulation techniques have helped to understand technical problems and therefore plan experimental work more efficiently. Smart interfaces help run and control experiments efficiently and effectively. In one of the organizations, it was observed that smart interfaces have enabled scientists across great distances and borders to conduct R&D experiments as a team, since the experimental data are collected and transmitted electronically to remote locations where the information is processed.

Computer-aided design (CAD) has already made a great impact in technical decisions. In almost all fields of manufacturing, computer-aided design and engineering are providing a variety of benefits. These include:

• a cost effective method for developing technical solutions;
• an increased level of flexibility in the manufacturing process; and
• integration of design information with manufacturing leading to

DECISION OBJECTIVES AND OTHER ISSUES	TECHNOLOGY DEVELOPMENT	TECHNOLOGY APPLICATION	TECHNOLOGY LAUNCHING	APPLICATION GROWTH	TECHNOLOGY MATURITY	DEGRADED TECHNOLOGY
Decision makers	Mainly R&D Executive	R&D, and Engineering Marketing	Mainly marketing	Marketing R&D and Engineering	Marketing	R&D Marketing
Information sources	Mainly technical	Technical and commercial	Commercial	Commercial and technical	Commercial and technical	Commercial and technical
Examples of Information technologies	Bibliographic databases	Modeling & Simulations Process control	Business oriented management information systems	Modeling & Simulations Process control	Business oriented management information systems	Business oriented management information systems
Requirements for interaction	Mainly among technical people with some input from marketing	Needs extensive interaction among marketing and technical people	Needs interaction among marketing people with some input from technical personnel	Needs extensive interaction among marketing and technical people	Needs interaction among marketing people with some input from technical personnel	Needs interaction among marketing people with some input from technical personnel
Customer involvement	Lead user gets involved	Customer is involved	Customer is involved greatly	Customer input is important	Customer input is important	Customer input is important

Table 3: Scope of information technologies and decision requirements at stages of the technology life cycle

better inventory control, materials planning, quality, etc.

Fjermestad and Chakrabarti (1993) have pointed out that computer integrated manufacturing (CIM) provides a firm not only the obvious benefits of labor efficiency, but also an opportunity to be more innovative in products and processes. In the domain of technical decision making, computer-aided design technology has become indispensable.

Organizational Aspects

Information technology has provided a great opportunity for communication. It is expected that the advances in communications technologies in the near future will be increasingly more user-friendly and effective (Huber, 1988). As the cost of these technologies declines and people become more familiar with them, their adoption will rapidly increase. The US is fast becoming a "networked nation" (Hiltz and Turoff, 1993). With the increased adoption of communications technologies by a larger proportion of people, business culture is changing.

Other types of technologies have also had significant impacts on the organizational culture of firms as it has facilitated communication between R&D, marketing, other functional units, customers. For example, one firm has used modeling and simulation techniques to understand the furnace conditions of its customers including thermal distribution and impurities in gas flows. With this understanding, R&D personnel have designed experiments to seek the solution for the specific problems of the organization's customer. This type of information is then used to facilitate discussions between marketing, R&D and customers.

A key organizational issue facing transnational firms is that they often have their R&D organizations located in many countries. Integrating the activities of these organizational units spread over wide geographical areas clearly requires the use of information technology. With the use of video conferencing, satellite communication and computers, scientists and technologists can work together on joint projects, exchange ideas and results of their work, and discuss the implications with their customers across continents. Organizational integration and development of a collegial environment are only possible through effective use of information technology.

The specific mechanisms of R&D coordination are, of course, determined by many factors. Since local conditions vary greatly, the central R&D personnel in a multinational firm may not be fully cognizant of the critical problems faced by the various divisions. Consider the case of Asea Brown Boveri (ABB). According to Chief

Executive Officer Percy Barnevik, ABB is a "multi domestic" organization rather than a "multinational" company with all of the usual connotations. Based on this notion, the different ABB units or subsidiaries maintain a certain cultural orientation of their host environments, yet are integrated together to form the corporation called ABB with its own unique identity. Developing such a matrix organization and culture requires intensive communication among the units (Bartlett & Ghosal, 1990).

Control of R&D

Control of R&D projects poses many difficulties; projects often take long periods of time for completion, myriads of people get involved in the projects at different phases, and keeping track of resources and progress is difficult. Computer based project management systems facilitate allocation of scarce resources among different projects and the tracking of the progress of individual projects. They are also useful in determining the trade-offs among various resources and time.

Project management systems facilitate control by identifying the responsibilities of various organizational entities and persons reporting progress against milestones. These control systems also help to develop databases for the project which may be useful for other management purposes. By integrating the control system with other management information systems, one gets the benefit of a system which may satisfy the needs of other organizational units.

Project management and control becomes extremely complex when some of the team members may be working across a continent or an ocean. When Honda started to work on the 1994 Accord model, both American and Japanese personnel needed to work together. The need to achieve close collaboration through integrated information technology was clear to this organization.

R&D IN THE GLOBAL SETTING

Most organizations are now competing in a global market place. Even if a firm does not sell its products or services outside the US, developments abroad greatly affect the firm's competitive posture. Transnational firms serve international markets. Manufacturing facilities, R&D, and marketing are spread around the globe. It is becoming an increasingly difficult challenge to manage such a vast network of organizations in different countries.

Many firms have to set up R&D facilities in different countries due to the local regulations of the host countries. It is also prudent practice to locate some R&D facilities somewhat near where a firm is selling its products. As noted earlier, information technology is essential to the integration of activities of the R&D organization scattered around the world.

To maintain competitive strength, a firm also needs to keep abreast of the technical progress made by its competitors around the world. Many firms have formed strategic alliances with their competitors, vendors and customers to gain access to technology, market niches, and manufacturing capabilities. Nurturing such diverse alliances and collaborative arrangements requires better communication and control. Information technology is being used as a powerful tool to manage these alliances.

The growth of the microelectronics industry in Japan exemplifies the value of global alliances. The path to technological development in microelectronics in Japan was based on access to American technology and know-how. The Japanese controlled the access to their domestic market, and used this as the springboard for an assault on the international market. It is no accident that the majority of the top ten microchip manufacturers are Japanese firms (Borrus, 1988). Although the Japanese model is not likely to be duplicated due to various sociocultural reasons, firms are increasingly using multiple types of strategic alliances to facilitate new product development and introduction.

SOME ISSUES AND CONCERNS

Information technology has been portrayed here not only as a powerful tool for managing the R&D function within a firm but also as an omnipotent resource for organizational integration. The author shares the optimism of the R&D executives of the three firms interviewed for this chapter who felt that advances in technology will make systems and software more user-friendly and efficient. Advances in optoelectronics have already contributed significantly to the development of CD (compact disc) based multimedia systems. Further developments will enhance our capability to store, process, and retrieve data, images and voices. Consider the CD/ROM (compact disc, read only memory) based journal databases available commercially. At a fraction of the cost and space required for the journals in paper format, one can build a substantial collection of technical journals. Retrieval of information from such a system would greatly enhance the productivity and effectiveness of development teams.

Advancements in computing are also expected to enhance modeling capabilities. In many design problems, computers have eliminated the need to build physical models. Many complex problems can be more efficiently investigated using simulation models. In the pharmaceutical industry, for example, computer models are being used effectively to design specific drugs.

Global R&D is, of course, not without its problems. There are a number of important concerns related to effective implementation of information technology that are readily identifiable:

(a) Since many of the forms of information technology can be viewed as "enabling", it has proven difficult to justify their benefits in the R&D environment using standard financial methods.

(b) Rapid changes in hardware and software has created problems of obsolescence in the R&D domain. One executive said, "you can never be sure to put all your eggs in one basket, you must invest in different systems such as Apple and IBM, UNIX, etc.". Global companies, with operations in different countries, are particularly susceptible.

(c) Incompatibility between different hardware and software creates problems of conversion of data into acceptable formats. This is particularly a problem if one wants to build up archives of information. Since the standards for video and other signals vary greatly between the USA, Europe, and Asia, incompatibility is a formidable problem for global firms.

(d) At present, technical standards vary both within industries and even across many firms. Incompatibility of standards creates problems in communication.

Effective implementation of information technologies also needs top management support and commitment. Many users are likely to be "amateurs" in the sense that they may not have the proper training and background knowledge to effectively use current and developing systems. Proper support and training will be required to make the end users of R&D information efficient and effective. It is a prevailing thought among the executives interviewed for this chapter that many scientists and technical people spend their valuable time in programming activities in somewhat amateurish ways. Many firms are not channeling adequate resources into training and support activities to prevent this.

ENDNOTES

[1] I thank the executives from three companies who have participated in a study related to the preparation of this chapter. Due to the terms of confidentiality, their identities remain anonymous. I am also indebted to Dr. Kirk Karwan and Dr. Candace Deans for their support.

REFERENCES

Bartlett, Christopher A. and Ghosal, Sumantra. "Matrix management: Not s structure, a frame of mind",*Harvard Business Review*, July/August, 1990, pp. 138-145.

Borrus, Michael J. *Competing for control: America's stake in microelectronics*, Cambridge, MA: Ballinger, 1988.

Brockhoff, Klaus and Chakrabarti, Alok K. "R&D/Marketing interface and innovation strategies: Some West German experience", *IEEE Transactions on Engineering Management*, Vol. 35 No. 3, 1988. pp. 167-174.

Diebold, John. "The changing information environment: Suggest future directions", *Vital Speeches*, Vol. 55, No. 5, Dec. 15, 1988, pp. 138-145.

Ford, D. and Ryan, C. "Taking technology to market",*Harvard Business Review*, March/ April, 1981.

Fjermestad, Jerry and Chakrabarti, Alok K. "Computer integrated manufacturing: A literature review towards a framework for strategy implementation and innovation",*Technology Analysis and Strategic Management*, 1993 (in press).

Hiltz, Star Roxanne and Turoff, Murray. *The network nation*, Cambridge: MIT Press, 1993.

Holland, Chris, Lockett, Geoff and Blackman, Ian. "Planning for electronic data interchange",*Strategic Management Journal*, Vol. 13, No. 7, 1992, pp. 539-550.

Huber, George P. "The nature and design of post-industrial organizations", *Management Science*, Vol. 30, No. 8, 1984, pp. 928-951.

Huseman, Richard C. and Miles, Edward W. "Organizational communication in the information age: Implications of computer-based systems",*Journal of Management*, Vol. 14, No. 8, 1988 pp. 181-204.

Myers, Sumner and Marquis, Donald G. *Successful industrial innovations*, Washington DC: National Science Foundation, Publication 17-69, 1969.

CHAPTER 19

Opportunities or Threats? Information Technology in Developing Countries

XIAOBO WU
WEIQIANG WANG
QINGRUI XU

Zhejiang University

As information technology develops explosively in recent years, the techno-economic paradigm is shifting and a new international economic competitive pattern is forming. It is considered that the influence of IT is so pervasive that developing countries (LDCs) is facing much more rigorous situation in the global marketplace as is compared with developed countries (DCs) which is gaining benefits with it. This chapter examines the impacts of IT on LDCs competitive conditions, especially the impacts on intra-firm's organizational structure and the indigenous technology capacity formation as well as technological innovation, as new paradigms of technological innovation and system integration emerge. Further the transition of sources of competitive advantage are explored and some strategic implications for firms of LDCs to enter global marketplace with full playing of their comparative advantages, such as the so-called Later-Comer's Advantages, are made. It is indicated that under threats of raised threshold to enter global marketplace, caused by the flourishing of IT, developing countries do still have their comparative advantages as a later-comer of global market. The key issue for LDCs to enter the market is to find ways to make full use of their comparative strong points in secondary innovation and offset their weakness in poor infrastructure.

INTRODUCTION

There are a lot of studies concerning the flourishing of information technology (IT) in recent decades. However the position of developing countries (LDCs) in the global marketplace under new situations of techno-economic paradigm shifting, and the strategies for LDCs to enter global marketplace, are still underexplored. In the changing world, it is very difficult for LDCs to keep pace with the twin challenges of vigorous global competition and the rapid technological change (Hill, 1992).

The goal of this chapter is to examine the pervasive influence of IT on the competitive positions of LDCs in the global market, the focus is put on the aspects of the changes in intra-firm's organizational structure and the pattern of information linkage between R&D, manufacturing and marketing, and to induce strategic issues for LDCs to enter the global marketplace by making full use of IT when the main sources of comparative advantage are shifting. It is started with a description of the shifting of techno-economic paradigm, especially the shifting of R&D paradigm and manufacturing paradigm, as IT penetrating the whole economy. It is indicated that the wide application of IT has profound impacts on the restructuring of firms' organizational structure, particularly in the integration of functional sub-organizations in firm, such as R&D, manufacturing and marketing, no matter in DCs or LDCs. Further section III discusses the nature of evolutionary process of secondary innovation in LDCs, and the availability of IT as a favourable weapon to improve the efficiency of innovation. The impacts of IT on the shifting of main sources of competitive advantages are examined in section IV. While in section V, the opportunities and threats provide by the swift development and wide application of IT, such as the raised threshold of entry to global marketplace, are analyzed, and the changes in comparative advantages and disadvantages of LDCs as later-comers in the global market competition are described. Finally some strategy implications for LDCs to enter global market are induced. As a LDC, one might well advised to stop bemoaning the coming rough days and start looking for creative ways to live with it.

PARADIGMS SHIFTING

As Kuhn did the pioneering work on proving paradigm change in science, many researchers in a diversity fields use the term of 'paradigm' to describe the dominant feature of people's behaviour. When the IT revolution is becoming the dominant force governing modern societies, a knowledge-based social order is now evolving, in which homes, offices, schools, and communities become interwoven into a web of intelligent communication services offering unparalleled opportunities for accelerating scientific progress, economic development, education, and other revolutionary changes(Halal, 1992). The impacts of the revolution are so pervasive that, in the increasing competitive global marketplace, the need of producing products with improved quality at competitive prices and introduce them as quickly as possible to the market, has forced organizations to look for new approaches in engineering and management practices (Venkatachalam, 1992), and forced organizations to wake up and take a cold, hard look at how their products are made. It is asserted that the new techno-economic paradigm is forming. Particularly the paradigms of technology, R&D, Manufacturing etc. are all in changing.

R&D Paradigm Shifting

The explosive development of IT is leading about the revolution in R&D practice and management. Some literatures described the paradigm shift in R&D, such as Steele(1991), Nelson(1991) and Mitchell(1992), in recent years. As is pointed out by Dr. Nikolajew (1991), in the new era, R&D is grown into production, and the increasing flexibility required of economic performance in order to master both the introduction of innovations and the structural adaption needed to accommodate the changes.

The classical paradigm of industrial R&D emphasizes discovering and inventing in house, so called in-house creativity, to create an entirely new kind of capability or to establish a new level of capability, so that R&D was not particularly sensitivity to the infrastructure and fit with resources that were needed to turn an invention into a successful innovation. And the role of elites and the autonomy of R&D labs were over emphasized. The subtleties and uncertainties inherent in the R&D process were such that searching questions about effectiveness and productivity were usually regarded warily as potentially counterproductive(Steele, 1991).

Now the research management agenda has evolved and broadened from the 1970s' concern with managing the research function to today's challenges of global competitiveness. As pointed by Mitchell(1992), in 1990s, the overall business objective is 'global competitive advantage', one of the key issues is IT, and one of the focuses and accomplishments is the need for new paradigms for industrial research(Mitchell, 1992). In recent years, the research cycle would include an iterative computational step between idea generation and experimentation, as great progress has made in R&D computing over last ten years. The faster computing machine allow us to look at phenomena on greatly expanded or compressed time scale(Nelson, 1991).

So some specific changes in viewpoints may become necessary in contrast with the old paradigm: two changes are particularly important - the need for unembarrassed differentiation of paradigms and the need for greater interdependence, rather than autonomy. This interdependency applies not only to other functions in a business, but to external agencies as well(Steele, 1991). Such as some firm's functions used to be regarded as peripheral may require more careful attention, i.e., managing access to external technology, managing innovation networks, supervising career development, are becoming a repository for the intelligence-based practice, which has its special significance to LDCs. Implementing these changes will require important modifications in the current work of managing R&D. Clearly, the implementation should result from a continuing dialogue with corporate management, but a dialogue in which R&D management should take the lead.

In LDCs, the system constraints, cost and market requirements are dominant, therefore market-driven, mostly incremental, advances are likely to be the key to survive and success. So that choosing a paradigm appropriate to the stages of country's social-economic-technological development is crucial. Furthermore, managing the transition from one stage to another, a process that may extend over years, is perhaps the most difficult task in R&D management in LDCs.

Manufacturing Paradigm Shifting

The current transition in manufacturing has been explicated in detail in a recent book entitled 'The Machine That Changed The World,' by James Womack et al(1990). They pointed out that current transition in manufacturing is from mass production to what they called 'lean production.' And IT might be key to the functioning of lean production organization (Hill, 1992).

In the 'new era of industrialization,' as stated by Hill(1992), technologies are considerably more dependent on advances in scientific understanding and on the availability of information than were the 'old era' revolutionary technologies. Such as flexible production, short production runs, high product variety, and frequent product change, the key characteristics of new era industrialization, are all required considerably greater access to information and greater coordination within production system at all levels. Further the integration of functions, decentralization of responsibilities, and worker empowerment also demand extensive networking of groups and individuals. In which IT should play a key role.

In fact, the new manufacturing paradigm is mainly supported by IT development in recent years, such as improved computer capabilities, computer numeric control tools and flexible manufacturing systems. The integration of product design and process design into intelligent CAD systems is paving the way for the integration of CAD and CAM. And this is a direction on which many organizations presently seem to focus to achieve automation in the manufacturing arena.

It is generally considered that design changes, as reflected in engineering change orders, are costly. And the later the changes, the more costly the implementation. The key to success is the ability to remove the artificial barrier between the design engineers and manufacturing engineers. Now supported by IT, a new form of engineering - 'concurrent engineering' is forming, which is the simultaneous engineering, and producibility engineering. And it is a people and communication issue, not engineering technology (Grant et al. 1992). The well-known Japanese team approach and consensus orientation is its basis. It is noticed that Japan's emphasis on R&D in process rather than product is complementary to the practice(Grant et al, 1992). In the engineering the design changes could occur much earlier in the development-production cycle with low cost, in which the engineering and manufacturing, as disciplines, could share in the design process *vice versa*, that engineering and manufacturing may share the same information and have input to the concurrent engineering design criteria. Such as the use of CAD/CAM lowered the cost of design changes in manufacturing and to enhance the manufacturability.

So that the traditional sequential engineering shifts to concurrent engineering, which permit the separate tasks of the product development process to be carried out simultaneously rather than sequentially. Product design, testing, manufacturing and process planning through logistics, for example, are done side-by-side and interactively. Potential problems in fabrication, assembly, support and quality could be identified and resolved early in the design process. Generally, it results in the form of ability to get high-quality products to market faster and at lower cost (see fig.1.). Finally with the new manufacturing paradigm, the simultaneous involvement of design and manufacturing functions lead to design improvement through analyzing and modifying designs based on cost and manufacturability evaluation even before a product is actually made(Venkatachalam, 1992). The linear production system is changing to non-linear dynamic system.

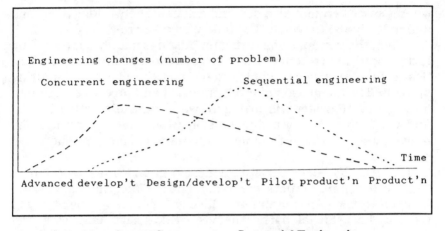

Figure 1: Problem Curve: Concurrent vs. Sequential Engineering (Izuchukwu, 1992)

Intra-firm System Integration

Before computerization, the Industrial Age demanded conformity to decisions flowing from the top of a hierarchy in order to keep the production lines running. But, now the Information Age encourages the creative use of knowledge because the need to solve tough new problems is becoming the central function. As management expert Peter Druck says, 'Leadership throughout the developed world no longer rests on financial control or traditional cost advantages. It rests on brain power.'(Halal, 1992)

A number of studies have shown that a low degree of integration or none at all between the marketing and R&D has been one of the most significant causes of market failure of new products. But until recently, particularly in LDCs, we operate under the assumption that large complex problems could be effectively dealt with by working on smaller pieces. Most of our work has been based upon 'reductionism,' or the practice of decomposing a problem into smaller, more manageable pieces (with the implicit assumption that the collection of solutions to these smaller problems will somehow combine to yield a solution to the larger problem - a typical linear viewpoint). Now, as we head into a new era of information society, this paradigm is been abandoning in favour of one which recognizes a need for explicit treatment of integration.

In accordance with the paradigms shifting, integrated efforts for product development have become more important, mainly, because of increased competition, faster technology progress, more sophisticated customers, shorter product life cycle, need for quick product development, and greater need to evolve external organizations in the process. To succeed in today's global marketplace, organizations must change from a segmented functional structure to an integrated one(Gupta & Rogers, 1992). The advantage derives partly from the inherent attributes of technology at a given stage of maturation, but also from the characteristics of competition, and from effective integration with other capabilities in an enterprise(Steele, 1991). Now most new innovative-oriented organizations are designed to enhance flexibility: static flexibility to adjust to changing market conditions, and dynamic flexibility for steadily increasing productivity through improved production processes and innovation(Grant et al, 1992).

Manufacturing flexibility provided by flexible manufacturing technology, however, has challenged the conventional wisdom about the trade-off in product and process (Chen et al, 1992). It now appears that manufacturing flexibility has pushed the technological constraints downward to the left corner of the matrix (see fig.2. & fig.3.). In other words, offering high product variety with relatively low process variety has increasing become viable. Thus, manufacturing flexibility, particularly process flexibility, can be expected to bring a substantial increase in harmony between this potential marketing-manufacturing conflict. We may much more understand the great significance of this tendency in the later section about the evolutionary process of secondary innovation in LDCs.

IT and Optional Organizational Structure in R&D

Early in 1986, Allen proposed three parameters, the rate of change of the knowledge base (dK/dt), the interdependency among subsystems and problem areas within the project (Iss), and project duration (Ti), which can be used to characterize project situations

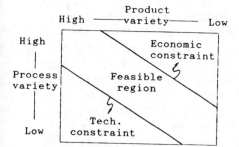

Figure 2: Classical product - process trade-off

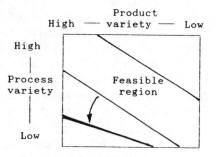

Figure 3: The impact of manufacturing flexibility on the trade-off

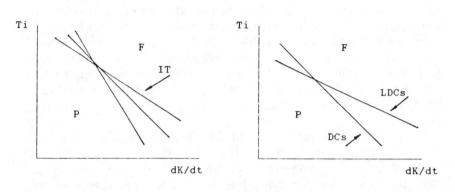

Figure 4: The effect of IT   Figure 5: Comparison of DCs & LDCs

and guide the decision on organizational form (Allen,1986). And it was pointed out by Allen that there is possibility that improvements in IT will be able to substitute for one of the two organizational forms, project vs. functional organization, and allow greater use of the other, thereby easing the organizational trade-off (see fig.4. & fig.5.).

And here we should suggest that, taking the situations of LDCs into consideration, the project organization might be more appropriate due to their rather poor information infrastructure.

From Mechanical to Organic

While most firms of LDCs are still in pursuing scale economies, DCs' factory systems and technology evolves from simple scale economies, as in conventional mass production, to scope economies, efficiencies are gained in the design and production of multiple products(Cusumano, 1992). And as an open system, firms are typically engaged in webs of strategic alliances and joint ventures, both domestically and internationally. These networks extend not only to suppliers and downstream customers, but also to competitors, universities, and government laboratories. They may focus on production, R&D, and information sharing. Effective use of external networking requires a complementary internal network structure to manage and act on the information that cross the firm's boundary from the external networks. External networking is not effective when it is connected to an administratively hierarchical internal organization. For example, new communication technologies facilitate, and then compel, decentralization of authority, and that in turn demands networking inside and out(Hill, 1992).

In recent years, there has been a move away from sprawling

conglomerates based on hierarchical structures towards more fo-cused, flexible firms based on network structures of organization. The 1970s' strategy of risk spreading by being big and diverse is giving way to the 1990s' strategy of being focused and flexible by subcontracting, engaging joint ventures, and disentangling con-glomerate divisions to function as entities within themselves (Barnatt & Wong, 1992). Finally organizations are becoming more and more organic rather than mechanic(see fig.6. & fig.7.).

The shift towards network forms indicates a shift within the marketplace for organizational processes to determine organiza-tional structure, rather than organizational structure determining processes.

But it should be mentioned that the network conglomerates have become feasible only in the past few years due to advances in IT. Organizations with the support of modern IT, for the first time, have the opportunity to become organic for more dynamic horizontal and structural communications linkages. So that it might need time for most LDCs to cope with the trend.

THE EVOLUTIONARY PROCESS OF TECHNOLOGICAL INNOVATION

In contrast to DCs, industries in LDCs initially used to begin at the mature stage of an industry(Kim & Dahlman, 1992), and reverse their evolutionary direction proceeding on to the other stages. It is suggested that LDCs have their unique evolutionary nature in their industry development and technological innovation.

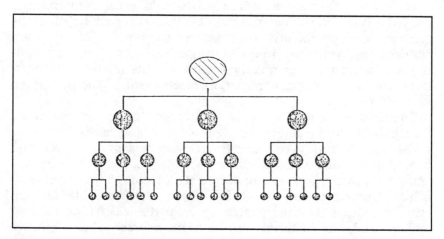

Figure 6: The rigid bureaucracy

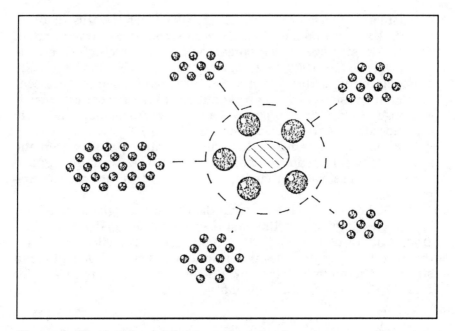

Figure 7: The loosely coupled organic network

Shortening Product Life Cycle

Traditionally, the product development life cycle activities are considered sequential, such as from design, fabrication, assembly, testing, to marketing and service. Now as the paradigm shifts in R&D and manufacturing, the activities should be done as concurrently as possible to avoid delays. And true concurrency is becoming possible to achieve with the support of IT, which is building the infrastructure needed. The improved coordination between different stages of the product development processes reduces the number of necessary changes and revisions, thus resulting in not only shortened lead-times, but also higher-quality products. This aspects makes it necessary to consider coordination mechanism in the integrated system (see fig.8.).

The shortening product life cycle in most industries, mainly in DCs, makes it important to treat time a critical source of competitive advantage. Currently, reducing the product development cycle and trimming manufacture lead-times becoming as important as managing cost, quality, or inventory(Shaw et al, 1992). However, it is also bringing unprecedented threats to LDCs, i.e., it is more difficult than ever for traditional industry intensive countries which take low-cost labours and raw materials as the main sources of comparative advantages to play roles in the global marketplace.

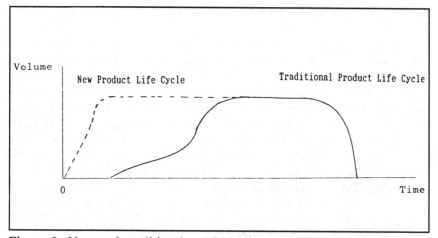

Figure 8: New and traditional product life cycle (Grant et al, 1992)

Integrated Technological Innovation Process

The changes described above make the technological innovation process more integrated than ever, which never as sequential as before. More and more studies assert that innovation is not a linear process.

The Japanese corporates' innovation activities are most typical in this nature. The Japanese corporates' innovation process is highly interactive and involves comprehensive organizational intelligence, quick organizational learning, rapid technology diffusion, horizontal information flow systems, fusion of different technologies to obtain innovations quickly, concurrent engineering and quick utilization of core competence for new business development. The innovation system is quick to response to competition and concentrates on developing core competence that is used for commercializing new products quickly. As is described in concurrent development model(Bowonder & Miyake, 1992), one of the five dominant elements in Japanese innovation system, is the extensive information sharing about the nature of technology and product through long term semi-fixed relationship between the users, suppliers or between the affiliated firms, subcontractors, and vendors.

As IT rapidly disseminates in firms, horizontal information flow structures, such as the establishment of management information systems, become one of the most important factors in successful technological innovation. They are used for accelerating the rate at which new ideas are generated, synthesized, and upgraded, and help to develop comprehensive systems for collection of technical and commercial information for decision-making. So the phases in technological innovation process are much overlapped.

Secondary Innovation in Developing Countries

Usually people think there are few technological innovations made in LDCs. And even if there are any, they might be characterized as begin at the later phase of normal innovation process, i.e. the phase of development not the research. So the technological innovation made in LDCs are commonly simple and lack of advantages. However, we should not ignore the fact that some former LDCs, such as Korea, Singapore etc., did successfully win the competitive advantages in the global marketplace, become newly industrialized countries (NICs), with rapid indigenous technological capability formation. Things are not so simple as some people thought about the nature of technological progress in LDCs. Technological innovations in LDCs is also a dominant factor of business success, though with the nature somewhat different from DCs.

It is pointed out by some researchers, such as Lee et al(1988), that almost all LDCs acquire the necessary technologies from DCs, while DCs develop their technologies mostly by their own R&D efforts. Starting with a LDCs' standing point, we studied the evolutionary nature of technological innovation in China, and a model of 'secondary innovation' process was proposed(Xu & Wu, 1991) and verified(Wu & Wang, 1991) to reveal the nature.

The proposed concept of secondary innovation is defined as the innovations made to the imported technologies along with the established trajectories which are determined by their primary technological paradigm (the concept was proposed by Dosi) developed by the 'first innovation' wich is made in the donor's country, i.e. usually a developed country, which created the paradigm and dominated the development trajectories of the technologies.

Further studies found that stronger evolutionary nature is embodied in the preceding of secondary innovations, which is very outstanding with remarkable characteristics of reverse directed evolutionary process. It is noted by the conceptual model of secondary innovation process (Xu & Wu, 1991), this kind of innovations evolves from technology acquisition, imitation, adaptation, improvement, to generation while the recipient's technology capacity accumulates.

Studies that simply note the number or size of firms that acquired technologies over time overlooked the factor that the sizes, profitability, technology capacity, such as the capacity in R&D, manufacturing and marketing, and the competitive advantages of these firms do in fact changes, sometimes quite significantly, during the evolutionary process in which secondary innovation is embedded.

A new perspective on the role of secondary innovation *per se* in the process of technical change, and thus bring into focus a number of previously disparate elements of the picture. The first observation is that much improvement has been made to the process technology during the reverse evolutionary process after technology acquisition. The characteristics of the evolutionary process of secondary innovation are described in Table 1.

Secondary innovation usually means incremental changes in technological trajectories. Which is much significant, as is noted by Silverberg(1991), a change of technological trajectory entails, first of all, a quantum jump in uncertainty, not so much with respect to the relative merits of competing technologies at a given time, but rather concerning the rate and extent of future developments, since extrapolations from past experience, which may have been specific to the old trajectory, lose their validity.

It may be induced that IT could play a key role in secondary innovation, both as a means of managerial tool, such as the establishment of MIS and techno-economic information collection and monitoring system, and as a means of productive tool, such as CAD/CAM etc. As is discussed above IT makes concurrent engineering, and concurrent development possible, which can speed up the creative imitation and promote the assimilation of imported technology more efficient, as secondary innovation is rather process focused, especially in the first phases of evolution.

It is argued that as the continuous inflow of foreign technology sustains, the formation of well-trained human resource with the absorptive capacity to undertake secondary innovation is one of the most important factors for most LDCs to speed up the evolution. This is validated by the experience of some newly industrialized countries, such as Korea' rapid development through the 1970s(Kim & Dahlman, 1992). And it should be noted that reverse engineering is the concrete activities to complement the evolutionary processes of secondary innovation in LDCs, however, it takes low-cost, but well-educated and well-trained, human resource as its prerequisite.

THE SOURCES OF COMPETITIVE ADVANTAGES

The rapid development of IT is leading to an significant shift in perspectives on the sources of competitive advantage. In recent years, competition between manufacturers is based less on price and more on the product quality, the range of product functions, and on the timeliness with which new and improved products are brought to market(Hill, 1992). New era industrialization tends to be less dependent on the availability of low-cost raw materials than before. However, it might not be so good a piece of news to most LDCs.

Stage Characteristics	Aquisition	Imitation	Adaptation	Improvement	Generation
1. Goals	Obtain "hardware" and "software" from donor	Mastery of operation technology	Localization	Make full use of opportunities	Compete in the world Open new market
2. Major activities	Investigation Feasibility analysis	Operation training Functional performence	Coordinate with existing technologies	New applications	Radical innovation
3. Key roles	Government officials Managers & engineers	Engineers Workers	Engineers and Managers	R&D personnel Engineers	R&D personnel Scientists. Engineers
4. Focus of efforts	Identify potential opportunities	Using the technology acquired	Stable production after localization	New product development	R&D and Seeking new markets
5. Vehicles of tech. transfer	Human, blueprints equipment, materials	Rules of operation Individual equipment	Complete set of facility	New products Improved process	Products and Processes new to the world
6. Critical events	Acquisition transactions made	Operation capacity formed	Acquired technology localized	New products are developed	Absolute new innovation are made
7. Nature of technology accumulation	Learning by awaring	Learning by using	Learning by doing Structural understanding	Functional understanding	Generating
8. Degree of design technology	None	Very low level	Medium level	High level	Very high level
9. Innovations	None	Few Management and Organization innovation	Mgt. innov. Org. innov. Process innov.	Incremental innovation	Radical inovation
10. Problem encountered	Information deficiencies	Unfamiliar to basics	Conflict with existing technology	Auxiliary technology deficiencies	Communication block Market deficiencies
11. Government influence	Great	Weak	Great	Medium	Weak

Table 1: The Evolutionary Process of Secondary Innovation

Speed-to-Market

In so called speed-to-market companies in DCs, process engineers use concurrent engineering to transform traditional trade-offs between efficiency and flexibility in manufacturing operations, see fig.9. & fig.10.(Grant et al, 1992)

Speed -to-market means higher profit. A McKinsey & Co. study showed that a product six months later to market misses out on one-third of the potential profit over the product's lifetime (Grant et al, 1992). Key to the success in speed-to-market or time-to-market is concurrent engineering which gives manufacturing managers a say in designing the production and ensuring that flexibility and efficiency are available in the product phase of product development(Vesey, 1991). However the conditions for LDCs to enter global marketplace become rougher than ever.

In relation with secondary innovations in LDCs, the key problem is to nurture the indigenous technological capacity so as to speed up the evolution as quick as possible, though it might be difficult. Though speed-to-market usually requires a major or total change in traditional operations, the quantum jump of secondary innovation never lose its significance in LDCs' coping with the changes, especially when technological advances in IT provide the powerful weapon in the innovation process.

However, the value of time as a competitive weapon is being

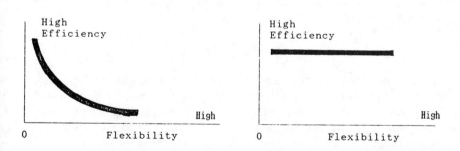

Figure 9: Historical trade-off between efficiency & flexibility

Figure 10: Relationship of efficiency & flexibility in the Accelerators'

recognized with a vengeance. The efforts to direct the power of technology toward reducing cycle time, speeding throughout, and even accelerating innovation itself are just beginning(Steele, 1991). When we refer to Japanese experience of success in the creative, market-sensitive using of existing technologies, it could be found that the somehow later modest refinement of secondary innovation can also be a potent powerful weapon. With the support of IT, firms in LDCs may be more sensitive to market, more effective in shortening the product development cycle to commit secondary innovation.

Information Networks

The newly emerging phenomenon of electronic interaction goes beyond the idea of the 'global village,' which focused on a sense of global awareness created by the advent of mass media like TV. The virtual community transcends mass communication to provide electronically mediated relationships that actually turn the earth into a single global community. To carry this line of thought further, a close similarity exists between the information networks now forming a virtual community and the brainlike quality of the computer architecture emerging for the future-neural networks. If the individual operating a computer can be thought as analogous to a single nerve cell, then the emerging web of information networks operated by billions of educated people around the world become analogous to a massive 'global brain' possessing the capacity for an unprecedented form of 'global intelligence'(Halal, 1992).

The rapid progress in information network building made it possible for LDCs to monitor the technological progress in DCs, sharing the worldwide technology pool, to learn the accumulated knowledge and experience, which might last DCs for years, more efficiently and conveniently, and to find market niches more quickly. So that faster organizational learning can be reached, and the comparative advantages can be obtained, by the lagging behind countries.

Productivity

It was commonly known that productivity is a function of specialization. In this thought work is typically specialized by functional sectors such as R&D, manufacturing, marketing, or finance etc. And further specialization in those sectors might be made as possible. But, in recent years, the mechanism of learning effect is much changed, though the appearance of the learning curve changed a little. However, the traditional thought of productivity is still popularly and deeply embedded in most LDCs' economic and managerial thinking, while it is changing in DCs.

As rapid technical advances are made in IT, the speed of information processing and the complexity of cross-functional processes are raised, and the 'lean production' is emerging, so that most traditional sources of productivity improvement are becoming depleted or irrelevant. It is noted by Istvan(1992), a new era of productivity potential is being realized in organizations that see themselves as overlapping sets of dynamic, nonlinear systems.

Though the market is often rather isolated with the protection of high tariffs, the firms of LDCs have to adapt to the changes in productivity causation in the global marketplace, otherwise LDCs might be LDCs forever. In the 'global village' of information time, the global market provides merciless judgement on business managers of every member no matter DCs or LDCs.

However, it should also be pointed out that the comparative advantages could be found in the deficiencies in specialization in LDCs, because the large sum of investment formerly planned to put in mechanical capital assets could now be transferred to buy IT-intensive assets in time. The weakness might be turn into good points while the managers could change their minds in time. The heavy losses in the transfer of production system, which some large companies of LDCs are suffering, could be avoided by adopting IT both in management and in production process, which offers the greatest potentials for productivity improvement in LDCs.

LATER-COMER'S ADVANTAGES AND DISADVANTAGES

According to classical Schumpeterian viewpoint, first movers do derive the largest net benefit, in terms of ultimate gains in market share, from introduction and diffusion of the new technology. But for intermediate values, however, a second mover or imitator may be able to capture more of the benefits by letting early innovators bear an excessive share of the development costs(Silverberg, 1991), as most NICs did in 1970s. It is argued that, as second movers, LDCs can gain their later-comer's advantages in the evolutionary process of secondary innovations, though they might also endure disadvantages at the same time. It is argued that the advantages and disadvantages tends to be more polarized than before in LDCs, under the impacts of IT adoption.

When IT offers enormous promise to the world, the key sources of competitive advantages are changing from price, which is the most important source of advantage in LDCs, to speed-to-market and quality. LDCs' competitive circumstances are getting worse. In fact, most LDCs have to content themselves with performing niche roles in current international division of labour. They often act as sites for transfer of 'dirty' production, as depots for waste products or as providers of cheap raw materials (Nikolajew, 1991).

IT Infrastructure

As is noted by Nikolajew(1991) that the building of information structure typifies the new technological paradigm and IT development is the precondition for modern economic development. Quite different from DCs which enjoy well constructed information networks have a qualitatively different starting point for decision making, the most important as well as the most difficult problems in LDCs may be not only the huge investment needed to acquire the information assets, but also making changes in institutions and firm's organizational structure.

The deficiencies in infrastructure to support the effective acquisition and adoption of IT might be the most important restraint to LDCs' development, and with which almost all the competitive disadvantages could find their causal relationship. The problems roots in both scope and depth, such as the information networks of telecommunication and business deals, professional collaboration, scientific research, and engineering, generic technologies, R&D facilities, financing institutions and the likes, which are not so virtually engaged in LDCs. In summary, the key barriers to LDCs' IT infrastructure building are as follow:

1. The traditional hierarchical organizational structure with poor technology capacity is still the dominant organizational structure in most firms of LDCs. Underdeveloped information networks in firms are insufficient and uncoordinated to support absorbing new technologies.
2. Underdeveloped communication networks including both structured communication channels and information facilities, as well as the managerial thought with little system thinking, lead to poorly worked out complementary roles in R&D for industry, government, universities, and other institutions, and even intra-firm's functional sectors.
3. Insufficient attention is paid to certain technical factors in global market entry, such as overemphasized hardware acquisition, labour-intensive and heavy raw material-dependent production system building.
4. Insufficient operation of financing institutions. Such as, the huge indirect social benefits or the good external economies of IT investment are frequently distorted and overlooked under their underdeveloped domestic market mechanism, though the government has great influential power on the investment orientation.

As a characteristic of technology infrastructure is that it depreci-
ates slowly, but it requires considerable effort and long lead times to
put it in place and maintain, time, patient, and persistent efforts are
needed for LDCs to mend the IT infrastructure.

Threshold in LDCs' Global Market Entry

Generally it is considered that technological innovation is an
important gateway to market entry, however it is just the main
weakness lying in LDCs when the innovation is scarce in
Schumpeterian meaning. So, in practice most LDCs take Porter's
generic strategies, such as low-cost or differentiation, as their
gateway to enter global market. However, as IT invaded in the world
competition, those strategies might be deficient and tending to be
weaker than before.

The threshold of global market entry used to be determined by
factors including scale economies, capital and labour intensity, R&D
intensity and marketing etc. However, in recent years, scale and
capital barriers may not be significant barriers to the entry, particu-

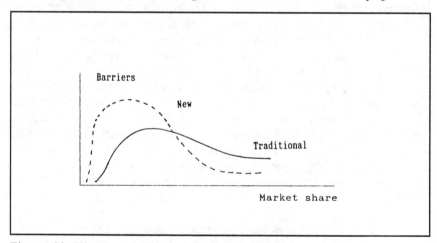

Figure 11: The threshold of global market entry

larly in high technology industries(Mansfield et al, 1977). Now the
entry relies more on R&D intensity and innovations to produce
timeliness and high quality products, relies on intelligence-based
factors, in which IT is playing an even more important role as the
core. Relevantly, LDCs' weakness in R&D and technological infrastructure, especially IT infrastructure, makes them more difficult to
enter global market. In other words, the threshold of LDCs' global
market entry has been raised.(see fig.11) But once the IT adoption
capability is established, the further capital assets needed may be
less.

Resources

As information becomes the primary source in recent years, great attention has been paid to the educated human resource who develops and utilize IT. Unlike DCs which assemble new systems and have the diverse resources required to introduce the new paradigm with full play of IT, LDCs lack of the resource and the skills to effect needed paradigm changes. Particularly, the first thing for LDCs to do might not be investing in technology facilities but be investing in the establishing of well educated human resource.

Such as in China, though the computer sets in using increase at a rate of more than ten percent per year in recent years, especially the personal computers, a large amount of them are used just as typewriters, few of them are linked in networks. Their efficiency in application is very poor due to the lack of qualified programming technicians. It is estimated that 1.2 million newly trained computer operators are needed in the year 1995, and this number will reach 2.3 million in the year 2000, in China(Yuan, 1993). Qualified human resource is the most scarce resource in LDCs, its formation needs generations' efforts. In fact, some later-comers' success in catching up with DCs, such as Japan, Singapore, Korea etc. is conditioned by the formation of educated human resource, in the final analysis.

For instance, even during the labour-intensive period of the 1960s, Korea government acted on its vision of an industrialized country by establishing a science and technology infrastructure at a time when demand for such an infrastructure was little in evidence. Heavy investment were made in human resource development, despite its low per capita income, that laid an important foundation for the sequential industrialization and made it possible to acquire technology capacity rapidly by rapid adaptation of imported technology and reverse engineering of foreign products(Kim & Dalman, 1992).

Secondary Innovation

As is noted above, though LDCs are not good at the Schumpeterian 'first innovation', they do have the great chances to make secondary innovation to existing product and process technologies to win their competitive advantage as later-comers. In LDCs, secondary innovation is no less significant than the discontinuous radical innovations in DCs, as to adapt to global competition.

By creative, market-sensitive, disciplined use or modest refinement of existing technologies, at one hand, secondary innovation saves high pioneering expenditure and bears less risks, such as the saving of high R&D expenditure in the funding of new technological paradigms' introduction and market exploration expenditure, which could hardly be borne by LDCs; at the other hand, secondary innovation enables LDCs to gain experience and knowledge which are accumulated for years in DCs, in a much shorter period.

Further, since secondary innovation takes foreign technology as its main source, to monitor the development of, and get sufficient information about, the primary technology in time becomes the key issue. So that a well structured IT network will be the dominant precondition for LDCs to make successful secondary innovation to get later-comer's competitive advantage.

Organizational Learning

The role of IT in LDCs should be not only monitoring the advances in DCs' technologies, but also adapting recipients' production systems to the changing global market circumstances. In which the key issue may be 'organizational learning'.

Traditionally, learning curve indicates that productivity is an exponential function of experience, which may be adequate in the linear environment. But as we are entering the new era of information, the over-emphasized learning curve effects, the persisting in pursuing specialization, might be the restraint for firms to adapting to swiftly changing circumstances in a nonlinear dynamic environment. While paradigms shift, firms' 'learning by doing', 'learning by using' and 'learning by R&D' etc., have their new contents to harness the collective genius of the people in organizations. As is noted by Senge(1990), 'The old model, the top thinks and the local acts, must now give way to integrating thinking and acting at all levels.' Learning from the experience of both foreign competitors and successful firms at home, firms have to adopt new structures, new ways of relating to customers, suppliers, and the community, and to adopt new ways of doing business. In which the building of well structured information networks is the precondition, and the efficient application of modern IT might play a key role.

Since the 'public learning' or the 'leak out' of the collective learning exists(Silverberg, 1991), when the scientists and engineers are quite willing to publish and exchange operations data on technological progress, with the support of IT, firms of LDCs could transform accumulated information into in-house knowledge, pool the accumulated experience and share the latest research results, so as to avoid the mistakes formerly committed in DCs and to direct efforts in the right direction. IT will be the core weapon to enhance LDCs' absorptive capacity.

STRATEGY IMPLICATIONS

It is noted that existing strategic planning systems and management approaches need to be extended to encompass the pervasive and rapidly changing impacts of IT(Nelson, 1991). The adaptation to the new paradigms may be painful, but it appears necessary. For LDCs, the relevant key strategic issues might be as follows.

Strategic Goals

Generally, to make major breakthroughs are not the highest goal of R&D for LDCs. But as later-comers, the firms of LDCs always not only had to produce new products based upon acquired technologies, which might be much different from the using technologies in the firms, but also had to adapt to the changed processing methods of marketing, servicing, manufacturing, and designing. The skills, attitudes and assumptions which undergird successful strategy in the former domestic technology need to be changed in ways both major and subtle to bring about successes in catching up with advanced economies in global market. Apparently, this is very difficult to do for most firms of LDCs.

As IT brings both new advantages and disadvantages to LDCs, the successful strategic goals for the firms of LDCs shifts. Traditionally, the most effective strategic goals of LDCs are low-cost and market differentiation, particularly the former, which played LDCs advantages in low price labour and raw materials. However, in the new era, while the basis of competitive advantage has shifted from manufacturing cost and product reliability towards speedily introduction of innovative design features(Vesey, 1991), the strategic goals of LDCs have to be shifted in accordance.

Secondary Innovation

It is argued that secondary innovation is the dominant pattern of technological progress in LDCs and is also the potential weapon for LDCs to gain later-comer's advantage in global marketplace. And the secondary innovation is also an important strategic issue for LDCs, as to counteract their weakness in R&D ability and technological infrastructure. However IT could provide much more opportunities to LDCs' secondary innovation.

As LDCs usually lack of pooled resource of latest knowledge, skills, and modern facilities, secondary innovation places more emphasis on monitoring external advances, and building the aggressive capability of absorbing and assimilating those advances. And then it is needed to assemble and manage R&D networks to accomplish systemic transition. In the evolutionary process of secondary creative activities, IT might play the most important role in either administrative application or productive utilization. As people are becoming more aware of the critical importance of the strategic management of technology in today's global market competition, the well understanding of secondary innovation might be one of the most important basis of strategy making, particularly for LDCs.

Collaborative R&D

In recent years, competitive advantage increasingly rely on the power and effectiveness of the allied network. Tough R&D is weak in most LDCs, the pervasive application of IT makes it possible for researchers in LDCs to be involved in researches being made in DCs. As IT develops fast, multinational corporations are now able to conduct their business around the world with ease(Halal, 1992), not only in DCs but also in LDCs.

Generally, there are two optional collaborative R&D strategies such as the vertical integration and the horizontal integration. In fact,most R&D activities in LDCs are accomplished vertically as follow-up work to researches done in DCs. So the linking chains are almost solely determined by DCs. They are easy to be broken, when technology is formally transferred from DCs to LDCs. While horizontal R&D integration takes the firm as an open system, the R&D activities are done almost in the same technology level. The horizontal information flow enables different R&D units, both in DCs and LDCs, to make full and creative use of each other's updated ideas and accumulated knowledge, but which demands the shorter technology distance between the R&D units. In LDCs, the R&D capability evolves reversely from imitation, development, application research to fundamental research, so that their collaborative R&D strategies might be dynamic to match their expectation and the capability, and to reconcile economic competition with collaborative R&D and technology targeting.

Entry Strategy

It is noted that in today's market, new entrants relies more and more on technological innovation rather than scale and capital to overcome the entry barriers(Dowling, 1992). The circumstances tend to be more rigour to LDCs which are weak in technology capacity, as the traditional low-cost becomes weaker and incompetent.

However, despite the inability in radical innovation, firms of LDCs could make more process focused secondary innovations even more successful, which tend to be more efficient with the application of IT.

By reconfiguring the production system acquired from DCs to link together with existing domestic components in a new way, just as Henderson's(1990) architectural innovation which is often triggered by a change in a component, and even improving the acquired technology with micro-radical changes, the firms of LDCs could gain their later-comers' advantage with not only low-cost, low risk but also innovative production system to overcome the entry barriers of global market, just as some succeeded Japanese companies done.

It is suggested that LDCs, while they make their entry strategies, should turn more attention from labour-intensive production of low-cost to make existing products and production system something new, i.e. make secondary innovation.

Dynamic Strategy Adoption

Further our point is that as the competence in global marketplace is much more affected by the changes, the innovation was strategically radical in the market in terms of the competitive dynamics; and as was asserted by Silverberg(1991) that dynamic appropriability of an innovative strategy is very much a function of the rates of learning, both internal and public; and as secondary innovation is embodied with stronger significance of production system's evolution; in LDCs, the strategies should be adopted dynamically in accordance with the phases of firms' evolutionary process. In which IT could do much more things than ever as a critical supporting force.

CONCLUSION

In summary, this chapter first examined the role of IT in the paradigms shifting and their impacts on LDCs' fortune in the coming new era. And the arguments was presented that as the paradigms are shifting, the basis of comparative competitive advantages are changing simultaneously from manufacturing cost towards speed-to-market. LDCs' competitive circumstances are comparatively getting worse. Otherwise, when the threats increase, IT does provide potential weapon to LDCs to gain new sources of later-comer's advantage by quickening organizational learning, accelerating technological evolutionary process and supporting secondary innovation, so the opportunities increase too. These findings suggest that, for LDCs, the traditional entry strategies of labour-intensive low-cost, under the assumption of linear environment, may be inappropriate in the new era. In such cases, strategies designed to take advantages of IT in the nonlinear dynamic environment, and focus on secondary innovation, may be more fruitful. Further study, especially empirical study, is needed, particularly in the interaction of IT and institutional change in LDCs. In addition, it should be noted that the most important thing, and might also the most difficult thing, for LDCs to do is to find ways to accelerate the formation of educated human resource.

REFERENCES

Allen, T.J.(1986). Organizational Structure, Information Technology, and R&D Productivity, *IEEE Transaction on Engineering Management,* 33(4), 212-217.

Barnatt, C. & Wong, P.(1992). Acquisition Activity and Organizational Structure, *Journal of General Management,* 17(3), 1-4

Bowonder, B. & Miyake, T.(1992). A Model of Corporate Innovation Management: Some Recent High Tech Innovation in Japan, *R&D Management,* 22(4), 319-335.

Chen, I.J. Calantone, R.J. & Chung, C.H.(1992). The Marketing-Manufacturing Interface and Manufacturing Flexibility, *OMEGA,* 20(4), 431-443.

Cusumano, M.A.(1992). Shifting Economies: From Craft Production to Flexible Systems and Software Factories, *Research Policy,* 21, 453-480.

Dowling, M.J. & Ruefli, T.W.(1992). Technological Innovation as a Gateway to Entry: The Case of the Telecommunications Equipment Industry, *Research Policy,* 21, 63-77.

Grant, R.M., Krishnan, R., Shani, A.B. & Baer, R.(1992). Appropriate Manufacturing Technology: A Strategic Approach, *Engineering Management Review,* Summer, 13-17.

Gupta, A.K. & Rogers, E.M.(1992). Internal Marketing: Integrating R&D and Marketing within the Organization, *Engineering Management Review,* Spring, 29-36.

Halal, W.E.(1992). The Information Technology Revolution, *The Futurist,* July-August, 10-15.

Henderson, R.M. & Clark, K.B.(1990). Architectural Innovation: The Reconfiguration of Existing Product Technologies and the Failure of Established Firms, *Administrative Science Quarterly,* 35, 9-30.

Hill C.T. (1992). New Manufacturing Paradigms/New Manufacturing Policies? *Technological Forecasting and Social Change,* 41, 351-363.

Istvan, R.L.(1992). A New Productivity Paradigm for Competitive Advantage, *Strategic Management Journal,* 13, 525-537.

Izuchukwu, J.(1992). Architecture and Process: the Role of Integrated system in Concurrent Engineering Introduction, *Industrial Management,* March/April, 19-23.

Kim, L. & Dahlman, C.J.(1992). Technology Policy for Industrialization: An Integrative Framework and Korea's Experience, *Research Policy,* 21, 437-452.

Lee, J., Bae, Z.T. and Choi, D.K.(1988). Technology development processes: A Model for a Developing Country with a Global Perspective, *R&D Management,* 18, 235-250.

Mansfield, E. et al.(1977). *The Production and Application of New Industrial Technologies,* New York: Norton.

Mitchell, G.R.(1992). The Changing Agenda for Research Management, *Research/technology Management*, Sept.-Oct., 13-21.

Nelson, G.R.(1991). The coming Revolution in R&D/Technical Computing, *Research/Technology Management*, Nov.-Dec., 29-30.

Nikolajew, V.(1991). The New Technological Paradigm of Intelligence-based Production - Global Challenges, *Futures*, Oct., 828-848.

Senge, P.M.(1990). The Leader's New Work: Building Learning Organizations, *Sloan Management Review*, Fall, 7-23.

Shaw, M.J., Solberg, J.J. & Woo, T.C.(1992), System Integration in Intelligent Manufacturing: An Introduction, *IIE Transactions*, 24(3), 2-6.

Silverberg, G.(1991). Adoption and Diffusion of Technology as a Collective Evolutionary Process, *Technological Forecasting and Social Change*, 19, 67-80.

Steele, L.W.(1991). Needed: New Paradigms for R&G, *Research-Technology Management*, July-August, 13-21.

Venkatachalam, A.R.(1992). Design for Manufacturability: A Survival Strategy for the American Manufacturing Industry, *Industrial Management*, May/June, 7-10.

Vesey, J.T.(1991). The New Competitors: They Think in Terms of 'Speed-to-market', *Engineering Management Review*, Winter, 12-21.

Womack, J., Jones, D.P. and Roos, D.(1990). *The Machine That Changed the World*, MA Cambridge: Rawson.

Wu, X.B. and Wang, S.L.(1991). An Empirical Analysis of Element of Technological Innovation in China, *Industrial Management*, Beijing, International Academic Press.

Xu, Q.R. and Wu, X.B.(1991).A Model of 'Secondary Innovation' Process, *PICMET'91*, Protland, IEEE Inc.

Yuan, M.D.(1993). Personal Computer: The Shock Wave in 1990s. *New Century Newsweek* (in Chinese), 51, 88-95.

SECTION 7

Global Human Resource Information Systems and Technology Applications

The Human Resource (HR) function takes on added complexity in the context of international business operations. A culturally diverse and globally dispersed workforce intensify the demands placed on information systems designed to support the organization's HR activities. Practical applications and recent literature citations support the growing significance of human resource information systems (HRIS) within the organization. These systems are becoming essential for the tracking of employee data relating to recruiting, compensation, benefits, payroll, training, and performance. For multinational organizations, the data and information requirements become increasingly complex and require more sophisticated systems that incorporate different currencies, international taxation, expatriate data, and varying laws and regulations.

The consequences for failure, both human and financial, are frequently more severe in an international setting. Although cross-cultural training programs help reduce the risks, better tracking of data and information will also aid in these efforts. The design and development of an effective international HRIS that meets the needs of diverse global organizations is clearly a challenge and one that is likely to be met by international constraints. Those companies that develop effective information systems to meet the HR needs of the organization and its foreign affiliates will likely reap competitive advantage and resulting opportunities.

In the first chapter of this section, Carol Agocs and Peter Suttie provide a conceptual argument for the need for a new paradigm to support the role of the HR function in the context of the "learning organization" that proactively responds to a dynamic global environment. This emerging paradigm is being driven by changing organizational forces and external environmental factors. The authors suggest that the HRIS will make a significant contribution to this new paradigm of HR management. In addition, the authors stress the importance of linkages between the HR function and strategic initiatives of the global organization. Success, they contend, will depend on the capabilities of information technology advancements.

In the second chapter, John Boudreau, Renae Broderick, and Vladimir Pucik begin with a hypothetical vision of the future for the international HRIS within the organization. The authors then provide a framework describing linkages between the firm's international objectives and HRIS applications. They propose the use of this framework to pinpoint areas of greatest potential for enhancing decision making, meeting the HR function's objectives, and matching the objectives of the organization. This framework further demonstrates the power of HRIS in the organization's efforts to coordinate its HR programs internationally.

In the third chapter, Kline Harrison and Candace Deans shift emphasis to a more focused examination of the organization's international human resource information system (IHRIS). They provide detailed descriptions of specific modules to be incorporated into the overall IHRIS and describe the additional information requirements necessary to support the international HR function. They conclude with a discussion of implementation issues that are relevant to the design and development of international information systems.

CHAPTER 20

Managing Human Resource Information in the Learning Organization: Strategic Responses to the Global Environment

CAROL AGÓCS
University of Western Ontario

PETER SUTTIE
University of Western Ontario

The survival and effectiveness of the organization in an environment that is both global and turbulent requires a transformation of the traditional human resource management function, which in many organizations still reflects the scientific management paradigm. Under the new paradigm of the learning organization, human resources management has become an information-based function that is increasingly dependent on human resource information systems (HRIS). Currently available HRIS capabilities have evolved beyond traditional transaction processing systems and management information systems to include expert systems and executive information systems applications that can support strategic decision making at the corporate level and widely distributed access and flexible use of human resources information by a variety of stakeholders. Yet these capabilities are still rarely used in organizations, perhaps because the human resources management function itself has not yet been recognized as an equal partner with the other key organizational functions, with a potentially critical relationship to the organization's strategic goals. As organizations adopt new information-based approaches to human resource management, several challenging issues will need to be addressed.

INTRODUCTION

Human resource information systems (HRIS) are powerful applications of information management technology that can support many new forms of human resource (HR) planning and decision making that are essential to organizational effectiveness in a context of global transformation. HRIS can also strengthen the organization's strategic planning and management capability if HR management is acknowledged as the peer of operations, marketing, finance, and other functions long recognized as critical to organizational survival. However, if the capabilities of HR information management are to be fully used to the organization's advantage, changes in the organizational role and meaning of the HR function itself must first occur. A transformation of the traditional HR management function is now occuring in many organizations and a new paradigm for HR management is taking shape--a vantage point from which to coordinate and focus organizational resources on meeting the challenges arising from a changing environment.

The purpose of this chapter is to examine the potential role of information management in the context of a new paradigm for human resource management that guides the "learning organization" —the kind of organization that proactively responds to a global environment characterized by rapid and unpredictable change (Wright and Morley, 1989; Senge, 1990). We begin with a discussion of the emerging role of HR management in the learning organization, and the new paradigm that might guide that role. Unfortunately, evidence we review suggests that an outdated scientific management paradigm characteristic of the early development of the HR function remains dominant, and as a result, the potential that information management applications offer for human resource issues has yet to be fully used. We explore some of the contributions HRIS might make to the management of human resources under the guidance of a new paradigm that is appropriate to a global environment of unprecedented change. In conclusion, we point to some issues that need to be addressed as organizations move toward the adoption of new information-based approaches to the management of human resources.

HUMAN RESOURCE MANAGEMENT IN THE 21ST CENTURY: A NEW ROLE AND AN EMERGING PARADIGM

The Changing Organizational Environment

The contemporary organization, whether in the private or public sector, is an open system in a turbulent and expanding environment. Significant and inter-related elements of this environment include a political economy whose reach is global, a changing population, a trend toward increasing levels of regulation by governments and a continued expansion of the service sector accompanied by a parallel focus on customer or client-driven management systems.

A Changing Population and a Global Marketplace

The demographic profiles of the U.S. and Canada have changed significantly over the past generation and these changes will accelerate in the future. The population is aging, becoming more racially and ethnically diverse and more highly skilled and educated and, in addition, traditional family and household patterns are changing. Women, racial minorities and immigrants make up the majority of the workforce and the customer and client populations. The typical employee is now culturally and socially different from the traditional white male employee of North American or European heritage (Teasley and Williams, 1991; Johnston, 1991) for whom the human resource management systems of most organizations were designed. Moreover, many organizations are learning to operate across cultural and national boundaries and to conduct their business on a global scale. The organization's ability to perform competitively and effectively in this environment will depend upon its capacity to respond to a labour market, client or customer population, and workforce that is increasingly diverse and complex.

Government Regulation

Organizations face increasing requirements to comply with regulations and legislation as governments respond to changing public expectations and growing concerns about racial and gender equality, health and safety, and the environment. Compliance frequently requires organizations to collect and report workforce data and to monitor change over time. In medium and large organizations these requirements necessitate the use of automated information management and reporting systems.

Expanding Service Sector and a Customer Focus

Post-industrialism has brought a shift in the structure of the labour market: most workers are now employed not in direct production but in service functions. Advanced information management technologies have stimulated increases in professional, administrative and clerical employment in manufacturing. The expansion of employment in public administration, health, education and welfare, as well as the retail, business and personal services, has contributed to the growth of the service sector. In recent years, consumer and retail services have been the major source of new employment. While the majority of men still work in goods production and distribution, women are heavily concentrated in social and commercial services (Boyd, Mulvihill and Myles, 1991). In the post-industrial world, organizational survival and productivity require a highly educated and skilled workforce capable of responding to a complex and changing service environment.

Structural transformation in the labour market has been accompanied by a growing emphasis on service to the customer or client as a strategy for organizational success in a competitive business environment. Information management systems, including HRIS, can assist organizations to serve customers more effectively by linking specialized customer needs with the people in the organization who are best able to respond.

A New Strategic Role for Human Resource Management

These changes in the organization's environment present new challenges to the human resource management function. For example, HR is responsible for assisting the organization to develop the capability to work effectively with a more diverse work force, to respond to government regulations and to develop staffing and training procedures that are responsive to new customer and client expectations within a service environment. Identifying, attracting, developing and retaining the employee characteristics the organization needs in order to attain its productivity and service goals has been recognized as the critical strategic role of HR management (Schuler, 1987; Walton, 1985).

In addition, the HR function can assist the organization to become more responsive, flexible and effective by providing expert support to employees as they work with an array of stakeholders in the environment. In facilitating the organization's interface with its communities, including governments, suppliers, the labour market, customer or client groups, interest groups, and organizations that are potential competitors or collaborators, HR management can serve as one of the organization's feedback and guidance systems. As well, HR's expertise in the management of change is a key resource as the organization works to break down limiting boundaries that separate it from external suppliers, competitors and other stake-holders (Jick, 1990), as well as dissolve internal barriers that interfere with working relationships among departments and functions. HR's role in helping the organization to learn and redefine itself as it adapts to a changing environment means that the human resource function itself will be both challenged and transformed (Beer and Spector, 1985).

THE PERSISTING INFLUENCE OF THE SCIENTIFIC MANAGEMENT PARADIGM IN HUMAN RESOURCE MANAGEMENT

From its emergence as a profession in the early twentieth century through the early to middle eighties, "personnel" has often been viewed as a cost centre and support function to the line and other staff functions in the organization (Devanna, Forbrun and Tichy, 1981; Evans, 1984; Watson, 1977). Furthermore, in many organizations HR management still bears the stamp of the era in which the function originated -- the world of scientific management, as conceptualized by Fredrick W. Taylor in the early years of this century.

Under the scientific management paradigm, as enacted within large bureaucratic organizations characterized by an elaborated division of labour and adversarial labour-management relations, the purposes of human resource management were to maximize efficiency and management control over the labour force (Goldman and Van Houten, 1980; Walton, 1985). Although the scientific management paradigm has been subjected to a sustained critique for several decades, the two priorities of efficiency and management control continue to be central to HR management practices in many organizations.   Comparative data from seven countries suggest that participation in decision making still tends to be restricted to managerial and professional employees, and that "Fordism" remains the dominant paradigm for managing people, in practice if not in theory (Boreham, 1992).

A survey of almost a thousand private sector firms in Canada found that almost three quarters of the responding organizations had introduced computer-based technological change from 1980 to 1985, primarily in applications related to production and administration, but only 35 percent introduced joint decision making or problem solving (Newton, 1989). A gap between technical and organizational innovation is apparent in a majority of organizations, despite widespread lip service to the need for more flexible and less hierarchical organizational structures and more participatory decision-making processes.

HRIS IMPLEMENTATION IN HUMAN RESOURCE MANAGEMENT: UNREALIZED POTENTIAL

In the human resource management function, the research literature documents a further gap between the potential capabilities of new information technologies and the use of that potential in support of new approaches to HR management, and suggests that failure to fully use the capabilities of HRIS is due more to organizational than to technical impediments (Sept, Westmacott, Agócs and Suttie, 1989). The under-utilization of HRIS may be rooted in the persistence of traditional views of the contribution of human resource management in organizations. To the degree that human resource management is seen as a service and control oriented function playing, at best, a supporting role in the activities central to the organization's mission, the implementation of HRIS may not be viewed as a priority. A recent Canadian study (Finegan, Agócs and Suttie, 1992) suggests that the failure of organizations to implement HRIS and to make use of their potential is linked to the powerlessness and low profile of the human resource management function within the organization.

In order to play a strategic role in the learning organization, human resource managers require access to large amounts of relevant and current information about the existing and potential workforce and labour market and the capability to manipulate this information so as to provide analyses relevant to strategic planning and decision-making. They also require the power to influence organizational decisions at the strategic level. Finally, the HR function must be capable of implementing state of the art HR management practices and must be supported and encouraged to do so by the organization. If the human resource management function lacks the power to use its expertise to the organization's strategic advantage and if it is unable or unwilling to implement leading edge HR practices, or to use the capabilities of new information technology, the organization's ability to orient itself to a changing external environment may be impaired.

HRIS can significantly enhance the organization's capacity for planning and decision-making regarding its crucial resource—human talent, skill and energy. However, whether and how HRIS are used depends upon the relationship between the human resource management subsystem and the larger organizational system of which it is a part. There is evidence that few organizations have implemented HRIS in ways that use the full spectrum of capabilities that existing technologies will support (Broderick and Boudreau, 1991). Furthermore, the HRIS applications that have been implemented in organizations often suggest the influence of the scientific management paradigm rather than the emerging paradigm for HR management in a learning organization.

Reflecting the scientific management paradigm, the central objectives in the early stages of implementing information management technologies in the HR function appear to have been to maximize efficiency and control. Early applications in "personnel" involved automating existing paper-based systems for administering payroll, pensions and benefits, and keeping records on transactions. These still appear to be the predominant uses of information technology in HR management (Cholak and Simon, 1991; Broderick and Boudreau, 1991; Finegan, Agócs and Suttie, 1992).

HRIS are commonly used to maintain data on employees (Thompson, 1991), prepare and distribute routine and customized reports (Bergin and Seesing, 1991), facilitate in-house payroll administration for small and medium sized organizations (O'Connell, 1991), provide routine information to employees (Greene, 1991), and administer compensation and benefits (Cholak and Simon, 1991). These applications of information management technologies to the HR function are typically justified by their contributions to reducing costs (Spirig, 1989). For example, the growing cost of benefits, now estimated to amount to 37% to 39% of employee salary, on average, has induced many large organizations to move to HRIS-supported flexible benefits programs (Stamps, 1990; Stylianou and Madey, 1992). Costs of compliance with government legislation and regulations have also prompted HRIS development (Cholak and Simon, 1991). There is evidence that HRIS applications reduce costs in many ways. For example, HRIS can a) save the time of HR counsellors in responding to employees' requests for information; b) improve efficiencies in payroll processing and HR operations associated with hiring, placement, and retention of employees; and c) provide leverage in negotiations with suppliers of employee benefits through economies of scale that are achieved when integrated corporate flexible benefit plans replace divisional plans (Curley and Henderson, 1992: 91).

James Beniger (1986) has argued that the "information society" — the widespread application of information processing technologies to management—is not a recent development, but has its roots in the "control revolution" that began a century ago. The development of information management capabilities within HR management to date might be viewed within this context, in light of the historical association between "personnel" and scientific management. In today's organizations, many applications of HRIS are directed toward enhancing management monitoring and control of employee time and activity, thereby reducing labour costs. For example, HRIS are used to monitor absenteeism in order to identify and control abuse of sick leave (Gardiner, 1992); assist line managers to monitor and reduce personnel costs (Richards-Carpenter, 1991); keep track of employees' working time and schedules (Smith, 1991; Stamps, 1990), including flexible scheduling, job-sharing, home-based work and part time programs; electronically monitor employees' performance (Safayeni et.al., 1992); locate qualified candidates within the organization before advertising a vacancy, or identify capabilities available in-house before contracting for external services (O'Connell, 1990).

Michael Hammer (1990: 104) has observed,

... heavy investments in information technology have delivered disappointing results—largely because companies tend to use technology to mechanize old ways of doing business. They leave the existing processes intact and use computers simply to speed them up. But speeding up those processes cannot address their fundamental performance deficiencies. Many of our job designs, work flows, control mechanisms, and organizational structures came of age in a different competitive environment and before the advent of the computer. They are geared toward efficiency and control. Yet the watchwords of the new decade are innovation and speed, service and quality. It is time to stop paving the cow paths.

HOW CAN HRIS CONTRIBUTE TO A NEW PARADIGM FOR HUMAN RESOURCE MANAGEMENT?

HRIS applications that reflect the scientific management priorities of efficiency and control in HR management may be relatively easy to sell to organizational decision makers, yet do little to enhance organizational effectiveness in a changing environment. Used in ways that support innovation and organizational responsiveness, the new technologies of information management have the potential to assist organizations as they shift into a new "post-Fordist" paradigm (Boreham, 1992). The HR management paradigm for the learning organization gives central importance to employees' capacities to innovate and learn, to participate in decision making and problem solving, and to work effectively with a diversity of internal and external stakeholders. New technologies of information management, including HRIS, have potential uses that can challenge traditional managerial hierarchies and systems of top-down control, while contributing to more flexible, responsive and participative approaches to HR management. HR information is essential to implementing corporate-wide productivity and service-oriented approaches involving performance measurement such as Total Quality Management and customer/client service programs (Eccles, 1991). Information management technologies and the applications they make possible will be at the centre of the redefined human resource management function as it moves into the twenty-first century.

In order to play the role within the organization that is envisioned in the new paradigm of the learning organization, the HR function will need to take on new and more complex activities that are linked to the mission and strategic goals of the organization. This will require HR to take its place at the corporate strategic planning and decision-making table. For this to occur, HR must develop an ever-expanding capability to store and use information concerning the organization, its sub-units, individual employees, and the changing relationship between employees and the organization -- and to use this information to support strategic decision making. Moreover, HR's information management capability will need to be highly flexible, dynamic, and available for distributed use in a variety of ways by various stakeholders within the organization.

Some information management applications now being mentioned in the literature foreshadow the new role of HR management. These applications, which began to come on-stream in the late 80's, go far beyond traditional record-keeping and information processing activities to include analysis, coordination and integration of information at the level of the work unit or the organization as a whole, and reporting in a wide variety of formats to meet differing and continuously changing user needs.

Broderick and Boudreau (1991) provide strong support for this thesis. Their review of the literature on the use of computers in HR revealed the lack of a theoretical foundation in the HRIS area. They therefore developed a model for the evolution of computer applications in HR that was based on research in organization theory and management information systems. The model proposes a sequence of three stages in the evolution of computer usage: threshold, growth, and consolidation and strategic expansion (Nolan, 1979). The model also proposed four generic types of computer applications, with each type best supporting a different level and type of decision making: transaction processing, management information systems, expert systems, and decision support systems (Laudon and Laudon, 1988).

To test the model, Broderick and Boudreau (1991) conducted an exploratory study of ten firms in the United States who were considered leaders in HR management and HRIS implementation.

All firms were well into the growth stage and were re-evaluating their systems to consolidate and capitalize on their investments. The anticipated third stage for the HRIS in these firms included the further integration of systems and data within the HR area, an increased use of computer applications by current users, new users at the operational and tactical levels of the organization in both HR and non-HR functional areas, and cooperation in corporate-wide activities in technology development, which they labelled as a strategic initiative.

In their discussion, Broderick and Boudreau (1991) do not mention the desirability of a strategic role for HR managers, as we have proposed. However, there is an expectation that key HR decision makers will move into other functional areas, perhaps foreshadowing more HR activity at the strategic management level.

As has been observed in other studies, Broderick and Boudreau (1991) found that the majority of the HRIS applications were transaction processing systems and management information systems, both of which were extremely well developed. [It is important to point out that the MIS category described by Broderick and Boudreau is often referred to as information reporting systems by other authors in the computer field (e.g. O'Brien, 1991), denoting the more structured and prespecified nature of the decisions that are supported]. Broderick and Boudreau also found some relatively simple expert HRIS that were used by both employees and managers to support (but not make) decisions, thus indicating some movement towards empowering all levels in the organization. The decision support systems applications provide interactive support for ad hoc and/or less structured problems; some HRIS decision support applications were identified. There was also an interest in some organizations in providing HR information to an executive information system, but again, the purpose was to supply information to the corporate level, not to enable HR to participate in decision making.

The study by Broderick and Boudreau demonstrates that the HR area is aware of the levels and types of decisions that can be supported by information technology. But it also shows that HR lags significantly behind other functions in its impact and participation at the corporate level, and in the sophistication of system applications; that is, expert systems were rare and simple and there were few decision support applications.

It should be emphasized that the Broderick and Bordreau study shows that the HRIS transaction processing systems and information reporting systems in use are efficient and effective. In addition, such systems in HR are probably as sophisticated as systems in other functional areas, and thus could form a strong base for the development of HRIS in the decision support, expert, and executive information systems categories, as has occurred in other functions.

It is useful to describe some HRIS applications in order to demonstrate their capabilities and potential for expansion within the HR function, in other areas, and at the corporate level, as well as the possibilities for empowerment of employees. Examples of a range of applications follow:

a) Individual employees are potential direct users of HRIS (Witkin, 1989; Curley and Henderson, 1992). For example, any employee can log onto the mainframe through a personal computer and access personal data on total compensation, pension and other benefits, as well as information about financial planning, training and development, and date of next performance review (Laabs, 1991). Other applications in which individual employees use HRIS include employee entry of data on completion of continuing education and training programs or changes in benefits status or options, and exchange of information about social activities, carpooling, or family care. Such uses of HRIS reduce costs by saving the time of HR counselling staff, and contribute to employees' effectiveness and satisfaction.

b) Coordination of data on positions and individuals can facilitate career planning, career pathing and succession planning from the perspectives of the individual employee, the organization, and line management in specific functions.

c) Using distributed systems, line management in any branch or region can access the HRIS, enter data (such as performance review information), and initiate enquiries and requisitions (Sheehan, 1991; Richards-Carpenter, 1991).

d) HRIS can provide data for screening and selection, including capabilities for on-line entry or optical scanning of applications for employment, skills inventories and performance appraisal information to support the matching of individual employees or applicants to suitable projects, vacancies, or franchise opportunities, or for planning to meet educational or training requirements for future projects or positions ("Solving the People Puzzle", 1991; Wexler, 1990; Frye, 1990; Curley and Henderson, 1992).

e) Computer-based job evaluation can be both centralized and decentralized, can accommodate both individual and organizational requirements, and can help to identify and reduce impacts of gender or racial bias (Murlis and Pritchard, 1991). Such information can also support pay equity or performance-based reward programs.

f) HRIS can provide information for planning, monitoring, and reporting on affirmative action or employment equity results in relation to goals, for use in organizational planning or for compliance with government requirements. In similar fashion, employee health and safety or workers' compensation data can facilitate monitoring, reporting, or planning.

g) HRIS can link organizations directly to external suppliers of benefits and other HR services. For example, cost reductions have been achieved by electronically linking employee and dependent claims to the health insurance provider (Curley and Henderson, 1992: 94).

h) Information on absenteeism, turnover, grievances, overtime, and other indicators can be monitored as an aid to identifying and solving potential management or scheduling problems.

Examples of decision support applications of HRIS include the following:

a) HRIS can be a resource in managing organizational change, for example by forecasting potential impacts of growth or down-sizing, or of introducing new technology, or of investment in training and development (Spirig, 1991). HRIS can provide what-if scenarios to aid decision makers in evaluating proposals to develop new product lines, services, or business activities, or to initiate mergers, acquisitions, divestitures, organizational restructuring, or other changes having implications for HR planning and budgeting (Kolodziej, 1990; Stamps, 1990; Frye, 1990).

b) Decision support information can facilitate the ability of HR or line management to plan and implement training that is specifically directed toward organizational and employee needs, and that is cost-effective (Ganger, 1991).

c) Forecasts or scenarios using HR data can be used in human resource planning, productivity assessments, budgeting, collective bargaining, and other kinds of strategic decision making at the corporate level.

HR management can most effectively use the capabilities afforded by the new information management technologies to benefit the organization if it becomes part of the strategic management, decision-making and planning process at the corporate level, alongside operations, finance, marketing, and other key organizational functions. For this to occur, HR managers must demonstrate that they can contribute at this level and they must have access to strategic HRIS support. The strategic role of HR information has only recently been acknowledged and the development of computer applications to support this level of HR decision making has lagged far behind such applications in other functional areas (Sept et al, 1989).

Access to information is an important source of organizational power in the "information society" and is likely to reflect traditional or emerging power dynamics, as well as central values within the organization's culture. Integrating HRIS into the organization's information management, decision making, and strategic planning systems can raise the profile of the HR function, even as it enhances the organization's productivity and ability to orient itself to a changing environment.

For example, in a case study of HRIS implementation in a large multi-national company, Curley and Henderson (1992: 93) report:

> . . . a divisional HR manager told of using the decision support capability of the HRIS to plan divisional staff reductions that were in line with the company's commitments to EEOC [affirmative action] guidelines while meeting cost reduction objectives and maintaining a required skills base. She demonstrated this capability to senior management during a high level meeting with a series of 'what if' queries that were done on line at the meeting. Management was very impressed, and the division manager felt that this one demonstration of decision support had elevated the importance of the HRIS to top management. At the same time, this manager perceived that her own status had been elevated and she felt proud of the fact that she could make a valuable contribution to an important strategic decision. The 'what-if' capability of the system also allowed for long range HR planning and the investigation of various HR initiatives such as elder care, English language training etc. that would meet the needs of a specific workforce while also meeting the division's guidelines for profitability.

Whether and how HRIS are implemented and used appears to depend in large part upon the role and power of the HR function in the organization, which in turn may reflect the value the organization places on its human resources. For example, in making strategic decisions about initiatives such as mergers, acquisitions or divestitures, does top management consider only financial and marketing projections, or is human resource planning information also considered? It is becoming clear that the success of such initiatives often depends upon human resource issues such as "fit", overlap, or gaps between the cultures and expertise of people in the organizations involved, or on the long-term availability of essential skills or knowledge.

Under the new paradigm of the learning organization, innovation and decision-making are not the exclusive prerogative of the core members of the executive: they are widely distributed throughout the organization. Likewise, human resource administration, planning, analysis and decision-making are carried out not only by HR specialists, but also by line managers at all levels and their administrative staff, specialists in various staff functions (e.g. employee health and safety, employment equity), as well as by employees and consultants. This requires that HR information be widely distributed and available in a variety of forms to meet specific needs (Naroni, 1991). Curley and Henderson (1992: 94) report that in a multinational company in which an integrated HRIS was implemented across 14 divisions, there was "a change in the overall process of human resource management through every level in the corporation." Furthermore, "increased use of the HRIS by employees and line managers will continue to redefine the job of the HR specialist and will require a new and broader definition of HR management functions within the responsibility of line managers."

ISSUES FOR THE FUTURE: MANAGING INFORMATION WITHIN A NEW HR MANAGEMENT PARADIGM

The implication of the argument presented above is that HRIS are not likely to be fully implemented and will not make the contribution to strategic management that they are capable of making, unless the role of the human resource management function is redefined, and its power enhanced. There is some evidence that the function is indeed undergoing transformation, especially in larger organizations, and that HRIS are contributing to this development. As the human resource management function changes and makes increasing use of advanced technologies for managing information, general issues concerning how HRIS will be used, and by whom, need to be addressed. In the paragraphs that follow we discuss several of the issues involved in the implementation of HRIS—from system design and development through testing, documentation, training, and developing the capacity to apply the system to assist in the solution of various kinds of organizational problems.

Is HRIS an end in itself?

Like any new managerial fad or technical capability, HRIS may come to be viewed by some as an end in itself, rather than as a resource that has the potential to enhance organizational performance if it is strategically used. Implementing an HRIS, in itself, is not likely to change or enhance the profile or strategic role of the human resource function in the organization or directly contribute to the attainment of organizational goals. HRIS are likely to realize their potential only if their implementation is part of a long-term strategy for defining (or redefining) the role and contribution of the human resource function in the organization.

It will be difficult for the HR function to gain support for investment in new HR information management capabilities if HRIS is seen as an end in itself, or merely as a means to enhance the efficiency of traditional HR operations. There is also the danger that if investment in HRIS is associated with a change in the culture of the HR function, such that data management and quantitative analysis become central HR operations rather than tools to support a range of HR applications, the result may be a "rationalization" of the HR function (Broderick and Boudreau, 1991). If HR management becomes overly analytical and focussed on measurement, and there is undue "reliance on quantitative standards in evaluation of HR policies and programs" (Broderick and Boudreau, 1991: 495), expertise based on understanding of human relations, communication, and organizational development may be devalued and pushed into the background. It is important, then, not to allow HRIS application to become an end in itself, to the detriment of a balanced approach to the role of the HR function in the organization.

Who should participate in HRIS implementation?

One might speculate that the HRIS is most likely to become an end in itself, rather than a means to accomplish the organization's strategic goals, if it is implemented by HR managers with minimal input from other stakeholders. The HR function may consider the implementation of an HRIS to be a proprietary process in which it has an overriding interest and one that it should control. This may be especially likely if the HR function has traditionally been marginalized within the organization and confined to a relatively circumscribed and powerless role (Kanter, 1979), or if there is conflict between systems and human resource experts about the control of HRIS development. In this case the HR function may view its control over the implementation process as an enhancement or assertion of its organizational power.

Yet theoretical notions of organizational power (e.g. Kanter, 1979; Pfeffer, 1981) suggest that power is most likely to grow and to enhance performance if it is shared. Moreover, the literature on organizational change clearly indicates that widespread participation in change, including the implementation of new technology, contributes to support for the innovation and ensures that it will meet demonstrated needs within the organization. HR managers who seek the participation of all of the key stakeholders in HRIS implementation, including not only systems experts and top management but also line managers, leaders of unions and employee associations, and staff experts in various functions (e.g. employee health and safety), may be most likely to end up with a system that enhances their profile by making a clear contribution to organizational performance in a variety of areas.

Curley and Henderson (1992:89-90) discuss successful implementation of an HRIS that brought together 14 divisional payroll and HR information systems in a large US pharmaceutical company. Among the key success factors were top management commitment sustained over time and involvement of other key stakeholders (corporate and divisional DP/MIS staff, line managers, and HR staff) throughout the project. This was accomplished by appointing a multiple stakeholder steering committee mandated to define the objectives of the system and to choose hardware and software, within the framework of business needs at both the divisional and corporate levels. Another key success factor was that the entire project was focussed on a common corporate-wide definition of the individual employee, a vision that placed the employee at the centre and that gave the disparate divisions a common goal and a way to arbitrate conflict.

Users of HRIS: Who are they? What are their interests?

The argument that there should be widespread participation in HRIS implementation, especially in identifying the objectives and uses of an HRIS, can be easily extended to include participation in its use. How could HRIS be used to facilitate authentic decentralization of decision-making and power—goals that many organizations now claim to espouse? HRIS, like other information management and decision support systems, can make use of networks and microcomputer technologies that are capable of supporting a highly decentralized community of users.

It is possible to envisage that nearly every employee, and certainly every manager involved in making personnel decisions and every union officer, might have uses for some applications of HRIS. These applications are potentially very broad, as noted earlier, and at a minimum, they can affect everyone having an interest in hiring, promotion, training, development, job assignment, and career and succession planning. Users could conceivably include both potential applicants for employment opportunities and those who make decisions related to human resource management, with beneficial results for the individual and the organization. If there were a free market in information such that costs of acquiring information were very low, and information were fully accessible both to potential applicants and to those responsible for selection decisions, perhaps the probability of suitable matches would be enhanced.

There are at least two important issues that arise from such a scenario. One concerns the protection of the privacy of individual employees: what would be the limits on the circulation of information, and how would they be set? Another concerns the impact on the power and role of the human resource management function: would it be diminished, enhanced, or simply changed, if it did not have a monopoly on access to information needed to support human resource management decisions?

Aside from transactions between individuals and the organization, one might further envision relatively widespread participation in macro-level applications of HRIS. Uses such as scheduling of meetings, appointments and consultations may pose few issues of concern beyond ensuring that the information in the system is current and accurate. Other applications might involve the union and management as users of the same information to support joint decision-making, as part of the collective bargaining process, in joint committee or other working groups, in dealing with grievances, or in on-going problem-solving. For example, joint union-management decisions might be made based upon:

(1) projections of the impacts of changes in compensation, staffing levels, job classifications, job evaluation systems, restructuring, new ventures, and other scenarios;
(2) monitoring of patterns and changes in job and/or shift assignments, absenteeism, turnover, grievances, workplace injuries or illness;
(3) supporting voluntary or mandatory joint union-management negotiations and agreement on such initiatives as pay equity, employment equity or affirmative action, or safety programs.

Applications such as these suggest the potential for HRIS to contribute to more equitable and harmonious labour relations, with union and management both working from the same information base. What would be the impacts on the collective bargaining process? On the incidence and management of grievances? Would the roles or the concerns of unions and management change? Under what circumstances might management consider giving up some of the power it now holds by virtue of its unilateral control of information? Would the union be willing to take on the increased responsibilities that might accompany joint decision-making on the basis of full and equal sharing of information?   Would this kind of HRIS application help to overturn the regime of scientific management with its program of managerial monopoly and control of information about the labour process?

New technologies of information management, notably HRIS, have potential uses that could challenge traditional systems of managerial hierarchy and control, at the same time as they can contribute to more flexible, responsive and participative approaches to human resource management and decision making. On the other hand, if the use of these systems remains a management monopoly, they can contribute to the further entrenchment and expansion of managerial control. As Michael Schrag (1992) notes, "networks don't destroy hierarchies; they reshape them. Organizations that run on power and influence do not take the 'participatory management pledge' simply because they've invested a fortune in network technology".

CONCLUSION

The entrapment of HR management in a scientific management paradigm, and the failure of HR to make use of the potential offered by the new technologies of information management, appear to be aspects of a vicious cycle. Canadian surveys in 1987 (Agócs, 1990) and 1989 (Finegan, Agócs and Suttie, 1992) found that a majority of responding organizations had not yet implemented progressive HR management practices such as succession planning, HR planning, flextime, and employment equity programs. It appears that the issue is not simply whether organizations are using the potential of HRIS technologies that are widely available on the market, but whether they are implementing current and effective human resource management practices— the kinds of practices that assist the organization to operate effectively in a changing environment, and that necessitate the use of advanced information management technologies. Unless the HR function itself is redefined to complement the needs of the learning organization, the full potential of HRIS is unlikely to be recognized and used.

The organization's ability to orient itself to a changing environment may be impaired unless the HR function develops the power and the will to use its expertise to the organization's advantage. This will occur if HR has an opportunity to contribute to strategic planning and decision making at the corporate level and to implement leading-edge HR practices that are dependent upon the advanced capabilities of new information technology.

REFERENCES

Agócs, Carol (1990). Employment Equity Activity Among Federal Contractors in Ontario, *Industrial Relations Issues for the 1990's*, Proceedings of the Canadian Industrial Relations Association, 517-529.

Beer, Michael and Bert Spector (1985). Corporatewide Transformation in Human Resource Management. In Richard Walton and Paul Laurence (Eds.), *Human Resource Management Trends and Challenges*. Boston: Harvard Business School, 219-253.

Beniger, James (1986). *The Control Revolution: Technological and Economic Origins of the Information Society*. Cambridge: Harvard University Press.

Bergin, Greg and Kathy Seesing (1991). CARD Deals with Report Distribution, *Personnel Journal*, 70(11), 109-113.

Boreham, Paul (1992). The Myth of Post-Fordist Management: Work Organization and Employee Discretion in Seven Countries, *Employee Relations*, 14(2), 13-24.

Boyd, Monica, Mary Ann Mulvihill and John Myles (1991). Gender, Power and Postindustrialism, *Canadian Review of Sociology and Anthropology*, 28(4), 407-436.

Broderick, Renae and John Boudreau (1991). The Evolution of Computer Use in Human Resource Management: Interviews with Ten Leaders, *Human Resource Management*, 30(4), 485-508.

Cholak, Paul and Sidney Simon (1991). HRIS Asks, 'Who's the Boss?' *Personnel Journal*, 70(8), 74-76.

Curley, Kathleen and John Henderson (1992). Assessing the Value of a Corporate Wide Human Resource Information System: A Case Study, *Journal of Management Systems*, 4(2), 85-96.

Devanna, Mary Anne, Charles Fombrun, and Noel Tichy (1981). Human Resources Management: A Strategic Perspective, *Organizational Dynamics*, 51-67.

Eccles, Robert (1991). The Performance Measurement Manifesto, *Harvard Business Review*, January-February, 131-137.

Evans, Paul (1984). On the Importance of a Generalist Conception of Human Resource Management A Cross-National Look, *Human Resource Management*, 23, 347-63.

Finegan, Joan, Carol Agócs, and Peter Suttie (1992). The Introduction of Human Resource Information Systems: Problems and Consequences, *The Journal of Management Systems*, 4(2), 29-40.

Frye, Colleen (1990). HR Professionals Moving Up Org Chart, *Software Magazine*, 10(11) 103 ff.

Ganger, Ralph (1991). HRIS Logs On to Strategic Training, *Personnel Journal*, 70(8), 50-55.

Gardiner, Richard (1992). Tracking and Controlling Absenteeism, *Public Productivity and Management Review*, 15(3), 289-307.

Goldman, Paul and Donald Van Houten (1980).   Bureaucracy and Domination: Managerial Strategy in Turn-of-the-Century American Industry.   In P. Dunkerly and G. Salaman (Eds.), *International Yearbook of Organizational Studies*. London: Routledge and Kegan Paul.

Greene, Alice (1991). Managing Human Resources with Systems, *Production and Inventory Management Review*, 11(1), 22, 29.

Hammar, Michael (1990). Reengineering Work: Don't Automate, Obliterate, *Harvard Business Review*, July-August, 104-112.

Jick, Todd (1990). Customer-Supplier Partnerships: Human Resources as Bridge Builders, *Human Resource Management*, 29(4), 435-454.

Johnston, William (1991). Global Work Force 2000: The New World Labor Market, *Harvard Business Review*, March-April, 115-127.

Kanter, Rosabeth Moss (1979). Power Failure in Management Circuits, *Harvard Business Review*, July-August, 65-75.

Kolodziej, Stan (1990). Service Firms Begin to Eye Strategic Benefits of MRMS, *Software Magazine*, 10(1), 87-93.

Laabs, Jennifer (1991). OLIVER: A Twist on Communication, *Personnel Journal*, 70(9), 79-82.

Laudon, K.C. and J.P. Laudon (1988). *Management Information Systems: A Contemporary Perspective.* New York: MacMillan.

Murlis, Helen and Derek Pritchard (1991). *Personnel Management*, 23(4), 48-53.

Naroni, Ren (1991). Planning Promotes HRIS Success, *Personnel Journal*, 70(1), 61-65.

Newton, Keith (1989). Technological and Organizational Change in Canada, *New Technology, Work and Employment*, 4(1) 42-47.

Nolan, R.L. (1979). Managing the Crisis in Data Processing, *Harvard Business Review*, March-April, 115-126.

O'Brien, James (1991). *Introduction to Information Systems in Business Management*, Irwin, sixth edition.

O'Connell, Sandra (1991). Payroll and HRIS on a PC?, *HR Magazine*, 36(11), 31-34.

O'Connell, Sandra (1990). Using the Computer to Manage Costs in Tough Times, *HR Magazine*, 35(12), 27-31.

Pfeffer, Jeffrey (1981). *Power in Organizations*. Boston: Pitman.

Richards-Carpenter, Colin (1991). Maximising the Value of a CPIS, *Personnel Management*, 23(5), 25, 27.

Richards-Carpenter, Colin (1991). Controlling Manpower Costs, *Personnel Management*, 23(11), 1-25.

Safayeni, Frank, Ric Irving, Lyn Purdy and Chris Higgins (1992). Potential Impacts of Computerized Performance Monitoring Systems: Eleven Propositions, *Journal of Management Systems*, 4(2), 73-84.

Schuler, Randall (1987). Personnel and Human Resource Management Choices and Organization Strategy. In R. S. Schuler, S. A. Youngblood and V.L. Huber (Eds.), *Readings in Personnel and Human Resource Management*. St. Paul: West Publishing, 3rd edition.

Schrag, Michael (1992). Toronto: *Globe and Mail*, October 13: B18.

Senge, Peter (1990). *The Fifth Discipline: The Art and Practice of the Learning Organization*. New York: Doubleday.

Sept, Ron, Penny Westmacott, Carol Agócs and Peter Suttie (1989). Human Resource Information Systems: Organizational Barriers to Implementation, *The Journal of Management Systems*, 1(2), 23-33.

Sheehan, Michael (1991). Paperchase Ends for Human Resources Department, *Systems 3X/400*, 19(3), 64-68.

Smith, Michael (1991). Tapping Voice Response as an HR Information Option, *Human Resources Professional*, 4(1), 21-25.

Solving the People Puzzle (1991). *Franchising World*, 23(1), 28, 30.

Spirig, John (1989). HRIS Topics, *Employment Relations Today*, 16(3), 249-52.

Spirig, John (1991). The HRIS Investment is Cost-Effective in Managing Change, *Employee Relations Today*, 18(2), 193-202.

Stamps, David (1990). Human Resources: A Strategic Partner or IS Burden? *Datamation*, 36(11), 47-52.

Stylianou, Anthony and Gregory Madey (1992). An Expert System for Employee Benefits Selection: A Case Study, *Journal of Management Systems*, 4(2), 41-59.

Teasley, C.E. III and Lee Williams (1990). The Future is Nearly Now: Managing Personnel in the Twenty-First Century, *Review of Public Personnel Administration*, 11(1-2), 131-138.

Thompson, Carolyn (1991). The Reluctant Revolution, *Credit Union Management*, 14(11), 10-13.

Walton, Richard (1985). Toward a Strategy of Eliciting Employee Commitment Based on Policies of Mutuality. In Richard Walton and Paul Laurence (Eds.), *Human Resource Management Trends and Challenges.* Boston: Harvard Business School, 35-65.

Watson, Tony (1977). *The Personnel Managers: A Study in the Sociology of Work and Employment.* London: Routledge & Keegan Paul.

Wexler, Joanie (1990). Johnson Wax: Planning 'Skill Connection' with IS, *Computerworld,* 24(51), 1, 63.

Witkin, Elliott (1989). Emphasize the Human in HRIS, *Personnel Journal,* 68(9), 75-77.

Wright, Susan and Morley, David (eds.) (1989). *Learning Works: Searching for Organizational Futures.* Toronto: York University, Faculty of Administrative Studies.

CHAPTER 21

Just Doing Business: Human Resource Information Systems in the Global Organization

JOHN W. BOUDREAU
RENAE BRODERICK
VLADIMIR PUCIK

Cornell University

Today's organizations face many paradoxes. The demands of globalization and flexibility require ever-increasing levels of communication, shared goals, and cross-boundary alliances. The power of technology is increasing, while the price plummets. Today's technology is quite capable of creating a true global network in which information to manage human resources is readily available to those who need it. Yet, evidence suggests that human resource information systems (HRIS) remain largely focused on administrative efficiency, and are often unconnected to the strategic international decisions of most organizations. Vast potential for improvement exists, yet progress is slow. This chapter suggests a future view of international HRIS. We begin with a hypothetical peek into the future. Then, we demonstrate how principles of global competitiveness can be linked with a taxonomy of HRIS applications to suggest new directions for HRIS development. This linkage provides a framework for developing future HRIS contributions to the global organization, and for understanding the nature of the value they can add. We conclude by briefly discussing the importance of demonstrating value, ensuring privacy, and managing international data transfer.

A DAY IN THE LIFE... A GLOBAL HUMAN RESOURCE EXECUTIVE, 1995 OR 2000?

Imagine the HR executive of the future. The future may be tomorrow, the year 2000, or perhaps a "2020 Vision". This HR executive works in a fully-integrated multi-national organization, with products and markets throughout the world. Successfully balancing the tradeoffs among its international goals, monitoring their achievement, and dealing with the paradoxes they create requires managing the human resources with the same diligence as the financial, marketing and production resources. The organization's top decision makers agree with leading strategic thinkers (e.g., Prahalad & Hamel, 1990) that identifying and nurturing the core competencies and capabilities of the organization may be the most important task facing the organization.

HR executives enjoy an enviable position of visibility, being called upon to help form and implement organization strategy. Along with this visibility, however, comes the responsibility to maintain a world-class level of quality in the way the organization's global workforce is managed. The far-flung and constantly-changing human resource needs of the organization make it absolutely imperative to rely on information technology. Let's take a peek into the daily routine of the future HR executive.

Atlanta, 6:30: Log into the corporate system to check Human Resource (HR) issues status. A world map appears on screen, showing regions and countries highlighted in green (no action necessary), yellow (no immediate action required, issues of low current importance), or red (action required, new, critical issues). Clicking on a red image of Singapore shows 25% versus 15% annual growth now forecast for a new joint venture's market. Local HR and line managers are using the on-line HR planning system to identify surplus talent, worldwide, and compare costs for moving talent internally and hiring from outside. The HR executive dictates a message to the voice-recognition system alerting the Singapore region HR manager of a new relocation-costing system developed and now being tested in Limerick, Ireland.

8:00: Check the corporate HR issues system again. No red areas. Clicking on a yellow Midwestern U.S. shows a week old request to keep a key engineering team together for another six months. The Midwest HR and line managers have used an expert system to identify new career paths for the engineers that preserve the competency-development career goals of team members, but delay the team dispersal for six months. These plans require cooperation from the Latin American division,because many of the new career paths will require involving team members in the new Latin American manufacturing process.

Clicking on a yellow Czech Republic recalls a dilemma of keeping R&D scientists in Prague. Low local compensation levels cause R&D scientists to pursue career opportunities in other parts of the world either within the firm or with other firms. Local HR managers have scanned the worldwide data base for examples of non-pay recognition systems, and have developed several alternatives. It's time for the executive to join a computer-assisted brainstorming and evaluation session with HR and line managers in the Western European divisions, by linking the groups through the automated group facilitation program.

12:00: Break for lunch after programming the HR search system to identify the latest published reports on the anticipated effects of new tax law and inflation on expatriate pay. The online citation data base automatically searches for publications reflecting the practices of a set of "benchmark" organizations, previously identified as leaders.

13:00: The "Personal Opportunity" icon flashes on the corporate HR system screen. Most company employees have online files listing their personal career goals and the competencies needed to achieve them. When a vacancy for a job, task force or team is identified, the competencies required to fill the vacancy and the associated development opportunities are input to the global staffing system and matched with individual files. The HR executives's file contains a goal of "building financial skills." Clicking on the "opportunity" icon shows an opportunity to serve as liaison between top corporate finance and marketing managers on a new task force to identify promising joint ventures. The HR executive clicks on the box indicating interest, knowing that a copy of his qualifications will be forwarded to the group selecting task force members.

13:30: Time for the one-on-one appraisal and development meetings scheduled with the HR executive's immediate staff. Top staff members have completed a major project, collaborating with cross-national teams to update the set of core competencies that all units use for career planning and performance assessment. It's time to identify new opportunities for this top group. Clicking on the "Staff Advising" icon calls up an on-screen image of each staff person. By clicking on each image, the executive receives a summary of the person's career goals, the competency gaps between the person's current qualifications and those needed to reach goals, and recommended options and time lines for achieving those goals. The summary includes highlighted worldwide vacancies that can contribute to each individual's career growth. The meetings will be held in person for the local managers; by teleconference for those not in the office.

15:00: Meetings completed, the HR executive sees a mail icon flashing on the corporate HR issues system map near Thailand. The message from the regional HR manager describes an expatriate pay calculation application that his staff developed on a PC. Expatriate pay calculations for incoming and outgoing employees were previously done manually, but the new application allows the HR manager to input relevant information and automatically calculates a recommended package. The HR executive forwards the message to the electronic mail "node" assigned to expatriate pay, so that HR and line managers around the world can consider using the new application or improve their own.

15:30: Another mail message, this time from the Northeastern U.S. manufacturing group. The group manager is forwarding a copy of her appraisal of HR support for the manufacturing division. It seems the group was considering layoffs due to rising costs. However, their HR representative used the worldwide talent status system to identify units in the Southwestern U.S. and Canada that were searching for the same skills that the Northeastern U.S. group had in surplus supply. They also tapped the electronic mail "node" devoted to sharing strategic staffing issues, and learned of an innovative work-sharing program designed in Mexico City that helped them lower costs without layoffs.

16:00: The "Personal Opportunity" icon is flashing again. The HR executive is one of three finalists for the joint-venture liaison vacancy. A teleconference interview with the other task force selection team is scheduled. The executive opens up the HR "succession planning" application to review the list of successors for his present job. There are three people "ready now" to take the job, and two are listed as available (one in Sydney, Australia, and one in Toulouse, France). The executive reviews the candidates' online files, knowing that the teleconference interview will include a discussion of his replacement.

16:30: The HR issues screen flashes a reminder of a meeting scheduled with the HR Vice President of a major customer who is interested in learning more about the company's global HRIS. A meeting file, including notes on the VP's background and current press coverage of the HR activities in both companies, is automatically printed. The HR executive picks them up on the way out of the office.

REALIZING THE POTENTIAL OF GLOBAL HUMAN RESOURCE INFORMATION SYSTEMS

1995, 2000 or 2020? Surprise. Today's information technology can already support global HR information systems (HRIS) like those depicted in our vignette. Still, while the technology exists and is applied on a piecemeal basis, there are no examples of companies incorporating HRIS seamlessly into the strategic and operational business activities of a global organization. There are many reasons for the limited development of global HRIS. We believe that one of the most important reasons is a lack of vision about the value and power of HRIS to support global business objectives. The primary purpose of this chapter is to begin creating such a vision, by linking ideas about global competitiveness, HR management, and information technology. This linkage suggests the power of global HRIS, and provides a framework for describing and planning future systems. Without such a vision, the time horizon for our scenario may be pushed even beyond 2020.

The linkages we will describe emphasize the importance of three controversies: Convincing key decision makers to invest in HRIS, privacy, and international data transfer. These issues are not necessarily unique to global HRIS, but take on added importance in a global context.

HUMAN RESOURCE MANAGEMENT THAT SUPPORTS GLOBALIZATION

The globalization of a business rarely occurs instantly, but rather proceeds in stages. Pucik (1984) describes a continuum of four transition stages: International division, Global products division, Global-matrix structure, and Global-culture driven structure. The global focus of HR objectives and the associated demands made on HR management increase with each stage. In the international division stage foreign assignments are viewed as an expensive side-track in an individual manager's development, and the role of HR is often simply to facilitate such movements with the least cost. However, in the global-culture stage, building a cadre of executives who naturally think and act to manage global resources is the core of HR's management development activities. HR management must coordinate staffing, development and reward policies to create a synergy that supports an international mind-set.

Although these four evolutionary stages are useful in describing globalization, different business functions evolve at different rates. For example, product marketing may reflect matrix structures, while manufacturing continues to see international operations as separate divisions. Pucik (1992) suggests that companies think about globalization as a final objective, so that each functional area is developing the structures and skills needed to support a fully global organization. Human resource managers must focus on objectives that support the core competencies required by a global organization.

As organizations globalize, they increasingly rely on key core competencies necessary to compete (Prahalad and Hamel, 1990).

These core competencies do not relate to a particular product or market, but rather create the glue that holds the product, market and financial strategies together. They reflect the underlying organizational capabilities necessary to foster growth and innovation. An example is Honda's competence in engine technology leading the company from motorcycles to cars and power products; or ATT's account management skills that allow the company to rapidly enter the credit card business. The challenge is to deploy these capabilities on a global scale.

Like marketing, finance, and manufacturing, HR must set and meet objectives that foster and sustain a competitive global culture. The workforces of many companies are already becoming global. Hewlett Packard opens computer plants in Guadalajara, Mexico; 3M has employees in Bangalore, India; General Electric makes headlamps in Budapest; Quarterdeck employs customer assistants in Limerick, Ireland. Sometimes these arrangements aim to cut costs, but more frequently they reflect the availability of top-notch talent outside of the U.S. (O'Reilly, 1992). Competing with such organizations requires the ability to exploit worldwide labor markets, and to use global human resources more creatively than competitors.

Three core competencies are critical to achieving a global culture in organizations. These competencies define essential goals and standards for HR activities (Pucik, 1992). Table 1 lists the three core global competencies and the HR objectives in each of the major functional role areas of HR management: Organization Design, Staffing and Selection, Performance Appraisal, Rewards, Management Development, and Communication.

The three competencies are continuous improvement, organizational learning, and competitive culture. **Continuous Improvement** reflects the organization's ability to improve existing processes and achieve greater efficiency, so that slack resources are made available without sacrificing competitive position. **Organization Learning** makes use of the slack resources by emphasizing the importance of related but new opportunities to experiment with new markets, and to foster continuous learning. **Competitive Culture** reflects a common set of worldwide organization values: to compete, to be part of a winning team, to strive always to be the best.

In order to deploy and sustain global organizational competencies, HR goals and evaluation criteria must align with the requirements of globalization. For example, to promote global continuous improvement processes, the organization needs to put an emphasis on task forces, teams and inter-unit communication. This means that the ability to "get things done" in a foreign country is a key consideration in international staffing. Allowing international employees to acquire these implementation skills will probably require slower career mobility, performance appraisals that measure cost and quality

HR ROLES	CORE COMPETENCIES		
	CONTINUOUS IMPROVEMENT	ORGANIZATION LEARNING	COMPETITIVE CULTURE
ORGANIZATION DESIGN	Task forces and teams Flexibility	Integrated network	Flat and lean Empowerment
STAFFING AND SELECTION	Implementation skills	Slack resources Organizational competence	Leadership Cross-cultural interactions
PERFORMANCE APPRAISAL	Customer focus Cost/Quality	Teamwork Initiative	Risk taking Values and behavior
REWARD SYSTEM	Process improvement Recognition	Cooperation Information sharing	Global sharing of rewards
MANAGEMENT DEVELOPMENT	Operations Slower mobility	Multifunction and multicountry careers	Socialization Global opportunities
COMMUNICATION	Workshops and conferences	Cross-boundary linkages	Shared mission and culture

Table 1: Three Core Competencies for Global Management and HR Implications

Source: V. Pucik (1992). "Globalization and human resource management," In V. Pucik, N. Tichy, and C. Barnett, *Globalizing Managment: Creating and Leading the Competitive Organization.* Copyright © 1992, John Wiley & Sons. Reprinted by permission.

improvement, and reward systems that recognize the balance between means (the quality of organizational processes) and ends (financial results).

INFORMATION TECHNOLOGY SUPPORTING GLOBAL HUMAN RESOURCE MANAGEMENT

The opening of this chapter illustrated how information technology could help HR support global competition. When talent was needed to staff new initiatives, the organization did not focus on particular jobs, career paths or single-country talent pools. Rather, it used competency-based data to identify appropriate talent everywhere in the world, and then track the movement of that talent to ensure that rewards, training and appraisal support not just performance but also development. The system naturally fosters global cooperation because the underlying data model reflects a global mindset. It also fosters empowerment, by placing the tools for managing human resources in the hands of the managers *and the employees*. For example, when creating an incentive package for international transfers, it is the line managers who use the expatriate compensation calculation program. The program captures the expertise of the managers who had previously developed the calculation, and makes this knowledge accessible to less-experienced managers.

The potential for integration between HR goals and HR information is intriguing. Unfortunately the power of information technology appears to be consistently underutilized in HR management. A recent survey of world-wide executives, consultants and researchers in human resource management (Towers-Perrin, 1992) depicts both the increasing importance and current limitations of human resource information systems (HRIS). The survey identified some benefits of HRIS's that are currently critically important, but offer limited potential for improvement in the next decade, including "lowering administrative costs" and "greater manpower cost control". Other areas had improvement potential, but a relatively low level of current importance, including "improved planning and program development using decision support software," "better understanding of employee attitudes through improved surveys," and "enhanced communication through customized documents, greater use of graphics, touch screens, interactive phone systems, electronic bulletin boards, etc.". The survey also suggested that computer literacy will be a fundamental skill for success among human resource managers in the future, and that human resource information will be made much more available in the future, not only to human resource professionals, but to line managers, executives and employees as well.

The Towers-Perrin study also presents a paradox. When asked to name the largest impediments to achieving the potential of HRIS, the most important impediment named by line executives, consultants and academics was a "lack of applications", and HR managers ranked this impediment second only to "lack of top management support." With thousands of HR software packages on the market, and thousands more internally-developed corporate HRIS systems, how is it that a lack of applications remains an impediment to fulfilling HRIS potential? We believe the key lies in examining the strategic value of existing applications.

Broderick & Boudreau (1992) suggested that the way users interact with HRIS spans a continuum ranging from "Transaction Processing and Reporting/Tracking Systems," which focus primarily on creating administrative efficiencies by cutting the costs of routine calculations and reports; to "Expert Systems" which capture the knowledge and experience of experts through mathematical models or decision rules, and distribute that expertise to other decision makers; to "Decision Support Systems", which provide an unstructured gateway to information, allowing the decision maker to freely explore relationships in an intuitively appealing environment. They reported that the vast majority of HR information applications were devoted to transaction processing and reporting. HR systems that focus too much on cost reductions run the risk of missing key opportunities. Administrative efficiency is important, but global competitiveness also requires improving key decisions, even when that means investing more resources. HR systems must add value, not merely cut costs (Boudreau, 1992). This is especially important in supporting globalization, where unique situations in different nations may make it difficult to achieve the huge economies of scale traditionally available by automating U.S. procedures. Instead, the true payoff from international HRIS may come from sophisticated expert systems and decision support systems.

BEYOND ADMINISTRATION: LINKING GLOBAL HR OBJECTIVES TO INFORMATION TECHNOLOGY

Table 2 links HR functional areas, globally driven HR competencies and specific HRIS applications. The HRIS applications span the range from Transaction Processing to Decision Support Systems. A few examples will illustrate the nature of the relationships.

The Organization Design Role requires creating flexible, flat and team-based structures. This means fewer hierarchical layers devoted to transmitting and amplifying communications across units. Teams and individuals must communicate directly, share goals and

HR Roles	International Objectives	HRIS Implications

Organization Design	Integrated Network
	Flexible Teams
	Flat Structure
	Empowerment
		Electronic Multilingual Communication
		Competency-Based Planning ES for Team
		   Building
		Online HR Information to Non-HR
		   managers
		ES for HR Issues of mergers/acquisition

Staffing and Selection	Efficient
	   Implementation
	Build Organization
	   Competence
	Create Slack for
	   Learning
	Leadership
	Cross-Cultural
	   Connections
		Online Relocation Costs
		Links to External Data
		International Candidate Data Bases
		ES for Competency-Based Selection
		Multimedia Leadership Tests
		Online Archive of Effective HR
		   Across Nations

Performance Assessment	Teamwork
	Initiative
	Customer Focus
	Cost/Quality
	Risk Taking
	Values
		Comprehensive and tiered online MBO
		   tracking
		Online Customer Satisfaction Linked to
		   HR Activities
		ES for Competency-Based Assessments

Reward System	Global Equity
	Recognition of Cross-
	   National Synergy
	Motivating
	   Information Sharing
	Motivating
	   Cooperation
		Calculation of expatriate pay packages
		Tracking international contacts
		Online summary of long-term career and
		   pay relationships

Management Development	Multifunction and
	   Multicountry
	   careers
	Facilitating Learning
	   While Building
	   Operational
	   Credibility
		Online Multi-Country succession data
		base
		Online cost calculations for
		   cross-country movements
		Competency-based Succession planning
		ES for identifying "best" career
		   movements

Communication	Cross-Boundary Links
	Shared
	   mission/culture
	Global Interaction
	   Opportunities
		Global village communications
		Online mission, policy and
		   culture information

Table 2: Links Between HRIS and International Objectives

information, and quickly identify needed talent to achieve their goals. Transaction-Processing applications would include improved multi-lingual communication links, that cut the costs of communicating across boundaries, and online information about the availability, costs, and competencies of human resources across national boundaries. Expert systems might capture the decision rules used by experts to build multi-cultural teams, or to evaluate the value of human resources for mergers and acquisitions. Finally, decision support systems might reflect competencies, rather than jobs or headcount levels. Analysts could examine the relationships between competency levels and regions, workforce demographics, and HR programs. This would help planners ensure that HR programs build competencies to support shared values and flexibility.

The Staffing/Selection Role requires moving employees through the organization in a way that provides cross-cultural learning opportunities, but also places individuals in roles where they can add immediate value. Such movements are a key tool for gaining cross-cultural awareness of innovations. At the Transaction-Processing level, applications that calculate relocation costs or scan international data bases to find candidates meeting certain minimum qualifications can greatly enhance the efficiency of cross-border movements. Multimedia tests of leadership or cultural sensitivity may assist in finding people with the appropriate competencies. An online archive of HR innovations across nations would allow managers to quickly identify when someone else had already invented the "wheel" that they need, and to contact the right people to get it. Expert Systems might capture the decision rules necessary to identify the best candidates from different cultures for assignments to teams or task forces. Decision-support systems could allow planners to project the growth of labor markets and skills under different future conditions, and to assess the potential of new or unknown labor markets.

The Performance Assessment Role requires linking performance to the three core competencies, and providing employees and their managers with tools to effectively track contributions to quality and innovation. Transaction Processing applications would include systems that allow employees to get online explanations of organization and regional goals, and then to link their own personal performance goals directly to them. Drawing on these individual development plans, the HRIS could provide managers at each level with an overall view of goal attainment, and automatically highlight gaps needing attention. Today's computer applications already allow managers to establish goals for their unit, company, or department, and then assign these goals to individuals and teams. A "people-planning" module then assists managers to periodically assess progress, track progress (by coloring goals green for on-track, yellow for behind, and red for critical), document performance discussions, and even suggests rewards for between pay raises, such as sports tickets or dinner for two (Mossberg, 1992). Expert Systems can be constructed to guide international managers as they evaluate performance, and help them record performance achievements in ways that will be useful to others. For example, in a competency-based planning system, appraisals should reflect the development of competencies, as well as the attainment of work goals. An expert system can help managers identify and record the progress of individual competency development. Decision-support systems could support exploring the relationship of goals and goal attainment across regions, teams, and markets. Planners might examine the effects of different performance assessment processes in different countries to determine which is more effective at enhancing critical competencies.

The Reward System Role requires maintaining perceptions of equity at the local and multi-national levels. This role also requires creating reward structures that motivate people to accept mobility opportunities appropriate to building competencies and enhancing cooperation. Transaction Processing applications might include expatriate pay calculators, and programs to track the frequency of contacts between countries. Expert Systems might be constructed to assist managers in linking rewards to competency development. Decision Support Systems could access data on cross-national pay and benefits, categorized by hierarchical level. Analysts could explore whether pay and benefit levels are closely related to changes in critical skills, and whether different reward systems may better motivate desired career paths for building needed skills.

The Management Development Role requires building careers across countries and functions, and creating employees who not only provide strong contributions, but who also get the opportunity for positions where they can learn new cultures or skills. Transaction-Processing systems can calculate the costs of cross-country movements and allow "what-if" analysis to determine how to reduce such costs. Expert Systems can capture the methods used by in-house experts to identify career movements that most efficiently build critical competencies. The example at the beginning of the chapter showed how the HR manager was identified as a candidate for a position that would build financial skills. Decision-Support Systems could provide information on the patterns of movements across work roles and international boundaries. Bottlenecks could be identified where upward movement is impeded by entrenched employees, suggesting the need to provide inducements to remove the blockages.

Finally, the Communication Role requires that the HR function establish cross-boundary linkages, communicate a sense of shared mission, and help units identify opportunities to interact and cooperate. Electronic mail and multimedia communication provide good examples of technology improving transaction processing in this area. Expert Systems can embody the rules used by the best organizational experts in tracking new ideas and worldwide information, to identify what is most relevant to particular units. Recall the example at the beginning of the chapter, in which the HR manager programmed the system to find the latest effects of tax laws and inflation effects on expatriate pay. Such systems can also track innovations from around the world, and alert units in one area to relevant innovations by units in other areas. Decision-Support systems could allow graphical analysis of interactions between teams and nations. These graphs would provide data-based evidence of the formation of alliances, teams and cross-national resource linkages. Where such linkages abound, further investigation might determine the variables that seem to nurture them.

EMERGING CONTROVERSIES AND TRADITIONAL CHALLENGES

The potential for HR systems to enhance global strategic management is clear. The technology to implement these contributions is already available. However, for most organizations, few cross-national data bases exist, little automated communication occurs, and existing systems hinder rather than support the kind of cross-national networks necessary to ensure strategic competitiveness. While there are many challenges to be overcome, we will highlight three: Convincing Key Decision Makers, Privacy and Security, and International Data Transfer.

Convincing Key Decision Makers

Any HR information system requires resource investments, and global HR systems are likely to require even greater resource commitments than traditional single-nation systems. Moreover, because the "clients" for such systems are likely to be nationally diverse and facing very different challenges, it will be even more important to demonstrate added value. HR systems add value in two general ways: Decreasing costs of activities through improved efficiency, and enhancing decisions.

Cutting Administrative Costs

Consider the typical HRIS applications. The first candidates for automation often include: Payroll processing, benefits tracking, job evaluation, applicant tracking, and employee record-keeping. Such applications enhance "administrative efficiency" as they reduce the costs or increase the speed of administrative tasks. They create very real and tangible value for organizations, that can be documented fairly easily. For example, suppose that in the past a regional payroll report was prepared by two people working full-time for two weeks (80 hours), at a pay rate of US $15/hour. The cost of employee time alone for each payroll report produced would be US $1,200. If we have 10 regions for which such reports must be created, the cost is US $12,000 per year. An investment of even US $20,000 to purchase and set up an automated payroll-budget accounting system can easily be justified based on a four-year payback if it cuts the costs by only half. Of course, if the cost cuts are even more dramatic, then the system is even more easily justified. Even a rudimentary estimate of the costs of processing human resource information is often enough to convincingly demonstrate substantial cost savings from more efficient administration of human resource processes. Such applications have become the bread and butter for countless software companies and consultants.

Enhancing Decisions

The value of enhanced decisions is often viewed as difficult to measure and quantify. Yet, we have seen that decision-support frequently holds the key to some of the most innovative and potentially revolutionary HR information system applications. Can we quantify the value of better decisions? The value of information is greatest when:

1. The information improves a large number of decisions.
2. The improved decisions have a large impact on the goals of the organization.
3. The cost of gathering and using the information is kept low.

Consider an automated system to provide job evaluation information to job analysts, designing an international pay structure. Suppose they analyze 100 jobs per year, and of these job evaluations about 20 are incorrect because they are based on outdated or nonexistent information. Suppose an automated system will correct 18 of these 20 wrong evaluations per year. The quantity of corrected decisions (Factor #1) is 18. Further, suppose that when an average job is mis-evaluated, the mistake increases the pay of 10 job incumbents by US $2,000 per year, and it takes two years to discover the mistake. Each mis-evaluated job costs, on average, US $40,000 (that is, 10 employees times US $2,000 times 2 years). The value of correcting each decision (Factor #2 above) is US $40,000. Finally, suppose that automating the current system to improve the 18 decisions will require an up-front cost of US $700,000 plus US $60,000 per year to run the new system. If we evaluate the system over a five-year period, the total cost will be US $1 million (or, US $700,000, plus 5 times US $60,000).

Is automating this job evaluation system worth the US $1 million investment required? The yearly value of the system can be estimated by multiplying the number of corrected decisions in each year by the value of each corrected decision, or a yearly value of US $720,000. Over a five-year period, the new system will provide roughly five times this value, or US $3.6 million dollars, at a cost of US $1 million. This is a substantial return on the automation investment. Of course these numbers can never be estimated precisely, and it's quite likely that the human resource manager who presents such an analysis will be challenged on the "softness" of the estimates. However, the *decision* to invest in automation doesn't depend on the exact figures. In this example, the investment would still pay handsome dividends even if the system cost is substantially higher, or if the number of corrected decisions or the value of each corrected decision is smaller.

International HRIS can add value by correcting many decisions, though each decision has a relatively limited impact. Providing employees with automated information about their benefits, corporate savings accounts, pensions, and payroll through telephone or interactive terminals affects thousands of individual employees, though the effect on each individual employee's decision may be less than one hundred dollars. Or, international HRIS can produce value by correcting a few very strategic decisions. A computerized top-management succession planning system may be used only once or twice per year, but if it produces even one better candidate for a top corporate position, the value may be millions of dollars.

Which Decisions to Enhance?

Broderick and Boudreau (1991) interviewed leading U.S. organizations to find out what worked and what did not work in designing HRIS. They identified four "Dimensions of Computer Use" that reflect attributes of the HRIS itself, including how much data is included, how widely available is the data, how much decision support is provided, and the degree of integration among the different data base components. They also identified three "HR System Characteristics" that reflect the structure and composition of the HRIS staff, the link between the HRIS technology strategy and that of the larger organization, and the impact of the HRIS staff's efforts on the personnel and the culture of the larger organization. Two profiles emerged.

Profile #1, "Centralized Mainframe," included organizations that computerized their HRIS early, when centralized mainframes (very large computers requiring a maintenance staff, climate controls, etc.) were the state-of-the-art. The organizations centralized their HR decisions, so the highest value-added for HRIS was in processing large amounts of data for a relatively few high-level executives, and efficiently accomplishing administrative tasks. In terms of the two aspects of information value, such systems support a few decisions, but each decision has very large consequences for the organization. Thus, Profile #1 systems typically contained comprehensive data, were available to both HR and Non-HR users at the corporate level, focused mainly on administrative decisions and top-management support, and were integrated on a large centralized computer. The HRIS groups in Profile #1 were situated at the corporate headquarters, and had strong links to the organization's information systems group and formal links to the organization's existing technology base.   Because the corporate staffs generally pre-approved the system, there was little effort devoted to trying to build enthusiasm or skills among the HR managers in the organization. Central staffs usually handle the day-to-day computer work, and the corporate HR decision makers request analysis from these staffs.

Profile #2, "Decentralized PC-Based," described organizations where the key HR decisions were made at each individual business unit (such as a division or even a single marketing region or manufacturing plant). Here, the HRIS created value by allowing users to develop applications for their own units, even if such applications don't apply to every other unit in the organization—and even if top management doesn't use them. Organizations following this profile had many separate data bases, each designed to support a particular unit's needs, or even a single HR activity within a unit. Data availability was limited. Most people had a PC, but had access only to the data bases and applications created for their unit. The decisions supported by the applications ranged from simple transaction-processing to sophisticated expert systems. Some units concentrated on administrative support and gap analysis, while others experimented with expert systems and data excursions. It depends on what the unit needed and was willing to pay for. The applications typically stood alone, and were often not tied together in any way, certainly not through a centralized data base. Support for the HRIS consisted mainly of HRIS "experts" within each unit, usually people with HR backgrounds who have learned how to use PC's. There were few formal links between units' technologies and the organization's overall technology base. Some units used Apple computers, some IBM's, and some use workstations. Finally, Profile Two organizations spent more resources building enthusiasm and support for computer systems.

The interviews revealed a third emerging profile, that attempted to build the best of both worlds. In Profile #3, a core set of HR data, common to all unit data bases, is available to all units and can be aggregated by corporate decision makers to track overall strategic trends. Yet, each unit is also free to develop additional data elements and applications, which can be shared with other units via a client-server system. HR data resides not on a central computer, but within the combination of linked systems across different units. Both Profile #1 and Profile #2 organizations were evolving to this new paradigm. Profile #1 organizations were frustrated by the limited use being made of their large and fertile data bases, and by the lack of enthusiasm for computer systems among business-unit HR managers. They were reaching out to make access easier for employees and HR managers in the business units, and encouraging more HR managers to develop their own ways to use HR data. Profile #2 organizations were frustrated by the lack of coordination, the tendency to reinvent the wheel across units, and the inability to pull all the data together. So, while preserving unit independence, they were encouraging units to link together, and to adopt data standards that would allow more sharing across units. The corporate HRIS staff was taking on a stronger role in coordinating cross-unit efforts, and in training and motivating HR professionals to support the new system. This client-server profile would have been impossible ten years ago, but recent advances in computer networks and user-friendly software now allow organizations to adopt this profile.

It seems possible that we will see these three profiles emerge among international organizations. To fully implement the global matrix culture will require systems designs that resemble the Client-Server Profile, but it may be necessary first to build systems resembling Profiles #1 or #2. Organizations whose international structures reflect centralized control may tend toward the characteristics of the "Centralized Mainframe" profile. Those that have evolved to have fairly independent units may find the "Decentralized PC-Based" Profile to be the appropriate starting point. In any case, the value of the system must be measured according to its proven ability to enhance decisions that lead to improving the core competencies of the organization.

Privacy and Security

While the benefits of ready access to computerized HR information are often compelling, this technology creates new obligations and responsibilities for the HR professional. The data stored on computerized systems is often confidential and private and should be accessible only to approved individuals under controlled conditions. When HR data resided on mainframes, controlling access was somewhat easier. Cumbersome access procedures, for all their disadvantages, served to reduce the chance that unauthorized persons could see the data. Today, even a novice computer user may combine information in ways no one anticipated. For example, information on marital status, medical claim history, and age might be used to identify potential AIDS victims. Because HR professionals increasingly lead the development of HRIS, they will undoubtedly be expected to shoulder the responsibility for achieving equity objectives by ensuring the privacy of personal information, and access to that information only by those with a legitimate need to know. A Louis Harris poll in 1990 showed that 79% of U.S. citizens believe that privacy ranks with life, liberty and happiness as a fundamental right (Amidon, 1992). To enhance privacy, consultants recommend attention to: *Management considerations*, such as who is authorized to use PCs, user training, inventories of equipment, and procedures for special events like power outages; *Physical security*, such as access to PC areas, diskette handling, and secure housekeeping; and *Information Security*, such as locking diskettes and hard drives, documenting PC applications, back-up procedures and network safety precautions (Adams, 1992; Harris, 1987).

Of course, even privacy can be taken to extremes. One Australian HR manager tells of a long and drawn-out meeting in which several of the organization's technical computer staff stubbornly insisted on very costly and restrictive security procedures as a prerequisite to approving a new HRIS. The HR professionals suggested that more modest security might be adequate. To illustrate their point, the HR professionals escorted the technical staff into a public hallway lined with unlocked filing cabinets containing the paper HR records the new system was designed to replace. Sometimes, even moderately secure PC systems can improve security over the status quo.

International Data Transfer

Organizations with operations in multiple countries could use the power of HRIS to better coordinate HR programs, identify talent across national boundaries, facilitate cross-national learning, and more effectively track and manage the quality and quantity of the multi-national workforce. All of this presumes that the data an organization produces on its employees can be communicated across national boundaries. This ability may be severely restricted by the privacy initiatives proposed by the European Community (EC) Council Directives introduced in 1990. The guidelines require that any organization communicating data must notify the subject of the data and the supervisory authority of the country, and cease the communication if the subject objects. This includes the personnel records of employees. If the country receiving the data (such as the U.S.) does not have privacy protection deemed adequate, it may have to negotiate with an EC commission (Amidon, 1992). Implementation of these guidelines is far from imminent, but HR managers must monitor such developments or risk losing access to key information resources.

CONCLUSIONS

The future is possible now. The information structures and applications discussed here are technologically feasible. Undoubtedly, organizations are even now at various stages of making this vision a reality. In this chapter we have endeavored to show how the core competencies necessary for globalization can be enhanced by human resource information systems that focus not only on improving transaction efficiency, but on enhancing key decisions. This framework provides the basis for identifying and classifying HR system applications according to the functions they support, and they nature of the value they add. A fundamental proposition of this chapter is that organizations will prosper by using this framework to pinpoint the areas of greatest potential. To date, it appears that most organizations have focused heavily on incremental changes designed to cut costs, enhance administration, and support a single-nation strategy. Our hope is that the frameworks outlined here will motivate managers, researchers, and planners to think beyond the short-term, and begin devising systems that live up to their potential.

REFERENCES

Adams, L. E. (1992). Securing your HRIS in a microcomputer environment, *HRMagazine*, February, pp. 56-61.

Amidon, P. (1992). Widening privacy concerns, *ONLINE*, July, 64.

Boudreau, J. W. (1992). HRIS: Adding value or just cutting costs? *HR Monthly*. May, 8-13.

Broderick R. & Boudreau, J. W. (1991). The evolution of computer use in human resource management: Interviews with ten leaders. *Human Resource Management Journal, 30* (4), 485-508.

Broderick, R. & Boudreau, J. W. (1992). Human resource management, information technology, and the competitive edge. *Academy of Management Executive.* 6, May, 7-17.

Harris, D. (1987). A matter of privacy: Managing personal data in company computers, *Personnel,* February, 34-43.

Mossberg, W. S. (1992). Personal technology: PC program lets machines help bosses manage people", *The Wall Street Journal,* December 24, 7.

O'Reilly, B. (1992). Your new global workforce, *Fortune,* December 14, 52-66.

Prahalad, C. K. & Hamel, G. (1990). The core competencies of the corporation, *Harvard Business Review*, May-June, 79-91.

Pucik, V. (1984). The international management of human resources, Chapter 23 in Fombrun, C., Tichy, N.M., & Devanna, M.A. (eds.), *Strategic Human Resource Management*, New York: John Wiley & Sons.

Pucik, V. (1992). "Globalization and human resource management", In V. Pucik, N. Tichy, and C. Barnett, *Globalizing Management: Creating and Leading the Competitive Organization*, New York: John Wiley & Sons.

Towers-Perrin (1992). *Priorities for Competitive Advantage*, New York: Towers-Perrin, Inc.

CHAPTER 22

The Design and Development of Modules for an International Human Resource Information System (HRIS)

J. KLINE HARRISON
Wake Forest University

P. CANDACE DEANS
Wake Forest University

Despite the increasing reliance on information systems in Human Resource Management, only recently have these systems been extended to include the international component. These extensions are timely given the increased emphasis on global competition and the need for integration of applications across national boundaries.

In this chapter, an initial review of the current state-of-the-art in development of human resource modules to support the firm's human resource information system (HRIS) is provided. Key international modules are identified and extended to include necessary information requirements to support the unique decision making processes of multinational firms coordinating human resource (HR) activities for non-U.S. operations. A modular approach to implementation allows for flexibility in the design of the firm's international human resource information system (IHRIS). The organization structure, policies, programs and philosophy will dictate the most appropriate system design to effectively meet the needs of the organization and its end users.

INTRODUCTION

The last decade has witnessed significant changes in the field of Human Resources Management (HRM). Perhaps the most significant change has been the development of Human Resource Information Systems (HRIS) (Kavanaugh, 1990) to support the decision making processes of the human resource (HR) function. For multinational firms, the demands of managing in the international operating environment have enhanced the need for increased coordination and integration of all business activities (Bartlett & Ghoshal, 1988) including human resources. As a result, firms are looking to information technology applications to provide solutions for worldwide managerial challenges in order to remain competitive globally.

An international human resource information system (IHRIS) should be viewed as an extension of the firm's domestic (U.S.) HRIS and is designed to identify and integrate pertinent human resource information across national boundaries. HRIS systems are typically designed using a modular approach in which each module supports a specific HR function (e.g., payroll, recruitment, benefits). International modules may, likewise, be developed and incorporated selectively in a manner that best supports the needs of the organization and conforms to the firm's resource constraints.

The development of an IHRIS that supports the information needs and decision processes of international HR management is clearly a difficult and challenging task. The IHRIS incorporates unique data needs and information requirements that reflect government regulations, legal restrictions and reporting requirements that may vary from one country to another. Design, development and implementation will certainly be met with additional complexities and obstacles in an international environment. Firms that are successful in developing an effective IHRIS will be building an information resource that will strengthen their position in the global marketplace and possibly provide the firm with a competitive advantage.

In this chapter, the development of modules that incorporate the unique information requirements for international HR management is proposed as one means by which to design an IHRIS. The contribution of this work is in the identification of these key modules and their corresponding international information requirements. Clearly, implementation barriers will impede the process, but progress can only be made when companies take the initial steps to respond to the changing needs of organizations that are becoming increasingly information-based.

The primary objectives of this chapter are threefold: 1) to provide a basic background understanding of the development of information systems that support the firm's HR function; 2) identify international HR modules and unique information requirements specific to the firm's international operations; and 3) discuss the resulting challenges and benefits for IHRIS implementation.

BACKGROUND

Given the dramatic trend in globalization of business, it has become increasingly imperative that organizations engage in Human Resources Management (HRM) on an international scale. Decisions must be made concerning (1) the numbers and proportions of host-country nationals and expatriates in staffing organizations through-out the world; (2) where and how to recruit these individuals and how to compensate them; and (3) whether personnel practices will be uniform across all locations or tailored to specific locales (Dowling and Schuler, 1990).

Based on the literature citing similarities and differences between international and domestic HRM, several differentiating factors have been identified. According to Dowling and Schuler (1990), these factors include:

1) International HRM departments must engage in more activities than in a domestic environment such as international taxation, international relocation and orientation, administrative services for expatriates, and host government relations.
2) International HR managers design and administer programs for more that one national group of employees.
3) For the selection, training, and effective management of expatriate employees, a greater degree of involvement in employees' personal lives is necessary.
4) The human and financial consequences of failure in the international arena frequently are more severe than in domestic business.
5) International HRM must contend with more external influences such as the type of government, the state of the economy, and the generally accepted practices of doing business in each of the host countries in which the business operates.

A key building block in the foundation of all human resource activities, domestic or international, lies in the effective development of a HRIS. A HRIS is defined as a systematic procedure for collecting, storing, maintaining, retrieving, and validating certain data needed by an organization regarding its human resources, personnel activities, and organization unit characteristics (Walker, 1982; Milkovich and Glueck, 1985). The focus of HRIS may be "to facilitate or support strategic, tactical, and operational decision making (e.g., to compare compensation strategy alternatives), to avoid litigations (e.g., to identify discrimination patterns), to evaluate programs, policies, or practices (e.g., to monitor the cost of sick leave policy), and/or to support daily operations (e.g., to remind of pay increases and to ensure employees are paid on time)" (Kavanagh et al., 1990).

Unfortunately, surveys indicate that a large number of companies and public agencies, particularly those of medium size, have yet to install HR computer systems. According to Kavanagh et al. (1990), the primary reasons for the slowness of HR departments to adopt HRIS are:

1) Lack of support by top management.
2) Many HR managers are satisfied with the status quo.
3) Some HR managers are defensive about revealing their operations.
4) Most HR managers are poorly prepared to develop and implement an HRIS because they lack appropriate knowledge and skills.

These problems become even more complex as one moves to the international realm. Multinational firms are just beginning to address the issues associated with the development of human resource information systems that support business activities on a worldwide scale.

From a broad perspective, U.S.-based multinational companies face many unique obstacles in the development and implementation of international information systems. Currently, the most pressing problems are technological in nature and relate to the firm's efforts to develop an integrated worldwide technological infrastructure. The proliferation of products, multiple vendors, and rapid changes in technology all complicate the integration of technology and the implementation of applications across nations (Deans and Kane, 1992).

The importance of designing and implementing an effective international HRIS can be seen from four primary perspectives:

1) MNCs have additional information requirements regarding HRM not necessary in domestic organizations (Dowling and Schuler, 1990). For example, identifying cross-cultural training needs is an additional requirement.
2) The data collected by MNCs varies in terms of measurement units and therefore, must be converted into appropriate units by managers in the home country (Asheghian and Ebrahimi, 1990). For example, differences in currency units affect wage administration.
3) The application of data must be tailored to specific locations (Harris and Moran, 1987). For example, staffing formulas for forecasting HR supply may be inappropriate for some cultures.

4) HRM must maintain a proactive role in the strategic management of MNCs (Lorange, 1986). For example, projected head counts and payroll costs may be solicited by top management for consideration of multinational expansion.

The increased role of human resources in international management, globalization of markets and organizations, and technological advancements provide MNCs with little choice but to develop an IHRIS for information flows. Those that do not respond to these changes may loose their competitive position.

DESIGNING IHRIS MODULES

The design of modules to support a specific HR function, typical of most HRISs to date (Sept, Westmacott, Agocs, and Suttie, 1989) is likewise, highly appropriate for an IHRIS because it allows for the incremental development of modules as the need arises and resources permit. As multinational organizations begin to expand their HRIS to include an international component, certain functions will need more immediate attention. For example, modules involving compensation and payroll may take precedence over modules on recruiting and applicant tracking because of the more immediate impact they have on both human and financial resources. Furthermore, as the efficient use of financial resources becomes more imperative in the world economy, the incremental development of IHRIS modules must be applied in areas that show immediate returns to the overall organization such as the more effective administration of compensation and payroll.

A variety of IHRIS modules can be developed by a multinational organization. There is no proper set to be used because each IHRIS should be tailored to meet the needs of the firm. Depending on the organizational structure, policies, programs, or philosophy, the IHRIS should be designed to best correspond to both the organization and the users.

Typical modules in a domestic HRIS include (Ceriello, 1991; Gallagher, 1991; Kavanagh et al., 1990):

Applicant tracking	Attendance
Basic employee information	Benefits
Career development/planning	Compensation
Employee/labor relations	EEO/AA
Health and safety	HR planning
Job descriptions	Medical records
Payroll	Pension administration
Performance management	Position control
Recruitment	Training and development

Of these modules, twelve are considered predominant based on applications in operation at a variety of companies, vendor products, prototypes, and expert suggestions (Kavanagh et. al., 1990). These twelve modules are described in the following sections along with their relevance in an international context.

Basic Employee Information Module. This module is used to maintain a profile of employees within the firm. Information provided in this module includes personal facts such as name, date of birth, social security number, address, phone number, gender, marital status, and next of kin. In addition, employment data such as job information (level, title, division), hire date, employment status (full-time, part-time, on leave), and wage level is included. Citizenship status is also necessary because Federal law mandates that employers verify that employees have a legal right to work in the U.S. (Ceriello, 1991). Furthermore, security clearance can be an important information element given the increasing security-level work required within many organizations. The basic employee information module is always a module in a HRIS and often the first one developed because it serves as the core of the overall system (Kavanagh et al, 1990). Information provided in this module is often used as component data in other modules. To maintain this module, data is collected during the hiring process and then updated throughout the employee's tenure.

In developing an IHRIS, this module is particularly important for accurate data on expatriates. Not only should it be the first module developed, it also should be verified frequently for several reasons. Given the geographic separation between the expatriates and their home office, information such as next of kin and home telephone number becomes more vital for emergency situations. Also, citizenship status and security clearance become increasingly important on an international scale. Finally, additional elements might be included for international operations such as fluency in foreign language and experiences (e.g., travel or residency) in different cultures.

Applicant Tracking Module. The applicant tracking module is used to identify applicants who qualify for job openings, to identify job openings for which people can apply, and to provide support for EEO/AA compliance (Kavanagh et al, 1990). A basic data element in this module is whether the individual is an internal or external applicant. Necessary information on internal applicants is retrieved from their basic employee information file. For external applicants, data must be input. This data includes name, address, gender, ethnic category, and phone number. Although gender and ethnicity cannot be used in hiring decisions, it is necessary for EEO/AA compliance.

In addition to this basic information, source codes and occupation codes also are included (Gallagher, 1991). The former relates to how the application arose (e.g., advertisement or referral) and the latter to occupation classifications within the organization to which the individual is applying. Finally, application status is a necessary data element. This element includes actions taken (such as testing and interviews scheduled or conducted) and decisions made (e.g., applicant rejected, offer made, offer rejected) (Ceriello, 1991).

If an external applicant becomes an employee of the organization, the data collected in the applicant tracking module feeds the basic employee information module. Furthermore, this module often shares data elements with an EEO/AA or a recruiting module and is frequently incorporated with one of the two depending on the organization (Kavanagh et al, 1990).

Application of this module in an IHRIS is important from three primary perspectives. From an employee selection perspective, it enables the MNC to identify applicants who may be most appropriate for an international assignment. By enhancing the application process to include information on international skills and interests, the MNC can identify and select valuable employees. From a recruitment perspective, it identifies job opportunities in different cultures that may be of interest to applicants. By expanding the data base to include opportunities abroad, the MNC may develop a larger pool of candidates from which to choose. Finally, from an EEO/AA perspective, this module ensures that applicants have equal opportunity in international assignments as well as domestic openings.

Recruiting Module. As mentioned previously, the recruiting module is closely associated with the applicant tracking module and is sometimes combined with it. The primary distinction with this module however, is that it tracks recruiting costs and analyzes recruiting-source effectiveness.

Recruitment sources include newspaper ads, trade journals, job fairs, college placement services, agency referrals, and current employees. With most of these sources comes an associated cost (e.g., the fee for a newspaper ad). Furthermore, some of these sources tend to be more effective for some jobs and organizations than others. By maintaining records of these sources, the organization can assess the effectiveness of the various media. For example, if certain newspapers are attracting primarily unqualified candidates, the organization can drop those publications. Conversely, if certain college placement services tend to provide candidates that become high job performers, the organization can allocate more resources or expand quotas for these colleges.

The degree of importance that a recruiting module has in a HRIS is related to the level of recruitment, the response to recruitment efforts in terms of the number of applicants, and the level of internal staff movement (Gallagher, 1991). As the level of recruitment activity and responses increases, the need for information management also increases. Therefore, this module can, not only determine the effectiveness of recruiting efforts, but also streamline the corresponding administrative procedures.

From an international perspective, as global expansion continues to escalate, qualified employees will increase in value. Therefore, recruitment will become increasingly important as MNCs try to attract and hire those individuals. Efforts to determine the effectiveness of these recruiting efforts will be imperative, thus making this module more essential. Furthermore, as the scope of recruitment efforts increases along with global expansion, recruitment costs must be monitored to ensure effectiveness from this standpoint as well.

EEO/AA Module. A major part of the EEO/AA module is report creation (Ceriello, 1991). This module monitors the hiring, promotion, and firing patterns of an organization in order to ensure compliance with EEO/AA guidelines and provide necessary reports to federal agencies. Because of the extensive data maintenance, manipulation, analysis, and reporting associated with EEO/AA activities, this module is a crucial element in a HRIS (Kavanaugh et al, 1990).

The EEO/AA module receives virtually all of its data from other HRIS modules such as basic employee information, applicant tracking, payroll, compensation, and training (Ceriello, 1991). In addition to employee demographics (from the basic employee information module) and the number and type of applicants for each job (from the applicant tracking module), every promotion, demotion, and termination must be recorded. Also, the federal government has established twelve job categories into which each job in an organization must be placed for filing standard EEO reports. As a result, job information must be maintained regarding the appropriate category for each job.

At first glance it may seem that an EEO/AA module is irrelevant for international operations, however, these issues must be addressed for employees in all employee locations. This module is important not only for domestic compliance with EEO/AA, but also for relevant laws in host cultures. Whereas the United States has one comprehensive statute (Title VII of the Civil Right Act of 1964) to cover most EEO situations, many other countries have separate laws to cover different types of discrimination such as racial or sex discrimination, still other countries have little or no EEO legislation (Dowling and Schuler, 1990).

Therefore, from an international perspective, the value of an EEO/AA module is twofold. First, it provides necessary reports to ensure compliance regarding expatriate opportunities and actions. Second, it provides accountability for the MNC in complying with the laws of its host culture.

Position Control Module. The position control module enables an organization to track its job positions for purposes of monitoring, budgeting, planning, and control. It involves identifying the types of jobs that are performed in the organization, how many people perform these jobs, and at what level or range of pay (Ceriello, 1991).

More specifically, characteristics about positions (e.g., title, salary, skill requirements, level, and location) are maintained, with each position being assigned a code. Also, the status (e.g., vacant, filled, frozen, or planned) of each position is monitored. Finally, for planning purposes, similar positions across departments are compared, variances between authorized and actual staffing are examined, and previous, current, and projected position budgets are compared (Kavanagh et al, 1990).

By identifying each job and each position within an organization, the position control module enables the firm to better define its internal structure. Moreover, it aids the organization in developing realistic budgets and controlling salary costs (Ceriello, 1991).

The most prevalent use of this module has been in the public sector where budgets and authorized head counts are tightly controlled. Nevertheless, firms in the private sector can use the position control module to resolve anomalies in organizational structure and improve administration of fiscal operation (Ceriello, 1991).

As the number and type of jobs increase when organizations expand globally, the need for effective tracking of positions also increases. The position control module enables MNCs to remain fiscally responsible as well as cope with the complexity of a multitude of positions worldwide.

Although this module has been most prevalent in the public sector, it can benefit the MNC in several areas. Primarily, the module can aid the organization in maintaining an appropriate global structure as well as controlling transnational financial resources. In addition, it can feed the recruiting module by identifying positions abroad that need to be filled and that may be of interest to prospective expatriates. Furthermore, this module enables MNCs to ensure comparability of jobs across national boundaries for employees making transitions.

Performance Management Module. The basic purpose of the performance management module is to monitor or track employee performance. In addition, it can be designed to list forthcoming performance reviews and record key performance events. Furthermore, data on employee performance enables the organization to identify trends in ratings by manager, job type, or department (Kavanagh et al, 1990).

Because the performance management area is very comprehensive, a module in this area includes such elements as performance appraisal, unit productivity, time and attendance, discipline, and grievances. Performance appraisal is an evaluation of employee performance according to standards established in the job descriptions and is important for administrative and motivational purposes. Unit productivity is an evaluation of unit performance according to organizational expectations and is used for comparison among units. The time and attendance element is a record for all employees which is used for pay and disciplinary purposes. The discipline element identifies established procedures, thus guiding managers through appropriate steps and ensuring that actions are recorded. Lastly, the grievance element identifies appropriate procedures for employees to follow in filing a grievance (Kavanagh et al, 1990).

On an international scale, the performance management module can be important from two basic perspectives. From a corporate management perspective, it allows top management to look at such trends as expatriate managers' ratings of host country employees compared to expatriate employees, and the performance of similar units in one country compared to another country. From an expatriate manager's perspective, this module can aid, not only in conducting performance appraisals for host country and expatriate employees, but also in ensuring that relevant cultural constraints are incorporated into disciplinary and grievance procedures to avoid costly mistakes.

Compensation Module. The compensation module is basically used to monitor compensation costs, policies, and programs as well as ensure legal compliance, develop salary structures, and support future compensation decisions. Furthermore, it enables the organization to make comparisons across jobs and with other companies, thus providing useful information for maintaining internal and external pay equity (Kavanagh et al, 1990).

Data elements included in this module are salary, bonus, employee type, data of last raise, hours worked, deductions, and tax status. In addition to this data, the module must interface with the payroll, benefits, and basic employee information modules in order to generate the information and reports needed by the organization (Kavanagh et al, 1990). Because compensation data involves dollar amounts, improvements in speed and accuracy through HRIS can improve organizational productivity and reduce potential sources of error (Ceriello, 1991). As a result, the compensation module is one of the most common and general HRIS applications (Kavanagh et al, 1990).

When designing this fundamental module for an IHRIS, special forms of compensation associated with expatriates must be included among the data elements. These special forms include home leave travel pay, hardship pay, special duty pay, car allowance, and servant reimbursement (Ceriello, 1991).

After tailoring the compensation module to address these special forms of compensation, its application can have significant benefits to the MNC. It enables the organization to ensure comparability in compensation with other MNCs and thus, remain competitive for qualified employees. It also helps the organization maintain internal equity across expatriate jobs. Finally, this module enables the MNC to administer or use financial resources efficiently, which is imperative in global expansion.

Payroll Module. The purpose of the payroll module is to calculate gross-to-net pay based on wage and salary policies and procedures, taxes, and other deductions (Ceriello, 1991). This module is used therefore, to verify hours worked, tax calculations and other deductions, payroll budgets, filing of state and federal reports, and compliance with company policies.

Because payroll must be accurate and timely, a HRIS can aid in the process. These two functions however, have traditionally operated independently. Nevertheless, they can be linked in either an interfaced system or an integrated system. The former provides a regular link between payroll and HRIS whereas the latter incorporates both into a single system. The trend in companies is towards an integrated system in order to streamline operations and manage information needs (Kavanagh et al, 1990).

Elements of the module consist of data included in several other modules. The basic employee information module provides the employee's name, address, social security number, employee category, and employee status. The compensation module provides data on pay type, pay rate, and pay frequency. Data on employee contributions for benefits come from the benefits module and the time and attendance is obtained from the performance management module. The payroll module supplements this existing data with taxes and other deductions in order to calculate gross-to-net pay.

This module has important implications for a MNC for two basic reasons. When operating in a foreign country, an organization must contend with host country taxes. Not only must the firm determine the appropriate taxation for its expatriates, it must also address tax protection or tax equalization for these individuals. Moreover, the MNC must contend with currency fluctuations in paying salaries to expatriates (who are not paid in their home currency) as well as to host country employees. Because of these complexities, a payroll module can aid significantly in the accurate and timely administration of a MNC's pay administration.

Benefits Module. The benefits module is used to ensure compliance with legislative requirements, administer programs and traditional benefits, provide advice on benefits choices, and monitor costs. The various benefits offered by employers can be divided into five broad categories: mandatory benefits (social security, unemployment insurance, and workers' compensation), pension plans (contributory and noncontributory), insurance protection (health, life, and accident disability), paid time off (holidays, vacation time, and sick leave), and employee services (educational assistance, parental leave, and child care).

As with compensation, benefits are one of the areas in HR of greatest expense to organizations (Ceriello, 1991). For example, benefits costs as a percentage of payroll are about 39 per cent (Dessler, 1991). Furthermore, this functional area involves a massive amount of paperwork and record keeping. Therefore, a benefits module enables the organization to, not only better process the quantity of information, but also maintain more accurate monitoring of expenses in order to effectively contain costs.

The application of a benefits module involves interfacing with other modules such as basic employee information and payroll. Additional data that must be maintained are benefits elections (e.g., various insurances, level of coverage, and optional policies), notification dates, employment history, dependent information, pension and deferred compensation agreements, pension status (e.g., vesting), and miscellaneous benefits (e.g., discounts, memberships, and company car usage) (Kavanagh et al., 1990).

A benefits module is important for MNCs because they must cope with a complicated set of benefits tasks. For example, because the level of state-provided health care programs varies from one country to another, employees working in countries without government health programs need different coverage than those in countries with state support. Furthermore, tax laws and retirement fund regulations vary among countries, thus necessitating separate retirement benefits for host country employees who pay taxes in that country (Ceriello, 1991). As a result, a benefits module can facilitate the management of such complexities.

Training Module. The training module is used to track the training experiences of employees, to identify training courses available, and to maintain training costs, enrollment figures, and training evaluation data. With this module, management can determine who received certain types of training, their performance improvement (if any), specific courses they completed, and when and where they received the training (Ceriello, 1991).

The advantages of incorporating the training module into a HRIS, beyond easier tracking and scheduling of courses and participants, include better matching of employees with appropriate training and easier generation of an employee's training history (Ceriello, 1991). Furthermore, this module provides more accurate information retrieval of training results. Management can identify the most cost effective and popular courses, as well as target those courses needing improvement based on course evaluations (Kavanagh et al.,

1990).

From an international perspective, research indicates that training can significantly improve the adjustment and performance of expatriates (Black and Mendenhall, 1989). Therefore, MNCs should track which expatriates have received training, how they subsequently performed, and which courses proved most effective. Unfortunately, cross-cultural training with MNCs is very limited (Black, Mendenhall, & Oddou, 1991). The most prevalent reason given for this lack of training is that top management considers it unnecessary or ineffective (Black and Mendenhall, 1989). Therefore, a training module in an IHRIS can be used to support the proliferation of cross-cultural training, in addition to tracking trainee and course effectiveness.

Career Development/Skill Inventory Module. The purpose of the career development/skill inventory (CD/SI) module is to provide advice regarding career opportunities and to suggest career development activities for employees. It combines data from the basic employee information and performance management modules with additional data listing the skills, experiences, interests, and aspirations of employees.

This module can produce a career development plan listing target positions, a career profile describing individual employees, a potential candidates report identifying high-potential employees, and a skills retrieval report indicating employees with specified skills. Furthermore, a comprehensive CD/SI module can help an organization plan for expansion or reorganization, succession planning, and other training and development needs (Ceriello, 1991).

The importance of this module can be seen from two perspectives. From an organizational perspective, it can be used for internal movement of employees, thereby avoiding costs associated with external hiring. From the employees' perspective, it enables them to see exactly where they can expect to progress within the organization (Kavanaugh et al., 1990).

As part of an IHRIS, the CD/SI module can identify employees who are qualified and interested in international careers, as well as those fluent in foreign languages. It can also provide prospective expatriates with a listing of available positions which they might target in other countries. As a result, it can minimize costs for the MNC in seeking candidates from external sources. Furthermore, as many organizations expand and reorganize in order to pursue global opportunities, this module can facilitate staffing plans and requirements.

Human Resource Planning Module. The human resource planning module is used to estimate future labor supply and demand by analyzing current staffing levels, skill mixes, turnover, promotions, and other employee movements. It attempts to identify and implement appropriate activities that ensure HR is supporting the organization's mission (Kavanagh et al., 1990).

In addition to drawing data from the basic employee information, applicant tracking, compensation, and benefits modules, the human resource planning module uses data from external sources, such as unemployment rates, economic forecasts, and labor market statistics. Nevertheless, this module focuses more on manipulating data rather than accumulating it (Ceriello, 1991).

Some common applications of this module include labor relations planning, personnel planning, organizational charting, turnover analysis, and succession planning. For example, these applications can help the organization determine if there are gaps or surpluses in staffing (e.g., too many middle managers), if corporate policies are being followed (e.g., hiring from within), and if newly implemented programs are effective (e.g., a turnover reduction program) (Kavanagh et al., 1990).

These types of planning activities play a key role in the success of MNCs. Unfortunately, the contributions of HR in corporate strategic planning are often very limited (Fombrun and Tichy, 1984). This is unfortunate given the interdependence of HR with other functional areas. Nevertheless, by incorporating a human resources planning module into a IHRIS, HR can enhance the significance of its contributions and provide substantive support for its greater inclusion in the corporate planning process.

IMPLEMENTATION ISSUES

Many of the obstacles relevant to the development and implementation of corporate-wide international information systems will also be relevant to the development of information subsystems within the organization. The problems may be more pronounced for functions such as HRM. For example, the nature of much of the data that is transferred through the IHRIS is name-linked and this has been known to cause particular problems for MNCs operating in some countries (Kane and Ricks, 1989). An array of issues both technical and managerial may complicate the development and implementation of the firm's IHRIS.

Technical Issues

Deans et al. (1991) identified many technological issues that currently pose problems for MNCs when implementing information systems outside U.S. borders. The lack of global standards for telecommunications is a significant factor hindering the development of global information systems. Another major obstacle lies in the restrictive policies imposed by the Postal, Telephone and Tele-graph (PTTs) companies in other countries. In effect, the PTTs make it very difficult for foreign MNCs to compete in local markets. Restrictions range from prohibiting certain types of equipment in the country to imposing excessive tariffs for a variety of communication services. The available telecommunications infrastructure in some countries will limit the available technological alternatives. In addition, the availability of vendors and service quality is limited in some foreign locations. Data security also becomes increasingly important as more information is transmitted over shared lines.

Transborder data flow restrictions may pose particular problems for the implementation of an IHRIS due to the nature of the data being transferred. Many countries have established legislative restrictions on the transfer of data from one country to another. Privacy protection is one of the major reasons for legislation in many countries. In these countries name-linked data is not permitted to leave the country. Although currently most MNCs do not perceive this issue to be a pressing problem, that could change if substantial amounts of name-linked data are being transferred via databases across national boundaries.

Managerial Issues

There are also an array of managerial issues that add to the complexities of implementing international information systems (Deans et al., 1991). As companies become more familiar with the technology and begin to overcome some of the technical barriers, managerial and control issues tend to take on added significance. Cultural constraints and language barriers must be considered when implementing or transferring any technology internationally. It will be necessary, for example, to print reports and other output from the IHRIS in the native language. These added complexities will increase cost structures and place added constraints on systems development and implementation. End-user computing may also become a significant issue for the implementation of IHRIS. If name-linked data cannot leave the country it may be necessary to decentralize data processing in that country and delegate more responsibility and control to local employees and expatriates in that country. These issues will surface as more companies set up IHRIS systems to meet the needs of their foreign subsidiary operations.

Software development for international systems will clearly become more complex as additional variables and information gathering and reporting requirements come into play. Standardization of software applications will also depend on many of these aforementioned factors.

Education and support of top level management will become even more significant in an international context. This support will be of utmost importance for the allocation of resources to successfully implement an IHRIS. Many unforeseen obstacles are likely not yet even apparent. As companies accept the challenges and risks of new endeavors they pave the way for future success for all involved.

Organizational Issues

There are a number of organizational characteristics that will clearly play a part in the difficulty a firm may encounter in the process of implementing an IHRIS. Specifically, other studies (Deans and Ricks, 1993) suggest several moderating variables that may play an important role in this context. In particular, the number of foreign subsidiaries, the location of those subsidiaries and the number of countries in which the firm does business will influence the importance of various obstacles and barriers to implementation of IHRIS.

Additional factors such as international business experience and experience with the international transfer of technology will, likewise, impact the degree of difficulty a firm is likely to encounter in the implementation of its IHRIS. Furthermore, the type of industry in which the firm competes globally, its international organization structure, and the degree to which its data processing operations are distributed represent additional factors that will come into play in the design of the firm's IHRIS.

This combination of organizational characteristics as well as internal and external influences will impact the degree of information technology (IT) support that is necessary and the design features that are realistic. As companies strive to develop systems that meet the needs of changing organizational structures, its end users, and an evolving international business environment, the challenges are immense. At the same time, the benefits may be substantial for those that successfully find the means by which to achieve these objectives. A well developed IHRIS will aid in maintaining the firm's competitive position and provide the means by which to respond to the needs of managing globally. An IHRIS will provide the firm with flexibility in meeting the local needs of host cultures while at the same time enable it to respond to the demands of operating globally. Organizational benefits may also accrue in terms of improved accuracy and efficiency for the firm's international operations.

CONCLUSIONS

A challenging, changing international business environment demands proactive decision making in order to respond to the competitive forces of global management. The human resource function plays a central role in the effective operations of the multinational corporation. It provides the MNC with one of its most valuable information resources. It is imperative that this resource be effectively managed in order to provide the firm with maximum benefits. One means by which to obtain these objectives is through the effective implementation of an IHRIS. A well developed IHRIS will provide the infrastructure for effective management of the firm's HR activities and a means by which to meet the needs of the organization and its end users.

REFERENCES

Asheghian, P. & Ebrahimi, B. (1990). *International Business*. New York: Harper and Row.

Bartlett, C. & Ghoshal, S. (Fall 1988). Organizing for Worldwide Effectiveness: The Transnational Solution. *California Management Review*, 54-74.

Black, J.S. & Mendenhall, M. (1989). A Practical but Theory-based Framework for Selecting Cross-Cultural Training Methods. *Human Resource Management*, 28(4), 511-539.

Black, J.S., Mendenhall, M. & Oddou, G. (1991). Toward a Comprehensive Model of International Adjustment: An Integration of Multiple Theoretical Perspectives. *Academy of Management Review*, 16(2), 291-317.

Boddewyn, J.J., Halbrich, M. B. & Perry, A.C. (Fall 1986). Service Multinationals: Conceptualization, Measurement and Theory. *Journal of International Business Studies*, 41-58.

Cerillo, V. R. & Freeman, C. (1991).*Human Resource Management Systems*. New York: Lexington Books.

Deans, P. C., Karwan, K. R., Goslar, M. D., Ricks, D. A., & Toyne, B. (Spring 1991). Identification of Key International Information Systems Issues in U.S.-Based Multinational Corporations. *Journal of Management Information Systems*, 27-50.

Deans, P. C. & Ricks, D. A. (1991). MIS Research: A Model for Incorporating the International Dimension. *The Journal of High Technology Management Research*, 2(1), 57-81.

Dessler, G. (1991). *Personnel/Human Resource Management*. Englewood Cliffs, New Jersey: Prentice Hall.

Dowling, P. J. & Schuler, R. S. (1990). *International Dimensions of Human Resource Management*. Boston, Massachusetts: PWS Kent Publishing Company.

Dowling, P. J. (1988). International and Domestic Personnel/Human Resource Management: Similarities and Differences. In Schuler, R.S., Youngblood, S.A. & Huber, V.L. (Eds.) *Personnel and Human Resource Management*. St. Paul, Minnesota: West Publishing Co.

Fombrun, C. and Tichy, N. (1984). Strategic Planning and Human Resource Management: At Rainbow's End. In Robert B. Lank (Ed.), *Competitive Strategic Management*. Englewood Cliffs, New Jersey: Prentice Hall.

Gallagher, M. L. (1991). *Computers and Human Resource Management*. Oxford, England: Butterworth - Heinemann Ltd.

Harris, P. R. & Moran, R. T. (1987). *Managing Cultural Differences*. Houston, Texas: Gulf Publishing Co.

Horsfield, D. (Summer 1987). Homegrown Documentation. *Computers in Personnel*, 51.

Kavanagh, M. J., Gueutal, H. G. & Tannenbaum, S. I. (1990). *Human Resource Information Systems: Development and Application.* Boston, Massachusetts: PWS Kent Publishing Co.

Lorange, P. (1986). Human Resource Management in Multinational Cooperative Ventures.*Human Resource Management*, 25(1), 133-148.

Milkovich, G. T. & Glueck, W. F. (1985).*Personnel/Human Resource Management: A Diagnostic Approach.* Plano, Texas: Business Publications, Inc.

Phatak, A. V. (1992). *International Dimensions of Management.* Boston, Massachusetts: PWS-Kent Publishing Company.

Saudagaran, S. M. (Spring 1988). An Empirical Study of Selected Factors Influencing the Decision to List on Foreign Stock Exchanges. *Journal of International Business Studies*, 19(1), 101-127.

Sept, R., Westcott, P., Agocs, C. & Suttie, P. (1989). Human Resource Information Systems: Organizational Barriers to Implementation. *Journal of Management Systems*, 1(2), 23-33.

CHAPTER 23

Information Systems Personnel, Human Resource Management and the Global Organization

FRED NIEDERMAN
University of Baltimore

Information Technology (IT) and human resource management (HRM) work together to support international commerce. Management Information Systems (MIS) and IT support global operations and, at times, help shape emerging industries. Skilled employees are needed to design and implement organizational actions. This chapter discusses (1) the emergence of both MIS and human resource management as important international business issues; (2) the potential for MIS and IT to support firms implementing international human resource management; and (3) the role of MIS and other technical professionals as employees in the global environment. Special attention is given to issues such as the consideration of MIS personnel as expatriates and the contrasting of MIS employees working in different countries.

INTRODUCTION AND OVERVIEW

Over the past three decades, both new information technology (IT) and global commerce have grown at a remarkable rate. It is not clear to what degree new information technologies have fueled global business growth or burgeoning trade has pushed firms to invest in more sophisticated information technology. It can be argued, however, that the simultaneous growth of information technology and global commerce are related phenomena. For example, near instantaneous transfer of capital from banks in Europe to projects in the US rely on telecommunications networks for transmission of data and also upon computer-based information technology at both ends to send and process that data correctly. These technologies require highly trained technical and managerial personnel for their efficient and effective planning, installation, operations, and maintenance.

In recent decades, some organizational theorists have taken an information processing view of the firm (Dunning, 1988). To some extent, the distribution and ownership of computing resources (hardware, software, and personnel), the ability and cost of performing transactions resulting from such assets, the potential for integration of border spanning activities through the use of computing and communications technologies, and the integration of centralized data processing with local production, distribution, and financial activities all affect the environment of a firm with multinational operations. It is reasonable to expect a high correlation between the approach to managing a set of foreign subsidiaries and the manner of gathering and distributing information and expertise throughout the organization. For example, it can be expected that a strategy of decentralized management and local autonomy would emphasize local or regional data collection and processing; centralized management and tight coupling of production or service across national boundaries would emphasize integrated information systems.

The head office in a multinational corporation (MNC) is faced with the dilemma of wanting local offices to take advantage of local opportunities while operating in coordination and harmony with overall organizational goals. Prahalad and Doz (1981) argue that head offices must recognize conditions which lead to loss of control and assert influence over: 1) what information managers collect and use in decision making; 2) the basis upon which managers compete; 3) which people have the power to commit strategic resources; and 4) the basis for administrative procedures such as career progression. The authors maintain that there are three mechanisms to assert such influence: 1) "data management systems" through managerial or cost accounting systems and the associated underlying MIS technology; 2) "manager management mechanisms" through the assignment of managers to key tasks, development programs and performance evaluations; and 3) through conflict resolution mechanisms such as matrix structures and task forces.

Following the Prahalad and Doz view, both MIS and human resource management are central to implementing head office policy throughout the MNC. Senior executives signal what they view as key production or service items for measurement and tracking; MIS provides the technology for collection, storage, processing, and distribution of this information. Human resource management, in a narrow sense, will involve the operational tasks of tracking middle level managers through their variety of assignments and providing data for assignments and performance evaluation and, in a broad sense, involve their recruiting, socialization, and ongoing skill development.

While global commerce increasingly relies on information technology, MNC strategies are also coming to rely on sophisticated global human resource management (Black, Gregersen, & Mendenhall, 1992; Brandt, 1991). As expressed by Broderick and Boudreau (1992, p. 7), there is a tight relationship between human resource management, information technology and firm strategy:

> To pull into the lead in global competition, managers must control labor costs, motivate employees to high quality, customer-oriented performance and continuously search out new and better ways of doing both. These objectives must be met in the face of shrinking head count and a global environment in which employees are more culturally diverse and located throughout the globe.

In the past, international business theorists have focused largely on explaining patterns in the movement of firms from exporters to global entities and in explaining what advantages are sought by expanding from domestic to multinational trade (Ricks, Toyne, and Martinez, 1990). However, more recently an increasing interest has been shown in the areas of strategy (e.g., Rosenzweig & Gingh, 1991), human resource management (e.g., Black, Gregersen, & Mendenhall, 1992), and information systems (e.g., Selig, 1982; Ives & Jarvenpaa, 1991; Roche, 1992). Researchers in each of these areas have been searching for better understanding of how to match global strategy with various structures of multi-national firms and with both the human resource management and information systems platforms to effectively support them.

MIS practitioners have also demonstrated a high interest in human resource management. The issue of staffing multinational enterprises with MIS personnel is recognized as a key issue in global information systems by multinational MIS managers (Deans et. al., 1991). This result is not terribly surprising in that human resource issues are generally viewed by MIS managers as highly important. In a broad survey of MIS managers (Niederman, Brancheau, and Wetherbe, 1991), human resource issues were ranked fourth out of 25 key MIS issues in the 1990s. In fact, since 1980, in a series of surveys conducted approximately every three years, human resource management has been ranked 7th, 8th, 12th, and most recently 4th (Niederman, Brancheau, Wetherbe, 1991).

This chapter will continue by discussing a number of international human resource management issues and the potential for management information systems to support these management functions in MNCs. The following section will then focus on MIS specialists, including attributes differentiating these from other personnel in the organization, the issue of turnover, and comparisons of MIS personnel currently active in different countries.

GLOBAL HUMAN RESOURCE MANAGEMENT AND INFORMATION SYSTEMS

Global human resource management is concerned with the traditional issues of selecting, training, evaluating, and compensating employees, including both expatriates assigned to serve outside of their country of origin and host country nationals. As pointed out by Cash, McFarlan, McKinney, and Applegate (1992, p. 548),

Financial and human resources for global operations require extremely coordinated management. Many firms have growing pools of staff that require extensive global coordination and development and their electronic support. Finally, technology skills, expertise, and intelligence all require much tighter coordination in the multinational realm. Information technology is central to accomplishing this.

Milliman, Von Glinow, and Nathan (1991) argue for viewing human resource management in an MNC as a series of "fits" between the organizational life cycle, the external environment, and the internal human resource department. The authors also point out the need for a fit between human resource departments among foreign subsidiaries, not only within their environments, but also with their corporate offices. They note the tendency to look at fit as existing on the opposite end of a continuum from flexibility. From a dynamic perspective, a firm may benefit from the flexibility to change by fitting policies to the environment at a series of points of time. The authors also provide an interesting review of different approaches to the dynamics of organizational change and propose that firms designed for international commerce will proceed differently in adapting to their environments than organizations that move from a domestic to an international focus. One implication of this view is that information systems may: 1) reflect the state of human resources at subsidiary and headquarters levels or 2) influence and expedite the sharing of information to smooth differences or bring about a good fit. Information systems may monitor subsidiary environments including changing consumer and labor markets in order to speed the awareness of new environmental demands to which human resources should be adjusted to create fit.

Two key issues stand out in the area of global HRM. The first of these involves developing cross-cultural skills and attitudes among senior managers. Adler and Bartholomew (1992) argue the importance of developing transnational capabilities among senior management of firms with transnational business strategies. This requires personnel recruiting, development, retention, and utilization strategies that create an appropriate mix of executives from various cultures and a set of skills among these executives to deal with cross-cultural and multi-cultural information exchange. It is interesting to consider the degree to which internationalization should permeate the organization or should focus on senior management; the degree to which it would affect technology specialists; and the ways that information technology can support internationalization of the human resource function.

The second area that warrants special attention is that of expatriate issues. Expatriates are workers sent from their country of origin to serve the organization in another country. They play an important role in transferring technological knowledge and managerial skills (Martinez and Ricks, 1989) from the country of origin to the host country. MNC headquarters will most likely opt to send expatriate managers when the subsidiary is of importance, where the subsidiary has low need of resources from headquarters, and where headquarters has less trust in the general manager of the subsidiary (e.g. after several periods of poor financial performance).

Research on expatriate employee assignments has included both development of a model for understanding adaptation to new environments and prescriptions for better selection and training for overseas assignments. A general model for understanding expatriate adaptation is presented by Mendenhall and Oddou (1985, 1986). They propose three dimensions (self-orientation, others-orientation, and perceptual-orientation) to differentiate skill levels in potential expatriate employees and create a taxonomy of potential personality types by varying high and low levels of skill in these three areas. These categories can be used in fine-tuning understanding of expatriate experiences and tailoring training programs even though the authors stress that all potential expatriates should receive training prior to assignment overseas. The length and intensity of prior training, however, can vary according to expected length of stay, type of involvement in the culture, cultural toughness of the host country relative to the country of origin, family differences, expected interaction with host-nationals, and likelihood of future overseas assignments. Using existing database technology, information systems can potentially be used to store data concerning individual employees and their appropriateness for expatriate assignments; for tracking employees' careers and documenting both costs and benefits of expatriate assignment.

Tung (1981) presents a model for selection and training of personnel for overseas assignment. She suggests matching the personal characteristics of the employee with the nature of the task and of the host-country environment. She also presents five levels of training: (1) area studies (data regarding the history and culture of the host country); (2) culture assimilator (simulation of the host culture through critical incidents and scenarios); (3) language training; (4) sensitivity training; and (5) field experiences. Training programs for personnel with longer assignments requiring more interaction with host country personnel generally ought to have higher levels of training types 3, 4 and 5. Tung also discusses results of a survey of training programs for overseas personnel used by a sample of organizations.

Information systems can potentially help a firm in implementing expatriate programs. Human resource management systems can help screen a wider array of candidates for overseas work, can track their progress through a range of assignments, and monitor openings throughout the firm to assist the employee at the end of their assignment. Additionally, computer-based instruction can potentially be used to deliver or enhance training. Area studies can make large volumes of data regarding the culture, history, and geography of the host country as well as information regarding the firm's activities in the host country readily available to employees— possibly annotated by others within the firm who have worked in these locations. Language skills can be reinforced through computer-aided instruction drills and new multi-media presentation offers the potential for accelerated spoken language training. Cross-cultural simulations can also potentially be provided through electronic media.

HUMAN RESOURCE ISSUES FOR INFORMATION SYSTEM PERSONNEL

Thus far, this chapter has focused on how MIS can support the global human resource management function. We now turn to a discussion of how the multinational MIS function requires labor from an exceptional type of employee.

MIS Personnel Compared to Other Employees

A significant body of evidence has been compiled suggesting that MIS professionals systematically differ from non-MIS counterparts (Couger and Zawacki, 1978a; Couger and Zawacki, 1978b; Couger and Zawacki, 1979; Couger, Zawacki, and Oppermann, 1979; and Bartol and Martin 1982). MIS professionals were primarily distinguished from non-MIS employees by higher levels of need for individual growth and lower levels of social need. Couger and his colleagues also found that MIS personnel rated their jobs significantly higher on core job dimensions of skill variety, task identity, task significance, and autonomy. An assignment overseas might provide an MIS professional with a high level of individual growth by presenting a new culture and a new set of problems, or perhaps even a period of exile from the latest technologies (if the assignment moves them to a less developed country). Lower levels of social need might allow MIS employees to focus on the task at hand without experiencing too high a level of discomfort not being able to communicate in another language although, on the other hand, a low social need might also engender a low sensitivity to the needs and interests of host country colleagues.

To the extent that existing studies show that true differences can be found in the workplace, an opportunity is presented for firms to differentiate human resource policies based on different job categories. Of course, failing to differentiate policies can create anomalies or problems. Research has yet to address questions such as: the degree to which MIS professionals and other technically oriented employees are actually sent abroad, whether there are differences in personnel policies between these employees and general managers (e.g., shorter periods of work abroad), and exactly what sort of human resource policies would be most appropriate for information systems professionals as expatriates.

Although a number of studies have supported the idea that information systems professionals display different motivational characteristics compared to other employees, studies by Ferratt and Short (1986, 1988), however, found no differences between MIS and non-MIS employees 1) in the pattern of motivational factors that would influence productive work 2) in the way in which they were managed; nor 3) in levels of productivity based on differences in the work-unit environment (as a surrogate for management style). The researchers did find, however, that regardless of manager-type highest performance followed from high levels of support and attention to production; lowest performance was from high attention to production with low levels of support.

The differences in findings between the works of Couger and Ferratt and Short may be the result of differences in their studies: questionnaires were administered in different time periods; the instruments and samples from the population of MIS professionals were drawn differently. Couger's sample must have been drawn in the mid-1970s whereas Ferratt and Short's was probably drawn in the 1980s. As a result it may be that over time MIS professionals have come to resemble other managers, particularly with the increasingly wide distribution and use of personal computers. Duliba and Baroudi (1991) argue that, "MIS personnel perform work today which differs dramatically from work performed twenty years ago (1991, p. 114)." Additionally, Couger polled high level MIS professionals from lists derived from the Society for Information Management, whereas Ferratt and Short sampled from employees in the midwest region of the United States of America in the insurance industry.

While MIS professionals generally focus more on technology than their general management counterparts, MIS professionals vary greatly among themselves. Studies often distinguish between programmers and analysts or between data processing "operations" and "development" personnel (Couger, Zawacki, and Oppermann, 1979; Chadwin and Cross, 1983). Myers (1991) adjusted for the volatility of the MIS field by contrasting not only MIS professionals against non-MIS professionals, but also by sub-dividing MIS into "traditional" and "non-traditional" job categories based on tools used and tasks performed (1991, p. 34). Traditional MIS professionals were those whose tasks more closely resembled the more prominent tasks of the 1970s data processing shop. This study supported Couger et al. as far as distinguishing traditional MIS professionals from non-traditional MIS professionals and non-MIS professionals; but also supported Ferratt and Short in that the combined traditional and non-traditional MIS professionals did not differ from non-MIS professionals.

MIS Personnel Around the World

There are many dimensions along which workers within varying cultures may differ. Pearce (1991), for example, presents a rather bleak picture of organizations in Hungary and the dysfunctional behavior that grew from political allocation of scarce resources. Difficulties reported include: 1) the weak performance pressures on Hungarian managers stemming from labor shortages and a lack of formal performance appraisal; 2) substantial pay-at-risk which generates significant amounts of bargaining, cheating, and politicization of the work environment; 3) promotion through connections resulting in widespread distrust as well as people with inadequate skills for the job; and 4) ambiguous responsibilities which truncate lateral and downward communication; generate widespread avoidance of responsibility; substitute credentials for performance in management selection; and generally foul up communications. This snapshot of worker life in Hungary suggests both the large amount of adjustment required of MIS professionals (as well as others) brought to work there from Western Europe and the potential for significant differences in motivation, training, and business understanding among MIS professionals in different countries.

Sullivan and Nonaka (1986) test the relationship of senior management culture (Japanese versus American) in terms of adherence to particular theories of management (rational, social, or informational). Some evidence is presented that Japanese managers more often hold informational theories of management and that Japanese senior managers are more likely to generate uncertainty (or amplify variety) which tends to correlate with economic success with junior managers acting to reduce uncertainty using rational, purposeful, deductive and integration methods. This merges interestingly with decision theories that hold both information search or divergent thinking and equivocality reduction or convergent thinking as important in problem solving, particularly in early problem formulation stages.

Cultural Differences Between MIS Personnel Across Borders

In a series of studies, Couger and colleagues (1986, 1989, 1992) compared attitudes of MIS professionals in several countries. One study (Couger, Borovits, and Zviran, 1989) compared MIS professionals in the U.S. to their Singaporean and Israeli counterparts. The study indicated significant differences on several dimensions. Singaporean MIS professionals rated their jobs lower than Americans on four dimensions (skill variety, task significance, autonomy, and feedback from the job). Israelis also rated task significance lower, but rated feedback from the job significantly higher than Americans. This might be explained by MIS work differing between countries; by people in different countries perceiving differently essentially the same work; or by some combination of these. Both Israeli and Singaporean MIS professionals rated satisfaction with pay/benefits significantly lower than did U.S. counterparts. This could signal different pay rates, different expectations among workers, or different labor supply curves in different countries. Israelis also indicated higher levels of goal clarity and feedback on goal accomplishment and lower levels of goal difficulty.

In a follow up study contrasting MIS workers in six Pacific Rim countries (Couger, 1992), Australians showed higher levels than American employees on both growth need strength and job motivating capacity, however, respondents from Hong Kong, the People's Republic of China (PRC), Singapore, Taiwan, and Thailand all showed significantly lower levels of job motivating capacity and both the PRC and Thailand showed significantly lower levels of growth need strength among employees.

These findings suggest important new questions regarding the degree to which MIS jobs and personnel differ across borders. To the extent that these effects are due to differences in the jobs themselves, then MIS expatriates need to be prepared for either adapting to changes (perhaps subtle changes) in their overseas work or to rearranging their work environment. To the extent that these effects are due to differences in the employees (whether resulting from culture, training, or some other source) MIS needs to be prepared for operating in new ways (or in spite of new ways). Of course it is possible that there is influence from both differences in jobs and in employees (perhaps there is a feedback loop where employees of different culture or background are inclined to arrange their jobs differently which in turn reinforces different cultural norms) and so the MIS expatriate would be wise to anticipate adjusting to both different jobs and ways of working.

In spite of problems facing workers in general and MIS professionals in particular in developing countries, an increasing amount of professional information systems work is being done outside of the U.S. and Western Europe. Press (1991) reviews the state of the software development industry in Chile, Eastern Europe, India, Ireland, and the Far East. A major contention is that some conditions suggest the possibility of a growing internationalization of software development, particularly in light of widespread diffusion of PC technology. This is in the form of (1) reduced export of U.S. software and more local development; (2) sub-contracting of off-shore software developers for U.S. applications; and (3) penetration of U.S. market by innovative software developed overseas. Yourdon is referenced as predicting widespread layoffs and rendering obsolete of U.S. software developers. Senn (1991) notes some of the trade-offs in outsourcing programming projects to India where there are many highly trained personnel but often a dearth of the latest computer and telecommunication equipment. However, firms willing to make the investment can potentially overcome these obstacles to employ Indian programmers, as Deere and Company is in the process of doing (Halper, 1993).

Kim, Westin, & Dholakia (1989) provide an overview of trends and issues in the diffusion of software industry technology and jobs from "advanced countries" to "newly industrialized countries." They also offer an analytic framework for assessing the resources available for influencing software activities in a country or region. The categories of framework elements are technological resources, human resources, traits of the relevant culture, and traits of the culture of the specific corporation.

The Expatriate-Host Country Mixture

Formulating the correct blend for staffing foreign offices with host country nationals versus expatriates is difficult in general and may be more difficult for the information systems specialist or for the technical professional (Niederman, 1992). Moreover, that blend of expatriates can include either senior managers sent abroad to oversee operations or contract programmers brought from lower-wage countries for their flexibility and productivity (Durand and

Iyengar, 1991; Senn, 1991).

Misa and Fabricatore (1979), in a widely cited article, open a discussion regarding true evaluation of the costs of sending employees across borders. Developing accounting information systems for tracking both costs and benefits of expatriate activities may be instrumental in producing the optimal (or even improved) combinations of domestic and imported labor for a particular information systems task.

Cross-National Development Projects

One implication of these differences in the nature of MIS professionals in different countries pertains to the development of large scale applications programs for use in multiple countries. Clearly, multi-national firms can take any of a number of approaches to the design of international systems. For example, they can assign systems engineers in one country to develop such a system and mandate its use worldwide (or regionally); they could make a version in each and build an interface to integrate key data for headquarters use; or they could create a single multi-national design team to build a system to meet the range of requirements (Ives and Jarvenpaa, 1991). If there are systematic differences between MIS professionals or between their different jobs, these could provide clues for managing cross-national development operations, particularly when using multi-cultural design teams.

Transfer of Technology

There are also some tasks which are often associated with international commerce, such as transfer of technology, that present both human resource and information technology problems. Ehrlich (1985) presents alternative models of technology transfer: the "pipeline" model which is efficient at moving from ideas to development and the "partnership" model where various stakeholders in the process act as partners. Identified problems in technology transfer include: communication among stakeholders with different skills, knowledge, and goals; the persistence to continue a long project to completion; and timing to bring the product to production neither before it is ready nor after its maximum market impact has passed by. Suggestions for ameliorating these problems includes small multi-disciplinary work groups; exposing groups (presumably user groups) to the technology; transferring personnel between research and development units; and cultivating "champions" to move the process to completion. There can well be a role in technology transfer for information technologies. Relevant technologies include those supporting organizational communication such as electronic mail, meeting support systems, and collaborative work technologies (e.g. Lotus notes). Information technology combined with quantitative analysis can also help with market forecasting and product introduction timing.

CONCLUSION

Both MIS and human resource management support the strategic, tactical, and operational activities of MNCs. The selection of strategic focus and the structuring of the multinational organization may both be related to preferences for and constraints in gathering and processing information. Of equal importance is the location of expertise and decision making at various points in the organization.

Global information systems management demands strategic collection, storage, processing, and distribution of information, as well as development and maintenance of the technological support enabling these activities. In addition to creating challenging new jobs, these tasks require individuals with skills to deal with increasing levels of complexity.

Both general managers and information systems specialists are living in an increasingly diverse population (Cox, 1991). As a result, the enhancement of cross-cultural skills and the ability to live and work outside of one's host country will become increasingly important. Although much research has been conducted to identify key characteristics for successful acclimatization to new environments, little has specifically targeted information systems professionals or other technical specialists (Niederman, 1992). To the extent that past research shows different motivational patterns differentiating information systems and other professionals (e.g. Couger, 1992), there would be value in extending the work of Tung (1984, 1981) and Mendenhall, Gregersen, and Oddou (1992) to specifically address effective treatment of technical specialists when they serve as expatriates. Moreover, the potential for cross-national information systems development teams and/or interface between host country and outsourcing staffs will generally require additional cross-cultural training even without large shifts of personnel from the home location. To the extent that attitudes of and the organization of work among information systems personnel differ from country to country, creating cross-national teams may turn out to be quite a challenge.

Global human resource management must be concerned with the traditional issues of selecting, training, evaluating, and compensating employees including both expatriates assigned to serve outside of their country of origin and host country nationals. Information systems can support global human resource management through automation of these traditional functions as well as through the use of decision support and expert systems (Broderick and Boudreau, 1992). This type of support will be particularly helpful in assessing the optimal mix of expatriate and host-country personnel at a given subsidiary or work site.

Managing the multinational organization is an enormous task that requires careful attention to strategy and organizational structure, to the control and coordination of the subsidiary-headquarters relationship, and to the gathering, processing, and utilization of information by well-trained professionals. It will be the fortunate firm, indeed, that can create excellence on a global basis without carefully working through expert general and technical managers and without providing the appropriate information technology for decision making and performance monitoring.

REFERENCES

Adler, N.J. and Bartholomew, S. (1992). Managing Globally Competent People, *The Executive*, 6, 3, August, 52-65.

Bartol, K.M. & Martin, D.C. (1982) Managing Information Systems Personnel: A Review of the Literature and Managerial Implications. *MIS Quarterly*, Special Issue, 6, 4, 49-70.

Black, J.S., Gregersen, H.B., and Mendenhall, M.E. (1992) *Global Assignments: Successfully Expatriating and Repatriating International Managers*, Jossey-Bass Publishers, San Francisco.

Brandt, E. (1991) Global HR. *Personnel Journal*, March, 38-44.

Broderick, R. and Boudreau, J.W. (1992) Human Resource Management, Information Technology, and the Competitive Edge, *Academy of Management Executive*, 6, 2, 7-17.

Cash, J.I., Jr., McFarlan, F.W., McKenney, J.L., and Applegate, L. (1992) *Corporate Information Systems Management: Text and Cases, 3rd Edition*, Chapter 12, Richard C. Irwin: Homewood Illinois, 547-570.

Chadwin, M.L. & Cross, E.M. (1983) Personnel Management for a Special Breed: The Data Processing Professional. *Personnel Administrator*, 28, 8, 53-59.

Couger, J.D. (1984) Blue Skies Ahead. *Datamation*, 30, 21, 107-110.

Couger, J.D. (1986) Effect of Cultural Differences on Motivation of Analysts and Programmers. *MIS Quarterly*, June, 1986, 189-196.

Couger, J.D. (1992) Comparison of Motivation Norms for Pacific Rim Programmer/Analysts Vs. Those in the United States. *International Information Systems*, 1, 3, in press.

Couger, J.D., Borovits, I. & Zviran, M. (1989) Comparison of Motivating Environment for Programmer/Analysts & Programmers in the U.S., Israel, & Singapore. *Proceedings of the 22nd Annual Hawaii International Conference on Systems Sciences*, 316-323.

Couger, J.D. & Zawacki, R.A. (1978a) What Motivates DP Professionals? *Datamation*, 19-20.

Couger, J.D. & Zawacki, R.A. (1978b) Compensation Preferences of DP

Professionals. *Datamation,* 94-102.

Couger, J.D. & Zawacki, R.A. (1979) Something's Very Wrong with DP Operations Jobs. *Datamation,* 149-158.

Couger, J.D., Zawacki, R.A., & Oppermann, E.B. (1979) Motivation Levels of MIS Managers Versus Those of Their Employees. *MIS Quarterly,* 3, 3, 47-56.

Cox, T., Jr. (1991) The Multicultural Organization, *Academy of Management Executive,* 5, 2, 34-47.

Deans, P.C., Karwan, K.R., Goslar, M.D., Ricks, D.A., and Toyne, B. (1991). Identification of Key International Information Systems Issues in U.S.-Based Multinational Corporations, *Journal of Management Information Systems,* 7,4, 27-50.

Deans, P.C. & Kane, M.J. (1992) *International Dimensions of Information Systems and Technology,* The Kent International Dimensions of Business Series (Ed. D.A. Ricks). PWS-Kent Publishing Company, Boston, MA.

Deans, P.C. & Ricks, D.A. (1991) MIS Research: A Model for Incorporating the International Dimension. *The Journal of High Technology Management Research,* 2, 1, 57-81.

Duliba, K.A. & Baroudi, J. (1991) IS Personnel: Do They Form an Occupational Community? In T.W. Ferratt (Ed.), *Proceedings of the 1991 ACM SIGCPR Conference,* 111-118.

Dunning, J.H. (1988) The Eclectic Paradigm of International Production: A Restatement and Some Possible Extensions, *Journal of International Business Studies,* 19, 1-31.

Durand D. and Iyengar, J. (1991) Exploratory Study of International Contract Programming for the Computer Industry: What? Why? Who? *Proceedings, Southeast Region Decision Science Institute,* Twenty-first Annual Meeting, Arlington, Virginia, February 27 - March 1, 324 and supplemental paper distributed at the conference.

Ehrlich, K. (1985) Factors Influencing Technology Transfer, *SIGCHI Bulletin,* 17, 2, October, 20-24.

Ferratt, T.W. & Short, L.E. (1986) Are Information Systems People Different: An Investigation of Motivational Differences. *MIS Quarterly,* 10, 4, 377-387.

Ferratt, T.W. & Short, L.E. (1988) Are Information Systems People Different? An Investigation of How They Are & Should Be Managed. *MIS Quarterly,* 12, 3, 427-443.

Halper, M. (1993) Deere's Faraway IS Solution *Computerworld,* February 15, 76.

Harris, P.R. and Moran, R.T. (1987) *Managing Cultural Differences, 2nd Ed.,* Houston, Texas, Gulf Publishing Company.

Ives, B. and Jarvenpaa, S.L. (1991) Applications of Global Information Technology: Key Issues for Management, *MIS Quarterly,* 15,1, March 32-49.

Kim, C., Westin, S., and Dholakia, N. (1989) Globalization of the Software Industry: Trends and Strategies, *Information and Management,* 17, 197-206.

Lyles, M.A. (1987) "Common Mistakes of Joint Venture Experienced Firms," *Columbia Journal of World Business,* Summer, 79-85.

Martinez, Z.L. and Ricks, D.A. (1989) Multinational Parent Companies' Influence over Human Resource Decisions of Affiliates: U.S. Firms in Mexico, *Journal of International Business Studies,* Fall, 465-487.

Mendenhall, M. Dunbar, E. and Oddou, G.R. (1987) Expatriate Selection, Training and Career-Pathing: A Review and Critique, *Human Resource Management*, 26, 331-345.

Mendenhall, M. and Oddou, G. (1986) Acculturation Profiles of Expatriate Managers: Implications for Cross-Cultural Training Programs, *Columbia Journal of World Business*, 21, 4, 73-79.

Mendenhall, M. and Oddou, G. (1985) The Dimensions of Expatriate Acculturation, *Academy of Management Review*, 10, 39-47.

Milliman, J., Von Glinow, M.A., and Nathan, M. (1991) Organizational Life Cycles and Strategic International Human Resource Management in Multinational Companies: Implications for Congruence Theory, *Academy of Management Review*, 16, 2, April 318-339.

Misa, K.F. and Fabricatore, J.M. (1979) Return on Investment of Overseas Personnel, *Financial Executive*, 47, April, 42-46.

Myers, M.E. (1991) Motivation & Performance in the Information Systems Field: A Survey of Related Studies, In T.W. Ferratt (Ed.), *Proceedings of the 1991 ACM SIGCPR Conference*, 32-37.

Niederman, F. (1992) Information Systems Personnel as Expatriates: A Review of the Literature and Identification of Issues, *Proceedings of the Association for Computing Machinery Special Interest Group Computer Personnel Research*, Cincinnati, Ohio, 232-240.

Niederman, F., Brancheau, J.C., & Wetherbe, J.C. (1991) Information Systems Management Issues in The 1990s. *MIS Quarterly*, 15, 4, 475-495.

Pearce, J.L. (1991) From Socialism to Capitalism: The Effects of Hungarian Human Resource Practices, *Academy of Management Executive*, 5, 4, 75-88.

Prahalad, C.K. and Doz, Y.L. (1981) An Approach to Strategic Control in MNCs, *Sloan Management Review*, Summer, 5-13.

Press, L. (1991) Personal Computers and the World Software Market, *Communications of the ACM*, 34, 2, February, 23-28.

Ricks, D.A., Toyne, B. and Martinez, Z. (1990) Recent Developments in International Management Research, *Journal of Management*, 16, 2, 219-253.

Roche, E.M. (1992) *Managing Information Technology in Multinational Corporations*, MacMillan Publishing Company, New York.

Rosenzweig, P.M. and Gingh, J.V. (1991) Organizational Environments and the Multinational Enterprise, *Academy of Management Review*, 16, 2, 340-361.

Selig, G.J. (1982) Approaches to Strategic Planning for Information Resource Management (IRM) in Multinational Corporations, *MIS Quarterly*, 6, 2, June, 33-45.

Senn, J.A. (1991) The Emerging Software Passage to India, *SIM Network*, 6, 1, January/February, 7.

Sullivan, J.J. and Nonaka, I. (1986) The Application of Organizational Learning Theory to Japanese and American Management, *Journal of International Business Studies*, Fall, 127-147.

Tung, R. (1981) Selection and Training of Personnel for Overseas Assignments, *Columbia Journal of World Business*, 16, 1, 68-78.

Tung, R. (1984) Human Resource Planning in Japanese Multinationals: A Model for U.S. Firms? *Journal of International Business Studies*, 15, 2, 139-149.

SECTION 8

Organizational Implications and Future Challenges

In this final section, we include four chapters which assess some of the broad organizational implications of information technology developments. The various themes that were discussed in Chapters 1 and 2, and then discussed in greater detail in terms of the functional areas in subsequent chapters, are tied back together in several different ways.

In the first chapter, Bill Chismar argues that the success of multinational business operations depends most heavily upon the ability of firms to enhance coordination of their various units, across functions, products, and geographic booundaries. Despite the promise of information technologies to provide for new methods of coordination, current evidence indicates that this is not yet happening on a widespread basis. Even global firms have demonstrated a reluctance to use IT to decentralize decision making for the purposes of enhancing the coordination of disparate groups.

K.S. Raman and Rick Watson then present an interesting piece which reminds us that it is too easy, in forums such as this book, to neglect or understate the effects of the variable known as "national culture". Organizational processes and the IS function and capabilities must be molded to reflect the realities of the national cultures that are being linked by the interests of the multinational corporation. The lessons that are being learned in each of the functional areas, i.e., that sensitivity to cultural differences is an important aspect to coordination and effectiveness, are essential also for IS managers attempting to facilitate and implement successful global applications.

In the third chapter, Terry Byrd, Chetan Sankar, and Jerry McCreary transcend the individual technology applications in the multinational firm to point out the risks associated with planning, developing and implementing systems in any of the functional areas. Risks are defined in terms of coordination, security, culture, and legal/regulatory requirements. The authors conclude, based upon comprehensive study of the international business and IS literatures, that coordination and legal issues seem to have a higher amount of risk on the strategic levels of IS management, whereas the risks due to security and culture seem to be greater for operational issues and activities that involve day-to-day management, development and implementation.

The final chapter in the book was written by Ed Roche and is the capstone piece in our argument that complex international information systems and technology support cannot be understood and developed without a good understanding at the application level. The chapter notes that, although categorization by business function is only one way to classify "applications", it is a meaningful and powerful way to get started since business is transacted by marketers, manufacturing employees, accountants, etc. rather than by general business people. Adding the international dimension and national differences to management situations makes it even more important that analysis be performed at specific application levels, even to the point of detailed, more focused sub-system applications that might be termed "application fragments". As the author indicates, failure to examine the effects of IS and IT development at these levels will only delay us from quickly attaining the goal of comfortably understanding "the relationship between organizational structure, decision-making, and information technology in the multinational".

CHAPTER 24

Information Technology and the Coordination of Global Organizations

WILLIAM G. CHISMAR
University of Hawaii

This chapter addresses the problems involved in using information technology in designing global organizations. It argues that technology plays a crucial role in allowing firms to implement global business strategies which depend on complex organizational and decision-making structures. These structures entail complex coordination problems and must cross functional, product, and geographic boundaries within the organization. With their sole functions being the processing and transmission of information, information technologies should be a prominent tool in facilitating new methods of coordination. While many managers agree with this conclusion, there is little evidence that information technology has been a major factor in the design of global organizations. This chapter investigates the reasons for this lack of prominence, considering technical and organizational barriers as well as the appropriateness of current technology to the coordination needs of global organizations. It also looks at the emerging technologies of multimedia information systems and photonics and discusses their potential impact on coordination in global organizations.

INTRODUCTION

A multinational corporation (MNC) operating in a global market faces an increasing number of competitive pressures, including

• Greater customer demands for integrated sales and service,
• Growing trends toward integrated product lines,
• Much shorter product development life-cycles and faster product delivery,
• Rapidly changing geographically based advantages, and
• The need to improve efficiency so as to reduce costs.

Adding to these pressures are the complexities of geographic and temporal dispersion of activities, cultural and market diversities, and a rapidly changing environment. As a result, managers of MNCs face complex coordination problems.

In response, MNC managers have attempted to develop business strategies which entail complex decision-making processes that cross geographic, functional, and product boundaries. The successful execution of these strategies relies on three critical capabilities that management must develop (Prahalad and Doz, 1987):

1. Efficiency in executing agreed upon strategies through a process of control of subsidiary actions.
2. Ability to change the nature of the headquarter-subsidiary, and subsidiary-to-subsidiary, relationships in order to allow required changes in strategic direction to take place.
3. Flexibility to bring subsidiaries together to compete in a coordinated fashion, to exploit government-controlled and non-conventional markets, and to take selective advantage of interdependencies across businesses (rather than to suffer from them).

The simultaneous development of these three capabilities represents a very difficult challenge for MNC managers. Activities carried out by different international units of the MNC must be more closely integrated while, at the same time, the MNC must be responsive to unique changes in local markets. The simplistic approach which considers only headquarter-subsidiary relationships must be expanded to include the many subsidiary-subsidiary relationships and a true network view of MNCs (Ghoshal and Bartlett, 1990). The wide range of available mechanisms for coordinating MNC activities provides managers with a plethora of options.

Because of their ability to directly address control and coordination issues, information technologies have long been touted as a means of enabling the necessary organizational changes within MNCs. As evident in the other chapters of this book, the operations of modern MNCs depend heavily upon information technologies. However, widespread integration of IT into international business strategy has not occurred (Chismar and Chidambaram, 1992). Rarely, outside of information intensive industries such as banking and finance, do senior managers explicitly include senior information technology managers in strategic planning. As a result, education of senior managers remains a very high priority concern of information technology managers (Ives & Jarvenpaa, 1992 and Deans, Karwan, Goslar, Ricks & Toyne, 1991).

Information systems within MNCs often do not provide the support necessary for company-wide international strategies. Most existing information systems were designed for individual geographic, functional, or product units within the MNC. This localized design is also reflected in the firm's telecommunication networks. Most MNCs have many different networks around the world, including LANs, domestic data networks, international data networks, and product/project specific networks. These systems and networks were typically designed to improve the decision-making within a particular business unit.

As a result of this situation, MNCs are currently confronted with a web of issues that includes: (1) increased communications that costs and complexity, (2) an inability to operationalize various global business strategies, such as coordinated manufacturing and customer service, and (3) an inability to quickly identify and respond to changes in the market place.

The solution to these problems requires an effective global organizational design based on a coordinated business and technology strategy. Thus, any global solution has two components: the organizational structure and the information technology architecture. It also requires an integrative approach that crosses departments, functions, geographic regions, and firms.

This chapter examines the coordination mechanisms that MNCs have been employing in attempting to better compete in global markets. It then discusses the potential coordination roles of IT and some of the barriers, both organizational and technological, that have slowed the widespread adoption of IT for coordination in MNCs. Ways to overcome these barriers are suggested.

COORDINATION WITHIN MULTINATIONAL ORGANIZATIONS

Choosing and developing appropriate coordination mechanisms for global operations represents a complex design problem. Empirical studies of MNCs have identified several approaches: changes in formal organizational structure, changes in formal decision-making structures, and development of informal mechanisms of coordination (Martinez and Jarillo, 1989).

Formal Organizational Structure

The basic hypothesis regarding formal organizational structure is that the complexity of global strategies, resulting from the need to balance multiple goals and perspectives, will require more complex organizational structures. Based on their study of MNCs, Stopford and Wells (1972) predicted that, in adapting to global competition, organizations progress through stages of structural change: starting with the use of autonomous subsidiaries, followed by the adoption of an international division, and concluding with the establishment of "global structures." They predicted the adoption of new, matrix organizational structures.

While many MNCs have experimented with matrix structures, very few have adopted these (Egelhoff, 1988, Pitts & Daniels, 1984). Galbraith and Kazan (1986) argue that the failures associated with matrix organizations are not because of inherent problems with a matrix, but because of management failures at implementing the matrix. Based upon their evaluation of companies which have successfully used this structure, they assert that the matrix can work and that it is "the only organizational form which fits the strategy of simultaneous pursuit of multiple business dimensions". They conclude that this is the best alternative for MNCs (pg. 50).

More recent studies of MNCs have found a shift away from formal organizational structure as a mechanism for control and coordination (Sullivan and Bauerschmidt, 1991). The reasons for this are apparent. The "fitting" of an organizational structure to a firm's strategy requires a fairly stable strategy. In the arena of global competition, few things remain stable. Accordingly, firms must maintain flexible strategies which "optimize efficiency, responsiveness, and learning simultaneously in their worldwide operations" (Bartlett & Ghoshal, 1987, p. 7). The need for more flexibility leads to a shift in emphasis from formal organizational structure to decision-making structures as coordinating mechanisms.

Decision-Making Structure

These formal mechanisms can be viewed as administrative tools for coordinating the activities in an MNC. In their extensive review of decision making structures, Martinez and Jarillo (1989, 1991) generate the following group of mechanisms: centralization, the extent to which the locus of decision making lies in the higher levels of the chain of command; formalization, the extent to which policies, rules, job descriptions, etc., are documented; planning, including budgeting, goal-setting, and the establishment of schedules intended to guide the activities of independent units; and output and behavior control, intended to evaluate the performance of units.

While easier to modify than formal organizational structures, and thus more flexible, these formal coordination mechanisms still rely on the headquarter to subsidiary relationships. But, global strategies are moving toward more integration of activities among the subsidiaries of MNCs. Among managers of MNCs there seems to be a growing common understanding of the "urgency and volatility of their competitive environment and the need to break with decision making based purely on hierarchical and functional authority" (Charan, 1991, p. 106). Work across boundaries must be coordinated at a pace that hierarchical decision making cannot handle; more lateral decision making is necessary.

Informal Coordination Mechanisms

In their study of MNCs, Martinez and Jarillo (1991) found that as the need for coordination increases, "the subtle (informal) mechanisms of coordination seem to play a serious role once the formal ones have been in place" (p. 441). They further conclude that:

A change towards a more integrated strategy, as most companies now plan, may be counterproductive if it is not supported by a concomitant increase in the amount and sophistication of international coordination....Country managers feel that, if they are to lose control over some critical parts of their operations to favor integration, there has to be much more flexibility and responsiveness in the overall company. And this calls for a more sophisticated level of coordination. (p. 442)

These informal coordination mechanisms span a wide range of options, from task forces, teams and committees, to personal visits, transfers of managers, and development of a corporate culture. Charan (1991) identifies the clear need for companies to create managerial networks to provide rapid, critical decision-making cuts across functional, geographic, and product boundaries. It seems that the ultimate goal is to create the ultimately flexible, "boundaryless" company (Hirschhorn and Gilmore, 1992).

INFORMATION TECHNOLOGY SUPPORT

What roles have information technologies played in supporting the coordination mechanism or in developing more "sophisticated" levels of coordination within MNCs? In answering this question, we first look at existing information technology architectures in MNCs.

Information Technology Architecture

At the applications level, most MNCs have developed a wide variety of information systems which have become critical to global operations. While many of the systems are quite sophisticated and span organizational and geographic boundaries, most are specific to a region, country, division, office, or even a person. Driven by localized requirements and multitudes of vendors, redundant and incompatible systems are scattered around MNCs. The integrated systems that do exist support data-driven, formal reporting and coordination within the MNCs. Such systems include accounting, sales reporting, and order processing systems.

At the network level, MNCs have numerous specialized data networks that were developed to provide straightforward, immediate solutions for linking a select group of individuals or computers. Most of these are private networks built on leased facilities (Roche, 1992). The growth of data networks has led to the widespread use of electronic mail. A recent survey of U.S. MNCs revealed that 70% of the firms used electronic mail for international communications (Chidambaram & Chismar, 1992). Obviously, the use of public voice networks abounds for telephone and facsimile communications. And, driven by dramatic decreases in cost, the use of video teleconferencing through public carriers is on the rise; currently at about 20% among U.S. MNCs (Chidambaram & Chismar, 1992).

As with applications systems, most data networks were developed in isolation. Now, in response to application demands for data accessibility, MNCs are using bridges, routers, and gateways to connect their local area networks, and various international data links to build global networks. The integration of global systems ranks high on the priorities of senior IS managers in MNCs; in a recent survey, the issue of integration was ranked third over all MNCs and first for MNCs with foreign sales greater than 25% (Deans, Karwan, Goslar, Ricks, & Toyne, 1991). With a multitude of vendors and network protocols associated with the individual networks, MNCs are creating very sophisticated and complex private networks that are a nightmare to most telecommunication managers, not to mention very costly to develop and maintain. But, managers have little choice; the current public networks lack the capacity and sophistication necessary to meet the needs of MNCs (Heldman, 1992).

In addition to their high costs, private networks have the disadvantage of being just that, private. Most large MNCs have a large number of relationships with other firms, not only with suppliers and customers, but with partners in cooperative ventures. Maintaining these "external" relationships is becoming more and more critical to the MNC (Ghoshal & Bartlett, 1990). Connecting to networks of other firms and to public networks entails another order of complexity and expense.

Coordination Roles

In their study of U.S. MNCs, Chismar and Chidambaram (1992) found no substantial evidence that telecommunications technology was being used to support new complex organizational structures. With respect to decision making structure, they found evidence that telecommunications technology was being used to centralize decision making across the functional areas in MNCs. Thus, rather than using the technology to distribute decision making authority, firms tend to use it to concentrate authority. While more empirical evidence is clearly needed, it would seem that the primary goal of the efforts to integrate information systems in MNCs is to improve the efficiency and reduce the cost of global operations. Common operational targets include customer support, data processing, and other back office functions.

The nature of informal coordination mechanisms makes it very difficult to assess the roles that information technology may be playing in facilitating new mechanisms. The high use of international telephone, fax, and electronic mail, which primarily support informal communications, clearly indicate an important role. But, it is also clear that this role is one of operational support. Normally, these technologies are not considered as important components in strategic planning or organizational design.

BARRIERS TO SUCCESS

In investigating the question of why information technology has not led to more rapid changes in organizational structures of multinational corporations, two sets of barriers come to light: technological and organizational. In addition, it may be the case that the technology available to date has not been appropriate for facilitating organizational change.

Technological Barriers

Many technological barriers slow progress toward global systems and networks. Not least among them is the large investment in existing, incompatible systems and networks. Many of these systems are critical to the operations of the MNC. The modification, necessary for the integration effort not only involves a large investment in systems development, but also entails a large risk of disrupting operations or possibly introducing bugs into existing systems.

From a technological consideration, the integration of isolated systems around the world can be a nightmare. Application systems, many of them custom built, run on a plethora of platforms, in a wide variety of languages. And the telecommunications side is just as eclectic. The lack of, or differing, technology standards, multiple vendors with a wide variety of unique products and services, and multiple PTTs all greatly impede any integration effort. And, if it's even possible, the integrated system consists of a complex network of gateways and translators, patching together the individual systems. On top of all of this, MNCs face the high costs of international linkages, varying government regulations, and the ever present rapid pace of technological change.

Organizational Barriers

In addition to technological barriers, formidable organizational barriers hinder a firm in achieving truly global systems and networks. Most of these barriers consist of tensions among managers of various business units, each with individual, possibly conflicting interests and authority. For example, conflicts can arise between a corporation and its subsidiaries, between senior executives and functional managers, and between technical managers and senior business managers. Conflicts on all of these levels must be resolved in order for a (systems integration project to succeed.

MNCs have long faced the issue of headquarter control versus subsidiary autonomy (Doz & Prahalad, 1981; Ghoshal & Bartlett, 1990). This is the basic trade off between control for the benefit of the company as a whole and responsiveness to local markets. In giving up autonomy and investing resources in an integration effort, subsidiary or division managers will require some compensation. Unlike the situation in purely domestic firms, the large physical and cultural distances between units in a MNC makes the power of the MNC's headquarters weaker (Ghoshal & Bartlett, 1990), thus making conflict resolution more important and difficult. Without a widely accepted management philosophy of global coordination, and an incentive system to support that philosophy, political obstacles will stop any global information systems integration effort.

Technological Appropriateness

Simply pulling together the isolated pieces of the information architecture in a MNC may not be sufficient in providing the necessary information support for global coordination. Most information systems in MNCs support formal coordination through the transfer and processing of data. However, the increased emphasis on informal coordination mechanisms brings an increased need for non-data types of information. In his analysis of global management networks, Charan (1991) emphasizes that the sharing of information is one of the most important success factors, but notes that data is in many respects the least important dimension of information. The network must also share openly and simultaneously each member's experiences, successes, and problems, soft information that can't be captured in databases and spreadsheets and that remains hidden for as long as possible in most traditional organizations. This is the kind of sharing that builds trust, empathy, and secure relationships. (p. 112)

While not specifically addressing MNCs, Daft and Lengal (1986) similarly note that "information processing in organizations is conceptually more than simply obtaining data to reduce uncertainty; it also involves interpreting equivocal situations" (p. 559). Dealing with this "equivocality" requires communications much more "media rich" than those provided by formal, data driven information systems. They go on to argue the equivocality is particularly high in organizations with a strong need for interdepartmental relationships and wide differences across departments. Therefore, within a MNC, a strong demand should exist for media rich modes of communication.

OVERCOMING THE BARRIERS

Technological

Given the complexities of integration and the pace of technological change, it is important that MNCs remain flexible in their development of global networks. Flexibility dictates a phased or evolutionary approach. First, the firm must set up the communication capability to move transactions among its related units. The aim should not be to get the best or optimal solution, but to get some solution to the problem of linking isolated systems. Many technical options exist for connecting dissimilar systems and the challenge involves getting some option to work without major disruptions to existing systems.

Once a network is in place, managers can then work on its evolution. This process involves the replacement of components of the system with new technology or services. It is during this ongoing process that detailed evaluations of alternative designs and products take place and the network adjusted accordingly. In order to maintain flexibility, the planning horizons and service contracts should be kept short.

Organizational

At the top of almost every survey of the priorities or concerns of senior information technology managers, including the surveys of MNCs (Ives & Jarvenpaa, 1991 and Deans, Karwan, Goslar, Ricks &

Toyne, 1991) is the need to educate senior business managers of the capabilities of technology. Since this concern also has long been, and remains a concern of domestic managers, it is likely that there is a serious gap between technology managers and senior business managers. If information technology is to assume a more prominent role in international business strategy, a closer relationship between these two groups of managers must develop.

Information technology managers must become more knowledgeable of and involved in the business, particularly from a strategic perspective. This is the flip side of trying to educate senior management about the technology. Technology managers who have been successful at becoming part of the business planning group often report that they began this process through more social contact with business managers, lunches, golf, and the like. Whatever the method, a relationship of trust must be established so that fast action can be taken to capitalize on opportunities to use information technology to enhance the MNC's competitive position.

New Technologies

Two ongoing advances in information technology deserve mention because of their great potential impact on international businesses: multimedia capabilities and photonics. These advances represent fundamental shifts in the nature of information management. As such, they will expand the options for coordination mechanisms, both formal and informal, available to businesses.

Multimedia Information Systems

Driven by the ability to digitize sound, images, and video, multimedia information systems provide access to information excluded from traditional information systems. In addition to being able to store, transmit, and view information, users will also be able to search, modify, compare the information. By providing this greater media richness, multimedia information systems open new possibilities for formal coordination within MNCs. In addition, multimedia opens new options for informal coordination within MNCs.

With multimedia capabilities, firms can integrate various voice, data, and video networks into a single network. Not only will this integration simplify the firms network operations, it will provide a media rich communication link. Electronic mail has been changing the way companies distribute information (Kiesler, 1986) and is very widely used in MNCs (Chidambaram & Chismar, 1992). The introduction of richer communication capabilities, such as on-demand video conferencing at the desk, should have great impact. At this point, it is difficult to predict the range of products and services that will be available, and even more difficult to predict the possible organizational impacts of such systems.

Photonics

Photonics refers to the use of light, instead of electricity, to transmit, store, and process information. Photonics represents a quantum advance in our ability to handle data and a means of realizing the potential of multimedia information systems. On the transmission side, fiber optic cable is now the telecommunications media of choice, with a large percentage of today's communications going over fiber networks. A major limiting factor in these networks is the use of electronic switches, but this may change within a few years. In 1990, Bell Labs fabricated the first photonic switch and, with intensive work continuing, such switches should be commercially available in a few years.

On the storage side, holographic storage devices promise orders-of-magnitude improvements over magnetic and optical-magnetic devices. Commercial products are scheduled to be released in 1994 which will provide tens of gigabytes of storage on a crystal a few cubic centimeters in size (Carey & Gross, 1993). On the processing side, optical computers also promise tremendous improvements in process performance and cost. In 1990, Bell Labs demonstrated the first digital photonic processor and in 1993, University of Colorado researchers demonstrated a version of the optical computer.

In the short run, perhaps over the next 5 years, the optical transmission and storage of information will provide MNCs opportunity to implement media rich, global information systems. In addition, photonics is driving a fundamental change in public communication networks. The capacity, speed, and reliability of these networks will improve significantly as they move toward all optical components. This fact is of particular importance to MNCs, which now rely heavily on their own private networks. With the growing sophistication of public networks, firms will no longer need to develop and maintain their own complex networks using leased lines, satellites, and microwaves to connect their separate networks.

These improved public networks will allow multimedia as well as dial-up video teleconferencing, which now require a 4 to 24 hour advance reservation through an operator. More importantly, these networks will eliminate the need for large capital investments in private networks, providing MNCs with greater flexibility and less risk in setting up global systems. Furthermore, such networks will allow MNCs the ability to implement sophisticated interorganizational systems.

All of the capabilities of multimedia and photonics add up to an ability for MNCs to implement systems to support informal coordination mechanisms which rely on soft or non-textual information. If the development of new organizational structures and coordination mechanisms has indeed been hampered to this point by the lack of media richness in existing information systems, removal of that constraint will surely allow more flexibility in the design of multinational organizations.

CONCLUSION

As multinational corporations continue to face fierce global competition, their reliance on more flexible and effective coordination mechanisms grows. The roles of information technology must change to support these coordination mechanisms and to generate new options for coordination. These options will provide the MNC with greater design opportunities with respect to the allocation of resources through the bundling and unbundling of information based activities. A number of shifts in the roles of information technology have begun and must continue.

First, and probably most important, is the shift from isolated to integrated global systems, pulling the pieces together. Global firms cannot afford to build geographic or functionally-centered applications and networks without considering the company-wide perspective. The ability to move data around the entire organization is critical to success of formal coordination mechanisms.

Second, there must be a shift from data driven systems to those which include other forms of information, including multimedia systems. While critical to the operations of an MNC, data driven applications cannot handle a large portion, or majority of the information needed for coordination. Currently this information is passed through documents and coordinating mechanisms such as face-to-face meetings and movement of personnel. The difficulties in moving this information around a global firm greatly limits the coordination options available to the firm; in turn, limiting the feasible strategic options. More media-rich information systems widen the set of coordinating options and improve the strategic flexibility of the firm.

Third, the use of the technology must shift from data processing to communication. Many of the coordination problems facing MNCs cannot be solved by gathering and analyzing more data; they require complex interactions among groups of people. Examples include most negotiation situations, the development of products for a world market, and the coordination of marketing plans across national markets. Closely related is the shift from formal to informal information systems. MNCs are increasingly relying on informal coordination mechanisms to deal with a dynamic environment.

Their formal information systems cannot provide the support needed and must also shift to more flexible and adaptable systems.

Finally, the shift from internal to external information systems must continue. Over the past decade or so there has been a major shift in international business to the use of firm alliances. These are not the traditional vertical integration relationships, but alliances among competitors and firms in formerly separate industries. These alliances run the range from short term contractual associations to pure equity joint ventures. Most large MNCs now have hundreds of such alliances. Information systems must move beyond the basic electronic data interchange (EDI) types of interorganizational systems to the more media rich, informal coordination type systems.

While this chapter has addressed information technology and MNC coordination issues, a number of related and important issues that have not been addressed should be mentioned. If information technology is an enabler to more complex global strategies, managers will not be able to apply the same methods of evaluation that they currently apply to individual, isolated applications. Evaluation of integrated systems by an individual business unit, no one of which receives the full "value" of the system, will fail to account for the true synergistic value of the system. Also, while it is generally assumed that providing greater information flows throughout a MNC via integration will provide positive benefits to the company, managers must still address the possibility that more communication may lead to detrimental outcomes. Even if the development and maintenance costs of the systems are ignored, it is possible these systems will have a negative value to the company!

REFERENCES

Bartlett, C. & Ghoshal, S. (1987). Managing across borders: new strategic requirements, *Sloan Management Review*, 28(4), 7-17.

Carey, J. & Gross, N. (1993). The light fantastic: Optoelectronics may revolutionize computers--and a lot more, *Business Week*, number 3318, May 10, 44-50.

Charan, Ram (1991). How Networks Reshape Organizations--For Results, *Harvard Business Review*, 69, September-October, 104-115.

Chidambaram, L. & Chismar, W.G. (1992). International telecommunication technologies: Use and investment patterns in U.S. multinational corporations, working paper, University of Hawaii, College of Business Administration.

Chismar, W.G., & Chidambaram, L. (1992). Telecommunications and the structuring of U.S. multinational corporations, *International Information Systems*, 1(4), 38-55.

Daft, R.L. & Lengel, R.H. (1986). Organizational information requirements, media richness, and structural design, *Management Science*, 32(5), 554-571.

Deans, P.C., Karwan, K.R., Goslar, M.D., Ricks, D.A., & Toyne, B. (1991). Identification of key international information systems issues in U.S.-based multinational corporations, *Journal of Management Information Systems*, 7(4), 27-50.

Doz, Y. & Prahalad, C.K. (1981). Headquarters influence and strategic control in MNCs, *Sloan Management Review*, 23(1), 15-29.

Egelhoff, W.G. (1988). Strategy and structure in multinational corporations: A revision of the Stopford and Wells model, *Strategic Management Journal*, 9(1), 1-14.

Galbraith, J.R. & Kazanjian, R.K. (1986). Organizing to implement strategies of diversity and globalization: The role of matrix designs, *Human Resource Management*, 25(1), 37-54.

Ghoshal, S. & Bartlett, C.A. (1990). The multinational corporation as an interorganizational network, *Academy of Management Review*, 15(4), 603-625.

Heldman, R.K. (1992). *Global telecommunications: Layered networks' layered services*, McGraw Hill, New York.

Hirschhorn, L. & Gilmore, T. (1992). The new boundaries of the "boundaryless" company, *Harvard Business Review*, May-June, 104-115.

Ives, B. & Jarvenpaa, S.L. (1991). Applications of global information technology: Key issues for management, *Management Information Systems Quarterly*, March, 33-49.

Kiesler, S. (1986). The hidden messages in computer networks, *Harvard Business Review*, 64, January-February, 46-60.

Martinez, J.I. & Jarillo, J.C. (1991). Coordination demands of international strategies. *Journal of International Business Studies*, 22(3), 429-444.

Martinez, J.I. & Jarillo, J.C. (1989). The evolution of research on coordination mechanisms in multinational corporations. *Journal of International Business Studies*, 20(3), 489-514.

Pitts, R. A. & Daniels, J.D. (1984). Aftermath of the Matrix Mania, *Columbia Journal of World Business*, 19(2), 48-54.

Prahalad, C.K. & Doz, Y. (1987). *The multinational mission: Balancing local demands and global vision*, The Free Press, New York.

Roche, E. M. (1992). *Managing Information Technology in Multinational Corporations: Theory, Measurement and Reality in the Global Environment*, Macmillan, New York.

Stopford, J. M. & L. T. Wells, Jr. (1972). *Managing the Multinational Enterprise: Organization of the Firm and Ownership of the Subsidiaries*, Longman Group, London.

Sullivan, D. & Bauerschmidt, A. (1991). The "Basic Concepts" of International Business Strategy: A Review and Reconsideration, *Management International Review*, 31, Special Issue, 111-124.

CHAPTER 25

National Culture, Information Systems, and Organizational Implications

K. S. RAMAN
National University of Singapore

RICHARD T. WATSON
University of Georgia

As organizations move beyond the confines of national boundaries, information systems (IS) managers face technical issues such as distributed databases and multiple national communications infra- structures, as well as major social issues arising from differences in national culture. Most MIS management knowledge is based on North American research and may not be applicable in other cultures. Consequently, Chief Information Officers (CIOs) responsible for global information systems and MIS managers facing foreign assignments need an understanding of cultural differences and their effect on MIS management. This paper raises some of the consequences of cultural differences for MIS. Two case studies are included to illustrate the effect of these differences.

INTRODUCTION

Theories and concepts of management information systems (MIS), like most management theories and concepts, are almost exclusively developed in the North American culture and context. Research shows that management theories, concepts, and practice developed in one culture may not be applicable in other cultures (Hofstede, 1991). Instances of the problems faced in applying North American management style in other cultures are illustrated by Daft (1991). For example, an American executive working in Japan offered a holiday trip to the top salesperson. Employees showed no interest in the award until the American manager changed the prize to a trip for the group if it achieved the sales quota. The group met its quota. Japanese are motivated in groups. It is a collectivistic culture in contrast to the individualism of North America.

We gain a quick understanding of differences between Eastern and Western cultures by examining some representative expressions from each society (see Table 1). The individualism and free will philosophy of the West contrasts with the collectivism and passive acceptance of outside forces by the East (Haglund, 1984).

An information system is an integrated user-computer system for providing information to support operations, management, analysis, and decision making functions in an organization. Since MIS is a support system for organizational functions, it draws from theories and concepts of organization, organizational behavior, management, and decision making (Davis and Olson, 1984). Therefore, the cultural differences that affect the applicability of management theories and concepts in other cultures are likely to affect the applicability of MIS theories and concepts. Cultural forces, like

The East	The West
What is possible depends on circumstances	All things are possible
One does not make the wind but is blown by it	Where there is a will, there is a way
The greatness of a person may be measured by ones humility, not by ones assertiveness	Nice guys finish last
The nail that stands above the board gets nailed down	He travels the fastest who travels alone

Source: adapted from Haglund [1984]

Table 1: Expressions representative of the differing views of the East and West

organizational forces, shape the use of computer technology. MIS managers who try to apply North American based MIS theories, concepts, and practice when they are not in phase with local culture and context, may create dysfunctional effects. Yet, national culture is a relatively neglected variable in the development of MIS theories, concepts, and practice.

THREE LEVELS OF CULTURE

Historically, use of the word culture has been reserved for nations, or ethnic or regional groups. More recently it has been applied equally to organizations and professions (Hofstede, 1980). For the purposes of this chapter, we identify three cultures—national, organizational, and MIS professional culture. In this section, we briefly define and discuss these cultures and the forces and influences they generate in organizations. In later sections, we discuss at length national culture and its potential impact on global management of the MIS function.

Culture as a Mental Program

Every individual has certain patterns of thinking, feeling, and acting which are learned throughout a lifetime. Hofstede (1980, 1991) calls these patterns of thinking, feeling, and acting a mental program. The sources of a person's mental program lie within the social environments in which that person grows up— family, school, work place, and community. In social anthropology, the word culture is used to encapsulate patterns of thinking, feeling, and acting, or the mental program.

Symbols, heroes, rituals, and values cover the total concept of culture. Symbols refer to language and jargon, accents of speech, dress, hair styles, food and eating, and status symbols. Heroes are persons real or imaginary, alive or dead, who possess characteristics highly prized by a culture and who serve as role models of behavior. Rituals are collective activities considered essential within a culture. Symbols, heroes, and rituals can be subsumed under the term practices. Values are broad tendencies of people to prefer certain states of affairs over others. Values are feelings that have a plus and a minus side.

Practices are manifestations of culture visible to outside observers. Values, on the other hand, are internal; they can only be inferred from the way people act under various circumstances. Practices are the outer, visible shell of culture that can undergo change. Values are the inner core or kernel of culture and are difficult to change.

National Culture

National culture is the common mental programming of a group of people who live or have lived in the same social environment. It is a collective phenomenon at the national level. It is the patterns of thinking, feeling, and acting that each person in the society inherits. Extending the social anthropology concept of culture as a mental program, Hofstede (1980, 1991) defines national culture as "the collective programming of the mind that distinguishes members of one group or category of people from another."

Research on social anthropology has shown that all cultures face very similar basic problems, but the answers differ across cultures. On the basis of a survey of literature on national culture, Inkeles and Levinson (1969) suggest that the following issues qualify as basic problems worldwide:

- relation to authority
- relationship between the individual and society
- the individual's concept of masculinity and femininity
- ways of dealing with conflicts.

Twenty years later, Hofstede (1980) analyzed a large volume of survey data about the values of IBM employees in over 50 countries and found similar common problems across countries, but with solutions differing from country to country. These common problems and differing solutions across countries have implications for the functioning of societies, and organizations and professions within societies. They also have implications for MIS management.

Organizational Culture

Organizational culture is a recent phenomenon relative to national culture. The term organizational culture first appeared in the literature in the 1960s (Blake and Mouton, 1964), and the more catchy term corporate culture was popularized by Deal and Kennedy (1982). There is no standard definition of organizational culture, but most authors on the subject seem to agree that organizational culture is: (1) holistic, (2) historically determined, (3) related to practices and values, (4) socially constructed, (5) soft, and (6) difficult to change. Hofstede (1991) extends the concept of culture as collective programming of the mind to organizations and defines organizational culture as "the collective programming of the mind that distinguishes the members of one organization from another."

Hofstede, Neuijen, Ohayv, and Sanders (1990) made a scientific study of organizational culture in 20 organizations in similar national cultures and identified the following six dimensions of organizational culture:

- process oriented vs. results oriented
- parochial vs. professional
- open system vs. closed system
- employee oriented vs. job oriented
- loose control vs. tight control
- normative vs. pragmatic

The first three dimensions are associated with values. The next three dimensions describe the organizational practices inculcated into employees; they have no links with values.

MIS Culture

The emergence of MIS as an academic discipline and a profession can be traced to the early 1960s. There is no systematic study of the professional culture of MIS yet, but we know that it is predominantly a product of North American culture and context. North American corporations such as Apple Computer, Digital Equipment Corporation, Hewlett-Packard, IBM, Microsoft, and the Yourdon Group are among the dominant developers and disseminators of concepts, methodologies, products, and technologies underlying MIS. Even when key concepts had origins in other regions, North American corporations were at the forefront of their popularization. For example, the genesis of structured programming was in Europe, but structured methodologies were evangelized by the New York based Yourdon Group through its seminars and text books.

North American text books have been and are a major force in transmitting MIS culture to the world. Seminal works, such as *Management Information Systems: Conceptual Foundations, Structure, and Development,* (Davis 1974, Davis and Olson, 1984), and the majority of Harvard MIS case studies (see Cash, McFarlan, McKenney, and Applegate, 1992) are based on North American research and experience. North American journals such as *Information Systems Research* and *MIS Quarterly,* and conferences such as the International Conference on Information Systems are the leading outlets for MIS research. Their gatekeepers are primarily North American scholars.

We are not exactly certain what MIS culture is—this is certainly an area for research—but we suggest it can be analyzed in terms of the practice and value dimensions of organizational culture. The practice dimension of MIS culture includes jargon, techniques, tools, methodologies, and standards. Regarding values, the MIS profession seems process oriented as opposed to results oriented; is more loyal to the profession than the organization; and operates a closed

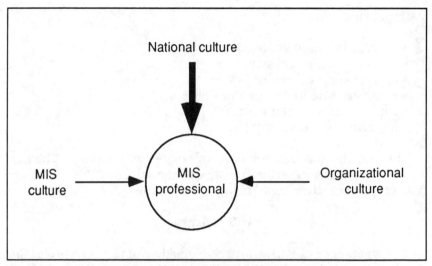

Figure 1: Cultural forces shaping the MIS professionals culture

system in which outsiders feel alien. The MIS culture also includes concepts such as data as a corporate resource, custodians vs. owners of data, and data security. Historically, MIS was seen an innovative profession; but in recent years, MIS departments have resisted innovations that empower users.

The MIS professional is subject to the three cultural forces, as shown in Figure 1, of which the national culture is dominant. The broader arrow in Figure 1 underlines its potency.

CULTURAL TRANSMISSION

The notion of cultural transmission parallels the notion of biological transmission. In biological transmission, certain features of a population are perpetuated across generations through genetic mechanisms. In cultural transmission, certain features of the mental programs of a group of people are perpetuated across generations through teaching and learning. For example, many features of the Chinese culture can be traced to the writings of Confucius, a Chinese philosopher of 500 b.c., and Western styles of thinking and values can be traced to the ancient Greek philosophers.

Cultural transmission can occur in three ways: vertically, horizontally, and obliquely. Vertical transmission (Cavalli-Sforza and Feldman, 1981) describes the descent or inheritance of parental cultural characteristics by offspring. Parents transmit cultural values and beliefs to their children; they are generally a major force in ensuring the transmission of national culture. In organizations and professions, superiors and mentors fulfill a similar role and are vertical transmitters of organizational and professional culture.

Horizontal cultural transmission refers to the process of learning from one's peers from birth to adulthood (Berry, Poortinga, Segall, and Dasen, 1992). National culture is learned from peers of the same ethnic group. Organizational culture is taught by one's fellow workers, and professional culture is transmitted by professional colleagues.

Oblique cultural transmission describes learning from other adults and institutions either in one's own culture or from other cultures (Berry et al., 1992). Oblique cultural transmission plays a key role in the development of organizational and professional cultures. Many organizations send recruits on a company training program to transmit their organizational culture (the way things are done here). Organizational culture is continually reinforced through such devices as periodic newsletters and annual get-together events. Professional culture is mostly developed during university education, particularly in established professions such as accounting, engineering, law, and medicine and is reinforced by professional societies, journals, conferences, and continuing education. MIS professionals receive their induction to the MIS culture while university students. They receive far less oblique cultural transmission than those in the established professions.

MIS managers need to understand that MIS professionals are subject to these three forms of cultural transmission. Development psychologists believe that by the age of ten most children have their vertically transmitted mental programs firmly in place. Therefore, by the time a MIS professional starts a career, although the forces vertically transmitting national culture might have been reduced (children move away from parental influence and assert individuality as they grow), they have had their effect. Vertically transmitted national culture is extremely persistent and changing its impact is beyond the influence of MIS managers.

There is scope to use horizontal and oblique techniques to transmit organization and MIS culture. Managers, as leaders, can be powerful disseminators of culture. They can also make extensive use of training to convey obliquely MIS culture. However, MIS managers should be aware that omnipotent national culture is likely to triumph in any clash of cultures. They should be prepared to modify MIS culture to avoid dissonance and stress when it conflicts with national culture.

DIMENSIONS OF NATIONAL CULTURE

Four dimensions of national culture—individualism, power distance, uncertainty avoidance, and masculinity—were identified by Hofstede during his international study of IBM (Hofstede, 1980, 1991). An additional dimension, long-term orientation, was discovered by Hofstede and Bond (1988) as a result of using the Chinese Values Survey. Hall's (1976) research adds two more dimensions, monochrony vs. polychrony and context, to national culture and extends the time dimension discovered by Hofstede and Bond (1988). Each of these dimensions is discussed in detail.

Individualism

Societies differ in their emphasis on individual rights and obligations to society. Individualism describes societies in which the ties between individuals are loose and people are expected to look after themselves and their immediate families. Collectivism describes societies in which people from birth are integrated into strong, cohesive groups that continue to protect the individual throughout life. The US is a highly individualistic society, and self interest is an implicit tenet of most management practice. Chinese societies (e.g., China, Hong Kong, Singapore, and Taiwan) are collectivist where individual behavior is governed by moral forces that put the well-being of the society and group above individual self-interest.

Power Distance

Power distance describes a culture's social relationship between superiors and subordinates. It is the extent to which the less powerful members of institutions and organizations in a culture expect and accept that power is distributed unequally. The US is a low power distance society. Thus, superiors and subordinates are usually on a first name basis and, and subordinates are generally unafraid to disagree with superiors and may question their orders and authority. Some societies (many Latin American, Arab, and East Asian nations) are marked by high power distance. Subordinates obey instructions unquestioningly and tend to be extremely deferential to high status individuals.

Uncertainty Avoidance

Uncertainty avoidance is the extent to which the members of a society feel threatened by uncertain or unknown situations and some societies take considerable pain to avoid uncertainty. For example, Germans are meticulous in their planning, and their legal system even has laws to cover the case when there are no laws. Other societies can handle a high degree of uncertainty and are less inclined to develop procedures and rules, and bother with detailed planning.

Masculinity

The masculinity dimension describes the extent to which social gender roles are differentiated in a society. This is reflected in the way jobs are distributed in a society. Very masculine societies, such as most of those in Latin America, tend to have few women in some occupations. High status positions are usually reserved for men. Feminine societies, such as the societies of Scandinavia, have a more equal distribution of social gender roles. For example, the current Norwegian government is headed by a woman and the cabinet is predominantly female.

Time Orientation

Time orientation can be described by a continuum with long-term orientation at one pole and short-term orientation at the other (Hofstede and Bond, 1988; Hofstede, 1991). Eastern and Western societies have different perceptions of time and time orientation. Eastern nations and organizations are more likely to invest in projects whose payoffs are quite distant. In contrast, American society and its organizations have a short-term time orientation and are driven by short-term goals. Capital is impatient and quarterly results are often a guiding principle for change agents.

Monochrony and Polychrony

Cultures vary in their attitude towards use of time. Perceptions of how late one may be for an appointment and task deadline flexibility vary from culture to culture. Hall (1976) and Hall and Hall (1990) take a broader view of people's attitudes towards time and identify monochrony and polychrony as two temporal styles that encompass the manner in which people separate or pool their activities in time. Monochronic people and cultures focus on one thing at a time; they emphasize tasks, schedules, and procedures. Polychronic people and cultures place importance on people and relationships and the completion of transactions rather than on rigid schedules. Western cultures such as the US tend to be monochronic; Latin American and East Asian cultures tend to be polychronic.

Context

Hall (1976) has observed that the proportion of explicit, coded information in communication varies across cultures. In many cultures, much information is contextual and bound with the event and not explicitly stated. Hall (1976) defines context as the information that surrounds an event. He posits that events and context are in different proportions in different cultures, which can be compared on a scale from high to low context. A high context communication (culture) is one in which most of the information is already in the persons involved and very little is in the explicit, coded part of the message. A low context communication (culture) is just the opposite; a mass of information is vested in the explicit code.

Hall (1976), and Hall and Hall (1990) do not offer any quantitative measures or scores for monochronic and polychronic, and low-context and high-context cultures. Nevertheless from the descriptions of these terms and anecdotal evidence offered by these researchers, it can be seen that strong power distance and weak uncertainty avoidance cultures tend to be polychronic and high-context.

National Culture as an Integrated System

The components of national culture fit together to create a relatively harmonious and integrated set of values, beliefs, and behavior. There are clearly some factors that are closely coupled. For example, the correlation matrix shown in Table 2 indicates that power distance correlates negatively with individualism and positively with long-term orientation. Societies such as Hong Kong, have high power distance, a long-term orientation, and low individualism. In such cultures, people are willing to suppress individual wants for the well-being of the society and are obedient to their leader. Also, collectivism appears to promote a longer-term perspective because individuals act to ensure the continued well-being of the society.

	Power distance	Uncertainty avoidance	Individuality	Masculinity	Time orientation
Power distance	1.0000	-0.0638	-0.7619	0.1489	0.3426
Uncertainty avoidance	-0.0638	1.0000	-0.1372	0.3137	0.1518
Individuality	-0.7619	-0.1372	1.0000	0.0091	-0.4135
Masculinity	0.1489	0.3137	0.0091	1.0000	0.0918
Time orientation	0.3426	0.1518	-0.4135	0.0918	1.0000

Data source: Hofstede [1980, 1991]

Table 2: Correlation coefficients of some cultural dimensions

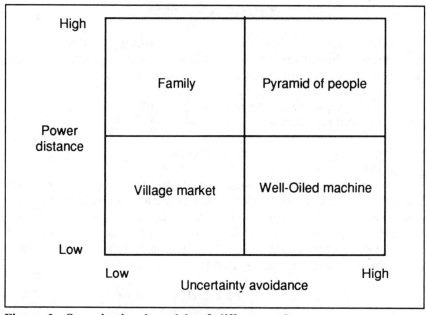

Figure 2: Organizational models of different cultures

ORGANIZATIONAL MODELS

The dimensions of national culture, especially power distance and uncertainty avoidance, affect the way organizations in different cultures handle the same type of problem. Based on the diagnosis and solutions offered by students from France, Germany, and Britain to an organizational problem in an international MBA course, Stevens (Hofstede, 1991) coined the terms Pyramids of People, Well-Oiled Machine, and Village Market for organizational models implicit in the minds of students from these cultures. A discussion of Steven's model with some Asian scholars led to the suggestion that the implicit model of organization in Asian cultures is the Family (Hofstede, 1991). The quadrants in Figure 2 map these four models of organizations.

Pyramids of People

The implicit model of organizations in strong power distance and strong uncertainty avoidance cultures is a pyramid of people, with the general manager at the top of the pyramid, and each successive level at the proper place below. France has relatively high scores for power distance and uncertainty avoidance. In this culture, the preferred approach to solving organizational problems at lower levels is to refer them to the common boss, who would issue orders for settling such issues in the future.

Well-Oiled Machine

Germany has weak power distance and strong uncertainty avoidance scores. In this culture, organizational problems are attributed to lack of procedures causing uncertainty. The solution is to establish procedures. In such cultures, the organization is viewed as a well-oiled machine in which management intervention is limited to exceptional situations.

Village Market

The implicit model of the organization in this culture is the village market in which the demands of the situation determine the solution. Each situation is handled ad hoc; neither hierarchy nor rules will determine the solution. Britain has weak power distance and weak uncertainty avoidance scores. In this culture, organizational problems are first viewed as human relations problems.

The Family

Many Asian countries have strong power distance and weak uncertainty scores. Organizations in these cultures operate as extended families, in which the manager is the omnipotent grandfather. Authority is concentrated in the supreme boss without structuring of activities.

CONSEQUENCES OF CULTURAL DIFFERENCES

The objective of the above analysis of national cultures is to understand the consequences of managerial actions in organizations. We are particularly interested in the consequences of cultural differences on management of the MIS function. On the basis of cultural differences, we make some conjectures on their effects on MIS. To provide direction for future research, we have stated some of our conjectures as propositions. We have used the North American MIS manager as a baseline for framing some of our surmises.

Management of the MIS Function

Anthony (1965) defines organizational management process in terms of strategic planning, management control, and operational control. Some management scholars (Hirschfield, 1983) use the term tactical planning for management control and operations planing for operational control. Daft's (1991) definition of management "... the attainment of organizational goals in an effective and efficient manner through planning, organizing, leading, and controlling organizational resources" is typical of those found in recent management text books. When considering management of the MIS function, we need only insert MIS before these definitions to have an apt definition of MIS management. Here, we adopt Hirschfield's modification of Anthony's definition of management to assess the consequences of cultural differences on MIS strategic planning, MIS tactical planning, and MIS operational planning in terms of the four organizational models discussed earlier.

Strategic MIS Planning

Strategic MIS planning refers to the process of identifying existing objectives of the MIS department; and deciding the changes in these objectives, the resources to be used to achieve the objectives, and on the policies that govern the acquisition, use, and disposition of these resources (McLean and Soden, 1977). Some important concerns of developing a strategic MIS plan are its alignment and fit with the organizational strategic plan; the management process within MIS; personnel development; and technology focus. The source discipline for organizational strategic planning is economics (Anthony, 1965), which is equally applicable to MIS strategic planning. We suggest that cross-cultural psychology and information technology are also key reference disciplines for MIS planning in the global organization.

MIS managers responsible for global MIS strategic planning will have to contend with varying attitudes to planning effort and project time horizon. Managers working in well-oiled machine cultures will need to provide very detailed and precise information to superiors and should anticipate meticulous planning from subordinates. They are likely to feel that there is too much planning and not enough action. In contrast, managers in family cultures will be exacerbated by the lack of planning and a bias for action. Further, organizations in these cultures have long-term orientation and are likely to invest their resources in projects with long term payoffs. An MIS manager attuned to quick payback periods might want to press for smaller projects with shorter time horizons. Our analysis suggests the following propositions:

P1. Cultural differences will be reflected in the level of detail and comprehensiveness of the strategic plans of MIS departments.
P2. The average systems development time of projects in long-term orientation societies will be longer than those in short-term orientation societies.

Tactical MIS Planning

Tactical MIS planning is the process by which resources are obtained and used efficiently and effectively in achieving the objectives of the MIS division. The critical resources are technology and people. The source discipline for organizational tactical planning is social psychology (Anthony, 1965). As in the case of global strategic MIS planning, cross-cultural psychology and information technology are additional reference disciplines for global tactical MIS planning.

Tactical MIS planning involves implementation of strategic MIS plans. This includes developing the MIS architecture to meet the host organization needs, identifying an application project portfolio, project implementation plans, and equipment acquisition projections. Here again, the time orientation dimension of culture will affect the project portfolio. Pyramids of people will pay meticulous care to implementation projections and equipment acquisition projections. Polychronic and family type of cultures will resist a rigid program development schedule of tasks, responsibilities, and deadlines. We suggest the following proposition:

P3. Projects in polychronic societies are less likely to finish on time when compared to similar projects in monochronic societies.

Operations MIS Planning

Operations MIS planning consists of allocating tasks in order to achieve the objectives of the tactical MIS plan. More specifically, it involves developing application systems using appropriate technology and methodology to achieve the tactical MIS plan. The effects of national culture require careful understanding and consideration when assessing MIS operational planning across cultures.

Determining information requirements is an important step in developing information systems. It is estimated that analysts spend 75 percent of their time on this activity (Vitalari and Dickson, 1983). In monochronic, low context, strong uncertainty avoidance, and pyramid cultures, determining information requirements is likely to take longer and will be more detailed. In high-context, low uncertainty avoidance, and family cultures, it will be difficult for an analyst who is not a part of the inner circle and network (i.e., someone who is not aware of the context) to determine information requirements satisfactorily. In such cultures, initial progress is likely to be rapid, but the system will continually undergo modifications.

P4. Systems change requests will be more frequent in a low uncertainty-avoiding culture.

Power distance and masculinity also require consideration in systems analysis. In strong power distance and masculine cultures, the interviewing systems analyst should be a male with a similar status to that of the interviewees.

P5. Systems analysis will be more successful when its execution is aligned with cultural norms.

MIS Personnel

People are a critical resource in developing global information systems. In addition to a sound technical background, MIS personnel with responsibilities extending beyond their national borders should receive cross-cultural sensitivity training. Furthermore, the recruitment and reward systems should be in harmony with the local national culture. In family cultures, recruiters are likely to first look for appointees from a network of contacts. For example, a software house in an East Asian country seeks its recruits from the brothers and sisters of existing employees.

In collectivistic cultures, it may be more appropriate to reward groups rather than individuals. Likewise, it is essential to pay attention to the relative roles of and status of men and women. Appointing a woman to a senior position in masculine societies is unlikely to be received positively. Indeed, we would expect most women in such societies to occupy less prestigious MIS positions.

P6. Women are more likely to be found in lower status MIS jobs in highly masculine cultures.

Application of Information Technology

The context dimension of national culture has implications for Decision Support Systems (DSS) and Executive Information Systems (EIS). These systems, which are widely used in organizations in low-context societies (e.g., USA), are not yet widely used in high-context cultures such as Japan. Managers in high context cultures believe that while a computer can capture the low-context, explicit information relating to a situation, it cannot satisfactorily reflect the full context. For a manager in a high context society, a DSS or EIS is a poor substitute for the meaning that comes from high context communication. For managers in a low context society, a DSS or EIS is ideal because for them all the information is vested in the code, and computer-based systems overcome the inefficiencies of manual information processing and low context communication.

P7. DSS and EIS will be more widely used in low context than in high context societies.

Global MIS managers should be mindful that varying attitudes to planning across cultures may also extend to specific technologies and methodologies. Consider, for example, group support and electronic mail technologies. The very purpose of group support technology is to change group behavior, the essence of culture. In strong power distance cultures, group support systems that are used to reduce status differentials are likely to create dysfunctional effects. Likewise, electronic mail in such cultures and organizations is likely to be used only for top-down communication. There is already some experimental evidence of varying effects for GSS technology in different cultures (Watson, Ho, and Raman, forthcoming).

P8. The effects of group communication technologies will vary in different cultural settings.

CASE STUDIES

We present two cases that illustrate the consequences of cultural difference on MIS. The first case describes the difficulties faced by a European insurance company in implementing the systems designed at its headquarters for an insurance company in Southeast Asia. The second case describes how the role of a highly successful and important MIS department in a large Southeast Asian company changed dramatically when expatriate top managers from low-context, strong uncertainty avoidance cultures were replaced by local managers.

Pacific Insurance

In the early 1980s, Pacific Insurance (not its real name), a successful insurance company in a Southeast Asian country with an annual premium income of $25 million and employing 40 people, set out to modernize and expand. It entered into a technical and managerial collaboration agreement with an European insurance company, which we will call Atlantic Insurance. In the process, Atlantic bought substantial equity in Pacific. One of the key items of the agreement was to introduce modern management practices and information systems into Pacific. Senior Atlantic and Pacific executives did not give a second thought to this after signing the agreement. Why should they? Atlantic had successfully accomplished this in Europe and the UK with companies ten times as large as Pacific. Why would Pacific be any different? Little did they know that Pacific was a high-context, strong power distance, polychronic, family type of organization, and this was going to make a world of difference to information systems.

A team of two Atlantic systems analysts arrived in Pacific with the mission to complete systems study and system specifications in six weeks. Prior to arrival, they had worked out a detailed schedule of appointments and interviews with managers and clerical staff of Pacific. After one week on the job, the Atlantic systems analysts began to sense that things in Pacific were going to be different and difficult. Although Pacific managers and staff kept their appointments with the Atlantic analysts, the interview sessions were highly inefficient and ineffective. There were frequent interruptions: phone calls; visitors dropping in with queries and problems; bosses asking for some information urgently, or dropping by to take some papers; and colleagues dropping in with a cup of coffee for a chat. The information and procedures so necessary to develop systems specifications were in the heads of people rather than documented and available in files. The polite, high-context manner of communication of Pacific people did not provide the detailed, linear information and logic required by the Atlantic analysts.

Calculations of premium payable on policies and amount to be paid for claims are the core of insurance systems. Premium calculation, which was a fairly routine process in Atlantic, turned out to be very complex in Pacific. Although Pacific had tables for computing premiums, in almost every instance there were exceptions, and the actual figure was provided by the managing director or his deputy, depending on the context. From their experience in Atlantic, the analysts knew that processing of claims and determining the claim amount to be settled was more complex than calculating premium. In Pacific there were additional dimensions of complexity. The hidden rules of claims processing, personal knowledge regarding the insured on the part of claims executives, and the high-context culture made it almost impossible for the Atlantic analysts to fathom how claims were processed in Pacific. For example, when going through files, they found several very similar claims some of which were expeditiously settled in full, some others partially settled after some delays, some totally rejected quickly, and some totally rejected after long delays. They never could find out the rationale and logic underlying these claim settlement decisions.

After six weeks, the analysts had bits and pieces of information, but were far from developing system specifications. They were frustrated and wondered how Pacific kept its act together and made good profits year after year. They realized that the systems in use in Atlantic companies would not work in Pacific. Their system solution strategy began to drift towards finding the appropriate technology. They speculated that expert system technology, which was not yet used in Atlantic, might meet the needs of the Pacific premium and claims systems. They started to worry about the daunting technical issues and problems in designing and implementing expert systems, and integrating them with traditional data processing systems.

Two years and half a million dollars later, the Atlantic analysts still had not understood how premiums and claims were computed in Pacific. They settled for a simple computer system into which manually computed premiums and claims were entered for further processing. The Pacific people privately mused: "Couldn't we have done this ourselves, perhaps more quickly and at lower cost?"

Peninsula Industries

Peninsula Industries (not its real name) is a medium sized manufacturing company in a Southeast Asian country. It is a subsidiary company of a multinational company with headquarters in London and manufacturing plants and sales offices in several countries. In the mid 1970s, Peninsula had annual sales of about $300 million and a workforce of about 1700 people, and was projected to continue its annual growth rate of 15 percent over the next few years. Historically, most divisional and senior level managers of the company were expatriates posted for periods of three to six years to this company, and the organizational culture appeared to be that of the parent company.

In order to cope with the projected growth through the 1970s, the expatriate managing director, who had attended top management courses on MIS offered by Diebold Consultants, Harvard, and IBM, decided to implement modern management information systems in Peninsula. He secured the support of the parent company who made the requisite systems expertise available to Peninsula from other parts of the group. An ambitious systems project covering all aspects of Peninsula's management and operations was launched and successfully completed over six years. The systems fully covered manufacturing, sales, accounting and finance, and human resource functions. A management support system was implemented to provide support to top management in strategic planning and management control. The expatriate managers fully used these systems in their decision making. Several middle management and staff assistant posts were eliminated, and the affected people were redeployed in line functions. MIS in Peninsula was considered so successful that several group companies adopted its system. The hardware vendor often brought prospective customers to Peninsula to show what its computer can do for a company.

In the mid 1970s, the parent company decided to gradually replace expatriate managers with local managers. The local managers had a good education in local or foreign universities. Peninsula sponsored them to attend overseas management courses as a part of their development and to give them exposure to modern management concepts. They were also attached to the group headquarters and manufacturing plants in the UK for transmission of corporate culture. Over a period of 10 years, most expatriate managers in Peninsula were replaced by local managers who were well educated and had considerable exposure to Western management concepts and practice, and management information systems.

This transition did not have any initial impact on the internal workings of Peninsula or its profits, but things began to change gradually. The new managers relied more on information elicited through their network of contacts in the company and outside the company. The production planning system, and the customer and supplier evaluation and reward systems, which incorporated sophisticated rules, were discontinued in favor of context-rich information obtained through the human network. Several support staff and intermediary posts were created to feed this context-rich information to managers for decision making and use of the management support system was quietly discontinued.

The systems analysts who had developed these systems left Peninsula for senior positions elsewhere. Over a period of five years, the role of the MIS department was transformed from one of providing support to management to that of processing routine, high-volume, low-context data. The MIS manager, who reported to the Director of Finance and was a member of several top management committees, left Peninsula. His position was filled by promoting the computer operations supervisor to the level of manager and designating him Computer Manager reporting to the Financial Accountant. The systems development unit became a COBOL program maintenance shop.

Peninsula continued to maintain the projected growth rates under local managers and the parent company continued to receive good returns on their investment in Peninsula. In 1987, after a few successful years on the job, the local Managing Director of Peninsula had this to say about computer systems:

"I have seen several highly successful management support systems during my visits abroad. In the management development program I attended at Harvard, there were some good sessions on management use of computers. But here, in my country and culture, things are different; we are used to operating in a highly flexible system of information gathering, processing, and use. That is why we depend on a network of people to provide information in a flexible manner. Information provided by a dedicated and loyal group of staff assistants is like a lump of putty. It is soft and can be massaged quickly and easily into any shape I need. Working with information provided by a computer is like working with a block of marble. I need an expert sculptor to get the shape I need. If there is a mistake in the process, we have to start all over again. Personal computers seem to be more flexible, but I guess they still have a long way to go before we can replace our human network."

CONCLUSION

A pair of insightful papers (Bostrom and Heinen, 1977), in an early issue of *MIS Quarterly*, put forward the socio-technical perspective of MIS. At that stage, the socio part applied to an organizations social system. The socio-technical viewpoint is still relevant, but we need to realize that the socio part encompasses both national and organizational cultures. MIS academics need to add yet another reference discipline, cross-cultural psychology, to the list of those from which they can draw. MIS managers and designers, when moving beyond their national boundaries, need to become sensitive to cultural differences. Cultural literacy is clearly becoming more pertinent as organizations begin managing MIS globally and developing global MIS systems. Organizations that fail to understand the importance of national culture are likely to increase the risk of project failure and ineffective use of information technology. They are likely to repeat the mistakes of the past if they fail to recognize the effect of an organization's social systems on project success.

REFERENCES

Anthony, R. N. (1965). *Planning and control systems: a framework for analysis.* Cambridge, MA: Harvard University.

Berry, J. W., Poortinga, Y. H., Segall, M. H., & Dasen, P. R. (1992). *Cross-cultural psychology: research and applications.* Cambridge, UK: Cambridge University Press.

Blake, R. R., & Mouton, J. S. (1964). *The managerial grid.* Houston, TX: Gulf.

Bostrom, R. P., & Heinen, J. S. (1977). MIS problems and failures: a socio-technical perspective: part I: the causes. *MIS Quarterly,* 1(3), 17-32.

Bostrom, R. P., & Heinen, J. S. (1977). MIS problems and failures: a socio-technical perspective: part I: the application of socio-technical theory. *MIS Quarterly,* 1(4), 11-28.

Cash, J. I. J., McFarlan, F. W., McKenney, J. L., & Applegate, L. M. (1992). *Corporate information systems management: text and cases* (3rd). Homewood, IL: Irwin.

Cavalli-Sforza, L. L., & Feldman, M. (1981). *Cultural transmission and evolution: a quantitative approach.* Princeton, NJ: Princeton University Press.

Daft R. L. (1991). *Management* (2nd), Fort Worth, TX: Dryden.

Davis, G. B. (1974). *Management Information Systems: conceptual foundations, structure, and development.* New York, NY: McGraw-Hill.

Davis, G. B., & Olson, M. H. (1985). *Management Information Systems:*

conceptual foundations, structure, and development. (2nd), New York, NY: McGraw-Hill.

Deal, T. E., & Kennedy, A. A. (1982). *Corporate cultures: the rites and rituals of corporate life.* Reading, MA: Addison-Wesley.

Haglund, E. (1984). Japan: cultural considerations. *International Journal of Intercultural Relations,* 8, 61-76.

Hall, E. T. (1976). *Beyond culture.* Garden City, NY: Doubleday Anchor Books.

Hall, E. T., & Hall, M. R. (1990). *Understanding cultural differences.* Yarmouth, ME: Intercultural Press.

Hirschfield. (1983). From the shadows. *Interfaces,* 13(2), 72-76.

Hofstede, G. (1980). *Culture's consequences: international differences in work-related values.* Beverly Hills, CA: Sage.

Hofstede, G. (1991). *Culture and organizations: software of the mind.* London, UK: McGraw-Hill.

Hofstede, G., & Bond, M. H. (1988). The Confucius connection: from cultural roots to economic growth. *Organizational Dynamics,* 16(4), 5-21.

Hofstede, G., Neuijen, B., Ohayv, D. D., & Sanders, G. (1990). Measuring organizational cultures: a qualitative and quantitative study across twenty cases. *Administrative Science Quarterly,* 35(2), 286-316.

Inkeles, A., & Levinson, D. J. (1969). National character: the study of modal personality and sociocultural systems. In G. Lindsey, & E. Aronson (eds), *Handbook of social psychology* (2nd) Vol. 4, Reading, MA: Addison-Wesley.

McLean, E. R., & Soden, V. S. (1977). *Strategic planning for MIS.* New York, NY: Wiley.

Vitalari, N. P., & Dickson, G. W. (1983). Problem solving for effective systems analysis. *Communications of the ACM,* 26(11), 984-956.

Watson, R. T., Ho, T. H., & Raman, K. S. (forthcoming). Culture: a fourth dimension of GSS research. *Communications of the ACM.*

CHAPTER 26

The Risks Associated with Planning and Implementing Global Information Technology Systems

TERRY ANTHONY BYRD
CHETAN S. SANKAR
JERRY D. McCREARY

Auburn University

The merging of computers and communications is having a profound effect on both public and private organizations. This integration of information technology (IT) is supporting the expansion of firms into global markets. While IT solves many problems, the implementation and operation of critical IT systems carry risks of their own. This chapter investigates the risks associated with planning and implementing international IT systems. A framework for risk analysis is presented. In the framework, four categories of risk are identified and examined from the strategic, tactical and operational perspectives. The risk categories are risks associated with IT coordination, security, culture, and legal/regulatory requirements. The framework provides a means for researchers to include risk as a factor in analyzing global information systems.

INTRODUCTION

The merging of computers and telecommunications is bringing profound changes to the ways that public and private organizations operate. Academics, consultants, politicians, business people, and others are hailing in a new era in which information technology (IT), i.e., computers, telecommunications, and automation, is creating a paradigm shift in organizations. Although many predicted that IT would cause changes in the ways that organizations operate, very few could see how human ingenuity and competitive pressure would usher in a completely new industrial era. Writers have labeled this era "the post-industrial era" (Huber, 1984), "the information society" (Katz, 1988), "the information revolution" (Robertson, 1990), and "the age of the smart machine" (Zuboff, 1988), among other tags. Organizations are encouraged to operate in this environment as "intelligent enterprises" (Quinn, 1992) "seamless enterprises" (Dimancessu, 1992), "virtual corporations" (Davidow and Malone, 1992) or "global organizations" (Porter, 1986; Peters, 1990).

As opposed to the old Tayloristic principle of the industrial revolution that extolled work separation, the genius of the new paradigm shift is the move toward unification. During the industrial revolution, work was separated into minute parts to support mass production. Each worker was charged with performing a very small piece of work in building the industrial products of the day. Although this work was laborious and monotonous, it was the most efficient way at the time to build a large number of the same type of product. However, IT has changed all that. The integration of computers, telecommunications, and automation has allowed organizations to fuse company departments, to tie customers and suppliers closely to them, and to establish strategic alliances with other organizations, sometimes even with competitors. This phenomenon, global as well as local and national, permits organizations to communicate - and carry on other aspects of business - with departments and companies that are halfway around the world as easily as if they were just down the hall.

It is almost unquestioned that IT provides such benefits as the potential to accelerate business processes, to replicate and disseminate scarce organizational knowledge, to create service excellence, and to reduce information float to organizations operating geographically dispersed units (Hammer and Mangurian, 1987). In fact, because of the power of IT to shrink time and distance, many large and small companies are combining global business strategies and IT very successfully to compete internationally and enhance their strategic positions within their industries (Peters, 1990).

Despite the many benefits inherent in utilizing IT to facilitate global business strategies, there are some risks that present unique challenges to managers of organizations using these global strategies. In fact, managing risk is one of the primary challenges of firms operating globally (Ghoshal, 1987).

Risk often carries with it a negative connotation. Managers generally associate risk with negative consequences in business outcome variables such as increasing costs, decreasing market share, higher losses, and worsening industrial relationships (March and Shapira, 1987). However, risk needs not be a negative factor. In most transactions in business, the higher the risk, the higher the potential payoff. Unfortunately, the greater the risk, the more one can lose on any particular business transaction. For this reason, and the tendency for human nature to dwell on the negative, risk is often viewed negatively.

Risk is actually associated with the term "uncertainty" in the management literature. Uncertainty refers to the unpredictability of environmental or organizational variables that impact corporate performance (Miles and Snow, 1978; Pfeffer and Salancik, 1978) or the inadequacy of information about these variables (Duncan, 1972). Increases in uncertainty about these variables also increase risk due to the higher unpredictability of corporate performance. Uncertainty can arise from exogenous shocks, unforeseeable behavioral choices, or combinations of the two (Lessard, 1988).

As organizations embark on global ventures, uncertainty about environmental and organizational variables tends to increase because of a larger scope and more diverse relationships. The inclination of many of these organizations is to use IT to reduce the uncertainty in the operations without realizing that the use of IT brings its own uncertainties or risks. The purpose of this chapter is to investigate, through IT research and business examples, the uncertainties, or risks associated with the planning and implementation of IT to orchestrate the global activities of organizations operating multinationally. The chapter will discuss the challenges for managers brought on by IT risks by using a two-dimensional framework with Anthony's (1965) familiar model on one dimension. Issues found in the IT literature to be especially important to global organizations occupy the other dimension.

THE FRAMEWORK

On one dimension, the framework uses Anthony's (1965) model of managerial activities to organize the challenges managers must face in using IT for their global operations. Anthony identified three types of activities that managers engage in: (1) operational management; (2) tactical management; and (3) strategic management. Operational management is the process of ensuring that specific tasks are carried out effectively and efficiently. Tactical management is the process by which managers ensure that resources are obtained and used effectively and efficiently in the accomplishment of the organization's objectives.   The final type of activities, strategic management or planning, involves deciding objectives, managing changes in these objectives, attaining the resources needed, and enabling the policies governing the acquisition, use, and disposition of these resources. The three types of activities are typically viewed as a hierarchy with managers at the bottom of the organizational ladder performing operational tasks, managers in the middle engaging in tactical activities, and top managers doing strategic functions. To effectively utilize IT in helping to manage a global enterprise, organizational personnel must be able to meet the challenges at all three management levels. These three levels are used as one of the dimensions in a two-dimensional framework in this discussion.

The other dimension reflects the IT issues found in the literature to be especially important to organizations using IT internationally. Table 1 presents a foundation for this dimension by citing a sampling of authors that have discussed these issues.   Table 2 categorizes these issues into four groups. The four categories on this dimension are: (1) coordination; (2) security; (3) culture; and (4) legal/regulatory.   Coordination is the current organizational connections between computer hardware and software, communications facilities, data facilities, computer applications, IT resources, and relevant personnel. Security is focused on protecting the computer environment from unauthorized intrusion and unwanted destruction. Culture is the set of key values, guiding beliefs, and understandings that are shared by members of a group, for example, an organization, a clan, or a country. The legal and regulatory aspect is simply the national and local laws and regulations that govern a country.

DEFINITION OF GLOBAL ORGANIZATIONS

Before getting into a detailed discussion of the framework introduced in this chapter, a step back is in order to consider a popular view of "global organizations" and to explain how the term is used. There have been various attempts by authors to categorize global organizations by type based, mainly, on mode of operation (e.g., Levitt, 1983; Perlmutter, 1983; Porter, 1986).   One of the most popular categorizations, and generally representative of most of the models, is the four basic types proposed by Bartlett and Ghoshal (1989).   Bartlett and Ghoshal argue for four basic types of global strategy that are distinguished by the organizational forces that organizations face.   The first type is characterized by a loose association of the various subsidiaries and is labeled multinational

AUTHORS	ISSUES CITED
Sethi and Olson (1992)	1. Privacy Concerns 2. International Standards 3. Network Security 4. Intellectual Property Rights 5. Regulatory Adjustments 6. Conflicts of National Laws 7. Sovereignty, Autonomy Concerns
O'Leary (1992)	1. Technical Standards 2. Unyielding Corporate Structures 3. Cultural Barriers 4. Nonexistent National Telecommunications Structures
Neo (1991)	1. Strategic Vision 2. IT Infrastructure 3. Host Government Regulations 4. Transfer of Strategic IT Applications
Palvia and Saraswat (1992)	1. IT Transfer 2. Cultural Differences 3. International Standards 4. IT Infrastructure 5. Global IT Applications 6. Global IT Policy
Sauvant (1984)	1. Personal Privacy Issues 2. Technical Matters 3. Legal Issues 4. Cultural Imperialism 5. Cultural Identity Issues 6. Data Vulnerability Issues 7. National Security Issues 8. TBDF Regulations
Buss (1984)	1. Lack of Uniform TBDF Laws 2. Privacy Issues 3. Cultural Sovereignty Issues 4. Lack of Accepted International Policy-Making Body 5. Lack of an Identifiable Person Responsible for Global IT Issues
Huff (1991)	1. Link to Corporate Strategy 2. Different Telecommunications Standards 3. Differences in IT Applications 4. Coordination of Data Center Operations 5. Differences in Hardware and Software Standards
Tsanacas (1985)	1. Cultural Infringement Issues 2. Privacy Issues 3. Security Issues 4. Cultural Imperialism
Keen (1992)	1. Organizational Design 2. Global IT Platform 3. Cultural Integration 4. Technology Adoption 5. Technology Constraints, Costs, and Opportunities

Table 1: A Sampling of Global IT Issues Cited by Various Authors

Coordination	Legal/Regulatory
IT Infrastructure	Regulaty Adjustments
International Standards	Conflicts of National Laws
Unyielding Corporate Structures	Host Government Regulations
Global IT Policy	TBDF Regulations
Global IT Applications	Lack of Uniform TBDF Laws
	Intellectual Property Rights
Security	
Privacy Concerns	**Culture**
Network Security	Cultural Differences
Data Vulnerability Issues	Cultural Imperialism
National Security Issues	Cultural Sovereignty Issues
	Transfer of Strategic IT Applications

Table 2. Categories of IT Global Issues

corporate strategy. Each subsidiary has strong local autonomy to make most of its business decisions with very little coming from a central authority. A second type, which Bartlett and Ghoshal called the global strategy, favors central control by a strong main center, thus enabling the firm to reap economies of scale. The third type is the international organization where innovations flow primarily from parent to subsidiaries for rapid deployment. The aim is to maintain a leading edge advantage in the industry's products while giving local business entities the flexibility required to be responsive to competitive forces. The last model is the transnational corporation. The transnational corporation is proposed as the ideal strategy because it combines many of the characteristics of the three previous types and therefore supersedes them. Such a company attempts to simultaneously maintain the local flexibility coupled with a strong center. Innovations and information are constantly flowing between the center and subsidiaries to compete effectively in the marketplace.

In contrast to the typologies advanced by others, a "global organization" is defined in this chapter as any firm that is driven to design, engineer, manufacture, purchase, assemble, market, distribute, and/or service its products or services internationally to achieve a competitive marketplace performance (Passino and Severance, 1991). Further a "global organization" is viewed as having significant operations and market interests beyond the geographical boundaries of their home countries (Hout et al., 1982; Anthony et al., 1984; Vernon and Wells, 1986; Neo, 1991).

IT can aid in overcoming some of the well-known difficulties of global organizations. Geographic distance becomes almost a non-issue with the correct use of IT. Some heretofore disadvantages, like operating across time zones, actually become advantages with the use of IT. One example of this "virtual" closeness is how Texas Instruments (TI) uses its engineers around the world to rapidly design new products for customers. A U.S. financial exchange asked TI to design and develop a new hand-held electronic tracking device for traders. To rapidly put together a design for the exchange, engineers in Texas began working on the problem the next day. At the end of the day, the engineers transmitted electronically their initial design work to engineers in Japan, who were just starting their day. The engineers in Japan continued the work on the design efforts started in Texas until the Japanese quitting time whereby they shipped their resulting design over telecommunications lines to designers in Nice, France, who still had a good portion of their work day to go. In like fashion, the engineers in France electronically dispatched their design to Texas at the end of the day. At the beginning of the work day for the Texas engineers, they were not only able to give a quote for the bidding device, but were able to demonstrate a computer-generated photo of a possible design.

Despite the value of IT in managing global organizations, there are many challenges for managers in using IT in this way. The payoff of IT can be huge; unfortunately, the downside risks can harbor great losses as well. The key is to be aware of the risks and to manage them intelligently and forcefully. While this will not guarantee success, it does give an organization a fighting chance to compete effectively in the global marketplace.

STRATEGIC RISK

Strategic management is defined as the set of managerial decisions and actions that determine the long-run performance of the corporation. It includes environmental scanning, strategy formulation, strategy implementation, evaluation, and control. The "strategy" term in strategic management refers to a comprehensive master plan stating how the corporation will achieve its mission and objectives. The focus of strategic management is always an all-encompassing view of the organization. The risks that are investigated first are at the strategic level. At this level, the challenges are IT issues that affect the organization as a whole. Each of the four categories - coordination, security, culture, and legal/regulatory - is discussed by looking at specific strategic challenges affecting them.

Coordination

Coordination indicates the desire to provide linkages among technologies used in an organization. This desire is expressed in an attempt to establish connectivity between powerful computers, telecommunications, data storage, information processing facilities, and the knowledge and experiences of the people utilizing these networks.

IT Architecture

The creation of an integrated IT architecture could be a high risk strategic issue since it defines the technology strategy that drives, shapes, and controls this coordination (Earl 1989). The elements that comprise the architecture are computing, telecommunications, data, and applications. The concept behind an IT architecture is to develop a strategy that will allow the IT resources to work together in a constructive and advantageous manner. The company's IT architecture specifies standards and locations for IT components. Specifically, it answers the questions about the types of hardware and software that will be employed; where specifically the people, equipment, data, and facilities will be located; how much application, data, and procedures compatibility will exist among locations; and how these locations will be connected, coordinated, and controlled (Passino and Severance, 1990). Keen (1987) states that"... the telecommunications (sic IT) architecture is generally the strategic drive for evolving a truly international capability". He goes on to say that the global IT architecture of an organization should serve as its backbone and become a true asset. His view is that decisions on IT architecture should not be left to be determined on a site-by-site basis.

Although an IT architecture can be easily defined and established in theory, gaining consensus on standards, policies, and procedures from the various stakeholders of the architecture in practice is another matter. The creation of an IT architecture to cover a worldwide organization is indeed a formidable task. Goodhue et al. (1992) came to several conclusions in their study that run counter to the development of an IT architecture for a global organization. First, they concluded that "strategic data planning" (SDP), a key component in developing an IT architecture, is a design methodology as well as a planning methodology. The significance of this finding is that, for maximum organizational effectiveness, the architecture developed by this task should be used in all IT designs and implementations. If this finding is true, then the most effective coordination schema is one where systems are totally integrated over the whole organizational domain. It does not take much imagination to see what an enormous task this is to subsidiaries that are spread over the world in different countries.

In fact, another finding by Goodhue et al. points out the difficulty of developing a global IT architecture. Their observation that "too large a scope spells trouble" is not compatible with the ambitions of organizations contemplating implementing a worldwide IT architecture. The authors claim that when the scope of the development is too large, planners get lost in a mountain of detail. If the task is broken into smaller parts and developed independently of each other, it is very difficult to fit the various pieces together in a cohesive architecture. Certainly this is not good news for global organizations.

Champion for Change

Goodhue et al. (1992) also concluded that the development process must have a strong champion if it is to have any chance at even a limited success. In fact, at one of their study sites, international groups of a corporation decided to split off from an integrated architectural effort and nothing could be done about it. Other organizations can expect similar outcomes when operating globally. In addition, Goodhue and his colleagues found that even if an integrated IT architecture could be developed, the effectiveness of having that architecture depended, understandably, on how well its use was enforced. In a global environment, the enforcement of such an integrated architecture on local subsidiaries is an extremely difficult task.

Aligning IT with Business Strategy

As more and more firms adopt a global business strategy, it is being increasingly recognized that IT must be closely aligned with the business strategy. The increased activity in the global arena has allowed some researchers to identify various models of global business strategy (e.g., Levitt, 1983; Rowe et al., 1986; Sankar et al., 1993). It was, however, later that a model was presented that linked business strategy with IT strategy. Ives and Jarvenpaa (1991) identify four business strategy-IT pairs for international organizations. The four types of IT infrastructures are: (1) independent global IT operations; (2) headquarters-driven global IT; (3) intellectual cooperation in global IT; and (4) integrated global IT. These were matched with the international business strategy types proposed by Bartlett and Ghoshal (1989). The independent global IT operations could be fitted with Barlett and Gloshal's multinational corporate strategy; the headquarters-driven global IT with their global strategy; the intellectual cooperation with Barlett and Gloshal's international strategy; and finally, the integrated global IT strategy with transnational.

For the last twenty years, astute corporate managers have been trying to match their domestic corporate strategy and their company's IT strategy. This has proven to be very difficult because of the many forces that have opposed change, including economic pressures, political pressures, incomprehensible technical language, personnel resistance and sabotage, and governmental interference. In addition, managers must be careful in not simply trying to take the existing domestic corporate strategy-IT match and trying to use it in the global setting. Take the example of Toys 'R' Us. After knocking off the competition in North America, Toys 'R' Us began to rapidly spread across Europe and Asia. However, in moving to these foreign markets, the company had to rethink its corporate and IT strategies. The domestic market is large, so Toys 'R' Us builds large scale systems consisting of corporate mainframes, minicomputers in the stores, and point of sales terminals tied to the local minicomputers and the remote mainframes for instant communications. The system was developed, of course, to support the high-volume, low-price business that Toys 'R' Us runs in the United States. The company found, however, that such a massive system would be overkill in virtually all overseas markets it was considering for expansion. One hundred stores are usually needed to justify such a strategy. Therefore, the company decided the best way to begin its overseas expansion was to organize itself into separate national business units. These units, which make use of IBM AS/400s and point of sales systems, are far smaller than the domestic counterparts.

Security

Lack of Security Concerns by Top Management

As more and more organizations develop transparent IT systems with their foreign subsidiaries, information about individuals, groups, institutions, corporations, and governments become more readily available to even the casual users of the systems in foreign countries. The alarming aspect of this phenomenon is that as vulnerability has been on the rise, awareness of the problem by senior managers has not. A study by Coopers & Lybrand (1988) concluded that in 95% of the cases studied, computer security was insufficient, although in 90% of these cases, top managers had the idea that security was adequate. The researchers concluded that management is insufficiently aware of the consequences of the vulnerability of their IT systems; in essence, there is no company security policy. This is surprising! Security is a problem for virtually any corporate resource. As the importance of a resource increases, so should the concern for the protection of that resource.

Increasing Vulnerability

As the complexity of a system increases, the vulnerability of that system does also. This should be a profound revelation for global organizations, for as the complexity of the operations grows, so does the complexity of the IT supporting those operations. A system is defined as complex, because it is coupled with other systems or the volume of the system is so extensive that a failure or unauthorized intrusion can have dire consequences. As a result, the vulnerability of global IT is typically much more than systems used domestically. Systems usually contain more information, are interconnected by networks over greater distances and through many vulnerable gateways, have integrated data, and are interdependent. All of these factors equate to the fact that a breach of security in a global IT system that results in interruptions and sabotage will have enormous and, probably, dire consequences for the system's corporate owner (Stoll 1989).

Culture

Cultural Backlash and National Sovereignty

One risk that might not be apparent to managers using IT in a global situation is the risk of a "cultural backlash". In analyzing this point, the issue of national sovereignty is involved. National sovereignty is a country's ability to influence the direction of its political, economic, social, and cultural changes. Many nations, rightly or wrongly, see their national sovereignty eroded to the extent that global communications, especially by new "rich media" (e.g., video, image, audio), are involved in the "migration of key decision-making functions" abroad. In addition, they see an influx of biases, norms, and behaviors being imported to their country along with the incoming global communications transmissions. Eger (1978) stated this sentiment well:

> "What many countries fear is cultural inundation or annihilation. They are resisting what they call 'electronic colonialism' or 'electronic imperialism'. They do not want their minds, banks, governments, news, literature, music, or any other aspects of their lives to be Americanized. Neither do they want to be Anglicized, Sovietized, or otherwise victimized by advanced technology and information that freely flows across their borders, thus possibly causing their own identities to become extinct."

The situation would seem to have become more acute since Eger wrote this in 1978. In 1978 and until fairly recently, most of the information flowing across national borders was what might be thought of as simple data. This flow has now taken on a richer flavor. Organizations using computers and telecommunications have increased the flow of information of all types - data, image, video, audio, graphical, and text - from country to country. It was mentioned earlier that Texas Instruments, the electronics company, frequently ships its product designs from engineers in one country to engineers in another county. The designs were once faxed between offices, but due to poor reproductions quality, many times vital information was lost in transmission.   Now, with the designs being transmitted electronically, much less information is lost and in fact, the engineers can attach written, voice, or video notes to any part of the designs to lessen communication problems that might occur between the engineers.   Because of the escalating richness of this communications flow, the effects of culture in foreign companies are becoming more profound.   This new richer information dramatically intensify the concerns of the host countries compelling many to strengthen their policies on information flow into their countries. This, in turn, increase the risks to global organizations operating within the countries' borders.

To further clarify this point, a study by Daft and Lengel (1986) found that a rich medium facilitates insight, rapid understanding, and transmission of personal feelings and attitudes. In their study, face-to-face communication was seen as the richest medium in relation to telephone and written notes. They noted that face-to-face interaction allows for timely adjustments and refocusing of the message and that physical cues such as head nods, smiles, tone of voice, and other nonverbal behaviors can be transmitted. As more and more companies use video and other rich media in their global communications, it is expected that this richer transfer of information could start an exchange of cultural attributes. Video conferencing, which is essentially a face-to-face meeting, is becoming more and more commonplace. Video and audio notes are being attached to more and more documents as multimedia continue to spread throughout the business world. Programs embedded with "intelligence" such as expert systems and decision systems also transmit biases and values of one country to another.

These new richer transmissions may also intensify cultural backlash from countries that feel vulnerable to the loss of national sovereignty. Managers using IT in an international setting must be aware of this potential development. Very recently (January, 1993), tens of thousands marched in the streets in Puerto Rico to protest the establishment of English along with Spanish as the official languages of the country. This illustrates the kinds of problems that can occur when people feel that their sovereignty is threatened.

Legal/Regulatory

Differing Laws

IT managers must try to assess the risk of operating in a country in conjunction with its legal and regulatory system. Policies of governments are also generally considered when deciding on the location of data processing centers and network nodes. Many policies such as operating regulations, price controls, trade restrictions, and export policies can be evaluated in advance of committing resources in a country. Not as obvious, but still important, are a company's needs to consider local environmental and work laws and regulations to establish the limits of liability to the local environment and workforce. Local laws and regulations concerning privacy of corporate and personal data need to be understood. Europeans have boards and administrative bodies to regulate privacy issues related to computer networks whereas, in the United States, there is no such regulation (Hoffman and Clark, 1991). *Restrictions on transborder data flow (TBDF)* could seriously affect the risk of locating data processing centers and network nodes. So far some of these restrictions have not been very effective for the enacting countries since the restrictions have been vague and therefore difficult to follow and enforce.

Changes in regulations and laws present one of the key challenges in that these cannot be seen prior to establishing a presence in a country. Significant corporate assets could be jeopardized by new policies which restrict a company's flexibility. At the extreme, the nationalization of strategic assets such as computing facilities and telecommunications systems by a host government could seriously affect a company both in loss of assets and the potential inability of the company to operate effectively.

TACTICAL RISKS

Tactical management involves the physical implementation of strategic plans. It concerns with such issues as vendor relations, optimal patterns of capital investment and expenditures, and decisions about facility utilization. Tactical or middle managers must also be aware of the risks and challenges associated with global IT.

Coordination

Management of Vendor Relationships

The management of vendor relationships falls to the middle manager in the global corporation, whether he or she is native or expatriate. These middle level executives must be concerned about high prices for local hardware and software, the absence of authorized distributors, long lead times in acquiring equipment and spare parts, software incompatibilities with American counterparts, and the use of unauthorized software within the local branch (Ives and Jarvenpaa, 1991).

Hardware and Software Prices

In Ives and Jarvenpaa's study, managers reported a problem with high hardware and software prices. For example, the authors reported that in Japan, local distributors double their prices over American distributors because the Japanese distributors are protected by regulatory conditions. Japanese distributors often hold a monopoly in their country and therefore are able to set whatever prices they see fit as long as they meet governmental regulations. Many times heavy tariffs and stiff regulations add to the cost of incoming hardware with the effect of making such a strategy too expensive. Companies usually have no choice but to buy from the locals at inflated prices. Brazil, for example, has severe limitations on assembled hardware from other countries entering their nation. Sometimes even without tariffs and regulations, hardware and software prices are increased by unexpected events. For example, a Canadian container company took more than a year for a software implementation in Italy because of the language translation of a computer manual (Huff 1991). Another example is the fact that many Asian languages require the use of two bytes of storage for each letter as opposed to one byte for each letter in English.

Absence of Authorized Distributors

The absence of authorized distributors is another problem often faced by local managers. Many software packages that are taken for granted in the United States are simply not available through authorized dealers in many foreign countries. Even when there are local distributors, a subsidiary of a global organization may still have problems.   First, there may be a long lead time in receiving the software or computer equipment ordered.

Secondly, software purchased from local vendors may be incompatible with other software sold in the United States or with foreign computer equipment used abroad. For example, Ikea, a $5 billion Swedish home-furnishings company, found it had to adapt Swedish systems to American requirements and vice versa. In one instance, the Swedes had to do some "keyboard mapping" so the company's North American staff could print reports with umlauts. Furthermore, a number of the American systems had difficulties generating reports on Euro-sized paper stock.

Use of Unauthorized Software

One final managerial headache that plagues many middle managers in foreign subsidiaries is the use of unauthorized software by employees in the local branch. In the United States, software piracy in most organizations is guarded against to some degree. Software companies in the United States have raided, with the assistance of the proper legal authorities, some corporations that had been illegally copying their software. This has made most corporations wary of piracy and, as a result, many corporations have established policies against software piracy in their organizations.

This is in direct contrast to many companies in Europe, the East, and many developing countries. In those countries, software is freely copied and even sold illegally for a low, low price. Governments are reluctant to crack down since, usually, the original copyright owner does not have an office in that country. In many countries, end-users have free access to the latest versions of software and these workers use the illegal software in their work. Illegal use of software by foreign subsidiaries can have at least two detrimental effects for the home corporations; (1) it can put the home organization at risk of being sued by software developers in this country, and (2) it pushes many software developers to actually withdraw from some foreign markets thus leaving the organizations there without an authorized dealer. Although the company might still obtain the software legally or illegally, the company has lost the local support for the software.

Security

Effective security of corporate data systems, in general, involves physical protection, training and personnel subsystems, technical protection of programs and communications, and management control and supervision (Carter, 1987). However, solutions which provide fine protection in the United States may be impossible to implement when the network expands overseas.

Electronic Thefts

Electronic thefts have been documented in every industrialized nation (Bequai, 1987, pp. 3). Hackers' undergrounds proliferate in North America, Europe, and Asia; an underground bulletin board in the UK was found to contain the access codes of over 400 telecommunications users including Barclay's Bank. Many perpetrators are even insiders (Bequai, 1987, pp. 122). In fact, a recent international survey (Harvey, 1990) reported 25% of disruptions to computer operations to be the result of human errors. This same survey found that 45% of disruptions could be attributed to deliberate actions. Through 1987, terrorists have bombed more than 600 computer sites and suppliers in Western Europe (Bequai, 1987, pp. 129). The problem exists in terms of international networks of criminals in one country attacking IT resources in another country.

Regime Changes

Stability of a country's government and its social structure affect the risk to a company's IT resources located in that country. Managers in these countries must be aware of the risks and take steps to lessen them. Regime changes may be particularly destabilizing in many countries. A company that is aligned with an unpopular regime may find little support or even hostility if a new government is put into power. Instability can cause unrest which, in turn, can result in demonstrations, strikes, or riots. This unrest is often accompanied by resentment of foreigners resulting in attacks and/or slowdowns against foreign companies. This divides the loyalties of local employees and can cause slowdowns and outages, or even destruction or loss of IT assets. The result to the company is a serious loss of communication, processing, and data.

Culture

Differences in Business Practices

Tactical managers must take culture into account when building relationships and establishing work operations with foreign subsidiaries and partners. One example of this is the case of Exabyte, a $250 million manufacturer of computer storage devices headquartered in Boulder, Colorado. Exabyte developed strategic partnerships with both Sony Corporation and Kubota, Ltd. in Japan. Exabyte claims it was ready and equipped to exchange CAD drawings and issue manufacturing change orders electronically with its strategic partners. However, due to Japan's consensus culture, the officials at Sony and Kubota have shown that they would rather confer with their counterparts at Exabyte instead of electronically exchanging drawings and change orders. In this case, managers insisted that a consensus be reached between parties before the developments proceeded further, and thus, negated some of the benefits of electronic transfer.

Another example features Federal Express. When Federal Express expanded to Britain, they found that they had to change their billing practices because of the cultural norms in that country. In Britain, customers do not pay from an invoice, but from a statement sent after the invoice. In invoicing, the Japanese also have their differences. Invoices must be sent within a specific time period after the sale and payment must be made within a specific time period after receiving the invoice. These illustrate the importance of culture in the establishment of business practices in foreign countries.

Legal/Regulatory

Transborder Data Flow

One task of tactical managers in a foreign subsidiary is to manage relationships with national and local governments. Companies using international data transmission are hampered by privacy and data protection laws. Many European countries, most notably Germany, place strong restrictions on the international flow of personal and financial information, including personnel records, bank statements, and even mailing lists. Other obstacles attributable to governmental forces include poor quality of transmission equipment, high costs of data transmissions, and the requirement by several countries that companies use locally produced computer and telecommunications equipment (Neo 1991). Despite the directive of the European Community Commission (ECC), the executive entity that administers the laws and regulations of the European Community, companies wishing to build networks to support their ventures in the EC must be prepared to accommodate different rules and regulations as well as varied service quality standards. At present, no European carrier is offering the full menu of services American businesses enjoy. For example, there are typically no Virtual Private Networks, Software Defined Networks, and Vnet in most European countries. These are telecommunications networks that can be totally controlled by any private organization.

Major Delays Due to Regulation

Many time specific approvals must be obtained to install new or nonstandard equipment. Users should expect major delays in implementing networks because of the still-varied regulations of European countries. Companies in the United States doing business in Europe need to hire local services to obtain telecom services in the respective country. A Peat Marwick study advises international users to enlist the aid of local network professionals in negotiating with regulatory officials, who are more open to dealing with people from their own country than with outsiders. Others (Wiggin, 1987; Buss, 1984) suggest that it is also advisable for companies operating in these foreign environments to become friends with the local state-owned PTT operators to build a more cooperative spirit.

OPERATIONAL RISKS

Operational management is associated with the allocation of tasks to each organizational unit in order to achieve objectives of the tactical plan. Operational managers focus on the day-to-day activities of the organization. Operational managers in foreign subsidiaries are also confronted with challenges in managing IT resources.

Coordination

Implementing an Integrated Global IT Architecture

The actual task of implementing architecture is really on the backs of operational managers, the ones responsible for the day-to-day activities inside an organization. The use of standards developed for the IT architecture must be promoted every day for applications development, database development, and telecommunications links. Otherwise, the developers of these systems will drift and move slowly but surely away from the architecture. One approach is to highlight the likely losses from limited business opportunities that result from fragmented development projects whether they be applications, database, or telecommunications.

Lack of Education/Training on Global Issues

Another important issue in the implementation of IT in a global environment is education and training. Operational managers must have the "news" to relay to their workers so their work can reflect organizational and technical mandates (Keen 1991). This helps local IT personnel understand their own "world" and its place in the global context. Without such a focus, it is very difficult to develop local applications, databases, and telecommunications links that will be compatible with those of other parts of the organization or to key external partners.

Managing People

Although an operational manager can be influential in implementing a mandated architecture, he or she will face many challenges. Roche (1992) outlined some of these in his study. For example, there are very few individuals, foreign or domestic, who truly have expertise in building large, complex international systems. Therefore, foreign managers must battle skill shortages in IT. Additionally, operational managers in foreign subsidiaries often do not have the financial support enjoyed by counterparts in domestic settings. A final challenge for these managers is maintaining a sense of local ownership and pride among the workforce. Although the systems that are being built must support certain standards, local workers can still be stroked and rewarded in line with their customs. From this standpoint, the manager must walk a thin line. On one hand he must follow standards, while on the other, he must allow his IT design and developers some freedom to express local software and management practices.

Security

Operational management in foreign subsidiaries must adjust to a new level of security. For example, cryptographic systems commonly available in the United States are illegal in many foreign countries (Hoffman and Clark 1991). Thus, in an international setting, communications are likely to be less secure. In fact, some countries such as Taiwan actually have a governmental policy of monitoring data transmissions. This, of course, lowers security considerably.

Security on Public Networks

Implementing international networks inevitably requires the use of public networks. Workstations/PCs connected to LANs which have gateways to E-mail/public/private networks (if telephone company circuits are being used) mean that there exists a physical path to a desk. This can be exploited. Further, there exists physical paths using the public networks for access to hosts. The **Cuckoo's Egg** by Stoll (1989) presents a classic example of how the public network can be used to penetrate supposedly secure private networks. In addition, the trend to electronic linkages between buyers and suppliers (i.e., EDI) points out the need to consider network vulnerability.

Access Control Restrictions

Common control for exposure to security threats include encryption, access control, user authentication, and traffic control. Encryption is a process that conceals meaning by changing intelligible message into unintelligible messages. Encryption can be by means of a code or a cipher. A code system uses a predefined table or dictionary to substitute a meaningless word or phrase for each message or part of a message. A cipher uses a computable algorithm that can translate any stream of message bits into an unintelligible cryptogram. The message is decoded or deciphered at its destination.

The purpose of access controls is to ensure that only authorized users have access to a particular system and its individual resources and that access to and modification of a particular portion of data are limited to authorized individuals and programs. User authentication is associated with access control in that a user is authorized through the use of a device, most commonly with a password, to gain access control over the network or at least some portion of the network. When the password is properly administered and used, one can expect reasonable control. However, with access needed from different countries, problem of language and cultural differences complicate management and administration. Further, effective local control of passwords will be necessary as more and more foreign employees gain computer user privileges.

Traffic control is normally used to prevent the detection of traffic patterns, i.e., who communicates frequently with whom. By knowing normal traffic patterns and being able to detect abnormalities, inferences can be made concerning strategic activities. Primarily the concern of military strategists, the increased computing power and sophistication of real-time software make traffic analysis capabilities generally available. The importance of international competition and the potential inability to prosecute offenders could make this an unrecognized risk. One common method to fight off offenders is with traffic padding, which involves filling in gaps in message traffic with irrelevant ciphertext, so that the traffic pattern is not readily observable.

Physical security of data processing centers and network nodes is complicated by differences in types of location and building codes. Local managers must become familiar with their circumstances and make judgments based on local conditions.

Fax and e-mail have become important components in being able to coordinate work at different locations. The careless sending of sensitive documents, drawing and contracts over unsecured telephone lines can do great harm to a company's competitive posture and, therefore, must be managed very carefully. Likewise, the increasing use of wireless communication, (e.g., cellular phones and, in the future, personal communication systems) has not been accompanied by the realization that the airwaves can be easily tapped and that these communications are not enciphered or coded (Vafaidis, 1989).

Culture

Creating Effective Dialogue

Operationally, managers need to interact with managers in other countries to perform transactions. Awareness of the culture of these managers is essential in establishing effective dialogue. In IT, as in other functions in a global organization, there is a decision to be made between centralization and decentralization. How much centralization of control is required to gain synergies and economies of scales sought by the global strategy? How much decentralization and local autonomy is needed to enhance successful execution of that strategy? One corporation, Ikea, the Swedish home furnisher, found the formula to success in the decision to maintain a strong Scandinavian identity and culture while subtly adapting to local markets. When operating in the United States, Ikea's management must acclimatize its American workforce to Scandinavian culture and use Americans to understand the American market. Although Ikea has a worldwide global communication network and could easily send messages to any of its operating facilities throughout the world, it does not use technology to teach Americans to work like their Swedish counterparts or for Swedes to understand Americans. Ikea does not manage suppliers centrally or use EDI, although it could. Instead, it relies on the "American trading partner" to maintain personal contact with suppliers.

Legal and Regulatory

Differing Liability Standards

Legal and regulatory issues at the operational level must include consideration of liability issues, environmental requirements and accounting differences. Different standards of liability between countries need to be understood and implemented correctly to protect the company. Environmental laws and regulations can impact IT. For example, restrictions on location and power output of satellite uplink stations and microwave transmitters can reduce the effectiveness of an IT system.

Differing Accounting Standards

Regulations regarding accounting standards differ between countries. Accounting standards in Eastern Europe differ so much from those in western, industrial countries that "almost any financial ratio or other economic indicator will not be directly comparable with its western equivalent (Verstraete, 1992)". In India, many strictly national businesses use single entry bookkeeping. This conflicts with requirements in most Western countries for double entry bookkeeping. This impacts on IT systems trying to reconcile the two systems.

DISCUSSION AND FUTURE RESEARCH

Table 3 summarizes the above discussion. The analysis of risks faced by global organizations in this discussion raises important questions and areas for future research. The coordination and legal/ regulatory issues seem to have a higher amount of risk on the strategic than at an operational level. In contrast, the risks due to security and culture seem to be higher at an operational level. For example, in coordination, a badly planned network is hard to work

Management IT Risks	Strategic	Tactical	Operational
Coordination	* Creation of integrated global IT architecture * Obtaining IT architecture * Aligning IT architecture with business strategies * Replicating domestic IT architectures globally	* Managing vendor relationships * High hardware, software, prices * Absence of authorized distributors * Use of illegal software	* Implementing integrated global IT architecture * Lack of education/ training on global issues * Managing People
Security	* Lack of security concerns at top management level * Increasing vulnerability	* Planning for security * Electronic thefts * Regime changes	* Lack of standards * Access control restrictions * Ability to tap communication lines
Culture	* Possibility of cultural backlash *Loss of national sovereignty	* Differences in business practices	* Creating effective dialogue
Legal/ Regulatory	* Restrictions on TBDF * Differing laws	* Delays in implementing networks	* Differing liability standards * Differing accounting standards

Table 3: Summary of Risks in Planning and Implementing Global IT

with, but telecommunications managers can route traffic around such network for a short period of time. In the course of time, however, lack of a properly integrated network could lead to substantial losses for an organization. Similarly, taking away regulation control from a country's regulatory agency will have longer-term implications rather than operational impact. In contrast, penetration of security systems at an international bank could lead to losses of millions of dollars. Similarly, conflicts in culture or religious issues could lead to strikes in a branch and the closing down of operations for long periods.

This direction of relative importance of risks has major connotations for management as IT goes through further changes in the next few years. Many middle management jobs are being lost as organizations flatten out. Such reorganization spreads the tactical risks to both upper management and to employees at lower level. It is important for top management and employees to be aware that these risks, which were earlier handled by middle management, still exist; it is just the people who handle them in the new organization that have changed. If the tactical risks are not properly considered, the organization might find itself in operational difficulties.

A tradeoff between risk and value needs to be struck to suit management's and shareholders' expectations and fears. A matching of these factors could lead to better informed decisions about the globalization strategies of a firm. This could be accomplished in the future by quantifying the benefits and risks in the strategic, tactical, and operational areas for a global company. A single measure needs to be derived to show the benefit/risk feature for each of these areas. The resulting measure will be similar to the "beta" used in stock markets. Beta measures the relative benefits provided by the stock (dividends and capital gains) versus the fluctuations of the prices (risk). A similar measure that evaluates the strategic, tactical, and operational benefit/risk of setting up an IS operation in a particular country would be of great benefit to management.

It may be possible to develop a comprehensive risk/value profile for each country (or blocks of countries). These profiles could be further clarified by discussions with top management and principal stakeholders. As decisions to expand into countries are made, the profile could be compared to check the alternatives to be pursued.

Another important research area is the evaluation of the relative importance of each global IT issue with the four types of organizations operating internationally (multi-national, global, international, and transnational; Barlett and Ghoshal, 1989). It may be hypothesized that different global issues are more important to manage in one type of these organizations than in others. It will be worthwhile to design and perform studies in this area.

CONCLUSION

This chapter classifies the risks involved in planning and implementing IT systems, identifies the major issues faced by global IT organizations, and classifies them under strategic, tactical, and operational categories. The classification scheme can help an organization delegate and manage its IT divisions effectively. As organizations continue to change, this framework may be of help top management in ensuring that the appropriate people have been assigned to manage the risks inherent in formulating and developing a global IT strategy.

REFERENCES

Anthony, R.N. (1965). *Planning and Control Systems: A Framework for Analysis*, MA: Harvard Business School.

Anthony, R.N., Dearden, J. and Bedford, N.M. (1984). *Management Control Systems*, IL: Irwin.

Bartlett, C.A. and Ghoshal, S. (1989). *Managing Across Borders: The Transnational Solution*, MA: Harvard Business School Press.

Bequai, A. (1987). *Technocrimes*, MA: Lexington Books.

Buss, M.D.J. (May-June 1984). "Legislative Threat to Transborder Data Flow", *Harvard Business Review*, 62(3), pp. 111-118.

Carter, R. (May 1987). "The Threats to Computer Systems - Learning the Rules of Risks", *Accountancy*, 99(5), pp. 124-124.

Coopers and Lybrand. (1988). "A Consolidated Report of Case Study Findings", Report No. 2.

Davidow, W.H. and Malone, M.H. (1992). *The Virtual Corporation: Structuring and Revitalizing the Corporation for the 21st Century*, NY: Harper Business.

Dimancessu, D. (1992). *The Seamless Enterprise: Making Cross Functional Management Work*, NY: HarperBusiness.

Daft, R.L. and Lengel, R.H. (1986). "Organizational Information Requirements, Media Richness and Structural Design", *Management Science*, 32(5), pp. 554-571.

Duncan, R.B. (1972). "Characteristics of Organizational Environments and Perceived Environmental Uncertainty", *Administrative Science Quarterly*, 17, pp. 313-327.

Eger, J. (November 1978). "Transborder Data Flow", *Datamation*, pp. 50-54.

Ghoshal, S. (1987). "Global Strategy: An Organizing Framework", *Strategic Management Journal*, 8, pp. 425-440.

Goodhue, D.L., Kirsch, L.J., Quillard, J.A., Wybo, M.D. (1992). "Strategic Data Planning: Lessons From the Field", *MIS Quarterly*, 16(1), pp. 11-34.

Hammer, M. and Mangurian, G.E. (Winter 1987). "The Changing Value of Communications Technology", *Sloan Management Review*, pp. 65-71.

Harvey, D. (September 1990). "Technology: Disaster Moves", *Director (UK)*, 44(15), pp. 123.

Hoffman, L.J. & Clark, P.C. (February 1991). "Imminent Policy Considerations in the Design and Management of National and International Computer Networks", *IEEE Communications Magazine*, 29(2), pp. 68-74.

Hout, T., Porter, M.E., and Rudden, E. (Sept.-Oct 1982). "How Global Companies Win Out", *Harvard Business Review*.

Huber, G.P. (August 1984). "The Nature and Design of Post-Industrial Organizations", *Management Science*, 30(8), pp. 928-951.

Huff, S.L. (Autumn 1991). "Managing Global Information Technology", *Business Quarterly*, 56(2), pp. 71-75.

Ives, B. and Jarvanpaa, S.L. (1991). "Applications of Global Information Technology: Key Issues for Management", *MIS Quarterly*, 15(1), pp. 33-49.

Katz, R.L. (1988). *The Information Society: An International Perspective*, NY: Praeger.

Keen, P.G.W. (1992). "Planning Globally: Practical Strategies for Information Technology Strategies in the Transnational Firm" in *The Global*

Issues of Information Technology Management, Palvia, S., Palvia, P, and Zigli, R.M., (eds.), PA: Idea Group Publishing, pp. 575-607.

Keen, P.G.W. (1991). *Shaping the Future: Business Design Through Information Technology*, MA: Harvard Business Press.

Keen, P.G.W. (1987). "An International Perspective on Managing Information Technologies, An ICIT Briefing Paper, International Center for Information Technologies, Washington, DC.

Lessard, D.R. (1988). "Country Risk and the Structure of International Financial Intermediation", in *Financial Risk: Theory, Evidence, and Implications*, Stone, C.C., (ed.), MA: Kluwer Academic, pp. 197-233.

Levitt, T. (May-June 1983). "The Globalizations of Markets", *Harvard Business Review*, 61(3), pp. 92-102.

March, J. and Shapira, Z. (1987). "Managerial Perspectives on Risk and Risk Taking", *Management Science*, 33, pp. 1404-1418.

Miles, R.E. and Snow, C.C. (1978). *Organizational Strategy, Structure, and Process*, NY: McGraw-Hill.

Neo, B.S. (1991). "Information Technology and Global Competition", *Information and Management*, 20, pp. 151-160.

O'Leary, M. (January 1992). "Globe Trotters", *CIO Magazine*, pp. 42-48.

Palvia, S. and Saraswat, S.P. (1992). "Information Technology and the Transnational Corporation: The Emerging Multinational Issues" in *The Global Issues of Information Technology Management*, Palvia, S., Palvia, P, and Zigli, R.M., (eds.), PA: Idea Group Publishing, pp. 554-574.

Passino, J.H., and Severance, D.G. (Spring 1990). "Harnessing the Potential of Information Technology for Support of the New Global Organization", *Human Resource Management*, 29(1), pp. 69-76.

Perlmutter, H.V. (January-February 1969). "The Tortuous Evolution of the Multinational Corporation", *Columbia Journal of World Business*, 4(1), pp. 9-18.

Peters, T. (1990). "Prometheus Barely Unbound", *Academy of Management Executive*, 4(4), pp. 70-83.

Pfeffer, J. and Salancik, G.R. (1978). *The External Control of Organizations: A Resource Dependence Perspective*, NY: Harper and Row.

Pfleeger, C.P. (1989). *Security in Computing*, NJ: Prentice Hall.

Porter, M.E. (1986). *Competition in Global Industries*, MA: Harvard Business School Press.

Quinn, J.B. (1992). *Intelligent Enterprise*, NY: The Free Press.

Robertson, D.S. (April 1990). "The Information Revolution", *Communication Research*, 17, pp 235-254.

Roche, E.M. (1992). "Managing Systems Development in Multinational Corporations: Practical Lessons from 7 Case Studies", in *The Global Issues of Information Technology Management*, Palvia, S., Palvia, P, and Zigli, R.M., (eds.), PA: Idea Group Publishing, pp. 630-654.

Rowe, A.J., Mason, R., and Dickel, K. (1986). *Strategic Management: A Methodological Approach*, MA: Addison-Wesley.

Sankar, C.S., Apte, U. and Palvia, P. (1993). "Global Information Architectures: Alternatives and Tradeoffs," International Journal of Information Management, 13, 84-93.

Sauvant, K.P. (June 25, 1990). "The Growing Dependence on Transborder Data Flows", *Computerworld*, 18, ID19-ID24.

Sethi, V. and Olson, J.E. (1992). "An Integrating Framework for Information Technology Issues in a Transnational Environment" in *The Global Issues of Information Technology Management*, Palvia, S., Palvia, P, and Zigli, R.M., (eds), PA: Idea Group Publishing, pp. 517-553.

Stoll, C. (1989). *The Cuckoo's Egg*, NY: Doubleday.

Tsanacas, D. (1985). "The Transborder Data Flow in the New World Information Order: Privacy or Control", *Review of Social Economy*, 43(3), pp. 357-370.

Vafaidas, N. (February 1989). "Cellular Radio: Vulnerable to Attack", *Telecommunications (International Edition)*, 23(5), pp. 55-56.

Vernon, R. and Wells, L.T. (1986). *Manager in the International Economy*, NJ: Prentice-Hall.

Verstraete, A. (1992). "Information Systems in the Soviet Union and Eastern Europe", in *The Global Issues of Information Technology Management*, Palvia, S., Palvia, P, and Zigli, R.M., (eds.), PA: Idea Group Publishing, pp. 55-72.

Wiggin, G. (October 1987). "The Golden Rules of Global Networking", *Datamation*, 33(19), pp. 68-73.

Zuboff, S. (1988). *In the Age of the Smart Machine: The Future of Work and Power*, NY: Basic Books.

CHAPTER 27

Finding Application Families and Application Fragments in Examining Global Systems

EDWARD MOZLEY ROCHE
Seton Hall University and New York University

Information systems in today's multinational corporations function to solve some of the problems which have been faced since the earliest organizations were set up to handle international trade. Although research on information technology in multinationals progressed rapidly in the 1980s, it is still inadequate in the sense that it relies on a set of high-level generalizations about the nature of international information systems. In this chapter, it is argued that recourse must be made to analysis of application families, such as "financial control" or "manufacturing", by decomposition into application fragments— defined as smaller applications which work together to support the overall application family. Once identified, application fragments can be categorized according to their functionality, geographic location, and role within the bureaucratic infrastructure of the multinational. Much research is needed to explore the nature of application families and their constituent parts in the domain of the MNC.

THE SEARCH FOR GLOBAL APPLICATIONS

Multinational Corporations and Information Systems

The multinational corporations (MNCs) of today - Exxon, Imperial Chemical Industries, Mitsubishi, and others - are descended in their form and function from the old trading companies and international organizations which have been at the heart of world trade since the seventeenth century. Just as the *Vereenigde Oost-Indische Compagnie*, the *Conselho do Impero*, the *Compagnie d'Occident* and others had to work hard at managing their control over foreign subsidiaries and the internal flow of information, we too see the same underlying patterns today - though in circumstances of completely different technology. (See Parry, 1967; Coornaert, 1967; Braudel, 1979.)

The multinational corporations of today operate in a very different environment, or so it seems. Encarnation's analysis (1985) demonstrated that more than 70 per cent of world trade today consists of the intra-firm transactions within multinational corporations. This means that internal trading is greater than external trading. If we look back to the time of the major trading companies of previous centuries, we also see the same type of dominance. Just as in the past, today's MNCs are the principal movers in the world's economy.

Although the multinational corporation is, in many ways, a "new animal", many of the themes in its management have remained constant. Firms must make major efforts to coordinate their activities between headquarters and subsidiaries. As in the past, it remains a challenge to keep far-flung subsidiaries under control. Furthermore, there continues to be an essential fragility of markets. Little in the market environment is constant, and the multinational must always be prepared to adapt to changes in the conditions under which it conducts business. This constant change drives the multinational to perform continual scanning for intelligence on market developments, changes in government policy, and on any other development or "bits" of information which may be relevant to its survival.

The constant need for information which is generated by the need to control large and diverse business operations drives the development of expanded communications systems capable of processing and correctly channelling the ever-expanding amount of information. As Egelhoff (1988) has pointed out, the multinational corporation can be thought of as a giant information machine in which all aspects of information are processed at one point or another.[1]

It was only natural that as information technology became available a little more than a quarter of a century ago, firms would quickly start to adapt it to their peculiar needs in international business. Information technology and telecommunications systems today form the vital nervous system of the global enterprise.

Analyses of Information Technology

Information technology, as it is used and distributed in the multinational of today, is a product of the late 1960s (Roche, 1992). For most, their foreign subsidiaries, reporting systems, factories, and many other aspects of their way of conducting business were well in place when information technology started to make its presence felt. Thinking back to that time, the computers used were startlingly different from what we have today.

In comparison with the present networked world, the first mainframes were barely functional. It was difficult to move information from one site to another, there was little telecommunications, and even no remote job entry for years. Talk of "global systems" were exercises in science fiction. The result was that individual data processing centers were placed in different locations around the world - isolated, unable to communicate, and in many cases left within specific and highly varied national contexts to develop on their own. They did develop, usually along different lines. Multinationals invested and up-graded information systems at different rates, depending on the economic priorities of the subsidiary locations where the machines were located, thus leading to development of even greater differences from one data center to another all within the same firm.

Technology continued to develop, and as the 1980s arrived, possibilities for global networking became reality, and companies woke up to find that they had inherited a tower of babel in their information systems. The process of global integration had to be started, but a very difficult task lay ahead. In general, we can say that the development of "global systems" has been throttled by developments in technological possibilities, particularly telecommunications systems. Imagination always ran ahead of technical realities, and still does today.

The academic view of these developments has been slow in coming. Studies of information technology in the multinational corporation proceeded along two tracks for a while (Deans and Ricks, 1992), with researchers like Egelhoff taking one view, and MIS researchers taking another. On the MIS side, one of the first tasks was to identify the different issues which were faced as the multinationals started this major integration effort. Deans et al (1991), Palvia et al (1993), Palvia et al (1992), also Palvia & Saraswat (1991) worked hard, with others, defining the different issues being faced. Others (Ein-Dor et al, 1992, Roche et al, 1992) worked at defining a framework to explain the reasons why environmental factors in the international system made demands upon the evolution of international information systems. Work by Daniels et al, (1991) even applied the stages of growth curve to the acquisition and management of information technology in the multinational corporation, with "global" representing the last and highest "wave" in the conceptual schema.

As the complexity and scope of the different international information systems became more apparent, some researchers (Konsynski 1993, McGee 1991, Roche 1993b) began to examine inter-organizational systems. It was clear from these efforts and others that the information systems being studied had considerable complexity, and that it was difficult to understand and model how large multinational corporations built information bridges between one another for specific purposes such as joint ventures or other specialized contractual arrangements. The field of EDI (Electronic Document Interchange) and similar systems also exploded with interest.

As the debate has continued and more researchers have joined the field, we have witnessed the persistence of several "models" or views of international information systems. Perhaps the greatest adjective applied was "global" - a concept which has never been adequately explained. So many models have emerged and the terminology to describe these is diverse; systems are described as global, centralized, decentralized, distributed, international, transnational, United Nations-type, Multi-domestic, replicated, and so on.

At this point, we need to consider more deeply what these popular models mean. Are they descriptions of entire systems or of individual applications? What are the empirical indicators which can be used to distinguish one system from another? How are we to decide? What do we do when we discover what type of system we have? In this chapter I wish to argue that we cannot understand the true nature of a complex information system within a multinational unless we examine the application level. We need to know much more about individual applications - how they function, how they are built, operated and maintained, how they are distributed throughout the global infrastructure of the MNC. The principal reason why it is necessary to examine applications on a one-by-one basis is that they are so highly varied in nature. A large multinational can have "global" and "local" and "multi-domestic" applications running simultaneously within the same system!

Lack of Analysis of Applications

There is virtually no published research on information systems in multinational corporations which takes an applications-driven approach in a systematic matter, yet there needs to be. If we are determined to collect information on how different applications operate in practice, it is possible to get insight from trade magazines, and perhaps a few specialized journals for individual economic sectors.[2] However, without a deeper look at individual applications, it will be impossible to understand the real functioning of information systems in the multinational.

AN APPLICATIONS-DRIVEN APPROACH TO EXAMINING GLOBAL SYSTEMS

We should keep in mind that multinational corporations have hundreds of data centers, sometimes located in more than 100 countries of the world. When we say that a firm has a "global" system, it is a huge generalization. It is as accurate as a medieval scholar saying that the universe is composed of spheres rotating within a system of pyramids, cubes and other geometrical shapes.[3] It is, in other words, a guess.

Some of the key questions we must ask about global applications include the following:

Size. What is the size of the application? There are several measurements which can be used: (1) the geographical extent of the application can determine whether its use is restricted to a specific location or it is used in many different parts of the firm; (2) the number of users can indicate the importance of the application, and if we know something about the types of users (e.g. position such as management, labor, etc.) being serviced, then it gives further important information about the nature of the application and its role in the business; (3) the number of display screens for the application can give an important picture of its complexity; (4) the number of inter-program linkages or a similar measurement can give an important picture of the organizational relevance of the application; and (5) the location of users - whether they are inside or outside the firm - can also give an important picture of the relevance of the application for inter-organizational systems.

Scope. The scope of the application can be measured by examination of its empirical extent as a ratio of the total application system being examined, or as any other relative measurement vis-a-vis the other applications being assessed. Some applications have very general purposes, others are highly targeted at specific points in the business. This assessment also tells us a great deal about the application, and gives us a clue as to its overall role in the organization.

Divisions of the Company. It is critical to understand that applications do not stand alone. They must also be examined within the organizational context of the multinational. In the case of a large diversified multinational corporation, there will be completely different portfolios of applications in use throughout different parts of the company. No systems are universally applicable. In the case of Imperial Chemical Industries, it is clear that application systems driving paint manufacturing are going to be very different when developed for plastics manufacturing in a completely different part of the world. This type of asymmetry occurs thousands of times throughout the bumpy terrain of multinational information systems, and makes generalization relatively tricky or even mis-leading.

Boundary Analysis. The purpose of boundary analysis is to come face-to-face with the myth that the information systems of multinationals are self-contained units that can be identified. In any multinational, we will find hundreds of points at which the information interfaces with outside systems - sources of information, depositories of information, mirrored counterpart processing operations (such as for EDI), or free-standing systems of joint-venture operations which must communicate both with the mother firm as well as with the foreign partner. Any industrial analysis shows the large number of inter-linkages between different companies. Therefore it is impossible to analyze multinational information systems from within a shell without reference to these important external linkages. The analysis of how specialized boundary-oriented applications function, therefore, helps to de-mystify this problem of the extended scope of the multinational information system. To ignore it is to bypass the realities of global business.

Repetitive Systems. A final type of analysis involves identification of those applications which are widely distributed, standardized and shared throughout the multinational corporation. Examination of repetitive systems, once they have been identified (research has not even been able to accomplish this yet!), will yield important insights into the key local functions of information within the multinational. We can assume that those applications which are most widely used, and are more systematically standardized, are high enough priority to have received a significant amount of attention from headquarters. This type of identification would be important for benchmarking since it helps distinguish possible points of reform.

Functional Classification of Applications

The most common way to identify the different families of applications is to use functional classifications. This leads to an analysis of the "financial" system, the "research & development" system, the "production and manufacturing" system, the "human resources" system, the "logistics and distribution" system, the "foreign exchange management" system, etc. For example, if you were analyzing a large multinational corporation such as General Motors, with its dozens of major data centers, and hundreds of smaller data centers, located around the world, then the identification of a specific application family, such as "logistics and distribution" would help you make a giant step towards simplification of your analytical problem. Providing you have determined from other forms of analysis that this particular application was critical to the profitability and efficient operation of the firm, this simplification of the problem will not destroy the validity of the analysis. Studying only the most critical applications, when faced with overwhelming complexity, at least leads the researcher in the right direction.

However, even after the problem has been thus been narrowed down in this way, there is still a vast amount of complexity which must be dealt with. Think of any major multinational corporation and, within that firm, a specific critical application family. For example, how long would it take to do an analysis of the financial control information systems for General Electric, or AT&T, or Hoffman-La Roche? The point is that even though you have greatly simplified the problem, one still needs a more detailed analysis and a set of tools with which to accomplish it. Examination of these major application families presents unique problems which need exploration. The most significant issue is how to break down application families into more manageable smaller parts which can be subjected to further analysis.

Application Families and Application "Fragments"

The major application families - logistics, finance, human resources, etc. - are giants in themselves in an organization as large as a multinational corporation. In general, we observe that these different families work together to encompass all the critical aspects of business operations and to compose, when taken all together, the global information system of the multinational. They may be considered to combine together to create this even larger information system.

Looking in the other direction, we can see that application families are composed of many smaller components. For example, if we were to examine the financial control family within a multinational corporation we would find that "financial control", as a general application family, was composed of many smaller applications and supporting systems. Each overseas subsidiary runs its own set of financial control programs. It also has special programs which prepare information for reporting to a corporate headquarters which itself is operating a special corporate-wide financial application able to support top management. It is also operating the associated financial reporting, i.e. generation of overall consolidated profit and loss statements. If the corporation has a regional center-headquarters operation, then one would expect to find still more specialized financial applications, yet all are part of the larger financial application "family". This type of analysis can be completed for any major application.

Thus, any larger application family is composed of many smaller applications components which operate as separate or semi-separate systems supporting the overall application. For definition purpose, we will use the term "application fragments" to signify such application sub-systems. It is interesting to note that some of these application fragments can be quite large, and can work at the international level and across national borders. The term "fragments" does not necessarily mean that they are small, only that they are small in relation to the larger application family.

In any case, we need to decompose applications families into their fragments, and it is necessary to have a technique for doing this. We can start by defining an application fragment as the smallest identifiable application which can operate independently with its own application program, database, processing location, and set of users.

Looking More Closely at Application Fragments

The definition and classification of application fragments is multi-dimensional, which means that we use those categories which are most relevant to the particular analysis under consideration, and discard or assume away, the others. For example, if we are examining national differences, we would pay particular attention to national variations among a similar class of fragments, and so on. The classification variables for fragments can be thought of as the "context parameters" for the application:

Geographical Placement. Fragments can be differentiated according to their geographical location, from one country to another. If an analysis concentrates on this factor, then the results will feed into the large and growing body of studies focusing on cultural differences, national barriers and regulations, and the over-chewed concept of adapting to local circumstances, one of the eternal themes of the management literature on the multinational corporation. For example, an inventory of application fragments distributed throughout a multinational and sorted by national presence would tell a great deal about investment priorities and business operations. Conversely, analysis of the entire inventory of application fragments on a nation-by-nation basis (a very large task!) would identify those fragments which are most widely used throughout the world system, and also those fragments which are highly customized to meet local conditions. Both of these analyses would give important clues regarding the optimization of the information system, or possible points for reform or re-engineering.

Bureaucratic placement. The characterization of application fragments as a function of their relative location within the hierarchical (bureaucratic) structure of the multinational corporation will yield another dimension of analysis. Some applications are located in subsidiaries, some in regional centers, some in headquarters, some in other places. Some applications operate in several locations simultaneously or throughout the entire corporation, e.g. a large centralized parts database accessible from anywhere via remote login. In addition, depending upon how the internals of the multinational are organized, it is useful to know in which managerial function the application fragment is serving. These two factors give both a horizontal and vertical dimension to the analysis.

Knowing the bureaucratic placement of a fragment helps to understand better its basic function, its relevance to the organization as a whole, how it supports the action of the its application family, and how it works to help the business win versus the competition.

Product/Division placement. It may be necessary, particularly in highly diversified multinationals, to characterize application fragments according to how they support a product/division structure within the company. This type of taxonomy would be necessary if the firm was engaged in several lines of business which were so different as to require highly differentiated types of information processing. Knowing the relationship with the unique nature of the product/division it is serving tells a great deal about an application fragment, in particular its relevance to the corporation as a whole, e.g., whether or not it is a specialized or generic fragment.

Infrastructure placement. A more complex but useful analysis is to characterize each application according to its relationship with the computing and telecommunications infrastructure of the multinational. Roche (1993c, d) has presented one model to do this, but there are surely other approaches as well which need to be tested. In the Roche model, application fragments are described according to the placement of their database, their software application, and their presentation, as measured by distribution of individual screens of data[4]. It has been observed that applications can have a number of variations for their infrastructure placement, and how they are placed within the infrastructure tells a great deal about their operation and how they support business. It should eventually help in understanding the underlying economics of global system change, particularly data center consolidation.

In this connection, the most peculiar aspect of studying infrastructure placement is that there appears to be only a weak relationship between computing infrastructure placement and bureaucratic placement. For example, a bureaucratically decentralized operation can be serviced by an infrastructure-centralized application. This should lead to a great deal of caution in any study of the relationship between information technology and organizational structure in the multinational.

Regardless of these different types of characterizations for the many different application fragments which must be explored, the practical realities are more down-to-earth. It is difficult to find fragments which do not work on single processors, usually minicomputer or mid-range computer systems. If this is not the case, then they are working as logical partitions of larger, almost inevitably mainframe-based application systems. This physical linkage between processor and application fragment gives important clues to the information structure of the multinational, since it is considerably easier for the researcher to locate computers within the multinational than to understand how they support a complex array of applications which can, as we see, have a variety of distribution patterns overlaying the physical computing infrastructure.

Understanding How Smaller Applications Link Together

Once the characteristics of the different applications fragments are understood, it then might be possible to study how the fragments work together to compose the larger family of the application.

Unfortunately, there is very little known about this area of research. Based on what we do know at this point about the differences between horizontal and vertical information flows in the multinational, two different classes of linkages can be hypothesized. Both of these have been only partially verified by case studies. Type I involves vertical flows of information in which different application fragments in different geographical locations link together to "report up" results and information to higher levels in the bureaucracy. This type of reporting structure is most characteristic of the financial reporting and control function. Each application fragment analyzes a great deal of data and then creates a summary report which is passed to the next higher application fragment. There is a "chain" or "ladder" (application chain or application ladder) of fragments which pass through and summarize the relevant information as it moves inevitably towards corporate headquarters.

A type II linkage involves the horizontal flow of coordination information between different fragments. Information is probably not summarized to the same degree (this needs to be measured), and the function is not so much to consolidate information as to share it. This type of horizontal linkage is characteristic of a manufacturing enterprise in which different plant locations must exchange data in order to keep the flow of parts and materials working smoothly to feed the overall manufacturing process.

Another characteristics of application fragments is that they may be distributed in equivalent or identical forms throughout the enterprise, but with little or no reporting or coordination function. Word processing and spreadsheet programs are like this. Although these applications do not work primarily in supporting the coordination between different geographic locations of the multinational, they have a very important part to play in supporting users at local levels, and no doubt represent in many cases very large investments of capital since they are so widely used.

ILLUSTRATIVE VIGNETTES

Research and Development Family

The nature of the R&D function within a multinational corporation is to develop new products, find better ways of using the technology and methods of work already employed, and to help the corporation to adapt to the unique characteristics found in different geographical locations. Corporations usually have a corporate headquarters laboratory which serves as the leader in the R&D effort and generally directs the operations of the different smaller research affiliate laboratories throughout the world.

The local affiliates are generally charged with collecting national adaptation information (standards, different tastes, field trial information) and reporting it back to the headquarters laboratory. In some cases, such as the IBM research laboratory in Zurich, Switzerland, the R&D operation may be a world-class basic research and development center, even though it is located away from headquarters[5]. In cases where a multinational is relatively weaker in technology, an R&D operation may be set up overseas to act as a technical "listening post" to monitor technology developments and to acquire technologies which are needed. For example, many companies and even governments have such operations in Silicon Valley, many of which are little more than thinly-disguised spying operations.

Although there are many differences, what we generally see in R&D is a highly decentralized operation, with a great deal of autonomy in different sites. R&D operations are heavy users of special purpose minicomputers (i.e., Digital Equipment Corporation VAX systems, Sun Sparcstations, IBM Risc 6000 AIX machines, etc.), and are generally heavy users of electronic mail. Under these circumstances, there is minimum amount of coordination between different sites as we would expect in a manufacturing environment, although the local sites generally report up to headquarters on a regular basis.

Logistics and Distribution Family

The nature of logistics and distribution is to coordinate and track the movement of goods throughout the world system of the multinational. This function is of critical importance in the manufacturing sector, where component parts and spares are constantly moved around the world in support of the business. The complexity of these logistics is befuddling, and it would be difficult for any researcher to fathom the entire logistics and distribution system of a major manufacturing operation. For example, the European Airbus is manufactured in three different major locations in the United Kingdom, France and Germany, with smaller "feeder" manufacturing operations in Spain and other countries of Europe. What do we imagine as the complexity and scope of the logistics and coordination systems which link together to support these operations?

Private companies such as Federal Express and United Parcel Service have shown the critical nature of information technology in providing tracking of individual packages, facsimiles of signatures, and delivery identification and verification all in real-time. The information system built to back up these operations is sophisticated and highly specialized to the logistics and inventory function. For these private companies, more competition is global in nature, and they are competing vigorously to maintain footholds in different parts of the world. One of the key elements in this strategy is working with distribution and package delivery companies in foreign countries. A critical and unstudied dimension of this is the set of challenges being faced in linking together their information systems with those of their partners in order to continue to provide the same level of information service to customers (e.g., delivery verification and real-time tracking).

A key element of logistics and distributions systems, either in specialized carriers such as UPS and Federal Express or within individual multinational corporations, is its apparent reliance on a highly centralized data processing operation. Its contrast to applications such as R&D could not be more complete. Logistics and distribution uses centralized processing with the use of digital packet radio scanners or on-line bar code scanning devices to track the movement of individual parts and packages throughout the system. Since the item always moves, only a centralized (inventory) system can efficiently handle the information processing requirements.

In terms of a logistics and distribution application fragment analysis, only the data screens and input forms have been distributed to the different geographical locations of the firm; everything else remains at the center. Access is distributed and processing is centralized.

Human Resources Family

The nature of the human resources function is to process benefits and payments for workers within the corporation. In addition, accounting must be kept of employee skills in order to aid in optimum distribution and utilization of talent. These systems are usually quite large, but suffer from under-study since they are rarely considered interesting from a corporate strategy point of view.

In terms of the optimum distribution of personnel and skills throughout the world, the type of database needed to handle this type of operation is inevitably centralized at corporate headquarters where major personnel decisions are made. This centralized system is supported by the individual personnel systems which operate at various overseas subsidiaries. Since a key element of the system is maintaining information on employees, there is always a risk of violating the privacy protection statutes of the various nations from which information is reported. For example, if the database is going to contain information on Swedish nationals, it is difficult to see how it could be legally maintained outside of Sweden.

A second element in the human resources application family involves processing of payroll and benefits statements for each of the employees of the corporation. In contrast to the personnel skills system mentioned above, payroll processing is most generally completely decentralized in nature. This is a natural outcome since taxation and other requirements are so different for each country in which the multinational is conducting business, not to mention the utilization of different currencies. Theoretically it is possible to construct a centralized system to handle these operations, but in practical terms it is more efficient to handle things locally.

Therefore what can we say about the human resources information systems in the multinational corporation? Are they centralized or decentralized? Obviously these characterizations are valid for individual fragments of the application, but are meaningless when applied to the application family as a whole. This is why it is necessary to distinguish fragments from families when studying systems as complex as those found in the multinational corporation.

CONCLUSIONS AND DIRECTIONS FOR RESEARCH

Probing Deeper Into Applications

Wherever research on the information and communications systems of multinational corporations leads in the future, it will be difficult to ignore the importance of applications. We may find that in many cases, a winning multinational has very large systems, but with only a tiny fraction of applications responsible for the most important business innovations. How narrowly do we focus the lens? Should we examine whole systems or only the critical parts? There are many questions which must be asked and so little is known about individual applications.

At best we have a series of case studies and story-tales of dramatic events within small portions of multinationals. No one has yet published a study of a complete global information system. We are lacking a coherent theoretical approach to examination of applications, we do not even know how many there are, or what their basic types are. Much more is needed in this respect, and until more information becomes available, much thinking about information technology and strategy must be put on hold.

Developing Tools to Examine Inter-Application Linkages

In the past, it might have been sufficient to categorize application linkages as "vertical", "horizontal", "cross functional", or "inter-departmental". Within an organization as complex as the multinational corporation, this type of categorization scheme is inadequate because it fails to appreciate the context-sensitive nature of applications. The way the accounting system operates in Tokyo, for example, will be very different from the way it operates in Chicago or Copenhagen. Therefore, generalizations about inter-applications linkages are considerably weakened, if meant to apply globally.

Inter-applications linkages can be considered as being fragments themselves making it possible for information to be transmitted from one type of processing area or platform to another. Inter-application linkages, for example, would exist for handling the transference of financial information from subsidiaries to headquarters. They are a type of "bridging" application.

In addition, inter-organizational systems (IOS) are dependent upon these inter-application linkages, and Konsynski's analysis (1993) leaves little doubt they should be studied as being a separate and unique class of application fragments, requiring new types of analysis. How do they work? When should they be used? What is their optimum design? These are but a few of the questions which must be answered in future research.

Employing Measurement and Mapping Tools to Verify Distribution

The study of applications in the multinational corporation is (for some time) going to be like a process of anthropological exploration. We need tools to analyze the complex systems of applications which are going to be encountered for the first time. There must be a way to link back what is found with the overall structure of the multinational and its corporate mission.

One such tool is the application of geographical theory and mapping to explore the relationship between the physical location of data, software, data centers, and terminal access with the corporation as a whole. Applications and their component parts cannot be viewed adequately without some appreciation of their location within the multinational and within the world economic system as a whole. Whether they are located at corporate headquarters, regional centers, local subsidiaries, in developing countries or at the inter-organizational interfaces between one firm and another must certainly color our view of their purpose and function. This type of approach has been explored at the general level by writers such as Bakis (1988) and Lorentzon (1993) who have been specifically interested in understanding how telecommunications and information technologies change the economic and managerial activities of large firms. Nevertheless, but considerably more research needs to be done.

In addition to the question of geographic space, research needs to concentrate on other techniques of measurement. The Roche model (1993 c and d) has suggested use of several infrastructure variables. There are no doubt other techniques of measurement. Until better measurements are made, we will remain in the dark regarding the true nature of applications.

Intelligent Design

Should we be able to learn more about the distribution of applications in multinational corporations - perhaps by making "maps" of how applications work and where they are located - then it should be possible to distinguish between applications which are the result of an intelligent design and those systems which are merely a default caused by historical accident. Some have argued that much of the current distribution and design of the information technology infrastructure in multinationals is the result of historical accident, since information technology came on the scene after the basic operational and managerial shape of the multinational was already set in place. This is probably true, but the situation must eventually change.

Current efforts at "re-engineering" are attempts to de-link the past from the future by completely re-thinking the way information technology operates within the multinational. In today's competitive environment (were not all historical periods "competitive environments"?) living with the "default" for systems is not sufficient. Some argue they must be completely re-designed from the ground up. This is certainly good business for management consultants, but it is the task of academics to determine if these implementors are truly successful at their efforts. By all means, the haphazard un-coordinated development of information technology systems which we have seen in the past must be replaced by a process of more intelligent design, guided in part by keen academic insight.

Further Studies in the MNC

We might do well to throw out the pre-conceptions that we have about information systems in multinational corporations. Certainly, when we examine systems at the level of applications and their components (fragments), concepts such as "global", "transnational", "international", "United Nations", and many of the other fashionable ideas become meaningless. The task is to understand these information systems at the operational level, a level more detailed than we have seen in the past several years. This should lead us closer to the goal of understanding the relationship between organizational structure, decision-making, and information technology in the multinational.

Eventually, perhaps it will be possible to develop ways of optimizing these systems, or even of comprehending them as a whole, but that will have to wait while further studies are made at the applications level. The high-level generalizations have served us well for a few years, but they only point the way to further study.

In the end, we know there is much to learn. We are swept along with the rapid rate of technological change in computer and telecommunications technologies. At the same time, we must think of the long-term secular trends, and the sometimes glacial pace of change in the underlying structure and functioning of the multinational corporation. There are many key differences between the operations of today's firms and those of old, but in terms of the fundamental role of information and the need to communicate ideas and control over vast geographic distances, things have not changed as much as we might fancy. In fact, there are many parallels with today's situation and the operations of the old trading companies of previous centuries. This need to coordinate world-wide operations has been a universal requirement for the multinational since its very beginning.

ENDNOTES

[1] One may wish to compare Egelhoff's ideas about information in the multinational with Steinbruner's cybernetic theory of decisionmaking.

[2] Examples would include *Wall Street Computer Review, Distribution, Chemicals*, etc. Each of the major economic classes has a variety of specialized journals. In addition, magazines such as *Datamation* or *Information Week* regularly carry specialized profiles on different information systems. Even given this information, no one has yet published a systematic analysis

[3] See Kepler, Johannes (1571-1630), *Mysterium Cosmographicum* published in 1596.

[4] The measurement of screens works when the application has a fixed set

of screens, such as a traditional 3270-based application program in a mainframe environment.

[5] The Zurich laboratory for IBM has produced several Nobel prize winners, and did the ground-breaking research on super-cold superconductors.

REFERENCES

Bakis, Henry. *Entreprise espace télécommunications - nouvelles technologies de l'information et organisation de l'espace économique.* (Caen, France: Paradigme, 1988).

Braudel, Fernand. *The Wheels of Commerce. Vol. II of Civilization and Capitalism 15th-18th Century.* (New York: Harper & Row, 1979).

Coornaert, E.L.J. European Economic Institutions and the New World: The Chartered Companies, in E.E. Rich and C.H. Wilson, Eds., *The Cambridge Economic History of Europe*, Vol. IV, The Economy of Expanding Europe in the Sixteenth and Seventeenth Centuries (Cambridge University Press, 1967), 223-275.

Daniels, J.L., S.A. Richards, R. Hanson, W.G. Seymour and G. Venters. (1991). *Becoming Global: Results of a Research Study on Global Companies.* Purchase, NY: IBM Corp.

Deans, P.C. et al Key International IS Issues in U.S.-Based Multinational Corporations. *Journal of Management Information Systems.* Vol. 7, No. 4, Spring 1991, 27-50.

Deans, P.C. and David A Ricks. (1993). An Agenda for Research Linking Information Systems and International Business. *Journal of Global Information Management*, Vol. 1, No. 1, 6-20.

Egelhoff, William G. *Organizing the Multinational Enterprise: An Information Processing Perspective* (Cambridge: Ballinger Publishing Company, 1988).

Egelhoff, William G. The implications of information technology for coordination and communication in MNCs. Unpublished manuscript. Fordham University Graduate School of Business Administration, 1992.

Ein-Dor, P., E. Segev, M. Orgad. The Effect of National Culture on IS. *Journal of Global Information Systems*, Vol. 1, No. 1, 33-44.

Ives, Blake and Sirkka L. Jarvenpaa. "Applications of Global Information Technology: Key Issues for Management", *MIS Quarterly*, March, 1991, 33-49.

Konsynski, B.R. "Strategic Control in the Extended Enterprise", *IBM Systems Journal*, Vol. 32, No. 1, 1993.

Lorentzon, Sten. The use of ICT at the Plant of ABB at Ludvika and at the plant of Volvo at Skövde in Sweden - a regional perspective, in Henry Bakis, Ronand Abler and Edward M. Roche, Eds., *Corporate Networks, International Telecommunications and Interdependence: Perspectives from Geography and Information Systems.* (London: Belhaven Press; New York: St. Martin's Press, 1993), 135-160.

McGee, James V. *Implementing Systems Across Boundaries: Dynamics of Information Technology and Integration.* DBA Thesis. Harvard University, Graduate School of Business Administration. 1991.

Palvia et al. "Global Information Technology Environment: Key MIS Issues in Advanced and Less-Developed Nations" in Palvia et al, eds. *Global*

Issues of Information Technology Management. (Harrisburg: Idea Group Publishing, 1992).

Palvia, Prashant, "Research Issues in Global Information Technology Management" in Mehdi Khosrowpour, Ed. *Challenges for Information Management in a World Economy.* Proceedings of the 1993 Information Resources Management Association International Conference, Salt Lake City, Utah, May 24-26, 1993 (Harrisburg: Idea Group Publishing, 1993).

Palvia, Shailendra, Satya Prakash Saraswat, "Information Technology and the Transnational Corporation: the Emerging Multinational Issues" in Palvia, Palvia and Zigli, Eds. *Global Issues of Information Technology Management.* (Harrisburg: Idea Publishing Group, Inc., 1991).

Parry, J.H. Transport and Trade Routes, in E.E. Rich and C.H. Wilson, Eds., *The Cambridge Economic History of Europe, Volume IV, The Economy of Expanding Europe in the Sixteenth and Seventeenth Centuries* (Cambridge University Press, 1967), 155-222.

Roche, E.M. S. Goodman, Hsinchun Chen. The Landscape of International Computing. *Advances in Computers,* Vol. 35, Spring 1992.

Roche, E.M. 1992. *Managing Information Technology in Multinational Corporations* (New York: MacMillan).

Roche, E.M. 1993a. "International Computing and the International Regime", *Journal of Global Information Management* (Vol. 1, No. 2).

Roche, E.M. 1993b. "Mesure des liens stratégiques à base de télécommunications entre les firmes et leurs clients, fournisseurs et partenaires commerciaux" (Measurement of Telecommunications-Based Strategic Linkages between Firms and their Customers, Suppliers, and Business Partners), *IDATE,* No. 9, 97-115.

Roche, E.M. 1993c. "The Geography of Information Technology Infrastructure in Multinational Corporations" in Henry Bakis, Ronald Abler, & Edward M. Roche, Eds. *Corporate Networks, International Telecommunications, and Interdependence - Perspectives from Geography, and Information Systems.* (London and New York: Belhaven Press), 181-204.

Roche, E.M. 1993d. "Theoretical Models of Information Systems in Multinational Corporations" *Union Géographique Internationale, Union Internationale de Sciences Politiques Telecommunications, Geographie Politique et Changement Global - Symposium Commun Union Geographique Internationale.* Issy-les Moulineaux, Paris, 10-13 May 1993.

Steinbruner, John D. *The Cybernetic Theory of Decision* (Princeton University Press, 1974)

Glossary

accounting cycle: the sequence of accounting procedures that are performed in a firm, beginning with the occurrence of economic events and continuing through the reporting of these events in the financial statements of the firm. The cycle includes recording, summarizing, and posting and varies in length among businesses from weekly to annual, with a monthly cycle common.

ANSI X12: a cross-industry Electronic Data Interchange standard developed by the American National Standards Institute which describes the content of an EDI transmission.

application family: a general class of applications within a multinational corporation which work together to support a single purpose. Examples would include financial reporting systems, human resource systems, logistics and distribution systems, sales and marketing systems, etc.

application fragment: an individual application which is self-contained and is an identifiable part of an application family. Many different application fragments work together to constitute a family. One example would be a local check processing and payroll system in an overseas subsidiary. It works independently, yet is part of the overall family of applications which service human resources within the multinational.

ASEAN: Association of Southeast Asian Nations, including Brunei, Indonesia, Malaysia, Singapore, Philippines, and Thailand.

Automated Clearing House (ACH): a computer-based system which clears payments by permitting banks to exchange debits, credits, and other financial information electronically instead of exchanging paper checks.

CAM-I (Computer-Aided Manufacturing International): CAM involves the use of computers and computer technology in all phases of manufacturing to cover the scheduling, processing, and quality aspects of products. CAM-I is a coalition of industrial organizations, accounting firms and governmental agencies formed in 1986 to define the role of cost management in the CAM environment.

CIFAR: the Center for International Financial Analysis and Research, Inc., an independent research group established in 1984. CIFARs address is 211 College Road East, Princeton, NJ 08540.

Clearing House Interbank Payments System (CHIPS): a computerized clearing system used by banks to settle interbank foreign exchange obligations.

competitive advantage: a strong, important sustainable benefit that a company may develop to provide it with a superior position in the marketplace relative to other companies that provide similar goods or services.

computer aided design (CAD): the use of computers in the design, modeling and drafting process for creating specifications for manufacture of goods.

computer integrated manufacturing (CIM): a combination of systems linked by computer technology to achieve greater efficiency and effectiveness in the transformation processes of materials and/or services into products that serve customer needs.

continuous improvement: the organization's ability to improve existing processes and achieve greater efficiency, so that slack resources are made available without sacrificing competitive position.

coordinate measuring machine (CMM): a machine used in manufacturing to measure and inspect assemblies and parts for a variety of features, and to improve the accuracy, flexibility, and productivity of measuring and inspection tasks.

country profile database: a collection of information that can provide a manager with a summary of the relevant market/marketing and environmental factors in a given nation.

digital data feeds: a data feed which can be decomposed and manipulated to support computations for real-time decision modeling and early warning alarms of key changes in the market. Discussed in section on financial services.

Dimensional Measuring Interface Specifications (DMIS): a set of standards developed by CAM-I, the purpose of which is to specify a direct interface between computer-aided design and manufacturing systems (CAD/CAM) and coordinate measuring machines (CMMs).

EC: the European Community, including the countries of Belgium, Denmark, France, Germany, Greece, Ireland, Italy, Luxembourg, the Netherlands, Portugal, Spain, and the United Kingdom.

EEA: the European Economic Area which is the single market with free movement of goods, services and capital between the EC (European Community) and the European Free Trade Association (EFTA).

electronic data interchange (EDI): the substitution of electronic messages for standardized commercial documentation so as to eliminate the need for actual physical copies of the documents. Facilitates flow of data from one firm to another.

environmental scanning: system for regularly monitoring external events that may be relevant to the management of the firm's competitive strategy.

eurocurrency: a currency deposited in a bank located in a country other than the country issuing the currency.

expert systems: software, applied within a specified domain, that incorporates the knowledge of experts in the domain and makes the knowledge available to nonexperts to aid in solving problems.

external reporting: the reporting of financial and accounting information by an organization to users outside the firm (e.g., customers, stock exchanges, the financial press, governmental units, the general public, etc.)

factory focus: the issue of linking an organization's manufacturing facilities to the appropriate competitive factors of its business(es), with the aim of enabling that company to gain a greater control of its competitive position.

Fedwire: a wire transfer system owned and operated by the US Federal Reserve System.

Financial Accounting Standards Board (FASB): an independent (US) organization that develops and issues statements of financial accounting standards which represent expressions of Generally Accepted Accounting Principles (GAAP).

flexibility: the ability of manufacturing or service processes to adapt to new (customer) requirements, either in terms of new products, changing volumes, or different product mixes. A confusing term unless the specific context is made clear.

flexible manufacturing system (FMS): a configuration of computer-controlled, semi-independent work stations where materials are automatically handled and machine loaded. The intent of FMS is to bring the benefits of numerical control (NC) to mid-volume manufacturing.

functional information system (or sub-system): a subset of a corporation's overall information system(s) tailored to meet the needs of a particular functional area such as marketing, finance, operations, etc.

GAAP (Generally Accepted Accounting Principles): the general guidelines used in financial accounting practice that are supported by the accounting profession as a whole. These are the result of a continuous, evolutionary process.

gap management: in financial management, the technique of assuring that cash in-flows match cash out-flows.

General Agreement on Tariffs and Trade (GATT): a global organization headquartered in Geneva, Switzerland, which organizes conferences periodically to reduce trade restrictions among its international members.

genetic algorithm: software program that learns from experience in a similar (though simplified) manner to the way in which biological systems learn.

global brand: a brand of product that is used by a global marketer in all of the national markets served.

global marketing: an approach to marketing that emphasizes similarities rather than differences between distinct geographical product markets served by a global marketer.

Global Positioning System: a system developed by the US Department of Defense that is based on a constellation of 21 satellites orbiting the earth at an altitude of 11,000 miles. It provides accurate positioning and navigation around the clock and at any place on earth, and can be used for surveying, vehicle tracking, air collision avoidance, and zero-visibiity landing assistance.

global sourcing: the consolidation of the purchasing function across organizational lines so as to prevent duplication and to take advantage of quantity discounts through order aggregation.

GLOBEX: the Chicago Board of Trade's electronic trading system that enables foreign exchange trading to continue outside the normal hours that the primary financial markets are in operation in the US.

hedging: once financial risks are identified and measured, the neutralization of overall risk by diversification across a breadth of complementary investments.

incremental innovation: a pattern of technological development that relies on small improvements in products or business processes through the relentless pursuit of "doing things better".

inference engine: component of an expert system that contains the inference strategies, and processes the elements of the knowledge base to solve a particular problem within the domain of application.

information technology architecture: a blueprint for a company's desired future for information technology, including components relating to beliefs or values, hardware, communications networks, applications, data structures, and the interrelationships among these.

International Accounting Standards Commission (IASC): a private sector organization formed in 1973 to develop international accounting standards and promote harmonization of accounting standards worldwide.

interpreter software: a computer program that maps the internal format of a company's business documents onto an accepted external standard, such as ANSI X12.

just-in-time (JIT): narrowly construed to refer to a system designed to produce or deliver goods or services as needed. More typically used to describe a philosophy that focuses on reducing inefficiencies and unproductive time in the production process.

knowledge base: component of an expert system that contains the rules and facts including the definitions of the objects and variables related to the application domain and the relationships among them.

latecomer's advantage: the advantage of a second (or later) entry into a particular market that is due to the first entrant/firm or innovator bearing an excessive share of development costs. Latecomers may then bring to bear more resources upon secondary innovation.

Manufacturing Automation Protocol (MAP): a communications standard that will enable manufacturing component technologies such as computers, computer numerical control (CNC) machines, and robots to be interconnected.

material requirements planning (MRP): a computerized scheduling and information system used to manage inventories and production of products made up of various components assembled in multiple steps.

multimedia information system: system which integrates voice, data, and video information in a single workstation or network.

NAFTA: the proposed North American Free Trade Agreement between the US, Canada, and Mexico.

national culture: the common mental programming of a group of people who live or have lived in the same social environment.

netting: a system used by multinational companies whereby the parent and its subsidiaries periodically "settle up" the net amounts owed or owing which have resulted from trade within the company. The process reduces transfer costs and exposure to foreign exchange risk and necessitates a regional netting center.

network architecture: the overall plan that governs the design of the hardware and software components that make up a data communications system.

neural nets: the network of sensory units (neurons) that give the brain a learning ability. With regard to computing, mathematical models that simulate these networks and their characteristics to provide for complex reasoning and decision making.

NOSTRO account: a clearing account at a foreign correspondent through which a bank pays or receives payment.

numerical control (NC): in a manufacturing process, the automatic performance of the set of required operations according to a set of coded instructions. Since NC systems are now typically controlled by computers, they are often described in terms of computer numerical control (CNC).

open applications: computer software which a group of firms develop jointly to resell in order to promote a system as a standard in the market and to defray the cost of developing the software.

organization learning: makes use of slack resources by emphasizing the importance of related but new opportunities to experiment with new markets, and to foster continuous learning.

organizational culture: the collective programming of the mind that distinguishes the members of one organization from another.

photonics: the use of light, instead of electricity, to transmit, store, and process information.

programmed trading: the simultaneous purchase or sale of at least 15 different stocks with a total value of $1 million or more (*Wall Street Journal*, March 17, 1993, p. C15).

psychographics: the technique of measuring life styles and developing lifestyle dimensions of target markets, using activity, interest and opinion measurements.

R&D management: comprises the tasks of planning, control, and origination of technology-based activities aimed at creating new ideas and bringing them to application.

re-engineer: to rethink and redesign business processes to realize improvement in performance measures.

regional processing unit (RPU): used by SWIFT. A computer facility which encodes or decodes messages and facilitates interbank transfer of messages.

secondary innovation: a pattern of technological development where incremental improvements are made to improve previous major or breakthrough innovations. A strategy followed by many firms that elect to wait until it is apparent that radical/new innovations will succeed in the market place.

SWIFT - Society for Worldwide Interbank Financial Telecommunications: a bank-owned cooperative electronic funds transfer system which transfers instructions behind payments from one member bank to another.

technology management: in its broadest usage, concerned with supplying and generating technological knowledge and providing the management capabilities for doing so. The latter includes planning and control activities as well as solving organizational and human resource issues. Technology management is frequently assumed to be identical with R&D management, but also includes the external acquisition and external use of technological knowledge.

time-based competition: placing priority upon development speed and fast delivery time in maintaining customers and winning new ones. Involves defining the steps and time involved to deliver a product or service and then analyzing to see whether time can be saved without sacrificing other competitive priorities.

transborder data flows: movement in information across national borders.

transnational: an organization which views itself as a single firm that spans many countries, in contrast to the multinational company which has a home country and any number of foreign "daughters" or locations.

UN/EDIFACT: a global Electronic Data Interchange standard developed by the United Nations which described the content of an EDI transmission. This standard is widely used in the European Common Market.

value chain: a series of stages in the production and distribution of goods or services carried out in such a way that each step adds benefits to the final product that will be used by the customer.

value-added network (VAN): a third party computer network provider. In the case of EDI the VAN acts as a clearinghouse for the EDI transactions.

video data feeds: video images (based on analog signals) of pages that contain data, about the market or a group of financial instruments (for example), in a fixed format.

Authors

THE EDITORS

Candace Deans is associate professor of information technology in the Department of World Business at Thunderbird - The American Graduate School of International Management. Prior to this appointment, she was on the faculty at Wake Forest University. She received her Ph.D. degree from the University of South Carolina with a major in information systems and minor in international business.

Dr. Deans' current research activities focus on international information systems issues and related curriculum development. She has published articles on this topic in the *Journal of Management Information Systems, Journal of Global Information Management, Journal of High Technology Management Research, Journal of Computer Information Systems, Journal of Information Systems Education* and others. She has also co-authored a book, *International Dimensions of Information Systems and Technology* (1992).

Dr. Deans developed and implemented a course in Global Information Systems and Technology Issues. She has also taught several faculty development seminars focusing on internationalizing the information systems curriculum.

Kirk R. Karwan is an associate professor of management science in the College of Business Administration at the University of South Carolina in Columbia. He holds bachelor's and master's degrees in engineering from the Johns Hopkins University and a Ph.D. in urban & public affairs from Carnegie-Mellon University. He has taught previously in the A.B. Freeman College of Business Administration at Tulane University and at the Fuqua School of Business at Duke University, and teaches regularly in the Master of International Business Studies (MIBS) program at USC. During the 1993-94 academic year he is teaching at the Institute for International Business Studies in Pordenone, Italy.

Professor Karwan has published broadly in information systems, operations management, engineering, operations research, and management. His articles have appeared in a wide array of journals including *The Journal of Applied Psychology, IEEE Transactions on Systems, Man and Cybernetics, IIE Transactions, Naval Research Logistics, Interfaces, Information and Management*, the *Journal of Management Information Systems*, and the *Journal of Operations Management*.

His on-going research is in the areas of technology/information technology strategy, the technology transfer process, and manufacturing/operations strategy. His recent work in technology transfer has been funded through the Department of Energy in conjunction with the South Carolina Universities Research Educational Foundation and the Oak Ridge Institute for Science and Engineering.

THE AUTHORS

Raj Aggarwal -- Dr. Aggarwal is Edward J. and Louise E. Mellen Professor of Finance at John Carroll University in Cleveland, Ohio. He has been a full-time academic since 1972 with experience as an engineer before that. His doctorate in finance is from Kent State University. He has lived and worked in Japan, India, and Singapore and has taught at Seton Hall and Toledo Universities. His work experience in addition to teaching includes research and consulting. He has authored or co-authored 11 books and his articles have appeared in the *Journal of Banking and Finance, Journal of International Money and Finance, Journal of International Business Studies, International Journal of Finance, Columbia Journal of World Business*, and *Journal of Portfolio Management*, among others. His consulting experience includes seminars given for the Government of Sri Lanka and the U.S. Securities and Exchange Commission, and other projects for Fortune 500 companies and banks. He has prepared instructional materials for the National Association of Accountants and given expert testimony in finance and banking.

Carol Agócs is an associate professor at the Centre for Administrative and Information Studies at the University of Western Ontario. She teaches organizational behavior, public administration and women's studies in undergraduate and masters of public administration programs. Her research and writing has focused on race and ethnic relations, employment equity policy and implementation, organizational change, and women in management. She is co-author of *Employment Equity: Cooperative Strategies for Organizational Change* (Prentice-Hall, Canada, 1992).

James C. Baker -- Dr. Baker is professor of finance and international business at Kent State University. He has taught full-time since 1965 and his doctorate in international business is from Indiana University. He has lived and worked in Korea, Germany, Spain, and Switzerland and taught at University of Maryland and San Francisco State University.

His research activities include authoring or co-authoring 13 books and monographs including his most recent, a definitive study of the International Finance Corporation (IFC), International Business Expansion Into Less-Developed Countries, published by Haworth. His articles have appeared in, among others, *Financial Analysts Journal, Columbia Journal of World Business, International Journal of Finance, Journal of World Trade Law, Journal of International Arbitration, The Banker, Journal of Global Business*, and *Accounting and Business Research*. His consulting activities include projects for banks and companies in Ohio, for the Cleveland World Trade Association, American Institute of Bankers, and the U.S. Regional Export Expansion Council.

Arun Bansal holds a Ph.D. in information systems from the Stern School of Business, New York University. He is currently working as a senior analyst at Bear Stearns and Company, Inc. in New York City where he specializes in developing management science models for risk management. He held a visiting position at the University of Connecticut, Storrs, for one year. His research interests include designing innovative models for pricing derivative financial securities, information economics, data quality analysis and control, and the application of neural nets and artificial intelligence models in financial forecasting. He has published articles in *JMIS* and *Information and Management*.

Giampiero Beroggi is an assistant professor in systems engineering, policy analysis and management at Delft University of Technology in the Netherlands. His research interests include operational control of large scale systems, risk and environmental management, decision support systems, and multicriteria models. He received his Ph.D. in urban and environmental studies and his M.S. in operations research and statistics from Rensselaer Polytechnic Institute, Troy, New York, and his Dipl. Ing. degree from the Federal Institute of Technology in Zurich, Switzerland.

John W. Boudreau is associate professor of personnel and human resource studies, at the Center for Advanced Human Resource Studies, School of Industrial and Labor Relations, Cornell University. He received his MSIA in management and his Ph.D. in industrial relations from the Krannert Graduate School of Management, Purdue University. Professor Boudreau's research includes human resource management decision making; applications of economic, accounting and financial theories to human resource decisions; personal computer applications to human resource management decisions; organizational staffing; and human resource strategic planning. His articles appear in scholarly and professional journals such as *Journal of Applied Psychology, Organizational Behavior and Human Decision Processes, Personnel Psychology, Industrial Relations, Personnel Administrator*, and *Computers in Personnel*. He has also authored numerous book chapters and presented papers in the United States and Europe, Australia and New Zealand. Professor Boudreau's textbooks, *Human Resource Management (6th Edition) and Personal Computer (PC) Exercises in Personnel/Human Resource Management*, written with George Milkovich, are widely used in university classes. Professor Boudreau has consulted and designed seminars in human resource management decision making and personal computer applications for companies including Mobil, IBM, Eastman Kodak, Corning Glass Works, NYNEX, and Schering-Plough. He is the coordinator of the IBM-ILR Personal Computer Education Project in Human Resource Management at Cornell University. Professor Boudreau serves on the editorial boards of *The Journal of Human Resource Management, Personnel Psychology*, and *Journal of Applied Psychology*.

Renae Broderick is a senior research associate with the Center for Advanced Human Resource Studies at Cornell. She conducts studies on the impact of compensation systems on employee and firm performance and on the evolution of information technology in human resource management. She has recently completed a research review of 'glass ceiling' and work force diversity issues.
Dr. Broderick has conducted large and small scale job evaluations, pay discrimination audits and labor market analyses for several Fortune 500 firms, and implemented gainsharing and profit sharing plans in smaller firms, both as an independent consultant and for The Wyatt Company (a multinational consulting firm). She has served as a consultant and writer on pay related studies for the National Research Council of the National Academy of Sciences. She has worked in corporate personnel policy planning and evaluation at General Motors, and in plant personnel and labor relations at Phillip Morris, U.S.A.
Dr. Broderick's teaching experience includes classes in human resource management, compensation administration, staffing, and fair employment practice regulation. Most recently (1984-1988), she taught MBAs and executives at the John Anderson Graduate School of Management, the University of California at Los Angeles.
Dr. Broderick has primarily published in the areas of compensation strategy, pay for performance, and pay discrimination. She speaks on these topics to academic and professional groups including the American Compensation Association, the Academy of Management, the Human Resource Planning Society, and the Industrial and Labor Research Association.
She holds a Ph.D. from the School of Industrial and Labor Relations at Cornell University, a M.A. in industrial relations from the University of Minnesota, and a B.A. in psychology from Macalester College.

Terry Anthony Byrd is associate professor of MIS in the Department of Management at the College of Business, Auburn University. He holds a B.S. in electrical engineering from the University of Massachusetts-Amherst and a Ph.D. in MIS from the University of South Carlina. His research has appeared in *MIS Quarterly, Journal of Management Information Systems, Interfaces, International Journal of Production Research, Annals of Operations Research, The Journal of Information Technology Management* and others. His research interests include technological innovations and organizational change, technology education and organizational learning, and information and knowledge processing in organizations.

Terry Campbell is professor of accounting and management control systems at the International Institute for Management Development in Lausanne, Switzerland. His research interests are eclectic; yet focused on decision making under uncertainty and measurement systems to assist and monitor such decisions. This emphasis has permitted research on compensation systems, differential diffusion rates of information technology, and emerging measurement systems for environmental activities, CEO compensation, and organizational learning. He is a member of the American Accounting Association, European Accounting Association, Decision Sciences Institute, and the Association for Computing Machinery. He received a doctorate from Indiana University with a double major in accounting and in business economics and public policy; an MBA from Southern Illinois University-Carbondale, and a bachelor's degree from Northwood Institute. He previously taught at the University of Central Florida, The Pennsylvania State University-University Park, and INSEAD. He has published over 150 articles in proceedings and in journals such as *Management Science, Accounting, Organizations and Society* and the *Journal of Accounting and Public Policy.*

Terry Campbell II is an MBA student at Wake Forest University where his emphasis is in international finance and strategy. He was a research assistant at the International Institute for Management Development in Lausanne, Switzerland in 1991-1992. He holds a bachelor's degree in economics from the Pennsylvania State University and expects to enter a doctoral program in finance in August 1994.

Dr. Erran Carmel is assistant professor in the Management Department at the American University. In addition to international information technology strategies, his research and publications focus on software design and the integration of research and development efforts in software organizations.

S. Tamer Cavusgil is currently professor of marketing and international business at Michigan State University. He also serves as executive director of the MSU Center for International Business Education and Research, a U.S. Department of Education-designated national center of excellence, and the Michigan International Business Development Center, a Small Business Administration supported international trade development center.

Cavusgil's teaching, consulting, and research activities have focused on marketing and international business. A native of Turkey, Cavusgil obtained his undergraduate training in business administration from the Middle East Technical University in Ankara, Turkey. Later, he studied at the University of Wisconsin, earning MBA. and Ph.D. degrees in marketing and international business.

Cavusgil serves as the editor of two professional publications, *Journal of International Marketing* (formerly *International Marketing Review*) and *Advances in International Marketing.* He is the author or co-author of more than one hundred publications in professional journals such as the *Business Horizons, Columbia Journal of World Business, European Journal of Marketing, Journal of Marketing Research, Journal of the Market Research Society, Journal of International Business Studies, International Trade Forum* and *Management International Review.*

Alok K. Chakrabarti is dean and distinguished professor at the School of Industrial Management at the New Jersey Institute of Technology (NJIT). He also holds the Sponsored Chair in the Management of Technology. Prior to joining NJIT, he was the William A. Mackie Professor of Commerce and Engineering at Drexel University in Philadelphia. He served as the associate vice president for research at Drexel in 1988 and was honored with the Research Achievement Award for "outstanding research contributions". Dr. Chakrabarti's research has been sponsored by the National Science Foundation, The Pew Charitable Trusts and the

Environmental Protection Agency. He has published in the area of technology and innovation management, and has co-authored a book with Martin Neil Baily, titled *Innovation and the Productivity Crisis*, published by the Brookings Institution. He serves on the editorial boards of *IEEE Transactions on Engineering Management*, the *British Journal of Management*, and the *Journal of Engineering and Technology Management*.

William G. Chismar, an associate professor of decision sciences at the University of Hawaii at Manoa, received his B.S. degree in philosophy and mathematics, his M.S. in system sciences, and his Ph.D. in industrial administration all from Carnegie Mellon University. His research interests include the economics of information systems, the role of information technology in international business, and the use of information technology in structuring organizations. His studies of international telecommunications have taken him through out East and Southeast Asia and Australia. In addition to academic publications and presentations, Dr. Chismar conducted seminars for managers and firms in Hawaii and Asia covering the management of international information systems and the use of information technology in reorganizing business process. In recognition of his teaching skills, he has received numerous teaching awards.

Dr. Sayeste Daser is a professor of marketing at the School of Business and Accountancy, Wake Forest University. Her current teaching and research interests are focused on issues of international marketing management. She has conducted several field study programs in Western Europe and has published on current developments in the European Community.

Vasant Dhar is associate professor of information systems at the Stern School of Business, New York University. His main interests are in understanding how symbolic and mathematical modeling techniques applied to large volumes of data and information can be coupled with business processes in order to design knowledge intensive systems. He has written over forty articles on symbolic and mathematical ways of representing knowledge, reasoning, search, and other topics related to artificial intelligence. Professor Dhar joined Stern in 1983. He is a member of the American Association for Computing Machinery, the Institute of Management Sciences, and the Society for Information Management.

Dr. Frank L. DuBois is assistant professor in the International Business Department at the American University in Washington, D.C. He has published in the areas of international manufacturing strategies and configuration decisions, manufacturing planning and control, and foreign direct investment.

Katherine Duliba is a doctoral student in information systems at the Stern School of Business, New York University, where she is studying re-engineering in financial services. She received her B. Comm. degree from the University of Alberta, Edmonton, Alberta. She has presented work at the Hawaii International Conference on System Sciences and the SIG Conference on Computer Personnel Research. Her dissertation work concentrates on the use of information technology in financial services. She is a member of the Institute of Management Sciences.

Cuneyt Evirgen is currently a third year doctoral student in the Department of Marketing and Logistics at Michigan State University. He did his undergraduate and master's studies at Bosphorous University, Istanbul, Turkey. Evirgen holds B.S. degrees in electrical engineering, and mathematics and an M.B.A. in marketing. His major research interests fall within the domain of international business and marketing, expert systems development, channel behavior, advertising strategy and marketing strategy. He has been actively involved in the expert systems project at MSU-CIBER as a research assistant for the last three years and is the author or co-author of a number of publications in various conference proceedings or professional journals. Evirgen is one of the co-authors of the article that received the best student paper award in the international marketing track at the AMA 1992 Summer Educator's Conference.

James E. Gauntt, Jr. is an associate professor of accounting at the University of Arkansas at Little Rock. He received his Ph.D. from the University of Mississippi and his MBA from the University of Chicago. He holds the CPA and CDP certifications.

Dr. Gauntt has worked with the Chicago office of Arthur Young as an audit manager, with the Amoco corporation, and with the Western Electric Company. He is a member of the American Accounting Association, the American Institute of Certified Public Accountants, and the EDP Auditors Association. He is on the editorial board of the *EDP Auditor Journal*.

Robert B. Handfield is an assistant professor of purchasing and operations management at Michigan State University. He received his doctoral degree in business from the University of North Carolina at Chapel Hill. His research interests include time-based competition, global sourcing strategies, and the purchasing/design interface.

J. Kline Harrison is an assistant professor of management in the School of Business and Accountancy at Wake Forest University where he teaches courses in organizational behavior and human resources management. He also oversees international management study tours to the Orient and France.

Dr. Harrison received his doctorate in management from the University of Maryland in 1987 with a major in organizational behavior and minors in human resources management and research methodology. He completed his undergraduate degree at the University of Virginia in 1980 where he majored in organizational management. Prior to his graduate studies, he served as a training program coordinator for the University of Virginia's Division of Continuing Education.

Dr. Harrison's research focuses primarily on international human resource development. His research appears in the *Journal of Applied Psychology*, *Journal of Management Education* and the *Journal of Management Development*. Also, he has co-authored a book entitled, *Personnel Human Resources Skills Modules*.

Prior to assuming his position at Wake Forest in 1990, Dr. Harrison was a management training consultant in Washington, D.C. for three years. Dr. Harrison is a member of the Academy of Management, the Organizational Behavior Teaching Society, the Society for Human Resources Management, the Institute for International Human Resources Management, the North Carolina World Trade Association, and Beta Gamma Sigma.

Robert J. Kauffman is NEC Faculty Fellow and associate professor of IS at the Stern School of Business, New York University, where he specializes in information technology in the financial services sector. Prior to completing a Ph.D. at the Graduate School of Industrial Administration, Carnegie Mellon University, he received an M.A. at Cornell University and was an international lending and strategic planning officer at a large money center bank in New York City. He has published articles in *MIS Quarterly*, *Journal of Management Information Systems*, *IEEE Transactions on Software Engineering*, *Information and Management*, and elsewhere. He also was a co-editor of *Strategic Information Technology Management: Organizational Growth and Competitive Advantage* (Middletown, PA: Idea Group Publishing, 1993). His current research focuses on developing new methods for measuring the business value of information technology in financial services settings, using techniques from finance, economics and management science.

Martha Larkin is an information systems consultant with Broughton Systems, Inc. in Richmond, Virginia. She holds a certificate in data processing from the Institute of Certification of Computer Professionals, and a certificate in production and inventory control from the American Production and Inventory Control Society. She earned a masters in business administration and a bachelor of science degree in mathematics from Virginia Commonwealth

University.

Kimball P. Marshall received his baccalaureate degree from the University of St. Thomas in Houston, Texas, and subsequently attended the University of Florida where he received his masters and Ph.D. in sociology. He has carried out postdoctoral research at Texas A&M and Syracuse Universities and served as director of social science computing services and director of business school computing services at Washington University (St. Louis) from which he received an MBA. Dr. Marshall has several years of marketing research and management experience in major companies in the telecommunications and computer industries and has published a variety of articles and a book related to marketing and social research. He is now working on a new book on marketing information systems. Dr. Marshall lives in Jackson, Mississippi where he serves as associate professor of marketing at Jackson State University.

Ann S. Marucheck is an associate professor of operations management at the Kenan-Flagler Business School at the University of North Carolina at Chapel Hill. She earned her Ph.D. in industrial engineering with a concentration in operations research from the University of Oklahoma. Her current research interests include the use of information technology in manufacturing and services, and the role of the knowledge worker in the operations of world class organizations.

Jerry D. McCreary is a Ph.D. student in MIS at Auburn University. He has a bachelor's degree in math and computer science. He was a naval officer and has worked in a variety of engineering and management positions for the MITRE Corp. and Martin Marietta Corp. His current research interests are telecommunications, technology management and information systems engineering.

Elliott Minor is associate professor of operations management at Virginia Commonwealth University, Richmond, Virginia. He received his Ph.D. in operations management from the University of South Carolina and a BA in Russian history from the University of Virginia. He has published articles in *European Journal of Operations Research, International Journal of Production Research, International Journal of Operations and Production Management,* and *Southwest Business Review.* His current research interests are focused on manufacturing and service operations strategy, both domestic and international.

Fred Niederman received his PhD in Management Information Systems from the University of Minnesota and is currently an assistant professor in the Information and Quantitative Sciences Department at the University of Baltimore. His research interests include group support systems, decision support systems, problem formulation, MIS personnel, and global information systems. He has previously published in *MIS Quarterly, Computer Personnel,* and the *Journal for Strategic Information Systems.* His affiliations include the Special Interest Group for Computer Personnel Research of ACM and Working Group 8.2 of the International Federation of Information Processing.

Vladimir Pucik is associate professor and academic director, international programs at The Center of Advanced Human Resource Studies at the ILR School, Cornell University. He was born in Prague, Czechoslovakia, where he studied international economics, law, and political science. Later, he received a master's degree in international affairs -specializing in East Asia - and a Ph.D. in business administration from Columbia University. Before joining Cornell, Dr. Pucik was a faculty member at the School of Business, University of Michigan, and spent three years as a visiting scholar at Keio and Hitotsubashi University in Tokyo. His research interests include management practices in global firms, transnational human resource policies, strategic alliance strategies, and comparative management with an emphasis on Japan. He has published extensively in academic and professional journals, as well as contributed to a number of books and monographs in the area of international business and personnel management.

Dr. Pucik's most recent major works are: *Globalizing Management: Creating and Leading the Competitive Organization* and *Management Culture and the Effectiveness of Local Executives in Japanese-owned U.S. Corporations*. He consulted and conducted workshops for major corporations worldwide, including BP, BASF, Dow-Corning, GE, GM, IBM, Kodak, 3M, Sony and Upjohn. Dr. Pucik also teaches regularly in a number of executive programs in the U.S., Europe, and Asia, including visiting appointments at Columbia University and INSEAD.

Dr. K. S. Raman is senior fellow and coordinator of information systems teaching and research, Department of Information Systems and Computer Science, National University of Singapore. His research interests include group support systems, information technology in small businesses, government policy and information technology, and cross national/cultural issues in information technology. His research papers in these areas have been presented in international conferences and published in international journals. Dr. Raman has wide experience in industry in information systems and was CIO of a large multinational conglomerate in the Asia-Pacific region before taking up his present position in 1984. He is on the editorial boards of the journals *MIS Quarterly* and *International Information Systems*, and is listed in *Marquis Who's Who in the World*.

Edward M. Roche is an associate editor for the journal *International Information Systems*, a contributing editor to *Transnational Data Report*, and a book review editor for *Journal of Global Information Management*. He serves on the IFIPS 9.4 working sub-committee on information technology in developing countries and has done field research on international information technology issues for more than 10 years. After completing an internship at the United Nations Centre on Transnational Corporations, he received an M. Phil and Ph.D. from Columbia University with a thesis on the international telecommunications systems of multinational corporations. He worked in management consulting for nine years with The Diebold Group and with Booz-Allen & Hamilton, Inc. He also holds a M.A. in international relations from the Johns Hopkins School of Advanced International Studies in Washington, D.C. He lives with his family in Manhattan.

Chetan S. Sankar is an associate professor of MIS at Auburn University's College of Business. He developed global telecommunications network management programs for multi-national companies while at AT&T's Bell Laboratories. He also developed the master's and Ph.D. programs in MIS at Temple University. His current research interests are global information technology management, career progression of technologists, telecommunications management, standardization of data dictionaries, and user interfaces. His a senior member of the IEEE and a member of TIMS, DSI, and IRMA. His papers have appeared in *Datapro Reports, MIS Quarterly, Information Management Review, Management Science, IEEE Transactions on Engineering Management, Decision, Journal of Database Administration, Decision Support Systems*, and *The Naval Logistics Quarterly*.

James A. Senn is director of the Information Technology Management Group at Georgia State University in Atlanta and vice-president for international affairs of the Society for Information Management, an organization of corporate information executives. He is known internationally as a dynamic speaker on management and information technology and on developing winning strategies for personal and corporate success. Senn consults widely with business and is the author of several leading books on information technology along with numerous articles and papers.

I. Peter Suttie is an associate professor and director of the Centre for Administrative and Information Studies, Faculty of Social Science at The University of Western Ontario. His undergraduate degree is in engineering physics from the University of Toronto and his graduate degrees are in computer science and management science from the Universities of Western Ontario and Waterloo. His research interests focus on the use of information technology to support decision-making in organizations.

Dr. Paul M. Swamidass is associate professor of management and the associate director of the Thomas Walter Center for Technology Management, Auburn University, Auburn, Alabama. His research and teaching interests are manufacturing strategy, manufacturing technology and international manufacturing. His publications have appeared in leading academic as well as practitioner journals including the *Management Science*, the *Academy of Management Review*, the *Journal of Management*, the *International Journal of Production Research*, and the *Journal of International Business Studies*. His study of the technology adoption practices of U.S. manufacturers was published as the monograph, *Technology on the Factory Floor* by the National Association of Manufacturers (1992). In the year 1993, Dr. Swamidass received a National Science Foundation grant to update his study of manufacturing technology adoption in the U.S. He is a member of several professional societies.

Dr. Charles A. Snyder is professor and head of the Department of Management at Auburn University. He has extensive management, research, and consulting experience. His more than 50 publications have appeared in leading journals such as *The Journal of Management Information Systems, Information & Management, The Academy of Management Review, Data Management, The International Journal of Man-Machine Studies, The Journal of Information Systems Management, IEEE Transactions on Engineering Management, Production and Inventory Management Journal*, and *Decision Support Systems*. His research interests include information resource management, computer integrated manufacturing, systems analysis and design, executive information systems, and telecommunications management. Dr. Snyder is a member of SIM, DSI, ACM, IEEE, IRMA, and other professional societies.

Veronique Duperret-Tran is a faculty assistant at the International Institute for Management Development in Lausanne, Switzerland. She has been involved in management and executive development activities since 1988 in a variety of capacities. She holds a degree in political science from the University of Lausanne. She expects to enter a doctoral program in the near future to further her research interests in cross-cultural decision making.

Alexander von Boehmer holds a master's degree both in mechanical engineering and in business administration from the Technical University of Berlin, Germany. He spent two years as a visiting fellow at the Sloan School of Management at the Massachusetts Institute of Technology. Currently, he is employed at the Institute for Research in Innovation Management at the University of Kiel in Germany, where he is responsible for a comparative study on the internationalization of research and development activities by U.S., British and German multinational corporations. This study constitutes his dissertation. He has published various journal articles and book chapters in the area of technology management.

William A. Wallace is professor of decision sciences and engineering systems at Rensselaer Polytechnic Institute. Professor Wallace has over 15 years experience in research on and in the development of decision support systems for industry and government. He is currently engaged in research on computer-based decision aids for emergency management, environmentally responsible design and manufacturing, and the process of modelling. Professor Wallace has authored and co-authored six books and over 100 articles and papers. He has held academic positions at Carnegie-Mellon University and the State University of New York at Albany, was a research scientist at the International Institute of Environment and Society in West Berlin, Germany, and a project engineer at the Illinois Institute of Technology Research Institute; was visiting professor at the Swiss Federal Institute of Technology, Zurich; and is a Navy veteran. His research has been reported on by national and international media including the Associated

Press, the *Christian Science Monitor* and *Business Week*. His educational background includes a B.Ch.E. from Illinois Institute of Technology and a master of science and doctorate in management science from Rensselaer Polytechnic Institute.

Steven V. Walton is completing his doctoral studies in operations management at the University of North Carolina at Chapel Hill. He has recently accepted a position as an assistant professor of business at North Carolina Agricultural and Technical State University. His research interests include the impact of EDI on the operations area and the strategic uses of information technologies in operations.

Weijiang Wang was born in Hangzhou, China, in 1966. He received B.Sc. in engineering management from Zhejiang University, Hangzhou, China. He was the director of factory's office of Hangzhou Instrument and Meter plant. He is currently an assistant professor of engineering management and is studying for the Ph.D. degree in engineering management at Zhejiang University. His research interests includes technological innovation and strategy management.

Richard Watson is an associate professor in the Department of Management at the University of Georgia. His Ph.D. in management information systems was awarded by the University of Minnesota. Dr. Watson joined the faculty of the University of Georgia in 1989. His current research interests are group support systems and information systems management. He coordinates a project in the US, Singapore, and Finland examining the effects of national culture on GSS use. He is also working with researchers in several other countries.

Bruce W. Weber is assistant professor in the Information Systems Department of the Stern School of Business at New York University. He teaches courses on financial information systems and managing information technology and systems in the school's MBA program. His research examines the impact of information technology on financial markets, the effects of information systems on industry and firm economic performance, and the valuation of technology investments. He has done consulting for the New York Stock Exchange, the London Stock Exchange, and several financial service firms, and has been a research contractor for the Congressional Office of Technology Assessment. He has an A.B. in applied mathematics from Harvard University, and M.A. and Ph.D. in decision sciences from the Wharton School of the University of Pennsylvania. Prior to joining the Stern faculty, he held a faculty position at the London Business School.

Allison McKinney Wilkins is a doctoral student in operations management at the University of North Carolina at Chapel Hill. She has accepted a position as an assistant professor of operations management at the University of Utah. Her research interests include operations and organizational behavior and interdisciplinary studies.

Xiaobo Wu was born in Hangzhou, China, in 1960. He received the B.Sc. degree in electrical engineering, and the M.A.Sc. degree in energy economics and the Ph.D. degree in engineering management from Zhejiang University, Hangzhou, China. He was formerly an assistant engineer and project official in Forest Ministry of China. He is presently an associate professor of engineering and technology management at Zhejiang University. His research interests include R&D management, technological innovation and organizational learning. He is an editor of *Chinese Journal of Industrial Engineering and Engineering Management*, which is published by Conducting Committee of State Education Commission of P.R. China.

Index

A

accounting 226, 243
accounting cycle 226
accounting information systems 243
accounting standards 225
Accredited Standards Committee (ASC) 315
ACH—Automated Clearing House 108
American Stock Exchange 139
applications-driven approach 544
artificial intelligence 176, 61
Assembly line diagnostic link (ALDL) 302
automation 189

B

bank 186
Bibliographic databases 366
business strategy 522
business value 186

C

CAD systems 379
centralization 269
centralized 348
Centre for International Financial Accounting Research 249
CHIPS—the Clearing House Interbank Payments System 108
client / server technology 22
comparative advantages 376

competitive advantage. 33
competitive strategy 362
Computer Aided Design 288, 289
computer integrated manufacturing (CIM) 264, 272, 294
computer literacy 431
Computer-Aided Manufacturing International (CAM-I) 271
concurrent engineering 379
core competencies 19, 425
country risk 168
cultural diversity 20
cultural Values 90
currency 243
currency risk 170
cycle time 296

D

data quality 177
data transfer. 424
database management system 174
decentralization 269
decentralized 348
decision making structures 482
Decision Support Systems 432
demand management 267, 298
Deregulation 95
developed countries 375
developing countries 88, 375
distribution 279
distribution of processing 226